Books for You

An Annotated Booklist for Senior High

Thirteenth Edition,
Covering Books Published from 1994–96

Lois T. Stover and Stephanie F. Zenker, Editors,

and the Committee on the Senior High School Booklist
of the National Council of Teachers of English

With a Foreword by
Chris Crutcher

NCTE Bibliography Series

National Council of Teachers of English
1111 W. Kenyon Road, Urbana, IL 61801-1096

NCTE Editorial Board: Pat Cordeiro, Bill McBride, Bobbi Fisher, Xin Liu Gale, Sarah Hudelson, Alleen Pace Nilsen, Helen Poole, Jerrie Cobb Scott; Karen Smith, Chair, *ex officio*; Michael Greer, *ex officio*

Manuscript Editor: Lee Erwin

Production Editor: Rona S. Smith

Series Cover Design: R. Maul

Cover Illustration: Raúl Colón. From the jacket illustration for *An Island Like You* © 1995 by Raúl Colón. Used by permission.

Interior Design: Doug Burnett

NCTE Stock Number: 03685-3050

About the Cover

The artwork on our cover was done in watercolor and colored pencil by Raúl Colón. It is from the front cover of *An Island Like You: Stories of the Barrio* by Judith Ortiz Cofer, published by Orchard Books. The art shows a neighborhood of great diversity—both genders, older people as well as young children—all of whom have a significant role to play in the lives of adolescents trying to figure out their place in the world. It shows very clearly the context in which the young people in the stories of *An Island Like You* are trying to move into adulthood—a context that is a complicated one, set in present-day urban New Jersey, but rooted in a Hispanic cultural past. It is, therefore, a fairly complex representation, one that reflects the growing sophistication of the adolescent readers of *Books for You*. We are grateful to Raúl Colón and to Orchard Books for allowing us to reprint this art on our cover.

It is the policy of NCTE in its journals and other publications to provide a forum for the open discussion of ideas concerning the content and the teaching of English and the language arts. Publicity accorded to any particular point of view does not imply endorsement by the Executive Committee, the Board of Directors, or the membership at large, except in announcements of policy, where such endorsement is clearly specified.

ISBN: 0-8141-0368-5

ISSN: 1051-4740

Contents

About the NCTE Bibliography Series

The National Council of Teachers of English is proud to be part of a tradition that we want to share with you. In our bibliography series are four different booklists, each focused on a particular audience, each updated regularly. These are *Adventuring with Books* (pre-K through grade 6), *Kaleidoscope* (multicultural literature, grades K through 8), *Your Reading* (middle school/junior high), and *Books for You* (senior high). Together, these volumes list thousands of recent children's and young adult trade books. Although the works included cover a wide range of topics, they all have one thing in common: they're good books that students and teachers alike enjoy.

How are these volumes put together? The process begins when an educator who knows literature and its importance in the lives of students and teachers is chosen by the NCTE Executive Committee to serve as booklist editor. That editor then works with teachers and librarians who review, select, and annotate hundreds of new trade books sent to them by publishers. It's a complicated process, one that can last three or four years. But because of their dedication and strong belief in the need to let others know about the good literature that's available, these professionals volunteer their time in a way that is commendable and serves as an inspiration to all of us. The members of the committee that compiled this volume are listed on pages 450–51, and we are truly grateful for their hard work.

As educators know, no single book is right for every reader or every purpose, so inclusion in this booklist is not necessarily an endorsement from NCTE. But it does indicate that the professionals who make up the booklist committee feel that the work in question is worthy of teachers' and students' attention, whether for its informative or aesthetic qualities. Similarly, exclusion from an NCTE booklist is not necessarily a judgment on the quality of a given book or publisher. Many factors—space, time, availability of certain books, publisher participation—may influence the final shape of the list.

We hope that you'll find this booklist a useful resource in discovering new titles and authors, and we hope that you will want to collect other booklists in the series. Our mission is to help improve the teaching and learning of English and the language arts, and we hope you'll agree that the quality of our booklists contributes substantially toward that goal.

Michael Greer
Senior Editor

Acknowledgments

From the beginning, this thirteenth edition of *Books for You* has been a collaborative effort. The committee of thirty-plus reviewers who met early in 1994 to make decisions about the organization and format of the text probably had little idea of the level of the commitment involved in actually generating it. But, for the past two years, these dedicated teachers, librarians, teacher educators, and curriculum supervisors have conscientiously given of their time to find books, to read them, to write about them, to mail them, to meet about them, and, in short, to create this manuscript. They gave of their energy on their own time, time squeezed out of days filled with planning lessons, grading papers, and attending meetings, because many of them had used previous editions of *Books for You* and were eager to share their enthusiasm for it as a resource with others. Their efforts are proof that those of us who care about connecting young people and books can work together across the sometimes artificial boundaries that separate us as professionals. To this crew of wonderful educators, we, the editors, say thank you. Especially, we must acknowledge the debt we owe to Rick Walters and Diane Freeman in particular. Rick was tireless in attempting to coax unwilling technologies into service, in tracking down lists of various kinds of information essential to the project, in editing the manuscript over and over again, and in helping us maintain our sanity throughout the final months of work. Diane managed to keep track of titles that won awards but that, without her efforts, would not have found their way into the text, and she reviewed over two hundred books as well.

We must also express our gratitude to the publishers without whom this project could not have been undertaken. Because they care about helping students, teachers, librarians, and parents find good books suited to their needs and interests, they freely gave us the almost four thousand young adult titles from which this booklist was generated. They are an important partner in our efforts to motivate the reading habit. Thank you.

Additionally, we want to say thank you to our liaisons at the National Council of Teachers of English. They were always willing to answer our questions, to forward books to us, and to help us in any possible way with our task.

Finally, we have to acknowledge the authors who have used their talents to write the books annotated in these pages. These creative souls believe in the power of story as a way of knowing, and demonstrate their commitment to helping young people extend their knowledge of the world through reading the written word, and without the results of their time and energy, our jobs as educators would be much more difficult.

We have had three rewarding years, and we hope everyone involved has found the experience just as enriching as we have.

Gratefully,

Lois T. Stover and Stephanie F. Zenker

Foreword

I t intrigues me to write about the importance of reading, because I have spent the last fifteen years, since the publication of my first novel, talking with students about the fact that I read only one book of fiction during my entire stay in high school. Tales of recycling my brother's book reports, and of making up titles and authors, are partly attention grabbers, which score high marks from the student population and a collective throat-clearing from teachers and librarians.

I pull myself out of the fire by discussing the importance of stories in my life, and examining what I cheated myself out of with my rebellious, developmentally appropriate behavior.

In 1956, when I was ten years old, television came to Cascade, Idaho. It was black and white, began its broadcast day at three in the afternoon, and woke my father on the couch to the strains of "The Star-Spangled Banner" or a particularly stirring recitation of "High Flight" well before midnight. My fifth-grade teacher, Minnie Byers, ran her finger over her grade book at the end of the year and estimated accurately, within three weeks, the date each of our families bought a T.V. My father told me television would change the social structure of the town, and he was right. The Roxy Theater closed before I reached junior high school, and groups such as the Civic Club and the Ladies' Auxiliary and the American Legion and the Masons and the Eastern Star either stopped meeting altogether, or cut back drastically on their meetings in order to accommodate Broderick Crawford on "Highway Patrol" or Ed Sullivan or Burns and Allen.

I loved television. It was hypnotic and magical. I took pride in my ability to recite the name of every program on every night of the week between 7:00 and 10:00 P.M. I raced home every day after school to watch Gene Autry or Roy Rogers gun down bad guys.

And I stopped reading.

I began writing stories for publication in 1981, at the age of thirty-five. I might well have started ten years earlier, but it took me that long to catch up on my reading and to realize that the benefit of good stories is interactive. A good storyteller puts his or her words on the page and challenges me to run those words through my imagination, to establish a relationship with the characters, to picture the places, to chase the plot. It is active; I play a part. Scout Finch or Bert Bowden or Kenny Watson or Tim O'Brien or Celie is a person with whom I have a relationship. They touch me because they see the world in a way that connects with the way I see the world. We have intimacy.

While some of this may also be true with T.V. characters and their stories, there is a big difference. Television shows me no respect. It does all the work. What I lost when I shifted my mode of receiving stories was the ability to participate, and to take the time I needed to savor the story, to process it in my head. So in general I robbed myself of stories at the age of ten, and didn't reclaim them until fifteen years later.

When I look at the kinds of stories I like to tell, I have only to go back to that one book of fiction I read in high school, *To Kill a Mockingbird*, considered a staple in the classroom now, but barely off the bestseller list then. My high school

English teacher assigned it, and I was delighted to discover informative front and back flaps and a teacher so excited about the story that she couldn't help giving away enough of the plot to allow me to slip through the tests, writing in generalities and in the evasive language at which I had become so proficient.

Then I made a mistake. I read the first few pages of this industrial-strength Shop-Vac of a novel and it sucked me, like a ping-pong ball in a tornado, into the heart and bowels of Scout Finch's South. It was a story that told the truth in its native tongue; it made me laugh, it sent me into rages, and when the black folks in the upper deck of the courtroom rose for Atticus's passing, I cried like a baby. I fell in love.

Unfortunately my English teacher followed that in machine-gun fashion with *The Scarlet Letter* and *Wuthering Heights*, one of which left me scrambling to discover which letter of the alphabet it might be without reading the book, while the other simply "wuthered" my brain and etched in concrete the belief that the only good book ever written was *To Kill a Mockingbird,* and, hey, I'd already read that.

I try to write stories that could stand up to being the next book a student like me might read following Harper Lee's story. I haven't done that yet, but I'm getting closer and, luckily, a lot of kids who read my stuff haven't read *Mockingbird* yet. So for now, I'm an opening act. I believe it's important to tell stories that ring of truth, to tell them in the language in which they exist—which is probably why I found myself on the *USA Today* list of ten most banned authors last summer. I believe there is only one way to respect your audience and that is to respect your characters—never to back off from telling the truth about them, never to sugar-coat a story, but to look for hope that exists within it. I believe it is important that any good literature reflect rather than model, and I will therefore never tell a story of what should be rather than what is. Teenagers do not like to be lied to any more than adults like to be lied to, and for the same reasons. I believe being a good storyteller carries with it as much responsibility as honor, and though I am aware that authors writing for young adults are often treated like the bastard siblings of "real" writers, as young adult novels are treated like the red-headed stepchildren of literature, neither of those truths is deserved. One cannot read Christopher Paul Curtis's wondrous new novel, *The Watsons Go to Birmingham—1963,* or the works of Terry Davis, Norma Fox Mazer, Will Weaver, Chris Lynch, Robert Cormier, Lois Lowry, Graham Salisbury, Walter Dean Myers, Richard Peck—to name a few and short-shrift many—without knowing that writing about younger people does not mean writing *down* to them. It is because of being in the company of writers like these that I continue to tell the stories I tell.

Chris Crutcher

Chris Crutcher writes novels that reflect real life as he sees it, and he's seen a lot of it, having been a lifeguard, a construction worker, a gas station attendant, a teacher, and the director of an alternative school, after roaming the country for a year after college. He now works in Spokane, Washington, as a child and family therapist in a mental health center, focusing on child-abuse cases. His novels, which include Running Loose, The Crazy Horse Electric Game, *and* Stotan!, *have won numerous awards, and his* Staying Fat for Sarah Byrnes *was praised by* School Library Journal *as "a masterpiece."*

Introduction for the Student

Sometimes you realize that ours can be a difficult and constantly changing world, a world in which there are no easy answers, a world in which it is difficult even to know sometimes what the questions are that need to be asked. Often, when you are confused, you phone a good friend and find solace in talking about the experience that has made you upset. Sometimes, though, you feel on top of the world, and you are especially glad to be alive. When times are good—when you've made the grade on an important project, when your team has played extraordinarily well, when you've found a terrific part-time job, when you find yourself involved in a relationship that feels great, or when you've been accepted at the college of your choice—you share the joy and excitement of the moment with your friends as well.

For those of us involved in the creation of this booklist, books are good friends. We turn to them when we need information, when we want to know that others have had similar experiences, and when we want to see how others deal with all the ups and downs of life. Sometimes we read just for enjoyment, just because we want to be transported into another place and time as a way to escape the particulars of our own. Sometimes we read because we love the way in which an author uses words and we value the craft and artistry involved in writing. And, because we enjoy the world of books for all these reasons, we want to share them with others in the hopes they, too, will be entertained, thrilled, informed, delighted, made wiser, and affected in a multitude of ways. In particular, we want to share with you the best the publishing world has had to offer over the past three years.

Since the end of 1993, the *Books for You* committee has read almost four thousand books copyrighted between 1994 and 1996. We then evaluated them, asked our students about their reactions to them, and talked about them with our colleagues in an effort to provide you with this list of titles. Of course, no one title will appeal to every reader. However, we have tried to show that, in the world of books, there is something for everyone. Some of you may fall in love with the poetry and photography combination of *Something Permanent* by Cynthia Rylant and Walker Evans. Some of you may thrill to the adventure of Lao Hong in Malcolm Bosse's *The Examination*. Some of you may find strength to confront your own fears as you read the grittily realistic depiction of Tish's response to abuse in *When She Hollers* by Cynthia Voigt. Still others of you may gobble up the statistics about a favorite sports event from a title such as Dan Gutman's *World Series Classics*, or may relish the joy of a romance like that of Lydia in Sid Hite's *Answer My Prayer*.

Because we want to make it as easy as possible for you to find the kind of books you want, we have tried to provide multiple ways into this booklist. The chapters are arranged alphabetically; some chapters revolve around a particular theme, such as "Friendship," while others focus on a particular topic of interest to many young adults, such as "Recreation, Travel, and Leisure Time Activities," while still others list books in a particular genre, such as "Poetry and Drama." Within each chapter, the books are arranged alphabetically by author's last name. The information you need to be able to find the book either at the library or the bookstore, such as the publisher, date of publication, and ISBN is also provided. At the end of each chapter we also list other titles which relate to that chapter but which have been annotated elsewhere. Thus, a book like *Much Ado about Prom Night*, by William D. McCants, which is primarily about students involved in a peer counseling program in their senior high, is annotated in the chapter title "School Stories," but because it has a subplot about romances related to the upcoming prom, it is cross-listed at the end of the annotations in the chapter titled "Dating and Sexual Awareness." Check out these lists, and also make sure you investigate topics and themes that overlap; if you are looking for information about a sports player, try both the "Sports and Sports Figures" chapter and the "Autobiography, Biography, and Collective Biography" chapter.

If you have a favorite author, you can find new books by him or her in the author index. If you know the title of a book and want to read about it, look it up in the title index. If you are interested in a particular topic but can't quite figure out which chapter might lead you to books about that topic, try the subject index. Additionally, there are appendices that list books written by authors from other countries and that provide titles in which there are characters reflective of the cultural diversity of both the United States and the world. When you are reading an annotation, just after the bibliographic information, you may see one of three sets of initials. **ER** means the title is easy reading; **WL**, short for "world literature," means that the title was written by an author from a country other than the United States or Great Britain; and **MC**, our abbreviation for "multicultural," is an indication that the characters in the book come from diverse cultural backgrounds.

We have reviewed newly released editions of previously published books, but you should know that there are many, many titles published earlier that are well worth your time. Previous editions of *Books for You* can provide you with information about these books. You should also be aware that we have not annotated every single title published during our time as the *Books for You* committee. Some publishers sent us many, many titles; other publishers sent us only a few of their new offerings, so that, in spite of our best efforts to provide you with some insight about the newest books, there are probably a few good ones that "got away."

Nevertheless, we hope you will find this edition of *Books for You* a valuable reference tool as you search for just the right book. We want you as young adults to enjoy all the wonders of the reading experience, and we hope that as you enter into these books your world will be made richer for the time you spend with them.

Yours in reading,

Lois T. Stover and Stephanie F. Zenker

1 Adventure and Survival

"Anyone can hold the helm when the sea is calm."
Publius Syrus

"It is always the adventurers who accomplish great things."
Montesquieu

1.1   Bosse, Malcolm. **Deep Dream of the Rain Forest.** Sunburst / Farrar, Straus and Giroux, 1993. 179 pp. ISBN 0-374-41702-4. Fiction.

Two young men whose lives could scarcely be more different are brought together in the jungle of 1920s Borneo. Harry Windsor, a fifteen-year old English boy whose interests run to rugby and cricket, finds his life entwined with that of Bayang, a member of a people who practice head-hunting. Bayang and his friend Duck Foot, a young girl ostracized by the tribe because of her webbed foot, abduct and then befriend Harry on their journey to fulfill the prophecy of a powerful dream, and the lives of all three are the richer for the adventure and lessons of the experience. MC

1.2   Bosse, Malcolm. **The Examination.** Farrar, Straus and Giroux, 1994. 296 pp. ISBN 0-374-32234-1. Fiction.

In sixteenth-century Ming Dynasty China, two teenage brothers travel from their home in the western province of Sichuan to the imperial capital of Beijing. Lao Hong is determined to see that his older brother Lao Chen passes the grueling government examinations, and this goal serves as the basis for a cross-country odyssey in which the brothers face floods, plagues of locusts, Japanese pirates, and their own self-doubts. Both brothers come to terms with their own views of the world and gain self-knowledge as they face the transition from home to the different futures upon which they finally decide. MC

ALA Best Books for Young Adults, 1995
Booklist Editor's Choice, 1995

1.3   Bosse, Malcolm. **Tusk and Stone.** Front Street, 1995. 244 pp. ISBN 1-886810-01-4. Fiction.

In seventh-century India, fourteen-year-old Arjun's life is drastically changed after the caravan in which he and his twelve-year-old sister are traveling is overrun by bandits. After his sister is carried off and Arjun is sold to the army, he eventually becomes a proud warrior in the elephant corps; still, he continues to search for his missing sister. India's ancient social order is described throughout the story. MC

1.4   Butler, Octavia E. **Parable of the Sower.** Four Walls Eight Windows, 1993. 299 pp. ISBN 0-941423-99-9. Fiction.

Lauren Olamina turns sixteen in the year 2025. She and her family are lucky to scrape by in their walled neighborhood, but she foresees that they will not long prevent the mayhem outside from overrunning their shaky haven. When this happens, she escapes with her survival bundle and her commitment to a new belief system. She is joined on her journey north by other refugees. The horrors they face from marauding gangs and the strength they show make an engrossing story.

ALA Best Books for Young Adults, 1995

1.5   Campbell, Eric. **The Shark Callers.** Harcourt Brace, 1994. 232 pp. ISBN 0-15-200010-0. Fiction.

Traveling around the world on their small sailing boat, Andy Thompson and his family have stopped on a small island off the coast of Papua New Guinea, when, because of the imminent eruption of a volcano, they are forced to evacuate. Once the volcano erupts, Andy and his family confront a 100-foot tidal wave, the destruction of their boat, and vicious sharks. At the same time, Kaleku, a native of the islands, has set off to start his life as a sacred Shark Caller, a hunter of the sharks that fill the waters around his island. Caught in the same tidal wave that affects the Thompson family, Kaleku must survive the shark-infested sea. The story weaves together the struggles to survive of these very different young men. ER MC WL

IRA Teacher's Choice Award, 1996

1.6   Carter, Alden R. **Between a Rock and a Hard Place.** Scholastic, 1995. 213 pp. ISBN 0-590-48684-5. Fiction.

Perhaps the title *Blood Is Thicker than Water* would be more appropriate for this adventure novel. Teenage cousins Mark and Randy are pushed into a family tradition: a canoe trip marking their transition into the adult world. Neither young man is happy about this situation, but they embark on their adventure in spite of mixed feelings about both the trip and each other. As they travel through Minnesota's lake country, they actually begin to enjoy the experience, until it turns into a life-and-death struggle for survival.

ALA Best Books for Young Adults, 1996

1.7   Cooney, Caroline B. **Flash Fire.** Scholastic, 1995. 198 pp. ISBN 0-590-25253-4. Fiction.

Danna and Hall Press, brother and sister, are at home when a wildfire flares up. Cooney paints the picture of the fire and all the events and actions that surround it in a quick-moving, minute-by-minute log of a fateful afternoon in the Los Angeles hills.

ALA Quick Picks for Young Adults, 1996

1.8   Crichton, Michael. **The Lost World.** Alfred A. Knopf, 1995. 393 pp. ISBN 0-679-41946-2. Fiction.

In this sequel to *Jurassic Park*, six years have passed since the disaster it described, which remains secret to all but those who had some direct part in it. It turns out that the dinosaur experiments were performed on another island as well. A team of American researchers, with two child stowaways, reaches the island to begin studies, only to be trapped by the beasts and a greedy corporate boss. Some strong language.

1.9   Cross, Gillian. **The Great American Elephant Chase.** Puffin Books, 1994. 193 pp. ISBN 0-14-037014-5. Fiction.

Reminiscent of *The Adventures of Huckleberry Finn*, this novel describes how fifteen-year-old Tad and his sister Cissie, a few years younger, find themselves drifting down the Ohio River of the late 1800s in a daring escape with, of all things, an elephant. Their goal is to reach a farm in Nebraska, while staying out of reach of the crooked Mr. Jackson and Esther. The story centers on how the orphaned Tad, unwanted and feeling worthless, gains confidence and self-knowledge during the trio's adventures.

1.10   Galloway, Les. **The Forty Fathom Bank: Novella.** Chronicle Books, 1994. 108 pp. ISBN 0-8118-0034-2. Fiction.

Twenty years after a disturbing incident on the sea that changed his life, the narrator looks back and tells his story. Down on his luck, the narrator had tried to make an instant fortune by shark fishing off the California coast. The deal he made with an experienced fisherman is at the heart of the narrator's feeling about this venture, feelings which turned from desperation to avarice to remorse.

1.11   Garland, Sherry. **Indio.** Harcourt Brace, 1995. 304 pp. ISBN 0-15-200021-6. Fiction.

Ipa-ta-chi is a fourteen-year-old Indian girl living in Mexico in the late 1500s. Her village is a peaceful and fertile farming village. A drought is plaguing the area, however, and Ipa goes to the hills to pray for rain. Upon her return to the village, the Apaches attack, killing many men. Ipa realizes that life in her community is going to change, but it is not until she meets the invading Spanish soldiers that she realizes how drastic that change will be. Enslaved by the Spanish along with her brother and cousin, Ipa assists in a dangerous escape attempt only to be accused of the murder of the slave foreman. MC

ALA Best Books for Young Adults, 1996

1.12   Hobbs, Will. **Far North.** Morrow Junior Books, 1996. 225 pp. ISBN 0-688-14192-7. Fiction.

Canada's Northwest Territories draw Gabe out of Texas; he wants to be nearer his dad, who works on drilling rigs. Gabe hears amazing tales of the frozen wilderness from his roommate Raymond, a native of the Dene tribe. Gabe sure wishes he'd paid better attention to those stories when they become stranded up the Nahanni River without a paddle as winter is about to hammer down. Hobbs's novel is a curious blend of mystical tribal teachings and harsh frontier reality. ER

1.13   Hobbs, Will. **Kokopelli's Flute.** Atheneum Books for Young Readers, 1995. 148 pp. ISBN 0-689-31974-6. Fiction.

Terp Jones and his dog, Dusty, climb Picture House, an Anasazi cliff dwelling, to view the moon's eclipse. While there, the two deter thieves from desecrating sacred burial grounds. When Terp finds and plays an ancient eagle bone flute the thieves leave behind, he experiences magical transformations, adventure, and a new awareness of the lore of the Southwest. Terp experiences a mystical encounter with Cricket, who reveals his true identity and that of the flute's owner, Kokopelli. ER MC

1.14   McCrumb, Sharyn. **She Walks These Hills.** Charles Scribner's Sons, 1994. 336 pp. ISBN 0-684-19556-9. Fiction.

Even in the Appalachian Mountains, still a place of wilderness and isolated communities, events ripple through many lives and cause waves on distant shores. Those touched by the tide include a local deejay transplanted from New England, an escaped convict with a life sentence for murder, his now-respectable ex-wife, a history professor obsessed with a girl who was kidnaped by Shawnee over two hundred years before, a woman aspiring to become a deputy sheriff, and the macho man she loves. Suspenseful and engaging.

School Library Journal Best Adult Books for Young Adults, 1995

1.15   Merino, José María. **The Gold of Dreams.** Translated by Helen Lane. Sunburst / Farrar, Straus and Giroux, 1994. 217 pp. ISBN 0-374-42584-1. Fiction.

Fifteen-year-old Miguel tells the story of his adventures during an expedition to find a legendary golden temple in the heart of sixteenth-century New Spain. His father, a Spanish conquistador, has disappeared years before in a similar adventure. In an expedition filled with danger from nature, hostile native peoples, and members of the expedition itself, Miguel must find strength to survive. MC WL

1.16   Mikaelsen, Ben. **Countdown.** Hyperion Books for Children, 1996. 248 pp. ISBN 0-7868-0252-9. Fiction.

Eliot, selected by NASA to be the first teen in space, connects with Vincent Ole Tome, a young Masai herder, via radio when the space shuttle on which he is a passenger becomes disabled. Both young men question their family traditions and learn about the true meaning of friendship and maturity in this exciting tale. MC

1.17 Oz, Amos. **Soumchi.** Translated by Amos Oz and Penelope Farmer. Harvest / Harcourt Brace, 1995. 71 pp. ISBN 0-15-600193-4. Fiction.

Amos Oz describes a day in the life of Soumchi, an imaginative eleven-year-old boy living in British-occupied Jerusalem. Much like Tom Sawyer, Soumchi has one continuously evolving adventure that starts when his eccentric uncle gives him a bicycle for a gift. Against his will, Soumchi trades this bicycle for a train set, which leads to his getting a dog and a pencil sharpener and then having a fight with his father and an evening with the girl with whom he is madly in love. MC WL

1.18 Parry, Glyn. **Monster Man.** Fawcett Juniper, 1995. 184 pp. ISBN 0-449-70444-0. Fiction.

Sixteen-year-old Melanie Spence is propelled out of her schoolgirl's life, a life overshadowed by the high-pressure tactics of a surfer-boyfriend, memories of an absent, sex-obsessed father, and an overprotective mother, into the twisted fantasy world of a kidnapper and killer. Taken from her own home, Melanie struggles to escape madman Curtis Lowe, who is striving to control the "monster" only he can see. This fast-paced, realistic account takes the reader into the minds of the abducted girl, the madman, the parent, and the police. MC WL

1.19 Paulsen, Gary. **Dogsong.** Aladdin Paperbacks, 1995. 177 pp. ISBN 0-689-80409-1. Fiction.

A fourteen-year-old Inuit boy undertakes a journey with a team of sled dogs to discover himself. Russell leaves modern ways behind in favor of the ways of the past, as he travels through the frozen north country. Mystic visions of himself in the past intertwine with the present adventure as life folds into dream and dream folds into life. MC ER

Newbery Honor Book in original edition

1.20 Paulsen, Gary. **Winterdance: The Fine Madness of Running the Iditarod.** Harcourt Brace, 1994. 256 pp. ISBN 0-15-126227-6. Nonfiction.

Gary Paulsen entered "a world beyond his knowing" when he decided to run the famous Iditarod dog sled race across Alaska. Tested both mentally and physically by the severe demands of the course and the weather, he came to know and truly respect the dogs who pulled him 1,180 miles. The experience was not only an individual victory for Paulsen, but was an event of mystical importance in his life and an adventure of the first rank. The chronicle begins with the author's first relationships with dogs and ends with the decree from his physician which forces him to abandon plans to run the Iditarod ever again. Color pictures taken by Paulsen on the race are included. MC

ALA Best Books for Young Adults, 1995

1.21   Pedersen, Ted. **True Fright: Trapped beneath the Ice! and Other True Stories Scarier than Fiction.** Tom Doherty Associates, 1996. 115 pp. ISBN 0-812-54395-5. Nonfiction.

This collection of fifteen ghostly tales all provide true accounts of mysterious happenings. An unidentified creature is spotted one foggy night by a local police officer in Florida. A young girl skating on a pond with her friend disappears beneath the ice. A French woman dies at sea and is buried, only to be found later—still alive.

1.22   Schulman, Audrey. **The Cage.** Algonquin Books of Chapel Hill / Workman, 1994. 228 pp. ISBN 1-56512-035-3. Fiction.

Though an accomplished photographer, Beryl Findham is chosen for an Arctic expedition primarily for her size: she can fit into a small cage to photograph polar bears. For a month, her companions will be David, a video photographer; Butler, a naturalist; and Jean-Claude, their guide. The trip is fraught with danger even before they leave Churchill, Manitoba, and grows increasingly hazardous. Which is more deadly, the cold or the bears?

ALA Best Books for Young Adults, 1995

1.23   Shusterman, Neal. **Dissidents.** Tor / Tom Doherty Associates, 1994. 179 pp. ISBN 0-812-53461-1. Fiction.

Fifteen-year-old Derek Ferretti has recently joined his mother, the U. S. ambassador to the Soviet Union, in 1989 Moscow after the stateside death of his father. A sometimes difficult person, Derek rebels against his inattentive mother and his situation and begins meeting the teenage daughter of a famous exiled dissident. He devises a plan to smuggle her out of the crumbling Soviet empire to be reunited with her father. In doing so, he learns much about himself and the importance of standing up for principles. MC

1.24   Sleator, William. **Dangerous Wishes.** Dutton Children's Books, 1995. 182 pp. ISBN 0-525-45283-4. Fiction.

Dom and his family were becoming very concerned about all the bad things that had been happening to them since their arrival in Thailand. Could bad spirits really be the cause of the accidents? Did the jade carving that his sister lost in a plane crash have anything to do with the family's mishaps? Dom knew that he had no choice but to find the carving and give it to the Erqwan shrine in Bangkok. ER MC

1.25   Smith, Roland. **Thunder Cave.** Hyperion Books for Children, 1995. 250 pp. ISBN 0-7868-0068-2. Fiction.

Jacob's mother has just died in an accidental death. His stepfather now is in charge of his future—unless Jacob can find his biological father, last known to be studying elephants in Kenya. On his quest for his dad,

Jacob links up with Supeet, a Masai youth, who is conducting a mission of his own. Together, the young men face lions, dehydration, and poachers in this tale of adventure and survival on the African plains written by a research biologist who has studied exotic animals for over two decades. ER MC

1.26   Staples, Suzanne Fisher. **Haveli.** Alfred A. Knopf, 1993. 259 pp. ISBN 0-679-84157-1. Fiction.

This sequel to the Newbery Honor Book *Shabanu: Daughter of the Wind* continues the tale of a courageous young woman from the desert of Pakistan. Now imprisoned in an oppressive marriage to a wealthy and influential older man, Shabanu must rely on her wits and her innate desire for independence as she battles the rigid and often cruel ways of her culture. As she struggles to guarantee a safe existence and an education for her young daughter, Shabanu encounters grave dangers as well as her first experience of love. A descriptive list of characters and a glossary of Pakistani terms are included. MC

1.27   Taylor, L. A. **Cat's Paw.** Ace Books, 1995. 211 pp. ISBN 0-441-00181-5. Fiction.

Miranda Glivven is married to the lightkeeper of the lighthouse in Gwynhead. Her husband has been gone for months and Miranda now is forced to leave her two sons in charge of the lighthouse while she searches for her missing husband. Miranda's only companion is a stray cat who seems intent on accompanying her on her journey. Magic and evil abound in this story of a love between a man and a woman.

1.28   Taylor, Theodore. **Sweet Friday Island.** Harcourt Brace, 1994. 173 pp. ISBN 0-15-200009-7. Fiction.

Fifteen-year-old Peg Toland and her adventurous father look forward to their holiday on remote and uninhabited Sweet Friday Island in the Sea of Cortez. Their peaceful vacation ends abruptly, however, when their boat is wrecked by a mysterious stranger intent on killing them. Struggling for survival, Peg must answer the question, "Are we capable of killing another human being to protect a loved one?" MC

1.29   Temple, Frances. **Tonight, by Sea.** Orchard Books, 1995. 152 pp. ISBN 0-531-06899-4. Fiction.

Set in 1980s Haiti, this novel traces the attempts of Pauli and her family and friends to build a boat so they can escape extreme poverty and governmental brutality. Initially, Pauli doesn't want to leave her homeland, but as she watches the people around her being threatened and killed, she embarks on a dangerous voyage to freedom in the handmade boat. MC WL

Notable 1995 Children's Trade Books in the Field of Social Studies

1.30   Turner, Megan Whalen. **The Thief.** Greenwillow Books, 1996. 196 pp. ISBN 0-688-14627-9. Fiction.

"It is not your intelligence I am interested in, but your skill," Gen is told. His skill is theft, and now he is being released from prison for stealing from the king so he can steal something very important *for* the king. The dangerous journey he and the king's scholar embark upon may win Gen his freedom, but it may also kill him. Tales of the old gods and goddesses not only entertain them on their trip, but reveal much about life to them in the process.

1.31   Wright, Richard. **Rite of Passage.** HarperCollins, 1994. 115 pp. ISBN 0-06-023419-9. Fiction.

Life in Harlem is good for fifteen-year-old straight-A student Johnny Gibbs until the day he is told that he is a foster child headed for a new home. Shattered by the news, he flees into the streets, where he is given shelter by a violent street gang. Feeling abandoned and empty, he launches into a life of crime. Wright's novel, written in the 1940s, is fresh, beautifully written, powerful, fast-paced, and compelling, even for the most reluctant reader. MC

Notable 1994 Children's Trade Books in the Field of Social Studies

Titles Annotated in Other Chapters Related to Adventure and Survival

Alder, Elizabeth. *The King's Shadow*. Historical Fiction.

Alexander, Lloyd. *The Arkadians*. Fantasy.

Anthony, Piers, and Roberto Fuentes. *Dead Morn*. Science Fiction.

Applegate, K. A. Animorphs series. Fantasy.

Avi. *City of Light, City of Dark*. Fantasy.

Brown, Mary. *Pigs Don't Fly*. Fantasy.

Bunting, Eve. *SOS Titanic*. Historical Fiction.

Burgess, Melvin. *The Cry of the Wolf*. Animals.

Carter, Peter. *The Hunted*. War.

Claremont, Chris. *Sundowner*. Science Fiction.

Cooney, Caroline B. *Emergency Room*. Horror.

Coville, Bruce. *The A. I. Gang: Operation Sherlock*. Mysteries.

DeChancie, John. *Living with Aliens*. Science Fiction.

Dickens, Charles. *Oliver Twist*. Classics.

Drake, David. *Igniting the Reaches*. Science Fiction.

Drake, David. *Through the Breach*. Science Fiction.

Farmer, Nancy. *The Ear, the Eye and the Arm*. Science Fiction.

Ferris, Jean. *All That Glitters*. Family.

Grant, Alan. *Batman: Knightfall and Beyond*. Myths.

Gregory, Kristiana. *Jimmy Spoon and the Pony Express*. Westerns.

Haggard, H. Rider. *She*. Classics.

Hughes, Ted. *The Iron Woman*. Science.

Jordan, Sherryl. *Wolf-Woman*. Animals.

Kagan, David. *Sunstroke*. Science Fiction.

Kipling, Rudyard. *The Jungle Book*. Classics.

Laird, Christa. *But Can the Phoenix Sing?* Holocaust.

Lasky, Kathryn. *Beyond the Divide*. Historical Fiction.

Lasky, Kathryn. *A Journey to the New World*. Diaries.

Levy, Robert. *Clan of the Shape-Changers*. Fantasy.

London, Jonathan. *Where's Home?* Family.

Merino, José María. *Beyond the Ancient Cities*. Historical Fiction.

Myers, Walter Dean. *Shadow of the Red Moon*. Fantasy.

Paulsen, Gary. *The Car*. Airplanes.

Plotkin, Mark J. *Tales of a Shaman's Apprentice*. Science.

Pohl, Frederik. *The Voices of Heaven*. Science Fiction.

Rinaldi, Ann. *The Secret of Sarah Revere*. Historical Fiction.

Salvatore, R. A. *Dragonslayer's Return*. Fantasy.

Service, Pamela F. *Storm at the Edge of Time*. Fantasy.

Stevenson, Robert Louis. *Treasure Island*. Classics.

Taylor, Theodore. *The Bomb*. Historical Fiction.

Taylor, Theodore. *Rogue Wave and Other Sea Stories*. Short Stories.

Taylor, Theodore. *Walking up a Rainbow*. Westerns.

Temple, Frances. *The Ramsay Scallop*. Historical Fiction.

Vornholt, John. *Star Trek Generations*. Science Fiction.

Walsh, Jill Paton. *Grace*. Historical Fiction.

Watkins, Yoko Kawashima. *My Brother, My Sister, and I*. Family.

Williams, Eric. *The Wooden Horse*. War.

Williams, Michael. *The Genuine Half-Moon Kid*. Family.

Wrede, Patricia C. *Talking to Dragons*. Fantasy.

2 Airplanes, Cars, Motorcycles, and Racing

"A camel makes an elephant feel like a jet plane."
Jacqueline Kennedy

"Whither goes't thou, America, in thy shiny car in the night?"
Jack Kerouac

2.1   Ballantine, Richard, and Richard Grant. **Richards' Bicycle Repair Manual.** Dorling Kindersley, 1994. 96 pp. ISBN 1-56458-484-4. Nonfiction.

Every bicycle enthusiast should own this book! It spans a variety of topics of interest to bicyclists such as the parts of a bike, care and maintenance, service schedules and suggestions, and an easy-reference troubleshooting chart. Did you ever think to use a twig as a temporary repair remedy for a broken chain? This is just one of several suggestions for emergency repairs offered in a special chapter. Colorful pictures and concise explanatory passages complete the appeal of this handy reference book.

2.2   Birkitt, Malcolm. **Harley-Davidson Electra Glide.** Osprey Automotive, 1994. 128 pp. ISBN 1-85532-402-4. Nonfiction.

This text provides a chronological history of Harley-Davidson's widely known Electra Glide model, covering engine developments, options, and accessories. The book includes many large color photographs, as well as reprints of older advertising materials. Technical and nontechnical information is well integrated so that the text is understandable.

2.3   Brownell, Tom, and Mike Mueller. **Chevrolet Pickup: Color History.** Motorbooks International, 1994. 128 pp. ISBN 0-87938-876-5. Nonfiction.

This text is a comprehensive history of Chevrolet trucks, from the company's 1918 entry into the light-truck market through the 1994 models. A parallel history of trucks manufactured by GMC, Chevrolet's sister company, is also given. The chronology of model years focuses on engines, body and cab developments, and design trends. Model evolution is described in technical terms (wheel-base, displacement) and nontechnical terms (chrome grilles, art deco styling). The early chapters are chronologically formatted, and then five chapters focus on unique models. The final chapter discusses technical aspects of the engines.

2.4 Campisano, Jim. **American Muscle Cars.** MetroBooks, 1995. 128 pp. ISBN 1-56799-164-5. Nonfiction.

This book chronicles the "muscle car" era from 1960 to 1974, describing model introductions and receptions, rivalries, popularity, slang, etc. Inserts focus on particular engines ("legends"), significant models, and calendars of model evolution. Color pictures as well as advertising reprints are included on almost every page. Three chapters cover periods, 1960–63, 1964–67, and 1968–74. One chapter, entitled "Ponycar Mania," focuses on the legendary Ford Mustang, and another chapter considers racing's impact on model evolution.

2.5 Chimits, Xavier, and François Granet. **Williams Renault Formula I Motor Racing Book.** Dorling Kindersley, 1994. 64 pp. ISBN 1-56458-627-8. Nonfiction.

Colorful and detailed pictures take the reader into the world of Formula I racing, describing all aspects of the sport from driver racewear to building a car to driving techniques. There is also a section on world champions of the sport and information on what has happened to some of racing's "greats," both the people and the cars.

2.6 Craft, John. **Vintage and Historic Stock Cars.** Motorbooks International, 1994. 96 pp. ISBN 0-87938-898-6. Nonfiction.

This model-by-model history of stock cars begins with a 1950 Oldsmobile and runs through 1994 Chevrolet, Pontiac, and Ford models. Each model is profiled and specifications are provided. Some NASCAR history is included as well as many color photos.

2.7 Cruickshank, Gordon. **Cars.** Dorling Kindersley, 1995. 160 pp. ISBN 0-7894-0217-3. Nonfiction.

This readable mini-encyclopedia of the automobile, part of the *Pockets Full of Knowledge* series, runs from past to future, exploring the vehicle inside out and covering luxury cars, everyday cars, sports cars, specialized cars, racing cars, and classic cars. A reference section includes a timeline, inventors, famous races and places, and amazing facts, followed by a list of resources and a glossary. This in-depth examination will fascinate novice and expert alike.

2.8 **Daytona 500: The Men and Machines of Speedweeks '94.** Autosport International, 1994. 160 pp. ISBN 0-929323-12-2. Nonfiction.

This collection of journalistic articles on Speedweek race events includes a pictorial narrative of the annual Daytona 500 stock car race and a pictorial yearbook of drivers and team owners. One article provides biographical information on 1994 race winner Sterling Marlin. Summary charts of race statistics, results, and driver/team field standings are included. The understandable descriptions given will appeal to the novice race enthusiast and yet are detailed enough to interest more informed readers.

2.9   Evans, Jeremy. **Motocross and Trials.** Crestwood House, 1993. 48 pp. ISBN 0-89686-821-4. Nonfiction.

This is a slim, brightly colored, nonthreatening book on motocross, being one volume in the Adventurers series. A contents page, a glossary, an index, and a list of international organizations devoted to motocross as a recreational hobby and a professional sport round out the large number of visuals. MC

2.10   Heasley, Jerry, and the automotive editors of *Consumer Guide*. **Mustang Chronicle.** Publications International, Ltd., 1995. 240 pp. ISBN 0-7853-1174-2. Nonfiction.

Heasley provides an in-depth history of Ford's ever-popular "ponycar" from the 1964$^1/_2$ original through 1995 models. He places the car's history in larger historical context (e.g., 1988: Manuel Noriega indicted, Chrysler profits drop for fourth straight year, only one change made to '88 Mustang). Three- to four-page chapter introductions are followed by calendar year/model year summary charts, then many color photographs with accompanying short explanatory entries.

2.11   Hilton, Christopher. **Ayrton Senna.** Patrick Stephens, 1994. 192 pp. ISBN 1-85260-483-2. Nonfiction.

This eloquent biographical tribute to deceased Grand Prix race-driver Ayrton Senna opens with a description of the crash that took the young champion's life. Responses to the tragedy, from prominent figures involved in the motorsport, are quoted. The biography then returns to the beginning of Senna's career, documenting his rise to fame. Quotations from Ayrton Senna and from family, friends, and colleagues are used to develop a portrait of the young man. A closing chapter provides Senna's full racing record from 1973–94.

2.12   Huff, Richard M. **Behind the Wall: A Season on the NASCAR Circuit.** Bonus Books, 1994. 291 pp. ISBN 1-56625-011-0. Nonfiction.

This is literally the "story" of stock car racing. Reporter and race fan Huff follows the race team of Billy Hagan and the career of NASCAR driver Terry Labonte through the 1991–93 race seasons. This insider narrative is all on-scene observation. With only a small black-and-white photo insert, the text is lengthy, but the up-close perspective is captivating. Detailed explanations and descriptions should interest both novices and knowledgeable enthusiasts.

2.13   Leffingwell, Randy. **Harley-Davidson: Myth and Mystique.** Motorbooks International, 1995. 192 pp. ISBN 0-7603-0031-3. Nonfiction.

Rather than presenting a technical overview of the company's engineering history, this account chronicles the evolution of the Harley-Davidson Motor Company's reputation. Combining people, places, and events with minimal but useful technical detail, the book should appeal to the motorcycle novice and expert alike. Additionally, many large color photos, concise captions, and the fluid prose style of the text will make it accessible to readers at many levels.

2.14 Look Inside Cross-Sections. Dorling Kindersley. 32 pp. Nonfiction. ER

Butterfield, Moira. **Bulldozers.** Illustrated by Chris Lyon and Gary Biggin. 1995. ISBN 0-7894-0012-X.

Butterfield, Moira. **Jets.** Illustrated by Hans Jenssen. 1996. ISBN 0-7894-0767-1.

Butterfield, Moira. **Record Breakers.** Illustrated by Chris Grigg and Keith Harmer. 1995. ISBN 0-7894-0320-X.

Johnstone, Michael. **Cars.** Illustrated by Alan Austin. 1994. ISBN 1-56458-681-2.

Johnstone, Michael. **Trains.** Illustrated by Richard Chasemore. 1995. ISBN 0-7894-0319-6.

Somerville, Louisa. **Rescue Vehicles.** Illustrated by Hans Jenssen. 1995. ISBN 1-56458-879-3.

This series successfully integrates technical information and historical data, combining detailed illustrations with interesting introductions to each diagram and informative captions surrounding the cross-sections. *Bulldozers* takes the reader on a trip through wheel loaders, excavators, and many other construction machines in addition to bulldozers. Ten jets are featured in detail in *Jets,* a book for aircraft lovers, while *Record Breakers* covers an assortment of speedy vehicles. *Cars* takes the reader from the Model T to Formula I racers. *Trains* includes views of locomotives from an early steam engine through a high-tech modern shuttle, and *Rescue Vehicles* includes unusual equipment such as paramedic bikes, and provides a survey of vehicles past and present. Appealing double-page illustrations, simple but informative historical timelines, helpful glossaries, and readable text render the series interesting and accessible. ER

2.15 Marselli, Mark. **Classic Harley-Davidson Big Twins.** Motorbooks International, 1994. 96 pp. ISBN 0-87938-922-2. Nonfiction.

This guide traces the Harley-Davidson "big twin," Harley's trademark engine, from the 1936 "Knucklehead" through the 1984 "Shovelhead." Color photographs of specific models and model-year-specific features have useful explanatory captions. The text body is unified and integrates technical and nontechnical information eloquently.

2.16 Moriarty, Frank. **Sunday Drivers: NASCAR Winston Cup Stock Car Racing.** Photographs by Rick Farnkopf. Howell Press, 1994. 175 pp. ISBN 0-943231-65-5. Nonfiction.

This is a detailed explanation of NASCAR, the National Association of Stock Car Auto Racing: autos, teams, tracks, crews, sponsors, money, rules, and drivers. Drivers are discussed as a group and as types, and individual drivers are introduced. The text closes with two chapters on the Daytona 500, the NASCAR "Super Bowl." Large color photographs are included throughout. The bulk of the writing is based on direct observation of events and includes many quotations from participants.

2.17   Paulsen, Gary. **The Car.** Harcourt Brace, 1994. 180 pp. ISBN 0-15-292878-2. Fiction.

Fourteen-year-old Terry assembles a car from a do-it-yourself kit after his parents abandon him at their Cleveland home, each thinking the other will care for him. That's just as well by Terry, as he then decides to drive his Blakely Bearcat across the country. He meets up with Waylon, a forty-five-year-old wandering Vietnam vet, and together they travel west on an adventure of learning.

ALA Quick Picks for Young Adults, 1995

2.18   Schleifer, Jay. **Daytona! Thunder at the Beach.** Crestwood House, 1995. 48 pp. ISBN 0-89686-818-4. Nonfiction.

This very easy and brief account of how the Daytona 500 stock car race got its start, part of the Out to Win series, also gives a sense of the excitement of the sport of racing in general. ER

2.19   Willson, Quentin, with David Selby. **The Ultimate Classic Car Book.** Dorling Kindersley, 1995. 224 pp. ISBN 0-7894-0159-2. Nonfiction.

This "gallery" of "classic" cars describes the aesthetic appeal of ninety unique examples. Though the collection is diverse, only an avid car-buff will recognize more than a few model names. Nevertheless, the pages of striking color photos are captivating, and the accompanying information is illuminating. The sophisticated text demands an accomplished reader, and while the coverage is broad, this is not a comprehensive reference. Still, the stylistic appeal is unmistakable.

2.20   Wilson, Anthony. **Dorling Kindersley Visual Timeline of Transportation.** Dorling Kindersley, 1995. 48 pp. ISBN 1-56458-880-7. Nonfiction.

This attractive, oversized book lives up to expected Dorling Kindersley standards, making it an appealing volume for browsing as well as reference. Plenty of illustrations accompany the text, which consists of concise descriptions of milestones in transportation of all sorts--outs and outriggers, roller skates and skateboards, spacecraft and hovercraft--all chronologically arranged with sociological impacts noted. The comprehensive index includes cross-references. ER

2.21   Wilson, Hugo. **The Encyclopedia of the Motorcycle.** Photography by Dave King. Dorling Kindersley, 1995. 320 pp. ISBN 0-7894-0150-9. Nonfiction.

This exhaustive reference capably overviews the motorcycle world and motorcycling history in alphabetical order. Loaded with large captioned color photographs and encyclopedic entries of fascinating technical and historical information, this volume makes for an exciting pleasure read or an unbeatable research tool. No background knowledge is assumed, and the book's comprehensive contents should attract dedicated enthusiasts and casual browsers both.

ALA Quick Picks for Young Adults, 1996

2.22   Wilson, Hugo. **The Ultimate Motorcycle Book.** Photography by Dave King. Dorling Kindersley, 1993. 192 pp. ISBN 1-56458-303-1. Nonfiction.

A history of motorcycles with emphasis on some of the more famous American, British, German, Japanese, and Italian motorcycle manufacturers is the main focus of this book, which includes photographs or drawings on every page. Technical aspects of motorcycle performance are highlighted, and a glossary of motorcycle terms is included.

Titles Annotated in Other Chapters Related to Airplanes, Cars, Motorcycles, and Racing

Harris, Jacqueline L. *The Tuskegee Airmen.* History.

Haskins, Jim. *Black Eagles: African Americans in Aviation.* Autobiography.

Hobbs, Valerie. *How Far Would You Have Gotten if I Hadn't Called You Back?* Family.

3 Animals and Pets

"Animals are such agreeable friends—they ask no questions, they pass no criticisms."

George Eliot

"Beasts of each kind their fellows spare.
Bear lives in amity with bear."

Samuel Johnson

3.1 Bauer, Peggy. **Wild Kittens.** Photographs by Erwin Bauer and Peggy Bauer. Chronicle Books, 1995. 80 pp. ISBN 0-8118-1012-7. Nonfiction. **Wild Puppies.** Photographs by Erwin Bauer and Peggy Bauer. Chronicle Books, 1995. 78 pp. ISBN 0-8118-1039-9. Nonfiction.

It is hard to resist picking up these lushly photographed books once the action shots on the front covers grab your attention. Each one explores the little-known world of the wild animal relatives of our favorite pets, exploring their natural habitats, their breeding and feeding habits, and their behavior. The detailed captions coupled with the incredible close-up photography provide readers with new appreciation for wild cats and dogs.

3.2 Burgess, Melvin. **The Cry of the Wolf.** Beech Tree, 1994. 128 pp. ISBN 0-688-13625-7. Fiction.

Their existence in a remote corner of England had been a secret for five hundred years until young Ben Tilley tells "the Hunter" about the wolves. Wanting recognition as the man who eliminated such a rare species, the Hunter begins the chase. Year after year, relentless and thorough, he focuses on his goal until the tarnished victory is his. Or is it? Unable to resist one more chase, the Hunter becomes the hunted and matches wits against a patient and equally determined enemy.

3.3 Chrystie, Frances N. Revised and updated by Margery Facklam. **Pets: A Comprehensive Handbook for Kids.** Illustrated by Gillett Good Griffin. Little, Brown, 1995. 279 pp. ISBN 0-316-14281-6. Nonfiction.

Want to know what to feed your salamander? Or how you should care for your budgerigar, water snails, or gerbils? You'll find the information you need in this comprehensive handbook. From canaries to chickens, tadpoles to porcupines, raccoons to finches, you'll find facts about first aid and common diseases, proper feeding and care, sleeping habits and training techniques for forty animals. An extensive index provides easy access.

3.4   Day, Nancy. **Animal Experimentation: Cruelty or Science?** Enslow, 1994. 128 pp. ISBN 0-89490-578-3. Nonfiction.

There are no easy, pat answers to the questions posed in this exploration of the issue of animal experimentation, part of the Issues in Focus series. Passionate animal rights activists make the case that experiments on animals are abusive, painful, cruel, and unnecessary. Scientists, just as passionate in their belief that human beings must use the methods available to find the causes and cures for diseases, make the case that such experimentation is a necessity. This "issues in focus" treatment of the topic explores both sides of the question, presenting persuasive arguments from both groups. Examination of the ethical and practical aspects of the issue is documented with facts and personal observations. Thus armed with the facts the reader is advised, "Decide for yourself."

3.5   Edney, Andrew, and David Taylor. **101 Essential Tips: Cat Care.** Dorling Kindersley, 1995. 72 pp. ISBN 1-56458-986-2. Nonfiction.

This easy-to-read handbook provides essential information for cat owners and lovers such as tips on housing and handling cats, safety, training, and health issues. The "how-to" information is well illustrated and easy to follow. ER

3.6   Farish, Terry. **Talking in Animal.** Greenwillow Books, 1996. 137 pp. ISBN 0-688-14671-6. Fiction.

Not only does Siobhan like animals better than people, she feels her dog Tree is the only one who truly understands her. She spends most of her time with Tree, and with a religious activist who rescues injured wild animals. However, rocky relationships and life's inevitable changes begin to work themselves out as Siobhan grows into a loving, courageous young woman.

3.7   Fogle, Bruce. **ASPCA Complete Dog Training Manual.** Training sequences by Patricia Holden White. Foreword by Roger Caras. Dorling Kindersley, 1994. 125 pp. ISBN 1-56458-487-9. Nonfiction.

Dr. Fogle provides the reader with step-by-step instructions on such topics as how to work with puppies, how to provide obedience training for your dog, and how to correct problem behaviors like aggressiveness, nervousness, car chasing, jumping up, food problems, and many more. The accompanying color pictures add further detail to the in-depth explanations. A must for dog owners!

3.8   Fogle, Bruce. **101 Essential Tips: Dog Care.** Dorling Kindersley, 1995. 72 pp. ISBN 1-56458-989-7. Nonfiction.

As a part of the 101 Essential Tips series, this minibook offers the dog owner a handy, concise guide to some of the most frequent quandaries they face: puppy care, dog grooming, training, play time, traveling with a dog, and health concerns. Colorful photographs accompany this brief text.

3.9   Grace, Eric S. **Apes.** Sierra Club Books for Children, 1995. 64 pp. ISBN 0-87156-365-7. Nonfiction.

Photographs, sketches, and maps highlight this book on different kinds of apes. How and where they live, eat, gather food, and communicate is covered for the reader in simple text. The author has simplified scientific study for the young researcher and provided interesting facts about each featured ape—chimpanzees, gorillas, and orangutans are discussed in detail—and the species in general. An index is provided for easy reference, making this book an excellent tool for young researchers.

3.10   Jennings, Patrick. **Faith and the Electric Dogs.** Scholastic Press, 1996. 146 pp. ISBN 0-590-69768-4. Fiction.

Jennings says of this first novel that it is "a story of language, friendship, and empathy." He tells the tale of Faith, who hates her new life, and who feels herself to be an outsider in New Mexico. So, Faith and her electric dog, Eddie, escape—by rocket—into a series of adventures that cause Faith to reevaluate her initial perceptions. ER MC

3.11   Jordan, Sherryl. **Wolf-Woman.** Houghton Mifflin, 1994. 162 pp. ISBN 0-395-70932-6. Fiction.

When she was only three, Tanith was brought by Ahearn, the leader of a clan of wolves, to live in his society. As a human being, Tanith must rise up against difficult obstacles to earn the respect of the wolves. And, when she is a young woman, she must choose between the world of wolves and that of humankind. Where does she belong? Where does her heart lie? Her first-person story is one of personal triumph as well as a penetrating look at the harsh and senseless brutality often inflicted on splendid animals by humans. MC WL

ALA Best Books for Young Adults, 1995

3.12   Koebner, Linda. **Zoo Book: The Evolution of Wildlife Conservation Centers.** Forge / Tom Doherty Associates, 1994. 192 pp. ISBN 0-312-85322-X. Nonfiction.

The mission of modern zoos is far from that evidenced in the old cramped cages which held beasts at bay for the amusement of humans. Today's zoos engage in the conservation of species and their natural habitats worldwide, actively researching behaviors, genetic makeup, dietary needs, reproductive requirements, and a myriad of other essential concerns. Lavishly illustrated with vivid color photographs, this volume addresses the past, present, and future of all facets of wildlife conservation in zoos.

ALA Best Books for Young Adults, 1995
IRA Teacher's Choice, 1996

3.13   Martyn, Elizabeth, and David Taylor. **The Little Cat Care Book.** Dorling Kindersley, 1991. 61 pp. ISBN 1-879431-62-9. Nonfiction.

This "tiny treasury of information" is packed with facts and ideas for cat lovers of all ages, beginning with historical information and taking the reader through sections on choosing the right cat, care and grooming, and special games and menus designed to pamper felines. "Cat Stars," a kitty horoscope, is a guide to indulging a cat according to the stars. This colorfully illustrated volume also includes a section for recording a cat's health history as well as an instructive "A–Z of Health and Safety" for cats.

3.14   Martyn, Elizabeth, and David Taylor. **The Little Cat Facts Book.** Dorling Kindersley, 1993. 61 pp. ISBN 1-56458-263-9. Nonfiction.

As any cat lover knows, cats are endlessly entertaining. This small compendium of feline facts presents an array of intriguing information, tracing cats through art and literature, war and the home front, on land and sea. Here the reader can learn about famous cats, humble cats, fat cats, rare cats, and courageous cats. Along with the colorful photographs and art, the book is sprinkled with cat anecdotes and history.

3.15   Monson, A. M. **The Deer Stand.** Beech Tree, 1994. 171 pp. ISBN 0-688-13623-0. Fiction.

The move from Chicago has been difficult for Bits. She misses her friends and all their shared adventures in the city. Bits hates everything about her new home and life in Wisconsin except for the one friend she has made. Buck soon becomes the center of her attention and she races home every day after school to be with him. Her devotion to Buck and the gifts she gives him ease his distrust and cement their friendship. When she reveals to a classmate that Buck is a deer and that she has trained him to trust her, Bits learns the terrible price Buck will probably have to pay for their friendship. ER

3.16   Nichols, Michael. **The Great Apes: Between Two Worlds.** Contributions by Jane Goodall, George B. Schaller, and Mary G. Smith. Photographs by Michael Nichols. National Geographic Society, 1993. 200 pp. ISBN 0-87044-947-8. Nonfiction.

True to *National Geographic* standards, the photography in this volume is outstanding and the text well-researched. Field research about the societies of various great apes reveals the need for protection against encroaching human activity. Information on apes in captivity—as pets, for entertainment, in biomedical research, and in zoos—is included. Notable researchers and conservationists such as Jane Goodall and Dian Fossey are given special attention.

ALA Best Books for Young Adults, 1995

3.17   Parker, Steve. **Natural World.** Dorling Kindersley, 1994. 192 pp. ISBN 1-56458-719-3. Nonfiction.

This volume in the Eyewitness series provides spectacular value for the price and is highly recommended for reference, classroom, or personal collections. Anatomy, habits, survival issues, extinction, and classification of wildlife are gloriously and engrossingly presented. A timeline, a glossary, and an index serve to enhance the usefulness of the book. ER

3.18   Pepper, Dennis. **The Oxford Book of Animal Stories.** Oxford University Press, 1994. 304 pp. ISBN 0-19-278134-0. Fiction.

Included in this anthology are stories old and new of animals and their relationship with humankind. Traditional myths and legends, fables and folktales are woven together with new works to present to readers a glimpse of a wide variety of animals including bears, cats, kangaroos, rabbits, tigers, crabs, horses, spiders, porpoises, and foxes. The beliefs and customs of many countries and cultures are also represented in these stories of wild beasts, domesticated working animals, and pets. Rich in content and language, this collection is a must for lovers of animals and lovers of literature alike. MC

3.19   Sharp, Ann. **The Koala Book.** Pelican, 1995. 160 pp. ISBN 1-56554-160-X. Nonfiction.

The koala—known for its soft fur, its gentle and appealing eyes, and its sweet nature—is the subject of this study, which considers the koala's evolution, its physical nature, its behavior, its interaction with the human race, the threat it faces as its habitat is destroyed, and efforts currently underway to help it survive. Sharp's incredible color photography adds depth and excitement to the story of this symbol of Australia.

3.20   Swanson, Diane. **Buffalo Sunrise: The Story of a North American Giant.** Sierra Club Books for Children, 1996. 58 pp. ISBN 0-87156-861-6. Nonfiction.

The story of a beloved North American giant, the buffalo, unfolds in this short but lovely book illustrated with beautiful photographs and enhanced by an index. Quick fact paragraphs add interest about legends of the herd, the buffalo horse, and the Wild West of Buffalo Bill. ER

3.21   Swanson, Diane. **Safari beneath the Sea: The Wonder World of the North Pacific Coast.** Photographs by the Royal British Columbia Museum. Sierra Club Books for Children, 1994. 58 pp. ISBN 0-87156-415-7. Nonfiction.

Although intended for a younger audience, this volume will nonetheless captivate teens with its large, vibrant color photographs on at least every other page. The text is simple but reveals a plethora of astonishing facts about sea creatures and plants. Ever heard of an animal that turns its stomach inside out, inserts it directly into its prey, and begins digesting, directly and immediately? Look forward to many more such fascinating bits of information. ER

NCTE Orbis Pictus Award for Outstanding Nonfiction for Children, 1995
ALA Quick Picks for Young Adults, 1995

3.22   Swinney, Geoff, and Kate Charlesworth. **Fish Facts.** Pelican, 1994. 48 pp. ISBN 1-56554-030-1. Nonfiction.

The world of fish is a large one indeed, as fish inhabit more than 70 percent of the surface of the planet. It is also a world largely unknown to most humans. This comic-book style paperback, which was first published by the National Museums of Scotland, gives the reader a whimsical and yet fact-packed peek into the life of fish. Each page is both a biology lesson and a comical insight into the imagined thoughts and humor of fish. A question index gives the reader the page numbers where the answers to such interesting queries as "Are fish noisy?" and "Sharks: Do they deserve their reputation?" are answered. ER

3.23   Tattersall, Ian. **Primates: Lemurs, Monkeys, and You.** The Millbrook Press, 1995. 72 pp. ISBN 1-56294-520-3. Nonfiction.

The roots of humankind's family tree include ancestors such as the orangutan, the gibbon, the owl monkey, the aye aye, and the chimpanzee. All of these primates and numerous others are included in this easy-to-read overview, offering details of their evolution, characteristics, habitats, similarities, and differences. Color photographs and illustrations highlight this introduction to over two hundred species representing our earliest relatives. ER

3.24   Tyning, Thomas F. **A Guide to Amphibians and Reptiles.** Little, Brown, 1990. 400 pp. ISBN 0-316-81713-9.

Species of many amphibians and reptiles are described in sections devoted to providing detailed information about each creature. A variety of frogs, salamanders, turtles, lizards, and snakes are introduced in a conversational style that allows for easy reading of the interesting facts. Each section includes black-and-white drawings and a quick reference chart.

3.25   Vogel, Colin. **The Complete Horse Care Manual.** Dorling Kindersley, 1995. 192 pp. ISBN 0-7894-0170-3. Nonfiction.

Precise advice by a veterinary surgeon who specializes in horse care is set forth with pictures, illustrations, charts, and text. This complete manual includes looking at the horse, general care, food and water, health, tack, and clothing. Helpful hints and tips are also included, as well as a glossary, useful addresses, and an index. All horse lovers will appreciate the information in this manual, and all horse owners will agree that this manual is essential to their collection.

Titles Annotated in Other Chapters Related to Animals and Pets

Carter, Alden R. *Dogwolf*. Choices.

Irwin, Hadley. *Jim-Dandy*. Historical Fiction.

Jacques, Brian. *The Bellmaker*. Fantasy.

London, Jack. *White Fang*. Classics.

McCaffrey, Anne. *Black Horses for the King*. Historical Fiction.

O'Donohoe, Nick. *Under the Healing Sign*. Fantasy.

Pringle, Laurence. *Scorpion Man: Exploring the World of Scorpions*. Autobiography.

Savage, Deborah. *To Race a Dream*. Choices.

Schulman, Audrey. *The Cage*. Adventure.

Scott, Peter W. *The Complete Aquarium*. Recreation.

4 The Arts: Art, Architecture, Music, Dance, Photography

"Architecture is frozen music."
   Johann Wolfgang von Goethe

"My mother adorned with flowers whatever shabby house we were forced to live in. And not just your typical straggly country strand of zinnia either. . . . Because of her creativity with flowers, even my memories of poverty are seen through a haze of blooms."

Alice Walker

"There are moments in our lives, there are moments in a day, when we seem to see beyond the usual. Such are the moments of our greatest wisdom. If one could but recall his vision by some sort of sign. It was in this hope that the arts were invented. Sign-posts on the way to what may be. Sign-posts toward greater knowledge."

Robert Henri

4.1   Ardley, Neil. **A Young Person's Guide to Music.** Music by Poul Ruders. Dorling Kindersley, 1995. 80 pp. ISBN 0-7894-0313-7. Nonfiction.

Photographs of young musicians playing instruments accompany the first part of this beautiful book-and-compact disc combination. Symbols tell when to listen to the CD, which begins with a piece written by Poul Ruders for the fiftieth anniversary of Benjamin Britten's *Young Person's Guide to the Orchestra*. Readers/listeners will learn how thirty-one instruments work and what they sound like individually and in combination. In the book's second part, the history of music is divided into eight time periods from the earliest times to the present day. It is followed by reference sections listing seventy composers, definitions and examples of musical forms, and a glossary of musical terms.

Notable 1995 Children's Trade Books in the Field of Social Studies

4.2   **The Art Book.** Phaidon Press, 1994. 512 pp. ISBN 0-7148-3032-1. Nonfiction.

This is an A-to-Z guide to the world's greatest painters and sculptors as selected by the staff of the Phaidon Press. Because it is organized alphabetically, Michelangelo falls between Metzu and Millais. Thus, traditional ways of thinking about art—by period or by genre—are violated, and the result is that the reader begins to search for the ways in which any piece of enduring art acts on a viewer. For each artist, there is a color plate of one representative work, which is analyzed in terms of craft and in terms of its relationship to other works by artists with similar aims. Cross-references to those other artists are provided, as are glossaries of artistic movements and technical terms.

4.3   Banyai, Istvan. **Zoom.** Viking, 1995. N.p. ISBN 0-670-85804-8. Fiction.

A book with many stories but no words, *Zoom* is an imaginative look at visual perception. After the opening close-up of a rooster's tail, each subsequent page presents another surprise. What begins as a farm scene ends up as something very different and far removed, with a look at many communities and cultures en route to the conclusion. For all ages, zooming with this book offers multiple stories full of action and prompts fascinating ideas for discussion. ER

4.4   Barber, Nicola, and Mary Mure. **The World of Music.** Silver Burdett Press, 1996. 94 pp. ISBN 0-382-39116-0. Nonfiction.

Colorful photographs and diagrams fill the eleven chapters of this book about music. There are three chapters about musical instruments from all over the world, one about electronic instruments, three telling the history of music in the Western world from 1100 C.E. to the present, one about the world's folk music, and two chapters about how music is put together with its pulse and rhythm, pitch and melody. Listening suggestions, a glossary of musical terms, a list of important composers, and an index make this a useful book for anyone who wants to learn about music. ER MC

4.5   Beckett, Sister Wendy, with Patricia Wright. **The Story of Painting.** Dorling Kindersley (in association with the National Gallery of Art, Washington, D.C.), 1994. 400 pp. ISBN 1-56458-615-4. Nonfiction.

"It seems to me that we are all born with the potential to respond to art. Unfortunately, not all of us have the good fortune to have this potential activated," Beckett writes. Her task in this volume is to help all viewers of art find it more accessible. She gives an overview of the characteristics and historical contexts of the major art movements and analyzes representative paintings from each period, giving information about the major artists and their works as well as sidebar commentaries on ways in which political activity affected art history during different periods.

4.6   Bennett, Cherie. **Wild Hearts.** Archway / Pocket Books, 1994. 199 pp. ISBN 0-671-86513-7. Fiction.

Jane McVay, a talented jazz drummer, thinks her world has ended when she and her family move from Manhattan to Nashville, Tennessee. How could anyone from the New York Performing Arts School survive at

"Hocum High School"? Jane hates country music, dresses in "vintage grunge," and embarrasses her sister. After a schoolmate named Savy, "a neon light among pastel people," recruits her to play in the school musical *Grease*, Jane learns more about music, friendship, and responsibility. ER

4.7 Boyd, Candy Dawson. **Fall Secrets.** Puffin Books, 1994. 216 pp. ISBN 0-14-036583-4. Fiction.

Jessie Williams lives in Oakland, California, where the 1991 firestorm burned most of her neighborhood. Hoping to become an actress like her grandmother, she knows she must succeed at her new performing arts school, where she earns a role in *Mufaro's Beautiful Daughters* and auditions for *Harriet Tubman*. But since the fourth grade, Jessie has been hiding a secret that makes her think that her dark African American skin is ugly and that her light-complexioned sister, Cass, is perfect. Can she tell the secret? ER MC

4.8 Brand, Stewart. **How Buildings Learn: What Happens after They're Built.** Penguin, 1995. 243 pp. ISBN 0 14 01.3996 6. Nonfiction.

Brand provides a study of how a building's appearance and usage are adapted and refined over time by its inhabitants. When buildings are allowed to evolve, they become better as they "learn" the needs of their occupants. This book uses many photographs to show the structural changes over time.

4.9 Brust, Beth Wagner. **The Amazing Paper Cuttings of Hans Christian Andersen.** Ticknor and Fields Books for Young Readers, 1994. 80 pp. ISBN 0-395-66787-9. Nonfiction.

As famous as Hans Christian Andersen is for his fairy tales, it is mystifying that he is not equally well known for his intricate paper cuttings, frequently pictured in this book, which are truly amazing. Andersen would fashion them extemporaneously as he told his tales to children, whom he loved. The story of his ambitious rise from pauper to world-renowned storyteller, told in very simple language, will interest many readers. ER

ALA Notable Books for Children, 1995

4.10 Burrows, Terry. **Play Country Guitar.** Dorling Kindersley, 1995. 80 pp. ISBN 0-7894-0190-8. Nonfiction. **Play Rock Guitar.** Dorling Kindersley, 1995. 80 pp. ISBN 0-7894-0189-4. Nonfiction.

These books are for anyone who wants to learn how to play a guitar. Each includes a history of the guitar, the instrument's parts (steel-string acoustic for country; solid-body electric for rock), and instructions about how to tune the instruments and how to keep time. Various sounds and special effects possibilities are also explained. CD symbols throughout the books indicate what track to play to hear the exercises or to play with a backing track. The books have colorful photographs, clear musical notation, and helpful glossaries and chord directories.

4.11 Bussell, Darcey, with Patricia Linton. **The Young Dancer.** Dorling Kindersley, 1994. 65 pp. ISBN 1-56458-468-2. Nonfiction.

Author Darcey Bussell, a dancer with the Royal Ballet of London, shares her experience in this easy-to-use text, which describes the basic positions and movements of ballet. Bussell includes much detail about the fascinating inner workings of ballet companies, a glossary of ballet terms, and a vivid description of the joys and challenges of being a professional dancer. The text is beautifully supplemented by photographs of both professionals and young dancers in training.

4.12 Camp, Jeffery. **Draw: How to Master the Art.** Dorling Kindersley, 1993. 250 pp. ISBN 1-56456-526-3. Nonfiction.

The premise of Camp's text is that anyone can learn to draw. He provides a complete overview of ways to delight in the medium of drawing, emphasizing copying as a strategy to develop drawing skill. Each double page is designed to present the experience and material for a period of drawing; thus, the reader can flip the text open to "Thin Bodies" or "Cats," read about technique, and be guided in copying the art of masters in creating a personal drawing. The book is filled with illustrations, both color and black-and-white, and is well-indexed by subject, artist, and title. *Draw* will help all its readers see the world in a different way and learn how to express themselves through art.

4.13 Capek, Michael. **Artistic Trickery: The Tradition of Trompe l'Oeil Art.** Lerner, 1995. 64 pp. ISBN 0-8225-2064-8. Nonfiction.

Is it real or did the artist play a visual joke with trompe l'oeil, meaning "fool the eye"? With pictures and text, this book tells about surprising works created with paint, clay, or mosaic tiles. Subjects are usually flat objects such as money, stamps, letter racks, or doors, but even food, animals, and bugs have been painted to deceive viewers. The ceramic work of Marilyn Levine, the art of the Peale family, and the wall murals of Richard Haas are featured. ER

4.14 Carle, Eric. **The Art of Eric Carle.** Philomel Books, 1996. 125 pp. ISBN 0-399-22937-X. Nonfiction.

Here is a beautiful book for those interested in art and alternative art techniques (collage with painted tissue) and for fans of *The Very Hungry Caterpillar* or other children's books by Eric Carle. The first half includes Carle's own comments on his life and his work as well as remarks by others, all enhanced by representative photographs. The last half is entirely made up of full-color illustrations from Carle's many publications, most of which he wrote as well as illustrated, and a gatefold spread showing how he composes his distinctive creations.

4.15 Chapman, Richard. **The Complete Guitarist.** Dorling Kindersley, 1993. 192 pp. ISBN 1-56458-711-8. Nonfiction.

With this book and lots of practice, you can play the guitar! You can also learn about the history of the instrument and study the book's detailed photographs of classical, steel-string, archtop, and solid-body guitars. Pages on playing include exercises, songs, background information, flatpick or finger style techniques, and instructions from simple chording to jazz progressions. A section on sound and amplification is followed by a glossary.

4.16 Chin, Steven A. **The Success of Gordon H. Chong and Associates: An Architecture Success Story.** Walker, 1996. 78 pp. ISBN 0-8027-8307-4. Nonfiction.

This architecture success story is one of the books in the Success series, which profiles companies owned and operated by minorities. Gordon Chong dreamed of becoming an architect when he was a child. He earned a master's degree in architecture, joined a firm to work in the field, and then struck out entirely on his own to establish his own firm. Today he has over fifty associates working for him. ER MC

4.17 Cole, Alison. **The Renaissance.** Dorling Kindersley, 1994. 64 pp. ISBN 1-56458-493-3. Nonfiction.

This book from the Eyewitness Art series focuses on the Italian and Northern European Renaissance from the early fourteenth to the mid-sixteenth centuries: a time of rebirth, intellectual adventure, and artistic experimentation in Western art. Various topics, such as an interest in naturalism, the demand for religious images, the rediscovery of classical themes, and the influence of the Reformation are illustrated with beautiful color reproductions and close study of selected masterpieces. The genius of Leonardo da Vinci and of Michelangelo are highlighted. A chronology, a glossary, and a list of featured works are included.

4.18 Cumming, Robert. **Annotated Art.** Dorling Kindersley, 1995. 104 pp. ISBN 1-56458-848-3. Nonfiction.

Forty-five of the world's greatest paintings from the Gothic period to the Impressionist and then Cubist movements are explored in this beautiful oversized book. Each page includes a large reproduction of the masterpiece; information about the artist; details about the subject, technique, symbolism, use of space and light, and historical style of the piece; and a personal interpretation. In looking at what makes a masterpiece, aspects of virtuosity, innovation, patronage, artistic vision, and the artist's role are discussed. A glossary and index are included.

ALA Quick Picks for Young Adults, 1996

4.19 Feelings, Tom. **The Middle Passage: White Ships / Black Cargo.** Dial Books, 1995. 70 pp. ISBN 0-8037-1804-7. Nonfiction.

In this beautiful book, Feelings tells the story of the Middle Passage through sixty-four narrative paintings. These paintings depict the painful voyage to the Americas made by captured Africans under horrifying conditions. With a historic introduction by Dr. John Henrik Clarke, this book traces the more than four hundred years of the brutal slave trade. MC

ALA Notable Books for Children, 1996
ALA Best Books for Young Adults, 1996
Coretta Scott King Honor Book (Illustrations), 1996

4.20   Feuer, Elizabeth. **Paper Doll.** Aerial / Farrar, Straus and Giroux, 1994. 186 pp. ISBN 0-374-45724-7. Fiction.

This story is about Leslie's talent as a violinist and her struggle with doting parents, not her disability from losing her legs ten years earlier in an automobile accident. To prepare for her Juilliard audition, Leslie is happy to spend hours practicing until she meets funny, confident Jeff, who has cerebral palsy, and who makes her feel that she no longer wants to be treated like her old paper dolls. Leslie's story includes conflicts between her brother and her father and decisions about sexual activity made by her friend Bobbie and ultimately by Leslie herself.

4.21   Garfunkel, Trudy. **On Wings of Joy: The Story of Ballet from the Sixteenth Century to Today.** Little, Brown, 1994. 194 pp. ISBN 0-316-30412-3. Nonfiction.

Ballet, after its beginnings several centuries ago, began to evolve into the professional dance form we recognize today in the court of Louis XIV. This interesting book traces the history and development of ballet, defined as a story and emotions conveyed through music and movement. Readers learn about works such as Tchaikovsky's *Sleeping Beauty* and Stravinsky's shocking *Rite of Spring*. "Entr'actes" tell about great dancers, ballet slippers, and a dancer's day. Half of the book is the fascinating story of twentieth-century ballets and performers.

4.22   Harris, David. **The Art of Calligraphy.** Dorling Kindersley, 1995. 128 pp. ISBN 1-56458-849-1. Nonfiction.

Beginning with a brief history of Western calligraphy, this guide gives suggestions for choosing equipment and learning to pen the various calligraphic scripts. Explanations of Roman, Insular, Nationalistic, Caroline, Gothic, Italian, Humanistic, and Post-Renaissance scripts are accompanied by colorful examples and reproductions of historical manuscripts. The work of influential twentieth-century calligrapher Edward Johnson is featured. The book ends with enlarged diagrams of Late Roman imperial capitals followed by a chart of all the scripts and a glossary.

4.23   Hewetson, Sarah. **Eye Magic: Fantastical Optical Illusions.** Illustrated by Phil Jacobs. Artists and Writers Guild Books / Western, 1994. N.p. ISBN 0-307-17625-8. Nonfiction.

Optical illusions are simply explained in this interactive pop-up book with thirty hands-on illustrations. It will provide entertainment and spark interest, but researchers into visual phenomenon will need other sources for in-depth information. This will prove more useful to art students than to science students. ER

ALA Quick Picks for Young Adults, 1995

4.24   Horton, James. **An Introduction to Drawing.** Dorling Kindersley, 1994. 72 pp. ISBN 1-56458-489-5. Nonfiction.

Written for a beginner, this guide to various drawing techniques, part of the DK Art School series, includes over three hundred photographs. In the beautifully illustrated introduction, drawing is discussed as a vital source of communication and pleasure involving a process of perception, interpretation, and selection. Eight chapters show how learning to make the most of materials is a matter of time, practice, and pleasure. Summaries, or gallery pages of form, composition, landscapes, and figures, show how artists have applied the various techniques explained. A useful glossary is included.

4.25   Howker, Janni. **The Topiary Garden.** Illustrated by Anthony Browne. Orchard Books, 1995. 63 pp. ISBN 0-531-06891-9. Fiction.

This delightful story, with its beautiful illustrations of the topiary garden and pictures of the main character Liz's sketchbook was first published in 1984 in Great Britain. Liz, who hopes to be an artist, is not interested in the motorcycle competition held in the fields of Carlton Hall. With her sketchbook she wanders through the fascinating topiary garden, where she meets the retired gardener, a ninety-one-year-old woman. Her story about long ago, when she pretended to be a boy, helps Liz realize who she is as an artist and young woman. ER

4.26   Jones, K. Maurice. **Say It Loud! The Story of Rap Music.** The Millbrook Press, 1994. 128 pp. ISBN 1-56294-724-9. Nonfiction.

Fans of rap will enjoy this overview of the development, controversies, and spread of this form of music. Many of their favorite artists are named and quoted, and lengthy notes, a glossary, a discography, and a bibliography round out the volume. The historical passages are not all as well documented as are the contemporary issues, but for enthusiasts reading for pleasure this will doubtless not present a problem. ER MC

ALA Best Books for Young Adults, 1995

4.27   Kent, Sarah. **Composition.** Dorling Kindersley, 1995. 64 pp. ISBN 1-56458-612-X. Nonfiction.

Composition, the way an artist arranges the elements of a work, is the key to understanding painting. This book, part of the Eyewitness Art series, includes information about artists' materials, sketches, and equipment, as well as memorable quotations and color reproductions of seventy works of art. Diagrams show various details about the role of geometry, the impact of diagonals, the placement of the vanishing point and the horizon, how a picture can unfold as a story, and the influence of photography. There are also a useful glossary and an index.

4.28   Krull, Kathleen. **Lives of the Artists: Masterpieces, Messes (and What the Neighbors Thought).** Illustrated by Kathryn Hewitt. Harcourt Brace, 1995. 96 pp. ISBN 0-15-200103-4. Nonfiction.

It would be hard to find a more interesting book about artists than this one. Nineteen artists are featured, from Leonardo da Vinci to Andy Warhol. Famous figures such as Vincent van Gogh, plus women artists and those from diverse cultures who should be better known, are included. Each biographical sketch has a full-page color illustration of the artist, an intriguing quotation from or about him or her, and information about his or her life, accomplishments, characteristics, and best-known artworks. Reading this book reminds one that artists are people, too. ER

4.29   Levine, Ellen. **Anna Pavlova: Genius of the Dance.** Scholastic, 1995. 132 pp. ISBN 0-590-44304-6. Nonfiction.

Anna Pavlova, who appeared before more audiences than any other performer of her day, was considered the world's greatest ballerina. Her determination to become a dancer began at age eight when she saw *The Sleeping Beauty.* This book tells her story from her birth in 1881 in St. Petersburg, Russia, through her years at ballet school, and through the difficulties of World War I. It describes her exciting performances all over the world until her death in 1931, and suggests that throughout her career, Pavlova believed she must help people everywhere forget life's sadness, if only for an hour. MC

Notable 1995 Children's Trade Books in the Field of Social Studies

4.30   Lloyd, Elizabeth Jane. **Watercolor Still Life.** Dorling Kindersley, 1994. 72 pp. ISBN 1-56458-490-9. Nonfiction.

This book, part of the DK Art School series, shows the essentials of watercolor still life painting, an art that stems from the sixteenth-century interest in motionless (still) nature (leven). Beautiful illustrations show detailed exercises, professional works in the making, and possibilities with colors, brushstrokes, paint types, and special effects. Gallery pages include works of artists such as Paul Cézanne, the master of modern still life.

4.31   MacDonald, Fiona. **A Sixteenth Century Mosque.** Illustrated by Mark Bergin. Peter Bedrick Books, 1994. 48 pp. ISBN 0-87226-310-X. Nonfiction.

Some of the finest achievements of Islamic art—the great mosques—and the life surrounding them are the subject of this book from the Inside Story series. The engineering feats of the architect Sinan Pasha

(1491–1588), who worked for Sultan Süleyman the Magnificent, ruler of the Ottoman Empire, are explained with drawings and text. Included are a history of the Islamic faith, detailed drawings of the mosque Sinan created for Süleyman in Istanbul, an index, and a glossary. ER MC

4.32   Marsh, Graham, and Barrie Lewis, editors. **The Blues: Album Cover Art.** Chronicle Books, 1996. 111 pp. ISBN 0-8118-1168-9. Nonfiction.

For the blues aficionado, seeing the way the colors and texts of these album covers combine to illustrate the vibrancy of this most American form of music makes this an interesting addition to the library. ER MC

4.33   Morley, Jacqueline. **Shakespeare's Theater.** Illustrated by John James. Peter Bedrick Books, 1994. 48 pp. ISBN 0-87226-309-6. Nonfiction.

This book, appropriate for elementary and middle school students but also of interest to older students and adults, is a very useful tool for understanding Elizabethan theater. The text and many colorful illustrations cover everything from the history of the first permanent theater to costuming to special effects to architecture to aspects of Shakespeare's life as an actor, writer, and businessman. Quotations from the diaries of actors and legal documents of the times lend authenticity to the text, although the book includes no documentation of sources. Part of the Inside Story series. ER

4.34   Mühlberger, Richard. **What Makes a Cassatt a Cassatt?** The Metropolitan Museum of Art / Viking, 1994. 48 pp. ISBN 0-670-85742-4. Nonfiction.

This book, organized in short chapters, contains beautiful photographs of Mary Cassatt's paintings and interesting facts about her life. Born in 1844 in Pennsylvania, but living most of her life in France, Mary was a pioneer among women artists. She had a lifelong interest in capturing human relationships, especially those between mothers and children, in her paintings. Readers will learn about her unique style, in which she combined themes of modern life with what she learned from other artists, including the Impressionists. ER

4.35   O'Donnell, Jim. **The Day John Met Paul: An Hour-by-Hour Account of How the Beatles Began.** Penguin Books, 1996. 179 pp. ISBN 0 14 02.5301 7. Nonfiction.

Based on eight years of research, the author recounts the events of the day in Liverpool when John Lennon met Paul McCartney, July 6, 1957. The two musicians met at a local church celebration. Lennon was seventeen and McCartney was fifteen. It was a day that not only changed the course of rock and roll, but also changed music history forever.

4.36   Opie, Mary-Jane. **Sculpture.** Dorling Kindersley, 1994. 64 pp. ISBN 1-56458-495-X. Nonfiction.

Sculptures in many Western and non-Western forms and materials, both ancient and contemporary, are shown in this book. Mesoamerican, Asian, African, Pacific Northwestern, Egyptian, Greek, Roman, and European works are included. Techniques are illustrated with details of works such as those of Michelangelo. The book ends with a glossary and a map showing where works are displayed.

4.37   Pellowski, Michael Morgan. **The Art of Making Comic Books.** Illustrated by Howard Bender. Lerner, 1995. ISBN 0-8225-2304-3. Nonfiction.

So you want to make comic books? This is the book for you. The development of plots and characters, the writing of scripts and storyboards, layout and approaches to drawing, and the opportunities for employment available to those who have honed these skills are thoroughly discussed and illustrated in this career guide. A brief history of the business of comics, a glossary, and a bibliography make this a valuable source of information. ER

ALA Quick Picks for Young Adults, 1996

4.38   Platt, Richard (written by). **Stephen Biesty's Cross-Sections: Castle.** Illustrated by Stephen Biesty. Dorling Kindersley, 1994. 28 pp. ISBN 1-56458-467-4. Nonfiction.

Richard Platt and Stephen Biesty, through text and illustrations, give a wonderfully detailed and comprehensive look at a fourteenth-century castle. Not only is the structure of the castle described but also its use as a means of defense for its inhabitants. The types of people who resided in a castle are portrayed, from the lord and his lady to the "gong farmer" (one who cleaned the latrines). Diet, wardrobe, and types of medieval entertainment are included. Besides being informative, the book has plenty of lopped-off heads adorning spikes to keep the attention of even the most reluctant teenaged reader. ER

IRA Teacher's Choice Award, 1996
Notable 1994 Children's Trade Books in the Field of Social Studies

4.39   Romei, Francesca. **Leonardo da Vinci: Artist, Inventor and Scientist of the Renaissance.** Illustrated by Sergio and Andrea Ricciardi. Peter Bedrick Books, 1994. 64 pp. ISBN 0-87226-313-4. Nonfiction.

Born in 1452 in Tuscany, Leonardo, the first "modern human," excelled in painting, sculpture, music, mathematics, engineering, and architecture. For him, art, with its ties to mathematics and science, required close study of the subject. This volume, part of the Masters of Art series, offers information about Leonardo's life in italicized sections on illustrated pages featuring city scenes and innovations of the Renaissance. Pages devoted to Leonardo's own art show details of his drawings about hydraulics and flight and of his famous works, such as the *Mona Lisa* and *The Last Supper.* ER

4.40   Salvi, Francesco. **The Impressionists: The Origins of Modern Painting.** Illustrated by L. R. Galante and Andrea Ricciardi. Peter Bedrick Books, 1994. 64 pp. ISBN 0-87226-314-2. Nonfiction.

In France during the second half of the nineteenth century a group of artists preferred to work outdoors, use bright colors, and paint everyday scenes. Called "Impressionists" and led by Claude Monet, these artists, including Paul Cézanne, Camille Pissarro, and, in the United States, Mary Cassatt, changed painting and sculpture forever. With illustrations and reproductions of masterpieces, this lovely book from the Masters of Art series shows the political, social, and artistic influences of the time, tells about individual artists' works and lives, and includes key dates and a guide to museums. ER

4.41   Sanmiguel, David. **Painting the Figure in Pastels.** Illustrated by Vicenç Ballestar. Barron's Educational Series, 1996. 63 pp. ISBN 0-8120-9398-4.

Written to help develop elementary skills in art, this book includes seven easy-to-follow, detailed exercises, such as how to draw a female bust, a reclining nude, or a male figure. Each step is clearly illustrated. The exercises include a list of specific materials needed and hints such as how to blend or refine strokes or make corrections. The book begins with an explanation of pastels, their use and related techniques, and why pastels are particularly effective for painting the figure, especially nudes.

4.42   Say, Allen. **The Ink-Keeper's Apprentice.** Houghton Mifflin, 1994. 149 pp. ISBN 0-395-70562-2. Fiction.

In the foreword to this reissue of a novel first published in 1979, Allen Say names himself as the narrator. Set in Tokyo, this autobiographical novel is about his apprenticeship to the great teacher (sensei) and famous cartoonist, Noro Shinpei. Nicknamed "Kiyoi," Say was thirteen when he courageously approached Sensei, from whom he learned that "to draw is to discover . . . and to be astonished." Kiyoi's adventures include drawing classes with nude models, riots with fellow apprentice Tokika, and strange lessons from his karate teacher. The author is a Caldecott Medal winner for *Grandfather's Journey*. MC WL

4.43   Silverman, Jerry. **Just Listen to This Song I'm Singing: African-American History through Song.** The Millbrook Press, 1996. 95 pp. ISBN 1-56294-673-0. Nonfiction.

This book tells about the experiences of African Americans from the 1860s to the 1960s as reflected in song. As he did in his book *Songs and Stories of the American Revolution*, Silverman introduces each song with an explanation of its significance. Each selection is accompanied by illustrations or photographs, full musical score for voice and keyboard, and recommendations for listening. Beginning with "Michael, Row the Boat Ashore" and ending with "We Shall Overcome," the book includes spirituals, folksongs, ragtime, blues, and jazz, plus a list of resources and an index. MC

4.44   Silverman, Jerry. **Songs and Stories from the American Revolution.** The
            Millbrook Press, 1994. 71 pp. ISBN 1-56294-429-0. Nonfiction.

Each song (printed on cream-colored paper) in this collection is introduced by pictures and a story (printed on white paper) explaining its
connection to the war. Interesting anecdotes illustrate how people felt
as the war progressed from 1775 to 1783. The presentations of the ten
songs include their multiple verses, melodies, and accompaniments for
keyboard or guitar. The stories about the war are chronological, ranging from the drum that called young men to war to the surrender, when
the narrative ballads were sung with feelings of nostalgic pride.

4.45   Smith, Ray. **An Introduction to Perspective.** Dorling Kindersley, 1995.
            72 pp. ISBN 1-56458-856-4. Nonfiction.

How can two-dimensional paintings portray our three-dimensional
world? With a brief history about how artists, beginning in Florence,
Italy, in the fifteenth century, have solved this problem, this beautiful
book with over three hundred photographs is a practical guide for learning the essentials of perspective. Gallery pages with works of masters
are interspersed with illustrated steps to help painters learn about one-
, two-, and three-point perspective, the horizon line, curves and circles,
reflections, and atmosphere perspectives. A glossary and an index are
included.

4.46   Smith, Ray. **Oil Painting Portraits.** Dorling Kindersley, 1994. 72 pp. ISBN
            1-56458-491-7. Nonfiction.

This book for beginners, part of the DK Art School series, shows what
materials and skills are needed to capture a person's likeness in an oil
portrait. Over three hundred photographs accompany step-by-step procedures for painting a self-portrait, a profile, and a double portrait with
dramatic light, and for painting in layers. Pictures and text show how
meaning results from choices about composition, color, pose, clothing,
setting, and tone. Six pairs of gallery pages show works by such masters as Picasso, Rembrandt, van Gogh, and Whistler. A useful glossary
is included.

4.47   Southgate, Martha. **Another Way to Dance.** Delacorte Press, 1996. 179
            pp. ISBN 0-385-32191-0. Fiction.

Stacey and Vicki are the only two African Americans selected to be a
part of a prestigious summer program run by the School of the American Ballet. They support each other during rigorous classes and in their
work. But Vicki in particular is aware that she will have to confront her
own prejudices toward the loud black teenagers she sees in the subway
on her way to school, while recognizing that she too must fight against
the prejudices often found within the highly competitive white world
of ballet. MC

4.48 Spence, Keith. **The Young People's Book of Music.** The Millbrook Press, 1995. 144 pp. ISBN 1-56294-605-6. Nonfiction.

In this lovely book, short chapters with pictures and sidebars tell about the music in our lives, its raw materials, and its many forms and definitions. Topics such as classical, romantic, and contemporary periods, church music, opera, ballet, and popular and folk music are interesting for those with and without a musical background. Anecdotes about musicians are included with historical and current information about orchestras, conductors, and instruments. Useful reference tools are included including a list of one hundred top composers, a glossary of musical terms, and an index.

4.49 Switzer, Ellen. **The Magic of Mozart: Mozart, *The Magic Flute,* and the Salzburg Marionettes.** Photographs by Costas. Atheneum Books for Young Readers, 1995. 90 pp. ISBN 0-689-31851-0. Nonfiction.

This beautiful book has three sections offering different perspectives on Wolfgang Amadeus Mozart's last opera, *The Magic Flute.* The story of Mozart's short life shows the hardships, joys, and accomplishments of this famous musician, who was born in 1756 in Salzburg, Austria. When his fame as a composer spread in Europe, Mozart, a poor musician with a young family to support, received the commission to write *The Magic Flute,* which became the last piece he conducted. The story of his fairy-tale opera is told in the second part of the book with beautiful photographs of the characters as performed by the Salzburg Marionettes. The history of these incredible puppets is told in the final section.

4.50 Trahant, Lenora Begay. **The Success of the Navajo Arts and Crafts Enterprise: A Retail Success Story.** Photographs by Monty Roessel. Walker, 1996. 78 pp. ISBN 0-8027-8336-8. Nonfiction.

The Navajo retail success story is one of the books in the Success series, which profiles companies owned and operated by minorities. Navajo weavers and jewelers have been creating beautiful pieces of art for a long time. Under the guidance of Ronald Smith, general manager of Navajo Arts and Crafts Enterprises, the Navajo artisans are experiencing the success they deserve. ER MC

4.51 Turner, Robyn Montana. **Dorothea Lange.** Little, Brown, 1994. 32 pp. ISBN 0-316-85656-8. Nonfiction.

This picture biography shows the determination of one of the first documentary photographers. Born in New Jersey in 1895, Lange had polio at age seven and was left with a limp. She grew from a child who did not even have a camera to an artist whose works were exhibited at the Museum of Modern Art before she died in 1965. Readers learn about how she combined the art of photography with perspectives on historical events, leaving lasting images of the Depression, migrant workers, and Japanese-American detention camps. Part of the Portraits of Women Artists for Children series. ER

4.52   Vernon, Roland. **Introducing Gershwin.** Silver Burdett Press, 1996. 32 pp. ISBN 0-382-39161-6. Nonfiction.

Born in 1898, the son of Russian Jewish immigrants, George Gershwin was a poor New York street kid who became a pioneer in twentieth-century music. As a pianist in Tin Pan Alley, he learned to mix his musical ideas with others' songs. With "Swanee," Gershwin became a popular songwriter, but he wanted to compose serious music. His remarkable achievements included writing *Rhapsody in Blue* in just ten days, winning a Pulitzer Prize with his brother, and combining his skill as a jazz composer and songwriter in his masterpiece *Porgy and Bess.* This biography includes colorful illustrations, boxed sections with historical information, a time chart, and a glossary. ER

4.53   Vernon, Roland. **Introducing Mozart.** Silver Burdett Press, 1996. 32 pp. ISBN 0-382-39159-4. Nonfiction.

This book traces the life of Wolfgang Amadeus Mozart, who became one of the most exciting composers in Europe by the age of twenty and yet died penniless at thirty-six. Mozart was born in Salzburg, Austria, in 1756, and became a master of every type of music he wrote. As a child star, he even astonished his father by remembering and copying every note of a piece he had heard in Rome. Mozart's incredible accomplishments, his best-known compositions, and his many disappointments are covered in this book, along with colorful illustrations, boxed sections with historical information, a time chart, and a glossary. ER

4.54   Voigt, Cynthia. **Orfe.** Scholastic Inc., 1994. 120 pp. ISBN 0-590-47442-1. Fiction.

This unusual story is a modern version of the Greek myth of Orpheus, but with a female protagonist, Orfe. When Yuri, the man she loves, returns to his use of drugs, Orfe tries to use her extraordinary songs to coax him from his underworld (his murky drug house). Orfe's friend Enny, the story's narrator, contrasts the power of meaningful, expressive songs with the devastation of drug addiction associated with the dark side of the rock music world. ER

Publisher's Weekly Best Book of 1992

4.55   Walker, Lou Ann. **Roy Lichtenstein: The Artist at Work.** Photographs by Michael Abramson. Lodestar / Penguin, 1994. 41 pp. ISBN 0-525-67435-7. Nonfiction.

Pop artist Roy Lichtenstein readily acknowledges that when his paintings first appeared in the 1960s both critics and other artists generally hated them and predicted that he would soon fade from the art scene altogether. Today, however, his work is very much in demand. How he produces his massive pieces, particularly his trademark Benday dots and crisp black diagonal lines, is explained briefly and simply, along with his philosophy behind the commonplace yet industrial-looking subjects he chooses. ER

ALA Quick Picks for Young Adults, 1995

4.56   Welton, Jude. **Looking at Paintings.** Dorling Kindersley, 1994. 64 pp. ISBN 1-56458-494-1. Nonfiction.

Browsing in this book, part of the Eyewitness Art series, is like taking a museum tour. The author invites you to have a dialogue with painting and explore the visual language of artists. Contributing to the dialogue are your expectations and imaginations along with the elements chosen by the painter. Each of twenty-eight topics (such as color, tempera, subject matter, or illusion and reality) is accompanied by vivid color photographs, clear illustrations of extracted details, and informative text. A glossary and a list of symbols are included.

4.57   Wilson, Elizabeth B. **Bibles and Bestiaries: A Guide to Illuminated Manuscripts.** The Pierpont Morgan Library / Farrar, Straus and Giroux, 1994. 65 pp. ISBN 0-374-30685-0. Nonfiction.

Manuscript: from the Latin "manus," meaning hand, and "cribere," meaning to write. *Illuminated:* from the Latin "lumen," meaning light. An illuminated manuscript of the Middle Ages was not only a source of information but was a work of art in its own right, its text copied by hand, its illustrations embellished with real gold and silver. In this well-documented, lavish text, Wilson introduces young adults to this important and fascinating part of medieval culture.

School Library Journal Best Books, 1995

4.58   Wolf, Sylvia. **Focus: Five Women Photographers.** Albert Whitman, 1994. 64 pp. ISBN 0-8075-2531-6. Nonfiction.

The five women covered in this book—Julia Margaret Cameron, Margaret Bourke-White, Flor Garduño, Sandy Skoglund, and Lorna Simpson—span the history of photography from its early days to the present, from photojournalism to portraiture to sheer zaniness. The biographies are brief and simple but informative about styles of both life and art. The accompanying representative photos are well-explained and intriguing. This would serve both browsers and researchers.

ALA Best Books for Young Adults, 1995
ALA Notable Books for Children, 1995
Booklist Editor's Choice, 1995

4.59   Wright, Michael. **An Introduction to Mixed Media.** Dorling Kindersley, 1995. 72 pp. ISBN 0-7894-0000-6. Nonfiction.

This practical guide from the DK Art School series offers over three hundred photographs and exercises to teach the essentials of working in mixed media, including choosing a support surface and drawing and painting materials. Techniques illustrated include charcoal with black ink or pastels, line and color, multilayered compositions, oil and soft pastels, unusual materials, resist techniques, and handmade paper. The works of masters such as Edgar Degas are featured on gallery pages and a useful glossary and an index are included.

Titles Annotated in Other Chapters Related to The Arts: Art, Architecture, Music, Dance, Photography

Begay, Shonto. *Navajo: Visions and Voices across the Mesa*. Poetry.

Bernotas, Bob. *Branford Marsalis*. Autobiography.

Bingley, Margaret. *A Dramatic Death*. Mysteries.

Brandenburg, Jim. *Sand and Fog: Adventures in Southern Africa*. History.

Camp, Jeffery. *Paint*. Recreation.

Ellis, Carol. *The Stalker*. Horror.

Garfunkel, Trudy. *Letter to the World: The Life and Dances of Martha Graham*. Autobiography.

Goodman, Joan Elizabeth. *Songs from Home*. Family.

Gravett, Christopher. *Castle*. History.

Hartnett, Sonya. *Wilful Blue*. Death.

Haskins, Jim. *The Harlem Renaissance*. History.

InsectAsides. Poetry.

Jones, Hettie. *Big Star Fallin' Mama: Five Women in Black Music*. Autobiography.

Kaye, Marilyn. *Dream Lover*. Romance.

Keillor, Garrison, and Jenny Lind Nilsson. *The Sandy Bottom Orchestra*. Family.

Kreischer, Elsie Karr. *María Montoya Martínez*. Autobiography.

Laughlin, Robin Kittrell. *Backyard Bugs*. Science.

Lawlor, Laurie. *Shadow Catcher: The Life and Work of Edward S. Curtis*. Autobiography.

Leroux, Gaston. *The Phantom of the Opera*. Classics.

Lewis-Ferguson, Julinda. *Alvin Ailey, Jr.: A Life in Dance*. Autobiography.

Llorente, Pilar Molina. *The Apprentice*. Historical Fiction.

Malone, Mary. *Maya Lin: Architect and Artist*. Autobiography.

Marshall, Mary Ann. *Now Hiring: Music*. College.

McGuigan, Mary Ann. *Cloud Dancer*. Family.

Menzel, Peter. *Material World: A Global Family Portrait*. Family.

Monceaux, Morgan. *Jazz: My Music, My People*. Autobiography.

Okimoto, Jean Davies. *Talent Night*. Choices.

Plain, Nancy. *Mary Cassatt: An Artist's Life*. Autobiography.

Robinson, Spider, and Jeanne Robinson. *Starmind*. Science Fiction.

Rosenberg, Liz. *Heart and Soul*. Friendships.

Rylant, Cynthia. *Something Permanent*. Poetry.

Sleator, William. *The Night the Heads Came*. Science Fiction.

Steiner, Barbara. The Dark Chronicles series. Horror.

Thesman, Jean. *Cattail Moon*. Family.

Thomas, Joyce Carol. *When the Nightingale Sings*. Choices.

Thorton, Yvonne S. *The Ditchdigger's Daughters: A Black Family's Astonishing Success Story*. Autobiography.

Turk, Ruth. *Lillian Hellman*. Autobiography.

White, Ruth. *Weeping Willow*. Family.

Willey, Margaret. *Facing the Music*. Family.

Yates, Janelle. *Woody Guthrie: American Balladeer*. Autobiography.

5 Autobiography, Biography, and Collective Biography

"Biography is the only true history."
Thomas Carlyle

"I would sooner fail than not be among the greatest."
John Keats

(Note: Autobiographies and biographies of sports figures may be found in the **Sports and Sports Figures** chapter.)

5.1   Alexander, Sally Hobart. **Taking Hold: My Journey into Blindness.** Macmillan, 1994. 165 pp. ISBN 0-02-700402-3. Nonfiction.

In this autobiography, Sally Hobart Alexander describes her loss of vision as a twenty-four-year old school teacher and her subsequent struggle to adapt to the world of the blind. Alexander includes poignant descriptions of how her relationships with her family and friends, including her fiancé, changed during this difficult period of her life.

5.2   Allen, Paula Gunn, and Patricia Clark Smith. **As Long as the Rivers Flow: The Stories of Nine Native Americans.** Scholastic Press, 1996. 328 pp. ISBN 0-590-47869-9. Nonfiction.

Jim Thorpe, Will Rogers, Louise Erdrich: the stories of these well-known Native Americans are presented in this collection of dramatic essays. But the stories of less frequently mentioned individuals important in Native American life, such as Wilmer Mankiller, first woman elected Principal Chief of the Cherokee Nation, are also told in this celebration of the contributions Native Americans have made to all aspects of American society. MC

5.3   Allison, Dorothy. **Two or Three Things I Know for Sure.** Plume, 1996. 94 pp. ISBN 0-452-27340-4. Nonfiction.

Dorothy Allison's reflections on her sometimes difficult life are presented here with wit and wisdom. From being raped at age five to acknowledging her lesbian sexuality, Allison describes her experiences as a way to depict the challenges all women face in coming to terms with life's realities. She says, "Two or three things I know for sure, and one of them is how long it takes to learn to love yourself, how long it took me, and how much love I need now."

National Book Award Finalist, 1995

5.4   Anderson, Margaret J. **Charles Darwin: Naturalist.** Enslow, 1994. 118 pp. ISBN 0-89490-476-0. Nonfiction.

Charles Darwin is best known as the author of *On the Origin of Species*. Although he originally set out to follow in his father's footsteps and become a doctor, Charles's greatest interest was in nature and his father soon realized that he would never become a doctor. Anderson's biography traces Charles's life from the time he was a mischievous child, through his five years as a naturalist on the *Beagle*, to his controversial yet significant career as an evolutionist.

5.5   Andryszewski, Tricia. **The Amazing Life of Moe Berg: Catcher, Scholar, Spy.** The Millbrook Press, 1996. 127 pp. ISBN 1-56294-610-2. Nonfiction.

Moe Berg loved major league baseball, languages, travel, and the United States. He was drafted by the major leagues as a catcher in the 1920s and played baseball until his country enlisted his help as a spy in World War II. Athletic, friendly, and intelligent, Moe Berg was an asset to sports and his country.

5.6   Archer, Jules. **A House Divided: The Lives of Ulysses S. Grant and Robert E. Lee.** Scholastic, 1995. 184 pp. ISBN 0-590-48325-0. Nonfiction.

This biography of the two Civil War giants has extraordinary scope for such a short book. The author manages to profile their personalities as much as their achievements. Liberally sprinkling the text with quotations from diaries and letters written during their lifetimes, the author creates two unbiased and compassionate portraits. Grant and Lee come across as complex and feeling men with weaknesses as well as strengths, making them very human.

5.7   Baldwin, Joyce. **DNA Pioneer: James Watson and the Double Helix.** Walker, 1994. 136 pp. ISBN 0-8027-8297-3. Nonfiction.

James Watson was always seeking answers, even as a youngster. So it was not surprising that upon graduation from college he would turn to biology and attempt to learn the mystery of DNA, the molecule that carries the genetic instructions for building an organism. Watson and his fellow researchers Francis Crick and Maurice Wilkins won the 1962 Nobel Prize for their discovery. In addition to this accomplishment, Watson wrote *The Double Helix*, a bestselling book about the search for the structure of DNA, and helped create the genre of popular science writing. MC

5.8   Barr, Roger. **The Importance of Malcolm X.** Lucent Books, 1994. 112 pp. ISBN 1-56006-044-1. Nonfiction.

In addition to presenting the life of African American activist Malcolm X, this volume places his life in historical context. The author discusses why Malcolm X continues to be an important figure in American history many years after his death and how today's youth culture has embraced his image and message. Part of The Importance of . . . biography series. MC

5.9   Bawden, Nina. **In My Own Time: Almost an Autobiography.** Clarion Books, 1994. 175 pp. ISBN 0-395-74429-6. Nonfiction.

Nina Bawden gives a gripping account of her life in England as a teenager during World War II, her problems with raising a schizophrenic son, and her ability to use the people and events in her life as subjects for her novels. A bestselling author of adult novels and children's books, Bawden pulls the reader into her life story with truthful insights and sensitivity that offer inspiration and help to young writers.

5.10   Beals, Melba Pattillo. **Warriors Don't Cry: A Searing Memoir of the Battle to Integrate Little Rock's Central High.** Pocket Books, 1994. 312 pp. ISBN 0-671-86638-9. Nonfiction.

As one of the "Little Rock Nine," Melba Pattillo Beals endured racial taunts, threats, and violence during the year she and her cohorts spent at Central High School in Little Rock, Arkansas. In this compelling story she reveals the personal and spiritual resources that gave her the strength to withstand that difficult time. MC

Notable 1995 Children's Trade Books in the Field of Social Studies

5.11   Bernier-Grand, Carmen T. **Poet and Politician of Puerto Rico: Don Luis Muñoz Marín.** Orchard Books, 1995. 118 pp. ISBN 0-531-06887-0. Nonfiction.

In 1898, José Luis Alberto Muñoz Marín was born in San Juan, Puerto Rico, the son of Luis Muñoz Rivera, a journalist and activist. Shortly thereafter, Spain ceded Puerto Rico to the United States and the elder Muñoz worked to give Puerto Rico a voice in its own government. Despite his father's hopes, José Luis was not interested in becoming a lawyer. Upon his father's death, he instead began a lifetime of pursuing his two passions—poetry and politics—becoming the first governor of the Commonwealth of Puerto Rico. ER MC

5.12   Bernotas, Bob. **Branford Marsalis: Jazz Musician.** Enslow, 1994. 112 pp. ISBN 0-89490-495-7. Nonfiction.

Branford Marsalis is the oldest of six brothers born to a musical family in New Orleans, the birthplace of jazz. Growing up in his household, it would have been difficult, if not impossible, to avoid music as an important part of his life. Marsalis did explore other options, but eventually turned to music as his career goal. Author Bernotas presents a spirited portrait of a multifaceted musician who is determined to follow his own mind even when his ideas differ from those of his jazz purist younger brother, Wynton. MC

5.13   Blue, Rose, and Corinne J. Naden. **People of Peace.** The Millbrook Press, 1994. 76 pp. ISBN 1-56294-409-6. Nonfiction.

This slim volume will be beneficial to students and faculty who need concise information, clear photographs, and / or a glossary of activists for peace around the world. The inclusion of Desmond Tutu of South Africa, Oscar Arias Sánchez of Costa Rica, and Williams and Maguire from Northern Ireland along with more well-known historical figures such as M. K. Gandhi, Dag Hammarskjöld, Andrew Carnegie, and Jane Addams enables students at a variety of study levels to become better acquainted with the issues and life forces which shaped these contributors to world improvement. ER MC

5.14   Blue, Rose, and Corinne J. Naden. **The White House Kids.** The Millbrook Press, 1995. 96 pp. ISBN 1-56294-447-9. Nonfiction.

Visit the living quarters of 1600 Pennsylvania Avenue and see it through the eyes of the "White House kids" in this easy-to-read collective biography. The stories of presidents' children and grandchildren are recreated through historical records, portraits, photographs, and personal interviews. This chronicle of the changing roles and lives of the White House children lends itself to both pleasure reading and research. ER

5.15   Bredeson, Carmen. **Henry Cisneros: Building a Better America.** Enslow, 1995. 128 pp. ISBN 0-89490-546-5. Nonfiction.

This volume, part of the People to Know series, is a profile of Henry Cisneros, former secretary of housing and urban development. Cisneros was educated at Texas A & M, George Washington, and Harvard universities. His work experience with the Model Cities Program, the National League of Cities, and the San Antonio City Council, as well as his service as mayor of San Antonio, Texas, prepared him for the task. The book does an excellent job of describing how, in his efforts to build a better America and renovate public housing, Cisneros developed the Creating Windows of Opportunity program. ER MC

5.16   Bredeson, Carmen. **Ross Perot: Billionaire Politician.** Enslow, 1995. 118 pp. ISBN 0-89490-545-7. Nonfiction.

Ross Perot seems to have been destined for success. His first job—selling newspaper subscriptions—his experience as an Eagle Scout, and his graduation from the U.S. Naval Academy were only the beginning. He became the top salesman for IBM and later founded Electronic Data Systems, which ultimately made him a billionaire. Perot is known to millions of Americans because of his 1992 presidential campaign. However, Bredeson reveals a man who is much more than a politician; he is a war hero, an entrepreneur, and a dedicated family man. Part of the People to Know series.

5.17   Bredeson, Carmen. **Ruth Bader Ginsburg: Supreme Court Justice.** Enslow, 1995. 128 pp. ISBN 0-89490-621-6. Nonfiction.

Ruth Bader Ginsburg, the second woman appointed to the United States Supreme Court, is an advocate of women's rights. This biography, part of the People to Know series, traces her life from birth to her current status as a justice of the Supreme Court. Ginsburg overcame discrimination in law school and the job market because of her gender. She argued for gender equality before the Supreme Court, became a professor at Rutgers University, and was granted tenure. This account provides a wonderful role model for young women and is supplemented with black-and-white photographs, an index, and a chronology.

5.18   Brown, Kevin. **Malcolm X: His Life and Legacy.** The Millbrook Press, 1995. 112 pp. ISBN 1-56294-500-9. Nonfiction.

Based on the bestselling book by Alex Haley, Brown gives a concise look at the life and times of Malcolm X. His early life, his conversion to Islam, and his tragic and suspicious death are detailed with quotations from personal interviews and insightful photographs. His deep religious beliefs and his dedication to the Civil Rights Movement of the 1960s make Malcolm X a hero for all who value integrity, commitment, and equality. MC

5.19   Bryant, Jennifer Fisher. **Lucretia Mott: A Guiding Light.** William B. Eerdmans, 1996. 175 pp. ISBN 0-8028-5098-7. Nonfiction.

Written in a narrative style, this book from the Women of Spirit series provides insight into the development of a pioneer for women's rights. Mott's affiliation with the Society of Friends (Quakers) and her family's values combined to form her lifelong belief in gender equity, and as early as 1845 she was speaking publicly for women's rights. She spoke out against slavery and poverty as well, and supported the causes she believed in despite outrage and opposition. Along with other women, such as Elizabeth Cady Stanton, she was a leader in the effort to give women economic, social, political, and educational opportunities equal to those enjoyed by men.

5.20   Cart, Michael. **Presenting Robert Lipsyte.** Twayne, 1995. 165 pp. ISBN 0-8057-4151-8. Nonfiction.

Lipsyte is a major figure in the world of young adult literature; his novel *The Contender*, written in 1967, is considered a groundbreaking book in the field. In recent years, he has turned to the writing of biographies of such diverse individuals as Jim Thorpe and Arnold Schwarzenegger. Michael Cart tells how Lipsyte became first a journalist writing sports stories on deadline for the *New York Times*, an author of books for young adults, a commentator for National Public Radio, a biographer, and a sports essayist for various networks. The well-chosen quotations from Lipsyte's work, the inclusion of an index and a chronology, and the care with which Cart deals with his subject make this biography a pleasure to read and a valuable reference tool.

5.21   Cartland, Barbara. **We Danced All Night.** Robson Books, 1994. 311 pp. ISBN 0-86051-925-2. Nonfiction.

We Danced All Night recreates a time when fashion, theater, and, of course, dancing were all-important. Cartland weaves her autobiography around a social history of the 1920s in Great Britain, and she provides in the process a "who's who" of royalty, prime ministers, authors, and actors. An index and pictures are included.

5.22   Chong, Denise. **The Concubine's Children.** Viking, 1995. 266 pp. ISBN 0-670-82961-7. Nonfiction.

The Concubine's Children provides a peephole into the lives of Chinese immigrants to Canada. A granddaughter of the family who found herself drawn to her past, Chong chronicles her family's triumphs and sorrows. Stretching over three generations, this autobiography allows the outsider to be enveloped in Chinese culture as well as to see its evolution within the modern-day world. MC

5.23   Chu, Daniel, and Bill Shaw. **Going Home to Nicodemus: The Story of an African American Frontier Town and the Pioneers Who Settled It.** Julian Messner / Silver Burdett Press, 1994. 96 pp. ISBN 0-671-88723-8. Nonfiction.

This is an interesting introduction to a period of American history about which not much has been written: the settling of the American West by African Americans. Chu and Shaw trace the history of Nicodemus, Kansas, from its founding twelve years after the Civil War to its status as a National Historic Landmark. Quotations from residents and original photographs are included to bring forth the community spirit of this town. The book also includes an index and chronology. MC

5.24   Cohen, Barbara. **David.** Clarion Books, 1995. 108 pp. ISBN 0-395-58702-6. Nonfiction.

This dramatic retelling of the story of King David of Israel, founder of Jerusalem, is based primarily on the Biblical books of Samuel but presented in modern language as interpreted by the author. David is portrayed as a man destined for and achieving greatness in spite of flaws that characterize the human condition. The legend of David, musician, poet, politician, soldier, king, father, and romantic, is documented in good storytelling fashion that traces the significant events of his life. ER MC

Notable 1995 Children's Trade Books in the Field of Social Studies

5.25   Cohen, Daniel. **Joseph McCarthy: The Misuse of Political Power.** The Millbrook Press, 1996. 128 pp. ISBN 1-56294-917-9. Nonfiction.

Just how did an undistinguished junior senator whose brief career seemed about to be voted to an end suddenly engineer a meteoric rise to a position as one of the most powerful and feared men of his time? Why were so many people so willing to believe him that lives were ruined because of innuendo? Although many questions remain unanswered, the damage done by hatred, even by small people, should be taken seriously, as Cohen's biography of McCarthy warns us.

5.26   Cole, Michael D. **John F. Kennedy: President of the New Frontier.** Enslow, 1996. 128 pp. ISBN 0-89490-693-3. Nonfiction.

John F. Kennedy overcame a sickly childhood and lackluster years as a student to embark on a highly successful political career, culminating in his election as the first Roman Catholic president of the United States. The author explores the influence of President Kennedy's father and the life-threatening illnesses Kennedy battled, as well as the influence his personal charisma had on his successes and achievements. Part of the People to Know series. ER

5.27   Collective Biographies series. Enslow, 1996. Nonfiction.
        Camp, Carole Ann. **American Astronomers: Searchers and Wonderers.** ISBN 0-89490-631-3.
        Jeffrey, Laura S. **American Inventors of the Twentieth Century.** ISBN 0-89490-632-1.
        Schraff, Anne. **American Heroes of Exploration and Flight.** ISBN 0-89490-619-4.
        Sheafer, Silvia Anne. **Women in America's Wars.** ISBN 0-89490-553-8.

Space, war, the heavens: this series tells of the achievements of American scientists, adventurers, and heroes. Beginning with a preface that gives an overview of the title topic, each book gives biographical detail about ten outstanding men and/or women in that field. Historically complete, the books begin with the lives and achievements of the pioneers in each field and continue to the present with the lives and accomplishments of today's newsmakers, scientists, and adventurers.

5.28   Cox, Clinton. **Mark Twain: America's Humorist, Dreamer, Prophet.** Scholastic, 1995. 224 pp. ISBN 0-590-45642-3. Nonfiction.

This biography follows Twain from birth to death, recounting his accomplishments, disappointments, and dreams. Throughout the biography, the reader sees the man behind the literature in both his public and his private life.

Notable 1995 Children's Trade Books in the Field of Social Studies

5.29   Davidson, Sue. **A Heart in Politics: Jeannette Rankin and Patsy T. Mink.** Seal Press, 1994. 183 pp. ISBN 1-878067-53-2. Nonfiction.

Two women who made a mark on the history of the U.S. Congress are Jeannette Rankin and Patsy T. Mink. Rankin, of Montana, was the first woman to run for Congress, and was elected to Congress twice, once in 1916 (before women's suffrage passed nationally) and again in 1940. Rankin worked hard for many issues but it was for being the only member of Congress to vote against the entry of the United States into World War II that she is best known. Patsy Mink of Hawaii was the first woman of color and the first Japanese American woman to be elected to Congress. She focused her efforts on social issues and on better opportunities for women in all aspects of American life. MC

5.30   Denenberg, Barry. **An American Hero: The True Story of Charles A. Lindbergh.** Scholastic, 1996. 255 pp. ISBN 0-590-46923-1.

Charles A. Lindbergh's historical flight is in this volume set within the context of his life experience and world events vividly enough to kindle awe and excitement even in those who hardly take note any longer of space shuttle lift-offs. Lindbergh's childhood, his captivation by dreams of flight during aviation's infancy, his serious study of its science, and his personal drive to fly across the Atlantic are well told and illustrated by black-and-white photographs. His place as grieving father in the "trial of the century" is also explored, as is his fall as a popular icon during World War II and his ultimate role as "ambassador of flight" prior to his death in 1974. This is an excellent selection for both research and pleasure reading.

5.31   Deschamps, Hélène. **Spyglass: An Autobiography.** Edited by Karyn Monget. Henry Holt, 1995. 308 pp. ISBN 0-8050-3536-2. Nonfiction.

What would you do if you were seventeen years old and your beloved country was invaded by an enemy force? Hélène Deschamps answered that question in 1940, when Germany invaded France, by joining the French Resistance and providing vital information to the Allies about German troop movements and personnel. She is captured and beaten, and devastated by her sister's death at German hands, but her autobiography shows that she remains true to her belief in her country and in an Allied victory. MC WL

5.32   Feinberg, Barbara Silberdick. **John Marshall: The Great Chief Justice.** Enslow, 1995. 112 pp. ISBN 0-89490-559-7. Nonfiction.

John Marshall served on the U.S. Supreme Court for thirty-four years, beginning in 1801. Marshall's years on the court during its infancy shaped that institution as an important entity of government. Marshall believed in a strong federal government and influenced cases that determined precedents that affect the court today. In this volume from the Justices of the Supreme Court series, Feinberg also discusses Marshall the man, a deeply devoted husband and father and an opponent of slavery at a time when that stance was not popular. ER

5.33   Ferber, Elizabeth. **Yasir Arafat: A Life of War and Peace.** The Millbrook Press, 1995. 134 pp. ISBN 1-56294-585-8. Nonfiction.

A good reference book for those studying Arafat and his leadership of the Palestinian Liberation Organization, this biography covers Arafat's life and describes his reasons for his early violent actions. The book also covers Arafat's more recent attempts at compromise and diplomacy. MC

5.34   Fleming, Robert. **The Success of Caroline Jones Advertising, Inc.: An Advertising Success Story.** Photographs by Michael Harris. Walker, 1996. 76 pp. ISBN 0-8027-8354-6. Nonfiction.

This advertising success story is one of the books in the Success series, which profiles companies owned and operated by minorities. As an African American woman, Caroline Jones is a role model for other young women trying to break into the male-dominated world of advertising. Caroline began as a secretary at an advertising agency and now owns her own successful ad company. ER MC

5.35   García, John. **The Success of *Hispanic* Magazine: A Publishing Success Story.** Photographs by Ricardo Vargas. Walker, 1996. 84 pp. ISBN 0-8027-8309-0. Nonfiction.

In this book, part of the Success series, which focuses on minorities who successfully own and operate businesses, we learn how *Hispanic* magazine covers music, fashion, sports, and travel from the Hispanic viewpoint. The founder of the magazine, Alfredo Estrada, feels that the Latino community needs a positive portrayal of itself, and that is exactly what the magazine accomplishes through the dedication of its staff. ER MC

5.36   Garfunkel, Trudy. **Letter to the World: The Life and Dances of Martha Graham.** Little, Brown, 1995. 87 pp. ISBN 0-316-30413-1. Nonfiction.

Martha Graham was a groundbreaker who took risks and challenged audiences to view dance in a new way. She was born to a Pennsylvania farm family in 1894 and always dreamed of being a performer. She eventually founded her own innovative dance company. Through her own strength and creativity, she performed until she was seventy-four years old and choreographed until she was ninety-six. Garfunkel describes the life and career of this dancer who challenged audiences to be honest and to be better people.

5.37   Goldenstern, Joyce. **Albert Einstein: Physicist and Genius.** Enslow, 1995. 128 pp. ISBN 0-89490-480-9. Nonfiction.

This biography of Albert Einstein, part of the Great Minds of Science series, focuses on Einstein's contribution to the world of physics. It also explores the question "What is genius?" and discusses Einstein in that context. The book includes activities that students can do that illustrate some of Einstein's work. ER

5.38   Gonzales, Doreen. **Alex Haley: Author of *Roots*.** Enslow, 1994. 128 pp. ISBN 0-89490-573-2. Nonfiction.

Alex Haley influenced the entire nation with his two major works, *The Autobiography of Malcolm X* and *Roots*. Malcolm X was portrayed in a sympathetic and understanding light for the first time, and *Roots* awakened the sense of family history in African Americans and challenged the way slavery was viewed. This book, part of the People to Know series, relates the life of Haley, who lived through segregation and poverty and became one of the most influential and celebrated writers and speakers of our times. Black-and-white photographs are included. ER MC

5.39   Gormley, Beatrice. **Maria Mitchell: The Soul of an Astronomer.** William B. Eerdmans, 1995. 123 pp. ISBN 0-8028-5116-9. Nonfiction.

Maria Mitchell, a self-taught astronomer who discovered Comet Mitchell, was the first woman inducted into the American Academy of Arts and Sciences. Born in 1818 in Nantucket, Massachusetts, the third child in a large Quaker family, she was greatly influenced by her father, who loved to observe the heavens and who taught her mathematics. Together they gathered information for whaling captains. Maria became a professor at Vassar College, where she introduced young women to the discipline and poetry of astronomy and to the women's movement. This biography shows the strength and independence of a remarkable woman.

5.40   Green, Henry. **Pack My Bag: A Self-Portrait.** Introduction by Sebastian Yorke. Penguin Books, 1994. 242 pp. ISBN 0 14 01.8793 6. Nonfiction.

Henry Green grew up in London under the care of his wealthy and prestigious family. He received the best classical education, first in boarding schools, then at Eton and at Oxford University, and decided to record his childhood experiences when faced with the possibility of death in World War II. Although he does not remember school as the best time of his life, his memories of adolescence return to him again and again. Green's autobiography explores the universal nature of young boys, from his fear of storms as a child to his yearning for freedom as a young adult.

5.41   Harris, Laurie Lanzen, editor. **Biography Today: Profiles of People of Interest to Young Readers.** Omnigraphics, 1995. 340 pp. ISBN 0-7808-0022-2. Nonfiction.

Do you want to know about the winner of the 1994 National Spelling Bee? How about the life of Steven Spielberg, Connie Chung, Jonas Salk, or Ed Bradley? These people and more than forty others are featured in this fact-filled book of current people of interest. You can learn new things about favorite actors, singers, athletes, and politicians, making this an interesting book to browse. ER

5.42   Haskins, Jim. **Black Eagles: African Americans in Aviation.** Scholastic, 1995. 178 pp. ISBN 0-590-45912-0. Nonfiction.

Haskins provides a series of short biographies of African American aviators, male and female, from the twenties to the Space Age. Bessie Coleman was the first African American female to receive her pilot's license. She received it in France in 1921 because lack of money and discrimination kept her from reaching that goal in the U.S. Against similar odds, a long line of aviators found triumphs, and yet many African American pilots never achieved status in the civilian sector. Only after black pilots brought a lawsuit to fight racial discrimination did the commercial airlines industry hire them as pilots. The book concludes on a more hopeful note by describing the achievements of African American astronauts. The book is supplemented by helpful photographs, a chronological chart, a bibliography, and an index. MC

Notable 1995 Children's Trade Books in the Field of Social Studies

5.43   Herda, D. J. Justices of the Supreme Court series. Enslow, 1995. Nonfiction. ER

Earl Warren: Chief Justice for Social Change. 104 pp. ISBN 0-89490-556-2.

Sandra Day O'Connor: Independent Thinker. 104 pp. ISBN 0-89490-558-9.

Thurgood Marshall: Civil Rights Champion. 112 pp. ISBN 0-89490-557-0. MC

Justices of the Supreme Court is a series that highlights Earl Warren, chief justice from 1953 to 1969; Sandra Day O'Connor, the first woman ever appointed to the Supreme Court; and Thurgood Marshall, the first African American justice. These are ideal books for school reports and research on the Supreme Court, civil rights, women's rights as influenced by law, and Americans who have had a great impact on the social conditions of the United States. A chronology, a bibliography, a glossary, and suggestions for further reading are included in each book.

Thurgood Marshall: Notable 1995 Children's Trade Books in the Field of Social Studies

5.44   Heyes, Eileen. **Adolf Hitler.** The Millbrook Press, 1994. 160 pp. ISBN 1-56294-343-X. Nonfiction.

The evils created by Adolf Hitler are a well-known part of history. This book explores how he rose to power as well as the conditions in his country and in the world that allowed him to conduct mass murder virtually unchecked for years.

5.45   Hockenberry, John. **Moving Violations: War Zones, Wheelchairs, and Declarations of Independence.** Hyperion, 1995. 371 pp. ISBN 0-7868-6078-2. Nonfiction.

John Hockenberry was a nineteen-year-old college student when an auto accident turned him into a paraplegic. Despite this life-changing event, Hockenberry was determined to overcome all obstacles. He kept pushing until he became a foreign correspondent for National Public Radio in places that challenged all journalists—the Middle East, Somalia, Iraq—despite having to do his work in a wheelchair. MC

School Library Journal Best Books for Young Adults, 1996

5.46 Hoig, Stan. **Sequoyah: The Cherokee Genius.** Oklahoma Historical Society, 1995. 142 pp. ISBN 0-941498-68-9. Nonfiction.

Hoig has written a very solid, well-researched biography of Sequoyah, whose invention of a Cherokee alphabet helped to preserve Cherokee culture. The appendices, endnotes, and black-and-white illustrations will make this volume useful to serious students and faculty with an interest in Sequoyah, the Cherokees, and written language development. The appendices address personal issues such as date of birth; a lineage of Sequoyah's family and descendants, developed through oral histories; and a chronological reconstruction of events. MC

5.47 Hopkins, Lee Bennett. **Pauses: Autobiographical Reflections of 101 Creators of Children's Books.** HarperCollins, 1995. 233 pp. ISBN 0-06-024748-7. Nonfiction.

Have you ever wondered where your favorite authors live or why they decided to write children's books? This collection provides a rare look at the lives, motivations, and dreams of 101 authors of children's books. Read about Scott O'Dell (*Sing Down the Moon, Island of the Blue Dolphin*), who lived in a house on stilts. Find out why *Cat in the Hat* was the biggest pain for Dr. Seuss. Readers who are thinking about writing for children, want to learn more about their favorite authors, or just want to read about creative, interesting people will be intrigued by this fascinating collection of reflections and remembrances.

5.48 Hughes, Libby. **Colin Powell: A Man of Quality.** Dillon Press, 1996. 171 pp. ISBN 0-382-39260-4. Nonfiction.

Guided by his beliefs in the value of hard work, the importance of family, and the need for honor, Colin Powell rose through the ranks of the U.S. Army to the position of chairman of the Joint Chiefs of Staff. From his modest beginnings as a child of middle-class immigrants from Jamaica, Colin Powell applied himself to every task he faced. His life's story, recounted in this People in Focus Book, is proof that hard work and perseverance are the keys to a successful life. MC

5.49 Ito, Tom. **The Importance of John Steinbeck.** Lucent Books, 1994. 112 pp. ISBN 1-56006-049-2. Nonfiction.

John Steinbeck decided to become a writer when he was a freshman in high school. After a disappointing period as a student at Stanford University, Steinbeck pursued his dream by moving to New York and accepting a job as a newspaper reporter. This proved to be another unsuccessful venture, so Steinbeck returned to his home in California.

Steinbeck's love and affinity for the land and people of his home state served as a source of inspiration, and he went on to write successful novels and stories that depicted the hopes and failures of American working people. In 1962, Steinbeck was awarded the Nobel Prize for literature. Today, his works are an integral part of American literature. Part of The Importance of . . . biography series.

5.50   Jones, Hettie. **Big Star Fallin' Mama: Five Women in Black Music.** Viking, 1995. 129 pp. ISBN 0-670-85621-5. Nonfiction.

Music is an essential part of African American culture. From this culture comes a legacy of music including blues, jazz, and spirituals. Hettie Jones traces the history of this music by sharing the lives of five great black women: Ma Rainey, Bessie Smith, Mahalia Jackson, Billie Holiday, and Aretha Franklin. The struggles and triumphs of these women despite their experiences of oppression are truly inspirational. ER MC

5.51   Karr, Mary. **The Liars' Club: A Memoir.** Penguin Books, 1996. 320 pp. ISBN 0 14 01.7983 6. Nonfiction.

A seven-times-married mother, a hard-drinking father, and life in a hardscrabble refinery town in East Texas are the cornerstones of Mary Karr's memoir. Tinged with raw-edged humor, she realistically recounts the turbulent events of her childhood from the lingering illness of her grandmother to being raped when she was eight. Energetic and disturbing, Karr's narrative shows a "terrific family of liars and drunks . . . redeemed by a slow unearthing of truth." Mature reading level and subject matter.

5.52   Katz, Jane, editor. **Messengers of the Wind: Native American Women Tell Their Life Stories.** Ballantine Books, 1995. 317 pp. ISBN 0-345-39060-1. Nonfiction.

Carole Anne Heart Looking Horse says her family name means "'When people see you they see something good.' My grandmother chose that name for me because she wanted me to be a good woman. She wanted people to see not only my exterior, but my interior. It's a name I have to live up to." The voices of these Native American women of North America combine to provide a portrait of a group of strong, proud women who reach back into their history to find the strength and power to forge new visions of the future. MC

5.53   Keene, Ann T. **Earthkeepers: Observers and Protectors of Nature.** Oxford University Press, 1994. 222 pp. ISBN 0-19-507867-5. Nonfiction.

Keene invented the word "Earthkeeper" to describe "men and women, past and present, who have had an enormous curiosity about the natural world in which we live and who have made major contributions to our understanding of nature." This collection of forty-six biographical sketches profiles such Earthkeepers as John James Audubon, Henry

David Thoreau, Rachel Carson, and Jane Goodall. Filled with photographs, watercolors, and a list of organizations promoting conservation, this collection tells the story of people committed to nature.

5.54   Keller, Emily. **Margaret Bourke-White: A Photographer's Life.** Lerner, 1996. 125 pp. ISBN 0-8225-4916-6. Nonfiction.

Margaret Bourke-White developed a love of photography as a teenager; however, for years, she planned a career in science. When her skills as a photographer became apparent to the staff at Cornell University, where she was enrolled, she was encouraged to pursue a career in architectural photography. Her pictures of steel mills in Cleveland led to her work with magazine tycoon Henry R. Luce at *Life,* and eventually Bourke-White's photographs were known around the world as she photographed some of the most important people and events of the mid-twentieth century. ER

5.55   Kent, Deborah. **Dorothy Day: Friend to the Forgotten.** William B. Eerdmans, 1996. 157 pp. ISBN 0-8028-5117-7. Nonfiction.

This biography, part of the Women of Spirit series, presents the life story of a strong woman who lived out her religious ideals and became a friend to the forgotten. Dorothy Day lived through turbulent times in America's history, but through it all, she continued to contribute to society through her faith. She opened houses of hospitality that provided food, shelter, and spiritual community for the poor. She made her voice heard in a fight against the injustices that cause poverty and suffering, and she was a powerful woman in the Roman Catholic church.

5.56   Kerr, M. E. **Me, Me, Me, Me, Me: Not a Novel.** HarperTrophy / HarperCollins, 1994. 212 pp. ISBN 0-06-446163-7. Nonfiction.

Her young adult readers constantly write to M. E. Kerr with questions about the origins of her characters and plots. In this series of vignettes, Kerr recounts various significant episodes from her childhood and adolescence and describes how these events are translated into her novels. Readers watch Marijane Meeker become Eric Ranthram McKay, become her own literary agent, and become Vin Packer, author of suspense novels for adults, and in the process see the chrysalis being spun out of which M. E. Kerr, writer of uncompromising, funny, and realistic fiction for young adults, eventually emerges.

5.57   Kessler, Lauren. **Stubborn Twig: Three Generations in the Life of a Japanese American Family.** Plume, 1994. 347 pp. ISBN 0-452-27301-3. Nonfiction.

This is the story of three generations of the Yasuis, who first came to the United States from Japan in the early 1900s to follow the American dream. Just as that dream was realized, it was crushed by their internment in Japanese "relocation camps." Too ashamed to live, Masuo Yasui committed suicide. His family endured and tells their stories here. Kessler reminds us, "Being an outsider is the quintessential American experience. . . . We cannot let ourselves forget this." MC

5.58   Kherdian, David. **The Road from Home: The Story of an Armenian Girl.** Beech Tree, 1995. 238 pp. ISBN 0-688-14425-X. Nonfiction.

Kherdian presents the biography of his mother, Veron Dumehjian, who was an Armenian living in Turkey in 1915. The government forced the Dumehjian family to march from their home to Syria. Veron was left an orphan after the march and was placed in an orphanage. She moved from school, back home with her grandmother, and finally to Greece and the United States as the Turkish government continued to destroy the Armenian population and their homeland. Through the specific story of Veron, readers see the horrific effects of racial conflict on all of us. MC

5.59   Kies, Cosette. **Presenting Lois Duncan.** Twayne, 1993. 139 pp. ISBN 0-8057-8221-4. Nonfiction.

Lois Duncan's books of mystery and suspense have made her one of the most popular writers for teen readers today, and in 1992 she won the Margaret A. Edwards Award from the American Library Association for her contribution to Young Adult Literature. This biography explores Duncan's early life and writing career, and gives considerable attention to the books that were considered turning points in her career. Kies devotes a special chapter to the harrowing episode in which Duncan's daughter was killed in what seemed like a plot from one of the writer's own novels. Part of United States Authors series.

5.60   Kort, Michael G. **Yitzhak Rabin: Israel's Soldier Statesman.** The Millbrook Press, 1996. 191 pp. ISBN 0-7613-0100-3. Nonfiction.

Kort intertwines the history of modern Israel with the story of the life of a remarkable young soldier and statesman who helped sharpen Israel's defensive forces to the point that they emerged victorious in the Six Day War of 1967. Rabin next served as ambassador from his country to the United States, and eventually served his country as Prime Minister, dying by assassination in that position as he continued his struggles to lead Israel into peaceful coexistence with its neighbors. MC

5.61   Kramer, Barbara. **Alice Walker: Author of *The Color Purple*.** Enslow, 1995. 128 pp. ISBN 0-89490-620-8. Nonfiction.

Born the youngest of eight children of a Georgia sharecropper, Alice Walker insists that she chose the field of writing "because the supplies were cheaper" than those required of an artist. This serendipitous choice led to a lifetime of dedication to literature as well as to the struggle of African American women. Wielding her pen to expose wife-beating husbands or practices of female circumcision, Walker's writing engages controversy with both commitment and concern, as described in this volume from the People to Know series. MC

5.62 Kreischer, Elsie Karr. **María Montoya Martínez: Master Potter.** Illustrated by Elsie Karr Kreischer and Roberta Sinnock. Pelican, 1995. 79 pp. ISBN 1-56554-098-0. Nonfiction.

In order for María Martínez to become a master potter, she had to be determined, courageous, and hardworking. As Kreischer describes in this biography of Martínez's life and work, Martínez uses her success to help her people and thus carry on the traditions and history of the American Indian. MC

5.63 Krull, Kathleen. **Presenting Paula Danziger.** Twayne / Simon and Schuster / Macmillan, 1995. 109 pp. ISBN 0-8057-4153-4. Nonfiction.

Paula Danziger is a superstar among young adult authors. From her 1974 hit *The Cat Ate My Gymsuit* to her most recent book about Amber Brown, Danziger has shown her ability to bring to life young people of all ages with humor, compassion, and dignity. Krull's biography captures the energetic and funny sides of Danziger, but she also describes some of the very difficult personal problems that have cast shadows over Danziger's life and career. Analyses of her books and details about how Danziger lives and works (she buys eight to ten pairs of shoes at a time!) make this a fascinating read for those who love Paula Danziger's books.

5.64 Lawlor, Laurie. **Shadow Catcher: The Life and Work of Edward S. Curtis.** Walker, 1994. 132 pp. ISBN 0-8027-8288-4. Nonfiction.

Edward S. Curtis was a renowned Seattle photographer in the late 1800s. By the early 1900s, he had begun to dedicate his life to preserving the images of over eighty Native American tribes which were then believed to be on the verge of vanishing, ultimately producing twenty volumes of text and photographs. Curtis incurred ruinous physical injury and immense hardship to accomplish his life's work, which was ignored or even destroyed over nearly fifty years, until awareness of Native American culture was renewed in the 1970s. The volume is lavishly illustrated with Curtis's stirring photographs. MC

ALA Best Books for Young Adults, 1995
Notable 1994 Children's Trade Books in the Field of Social Studies

5.65 Lawrence-Lightfoot, Sara. **I've Known Rivers: Lives of Loss and Liberation.** Penguin Books, 1995. 644 pp. ISBN 0-14-02.4970-2. Nonfiction.

By combining biography and autobiography, Lawrence-Lightfoot details the fascinating lives of six African American achievers. The subjects include a maker of documentary films, a professor of theology, a research chemist, and a former nun. The journeys that these storytellers have taken are full of love, triumph, loss, and sometimes difficult decisions about sexuality and identity. Readers will see hope and understanding in their stories. MC

5.66   Lazo, Caroline. **Jimmy Carter: On the Road to Peace.** Dillon Press, 1996. 128 pp. ISBN 0-382-39263-9. Nonfiction.

Jimmy Carter is a man of peace, looking to improve humankind's place in the universe. His life is traced in this biography from "Away Down South in Dixie" to "Habitat for Humanity," with "At Home in the White House" in between. His strong partnership with his wife, Rosalynn, is also illustrated. Numerous pictures, a bibliography, and an index add to the value of this People in Focus Book.

5.67   Lewis-Ferguson, Julinda. **Alvin Ailey, Jr.: A Life in Dance.** Walker, 1994. 84 pp. ISBN 0-8027-8239-6. Nonfiction.

Alvin Ailey Jr. was a world-renowned dancer and choreographer, and founder and director of the Alvin Ailey American Dance Theater. Ailey melded a variety of dance influences and his own creativity to bring the magic of dance to audiences around the world. Ailey was not content to create dance; he also established a school to ensure that his vision of dance for all cultures would continue into the future. MC

5.68   Lipsyte, Robert. **Arnold Schwarzenegger: Hercules in America.** HarperTrophy / HarperCollins, 1995. 90 pp. ISBN 0-06-446142-4. Nonfiction.

Arnold Schwarzenegger continues to dominate the action movie scene. Robert Lipsyte explores how an insecure boy who grew up in post-World War II Austria became one of the most recognizable figures in America, someone known by his first name. Lipsyte chronicles Schwarzenegger's "master plan" of achievement and points out the efforts he made to make his dreams come true. In this volume of the Superstar Lineup series, the author places the star in the context of his times and discusses what his success means for sports, entertainment, and society. ER

5.69   Mairowitz, David Zane, and Robert Crumb. **Introducing Kafka.** Kitchen Sink Press, 1994. 175 pp. ISBN 0-87816-282-8. Nonfiction.

Elaborately illustrated in comic-book style, this is a most unusual biography of Franz Kafka, supported by synopses of his works, also in graphic form. His relationships with his family, with women, and with government and his Jewish Bohemian background are explored, culminating with a discussion of the irony that Kafka kitsch is hawked in post-Communist Prague today.

ALA Quick Picks for Young Adults, 1995

5.70   Malone, Mary. **Maya Lin: Architect and Artist.** Enslow, 1995. 112 pp. ISBN 0-89490-499-X. Nonfiction.

Maya Lin was just twenty-one years old when she won a competition for the design of the Vietnam Veterans Memorial in Washington, D.C. This book from the People to Know series describes the controversy surrounding the design and the impact the memorial continues to have on its visitors. Maya Lin then went on to create another important design, for the Civil Rights Memorial at the Southern Poverty Law Center in Birmingham, Alabama. MC

5.71   Marrin, Albert. **The Sea King: Sir Francis Drake and His Times.** Atheneum Books for Young Readers, 1995. 168 pp. ISBN 0-68931887-1. Nonfiction.

This account of the legendary English seafarer Sir Francis Drake is particularly readable, illuminating, and objective. While Drake's exploits are revealed to be little more than those of a brazen pirate and thief, this reality is fit into its proper perspective, given the political, military, economic, and religious climate of the sixteenth century. Notes, a bibliography, and an index make this a good reference source as well as an interesting biography to be enjoyed by many, not just history buffs. ER

School Library Journal Best Books, 1995

5.72   McCall, Nathan. **Makes Me Wanna Holler: A Young Black Man in America.** Vintage Books / Random House, 1994. 416 pp. ISBN 0-679-74070-8. Nonfiction.

Nathan McCall, a journalist for the *Washington Post,* uses his memoirs to express his rage at racism. Although McCall was raised in a supportive working-class household, his admiration for the macho hustlers who "hung out" led him, by the age of twenty, to prison for armed robbery. His determination to win respect, sometimes misdirected, is told in frank language and reveals his intelligence and talent. He defines himself "a tourist in white mainstream" America and struggles for solutions to the inequities of color. MC

ALA Best Books for Young Adults, 1995

5.73   McPherson, Stephanie Sammartino. **Ordinary Genius: The Story of Albert Einstein.** Carolrhoda Books, 1995. 95 pp. ISBN 0-87614-788-0. Nonfiction.

Did you know that Albert Einstein played the violin? Loved to sail? Gave up his German citizenship twice? Was asked to be president of Israel? This biography is an account of both ordinary and extraordinary elements in the life of the twentieth century's most famous scientist. The author examines the human side of being a genius, chronicling Einstein's difficulty in school, his efforts to balance work and family, and his struggle against Hitler's Nazi regime. ER

5.74   Meachum, Virginia. **Janet Reno: United States Attorney General.**
             Enslow, 1995. 128 pp. ISBN 0-89490-549-X. Nonfiction.

Highlights of Janet Reno's life and career are listed in this concise biography of America's first woman attorney general, from the People to Know series. From her formative years near the Florida Everglades, to her college years at Cornell and Harvard universities, to her career in law and politics, Reno's life is an example of the positive effects of goal-setting and of a belief in one's self. ER

5.75   Mikkelsen, Nina. **Virginia Hamilton.** Twayne, 1994. 173 pp. ISBN 0-8057-4010-4. Nonfiction.

Over the last twenty-six years, Virginia Hamilton has published thirty books for young readers, and, in the process, she has won almost every major honor for her writing, including the Hans Christian Andersen Award and the Newbery Award. A folklore scholar, she draws on her background in that field to collect and write folktales, myths, and legends, but she also writes realistic fiction, historical fiction, and fantasy. In this critical biography, from Twayne's United States Authors series, Mikkelsen describes Hamilton's contributions to the field of literature, showing how she has broadened readers' knowledge of the African American experience through her books, which, because of their rich characterization, language, and plots, show the power of story as a way of knowing. MC

5.76   Mohr, Nicholasa. **In My Own Words: Growing Up inside the Sanctuary of My Imagination.** Julian Messner / Simon and Schuster, 1994. 118 pp. ISBN 0-671-74171-3. Nonfiction.

Being Puerto Rican in New York City is not easy, and Nicholasa Mohr realized that at an early age. Her family was large and poor, living in small apartments often shared with extended family members in distress. She writes without recrimination of the bigotry she experienced, focusing instead on the richness of her heritage. This successful author writes compassionately of the critical period of her life up to the age of fourteen, when her mother's death signaled the end of family life as she had known it. ER MC

ALA Quick Picks for Young Adults, 1995

5.77   Monceaux, Morgan. **Jazz: My Music, My People.** Foreword by Wynton Marsalis. Alfred A. Knopf, 1994. 64 pp. ISBN 0-679-85618-8. Nonfiction.

Large stylized drawings by the author accompany brief sketches of the great names in blues, jazz, swing, bebop, and scat, names such as Bessie Smith, Louis Armstrong, Duke Ellington, Billie Holiday, Ella Fitzgerald, Charlie Parker, Miles Davis, and the Modern Jazz Quartet. ER MC

ALA Notable Books for Children, 1995
ALA Quick Picks for Young Adults, 1995

5.78   Monseau, Virginia R. **Presenting Ouida Sebestyen.** Twayne, 1995. 132 pp. ISBN 0-8057-8224-9. Nonfiction.

Monseau traces Ouida Sebestyen's development as a writer for young adults from the success of her first effort, *Words by Heart,* in 1979, through her most recent book, *Out of Nowhere.* Sebestyen emerges as a very spiritual woman who writes carefully and poetically about the universal longing for love and understanding, and whose characters—young adult and adult alike—are more complex and multidimensional than those of many writers for young adults. Throughout this in-depth study of Sebestyen's books Monseau weaves her own critical perspective together with information drawn from extensive interviews about Sebestyen's life and writing habits.

5.79   Mori, Kyoko. **The Dream of Water: A Memoir.** Henry Holt, 1995. 275 pp. ISBN 0-8050-3260-6. Nonfiction.

As a writer and teacher of writing, Kyoko Mori uses her writing skill to reveal her conflicting feelings about her trip to Japan, the homeland she fled as a teenager to escape her abusive father and her calculating, cruel stepmother. Her mother's suicide needs no forgiveness, but does she even want to forgive her father? Can a family that was manipulated into painful division become reunited? MC

5.80   Morris, Jeffrey. Great Presidential Decisions series. Lerner. Nonfiction.
   The Jefferson Way, 1994. 128 pp. ISBN 0-8225-2926-2.
   The Truman Way, 1995. 128 pp. ISBN 0-8225-2927-0.
   The Washington Way, 1994. 128 pp. ISBN 0-8225-2928-9.

The books in this series look at significant decisions made by selected U.S. presidents, placing those decisions in historical and political context. The books include short biographical sketches of the presidents and they are richly illustrated with photographs and drawings.

5.81   Multicultural Junior Biographies series. Enslow, 1995. Nonfiction. ER MC
   Hajdusiewicz, Babs Bell. **Mary Carter Smith: African-American Storyteller.** 104 pp. ISBN 0-89490-636-4.
   Herman, Spring. **R. C. Gorman: Navajo Artist.** 104 pp. ISBN 0-89490-638-0.
   Riley, Gail Blasser. **Wah Ming Chang: Artist and Master of Special Effects.** 97 pp. ISBN 0-89490-639-9.
   Schleichert, Elizabeth. **Dave Bing: Basketball Great with a Heart.** 103 pp. ISBN 0-89490-635-6.
   Wade, Mary Dodson. **Guadalupe Quintanilla: Leader of the Hispanic Community.** 104 pp. ISBN 0-89490-637-2.

The books in this series tell of the lives of individuals from different ethnic backgrounds who have retained their native cultures while becoming important in the larger society. Their various backgrounds are described with respect and admiration. Reluctant readers will want to consider the books in this series when given a biography or nonfiction assignment because they are easy to read, tell about someone less likely to be already familiar, and give plenty of information for a report.

5.82 Nall, Jasper Rastus. **Freeborn Slave: Diary of a Black Man in the South.** Crane Hill, 1996. 106 pp. ISBN 1-881548-28-7. Nonfiction.

This diary provides a compelling picture of life for an African American man living in the Deep South during the early years of the twentieth century. Jasper Rastus Nall was a very determined man who believed in the importance of passing on family stories. Because of this determination, readers can learn the day-to-day details of life for slaves as told by Nall's relatives. Despite his humble beginnings, Nall went on to become a businessman and a leader in his community. MC

5.83 Neimark, Anne E. **Myth-Maker: J.R.R. Tolkien.** Illustrated by Brad Weinman. Harcourt Brace, 1996. 118 pp. ISBN 0-15-298847-5. Nonfiction.

Neimark tells the story of how J.R.R. Tolkien, soldier, scholar, and linguist, created fabulous worlds and peopled them with elves, dwarves, hobbits, and other fantastic creatures, developing an entire mythology beloved by modern readers. ER

5.84 Old, Wendie. **Marian Wright Edelman: Fighting for Children's Rights.** Enslow, 1995. 128 pp. ISBN 0-89490-623-2. Nonfiction.

As the daughter of a South Carolina Baptist minister, Marian Wright grew up with the idea that "service is the rent you pay for living, not something you do in your spare time." She is the recipient of many honors because of her commitment to that principle, serving not only African Americans but all people in need, especially children. The language and style of this book, part of the People to Know series, are very simple and the references to other people and historical events are carefully explained. ER MC

Notable 1995 Children's Trade Books in the Field of Social Studies

5.85 Peck, Richard. **Anonymously Yours.** Beech Tree, 1995. 122 pp. ISBN 0-688-13702-4. Nonfiction.

In this new paperback edition of his autobiography, prolific and award-winning writer Richard Peck tells how he came to spend his life putting words on paper and why he writes specifically for young adults. Listening is the skill he deems essential to the writer; Peck describes the people to whom he has listened in order to learn the craft of storytelling. The same blend of humor and poignancy that are hallmarks of Peck's best fiction is evident in these pages, as is his passion for writing and thus for reaching the readers of the world, "and through them, the future."

5.86   Plain, Nancy. **Mary Cassatt: An Artist's Life.** Dillon Press, 1994. 168 pp. ISBN 0-87518-597-5. Nonfiction.

Mary Cassatt was a talented young painter from Philadelphia who became a major artist in the Impressionist movement in Paris during the 1870s. Despite the rejection of the art establishment, Cassatt recognized the importance of the innovations of artists like Degas, Monet, and Pissarro. Cassatt's works, which depicted women and children, added a distinctively female perspective to the movement. A People in Focus Book.

5.87   Plowden, Martha Ward. **Famous Firsts of Black Women.** Illustrated by Ronald Jones. Pelican, 1993. 155 pp. ISBN 0-88289-973-2. Nonfiction.

African American women who achieved despite barriers against their race and gender are featured in this collection of biographical sketches. Their accomplishments represent many fields; the reader meets women from freedom fighters to modern politicians and diplomats. Well-known figures such as Harriet Tubman are included, as well as those more obscure. ER MC

5.88   Poynter, Margaret. **Marie Curie: Discoverer of Radium.** Enslow, 1994. 113 pp. ISBN 0-89490-477-9. Nonfiction.

Poynter has written much more than a biography about Marie Curie. This is a book about determination, perseverance, and ethnic loyalty. Curie attended school in Poland while Poland was part of the Russian Empire. Russians replaced the Polish teachers and Polish students were forced to speak and write Russian. Often the Russian teachers would give them lower grades than they gave the Russian students. Because women were not allowed to go to college, Marie attended "Floating Universities" in order to pursue her dream of becoming a scientist. Her triumph over tough times makes her story one worth reading. MC ER

5.89   Press, Skip. **The Importance of Mark Twain.** Lucent Books, 1994. 112 pp. ISBN 1-56006-043-3. Nonfiction.

What was it about Samuel Clemens, better known as Mark Twain, that inspired him to bring such unforgettable characters to life? In a direct and personal style, this well-organized book provides facts of Twain's life along with many lesser-known tidbits. The approachable format includes sidebars with quotations from Twain's books, providing insight into parallels between his life and his works. Black-and-white photographs as well as illustrations from Twain's books are included. Engrossing and fun! Part of The Importance of . . . biography series.

5.90   Pringle, Laurence. **Scorpion Man: Exploring the World of Scorpions.** Photographs by Gary A. Polis. Charles Scribner's Sons, 1994. 42 pp. ISBN 0-684-19560-7. Nonfiction.

Biology instructor Gary Polis's fascination with desert creatures began as a youngster when he was exploring around his Southern California home. In college, he started to focus on scorpions and today continues his research all over the world. The facts given about scorpions are often surprising, and the book includes plenty of good color photographs, often taken at night with ultraviolet lights. ER

ALA Quick Picks for Young Adults, 1995

5.91   Pushman, Muriel Gane. **We All Wore Blue.** Robson Books, 1994. 175 pp. ISBN 0-86051-940-6. Nonfiction.

When World War II breaks out, Muriel Gane is eager, as are many other young Englishwomen, to serve her country in the Women's Auxiliary Air Force. She leaves a secure home in the country to encounter the changing role of women in a country at war. She earns a commission as an officer and experiences the role of authority. The author recounts many stories, humorous and heartbreaking, about serving in the line of duty.

5.92   Reef, Catherine. **Walt Whitman.** Clarion Books, 1995. 148 pp. ISBN 0-395-68705-5. Nonfiction.

Whitman's life, times, and works are profiled in this biography featuring a number of black-and-white drawings and photographs. From his youth on Long Island to his uneven New York newspaper career to his days as a Civil War wound dresser to his final years in Camden, New Jersey, Whitman's life experiences exemplify his need to break away from traditional poetic forces.

Notable 1995 Children's Trade Books in the Field of Social Studies

5.93   Reid, Suzanne Elizabeth. **Presenting Cynthia Voigt.** Twayne / Simon and Schuster, 1995. 135 pp. ISBN 0-8057-8219-2. Nonfiction.

When She Hollers, Orfe, The Callendar Papers, Dicey's Song, Jackaroo—these very different types of young adult novels feature strong, finely drawn female characters. *Sons from Afar* and *A Solitary Blue* show Voigt's ability to craft interesting young men as well. Reid's critical biography tells the story of Cynthia Voigt, prolific and acclaimed young adult author, intertwining commentary and analysis with information about Voigt herself drawn from a rare and unpublished interview. Those who love Voigt's work will enjoy learning more about her craft and her life; those who have not yet read a book by Voigt will be compelled to do so after meeting her in these pages.

5.94   Rosen, Dorothy Schack. **A Fire in Her Bones: The Story of Mary Lyon.** Carolrhoda Books, 1995. 81 pp. ISBN 0-87614-840-2. Nonfiction.

Mary Lyons's fifty-two-year-long life is a testament to what one woman's energy, conviction, and persistence can accomplish. Today thousands of women, Mount Holyoke College graduates in particular, can thank Mary Lyons for her efforts to make education attainable at a time when girls were thought not to need much schooling. Sacrificing time with the family she cherished, Lyons paid dearly to learn all that she could. In turn, she opened schools and educated others.

5.95   Ross, Stewart. **Shakespeare and Macbeth: The Story behind the Play.** Illustrated by Tony Karpinski and Victor Ambrus. Viking, 1994. 44 pp. ISBN 0-670-85629-0. Fiction.

This book is a resource guide for those interested in Shakespeare in general and his play *Macbeth* specifically. The book covers Shakespeare's development of one of his most famous plays, including the sources he used, the actors who formed his troupe, and the conditions under which he was forced to work.

ALA Best Books for Young Adults, 1995

5.96   Rutberg, Becky. **Mary Lincoln's Dressmaker: Elizabeth Keckley's Remarkable Rise from Slave to White House Confidante.** Walker, 1995. 166 pp. ISBN 0-8027-8224-8. Nonfiction.

Rutberg dedicates this book to "those former slaves whose stories died with them." This true story weaves together the lives of Mary Todd Lincoln and her dressmaker Elizabeth Keckley after Keckley buys her own freedom and sets up a dress shop in Washington, D.C. The life stories of these two very different women are enhanced through photographs and explanations that provide a historical context for their fascinating friendship. ER MC

Notable 1995 Children's Trade Books in the Field of Social Studies

5.97   Sanford, William R. **Quanah Parker: Comanche Warrior.** Enslow, 1994. 41 pp. ISBN 0-89490-512-0. Nonfiction.

Sanford separates myth from reality in this biography about a great Comanche warrior. Parker's training began when he was able to ride a horse. Becoming a warrior was the most important goal in his life, and he was a man who accomplished whatever he set his mind to—from winning a wife to becoming one of the best Comanche warriors ever to live. Photographs from the Fort Sill Museum, the National Archives, the Smithsonian Institution, and the author himself enhance this volume, part of the Native American Leaders of the Wild West series. MC ER

5.98   Schmidt, Gary D. **Katherine Paterson.** Twayne, 1994. 152 pp. ISBN 0-8057-3951-3. Nonfiction.

Katherine Paterson has won critical acclaim and numerous awards for her writing, including the 1978 and 1980 Newbery medals. This study looks briefly at her life and more fully at how this skilled writer effectively explores universal themes of loss, redemption, and the search for family and acceptance.

5.99   Schraff, Anne. **Women of Peace: Nobel Peace Prize Winners.** Enslow, 1994. 112 pp. ISBN 0-89490-493-0. Nonfiction.

Nine women in the world have won the Nobel Prize for Peace and each of them engaged in a unique struggle that brought attention to her efforts and to the needs of those suffering from conflict or oppression. In this volume from the Collective Biographies series Schraff explores the personal and public lives of Baroness von Suttner, Jane Addams, Emily Greene Balch, Mairead Corrigan, Betty Williams, Mother Teresa, Alva Myrdal, Daw Aung San Suu Kyi, and Rigoberta Menchú, women who gave a great deal of themselves to help others. MC

Notable 1994 Children's Trade Books in the Field of Social Studies

5.100   Schuman, Michael A. **Bill Cosby: Actor and Comedian.** Enslow, 1995. 128 pp. ISBN 0-89490-548-1. Nonfiction.

Schuman's biography, part of the People to Know series, shows that Bill Cosby balances each setback in his life with a success. He dropped out of high school, but earned a doctorate from the University of Massachusetts. He paved the way for African Americans by starring in the hit television shows *I Spy* and *The Cosby Show,* but *You Bet Your Life* and *Cosby Mysteries* were not successful. This biography shows that through his perseverance Cosby has been a success as an actor, author, comedian, husband, and father. MC

5.101   Schuman, Michael A. **Eleanor Roosevelt: First Lady and Humanitarian.** Enslow, 1995. 128 pp. ISBN 0-89490-547-3. Nonfiction.

Eleanor Roosevelt accomplished many things in her lifetime, as described in this book from the People to Know series. She started Val Kill Industries to promote local artisans and taught at Todhunter School. While first lady, Mrs. Roosevelt was the eyes and hands for President Roosevelt. She visited farms, prisons, and coal mines, inspected troops, and met Prime Minister Winston Churchill and Queen Elizabeth. After the president's death, Mrs. Roosevelt's story continued. She was appointed a delegate to the United Nations and spoke out about the significant issues of the day in newspaper columns and several books. ER

5.102   Siegel, Dorothy Schainman. **Ann Richards: Politician, Feminist, Survivor.** Enslow, 1996. 112 pp. ISBN 0-89490-497-3. Nonfiction.

Ann Richards was born to a working-class family in Texas during the Depression. She excelled in debating during high school and went on to pursue her best subject in college. Siegel tells how, although she married early and had four children, Richards managed to become active in Texas politics, winning her first elective office in 1976. Richards did face some adversities as she pursued higher office and eventually became governor of Texas: she entered a treatment program for alcoholism and her marriage ended. However, humor, honesty, and optimism were her hallmarks, even when she lost the election for a second term as governor. ER

5.103 Sobel, Dava. **Longitude: The True Story of a Lone Genius Who Solved the Greatest Scientific Problem of His Time.** Penguin Books, 1996. 184 pp. ISBN 0 14 02.5879 5. Nonfiction.

Award-winning journalist and science writer Dava Sobel tells the dramatic tale of John Harrison, a solitary genius who managed to solve "the longitude problem" facing the great explorers by imaging a clock that would keep precise time at sea, succeeding "against all odds, in using the fourth, temporal, dimension to link the points on a three-dimensional globe."

5.104 St. George, Judith. **To See with the Heart: The Life of Sitting Bull.** G. P. Putnam's Sons, 1996. 182 pp. ISBN 0-399-22930-2. Nonfiction.

Sitting Bull established himself as a warrior among his people because of his courage in fighting enemies from other tribes. In time, his courage and leadership were put to the test as whites moved westward and sought to own the lands where Native Americans lived. Although Sitting Bull is best-known for the Sioux victory over Custer's troops at the Battle of Little Bighorn, for years after that skirmish he and other leaders fought a losing battle to maintain their way of life, all of which is chronicled in this biography of a great American Indian hero. ER MC

5.105 Stacey, T. J. **Hillary Rodham Clinton: Activist First Lady.** Enslow, 1994. 128 pp. ISBN 0-89490-583-X. Nonfiction.

Hillary Rodham Clinton is making a difference in the lives of Americans as first lady. This biography from the People to Know series traces her life from birth to 1994 and her role as a policymaker in the White House. The focus is her partnership with her husband, President Bill Clinton, and their impact on current issues such as health care. This work is highlighted by firsthand accounts of events by Hillary and Bill Clinton, as well as personal photographs of the public and private Hillary. ER

5.106 Steele, Phillip W., with George Warfel. **The Many Faces of Jesse James.** Pelican, 1995. 128 pp. ISBN 1-56554-097-2. Nonfiction.

Authors Phillip Steele and George Warfel draw on their years of research and close contacts with the descendants of Jesse James to present a unique and sympathetic portrait of the legendary outlaw. The authors explore the controversies that surrounded James in life and in death. They place James and his associates in their historical context, even providing political explanations as to why they turned to crime. ER

5.107 Stefoff, Rebecca. **Mao Zedong: Founder of the People's Republic of China.** The Millbrook Press, 1996. 128 pp. ISBN 1-56294-531-9. Nonfiction.

Mao Zedong grew up in the countryside of the Hunan province of China. Although his father was a landowner, Zedong tended to identify with the poorer peasants in his village. When he went to school, he fell in love with reading and this love changed his life. His restless mind caused him to try many areas before going to teachers' college, and in addition to teacher training Mao also gained experience as a political activist. These experiences remained important as Mao struggled for political power for the next thirty years. Finally, he achieved his goal of a Communist China in 1949, changing the history of world politics. Today, however, even former Mao loyalists question many of the tactics he used to bring change to China. MC

5.108   Stefoff, Rebecca. **Nelson Mandela: Hero for Democracy.** Rev. ed. Fawcett Columbine, 1994. 148 pp. ISBN 0-449-90570-5. Nonfiction.

Nelson Mandela sacrificed his law career, money, family, and even personal freedom in his fight for racial equality in South Africa. He is strongly opposed to violence and only resorted to it after numerous futile attempts to peacefully bring about changes in the Nationalists' "unjust, immoral, and intolerable" laws. People recognize Nelson Mandela today as the president of South Africa, but few know of the integrity and lifelong fight for democracy which make him worthy of that office. Stefoff, in tracing Mandela's personal and political life, also tells the tragic and triumphant history of South Africa. MC

5.109   Stefoff, Rebecca. **Saddam Hussein: Absolute Ruler of Iraq.** The Millbrook Press, 1995. 112 pp. ISBN 1-56294-475-4. Nonfiction.

Saddam Hussein was raised by his Uncle Khayiallah Tulfah, a political leader whose greed and cruelty earned him many enemies. Like his uncle, Hussein was cruel and greedy, only much more ambitious. He launched his career as an interrogator and torturer for the Baathist government, and Stefoff tells the story of a man so hungry for power that he would eliminate anyone who opposed him, even his most faithful followers. ER MC

5.110   Stewart, Whitney. **Sir Edmund Hillary: To Everest and Beyond.** Photographs by Anne B. Keiser. Lerner, 1996. 128 pp. ISBN 0-8225-4927-1. Nonfiction.

In 1953, Sir Edmund Hillary and Tenzing Norgay became the first people to reach the top of Mount Everest, something Hillary worked toward his entire life. Edmund Hillary was born to a New Zealand farming family. He was not a strong student academically, but early on he developed a love of adventure. Finally, Hillary had an experience with mountain climbing and decided what he wanted to do with his life, and Stewart chronicles his determination and eventual success in achieving his goal.

5.111   Streissguth, Tom. **Rocket Man: The Story of Robert Goddard.** Carolrhoda Books, 1995. 88 pp. ISBN 0-87614-863-1. Nonfiction.

In 1899, a bedridden boy named Robert Goddard read a magazine excerpt of *The War of the Worlds,* by H. G. Wells, and was transfixed by the idea of rocket travel. This biography chronicles Goddard's solitary, painstaking, and frustrating quest to design and build a liquid-fueled rocket that could venture beyond Earth's atmosphere. With the help of the Smithsonian Institution and supporters such as Charles Lindbergh, Goddard persisted, setting the stage for all future space travel by humankind. ER

5.112   Sullivan, George. **Matthew Brady: His Life and Photographs.** Cobblehill Books / Dutton, 1994. 136 pp. ISBN 0-525-65186-1. Nonfiction.

Photographer Matthew Brady was already world-famous by the time the Civil War began, but much of the photography we know him for today came out of that conflict. In one 1864 incident described by Sullivan, Brady was among Northern troops near Petersburg when he asked permission to photograph a battery of light artillery, and the troops obligingly assumed position. Southern batteries nearby began to fire, not realizing that the troops were playacting, but Brady calmly continued to photograph the scene. Brady also met many of the most notable people of his day, often in unusual circumstances. Many of Brady's most important photographs are reproduced here.

Notable 1994 Children's Trade Books in the Field of Social Studies.

5.113   Symynkywicz, Jeffrey. **Václav Havel and the Velvet Revolution.** Dillon Press, 1995. 184 pp. ISBN 0-87518-607-6. Nonfiction.

This easy-to-read biography, a People in Focus Book, is an excellent beginning reference for information on Václav Havel and the struggles of the Czech people in the twentieth century. The author chronicles in parallel fashion Havel's personal struggles and those of his people, enabling the reader to track the history behind the stories. This objective and realistic account concludes with the chapter "A Hard Road Ahead," a discussion of the large problems confronting Havel and the young republic. ER MC

5.114   Thornton, Yvonne S., M.D., as told to Jo Coudert. **The Ditchdigger's Daughters: A Black Family's Astonishing Success Story.** Plume, 1995. 261 pp. ISBN 0-452-27619-5. Nonfiction.

Donald Thornton, an African American laborer, and his wife, a cleaning woman, proclaimed that their five dark-skinned daughters would become doctors. Because Thornton knew his girls would have to work hard to succeed, he carefully chose their schools and insisted they study their hearts out. Yvonne, who did indeed become a doctor, tells about the remarkable achievements of her loving family. Earning money for college with their successful rhythm-and-blues band, the Thornton Sisters all became successful professionals. This inspiring book is sprinkled throughout with the father's wisdom and clearly shows his determination to overcome every obstacle. MC

ALA Best Books for Young Adults, 1996

5.115 Tilton, Rafael. **The Importance of Margaret Mead.** Lucent Books, 1994. 112 pp. ISBN 1-56006-039-5. Nonfiction.

Margaret Mead was a pioneer anthropologist and an early activist for increased opportunities for women. Her landmark studies of Pacific cultures changed her field, while her wide-ranging interests led her to write and speak out on a variety of topics. This book explores her life and discusses the impact she had on the important cultural subjects of her time. It also emphasizes how Mead's life and work continue to influence society today. Part of The Importance of . . . biography series.

5.116 Turk, Ruth. **Lillian Hellman: Rebel Playwright.** Lerner, 1995. 128 pp. ISBN 0-8225-4921-2. Nonfiction.

From her childhood in New Orleans until her death in 1984 at age seventy-nine, Lillian Hellman was a rebel. She wrote powerful plays and memoirs, created unforgettable characters, and courageously spoke out against political harassment. This biography includes information about her youthful restlessness, her two marriages, her European travels, her friendships with well-known authors, her survival of the McCarthy era, her husband Dashiell Hammett's influence, and her plays, such as *The Children's Hour* and award winners *The Watch on the Rhine* and *Toys in the Attic*. ER

5.117 Uchida, Yoshiko. **The Invisible Thread.** Beech Tree, 1995. 137 pp. ISBN 0-688-13703-2. Nonfiction.

When she was a young child, Uchida begged for a puppy. When her mother finally got one, the young girl filled her diary with descriptions of its exploits; when Brownie died, she used an entire page to draw a picture of his tombstone. Then she realized the power of writing for "holding on to the special magic of joyous moments" and for "finding comfort and solace from pain as well." Thus began Uchida's love affair with writing—a passion that helped her survive the horrors of living in U.S. internment camps for Japanese Americans during World War II, and that provides her a means of livelihood today as she writes books that, in her own words, will help the young people who read them "to dare to have big dreams" and "to celebrate our common humanity." MC

5.118 Underhill, Lois Beachy. **The Woman Who Ran for President: The Many Lives of Victoria Woodhull.** Penguin Books, 1996. 347 pp. ISBN 0 14 02.5638 5. Nonfiction.

Victoria Woodhull rose from poverty to become the first woman Wall Street broker, the first woman to testify before Congress on suffrage, a publisher, a popular public speaker, and, in 1872, the first woman to run for the American presidency. This biography gives historical and political background to the women's suffrage movement. The many aspects of the lives of Woodhull and her sister, Tennie Claflin, are explored, and figures such as Cornelius Vanderbilt, Susan B. Anthony, Elizabeth Cady Stanton, Harriet Beecher Stowe, and her brother, Henry Ward Beecher, come alive through the sisters' correspondence, photographs, and autobiographical writings.

5.119 Van Meter, Vicki, with Dan Gutman. **Taking Flight: My Story.** Viking, 1995. 134 pp. ISBN 0-670-86260-6. Nonfiction.

Vicki Van Meter, at age twelve, has flown a single-engine plane across the United States and the Atlantic Ocean. Van Meter uses maps, pictures, and diary entries written by her parents to tell of her training and trips. One of her main points in this autobiography is the importance of setting goals and then working to accomplish them. ER

5.120 Villaseñor, Victor. **Walking Stars: Stories of Magic and Power.** Piñata Books, 1994. 202 pp. ISBN 1-55885-118-6. Nonfiction.

Like so many young people, Victor Villaseñor grew up hearing family stories that he discounted as he grew older. However, when he decided to become a writer, he found himself drawn to the magic, power, and truth of the stories he had thought were no more than legends. When he begins to seek more information about the stories, even visiting the remote village of his mother's childhood, he begins to believe. Villaseñor presents nine stories from his life, and from the lives of his mother and father, that are both rooted in his Mexican heritage and full of the universal truths of family stories of all cultures. MC

5.121 Williams, Gregory Howard. **Life on the Color Line: The True Story of a White Boy Who Discovered He Was Black.** Plume, 1996. 285 pp. ISBN 0-452-27533-8. Nonfiction.

Growing up during the 1950s in Virginia, Williams believed he was white until he discovered that his father, who had always passed as Italian American, was actually half-black. In this memoir, Williams details his journey across cultures and brings to light the differences between the two worlds. His story describes his experiences of racism from both worlds, as well as moments of love and acceptance from both communities. MC

School Library Journal Best Adult Books for Young Adults, 1996

5.122 Worth, Richard. **Edith Wharton.** Julian Messner / Simon and Schuster, 1994. 154 pp. ISBN 0-671-86615-X. Nonfiction.

As this volume from the Classic American Writers series describes, there was no one better to write about the traditions and mores of America's late nineteenth- and early twentieth-century elite than Edith Wharton. Wharton was a member of that class who discovered her love of writing early in life and successfully used her experiences to create her short stories and novels. While her works were well received in literary circles, many in the social elite disapproved of her writing. Undeterred, Wharton continued to write, finally receiving the Pulitzer Prize for her novel *The Age of Innocence* in 1921.

5.123 Yates, Janelle. **Woody Guthrie: American Balladeer.** Ward Hill Press, 1995. 137 pp. ISBN 0-9623380-5-2. Nonfiction.

Life was not easy for Woody Guthrie. When he was six, he watched his beloved older sister die from burns, and shortly thereafter he watched his mother waste away in grief for her daughter. The family moved several times and Woody was a lonely child. As a young man, he hitched rides and found his way to railroad yards for the good conversation and the music offered there. From the migrant workers he learned the sentiments he later expressed in his more than a thousand songs. Part of the Unsung Americans series.

5.124 Zeinert, Karen. **Elizabeth Van Lew: Southern Belle, Union Spy.** Dillon Press, 1995. 160 pp. ISBN 0-87518-608-4. Nonfiction.

Elizabeth Van Lew's deeply held beliefs against slavery and secession compelled this Richmond woman to take a stand against popular beliefs and operate as a Union spy during the Civil War. At great personal peril, she led a spy ring, passed on coded messages, helped Union prisoners, and suffered the eventual rejection of the society in which she had been raised. Miss Lizzie's daring escapades are interspersed with brief biographies of historical figures and photographs and supplemented by a Civil War timeline in this People in Focus Book. ER

5.125 Zeinert, Karen. **Those Incredible Women of World War II.** The Millbrook Press, 1994. 144 pp. ISBN 1-56294-434-7. Nonfiction.

The women in this book have one thing in common—they wanted to serve their country in World War II. These women saw their chance to help, whether as pilots, combat nurses, Red Cross volunteers, journalists, or factory workers, and demanded their rights. Their stories range from capture by the Japanese to recording the liberation of the concentration camps to building war materials. The book illustrates that, despite prejudice and obstacles, they persevered in their struggle, and that they deserve thanks for America's victory. The book includes black-and-white photographs.

Titles Annotated in Other Chapters Related to Autobiography, Biography, and Collective Biography

Ashby, Ruth, and Deborah Gore Ohrn, eds. *Herstory: Women Who Changed the World.* History.

Ayer, Eleanor H., with Helen Waterford and Alfons Heck. *Parallel Journeys.* Holocaust.

Barboza, Steven. *Door of No Return: The Legend of Gorée Island.* History.

Beetz, Kirk H., ed. *Beacham's Guide to Literature for Young Adults, Volumes 6–8.* Reference.

Brust, Beth Wagner. *The Amazing Paper Cuttings of Hans Christian Andersen.* Arts.

Bryant, Jennifer Fisher. *Lucretia Mott: A Guiding Light.* Autobiography.

Carle, Eric. *The Art of Eric Carle.* Arts.

DeBartolo, Dick. *Good Days and Mad: A Historical Hysterical Tour behind the Scenes at* Mad *Magazine.* Humor.

Galt, Margot Fortunato. *Up to the Plate: The All American Girls Professional Baseball League.* Sports.

Gonzales, Doreen. *AIDS: Ten Stories of Courage.* Death.

Gourley, Catherine, in association with Mystic Seaport Museum. *Hunting Neptune's Giants: True Stories of American Whaling.* Diaries.

Green, Carl R. *Jackie Joyner-Kersee.* Sports.

Green, Carl R., and Roxanne Ford. *Deion Sanders.* Sports.

Green, Carl R., and William R. Sanford. *Allan Pinkerton.* Westerns.

Green, Carl R., and William R. Sanford. *Butch Cassidy.* Westerns.

Green, Carl R., and William R. Sanford. *The Dalton Gang* Westerns.

Green, Carl R., and William R. Sanford. *Doc Holliday.* Westerns.

Green, Carl R., and William R. Sanford. *Judge Roy Bean.* Westerns.

Green, Carl R., and William R. Sanford. *The Younger Brothers.* Westerns.

Gutman, Bill. *Emmitt Smith: NFL Super Runner.* Sports.

Gutman, Bill. *Larry Johnson: King of the Court.* Sports.

Gutman, Bill. *Reggie White: Star Defensive Lineman.* Sports.

Hilton, Christopher. *Ayrton Senna.* Airplanes.

Jones, K. Maurice. *Spike Lee and the African American Filmmakers: A Choice of Colors.* Television.

Klein, Aaron. *Deion Sanders: This is Prime Time.* Sports.

Krone, Julie, with Nancy Ann Richardson. *Riding for My Life.* Sports.

Krull, Kathleen. *Lives of the Artists: Masterpieces, Messes (and What the Neighbors Thought).* Arts.

Levine, Ellen. *Anna Pavlova: Genius of the Dance.* Arts.

Lipsyte, Robert. *Jim Thorpe: Twentieth-Century Jock.* Sports.

Malone, Mary. *Will Rogers: Cowboy Philosopher.* Westerns.

Marrin, Albert. *Unconditional Surrender: U.S. Grant and the Civil War.* History.

Marrin, Albert. *Virginia's General: Robert E. Lee and the Civil War.* History.

McKissack, Patricia C., and Fredrick McKissack, Jr. *Black Diamond: The Story of the Negro Baseball Leagues.* Sports.

Meltzer, Milton, ed. *Frederick Douglass: In His Own Words.* Diaries.

Mühlberger, Richard. *What Makes a Cassatt a Cassatt?* Arts.

Parks, Deborah. *Climb Away! A Mountaineer's Dream.* Sports.

Pious, Richard M. *The Young Oxford Companion to the Presidency of the United States*. Reference.

Plowden, Martha Ward. *Olympic Black Women*. Sports.

Rappoport, Ken. *Shaquille O'Neal*. Sports.

Rees, Bob, and Marika Sherwood. *The Black Experience: In the Caribbean and the U.S.A.* History.

Rivers, Glenn, and Bruce Brooks. *Those Who Love the Game: Glenn "Doc" Rivers on Life in the NBA and Elsewhere*. Sports.

Romei, Francesca. *Leonardo da Vinci: Artist, Inventor and Scientist of the Renaissance*. Arts.

Schon, Isabel, ed. *Contemporary Spanish-Speaking Writers and Illustrators for Children and Young Adults: A Biographical Dictionary*. Reference.

Sports Great Books series. Sports.

Sports Top 10 series. Sports.

Sullivan, George. *Pitchers: Twenty-Seven of Baseball's Greatest*. Sports.

Sullivan, Michael J. *Chris Mullin: Star Forward*. Sports.

Thwaite, Ann. *The Brilliant Career of Winnie-the-Pooh: The Definitive History of the Best Bear in All the World*. History.

Turner, Robyn Montana. *Dorothea Lange*. Arts.

Vernon, Roland. *Introducing Gershwin*. Arts.

Vernon, Roland. *Introducing Mozart*. Arts.

Walker, Lou Ann. *Roy Lichtenstein: The Artist at Work*. Arts.

Wolf, Sylvia. *Focus: Five Women Photographers*. Arts.

6 Choices and Transitions

"Grand griefs. And choices.
He feared most of all the choices, that cried to be taken."

Gwendolyn Brooks

"You're either part of the solution or part of the problem."

Eldridge Cleaver

6.1 Banks, Russell. **Rule of the Bone: A Novel.** HarperPerennial / HarperCollins, 1996. 390 pp. ISBN 0-06-092724-0. Fiction.

To escape his abusive stepfather, Chappie leaves home at fourteen to live with another young runaway and some degenerate bikers. Surrounded by drugs, crime, and sex, he moves from bad to worse, renaming himself Bone in honor of his new tattoo. Some peace finally comes when he hooks up with an old Rastafarian. Is this just another phase in his ruined life, or can Bone yet redeem himself? Rough situations and language illustrate the impoverishment of Bone's life. MC

ALA Best Books for Young Adults, 1996
School Library Journal Best Adult Books for Young Adults, 1996

6.2 Benedict, Helen. **Bad Angel.** Dutton, 1996. 293 pp. ISBN 0-525-94100-2. Fiction.

Living in one of New York's toughest neighborhoods, Bianca Diaz, a fourteen-year-old Dominican American mother, struggles with the demands of a baby daughter, a husband who abandons her, school lessons, poverty, and the yearning to be a happy-go-lucky teenager again. The author writes a sensitive story, though with some strong language, about a family that breaks apart in order to save the individual members. MC

6.3 Bennett, James. **Dakota Dream.** Scholastic, 1994. 182 pp. ISBN 0-590-46680-1. Fiction.

Floyd Rayfield has been shuttled among foster homes for most of his life. He feels as if he is being punished for something he didn't do and doesn't understand. Floyd holds onto a dream that came to him: that he is Charley Black Crow, Dakota Warrior. He needs to find the spirit of Black Elk to find his vision and make sense of his life. Floyd must struggle against the authorities, who think he is dangerous, and against himself to find his destiny. MC

ALA Best Books for Young Adults, 1995
ALA Quick Picks for Young Adults, 1995

6.4   Cadnum, Michael. **Taking It: A Novel.** Viking, 1995. 135 pp. ISBN 0-670-86130-8. Fiction.

Anna's kleptomania is finely tuned, and she never gets caught. Lately, however, the risks she is taking have been getting bigger. Soon she is finding things she doesn't even remember taking. Her cool, outward facade begins to crack as friends and family let her know just where they stand. Will Anna find her way back?

6.5   Carter, Alden R. **Dogwolf.** Scholastic, 1994. 231 pp. ISBN 0-590-46741-7. Fiction.

For Pete LaSavage, it is a summer that makes no sense and offers little comfort. Forest fires rage and threaten his home, while the "dogwolf," named by those not quite sure which it is, howls through day and night. Pete understands the animal's anguish, its desire to be free, its need to be either dog or wolf. Half-white and half-Chippewa, unsure of where he belongs, Pete moves restlessly between his two worlds, as does the dogwolf in its cage. With much sacrifice, both are released from their turmoil, but only one finds peace. MC

6.6   Castañeda, Omar S. **Imagining Isabel.** Lodestar Books, 1994. 200 pp. ISBN 0-525-67431-4. Fiction.

When she explores the tokens passed down through eleven generations of women, sixteen-year-old Isabel knows that her dying mother approved of her marriage to Lucas. She feels doubt and fear, however, as she leaves her traditional Mayan village to accept the government's invitation to attend a teacher-training program. Isabel successfully manages her studies, while still caring for her young sister, yet she is haunted by mysterious political events and people. Who is really in control of her and the people of Guatemala? This book is a sequel to *Among the Volcanoes.* MC WL

Child Study Association Book of the Year

6.7   Choi, Sook Nyul. **Gathering of Pearls.** Houghton Mifflin, 1994. 163 pp. ISBN 0-395-67437-9. Fiction.

When Sookan Bak leaves her family in Seoul to attend an all-girls' Catholic college in upstate New York, she embarks upon a journey that includes hardships and triumphs. Not only does Sookan feel the pressures from struggling academically and working in the dining hall every evening, but she also labors to fit into a new culture. Set in the 1950s, the novel explores the codes of dating, friends, and success in this time period as well as the contrasting values of Sookan's family in Korea. ER MC WL

6.8   Christiansen, C. B. **I See the Moon.** Atheneum / Macmillan, 1994. 116 pp. ISBN 0-689-31928-2. Fiction.

Bitte is not ready for all the changes that happen the summer of her twelfth year. Her friend Claire is reading romance magazines, but Bitte can't even determine a definition for love. Then there's her fifteen-year-old sister Kari's pregnancy. Bitte is excited to become an aunt and responds bitterly to Kari's decision to let the baby be adopted. When Bitte is sent to Uncle Axel's, although her beloved Aunt Minna is in a home for Alzheimer's patients, she learns not only how to cope with changes but also the meaning of love. ER MC

ALA Best Books for Young Adults, 1996
ALA Quick Picks for Young Adults, 1996
ALA Notable Books for Children, 1995
Notable 1994 Children's Trade Books in the Field of Social Studies

6.9   Cooney, Caroline B. **The Voice on the Radio.** Delacorte Press, 1996. 184 pp. ISBN 0-385-32213-5. Fiction.

Long ago, Janie Johnson was kidnapped (*The Face on the Milk Carton*). But life has settled down for her family, and sixteen-year-old Janie is doing okay except for the fact that Reeve Shields is away at college and she's lonely. As for Reeve, he's overwhelmed. When he takes over a spot on late night radio, he betrays Janie and her family and life will never be the same for any of them.

6.10   Danticat, Edwidge. **Breath, Eyes, Memory.** Vintage Books / Random House, 1995. 235 pp. ISBN 0-679-75661-2. Fiction.

At the age of twelve, Sophie has to leave Haiti; she is sent to New York to be with the mother of whom she has few memories, and once there she is enveloped in a painful web of shameful secrets. Sophie's search for healing takes her back to Haiti to be with the woman who had been the mother figure of her childhood. There she encounters the elements of the supernatural coupled with political violence that characterize the lives of the Haitian people, as well as the lushness of the countryside and the power of the bonds among women that ultimately give her the strength she needs to complete her journey of self-discovery. MC WL

6.11   Davis, Ossie. **Just like Martin.** Puffin Books, 1995. 215 pp. ISBN 0-14-037095-1. Fiction.

Stone is very active in the nonviolent Civil Rights movement advocated by Martin Luther King Jr. But everything he does encounters disapproval from his father, who has been emotionally scarred by his service in the Korean War. When Stone's Alabama church is bombed and two of his classmates are killed, Stone must confront his own anger, which takes him closer to the angry world of his father and further away from the freedom movement of King. MC

6.12   Dickinson, Peter. **Shadow of a Hero.** Delacorte Press, 1994. 294 pp. ISBN 0-385-32110-4. Fiction.

Restaur Vax brings his story to life for his granddaughter Letta and inspires her to help save the country of Varina from the control of its three domineering neighbors. After the fall of communism and the chaos prevalent in Eastern Europe, a determined few struggle to keep Varina from the tragic fate of Bosnia and Croatia. Although Varina is an invented country, this novel vividly portrays the struggles of a small country fighting for its independence. ER MC

6.13   Dorris, Michael. **Sees behind Trees.** Hyperion Books for Children, 1996. 104 pp. ISBN 0-7868-0224-3. Fiction.

In sixteenth-century America, Walnut has always felt himself to be an outsider because his eyes just don't work as they should. But at his coming-of-age ceremony, he discovers a gift for "seeing" that earns him the respect of his peers and the adults of the tribe. Eventually, his courage and his gifts are tested during a treacherous journey to the "land of water," a journey that turns out to be a true rite of passage for the young man. ER MC

6.14   Duong Thu Huong. **Paradise of the Blind.** Translated by Phan Huy Duong and Nina McPherson. Penguin Books, 1994. 270 pp. ISBN 0 14 02.3620 1. Fiction.

Hang, a young Vietnamese woman, narrates her life story, in which she journeys from a village outside Hanoi to a textile factory in Moscow. This coming-of-age novel details the horrors and the beauty of northern Vietnam from the 1950s to the 1980s through the story of three struggling women. Banned in Vietnam, the book combines an open account of the problems of political reform and a lyrical story of a girl fighting to be free. MC WL

6.15   Garland, Sherry. **Cabin 102.** Harcourt Brace, 1995. 243 pp. ISBN 0-15-200663-X. Fiction.

Twelve-year-old Dusty, who is deathly afraid of water, must spend his summer vacation with his father's new family on a Caribbean cruise. While continually trying to avoid participating in any of the family's planned water activities, Dusty encounters a mysterious sprite-like waif who entices him to explore the mysteries hidden in the history of the Arawak people and the Spanish invaders of the Caribbean. MC

6.16   Gunesekera, Romesh. **Reef.** The New Press, 1994. 190 pp. ISBN 1-56584-219-7. Fiction.

Young Triton's rise to an esteemed position in Mr. Salgado's household is described against the backdrop of turbulent politics on the island paradise of Sri Lanka. The charm of Miss Nili distracts the master from his scientific inquiry into the sea, but does not slow the tide of revolt outside their affluent social circle. The eventual erosion of their comfortable life parallels the growing threats within the larger context, forcing them to learn to direct their own destinies. MC WL

School Library Journal Best Adult Books for Young Adults, 1995
Booker Prize finalist, 1994

6.17   Haddix, Margaret Peterson. **Running Out of Time.** Simon and Schuster Books for Young Readers, 1995. 184 pp. ISBN 0-689-80084-3. Fiction.

In 1840, there is no cure for diphtheria. When the children of the small town of Clifton begin to die of this dread disease, Jessie's mother tells her the secret of the town: in reality, the year is 1996, and Clifton is a reconstructed village designed for tourists. To save the children, thirteen-year-old Jessie must face the outside world, risking her own life in the process. ER

6.18   Hamilton, Virginia. **Arilla Sun Down.** Scholastic, 1995. 296 pp. ISBN 0-590-22223-6. Fiction.

Woven with flashbacks of her childhood, Arilla tells the story of her twelfth year in a small Midwestern town. Arilla lives in the shadow of her older brother, Jack Sun Run, who embraces his Native American heritage while Arilla struggles to find her place in the white world. Jack has named Arilla after the moon, in one of his many attempts to display his dominance over her. Arilla doesn't know where she belongs until one day when Jack needs her help and she must decide between the two worlds in which she lives. MC

6.19   Hesse, Karen. **The Music of Dolphins.** Scholastic Press, 1996. 181 pp. ISBN 0-590-89797-7. Fiction.

At the age of four, Mila is lost at sea—and rescued by dolphins, who raise her as a member of their own family. As an adolescent, Mila is found by the Coast Guard, which takes her to be studied by researchers. At first Mila delights in being human. Then the doctors ask her to engage in behavior that is inconsistent with her dolphin nature, and she has to choose between her biological heritage and a life in which there are no secrets, no lies, and no fear. ER

School Library Journal Best Books, 1996

6.20   Hewett, Lorri. **Soulfire.** Dutton Children's Books, 1996. 231 pp. ISBN 0-525-45559-0. Fiction.

Set in Denver, this novel details the struggles of two young men to find their place in a chaotic environment. The narrator, Todd, lives with his mother and four siblings, one of whom is a drug dealer, Marcus. Todd's best friend, Ezekiel, the son of a prominent minister, is determined to prevent his young relative Tommy from joining Marcus's gang. A violent struggle between Ezekiel and the gang leads to a double shooting that leaves one person dead and another wounded. After the shooting, Todd searches his soul to understand his true feelings for Ezekiel, his love for a young woman, and what it means to be a man. MC

6.21 Jenkins, Lyll Becerra de. **So Loud a Silence.** Lodestar, 1996. 154 pp. ISBN 0-525-67538-8. Fiction.

Juan, visiting his grandmother's rural Colombia home, enjoys the treatment he receives as "el señor" but feels puzzled by the atmosphere of fear and suspicion that permeates the town. As the seventeen-year-old is caught up in the fighting between guerrillas and the army, he has to evaluate both his sense of who he is and his perceptions about the value of family. MC WL

6.22 Johnson, Scott. **Overnight Sensation.** Atheneum, 1994. 232 pp. ISBN 0-689-31831-6. Fiction.

Over the years, Kerry and Madeline have shared interests and commiserated over being unpopular, until Kerry returns from a summer in the country looking and feeling great. When they return to school in the fall, Kerry relishes her newfound popularity and is pulled away from Madeline by new friends. As she gets to know her new crowd, however, Kerry gets drawn into doing something that deeply hurts Madeline, and has to decide what's more important—popularity or real friends.

6.23 Killingsworth, Monte. **Circle within a Circle.** Margaret K. McElderry Books / Macmillan, 1994. 139 pp. ISBN 0-689-50598-1. Fiction.

Fourteen-year-old Chris runs away from a horrible foster home and hitchhikes a ride with Chopper, a Chinook Indian. Chopper is driving home in his souped-up Volkswagen bus to help save the Chinook tribe's sacred beach from being turned into a resort complex. Chopper and Chris team up to save the beach and face tremendous opposition and danger in the process. Both troubled individuals, Chris and Chopper teach each other much during their time together. MC

6.24 Klass, David. **California Blue.** Scholastic, 1994. 199 pp. ISBN 0-590-46688-7. Fiction.

John Rodgers, a distance runner and nature lover, is nothing like his family, especially his father. He lives in a lumber town in northern California where football and "the company" are supposed to be the most important things in a teenage boy's life. While running through the company forest, John discovers an unusual butterfly, which his biology teacher believes to be an undiscovered species. John must decide whether to work with his teacher to protect the butterfly or turn his back on its plight to please his dying father, who owns the lumber company with a vested interest in cutting down the forest.

ALA Quick Picks for Young Adults, 1995
School Library Journal Best Books, 1994
Notable 1994 Children's Trade Books in the Field of Social Studies
IRA Teacher's Choice Award, 1996

6.25   Krisher, Trudy. **Spite Fences.** Delacorte Press, 1994. 280 pp. ISBN 0-385-32088-4. Fiction.

Growing up in Kinship, Georgia, during the 1950s, thirteen-year-old Maggie Pugh knows all about the fences that separate rich and poor, black and white. When Zeke gives her a camera and teaches her about "never being afraid of the truth," Maggie is forced to question the fences and make tough decisions. ER MC

ALA Best Books for Young Adults, 1995
IRA Children's Book Award, 1995

6.26   Lipsyte, Robert. **The Chief.** HarperTrophy / HarperCollins, 1995. 226 pp. ISBN 0-06-447097-0. Fiction.

In this sequel to *The Brave,* Sonny Bear is about to give up on the heavyweight trail despite his golden gloves. But when Sonny, the Tomahawk Kid, hooks up with New York City cop Alfred Brooks and the loudmouthed Martin Malcolm Witherspoon, they form an unstoppable trio and find themselves enmeshed in a scheme to rescue the reservation from troubles involving the construction of a gambling casino. ER MC

6.27   Lynch, Chris. **Blood Relations: Blue-Eyed Son #2.** HarperCollins, 1996. 216 pp. ISBN 0-06-025399-1. Fiction.

In this compelling sequel to *Mick: Blue-Eyed Son #1,* fifteen-year-old Mick recovers from a brutal beating he received from his brother's friends because he was rejecting their narrow, alcohol-dominated lifestyle. As Mick recovers physically, he also becomes stronger emotionally and he makes some critical decisions about his future, including where he will live when his own home is no longer an acceptable choice.

6.28   Lynch, Chris. **Mick: Blue-Eyed Son #1.** HarperCollins, 1996. 146 pp. ISBN 0-06-025397-5. Fiction.

Fifteen-year-old Mick has spent all of his life on Sycamore Street, a blue-collar Irish neighborhood in a very segregated city. Mick learns that there may be more to life than getting drunk with his bigoted older brother Terry and terrorizing people just because they are not white and Irish. As Mick struggles to redefine himself, he meets new people who introduce him to life beyond his neighborhood. In moving out of it, however, Mick must fight against his brother and his brother's friends, who don't want him to stray.

6.29   Mead, Alice. **Adem's Cross.** Farrar, Straus and Giroux, 1996. 132 pp. ISBN 0-374-30057-7. Fiction.

Fourteen-year-old Adem is tired of living with oppression, terrorism, and beatings. He wants to fight the killers, the Serbians who have dominated his homeland of Kasavo for four and a half years. But the Albanian population, of which Adem is a part, is committed to a policy of nonviolence. When Adem's sister decides to read a protest poem in public, Adem's family is torn apart, and he faces difficult choices about his future. MC

6.30   Myers, Christopher A., and Lynne Born Myers. **Forest of the Clouded Leopard.** Houghton Mifflin, 1994. 112 pp. ISBN 0-395-67408-5. Fiction.

Set in the rainforest of the island of Borneo and narrated by Kenchendai, this is a story about difficult choices and cultural change. Kenchendai's family practices the traditional customs of their people, but he begins to question those beliefs in light of the modern education he is receiving at school. When his grandfather dies, Kenchendai follows his father into the rainforest to save him, to save his people, and to send his grandfather's spirit into the other world. MC

6.31   Okimoto, Jean Davies. **Talent Night.** Scholastic, 1995. 161 pp. ISBN 0-590-47809-5. Fiction.

Rodney Suyama wants to become an Asian rapper, and so, with the encouragement of Ivy, he enters a talent contest. In between classes, dances, and projects, Rodney and Ivy fall in love. The views of Rodney's mother, who was born in an internment camp during World War II, and his traditional Japanese uncle, who comes to visit, add suspense to this story as Rodney tries to come to terms with his mixed heritage. MC

6.32   Paterson, Katherine. **Jip: His Story.** Lodestar Books, 1996. 181 pp. ISBN 0-525-67543-4. Fiction.

Living in pre–Civil War Vermont, Jip knows he must be content on the "poor farm," and should be grateful to the town for taking care of him ever since he was found on the roadside as an infant. He works very hard and has a magical way with animals as well as with the other farm residents, especially simple Sheldon and the new "lunatic" Put, who provides great companionship between his seizures. Jip could not possibly have predicted the changes that are suddenly wrought in his circumstances. ER MC

School Library Journal Best Books, 1996

6.33   Paulsen, Gary. **Sentries.** Aladdin Paperbacks, 1995. 168 pp. ISBN 0-689-80411-3. Fiction.

This compelling story of four young people—an Ojibway Indian, an illegal Mexican migrant worker, a rock musician, and a sheep rancher's daughter—and three older people, veterans of past U.S. wars, deals with survival in adverse societies. Each chapter focuses on one of the seven characters, who are linked by their youth, their hopes, their fortitude, and their vulnerability in the face of nuclear disaster. Paulsen's beautiful descriptions juxtapose the physical and psychological challenges faced by the teenagers. MC

6.34   Pausewang, Gudrun. **Fall-out.** Translated by Patricia Crampton. Viking, 1994. 172 pp. ISBN 0-670-86104-9. Fiction.

Everything about Janna—her personality, her family, her town, her school—seems typical for a fourteen-year-old until dangerous amounts of radioactive waste escape from a nearby nuclear reactor. Janna is separated from all of her family except her younger brother, Uli. Together they set off to outrun danger and make it to their aunt's house in Hamburg. As their journey unfolds, Janna is faced with challenges, tragedy, and ultimately triumph. MC WL

German Literary Award for Children's Young Adult Books

6.35   Powell, Randy. **Dean Duffy.** Farrar, Straus and Giroux, 1995. 170 pp. ISBN 0-374-31754-2. Fiction.

Dean Duffy, promising young athlete, finds himself graduating from high school in a baseball-playing slump. Jack Trant, his mentor, arranges another chance for Dean with a full college scholarship starting in the spring. Dean uses the fall semester for introspection: Is baseball still important in his life? Is he willing to risk further playing failure? As Dean makes his decisions, he sees his family and friends also working toward their aspirations.

ALA Best Books for Young Adults, 1996
ALA Quick Picks for Young Adults, 1996

6.36   Rostkowski, Margaret I. **Moon Dancer.** Browndeer Press / Harcourt Brace, 1995. 180 pp. ISBN 0-15-276638-3. Fiction.

A summer hike through the canyons of southern Utah begins as an outdoor adventure for fifteen-year-old Mira, but she gets more than a physical workout. The magic of the mountains, the stories of the women who lived there, and a moonstruck romance with a handsome male guide lead her to a better understanding of herself and others.

6.37   Ruby, Lois. **Skin Deep.** Scholastic, 1994. 280 pp. ISBN 0-590-47699-8. Fiction.

At first, Dan Penner is just feeling down and powerless. Then he meets a group of skinheads. Their steel-toed Doc Martens with white laces seem cool. These guys are a part of something, he thinks. While his girlfriend Laurel conspires with the FemPower group at school to get Bella Donna Prozac (a ferret) elected homecoming queen, she loses her boyfriend to the neo-Nazis. In this tale of racism and hatred, Ruby explores the paranoia and insecurity at the root of one of the most destructive forces in America today.

6.38   Rumbaut, Hendle. **Dove Dream.** Houghton Mifflin, 1994. 119 pp. ISBN
        0-395-68393-9. Fiction.

        In this coming-of-age story, Dove, a thirteen-year-old Chickasaw Indian,
        spends a summer with her aunt in rural Kansas. This physical distance
        from her father's alcoholism and her parents' marital problems provides
        Dove with the opportunity to explore her Chickasaw heritage and ex-
        perience the trials and tribulations of being an adolescent. Living with
        her carefree and independent aunt, Dove works as a waitress, discov-
        ers a boyfriend, and finds the time to enjoy what it means to be a teen-
        ager. ER MC

        ALA Quick Picks for Young Adults, 1995

6.39   Savage, Deborah. **To Race a Dream.** Houghton Mifflin, 1994. 245 pp.
        ISBN 0-395-69252-0. Fiction.

        Being a girl in 1906 is not easy for Theo, who only dreams of driving
        the horses from the harness racing farm near her home. Bored with
        school, her classmates, and the small town of Savage, Minnesota, Theo
        sees no way out of her loneliness and oppression. Then she realizes that
        by disguising herself as a boy, she can rise above the societal restrictions
        placed on girls and make her dream come true. Horse lovers will par-
        ticularly enjoy this novel. ER

6.40   Sinclair, April. **Coffee Will Make You Black.** Avon Books, 1994. 239 pp.
        ISBN 0-380-72459-6. Fiction.

        Jean "Stevie" Stevenson is growing up amid the changes of the late
        1960s. Not only is her body changing as she approaches adolescence,
        but the Civil Rights movement is transforming her African American
        friends and family. Stevie copes with her potential for college, her
        choices of friends, the unrest in her community, and her sexuality and
        individuality with strength and insight. Mature themes and strong street
        language are used. MC

        ALA Best Books for Young Adults, 1995

6.41   Soto, Gary. **Jesse.** Scholastic, 1994. 166 pp. ISBN 0-590-52837-8. Fiction.

        Jesse and his older brother Abel work the fields to support their dreams
        for the future—for a college education, for a life less desolate and less
        poverty-stricken than that of their present. But in the turbulent politi-
        cal climate of the 1960s, these young men also know that the decisions
        they make, as members of a disenfranchised minority culture, will have
        a significant effect on the lives of others as well. MC

6.42   Strauss, Victoria. **Guardian of the Hills.** Morrow Junior Books, 1995.
        229 pp. ISBN 0-688-06998-3. Fiction.

        When Pamela moves to the post-Depression-era Flat Hills of Arkansas
        from Connecticut with her mother, she discovers a grandfather and a

heritage previously hidden from her. Not only does Pamela find she is an outcast in both white and Indian societies because of her mixed parentage, she also discovers that she is drawn to the sites of ancient mound builders. She grapples with the supernatural spirits that are unleashed by the archaeologists her grandfather calls in after she unwittingly makes a find at a mound.

6.43   Temple, Frances. **Taste of Salt: A Story of Modern Haiti.** HarperTrophy / HarperCollins, 1994. 179 pp. ISBN 0-06-447136-5. Fiction.

Set in Port-au-Prince, Haiti, in 1991, this book tells a compelling story of two teenagers struggling to survive. Djo is the victim of a firebombing, and Jeremie is a schoolgirl asked by an aide of President Jean-Bertrande Aristide to record Djo's story while he recovers. Together their dreams are woven with Aristide's in a world of romance, violence, politics, and change. ER MC WL

6.44   Terris, Susan. **Nell's Quilt.** Sunburst / Farrar, Straus and Giroux, 1996. 162 pp. ISBN 0-374-45497-3. Fiction.

At eighteen, Nell wants to go to college in Boston, but her family wants her to marry Anson Tanner. Since the year is 1899, it appears that the marriage plans will proceed and Nell has to determine how to regain and then retain control over her future.

ALA Best Books for Young Adults in original publication

6.45   Thomas, Joyce Carol. **When the Nightingale Sings.** HarperTrophy / HarperCollins, 1994. 148 pp. ISBN 0-06-440524-9. Fiction.

Fourteen years old and orphaned, Marigold works hard to please her demanding aunt and nasty cousins. Her only escape is to sing and write in her journal while in the Swamp, alone. Then one day, amidst a hurricane, Marigold's singing voice is discovered. She struggles to make her way to the Great Gospel Convention, where she meets Sweet Jimmy and Queen Mother Rhythm and realizes many of her secret hopes and dreams. MC

6.46   Tolan, Stephanie S. **Welcome to the Ark.** Morrow Junior Books, 1996. 250 pp. ISBN 0-688-13724-5. Fiction.

In an experimental program called the Ark, four gifted misfits are thrown together and discover that, collectively, their minds have incredible power, which they determine to use to save the world from the random violence now destroying it.

6.47   Vande Velde, Vivian. **Companions of the Night.** Harcourt Brace, 1995. 212 pp. ISBN 0-15-200221-9. Fiction.

When Kerry steals out of her house to retrieve her baby brother's stuffed bear from the laundromat, she has no idea she will be walking into a crime scene. Because she can identify the men involved, they are reluctant to let her go. As if that weren't scary enough, the laundry owner announces that one of the members of the group was a vampire. Suddenly Kerry finds herself involved in an adventure in which nothing is as it appears to be.

ALA Best Books for Young Adults, 1996
ALA Quick Picks for Young Adults, 1996

6.48 Voigt, Cynthia. **Izzy, Willy-Nilly.** Aladdin Paperbacks, 1995. 280 pp. ISBN 0-689-80446-6. Fiction.

Isobel, called Izzy by everyone, slips into unconsciousness just as doctors inform her that they will have to amputate her leg. Her life changed forever, this "nice" girl who has always had everything—a comfortable family life, many friends, a busy high school career—must recover from her injuries and learn to cope. Every day she faces new, difficult realities including just who her real friends are. An unlikely friend, Rosamunde, and Izzy's own inner strength prevail.

6.49 Voigt, Cynthia. **The Runner.** Scholastic, 1994. 281 pp. ISBN 0-590-48380-3. Fiction.

Set on Maryland's Eastern Shore in the late 1960s, this intense novel documents the thoughts and actions of a seventeen-year-old cross-country runner, Bullet Tillerman. A true loner, Bullet find his thoughts and actions are frustratingly entangled with a period of racial tension and fear of the draft felt keenly by his high school peers. Bullet's realization of his own racial bigotry, the depiction of the personal losses he faces, including death, and the chasm of poor family communication create a realistic though not cheerful coming-of-age novel.

6.50 Wangerin, Walter, Jr. **The Crying for a Vision.** Simon and Schuster Books for Young Readers, 1994. 279 pp. ISBN 0-671-79911-8. Fiction.

Waskn Mani (Moves Walking) is a Lakota teenager with eerie powers that lead him on a journey on which he must use all his strength and wisdom to save his tribe from Fire Thunder, the fierce warrior with the hidden wound. This coming-of-age epic blends Lakota folklore with fantasy, adventure, and myth. A glossary of Lakota words and phrases is included. ER MC

6.51 Wartski, Maureen. **Candle in the Wind.** Fawcett Juniper, 1995. 185 pp. ISBN 0-449-70442-4. Fiction.

Terri Mizuno, a Japanese American teenager, becomes the target of bigotry and violence after her older brother Harris is shot dead by an older white man who mistakes Harris for an intruder. The case divides the town between those seeking revenge for a crime they believe to be racially motivated and those seeking revenge for the threat they feel from "foreigners." Can Terri pull herself, her family, and her community back together? MC

6.52 Wurmfeld, Hope. **Baby Blues.** Puffin Books, 1995. 90 pp. ISBN 0-14-034870-0. Fiction.

Recently orphaned, Annie quits high school and finds a makeshift family with a dropout, graffiti-bombing gang. To escape her loneliness, Annie succumbs to Jimmy's sexual advances, but this leads to another dilemma when she becomes pregnant. Should she have an abortion? Put the baby up for adoption? Keep the baby? Herself having been given up at birth for adoption by a teenage mother, the author writes a sensitive story about two young persons who might have been her biological parents. ER

Titles Annotated in Other Chapters Related to Choices and Transitions

Alcott, Louisa. *Jo's Boys and How They Turned Out*. Classics.

Avi. *Sometimes I Think I Hear My Name*. Family.

Barrett, Elizabeth. *Free Fall*. Dating.

Bennett, Cherie. *Wild Hearts*. Arts.

Bennett, James. *The Squared Circle*. Sports.

Brooks, Martha. *Traveling on into the Light and Other Stories*. Short Stories.

Burks, Brian. *Runs with Horses*. Historical Fiction.

Cole, Sheila. *What Kind of Love?* Diaries.

Cottonwood, Joe. *Quake!* Family.

Cross, Gillian. *The Great American Elephant Chase*. Adventure.

Cushman, Karen. *The Midwife's Apprentice*. Historical Fiction.

de Trevino, Elizabeth Borton. *Leona: A Love Story*. Historical Fiction.

Frank, Lucy. *I Am an Artichoke*. Family.

Goodman, Joan Elizabeth. *Songs from Home*. Family.

Grant, Cynthia D. *Mary Wolf*. Family.

Haseley, Dennis. *Getting Him*. Friendships.

Herman, Charlotte. *What Happened to Heather Hopkowitz?* Religion.

Hyde, Margaret O. *Kids in and out of Trouble*. Political Science.

Johnston, Julie. *Adam and Eve and Pinch-Me*. Family.

Karas, Phyllis. *The Hate Crime*. School.

Kerr, M. E. *Deliver Us from Evie*. Dating.

Klass, David. *Danger Zone*. Sports.

Langone, John. *Tough Choices*. Drugs.

Lee, Gus. *China Boy*. Family.

Lee, Marie G. *Saying Goodbye*. Friendships.

Lester, Julius. *Othello: A Novel*. Classics.

MacLeod, Joan. *The Hope Slide; Little Sister*. Poetry.

Mahy, Margaret. *The Other Side of Silence*. Family.

McClain, Ellen Jaffe. *No Big Deal*. School.

Morrison, Toni. *The Bluest Eye*. Classics.

Myers, Walter Dean. *Slam!* Sports.

Neenan, Colin. *In Your Dreams*. Romance.

Orlev, Uri. *The Man from the Other Side*. Holocaust.

Oz, Amos. *Soumchi*. Adventure.

Paterson, Katherine. *Lyddie*. Historical Fiction.

Paulsen, Gary. *Dogsong*. Adventure.

Paulsen, Gary. *The Rifle.* Historical Fiction.

Pears, Tim. *In the Place of Fallen Leaves*. Family.

Ray, Karen. *To Cross a Line*. Holocaust.

Reynolds, Marilyn. *Too Soon for Jeff.* Dating.

Rinaldi, Ann. *Finishing Becca*. Historical Fiction.

Rinaldi, Ann. *Keep Smiling Through*. Historical Fiction.

Roybal, Laura. *Billy*. Family.

Shusterman, Neal. *Dissidents*. Adventure.

Southgate, Martha. *Another Way to Dance*. Arts.

Sutcliff, Rosemary. *Warrior Scarlet*. Historical Fiction.

Tamar, Erika. *The Things I Did Last Summer*. Romance.

Temple, Frances. *Tonight, by Sea*. Adventure.

Twain, Mark. *The Adventures of Huckleberry Finn*. Classics.

Wiggin, Kate Douglas. *Rebecca of Sunnybrook Farm*. Classics.

Wisler, G. Clifton. *Thunder on the Tennessee*. War.

Yolen, Jane. *Dragon's Blood*. Fantasy.

7 Classics

"A classic is something that everybody wants to have read and nobody has read."
Mark Twain

"What a sense of security is an old book which Time has criticized for us!"
James Russell Lowell

7.1 Achebe, Chinua. **Things Fall Apart.** Anchor Books / Doubleday, 1994. 209 pp. ISBN 0-385-47454-7. Fiction.

Okonkwo is the powerful son of a weak and poverty-stricken father in a small Nigerian village that is held together by its religious beliefs and social customs. With three wives and many children, he has gained all the respect his father never had, but his pride and fear of failure bring him troubles with his family and neighbors. Setting his story against the coming of the white missionaries, Chinua Achebe has crafted a delicate and ironic tale of the disruption of a formerly coherent world. First published in 1959. MC WL

7.2 Alcott, Louisa May. **Jo's Boys and How They Turned Out.** Little, Brown, 1994. 316 pp. ISBN 0-316-03110-0. Fiction.

The girls of *Little Women* have grown up, and a younger generation, several of whom Jo and her husband taught in *Little Men,* have also grown to adulthood. This, the final book in the March family trilogy, tells of the further adventures of "Jo's Boys" from Plumfield School. The volume is offered in a gift-book format (but without illustrations) from the original publisher of the Alcott classics. First published in 1886. ER

7.3 Alcott, Louisa May. **Little Men: Life at Plumfield with Jo's Boys.** Little, Brown, 1994. 332 pp. ISBN 0-316-03108-9. Fiction.

This is a new edition of the children's classic, the sequel to *Little Women.* The "little men" of the title are the students of Plumfield School, a progressive school run by Jo and her husband. First published in 1871. ER

7.4 Alcott, Louisa May. **Little Women.** Pocket Books / Simon and Schuster, 1994. 578 pp. ISBN 0-671-51764-3. Fiction.

This is a new paperback tie-in published to coincide with the theatrical release of the 1994 version of *Little Women.* Illustrated with black-and-white stills from the movie, the story of Beth, Meg, Jo, and Amy March comes to life for contemporary readers. First published in 1868. ER

7.5 Alcott, Louisa May. **Little Women or Meg, Jo, Beth and Amy.** Little, Brown, 1994. 502 pp. ISBN 0-316-03107-0. Fiction.

In this new, gift-boxed edition of the children's classic, reissued by the original publisher, a new generation of readers can experience the joys and sorrows of Meg, Beth, Jo, and Amy March as they come of age in nineteenth-century New England. First published in 1868. ER

7.6   Alcott, Louisa May. **Rose in Bloom: A Sequel to** *Eight Cousins*. Little, Brown, 1995. 302 pp. ISBN 0-316-03089-9. Fiction.

The story of Rose Campbell will be appreciated by Alcott fans but enjoyed best by those who remember *Eight Cousins* well. Rose returns from her Grand Tour of Europe with her beloved guardian Uncle Alec and her former servant, now friend and equal, Phebe, ready to reenter family and society as a grown woman and experiences some unavoidable complexities. The Victorian language is quaint and the situations sentimental, but the charm of the writing is timeless. First published in 1876.

7.7   Azuela, Mariano. **The Underdogs: A Novel of the Mexican Revolution**. Translated by E. Munguía, Jr. Illustrated by J. C. Orozco. With a new introduction by Ana Castillo. Signet Classics, 1996. 161 pp. ISBN 0-451-52625-2. Fiction.

Against the setting of the Mexican Revolution, Demetrio Macías changes from a peace-loving campesino to a military leader of the rebels. When his troops are unable to defeat the government's forces, Demetrio is no longer a hero in the eyes of his soldiers and his fellow peasants, demonstrating that the casualties of war do not all necessarily take place on the battlefield; war causes difficulties for those whose choices are contrary to their moral beliefs. Because of the graphic nature of the subject, the book does contain some profanity and explicit sexual scenes. First published in 1963. WL

7.8   Beneduce, Ann Keay (retold by). **William Shakespeare:** *The Tempest*. Illustrated by Gennady Spirin. Philomel Books, 1996. 32 pp. ISBN 0-399-22764-4. Fiction.

A retelling of Shakespeare's fantastical play *The Tempest*, this story's purpose is to introduce the reader to Shakespeare for the first time. The magnificent illustrations allow the reader to envision the story while reading the lyrical prose in which the story is written.

7.9   Boyd, James. **Drums.** Illustrated by N. C. Wyeth. Charles Scribner's Sons, 1995. 409 pp. ISBN 0-689-80176-9. Fiction.

This classic of the American Revolution tells the tale of a youth from North Carolina, Johnny Fraser, who is swept up in the fight for American Independence on John Paul Jones's *Bonhomme Richard*. First published in 1925.

7.10   Brontë, Charlotte. **Jane Eyre.** Puffin Books, 1994. 643 pp. ISBN 0-14-036678-4. Fiction.

In early nineteenth-century England young Jane Eyre, an orphan, endures a terrible childhood and life at Lowood School. At the school, she survives and becomes a teacher before being sent as a governess to the home of Mr. Rochester. Jane and Rochester fall in love, but Rochester's terrible secret threatens to keep them apart: what, or who, is being kept in the attic? First published in 1847.

7.11   Cather, Willa. **Twenty-four Stories.** Selected and with an introduction by Sharon O'Brien. Meridian, 1993. 340 pp. ISBN 0-452-00874-3. Fiction.

This is a collection of twenty-four of Cather's early stories, twelve never before published, that were written between 1892 and 1912, when the influences of Henry James and Sarah Orne Jewett were strong. The final story in the collection, "The Bohemian Girl," is the breakthrough story, in which Cather's mature voice can be heard for the first time. O'Brien's introduction is very useful for students doing research papers on Cather.

7.12   Dickens, Charles. **Oliver Twist.** Abridged by Robin Waterfield. Puffin Books, 1994. 346 pp. ISBN 0-14-036814-0. Fiction.

The classic story of the orphan Oliver Twist probably has more to say to modern readers than it did to Dickens's audience. Oliver is sold to an undertaker but escapes, only to fall in with a gang of pickpockets on the streets of London. It's a story of crime, poverty, abuse, murder, and redemption, as current as any story on "Inside Edition." First published in 1837–39.

7.13   Green, Roger Lancelyn. **King Arthur and His Knights of the Round Table.** Illustrated by Lotte Reiniger. Puffin Books, 1994. 330 pp. ISBN 0-14-036670-9. Fiction.

Many books retell the stories of King Arthur and his knights of the Round Table. This author's version attempts to weave the tales together rather than presenting them as disjointed stories. Based on a wide variety of sources from the famous tales of Sir Thomas Malory, first published in England in 1485, to different English, French, and German poems, this book demonstrates how the stories differ from country to country and genre to genre.

7.14   Haggard, H. Rider. **She.** Introduction by Regina Barreca. Signet Classics, 1994. 317 pp. ISBN 0-451-52584-1. Fiction.

For people who want to know where stories like *Raiders of the Lost Ark* and other modern quest adventures came from, this is the book. But in this tale of ancient Egyptian relics, sorcery, and the secret of immortality, first published in 1887, we also gain insights into the darker side of the Victorian Age and its attitudes toward female power, racism, Darwinism, and marriage. MC

7.15   Kipling, Rudyard. **The Jungle Book: The Mowgli Stories.** Illustrated by Jerry Pinkney. Afterword by Peter Glassman. Books of Wonder / William Morrow, 1995. 258 pp. ISBN 0-688-09979-3. Fiction.

Rudyard Kipling's classic tales of Mowgli, the lost boy who is raised by wolves in the jungles of India, is as captivating today as it was when written a hundred years ago. The nine stories follow Mowgli as he learns the ways of the jungle from the wise old bear, Baloo; the great black panther, Bugheera; and his faithful wolf friend, Gray Brother. The beautiful descriptions and fast pace make this a must to read aloud. Pinkney's eighteen illustrations show the beauty and the strength of the animals. MC

7.16   Lamb, Charles, and Mary Lamb. **Tales From Shakespeare.** Puffin Books, 1994. 346 pp. ISBN 0-14-036677-6. Fiction.

In this complete and unabridged version of the Lambs' classic retelling of Shakespeare's stories, all the wit and pathos, the tragedy and fun, of favorite tales come to life. The language is true to the poetry of the Bard, and the format allows for ease of access to some of Shakespeare's lesser-known works such as *Timon of Athens,* as well as to the very popular plays such as *A Midsummer Night's Dream, Macbeth,* and *The Tempest.* First published in 1807.

7.17   Lawrence, D. H. **Women in Love.** Introduction by Louise DeSalvo. Signet Classics, 1995. 542 pp. ISBN 0-451-52591-4. Fiction.

This sequel to Lawrence's *The Rainbow* follows the lives of two sisters, Ursula and Gudrun Brangwen, and their lovers, Rupert Birkin and Gerald Rich. The two love affairs take different paths: Rupert fears total commitment to Ursula, and her sister's affair leads to tragedy. As with most of Lawrence's works, there is some fairly explicit sex, and in *Women in Love* Lawrence adds elements of homoeroticism. First published in 1921.

7.18   Leroux, Gaston. **The Phantom of the Opera.** Puffin Books, 1994. 322 pp. ISBN 0-14-036813-2. Fiction.

Most people think they know *The Phantom of the Opera* because they have seen the Lon Chaney silent film, or any of the numerous sound versions, or the Andrew Lloyd Webber musical. But the true Phantom lies between the covers of the book. The classic horror-love story of the hideously deformed genius and the pupil he adores has taken on new meaning in the modern world. This new paperback edition features a highly readable typeface. First published in 1911. MC WL

7.19   Lester, Julius (as told by). **The Last Tales of Uncle Remus.** Illustrated by Jerry Pinkney. Dial Books, 1994. 156 pp. ISBN 0-8037-1303-7. Fiction.

This fourth and final volume in Lester's series includes favorites such as Brer Rabbit, Brer Bear, Brer Fox, and more. Updated to refer to microwaves, VCRs, recessions, and therapists, the stories still explain natural phenomena like why the earth is mostly water and why the opossum has no hair on its tail, as well as the basics of human nature. Color illustrations and ink sketches add to the stories, but the narrator's keen observations are what keep you reading. ER MC

Notable 1994 Children's Trade Books in the Field of Social Studies

7.20 Lester, Julius. **Othello: A Novel.** Scholastic, 1995. 151 pp. ISBN 0-590-41967-6. Fiction.

In this novelization of Shakespeare's famous play, Othello is an admired and powerful African general who serves the king in sixteenth-century England. When the black warrior falls in love with Lord Bertrand's beautiful white daughter, Desdemona, Othello becomes vulnerable to manipulation by a vengeful companion, Iago. The combination of Iago's treachery and Othello's own lack of faith in humanity brings a premature and tragic end to what otherwise might have been an inspiring example of interracial love and devotion. MC

ALA Best Books for Young Adults, 1996
ALA Quick Picks for Young Adults, 1996

7.21 Lewis, Sinclair. **Dodsworth.** Introduction by Michael Meyer. Signet Classics, 1995. 380 pp. ISBN 0-451-52598-1. Fiction.

While on an extended European tour with his selfish and shallow wife, Fran, Sam Dodsworth, retired automobile designer and manufacturer, discovers that he is no longer needed by his business partners or his children, and that his marriage has crumbled, but also that while one life may be over a new one can begin. This novel is a wicked satire about American business and European culture, as well as Nobel Prize–winner Lewis's spin on his own failed marriage. First published in 1929.

7.22 London, Jack. **White Fang.** Puffin Books, 1994. 271 pp. ISBN 0-14-036667-9. Fiction.

Jack London's "other" dog story follows the adventures of White Fang, who, as the lone survivor of his litter, must learn to live on his own in the primal world of the frozen wilds of northwest Canada. But in this book London reverses the trail Buck had to follow in *The Call of the Wild*, for here White Fang, a wild half-wolf half-dog, must adapt to being a domesticated house dog in California after having survived as a wild creature on his own. First published in 1905. MC

7.23 Morrison, Toni. **The Bluest Eye.** With a new afterword by the author. Plume, 1994. 216 pp. ISBN 0-452-27305-6. Fiction.

Eleven-year-old Pecola Breedlove is an African American girl living in Ohio in 1940. Her loathing of her own blackness and her desire for the badge of "true beauty," blue eyes, drives her ultimately to insanity. Nobel Prize–winner Toni Morrison's first novel is structured to show the reader the underside of the Dick and Jane readers all children read and judged their own lives against, in a harrowing story that includes vivid descriptions of rape, alcoholic violence, and child and wife abuse. This latest edition of the 1970 novel includes a new afterword by the author. MC

7.24   Ovid. **The Poems of Exile.** Translated by Peter Green. Penguin Books, 1994. 451 pp. ISBN 0-14-044407-6. Fiction.

The Roman poet Ovid is best known for his erotic verse, but was punished by the Emperor Augustus for his satirical slander and banished. These selections, "Tristia" and "Black Sea Letters," were his attempt to ingratiate himself with the unamused emperor. The extensive introduction and notes, provided by Green, are useful for background information and research. MC WL

7.25   Philip, Neil (retold by). **The Arabian Nights.** Illustrated by Sheila Moxley. Orchard Books, 1994. 157 pp. ISBN 0-531-06868-4. Fiction.

Sheherazade is desperate. If she can't do some quick thinking, she will meet the same deadly fate as King Shahryar's other brides. She hits upon the idea of spinning tales for the king, and over a thousand and one nights she entertains and enthralls him with her words. This lavishly illustrated edition captures all the magic and enchantment of well-known stories such as "Ali Baba and the Forty Thieves" and "Aladdin," and of lesser-known tales such as "The Wonderful Bag" and "The Fisherman and the Jinni." Readers of all ages will delight in this new version of a truly classic book. MC WL

7.26   Schmidt, Gary D. (retold by). **John Bunyan:** *Pilgrim's Progress*. Illustrated by Barry Moser. William B. Eerdmans, 1994. 76 pp. ISBN 0-8028-5080-4. Fiction.

Gary Schmidt retells John Bunyan's seventeenth-century morality tale of Christian's spiritual journey from the City of Destruction to the Heavenly Palaces. Schmidt's version emphasizes the "road epic" qualities of the story, and Barry Moser vividly brings the characters and the setting to life in watercolors that range in tone from political satire to fantasy/horror comic-book illustrations. ER

7.27   Shelley, Mary. **Frankenstein: Or, the Modern Prometheus.** Puffin Books, 1994. 282 pp. ISBN 0-14-036712-8. Fiction.

Written in 1817 by a nineteen-year-old woman, this is the most famous horror story ever written. The cautionary tale of Victor Frankenstein and his attempt to create intelligent human life is a classic story of science gone awry: Frankenstein's creature wants only to be like the people he sees in Victor's life, but goes on a murderous rampage when a normal life is denied him. First published in 1818.

7.28   Stevenson, Robert Louis. **Treasure Island.** Illustrated by François Place. Viking, 1996. 296 pp. ISBN 0-670-86795-0. Fiction.

What can be new about a famous classic first published in 1883? An edition in the new The Whole Story series. Pirates and suspense still abound, but so do informative illustrations and notes about sailing ships, nautical facts and lore, animals, seventeenth-century medical practices, and much more. In addition to a riveting story, readers now get every bit of background information they could ever want about this classic tale, first published in 1883. ER

7.29   Stevenson, Robert Louis. **Treasure Island.** Puffin Books, 1994. 298 pp. ISBN 0-14-036672-5. Fiction.

Here is a new paperback edition of the great pirate saga, first published in 1883, of Long John Silver and Jim Hawkins, the cabin boy who befriends him and then learns about the duplicitous and dark nature of some human hearts. Puffin has reissued several classics traditionally appealing to young readers in a series that features clear, user-friendly typefaces. ER

7.30   Stoker, Bram. **Dracula.** Puffin Books, 1994. 520 pp. ISBN 0-14-036717-9. Fiction.

Real estate agent Jonathan Harker travels to Transylvania to meet with a new client, Count Dracula, who has bought property in London. When Dracula comes to England, Harker's fiancée Mina and her friend Lucy come under the power of the centuries-old vampire. Told in the form of letters and diary entries, *Dracula* may be the scariest book ever written, and no movie has ever come close to its power. First published in 1897.

7.31   Twain, Mark. **The Adventures of Huckleberry Finn.** Illustrated by Steven Kellogg. Afterword by Peter Glassman. Books of Wonder / William Morrow, 1994. 348 pp. ISBN 0-688-10656-0. Fiction.

This new edition of an American classic is enlivened by illustrations that enhance its appeal to young readers. While the story of Huck's fleeing his drunken father and traveling down the river with the escaped slave Jim is intended for more mature students, the illustrations may also interest younger readers in the story. First published in 1884.

7.32   Verne, Jules. **Journey to the Center of the Earth.** Translated by Robert Baldick. Puffin Books, 1994. 291 pp. ISBN 0-14-036715-2. Fiction.

Set in 1863, this classic story follows the travels of Axel and his uncle, Professor Lidenbrock, from the time they decipher an old parchment in Germany to their exploration of the earth's interior by way of a secret passage through an Icelandic volcano. Scientifically oriented readers will be interested to see how Verne imaginatively creates scientific "facts" to suit the story and to explain how it might be possible. First published in 1864. WL

7.33   Wiggin, Kate Douglas. **Rebecca of Sunnybrook Farm.** Illustrated by Helen Mason Grose. Afterword by Peter Glassman. Books of Wonder / William Morrow and Company, 1994. 291 pp. ISBN 0-688-13481-5. Fiction.

This is a new edition of the perennial classic in quality hardcover gift format. Grose's original black-and-white line drawings and color illustrations are attractive, if old-fashioned. First published in 1903. ER

Titles Annotated in Other Chapters Related to Classics

Dangerous Journey. Religion.

Green, Roger Lancelyn. *Tales of the Greek Heroes*. Myths.

Hansberry, Lorraine. *A Raisin in the Sun*. Television.

Ito, Tom. *The Importance of John Steinbeck*. Autobiography.

Martin, Wendy, ed. *Colonial American Travel Narratives*. Recreation.

Pierce, Richard. *Frankenstein's Children, Book One: The Creation*. Horror.

Press, Skip. *The Importance of Mark Twain*. Autobiography.

Webster, Jean. *Daddy-Long-Legs*. Romance.

Wilde, Oscar. *The Fairy Tales of Oscar Wilde*. Myths.

8 College, Education, and Careers

"Education is a treasure and culture never dies."

Petronius

"As women, we need to be clear about our role as workers. We need to take ourselves seriously and be aware of our rights on the job. . . "

Susan Moyer

8.1 Armstrong, William H. **Study Is Hard Work.** David R. Godine, 1995. 148 pp. ISBN 1-56792-025-X. Nonfiction.

Each chapter of this book begins with an interest-measurement test to allow the reader to determine how well he or she listens, reads, writes, studies, and performs other skills. An explanation and helpful hints follow. This guide is written to help students study more efficiently and do well in school, to prepare for college and a job. A place should be made on the shelf next to the dictionary and the thesaurus for this guide. ER

8.2 Ballinger, Erich. **Detective Dictionary: A Handbook for Aspiring Sleuths.** Lerner, 1994. 144 pp. ISBN 0-8225-0721-8. Nonfiction.

An alphabetical listing of detective/mystery terms, this book is not to be taken altogether seriously; some entries are meant as jokes. There are secret codes and mysteries to be solved by the reader as well as descriptions of real-life detective work and mysteries. Entries about famous mystery writers and their fictional characters are also included.

ALA Quick Picks for Young Adults, 1995

8.3 Bonner, Staci. **Now Hiring: Sports.** Crestwood House / Macmillan, 1994. 48 pp. ISBN 0-89686-789-7. Nonfiction.

Even though there are only a relatively few athletes who earn huge salaries, there are many career areas in sports, and this book briefly interviews people in eight of them. These jobs include team community events organizer, coach, team logo salesperson, umpire, sports photographer, player agent, media director, and events coordinator. Related jobs are also listed, along with a sample résumé and a glossary of sports career terms. ER

8.4 Crisfield, Deborah. **Now Hiring: Travel.** Crestwood House / Macmillan, 1994. 48 pp. ISBN 0-89686-790-0. Nonfiction.

A thumbnail sketch of the travel industry, this book provides an overview of some of the jobs involved with it. There are seven interviews with people in such jobs as travel agent, tour guide, flight attendant, concierge, assistant cruise director, passenger service representative, and cruise ship entertainer. Related jobs are also listed, some from outside the travel industry. Also included are a sample résumé and a glossary of travel terms. ER

8.5   Cummings, Rhoda Woods, and Gary L. Fisher. **The School Survival Guide for Kids with LD (Learning Differences).** Free Spirit, 1991. 104 pp. ISBN 0-915793-32-6. Nonfiction.

Filled with information and sound advice for students labeled "learning disabled," this text explains LD in terms kids can understand, defines different kinds of LD, discusses LD programs, and emphasizes that kids with LD can be winners too. One of the most readable books available on the subject, it is the kind of book that children, parents, and teachers can browse for profitable insights and strategies. For students with a real reading problem, this book comes with a 96-minute audio cassette.

8.6   Jensen, Eric. **Student Success Secrets.** 4th ed. Illustrated by Tom Kerr. Barron's Educational Series, 1996. 245 pp. ISBN 0-8120-9488-3. Nonfiction.

From motivational tips, to secrets of assessing your optimal learning environment, to memory aids and strategies to evaluate literature or to take tests more successfully, this book offers students useful information in an easy-to-follow format that will help them take charge of their futures. ER

8.7   Marshall, Mary Ann. **Now Hiring: Music.** Crestwood House / Macmillan, 1994. 48 pp. ISBN 0-89686-793-5. Nonfiction.

For every famous performer in the music business, there are many other people behind the scenes. Some careers in this industry are briefly explored through interviews with people in these jobs: musician, engineer, band manager, lighting director, songwriter, assistant concert promoter, and producer. Related jobs are also listed. A sample résumé and a glossary of music industry terms are included. ER

8.8   McCutcheon, Randall. **Can You Find It? Twenty-five Library Scavenger Hunts to Sharpen Your Research Skills.** Free Spirit, 1991. 196 pp. ISBN 0-915793-38-5. Nonfiction.

As the book says, "Research. It's a dirty job, but someone has to do it. And someday that someone is bound to be you." This book takes you on an unorthodox tour of your favorite library. You are guided by cartoons, quotations, and cryptic clues to find the answer to twenty-five trivia questions, while at the same time developing effective research methods in libraries. This is a book every English teacher would want to put on his or her shelf, in the "most valuable teaching aids" section, and it is a book every student needs in order to develop skill in using the library.

8.9   Meltzer, Milton. **Cheap Raw Material**. Viking, 1994. 151 pp. ISBN 0-670-83128-X. Nonfiction.

The five million teenagers in America who work are an essential cog in our huge economy. They are the "cheap, raw material" of whom Milton Meltzer writes, and are part of a long and often abusive tradition of child labor in our country and our world. Meltzer tells the story of that tradition, from child slavery in ancient times to today's fast food restaurants, often letting the words of young workers bring to life the realities of exploitation, danger, and abuse. He makes a case for fundamental changes in how our society values and treats its children, and dedicates his book "to all those who seek to protect the health and safety of young workers."

Booklist Editor's Choice, 1995

8.10   Pope, Loren. **Colleges That Change Lives: Forty Schools You Should Know about Even if You're Not a Straight-A Student.** Penguin Books, 1996. 272 pp. ISBN 0 14 02.3951 0. Nonfiction.

Written by the director of the College Placement Bureau, this book describes forty smaller colleges that fully develop the potential of students from a wide range of backgrounds. The book encourages students to consider smaller, lesser-known schools, where they will receive more opportunities and individual attention. Each college is profiled by school climate, personality, students' opinions, and interviews with professors and administrators. ER

8.11   Powell, Stephanie. **Hit Me with Music: How to Start, Manage, Record, and Perform with Your Own Rock Band.** The Millbrook Press, 1995. 142 pp. ISBN 1-56294-653-6. Nonfiction.

The musician of any age at any stage of organizing a band of any kind (not just rock) would do well to read the advice in this book. It offers concrete suggestions on seemingly every aspect of the endeavor—creative, interpersonal, technical, and business. Within the appropriate chapters are suggestions of other helpful publications and groups for further information. This book is well-researched as well as well-written.

8.12   Schumm, Jeanne Shay, and Marguerite Radencich. **School Power: Strategies for Succeeding in School.** Free Spirit, 1992. 123 pp. ISBN 0-915793-42-3. Nonfiction.

The authors provide a visually appealing text full of recommendations for better ways for students to organize their time, keep track of assignments, listen with more comprehension, take better notes, and partici-pate in class. They include excellent sections on reading, writing, and test-taking strategies. The creative presentation coupled with straight-forward advice makes the text valuable for any student, but most of all for those students who need visual organizers as learning aids.

8.13   Vitkus-Weeks, Jessica. **Now Hiring: Television**. Crestwood House / Macmillan, 1994. 48 pp. ISBN 0-89686-783-8. Nonfiction.

Seven careers in the television industry are briefly discussed through interviews with people holding the following jobs: production assistant, camera operator, sound engineer, hairstylist, costume designer, and actor. Related jobs are also listed along with a sample résumé and a glos-sary of television terms. ER

8.14   Wilson, Erlene B. **Money for College: A Guide to Financial Aid for African-American Students**. Plume, 1996. 481 pp. ISBN 0-452-27276-9. Nonfiction.

Essentially a giant scholarship availability list, this publication is a re-source for African American students who are planning to attend col-lege or university and who are seeking financial aid. The process for applying for such aid is described and explained, and then lists includ-ing college scholarships by field, private scholarships, and athletic schol-arships are offered. Deadlines, monetary amounts, addresses, and phone numbers are also included. MC

Titles Annotated in Other Chapters Related to College, Education, and Careers

Ashabranner, Brent. *A New Frontier: The Peace Corps in Eastern Europe*. History.

Choi, Sook Nyul. *Gathering of Pearls*. Choices.

Freedman, Michael. *The Princeton Review Student Advantage Guide to Summer*. Reference.

Gillam, Scott. *Discrimination: Prejudice in Action*. Human Rights.

Lee, Marie G. *Saying Goodbye*. Friendships.

Narayan, Kirin. *Love, Stars, and All That*. Romance.

Soto, Gary. *Jesse*. Choices.

9 Computers and Related Technology

"Things are in the saddle and ride mankind."
Ralph Waldo Emerson

*"Our engines plunge into the sea
they climb above our atmosphere."*
Edna St. Vincent Millay

9.1   Cruise, Beth. **Computer Confusion.** Collier Books / Macmillan, 1994. 135 pp. ISBN 0-02-042784-0. Fiction.

This easy-to-read novel is the twelfth in a series based on a group of teenagers called the "Saved by the Bell" kids. The friends, Lisa Turtle, Jessie Spano, Zack Morris, A. C. Slater, Kelly Kapowski, and Screech Powers, who have known one another for years, are seniors at Bayside High School in Palisades, California. The novel is a whodunit that will pull readers in quickly with the intrigue of the mysterious computer virus that has been introduced into a brand-new software program developed by Zack's father. Zack and the gang try to solve the mystery of the computer spy who is bent on destroying Mr. Morris's young software company, Intelpro. Interwoven into the intrigue of corporate espionage are subplots that successfully address gender issues, job responsibilities, and decision making. ER

9.2   Darling, David. **Computers of the Future: Intelligent Machines and Virtual Reality**. Dillon Press, 1996. 71 pp. ISBN 0-87518-617-3. Nonfiction.

This latest edition to the Beyond 2000 series explains complex technology and procedures in very simple language for those with no acquaintance with the subject. Computer terms appear in boldface and are included in the glossary. Diagrams and color photographs also help to make the information clear to the novice. A bibliography and index are included. ER

9.3   Elliot, Joe, and Tim Worsley, editors. **Multi-media: The Complete Guide**. Dorling Kindersley, 1996. 192 pp. ISBN 0-7894-0422-2. Nonfiction.

This book is designed to be browsed through as the reader searches for information on topics ranging from CD-ROMs and interactive movies to 3D games, the Internet, and the World Wide Web. The script is generally jargon-free, and there are detailed color photographs and illustrations on every page. Descriptions and explanations are designed to help the reader understand multi-media from the stage of product creation through that of consumer use. ER

9.4   Judson, Karen. **Computer Crime: Phreaks, Spies, and Salami Slicers.** Enslow, 1994. 128 pp. ISBN 0-89490-491-4. Nonfiction.

This book, part of the Issues in Focus series, provides actual accounts of computer hacking, some unintentional and some very serious. Among those who are decidedly malicious are the "phone phreaks," those who steal long distance phone services; "spies," who steal information using unauthorized computer access; and "salami slicers," who steal small amounts from many bank customers, thus ultimately stealing a great deal of money. The book is interesting and easy to read, making it an excellent source of relevant information for young adult readers. The book includes a glossary, bibliographical references, and an index.

9.5   Marshall, Elizabeth L. **A Student's Guide to the Internet: Exploring the World Wide Web, Gopherspace, Electronic Mail, and More!** The Millbrook Press, 1996. 159 pp. ISBN 1-56294-923-3. Nonfiction.

Marshall describes strategies for gathering information from the Net, using newsgroups, e-mail, and the Web. She also provides tips for connecting with potential collaborators and for using the Net to expand the horizons of the reader's world. She concludes with "safety tips" to ensure that time spent on the Net is productive and not destructive.

9.6   Milner, Anna, and Terry Burrows, editors. **The Internet**. Dorling Kindersley, 1996. 128 pp. ISBN 0-7894-1288-8. Nonfiction.

In clear, precise prose, this slender volume, "a beginner's guide to the Internet for Windows 95 users," tells its readers how to get connected, explore the World Wide Web, exchange news, use e-mail, download software, and communicate online. Question boxes, warning boxes, and tip boxes, appendixes on topics such as "Troubleshooting" or "Useful Web Sites," and a useful glossary add to the value of this very helpful text.

9.7   Palfreman, Jon, and Doron Swade. **The Dream Machine: Exploring the Computer Age.** BBC Books, 1993. 208 pp. ISBN 0-563-36992-2. Nonfiction.

The computer, now commonplace in our lives, was not so long ago a phenomenon. It is no longer a machine cranking out pages of numbers for only experts to translate. Today the computer is a means of personal communication and expression, opening doors around the world in record time. *The Dream Machine* outlines the rise of computers from the earliest attempt at automatic calculating in the seventeenth century to our late-twentieth-century travels on the information highway. The human stories behind the machines are told, detailing the fascinating growth and sophistication of a product that continues to change almost daily. Numerous illustrations and a glossary are included.

9.8   Pedersen, Ted, and Mel Gilden. **Cybersurfers: Cybercops and Flame Wars**. Price Stern Sloan, 1996. 128 pp. ISBN 0-8431-3979-X. Fiction.

An Internet insult leads to big trouble for high school computer whizzes Athena Bergstrom and Jason Kane. Family credit ratings, phone bills, and criminal records are all altered by an anonymous computer hacker with an enormous ego and a strange sense of humor. A glossary of Internet signs and computer terms is included. ER

9.9   Pedersen, Ted, and Mel Gilden. **Cybersurfers: Ghost on the Net**. Price Stern Sloan, 1996. 141 pp. ISBN 0-8431-3979-X. Fiction.

A Halloween online séance in the high school computer lab is followed by mysterious cyberspace messages to Jason from his mom—but she died years ago. Jason and his friend Athena look into the strange events and focus their attention on MegaCorp, a secretive company working on computer-enhanced immortality. A spiritualist with a hidden past, a mad scientist, and a newspaper reporter are all involved in the final outcome. A glossary of Internet signs and computer terms is included. ER

9.10   Rubin, Charles. **The Little Book of Computer Wisdom: How to Make Friends with Your PC or Mac**. Houghton Mifflin, 1995. 311 pp. ISBN 0-395-70816-8. Nonfiction.

This easy-to-read book is chock-full of useful information about the different kinds of computers, how to choose them, how to set them up, how to operate them, what software is available, what the possible problems are, and more. As the title indicates, information is given for both PCs and Macs. Though not designated solely for young adult reading, the volume has a place among young adult readers as it provides important facts in a straightforward way. A glossary and an index are included.

10 Dating and Sexual Awareness

"I lose my respect for the man who can make the mystery of sex the object of a coarse jest, yet, when you speak earnestly and seriously on the subject, is silent."

Henry David Thoreau

"Answering questions is a major part of sex education. Two rules cover the ground. First, always give a truthful answer to a question; secondly, regard sex knowledge as exactly like any other knowledge."

Bertrand Russell

10.1   Barrett, Elizabeth. **Free Fall.** HarperCollins, 1994. 249 pp. ISBN 0-06-024465-8. Fiction.

Seventeen-year-old Ginnie Ryan is sent to spend the summer with her grandmother while her parents try to work out problems in their marriage. During the summer, Ginnie learns about love and romance after her boyfriend Denny breaks up with her and she meets a boy named Kris. Ginnie also learns about life and growing up and what it means to be an adult.

10.2   Bode, Janet, and Stan Mack. **Heartbreak and Roses: Real Life Stories of Troubled Love.** Delacorte, 1994. 158 pp. ISBN 0-385-32068-X. Nonfiction.

Authors Janet Bode and Stan Mack record interviews with a group of teens who tell their own stories of the confusion, obsession, and sometimes violence they experience as they try to establish love relationships. MC

ALA Best Books for Young Adults, 1995
IRA Teacher's Choice, 1996

10.3   Fiedler, Lisa. **Curtis Piperfield's Biggest Fan.** Clarion Books, 1995. 121 pp. ISBN 0-395-70728-5. Fiction.

Crushes, kisses, and Catholic school are C. C.'s life as she tells the tangled and humorous tale of her longstanding crush on a "younger man" and future rock star, Curtis Piperfield. Exploring her desire to French-kiss Curtis in her journal and her poetry, C. C. is as shocked as anyone when she finds herself actually kissing the heartthrob of St. Bernadette's School for Girls. ER

10.4   Garden, Nancy. **Good Moon Rising.** Farrar, Straus and Giroux, 1996. 229 pp. ISBN 0-374-32746-7. Fiction.

In this unconventional love story, high school actors Kerry and Jan face the cruelty of intolerance for those who challenge society's norms as they make decisions about their sexual orientation and their relationship that will greatly affect their future plans.

10.5   Johnston, Norma. **The Image Game.** BridgeWater Books, 1994. 160 pp. ISBN 0-8167-3472-0. Fiction.

Celia Pendergast will have to learn the hard way that people aren't always what they seem. Brock Peters is so good-looking and popular that Celia must win his affection. She is so busy thinking about Brock that she overlooks the "diamond," Zack, who is right beside her. Brock uses the expansion of a major chemical company to bring fame to himself, ignoring the fact that the plant is causing water contamination. Zack urges Celia to tell the truth even though she will lose Brock. What will she do? ER

10.6   Kerr, M. E. **Deliver Us from Evie.** HarperCollins, 1994. 177 pp. ISBN 0-06-024475-5. Fiction.

Evie Burrman lives with her family on a farm near a small Missouri town. When she meets rich and beautiful Patsy Duff at a party, Evie is forced to confront her homosexual feelings, and the two girls leave the town to live together. Soon everyone is talking about Evie, and their views on love and life change as a result of witnessing the courage Evie and Patsy exhibit.

ALA Best Books for Young Adults, 1995
ALA Quick Picks for Young Adults, 1995
Booklist Editor's Choice, 1995
School Library Journal Best Books, 1994

10.7   Pollack, Rachel, and Cheryl Schwartz. **The Journey Out: A Guide for and about Lesbian, Gay, and Bisexual Teens.** Viking, 1995. 148 pp. ISBN 0-670-85845-5. Nonfiction.

Teen homosexuality is examined with common sense in this book aimed at helping teens who are confused about their sexuality come to terms with their emerging feelings. Arriving at self-acceptance, sharing (or not sharing) with family and friends, discovering love and relationships, coping with prejudice, defining health and legal issues, and finding resources available to homosexual teens are some of the topics offered that help deliver the authors' message: "You are not alone."

10.8   Powell, Randy. **Is Kissing a Girl Who Smokes like Licking an Ashtray?** Aerial / Farrar, Straus and Giroux, 1994. 199 pp. ISBN 0-374-43627-4. Fiction.

It is May of his senior year and eighteen-year-old Biff, who looks fourteen, has been in love with Tommie Isaac for twenty-three months. The only problem is that he is too shy to ask her out. In fact, he can barely say "hi" without freezing up. And then his sister's friend introduces him to Heidi. Heidi smokes, talks tough, and has an attitude. Biff is fascinated with her and has never had so much fun. But what should he do about Tommie?

10.9   Reynolds, Marilyn. **Too Soon for Jeff.** Morning Glory Press, 1994. 222 pp. ISBN 0-930934-91-1. Fiction.

Jeff, a high school senior hoping to earn a debate scholarship to college, has tired of his freshman girlfriend, Christy. After a year, he is preparing to finally break up with her when she happily announces, "We're having a baby." Although Christy cannot escape the consequences of their actions, Jeff insists that he, nonetheless, is too young for parenthood. Since Christy rejects both abortion and adoption, Jeff must address some weighty decisions.

ALA Best Books for Young Adults, 1995
ALA Quick Picks for Young Adults, 1995

10.10   Sparks, Beatrice, editor. **It Happened to Nancy: By an Anonymous Teenager.** Avon Flare, 1994. 241 pp. ISBN 0-380-77315-5. Nonfiction.

This diary chronicles the experiences of an anonymous narrator from the end of her fourteenth year, when she meets an older boy, sees him secretly, and is date-raped, to shortly after her sixteenth birthday, when she dies of AIDS contracted from that encounter. This interval also includes friends, a boyfriend, school, shuttling between divorced parents, and both physical and emotional pain. The story offers encouragement to others that the suffering is somehow bearable. ER

ALA Quick Picks for Young Adults, 1995

10.11   Spinelli, Jerry. **Jason and Marceline.** Little, Brown, 1986. 228 pp. ISBN 0-316-80702-8. Fiction.

In this sequel to *Space Station Seventh Grade,* Jason Herkimer and Marceline McAllister enter ninth grade. They are becoming more than friends, but in the process their relationship changes. Jason thinks of kissing Marceline and compares their relationship to those of other couples. Marceline is different from other girls and she does not care what others think. As time goes by, Jason and Marceline begin to wonder if their budding romance will bring an end to their friendship.

10.12   Westall, Robert. **Falling into Glory.** Farrar, Straus and Giroux, 1995. 304 pp. ISBN 0-374-32256-2. Fiction.

Robbie is in his last year of school and seems to have it all—good grades, a good reputation, lots of friends, a winning rugby team, and a faithful girlfriend. In addition he gains the attention of a beautiful teacher in his school who is almost twice his age. Love and passion prevail, putting the futures of Robbie and the teacher at great risk.

Titles Annotated in Other Chapters Related to Dating and Sexual Awareness

Bauer, Marion Dane, ed. *Am I Blue? Coming out from the Silence*. Short Stories.

Bezzant, Pat. *Angie*. Romance.

Fitch, Janet. *Kicks*. Friendships.

Flanagan, Geraldine Lux. *Beginning Life*. Drugs.

Landolphi, Suzi. *Hot, Sexy and Safer*. Drugs.

McCants, William D. *Much Ado about Prom Night*. School.

Rodowsky, Colby. *Lucy Peale*. Romance.

Sinclair, April. *Coffee Will Make You Black*. Choices.

Singer, Bennett L. *Growing Up Gay/Growing Up Lesbian*. Diaries.

Sutton, Roger. *Hearing Us Out: Voices from the Gay and Lesbian Community*. Diaries.

Van Dijk, Lutz. *Damned Strong Love*. War.

Wiseman, Rosalind. *Defending Ourselves: A Guide to Prevention, Self-Defense, and Recovery from Rape*. Self Help.

11 Death and Dying

"Death is the supple suitor
That wins at last."

Emily Dickinson

"If we must die, O let us nobly die . . .
Pressed to the wall, but fighting nobly back."

Claude McKay

11.1 Block, Francesca Lia. **The Hanged Man.** HarperCollins, 1994. 137 pp. ISBN 0-06-024536-0. Fiction.

Nearly everyone tries to get seventeen-year-old Laurel to eat; she refuses. Her father is dead now. Their house in Los Angeles is quiet; no more sounds of breaking glass. Why, then, is Laurel feeling like the fragments are ricocheting inside her? At what cost are family secrets to be contained? Can Laurel "afford" the cost? What share is her mother willing to pay? ER Adult situations

ALA Quick Picks for Young Adults, 1995

11.2 Bode, Janet. **Death Is Hard to Live With: Teenagers Talk about How They Cope with Loss.** Illustrated by Stan Mack. Laurel-Leaf Books, 1995. 178 pp. ISBN 0-440-21929-9. Nonfiction.

Teenagers who have experienced firsthand the death of a parent, friend, sibling, relative, or classmate describe the painful experience. This book describes deaths of young persons as well as adults, and the impact they have had on teens. It also provides a multicultural perspective in its discussion of burial customs in different cultures. ER

11.3 Buffie, Margaret. **Someone Else's Ghost.** Scholastic, 1995. 227 pp. ISBN 0-590-46922-3. Fiction.

Sixteen-year-old Jessica reluctantly moves to a guest ranch in Canada with her parents. Her grieving, distant mother stays in her room and her reticent father works endlessly to make a success of the ranch; Jessica is left alone, also grieving for the death of her younger brother, Scotty. Apparitions that Jessica doubts and a hatbox of mementos from the Shaw family finally combine to resolve Scotty's death and the disconsolate spirits that cohabit the guest ranch. ER

11.4 Donovan, Stacy. **Dive.** Dutton Children's Books, 1994. 240 pp. ISBN 0-525-45154-4. Fiction.

What's lucky about a dog named Lucky that is almost killed, an alcoholic mother, a seriously ill father, a sister named Baby, a brother named Edward, and a friendship that is dissolving? These are exactly the kinds of questions V agonizes over in this novel. Just when the bottom is ready to drop out of V's world, Jane arrives at school. This new friendship between the two girls gives rise to other questions. What should V do and where will this relationship lead?

11.5   Dorfman, Elena. **The C-Word: Teenagers and Their Families Living with Cancer.** Foreword by John T. Truman. New Sage Press, 1994. 127 pp. ISBN 0-939165-21-X. Nonfiction.

Looking at cancer through the eyes of young people is very different from looking at it from an adult perspective. This author, a cancer patient, tells firsthand what life is like for the patient, the family, and close friends. Through personal interviews with five teenagers, we learn how parents, siblings, friends, and patients react to cancer and its treatments. Attitudes and perceptions are explained by teenagers, which makes a devastating illness like cancer a bit easier for us all to understand.

11.6   Draper, Sharon M. **Tears of a Tiger.** Atheneum, 1994. 162 pp. ISBN 0-689-31878-2. Fiction.

High school basketball star Rob Washington is killed in a car accident and Andy, fellow Tiger, can't get over the event; he was driving the car and the guilt is just too much to bear. Draper tells the story of Rob's death and the struggle of his friends to come to terms with it and to move on with their lives by juxtaposing letters, articles, homework assignments—including poetry—and dialogues written by those close to Rob and Andy over the months that follow the accident. MC

ALA Best Books for Young Adults, 1996
Notable 1994 Children's Trade Books in the Field of Social Studies

11.7   Ferris, Jean. **Invincible Summer.** Aerial / Farrar, Straus and Giroux, 1994. 167 pp. ISBN 0-374-43608-8. Fiction.

Robin Gregory's ultimate goal, to leave the farm and the town of Bennett when she graduates from high school, changes after she meets Rick. He helps her sort out the things in life that truly matter. The hospital, though, is where they meet and where they face their own mortality—together. MC

Awards to first edition, 1987:
ALA Best Book for Young Adults
Booklist Young Adult Editor's Choice
School Library Journal Best Book of the Year

11.8   Ferris, Jean. **Signs of Life.** Farrar, Straus and Giroux, 1995. 122 pp. ISBN 0-374-36909-7. Fiction.

Seventeen-year-old Hannah Flood struggles to make sense of her twin sister's death and feels that a family trip to see the extraordinary animal paintings in the caves of Lascaux, in France, is just an escape. But through a magical romance with Stefan Kremo, a Romani circus performer, and vivid remembrances of her sister that are triggered by visits to the caves, Hannah reconnects with her family and her own sense of happiness.

11.9   Fox, Paula. **The Eagle Kite: A Novel.** Orchard Books, 1995. 127 pp. ISBN 0-531-06892-7. Fiction.

Fourteen-year-old Liam Cormac unravels a web of excuses and half-truths as he makes peace with Phillip, his dying father. For three years, Liam has kept an angry silence about his accidental discovery of his father's homosexuality. When Liam's parents lie to him about the origin of Phillip's exposure to AIDS by saying he contracted the disease through a blood transfusion, his distrust grows into explosion.

ALA Notable Books for Children, 1996
School Library Journal Best Books, 1995
Booklist Editor's Choice, 1996
Publisher's Weekly Best Books, 1996

11.10   Fry, Virginia Lynn. **Part of Me Died, Too: Stories of Creative Survival among Bereaved Children and Teenagers.** Foreword by Katherine Paterson. Dutton Children's Books, 1995. 218 pp. ISBN 0-525-45068-8. Nonfiction.

Fry's collection of eleven accounts of children experiencing the deaths of others close to them and the process of grieving creatively demonstrates strategies to use to survive and heal after the death of a loved one. Selections of poetry, artwork, and writing serve as examples. These include a shared journal, a "Fears and Hopes" poem, a "Magic Shield," "Worry Stones," and a "Duo Drawing." The deaths these children experienced include those of a grandparent; parents, through disease, accident, suicide, and murder, including a sexually abusive father from cancer; and even a pet.

ALA Notable Books for Children, 1996
Publisher's Weekly Best Books, 1996

11.11   Gelb, Alan. **My Best Friend Died.** Archway Paperback / Pocket Books, 1995. 149 pp. ISBN 0-671-87273-7. Fiction.

Recognizing that Walt is drunk, Dave Hickock insists on driving his best friend back to his grandmother's to return her car. Walt's behaviors, a sudden patch of dense fog, and a single piece of ice change Dave's life in a split second. Where does a seventeen-year-old turn to deal with his best friend's death, which he believes he caused? Part of the Real Life series. ER

11.12 Gonzales, Doreen. **AIDS: Ten Stories of Courage.** Enslow, 1996. 112 pp. ISBN 0-89490-766-2. Nonfiction.

These are stories of the courage displayed by people who face death from AIDS. Profiles of celebrities in this volume from the Collective Biographies series include Arthur Ashe, Freddie Mercury, Rudolf Nureyev, Anthony Perkins, and Ryan White.

11.13 Gootman, Marilyn E. **When a Friend Dies: A Book for Teens about Grieving and Healing.** Edited by Pamela Espeland. Free Spirit, 1994. 109 pp. ISBN 0-915793-66-0. Nonfiction.

Any adolescent who has experienced a friend's death will find this an approachable and readable book. Following a concise question-and-answer format with quotations from grieving teens, this text encourages the reader to reflect on his or her feelings about losing a friend. A listing and explanation of supportive organizations ends the book. The author also lists additional readings on this topic. ER

ALA Quick Picks for Young Adults, 1995

11.14 Hartnett, Sonya. **Wilful Blue.** Viking, 1994. 156 pp. ISBN 0-670-85718-1. Fiction.

Guy Alexander Defoe, a gifted young artist, takes his genius for granted. While on an artist's retreat, he reveals to his friends that he wishes his life to be remembered for something that matters, but finds only disappointment in himself and in the world around him. His peers Jesse and Walt see him suffering from suicidal unhappiness, but do not discover this early enough to prevent a fatality. They must decide whether to console Guy's family or to be truthful to them. MC WL

11.15 Hesse, Karen. **Phoenix Rising.** Henry Holt, 1994. 182 pp. ISBN 0-8050-3108-1. Fiction.

A nuclear power plant accident in Vermont forces thirteen-year-old Nyle to adopt an isolated and inconvenient lifestyle in order to survive. With Gran as her "parent," Nyle lives and works on a sheep farm. But when Gran offers nuclear fallout victims a refuge at the farm, Nyle must deal with her feelings of loss and her fear of attachment. ER

ALA Best Books for Young Adults, 1995
ALA Notable Books for Children, 1995
School Library Journal Best Books, 1995
IRA Teacher's Choice, 1995
IRA Young Adult's Choice, 1996

11.16 Hurwin, Davida Wills. **A Time for Dancing: A Novel.** Little, Brown, 1995. 257 pp. ISBN 0-316-38351-1. Fiction.

Julie and Sam, close friends since childhood, spend hours planning how they will spend the summer before senior year. Dance will require a major time commitment that both are willing to make since it is their passion. But when Julie leaves rehearsal in pain, the girls' friendship begins a painful transition. Through alternating chapters, each reveals her feelings about their significant bond of friendship and how it is stretched and strained by their love of dance and their encounter with cancer.

ALA Best Books for Young Adults, 1996

11.17   Murphy, Claire Rudolf. **Gold Star Sister.** Lodestar Books / Dutton, 1994. 166 pp. ISBN 0-525-67492-6. Fiction.

Carrie is mature beyond her thirteen years. Her much-loved Gram has cancer, and although the impending loss is unthinkable to Carrie she gives Gram her unfailing attention. A long-buried box of old letters reveals that Gram's cherished brother Billy died in World War II, before he could keep a vow to a dying soldier. Carrie is determined to fulfill the promise, believing this quest to be equally meaningful to Gram. Murphy has written a moving story of a family coming together. ER

Notable Children's Trade Books in the Field of Social Studies, 1994

11.18   Nelson, Richard E., Ph.D., and Judith C. Galas. **The Power to Prevent Suicide: A Guide for Teens Helping Teens.** Free Spirit, 1994. 125 pp. ISBN 0-915793-70-9. Nonfiction.

Your best friend has confided in you that he or she has nothing to live for and is dropping out of school. Days later you learn that he or she has committed suicide. What could you have done to help change your friend's mind? Nelson and Galas provide straight talk for teens who care about their friends, and want to empower themselves with skills to prevent teen suicide. Through the use of discussion cues, questionnaires, and checklists, readers are able to identify at-risk behaviors, warning signals, prevention techniques, and accessible resources needed to conduct suicide analyses for themselves and their peers.

ALA Quick Picks for Young Adults, 1995

11.19   Nelson, Theresa. **Earthshine: A Novel.** Orchard Books, 1994. 192 pp. ISBN 0-531-06867-6. Fiction.

Twelve-year-old "Slim" Margery Grace is happily living with her adored actor / father, Mack McGranahan, and his friend / companion in Los Angeles after her parents' divorce. Mack has the unique ability to keep everyone around him laughing and happy. When his illness returns with belligerence, Slim must come to terms with the reality of AIDS and its impact on her life and her beliefs. ER

ALA Best Books for Young Adults, 1995
ALA Notable Books for Children, 1995
ALA Quick Picks for Young Adults, 1995
School Library Journal Best Books, 1995
IRA Young Adult's Choice, 1995

11.20 Rodowsky, Colby. **Remembering Mog.** Farrar, Straus and Giroux, 1996. 136 pp. ISBN 0-0-374-34663-1. Fiction.

Mog was murdered on the night of her high school graduation. Now it's her younger sister's turn to leave high school, and Annie's wondering how to go on with her own life when there's been no reconciliation to its loss within the Fitzhugh family.

11.21 Schwandt, Stephen. **Holding Steady.** Free Spirit, 1996. 176 pp. ISBN 0-915793-94-6. Fiction.

Brendon and his mother and brother are trying to cope after the accidental death of the father of the family. A summer vacation on Washington Island seems just the right answer. The summer starts slowly with boating and swimming, but adventure, romance, and a narrow escape await them.

11.22 Snyder, Melissa. **Souvenirs.** Avon Flare, 1995. 181 pp. ISBN 0-380-77805-X. Fiction.

Kendall is devastated by the drowning death of her older sister, Katie. The fact that Katie died trying to save Kendall herself from drowning creates a deep feeling of guilt on her part. Her family's inability to communicate about Katie's death make their grief unbearable, and Kendall is left pretty much alone to work through feelings she can barely understand. Gradually, though, she is able to handle her grief and her guilt and find a way to cope with her painful and personal loss. ER

11.23 Springer, Nancy. **Toughing It.** Harcourt Brace, 1994. 119 pp. ISBN 0-15-200011-9. Fiction.

With no identified father and a mother either too drunk or too busy with his half-siblings, sixteen-year-old Shawn treasures his relationship with Dillon. Dillon has charm, good looks, and girls. When Shawn witnesses Dillon's chance murder and chooses to act on his rage, he makes several discoveries about himself, his "family," and his friend. ER

ALA Best Books for Young Adults, 1995
ALA Quick Picks for Young Adults, 1995
Edgar Allan Poe Award, 1995

Titles Annotated in Other Chapters Related to Death and Dying

Cooney, Caroline B. *Driver's Ed.* School.

Creech, Sharon. *Walk Two Moons.* Family.

Doty, Mark. *Atlantis.* Poetry.

Dozois, Gardner, and Sheila Williams, eds. *Isaac Asimov's Ghosts.* Short Stories.

Gilbert, Barbara Snow. *Stone Water.* Family.

Hayes, Daniel. *Flyers.* School.

Porte, Barbara Ann. *Something Terrible Happened*. Family.

Sparks, Beatrice, ed. *It Happened to Nancy*. Dating.

12 Diaries, Essays, Journals, Letters, and Oral Histories

"I never travel without my diaries. One should always have something sensational to read on the train."

Oscar Wilde

"We can escape almost anything, with these stories we survive."

Leslie Marmon Silko

12.1 Alicea, Gil C., with Carmine DeSena. **The Air down Here: True Tales from a South Bronx Boyhood.** Chronicle Books, 1995. 134 pp. ISBN 0-8118-1048-8. Nonfiction.

Gil Alicea lives in a tough section of the Bronx—a place where drugs and gangs are familiar parts of the landscape. In spite of his own family difficulties, however, including the death of his mother, Gil maintains a positive outlook on life. His close relationship with his father gives him values and a sense of security that allow him to rise above the conditions around him. Gil's humor and warmth make his story a unique one of inner-city life. MC

12.2 Arnosky, Jim. **Nearer Nature.** Lothrop, Lee and Shepard, 1996. 176 pp. ISBN 0-688-12213-2. Nonfiction.

Arnosky vividly describes his domesticated animals and the natural life around his Vermont farm in short stories and essays accompanied by his own sketches. He explores the balance of life and death during the cycle of the seasons as he raises sheep, tends to crops, and tramps through the surrounding woods with an artist's/naturalist's perspective.

12.3 Artenstein, Jeffrey. **Runaways: In Their Own Words: Kids Talking about Living on the Streets.** Tom Doherty Associates, 1995. 171 pp. ISBN 0-812-51354-1. Nonfiction.

"I hope some readers will lose their innocence as I did," states the author, a counselor who works with runaway teens in Los Angeles. In matter-of-fact voices, ten young people describe the pain that precedes running away, and the tragedy that follows it. Life on the streets for these teens means betrayal, drugs, theft, and prostitution. Shelters like the one the author is associated with offer some hope, help, and skill development to these young people.

12.4 Atkin, S. Beth. **Voices from the Streets: Young Former Gang Members Tell Their Stories.** Photographed by S. Beth Atkin. Little, Brown, 1996. 132 pp. ISBN 0-316-05634-0. Nonfiction.

Saroem Phoung says, "There is a human to me." His cry is echoed throughout the interviews presented here to document the conflicts, hopes, and fears of young gang members who have managed to leave their gangs, supported by various individuals able to help them envision other possible lives. MC

12.5 Boyko, Carrie, and Kimberly Colen, compilers. **Hold Fast Your Dreams: Twenty Commencement Speeches.** Scholastic, 1996. 230 pp. ISBN 0-590-50956-X. Nonfiction.

Individualism, multiculturalism, patriotism, personal dedication, humanism, inspiration, advice, and humor are exemplified in this book of twenty commencement speeches by such notable people as Colin Powell, Billy Joel, Dr. Seuss, Jimmy Carter, Cathy Guisewite, and others. From the messages they contain to the way they are presented, the speeches offer much wisdom to the reader. MC

12.6 Cole, Sheila. **What Kind of Love? The Diary of a Pregnant Teenager.** Lothrop, Lee and Shepard, 1995. 192 pp. ISBN 0-688-12848-3. Fiction.

Val is fifteen, in love, and pregnant. Through her diary, she reveals her innermost feelings as she confronts her boyfriend, her family, and herself. She imagines a perfect family after she marries her boyfriend, but when he abandons her, Val must decide whether to keep the baby or give it up for adoption.

12.7 Desetta, Al, editor. **The Heart Knows Something Different: Teenage Voices from the Foster Care System.** Foreword by Jonathan Kozol. Youth Communication / Persea Books, 1996. 272 pp. ISBN 0-89255-215-8. Nonfiction.

The authors of the thirty-nine personal accounts in this collection have all lived in foster care. Their essays tell what it is like to be part of the system. Many write about parents who are temporarily out of order, about their own identity, and about looking into the future, and they offer advice to others. The teens' words show that writing helped them understand their feelings and discover ways to change their lives. The book includes a slang glossary, subject guide, and resource list. MC

12.8 Filipović, Zlata. **Zlata's Diary: A Child's Life in Sarajevo.** Introduction by Janine Di Giovanni. Translated by Christina Pribichevich-Zorić. Viking, 1994. 200 pp. ISBN 0-670-85724-6. Nonfiction.

Monday, October 4, 1994. Zlata writes, "Life in a closed circle continues. You wonder what that life is like, Mimmy. It's a life of waiting, of fear, a life where you want the circle to open and the sun of peace to shine down on you again." But Zlata lived a life of fear between October 1991, when the war began that has since torn apart her homeland of Bosnia, and December 1993, when she and her family were allowed to leave Sarajevo for Paris. In her diary, Zlata chronicles the ugliness of war and its effects on those who live through it with remarkable clarity and a courage well beyond her years. ER WL MC

ALA Quick Picks for Young Adults, 1995
Booklist Editor's Choice, 1995

12.9   Ford, Michael Thomas. **The Voices of AIDS: Twelve Unforgettable People Talk about How AIDS Has Changed Their Lives.** Morrow Junior Books, 1995. 225 pp. ISBN 0-688-05322-X. Nonfiction.

Twelve "Fast Facts" about HIV, AIDS, and safer sex are interspersed in this book with the stories of twelve people personally affected by AIDS. The author interviewed a variety of people—a gay teen, mothers whose daughters died of AIDS, a brother whose sister tested HIV-positive, and people of all ages who lost friends to the disease. In this collection of their honest answers to specific questions, teens will find much information and ideas about ways to help.

ALA Best Books for Young Adults, 1996
Booklist Editor's Choice, 1996

12.10   Gourley, Catherine, in association with Mystic Seaport Museum. **Hunting Neptune's Giants: True Stories of American Whaling.** The Millbrook Press, 1995. 93 pp. ISBN 1-56294-534-3. Nonfiction.

The author, in association with Mystic Seaport Museum, has collected excerpts from diaries, ships' logs, letters, and other written documents from people involved in the nineteenth-century whaling industry. They found adventure, along with danger, hardship, and sometimes death, but by the early twentieth century, the whaling industry was on the wane because whales had been hunted to the point of extinction.

12.11   Hinojosa, Maria. **Crews: Gang Members Talk to Maria Hinojosa.** Photography by German Perez. Harcourt Brace, 1995. 168 pp. ISBN 0-15-292873. Nonfiction.

Reporter Maria Hinojosa spent time with gang, or "crew" members, from New York City. "I kept asking myself what makes it so easy for a kid to rely on violence? What makes it so easy for a kid to pull out a knife and stab someone? Who asks what they feel and why? Who wants to listen, no matter how painful the answers might be? I wanted to listen. And I wanted to know why." The book includes a glossary of slang terms. MC

Notable 1995 Children's Trade Books in the Field of Social Studies

12.12   Hoobler, Dorothy, and Thomas Hoobler. The American Family Album series. Oxford University Press, 1994, 1995. 128 pp. ISBN (series) 0-19-509125-6. Nonfiction.

Pick up any of these five family albums and the pictures will entice you to read the entire book. The series includes *The African American Family Album, The Chinese American Family Album, The Irish American Family Album, The Italian American Family Album,* and *The Mexican American Family Album.* The black-and-white photographs convey a sense of time and place, making the people and events come alive. Each chapter is sprinkled with diary entries, interviews, and essays written by people from all walks of life. Volumes cover historical roots, immigration, "assimilation," and political movements. They offer a more personal view in chapters on family, neighborhoods, religion, schools, cultural celebrations, and work life. Stereotypes are explored. A prominent descendant of each heritage introduces each volume, and each volume includes a timeline, further reading suggestions, and the biography of a particular family. MC

12.13   Johnson, Venice, editor. **Voices of the Dream: African-American Women Speak.** Chronicle Books, 1995. 108 pp. ISBN 0-8118-1113-1. Nonfiction.

This beautiful book includes quotations from well-known African American women including Maya Angelou, Mary McLeod Bethune, Rosa Parks, and Alice Walker, and reproductions of paintings, drawings, and mixed-media art work by African American women artists. A brief biography section is included in the book. MC

12.14   Kuklin, Susan. **Irrepressible Spirit: Conversations with Human Rights Activists.** G. P. Putnam's Sons, 1996. 230 pp. ISBN 0-399-22762-8. Nonfiction.

Human rights activists working in China, Cuba, Bosnia, Rwanda, Brazil, the United States, Asia, Cambodia, Jamaica, Tajikistan, and South Africa tell their stories of human rights abuses and the struggle to achieve justice. A historical background on each country or area's abuses is given "In Brief," before the activist's personal history unfolds. The accounts are organized under the United Nations' "Universal Declaration of Human Rights" categories. There are many references to the Human Rights Watch organization, and a list of other human rights organizations is included. The activists' stories describe the evils of human nature, including tyranny, genocide, rape, poverty, slavery, torture, and political incarceration, but also the indomitable human spirit that strives to find a better way. MC WL

12.15   Lawlor, Veronica. **I Was Dreaming to Come to America: Memories from the Ellis Island Oral History Project.** Illustrated by Veronica Lawlor. Foreword by Rudolph W. Giuliani, Mayor, New York City. Viking, 1995. 39 pp. ISBN 0-670-86164-2. Nonfiction.

This brief composite of oral histories presents the remembrances of sixteen people of the moments at which they first arrived as young immigrants in the United States. Readers will feel both the wondrous amazement experienced by many immigrants, including Golda Meir, as they first saw the Statue of Liberty or took those first few steps on American soil and the overwhelmed feelings of those who remember only the shoes on their feet or being detained for illness or political reasons. Each vignette is accompanied by a marvelous illustration and supplemented by a detailed biography. ER MC

Notable 1995 Children's Trade Books in the Field of Social Studies

12.16　Lyons, Mary E. **Keeping Secrets: The Girlhood Diaries of Seven Women Writers.** Henry Holt, 1995. 180 pp. ISBN 0-8050-3065-4. Nonfiction.

Women in nineteenth-century America were often victims of tradition; few choices were available for them to assert their intelligence or independence. Keeping a diary was an acceptable feminine pastime, so many used this outlet to express their restricted emotions. These seven women, both black and white, chafed under society's expectations, but rose to prominence in their time. Much is revealed and still more extrapolated about Louisa May Alcott, Charlotte Forten, Sarah Jane Foster, Kate Chopin, Alice Dunbar-Nelson, Ida B. Wells, and Charlotte Perkins Gilman.

Notable 1995 Children's Trade Books in the Field of Social Studies

12.17　Meltzer, Milton, editor. **Frederick Douglass: In His Own Words.** Illustrated by Stephen Alcorn. Harcourt Brace, 1995. 220 pp. ISBN 0-15-229492-9. Nonfiction.

Frederick Douglass was an eloquent orator on injustice and inequality. He supported women's right to vote, and spoke from personal experience on the evil of slavery. These selections from Douglass's speeches and writings represent his extensive and developing views. Autobiographical writings are not included, as they are available elsewhere. Each selection has a brief but insightful introduction or explanation. Stephen Alcorn's powerful illustrations are the perfect complement to the evocative and impassioned words with which Douglass mesmerized listeners, then and now. MC

Notable 1995 Children's Trade Books in the Field of Social Studies

12.18　Michelson, Maureen, editor. **Women and Work: In Their Own Words.** NewSage Press, 1994. 191 pp. ISBN 0-939165-23-6. Nonfiction.

Women write about their jobs, which range from rodeo bronco rider to fisherwoman to restaurant worker to milliner. This is a revised and updated edition of the award-winning *Women and Work: In Their Own Words* published in 1986. Here are contemporary essays which are especially relevant to women's work in the 1990s. ER MC WL

12.19   Paulsen, Gary. **Father Water, Mother Woods: Essays on Fishing and Hunting in the North Woods.** Illustrated by Ruth Wright Paulsen. Delacorte Press, 1994. 159 pp. ISBN 0-385-32053-1. Nonfiction.

Paulsen fans may be especially interested in this semi-autobiographical book, which is a meditation on hunting, fishing, and the changing seasons in the northern woods. Paulsen describes the techniques, rituals, and superstitions that he and his friends employ while hunting and fishing. The book's climax is reached at the end, when Paulsen succeeds in killing his first deer with an arrow, and learns the finality of death and beauty.

ALA Quick Picks for Young Adults, 1995

12.20   Paulsen, Gary. **Puppies, Dogs, and Blue Northers: Reflections on Being Raised by a Pack of Sled Dogs.** Harcourt Brace, 1996. 81 pp. ISBN 0-15-292881-2. Nonfiction.

Experienced Iditarod racer Gary Paulsen presents personal essays about the birth and life of a litter of sled dogs born to the sport Paulsen has come to love. ER

12.21   *Read* Magazine. **Dear Author: Students Write about the Books That Changed Their Lives.** Introduction by Lois Lowry. Conari Press, 1995. 186 pp. ISBN 1-57324-003-6. Nonfiction.

The editors of Weekly Reader's *Read* magazine have collected letters written by junior and senior high school students to authors. Letters included address authors as varied as Maya Angelou, Ernest Hemingway, Anne Frank, Judy Blume, Alex Haley, and Toni Morrison, to name but a few, and they encompass topics such as grief and loss, self-discovery, war, and inspiration.

12.22   Robertson, Elizabeth W. **Weep Not for Me, Dear Mother.** Illustrated by Stephen McCall. Pelican, 1996. 168 pp. ISBN 1-56554-186-3. Nonfiction.

This book contains the correspondence of Eli Landers, a Confederate soldier serving in Georgia's infantry. He participated in many of the major campaigns of the war, from Pennsylvania to Georgia. His vivid accounts detail the daily life of a foot soldier, and are accompanied by interpretations and explanations by the author.

12.23   Scholastic Inc. Dear America series. 1996.

Denenberg, Barry. **When Will This Cruel War Be Over? The Civil War Diary of Emma Simpson.** 157 pp. ISBN 0-590-22862-5. Fiction.

Gregory, Kristiana. **The Winter of Red Snow: The Revolutionary War Diary of Abigail Jane Stewart.** 173 pp. ISBN 0-590-22653-3. Fiction.

Lasky, Kathryn. **A Journey to the New World: The Diary of Remember Patience Whipple.** 173 pp. ISBN 0-590-50214-X. Fiction.

Scholastic asked respected authors to create historically accurate, but fictional, diaries of young people living during different periods of American history. Supplementing the diaries are maps, pictures, photographs, facsimiles of pertinent documents, and afterwords containing historical notes. The goal of the series is to make history come alive for today's young adult readers by presenting historical events through the eyes of adolescents who lived long ago.

12.24   Singer, Bennett L., editor. **Growing Up Gay / Growing Up Lesbian: A Literary Anthology.** New Press, 1994. 318 pp. ISBN 1-56584-103-4. Fiction / Nonfiction.

Singer's is an essential book for straights, gays, everyone. Do you become gay, or are you born that way? Is the process of gaining family acceptance more difficult than developing self-acceptance? What are the advantages of coming out? Of keeping your differences private? Over fifty coming-of-age stories, both autobiographical and fictional, are as individual as they are moving. Readers will gain a much deeper understanding of what being gay means with this remarkable and interesting book.

12.25   Stepto, Michele, editor. **African-American Voices.** The Millbrook Press, 1995. 159 pp. ISBN 1-56294-474-6. Nonfiction.

Intense emotion permeates the selections printed here from the works of authors such as Paul Dunbar, Frederick Douglass, and Toni Morrison. These are authors who have achieved lasting international fame because their words have the power to move us, to educate us, to make us grow in spirit. They represent more than two hundred years of African American literary tradition. Readers will be inspired to explore these authors further as they become intrigued by the motifs—veil, water, sacred circle—that form a common thread throughout the volume, part of the Writers of America series. MC

12.26   Sutton, Roger. **Hearing Us Out: Voices from the Gay and Lesbian Community.** Photographs by Lisa Ebright. Foreword by M. E. Kerr. Little, Brown, 1994. 128 pp. ISBN 0-316-82326-0. Nonfiction.

Middle school to adult readers will contrast the pain and confusion that many of the teens in this book experience with the increased sense of confidence and satisfaction that the adults represented here have found. Over fifteen individuals, from all ages, races, and walks of life, share stories about high school, coming out to their parents, searching for role models, and finding acceptance and respect. Readers will be more likely to view gays as people, rather than stereotypes, after reading this. Highly recommended for everyone. MC

ALA Best Books for Young Adults, 1995
Notable 1994 Children's Trade Books in the Field of Social Studies

12.27   Tarpley, Natasha, editor. **Testimony: Young African-Americans on Self-Discovery and Black Identity.** Beacon Press, 1995. 272 pp. ISBN 0-8070-0929-6. Nonfiction.

Natasha Tarpley, a law student at Georgetown University, has in this volume collected essays, poems, and personal narratives written by young African Americans in which they explore their perspectives on their generation's shared experiences of racism and of being African American in this time period. These writers refer to their personal and family histories as they search for ways of being in the world and they claim historical figures from Phyllis Wheatley to Alice Walker as their models of how to find internal strength and pride. The book reflects what "Afrocentricity" means, but offers, too, a sense of hope and caring that these young writers and their peers can find their way. As Yao Bhoke Ahoto writes in "X 1 (Unknown),"

> for what is right
> for what is good
> is not to be wished upon
> it is to be practiced
> cared for
> every day.   MC

12.28   Thomas, Roy Edwin, compiler. **Come Go with Me: Old-Timer Stories from the Southern Mountains.** Pictures by Laszlo Kubinyi. Farrar, Straus and Giroux, 1994. 173 pp. ISBN 0-374-34382-9. Nonfiction.

Thomas has collected stories about the old days in the Appalachian, Ozark, and Ouachita Mountains as told by the people who hunted the coons and lived in the log-floored houses. Attitudes about parents, dating, food, and customs are revealed in these spirited interviews full of love, fun, and adventure. MC

12.29   **A World in Our Hands: Written, Illustrated, and Edited by Young People of the World in Honor of the Fiftieth Anniversary of the United Nations.** Tricycle Press, Peace Child International, and Paintbrush Diplomacy, 1995. 91 pp. ISBN 1-883672-31-7. Nonfiction.

This book is a compilation of an international span of authors and editors, ranging in age from twelve to twenty-five years old, focusing upon many different aspects of a single subject: the United Nations. Each of the four main sections of the book zeroes in on an important area such as "A Charter of Hope," "Once Upon a U.N.," "U.N. of the Future," and "We the Young People." Read and learn from the generation we will depend upon for our futures. ER MC WL

Titles Annotated in Other Chapters Related to Diaries, Essays, Journals, Letters, and Oral Histories

Blue, Rose, and Corinne J. Naden. *The White House Kids*. Autobiography.

Boas, Jacob. *We Are Witnesses: Five Diaries of Teenagers Who Died in the Holocaust*. Holocaust.

Bode, Janet. *Death Is Hard to Live With*. Death.

Bode, Janet, and Stan Mack. *Heartbreak and Roses: Real Life Stories of Troubled Love*. Dating.

Cook, Mariana. *Mothers and Sons*. Family.

Cushman, Karen. *Catherine, Called Birdy*. Historical Fiction.

Denenberg, Barry. *Voices from Vietnam*. War.

Emert, Phyllis Raybin. *Mysteries of Strange Appearances from Beyond*. Mysteries.

Hesse, Karen. *The Music of Dolphins*. Choices.

Holliday, Laurel, compiler. *Children in the Holocaust and World War II: Their Secret Diaries*. Holocaust.

Martin, Joseph Plumb. *Yankee Doodle Boy*. War.

Miller, Brandon Marie. *Buffalo Gals*. Westerns.

Morris, Juddi. *The Harvey Girls*. Westerns.

Rochman, Hazel, and Darlene Z. McCampbell. *Bearing Witness*. Holocaust.

Sparks, Beatrice, ed. *It Happened to Nancy*. Dating.

Towsend, Sue. *Adrian Mole: The Lost Years*. Humor.

Woodson, Jacqueline. *From the Notebooks of Melanin Sun*. Family.

13 Drugs, Alcohol, and Other Health Issues

"Health and cheerfulness mutually beget each other."
Joseph Addison

"A man who fears suffering is already suffering from what he fears."
Michel de Montaigne

13.1   Brynie, Faith Hickman. **Genetics and Human Health: A Journey Within.** Illustrated by Sharon Lane Holm. The Millbrook Press, 1995. 128 pp. ISBN 1-56294-545-9. Nonfiction.

Genetic researchers are modern-day detectives looking for clues within human cells to unlock the mysteries of the DNA molecule and its effect on inherited traits and genetically transmitted diseases. Easy-to-understand diagrams and personal case histories are used to detail the origins and complexity of DNA research. The successes of technological research and the ethical questions presented by genetic engineering are considered.

13.2   Fenwick, Elizabeth, and Richard Walker. **How Sex Works: A Clear, Comprehensive Guide for Teenagers to Emotional, Physical, and Sexual Maturity.** Dorling Kindersley, 1994. 96 pp. ISBN 1-56458-505-0. Nonfiction.

This user-friendly text, illustrated with detailed photography, provides everything the reader needs to know about the adolescent mind and body. Sexual myths, stereotypes, and prejudices are explored and the authors provide up-to-date information about timely topics such as AIDS/HIV and birth control. There is an emphasis on safe sexual practice throughout the book, and the emotional anxieties associated with making decisions about becoming sexually active are explored.

ALA Quick Picks for Young Adults, 1995

13.3   Flanagan, Geraldine Lux. **Beginning Life.** Dorling Kindersley, 1996. 120 pp. ISBN 0-7894-0609-8. Nonfiction.

By day twenty-five of a pregnancy the embryo's heart will start beating. With many such fascinating details this book provides an overview of the formation of life from conception to birth. Written in an easy narrative style to sharpen our understanding of these events, and illustrated with photographs, this book is a useful and valuable reference.

13.4 Flynn, Tom, and Karen Lound. **AIDS: Examining the Crisis.** Lerner, 1995. 72 pp. ISBN 0-8225-2625-5. Nonfiction.

This treatise on AIDS gives the reader basic factual information about the early emergence of the HIV virus, its transmission, prevention, and treatment, and the educational initiatives designed to inform the public about it. Statistical information is included, such as the medical costs involved, numbers of victims, and projected numbers of victims, as well as personal information about famous people afflicted with the disease. A glossary and a list of resources for further information about AIDS are included.

Notable 1995 Children's Trade Books in the Field of Social Studies

13.5 Harris, Robie H. **It's Perfectly Normal: A Book About Changing Bodies, Growing Up, Sex, and Sexual Health.** Illustrated by Michael Emberley. Candlewick Press, 1994. 89 pp. ISBN 1-56402-199-8. Nonfiction.

The title just about says it all. Everything adolescents may need to know about their changing bodies—reproduction, birth, sexuality, contraception, diseases, abuse—is told in clear, correct, affirming language, painstakingly explained and generously illustrated with drawings and lively cartoons. A very reassuring tone repeatedly reminds readers that all of these transformations are "perfectly normal." For those with specific questions, a good index is included. ER

ALA Notable Books for Children, 1995
School Library Journal Best Books, 1994

13.6 Hawksley, Lucinda, and Ian Whitelaw, editors. **101 Essential Tips: Yoga.** Dorling Kindersley, 1995. 72 pp. ISBN 1-56458-991-9. Nonfiction.

Clear illustrations and explicit explanatory text make this a useful introduction to yoga. As it admonishes early on, however, a qualified teacher would be the best means to achieve proper postures and breathing. Emphasis is on the physical exercises and benefits, with only passing mention of the philosophical basis or meditational aspects of yoga.

13.7 Himrich, Brenda L., and Stew Thornley. **Electrifying Medicine: How Electricity Sparked a Medical Revolution.** Lerner, 1995. 88 pp. ISBN 0-8225-15717. Nonfiction.

This informative book explores various ways that electricity plays a role in maintaining the body's equilibrium. With this knowledge, doctors have been able to use the power of electrical current to restimulate damaged organs and muscles. The layperson has observed the effects of electricity in the forms of the pacemaker and ventricular defibrillation (paddles applied to the heart region of the chest to restimulate it). Along with many successes, the authors also point out many misconceptions about how electricity can be used as a "healer" and offer hope for ways it can be used in the future. A glossary is included.

13.8   Hyde, Margaret O. **Know about Tuberculosis.** Walker, 1994. 106 pp. ISBN 0-8027-8338-4. Nonfiction.

Did you think tuberculosis was a disease of the past that had disappeared a long time ago? Think again. The World Health Organization estimates that one-third of the world's population is already infected with TB. In easy-to-read chapters titled "Can You Get TB by Riding the Bus?" and "Kids Can Get Tuberculosis," readers can learn how to protect themselves from this frightening disease. From the author of *Know about AIDS*, this book is another addition to the Know about . . . series. ER

13.9   Hyde, Margaret O., and Elizabeth H. Forsyth. **Know about AIDS.** Illustrated by Debora Weber. Walker, 1994. 97 pp. ISBN 0-8027-8345-7. Nonfiction.

In this revised edition of *Know about AIDS*, the authors provide the latest information and statistics about the disease. The authors stress that while most groups are taking the necessary precautions to prevent AIDS, HIV, the AIDS virus, is spreading most rapidly in adolescents. Geared toward this age group, this book describes the history of AIDS, how the disease is transmitted, how it can be prevented, the latest treatments for AIDS patients, and much more. ER

13.10   Landau, Elaine. **Teenage Drinking.** Enslow, 1994. 104 pp. ISBN 0-89490-575-9. Nonfiction.

The personal testimonies of young drinkers, interwoven with a thorough exploration of the causes, dangers, and treatment of teenage drinking, make a powerful statement about one of society's most critical problems. The risks of drinking alcohol, especially for teenagers, are documented, along with the penalties assessed for youthful offenders in many states. The chapter on treatment includes advice for families as well as an Alcoholics Anonymous twelve-question quiz for teens who drink and the Contract for Life between Parent and Teenager distributed by S.A.D.D. (Students against Driving Drunk). Also included is a resource directory of federal and state agencies involved in preventing substance abuse. This is part of the Issues in Focus series.

13.11   Landolphi, Suzi. **Hot, Sexy and Safer.** Perigee / Berkley, 1994. 162 pp. ISBN 0-399-51882-7. Nonfiction.

Suzi Landolphi began presenting the facts about sex and sexuality when she volunteered to work for an AIDS organization. Now, with a unique blend of wry humor and personal stories, Landolphi tells her readers how to talk openly about sex, how to get their partners to practice safer sex, how to begin to feel good about themselves as sexual beings, how to take care of themselves, and how to have more honest relationships. The text is explicit, but it is also readable, truthful, and important in today's society.

13.12   Langone, John. **Tough Choices: A Book about Substance Abuse.** Little, Brown, 1995. 122 pp. ISBN 0-316-51407-1. Nonfiction.

Do you know the difference between uppers and crack? Which is worse: drinking alcohol or smoking pot? Objective and understandable, Langone answers these questions and more. Substance abuse is one of the biggest problems in modern society, and this author figures that the more you know, the more able you are to make smart choices. ER

13.13   Littell, Mary Ann. **LSD.** Enslow, 1996. 112 pp. ISBN 0-89490-739-5. Nonfiction.

This thought-provoking book in the Drug Library series leads the reader through the history of this hallucinogenic drug and its societal and physical effects. Each chapter is written in a simple style, includes charts and pictures, and provides discussion questions to prompt the reader to better absorb the information. The effects on individuals and families, and the treatment and prevention of LSD use, are included, along with a section on where to go for help, a glossary, and an index.

13.14   Monroe, Judy. **Nicotine.** Enslow, 1995. 128 pp. ISBN 0-89490-505-8. Nonfiction.

Three out of four teens who think they can stop smoking within a year in fact cannot quit. Beginning with the history of the "golden leaf," this book from the Drug Library series tells about the effects of tobacco and nicotine, including smokeless tobacco and secondhand smoke—the health problems they create, governmental actions in response, who smokes, and reasons to stop. The difficulties involved in quitting are discussed and suggestions for how to quit are offered, including names and addresses of quit-smoking programs, and the volume also includes discussion questions, a glossary, and an index. ER

13.15   Moragne, Wendy. **Attention Deficit Disorder.** The Millbrook Press, 1996. 112 pp. ISBN 1-56294-674-9. Nonfiction.

Inattention, impulsiveness, and hyperactivity—these are three key categories of symptoms indicative of Attention Deficit Disorder, all of which make family life, schooling, and even friendships more difficult for the young person diagnosed with the disorder. In clear prose documented with case studies, Moragne explains symptoms, various therapies, and, most important, practical strategies for living productively with ADD.

13.16   Parker, Steve. **Medicine.** Dorling Kindersley, 1995. 64 pp. ISBN 1-56458-882-3. Nonfiction.

This book in the Eyewitness Science series explores the beginning of medicine in ancient Greece and during the time of the Roman Empire, and connects this history to the contemporary and future worlds of computers and technology. Short chapters, clear illustrations, and an index make this a reader-friendly text. Paragraph biographies of the men and women of medicine are included to show how they have improved human health, and the text also covers topics such as the use of plants in healing and the mind-body connection. ER

13.17 Preston, Richard. **The Hot Zone.** Random House, 1994. 300 pp. ISBN 0-679-43094-6. Nonfiction.

Few diseases strike fear like the mention of AIDS, but clearly its cousin Ebola is even more terrifying. Despite the common misconception that Ebola is confined to Africa, it could potentially ravage the globe virtually unchecked, and in fact was present in Reston, Virginia, in 1989. Descriptions of the gruesome and almost certain death it causes and the biohazard precautions necessary make this a must read for those interested in medical research or who just plain like to be horrified.

ALA Best Books for Young Adults, 1996
School Library Journal Best Adult Books for Young Adults, 1995

13.18 Pringle, Laurence. **Smoking: A Risky Business.** Morrow Junior Books, 1996. 128 pp. ISBN 0-688-13039-9. Nonfiction.

Pringle provides a history of tobacco farming, tobacco manufacturing, and tobacco use while discussing the ethical issues society faces as information piles up about its harmful effects. Sources of helpful information and tips on how to quit smoking are also included. ER

13.19 Robbins, Paul R. **Designer Drugs.** Enslow, 1995. 112 pp. ISBN 0-89490-488-4. Nonfiction.

The author explains the history, types, and characteristics of "designer" drugs, and recounts real-life situations and experiences from his clinical studies of drug addiction and abuse. The role of society, including family and friends, is also explained and at the end of the book the author provides a list of places to contact to get further information and help. Part of the Drug Library series. ER

13.20 Ryan, Joan. **Little Girls in Pretty Boxes: The Making and Breaking of Elite Gymnasts and Figure Skaters.** Doubleday, 1995. 243 pp. ISBN 0-385-47790-2. Nonfiction.

Joan Ryan provides an eye-opening expose of the appalling treatment of little girls which in any other setting would be called child abuse: starvation resulting in permanent bone damage, public ridicule and humiliation, competitions performed with broken bones, and worse. The topics covered (injuries, eating disorders, image, pressure, parents, politics, money, and coaches) are well documented. The text includes sixteen pages of black-and-white photographs, and it provides a fascinating read whether one is a sports enthusiast or not.

13.21 Silverstein, Alvin, Virginia Silverstein, and Robert Silverstein. **Diabetes.** Enslow, 1994. 128 pp. ISBN 0-89490-464-7. Nonfiction.

What is the relationship between the baseball player Jackie Robinson and the lead singer for the heavy-metal group Poison? They shared the same disease: diabetes. This book provides a simplified discussion of the characteristics of diabetes, its effects on teens and adults, its causes, treatments, management strategies, and prevention methods. Brief summaries of current research coupled with biographical sketches of young persons who have learned to cope with diabetes and live productive lives are offered throughout the text. ER

13.22 Slap, Gail B., and Martha M. Jablow. **Teenage Health Care: The First Comprehensive Family Guide for the Preteen to Young Adult Years.** Foreword by Dr. Benjamin Spock. Pocket Books, 1994. 530 pp. ISBN 0-671-75412-2. Nonfiction.

In one easy-to-use, authoritative volume adolescents can find information about the full range of medical, social, and emotional issues relevant to the preteen through young adult years. Readers will have help in interpreting symptoms and determining when and how to seek medical assistance. Growth and development, nutrition, sports, eating disorders, the brain, risk behaviors, sexuality, and conditions of the skin and hair are just some of the topics covered in this text, which is enhanced with tables, charts, and cross-references.

13.23 Vogel, Carole Garbuny. **Will I Get Breast Cancer? Questions and Answers for Teenage Girls.** Julian Messner / Silver Burdett, 1995. 191 pp. ISBN 0-671-88046-2. Nonfiction.

Breast cancer and related issues can be quite frightening for teenage girls, or for any female. The author allows the reader to learn about this critical health issue, without trying to scare anyone, by asking clear, essential questions while providing the latest information in age-appropriate responses. Some of the topics included are: "What Is Cancer?" "Who Gets Breast Cancer?" and "Diagnosis and Treatment." The book also provides a glossary and a bibliography for further reading about related subjects.

Titles Annotated in Other Chapters Related to Drugs, Alcohol, and Other Health Issues

Andryszewski, Tricia. *Abortion: Rights, Options, and Choices*. Reference.

Barrie, Barbara. *Adam Zigzag*. Family.

Block, Francesca Lia. *The Hanged Man*. Death.

Brewer, Sarah. *Body Facts*. Reference.

Christopher, Matt. *Shoot for the Hoop*. Sports.

Clayman, Charles, ed. *The Human Body*. Reference.

Dorfman, Elena. *The C-Word: Teenagers and Their Families Living with Cancer*. Death.

Ford, Michael Thomas. *The Voices of AIDS*. Diaries.

Gonzales, Doreen. *AIDS: Ten Stories of Courage*. Death.

Hipp, Earl. *Fighting Invisible Tigers: A Stress Management Guide for Teens*. Self-Help.

Johnston, Julie. *Hero of Lesser Causes*. Family.

Landau, Elaine. *The Beauty Trap*. Self-Help.

Mather, Cynthia L., with Kristina E. Debye. *How Long Does It Hurt? A Guide to Recovering from Incest and Sexual Abuse for Teenagers, Their Friends, and Their Families*. Self-Help.

Robbins, Paul R. *Designer Drugs*. Drugs.

Sonnenmark, Laura. *A Summer for Always*. Family.

Sherrow, Victoria. *The U.S. Health Care Crisis*. Human Rights.

Tate, Eleanora E. *A Blessing in Disguise*. Family.

Voigt, Cynthia. *Orfe*. Arts.

14 Family Relationships

"I do not love him because he is good, but because he is my child."

Rabindranath Tagore

"All happy families resemble each other; every unhappy family is unhappy in its own way."

Leo Tolstoy

14.1 Aitkens, Maggi. **Kerry, a Teenage Mother.** Photographs by Rob Levine. Lerner, 1994. 48 pp. ISBN 0-8225-2556-9. Nonfiction.

As she struggles to take care of her daughter and continue her education, nineteen-year-old Kerry faces long days with determination and perseverance. Having fun with friends is put on hold, while instead Kerry learns to deal with finances, public assistance forms, housework, and homework in her attempts to reach her goals—giving her daughter a good upbringing and going to college someday. ER

IRA Teacher's Choice, 1996

14.2 Avi. **Sometimes I Think I Hear My Name.** Avon Flare, 1995. 139 pp. ISBN 0-380-72424-3. Fiction.

Conrad's pressing need to see the parents who abandoned him three years earlier leads him on a journey to New York, where he does finally connect with them, as well as with some painful truths. During his one-week stay, he becomes involved in an unusual relationship with an affluent New York girl he had met in St. Louis. This relationship helps him clarify and resolve some important personal issues relating to love, acceptance, and the true meanings of parents, family, and riches.

ALA Quick Picks for Young Adults, 1996

14.3 Barrie, Barbara. **Adam Zigzag.** Delacorte Press, 1994. 192 pp. ISBN 0-385-31172-9. Fiction.

The reader quickly zigzags through the short chapters of this novel, as Adam Brody, a severely dyslexic young boy, reacts to the daily frustrations of growing up learning-disabled. Talented, supportive parents and a sometimes sympathetic older sister can't help him. After going from evaluation to evaluation and private school to private school, Adam faces the fact that he can't read. As a teenager, he has to decide if this is a challenge he is willing to meet on his own terms. ER

14.4 Blair, Cynthia. **Molly and the Great American Family.** Fawcett Juniper, 1994. 247 pp. ISBN 0-449-70428-9. Fiction.

Molly tells the story of her unique family as she and her four sisters struggle to cope with life when their mother goes to Japan for three months, leaving them in the charge of their absent-minded professor father. Molly has to complete a project describing her family for her "Today's Family" class. Unfortunately, she makes a bet with her enemy Candy Carlisle that she can prove that her family is a normal American family. As Molly attempts to videotape her family in action, she captures something wrong about each sister and her father. Lizzie has tremendous difficulties keeping a job, Emma has trouble living in the present, Ralph has baseball troubles, and young Clementine feels tremendously neglected. Moreover, their father must convince some hostile rivals into sharing a grant. By helping her family get through the many humorous and touching events that fill the book, Molly learns that while her family may not be typical, it is as American as any other family. ER

14.5   Bond, Nancy. **Truth to Tell.** Margaret K. McElderry Books, 1994. 325 pp. ISBN 0-689-50601-5. Fiction.

Adjust to living in New Zealand after growing up in Cambridge, England? This is the situation fourteen-year-old Alice Jenkins must face when her mother abruptly accepts a position in Dunedin to collaborate on a history of Florestan, a once magnificent mansion. Miss Fairchild, the mansion's mistress, acts as the catalyst as Alice attempts to unravel her "real" father's identity. WL

14.6   Brooks, Bruce. **What Hearts.** HarperTrophy / HarperCollins, 1995. 193 pp. ISBN 0-06-447127-6. Fiction.

Because of frequent moves, Asa has had to develop coping mechanisms in order to deal with all the chaos of his life. Asa endures his parents' divorce, his mother's remarriage and emotional instability, and his stepfather's bullying. Four chapters, like connected short stories, tell about Asa: his first move; his help to Joel so that Joel can succeed in a variety show; his use of baseball as a way to act out difficulties with his stepfather; his first experience of falling in love. Readers who enjoyed the story of Bix, in Brooks's *The Moves Make the Man*, might be especially interested in this one.

A Newbery Honor Book (original publication), 1992

14.7   Cadnum, Michael. **Zero at the Bone.** Viking, 1996. 218 pp. ISBN 0-670-86725-X. Fiction.

Cray's older sister doesn't come home, and his family's desperation begins. Hours turn into days, and days turn into months as the all-too-familiar plight of missing children is explored from the perspective of the family left to cope.

14.8   Case, Dianne. **92 Queens Road.** Farrar, Straus and Giroux, 1995. 162 pp. ISBN 0-374-35518-5. Fiction.

Growing up black in South Africa's Cape Town in the 1960s means growing up as a second-class citizen under apartheid. Kathy's daily life is one struggle after another. Kathy's world is controlled by her grandmother, who rules the home and all its occupants, including Kathy, her mother, and her Uncle Reggie. Nevertheless, Kathy manages to thrive, and this story, based on the author's life, is one of warmth, strength, and poignancy. ER MC WL

14.9   Casey, Maude. **Over the Water.** Henry Holt, 1994. 246 pp. ISBN 0-8050-3276-2. Fiction.

Fourteen-year-old Mary narrates the story of her difficult adolescence. As an Irish teenager living in England, Mary is desperately unhappy because her strict mother will not let her have any English friends or do the normal things teenage girls like to do. Mary's family may live in England, but they spend all their time preparing for their annual visits to Ireland, where Mary's mother's family runs a small farm. During this year's annual visit, Mary and her mother fight bitterly as Mary struggles to find a place for herself in her Irish and English worlds. During the rough visit, and through talks with her compassionate aunt, Mary comes to understand her mother better and eventually to make peace with her. MC WL

School Library Journal Best Books, 1994

14.10   Cook, Mariana. **Mothers and Sons: In Their Own Words.** Introduction by Isabel Allende. Photographs by Mariana Cook. Chronicle Books, 1996. 126 pp. ISBN 0-8118-1170-0. Nonfiction.

There are seventy-eight portraits of mothers and sons in this book—full-page, black-and-white photographs accompanied by written texts. Sometimes the words are a mother's essay, sometimes a young man's observations, and sometimes short poetic passages. The introduction is a beautiful essay by author Isabel Allende. Well-known people profiled within its pages include Bill Clinton, Steven Spielberg, Robin Williams, Mary Higgins Clark, and Supreme Court Justice Ruth Bader Ginsburg. There are touching and humorous portraits of many others, including musicians, restaurant owners, window washers, teachers, and farmers.

14.11   Cottonwood, Joe. **Quake! A Novel.** Scholastic, 1995. 146 pp. ISBN 0-590-22232-5. Fiction.

When her parents go to the 1989 World Series, fourteen-year-old Franny has the chance to spend some time at home with her old best friend Jennie, whom she hasn't seen in five years. Franny, Jennie, and Sidney, Franny's little brother, get the shock of a lifetime, however, when an earthquake shakes their home in the Santa Cruz Mountains outside San Francisco. These three learn important lessons as they struggle to find safety and shelter and to be reunited with their parents.

14.12 Creech, Sharon. **Walk Two Moons.** HarperCollins, 1994. 280 pp. ISBN 0-06-023337-0. Fiction.

In this 1995 Newbery Medal–winning novel, thirteen-year-old Salamanca Tree Hiddle tells the journey of her cross-country car trip with her free-spirited grandparents, a trip that retraces the mysterious one Salamanca's mother recently took. During the trip, Salamanca tells her grandparents the story of her friend Phoebe, whose mother is also involved in a mystery.

Newbery Medal, 1995
ALA Notable Books for Children, 1995
School Library Journal Best Books, 1994

14.13 Davis, Deborah. **My Brother Has AIDS.** Atheneum / Macmillan, 1994. 186 pp. ISBN 0-689-31922-3. Fiction.

Thirteen-year-old Lacy already suspects that her older brother Jack is gay. So what's the big deal about Jack's letter and his wish to return home? Reluctantly, her mother confirms Jack's illness to Lacy but cautions that no one is to know. Lacy, meanwhile, researches AIDS, as she watches her beloved brother fight each stage of the illness. How will Lacy be able to deal with her mixed feelings and go on with her daily routine while Jack dies? ER

Notable 1994 Children's Trade Books in the Field of Social Studies
IRA Teacher's Choice, 1996

14.14 de Vries, Anke. **Bruises.** Translated by Stacey Knecht. Front Street / Lemniscaat, 1995. 168 pp. ISBN 1-886910-03-0. Fiction.

The reader needs only to close his or her eyes and envision all the possible images associated with the word "bruises" to understand the impact of this book. Judith, a young girl, is victimized by verbal and physical abuse at the hands of her own mother. This compelling novel brings to light the importance of friends, teachers, and others who can and should respond to people who they feel may be in dangerous situations. Michael, Judith's friend, finds out the ugly truth behind Judith's sad life and is able to get Judith help. MC WL

14.15 Deem, James M. **3 NBs of Julian Drew.** Houghton Mifflin, 1994. 227 pp. ISBN 0-395-69453-1. Fiction.

An emotionally and physically abused teenager, Julian chronicles his feelings and events in a coded language. This fifteen-year-old writes to his dead mother, fighting to maintain his sense of self. To what degree is Julian successful in using his NBs to deal with the grim reality he faces? How is he able to balance his desire to be with his mother against his desire to live?

14.16 Derby, Pat. **Grams, Her Boyfriend, My Family, and Me.** Farrar, Straus and Giroux, 1994. 195 pp. ISBN 0-374-38131-3. Fiction.

Fifteen-year-old Andy does his best to cope with his four sisters. There's seventeen-year-old Dennie, defender of women's rights; thirteen-year-old Molly, blossoming intellectual; and six-year-old twins Alice and Anne, whirlwinds of curiosity. When Mom takes a job outside the home, life in the Halliday household becomes a jumble of schedules, missed appointments, and dull meals. Just when Andy thinks matters can't get any worse, in moves his widowed grandmother. All he needs is another female in his life. All things considered, everything runs surprisingly well until Grams decides to marry against the wishes of her son, Andy's father. Once again, the Halliday household is in an uproar. Can Andy and his sisters find a way to make everyone happy?

School Library Journal Best Books, 1994

14.17 Ferris, Jean. **All That Glitters.** Farrar, Straus and Giroux, 1996. 184 pp. ISBN 0-374-30204-9. Fiction.

Sixteen-year-old Brian is not having a good summer. Forced to stay in the Florida Keys with his uncool father while his mother honeymoons with her new husband, Brian is both uncomfortable with his father and unsure of himself and his relationship with Tia, the beautiful, confident daughter of his father's friend. As they search for Spanish treasure off the Florida coast, a violent hurricane provides the winds of change that help Brian come to terms with his father and himself.

14.18 Frank, Lucy. **I Am an Artichoke.** Holiday House, 1995. 187 pp. ISBN 0-8234-1150-8. Fiction.

When fifteen-year-old Sarah chooses to work as a mother's helper in exciting New York City in order to escape her boring suburban family, everything about the job looks great at first. The Friedmans live in a huge apartment in an expensive neighborhood. However, Sarah soon realizes that twelve-year-old Emily has an eating disorder and that her divorced parents disagree completely about how to handle her. Sarah struggles to find the maturity to deal with these serious problems. ER

14.19 Fraustino, Lisa Rowe. **Ash: A Novel.** Orchard Books, 1995. 171 pp. ISBN 0-531-06889-7. Fiction.

Half the advantage of having a brother named Ash is seeing what fun you can have with his name. Wes Libby enjoys teasing his older brother; then things start to change in the Libby household when the world starts to crumble around Ash, formerly smart and very popular at school. The journal he keeps about Ash during this time is the only thing that seems to keep Wes going, as he sees his brother struggling for sanity and watches the impact of his illness on the Libby family.

ALA Best Books for Young Adults, 1996

14.20 Frede, Richard. **The Boy, the Devil and Divorce.** Pocket Books, 1994. 374 pp. ISBN 0-671-77662-2. Fiction.

What possible power could a ten-and-a-half-year-old boy wield in his own parents' divorce? Justin Whitney surprises even himself when he decides to sue his own parents to stop their impending divorce. Love, anger, hurt, and hope propel Justin to act quickly and decisively. But what about the risks and the eventual cost of such an act? The surprising conclusion speaks loudly to the power of love and determination. Strong language.

14.21   Gantos, Jack. **Jack's New Power: Stories from a Caribbean Year.** Farrar, Straus and Giroux, 1995. 214 pp. ISBN 0-374-33657-1. Fiction.

In this sequel to *Heads and Tails*, Jack's family, after his father's business schemes have forced many moves, relocates to Barbados, a Caribbean paradise. His sister Betsy is still a know-it-all, Pete is a typical little brother, and Jack continues to learn life's lessons the hard way. Since Jack is only in junior high school, this may be most appealing to those in touch with concerns of young teens, though the story definitely is charming and the experiences have universality. ER

School Library Journal Best Books, 1995

14.22   Gilbert, Barbara Snow. **Stone Water.** Front Street, 1996. 168 pp. ISBN 1-886910-11-1. Fiction.

Grant and his grandfather have always been close. This closeness makes Grant the recipient of an envelope marked with instructions to open it only if Grandpa gets put "in the other wing" of the nursing home, the wing where Grandma lay for years before she died. Can Grant fulfill his grandfather's wish to help him die rather than be put on life support systems? Gilbert deals with weighty issues by masterfully interweaving various viewpoints.

School Library Journal Best Books, 1996

14.23   Goodman, Joan Elizabeth. **Songs from Home.** Illustrated by Joan Elizabeth Goodman. Harcourt Brace, 1994. 224 pp. ISBN 0-15-203590-7. Fiction.

Eleven-year-old Anna and her father are American expatriates living in Rome. They make their living by singing for tips at local cafés and restaurants; in their spare time, Anna's father gives her beautiful tours of Rome. Anna desperately wants to understand why her father will not return to America, but he refuses to talk about the past. Moreover, Anna is tired of having to hide her poor lifestyle from her schoolmates and of having to adjust to a new country whenever her father feels the urge to move. When someone appears in Rome from her father's home town and offers to fill in the blanks about Anna's past, Anna is forced to choose between life with her father and life back in America. MC

14.24   Grant, Cynthia D. **Mary Wolf.** Atheneum Books for Young Readers, 1995. 166 pp. ISBN 0-689-80007-X. Fiction.

Mary Wolf is an intense novel for older readers. Mary must meet responsibilities that normal teenagers do not face. The problems start when Mary's father loses his job and the family goes on an extended vacation. As the family wanders aimlessly, Mary attempts to keep the family together in spite of her father's drastically changed personality, in this tragic tale of contemporary life.

ALA Best Books for Young Adults, 1996
Notable Children's Trade Books in the Field of Social Studies, 1995

14.25 Hartnett, Sonya. **Sleeping Dogs.** Viking, 1995. 130 pp. ISBN 0-670-86503-6. Fiction.

The Willow family live a self-contained, self-sustaining life on their farm, keeping family secrets until fifteen-year-old Oliver unwittingly confides in his new friend, Bow Fox. Bow uses this information to "make an impression" and then faces the family's retaliation. He leaves suddenly, but not before Oliver's father kills one child and disappears with the remaining family members. Mature content. WL

14.26 Henkes, Kevin. **Protecting Marie.** Greenwillow Books, 1995. 195 pp. ISBN 0-688-13958-2. Fiction.

Fanny loves her father, a temperamental artist, but is unsettled by his moods. She also loves her new dog and goes to great lengths to ensure that it doesn't annoy her father, who would surely give it away and break her heart. Fanny must protect the dog just as she had once protected her homemade paper doll against being thrown away. Fanny's mother is a source of calm strength as father and daughter struggle to understand each other. ER

School Library Journal Best Books of 1995

14.27 High, Linda Oatman. **Maizie.** Holiday House, 1995. 180 pp. ISBN 0-8234-1161-3. Fiction.

Wishes are a dime a dozen for Maizie Musser, a teenage girl living on Welsh Mountain. Maizie wishes for her pa to stop drinking, for more money to help pay the bills, and for a strawberry roan pony, but most of all she wishes to know the reason her mama deserted her family. ER

14.28 Hite, Sid. **It's Nothing to a Mountain.** Henry Holt, 1994. 214 pp. ISBN 0-8050-2769-6. Fiction.

Coping with the loss of their parents is difficult enough for children, but moving in with grandparents in the mountains of Virginia further complicates the grieving process for Lisette, thirteen, and her nine-year-old brother. Nevertheless, they begin to heal as they discover new friends, the value of extended family, and the adventures the hills hold for them. ER

ALA Best Books for Young Adults, 1995
IRA Teacher's Choice, 1996

14.29 Hobbs, Valerie. **How Far Would You Have Gotten If I Hadn't Called You Back? A Novel.** Orchard Books, 1995. 306 pp. ISBN 0-531-09480-4. Fiction.

This is the bittersweet story of Bronwyn Lewis and her family, who leave their home in New Jersey to move to Ojala, California. Everything changes after the family buys a restaurant and Bron buys a car. She must grow up quickly and accept the family secret, but she also finds romance on a ranch and at a race track.

ALA Best Books for Young Adults, 1996

14.30 Hunter, Mollie. **A Stranger Came Ashore.** HarperTrophy / HarperCollins, 1995. ISBN 0-06-440082-4. Fiction.

On a dark and stormy night, a stranger appears. Finn Learson is the only survivor of a shipwreck. As charming as he appears to the Henderson family who offer to help this lone survivor, Robbie Henderson fears that danger for his sister and the rest of his family lurks beneath Finn's smile. Robbie recalls a dark memory from his grandfather's deathbed and is spurred on to "save" his sister. Adventure, mystery, suspense, and underlying love of family move this novel at a quick pace. ER MC

14.31 Ingold, Jeanette. **The Window.** Harcourt Brace, 1996. 181 pp. ISBN 0-15-201265-6. Fiction.

Mandy and her mother have always been close, especially since they have frequently had to move from place to place. Then Mandy finds herself blinded and without her mother after a fatal accident, but she also finds she can "see" things that took place in the past. This new gift, coupled with strength drawn from new friendships developed at a new school, help Mandy become ready to face the future.

14.32 Jenkins, Lyll Becerra de. **Celebrating the Hero.** Puffin Books, 1995. 179 pp. ISBN 0-14-037605-4. Fiction.

Camila Draper once found herself too busy to listen to the family stories about her Colombian background. Living in America, she wanted to leave the past behind her. After her mother's death, however, Camila is desperate to hear these stories that would connect her to the family's past. When she travels to Colombia to attend a ceremony honoring her late grandmother, Camila discovers a community reluctant to discuss her grandfather. What disturbing secret are they hiding? MC WL

14.33 Johnson, Angela. **Humming Whispers.** Orchard Books, 1995. 128 pp. ISBN 0-531-06898-6. Fiction.

Fourteen-year-old Sophy struggles to find her own identity in this story. She is now the same age as her older sister Nicole was when Nicole began suffering from schizophrenia, a debilitating mental illness that takes Nicole in and out of mental hospitals. Sophy fears that she too will develop the illness which has stolen Nicole's dream of being a dancer, a dream that Sophy herself still has. MC

14.34   Johnston, Julie. **Adam and Eve and Pinch-Me.** Little, Brown, 1994. 180 pp. ISBN 0-316-46990-4. Fiction.

Delete, move, change. Words familiar to anyone who has used a computer. Sara Moore, a fifteen-year-old foster child, uses these commands on her computer to delete, move, and change the reality of her world. Sara has been in a number of foster care homes and dreads the thought of going to live with the Huddlestons. When, with her trusty computer and the few belongings she has acquired over the years, she moves in with the family and their other two foster children, Sara soon discovers that it is not easy to delete, move, or change her "new life."

ALA Notable Books for Children, 1995
School Library Journal Best Books, 1994

14.35   Johnston, Julie. **Hero of Lesser Causes.** Puffin Books, 1994. 194 pp. ISBN 0-14-036998-8. Fiction.

Who would have imagined that a twelve-year-old's best friend could be her older brother? That is exactly the case with Keely and her brother, Patrick . . . until he becomes paralyzed with polio. It is 1946 and a vaccine is yet undiscovered. Keely grieves Patrick's loss; can her strength and determination encourage Patrick to "re-enter life," or will he choose an alternative exit? ER

ALA Notable Book (first publication), 1992

14.36   Keillor, Garrison, and Jenny Lind Nilsson. **The Sandy Bottom Orchestra.** Hyperion Books for Children, 1996. 263 pp. ISBN 0-7868-2145-0. Fiction.

At fourteen, Rachel Green wishes her parents weren't quite so different. They don't own a television, and they often express their passions publicly and alienate the other members of the small-town community in which they live. Rachel spends the summer trying to avoid having their weirdness rub off on her, seeking refuge in her violin, while struggling to come to terms with both the Green family and Sandy Bottom.

14.37   Kerr, M. E. **Linger.** HarperTrophy / HarperCollins, 1995. 213 pp. ISBN 0-06-447102-0. Fiction.

Gary's brother Bobby has enlisted in the army and is sent overseas to fight in the Persian Gulf War. Gary tells of life in his small Pennsylvania town without his popular brother, who is sending unrequited love letters to Lynn. Gary learns that Lynn is in love with his teacher, Mr. Raleigh, and is forced to keep her affair a secret. Other secrets fill this book; they all come to a head when Bobby returns injured from the war.

14.38   Klass, Sheila Solomon. **Next Stop: Nowhere.** Scholastic, 1995. 181 pp. ISBN 0-590-46686-0. Fiction.

Beth Converse, the adolescent narrator of this novel, takes the reader to Vermont, where she is living with her father, who is a potter, and who constantly complains about New York City. Beth used to live in New York City until her mother decided to marry and go to Europe. Actually, things were not going all that smoothly between Beth and her mother, but the necessity of another adjustment has taken her off guard. She is a resourceful loner, however, who becomes savvy through her adjustments to parents, to different settings, and to a young male admirer.

14.39   Koertge, Ron. **Tiger, Tiger, Burning Bright.** Orchard Books, 1994. 179 pp. ISBN 0-531-06840-4. Fiction.

Eighth grader Jesse loves his grandfather Pappy, an old rancher who teaches him the ways of the desert surrounding their central California home. However, Jesse can't yet understand the danger his single mom sees in her father's forgetful behavior, which is caused by Alzheimer's disease. The funny, clever conversations between Jesse and his best friend Kyle keep the story upbeat, and concern for Pappy keeps the reader turning pages.

ALA's Best Books for Young Adults, 1995
ALA Notable Books for Children, 1995

14.40   Lawson, Julie. **Danger Game.** Little, Brown, 1996. 213 pp. ISBN 0-316-51728-3. Fiction.

Chelsea is a pyromaniac; that's the way she's coped with the sexual abuse she's experienced for years at the hands of her mother's boyfriend. But after setting a fire at school, she is sent to live with her long-absent father, who has a serious accident two weeks after she arrives. Sent next to stay with relatives on a Canadian island, she begins to develop a strained friendship with her younger cousins through their childishly daring "danger game," which she soon forces to an intense and serious level.

14.41   Lee, Gus. **China Boy.** Plume, 1994. 322 pp. ISBN 0-452-27158-4. Fiction.

Kia Ting is horribly unprepared for the brutal violence of the San Francisco streets of the 1950s. The only American son of an aristocratic mandarin family that fled China in the wake of Mao's revolution, Ting was being trained to be a scholar until his mother died. At seven years old, the frail, sensitive boy is locked out of his home every afternoon by his abusive stepmother. The streets are menacing, full of toughs who delight in beating the "China Boy." A mixture of memory, tradition, luck, and humor guides Ting through his fight for survival of body and mind. MC

14.42   Levine, Beth. **Divorce: Young People Caught in the Middle.** Enslow, 1995. 128 pp. ISBN 0-89490-633-X. Nonfiction.

This Issues in Focus book balances issues faced by children caught in the middle of a divorce with individual vignettes of adolescents and their families. Issues explored include shame and guilt before the divorce, economic effects, custody and visitation rights, the disappearance of fathers, and the possibility of step families.

14.43   London, Jonathan. **Where's Home?** Viking, 1995. 89 pp. ISBN 0-670-86028-X. Fiction.

Fourteen-year-old Aaron hitchhikes to San Francisco with his father to find a new life on the West Coast. With little money and few prospects, however, the two become homeless. This short book chronicles the father and son's attempts at making a stable life for themselves. ER

14.44   Lynch, Chris. **Gypsy Davey.** HarperCollins, 1994. 179 pp. ISBN 0-06-023586-1. Fiction.

Twelve-year-old Gypsy Davey likes himself best when he is traveling on his bike, a gift from his estranged dad, Sneaky Pete. Struggling to care for a tired mother, a seventeen-year-old sister, and ultimately an infant nephew, Davey precariously balances his carefully protected emotions. How much more can Davey give without getting anything in return? ER

ALA Best Books for Young Adults, 1995
ALA Quick Picks for Young Adults, 1995

14.45   Lynch, Chris. **Iceman.** HarperCollins, 1994. 181 pp. ISBN 0-06-023340-0. Fiction.

Adolescence is a time of searching for self; fourteen-year-old Eric conducts his search on the ice, around the dinner table, and in the mortuary. Struggling to connect with a family he finds emotionless and unreal, Eric takes his frustration to the ice, but his disillusionment is only heightened as Eric limps away from a vicious opponent's attack during his final game of the season. Between the overt physicality of hockey and a seemingly unapproachable family, can Eric find a sense of himself and finally "get happy," as his mom so desperately wants?

ALA Quick Picks for Young Adults, 1995
Booklist Editor's Choice, 1995

14.46   Mahy, Margaret. **The Other Side of Silence.** Viking, 1995. 170 pp. ISBN 0-670-86455-2. Fiction.

Twelve-year-old Hero, who has chosen to be mute, tells the story of her eccentric, intellectual New Zealand family and her relationship with a bizarre older woman who has a mysterious estate in the woods. The closer Hero gets to solving a mystery involving the older woman, the closer she gets to merging her "true" fantasy life with her real life, finding her place in her family and discovering why she has chosen not to talk. MC WL

14.47   McColley, Kevin. **Pecking Order.** HarperCollins, 1994. 215 pp. ISBN 0-06-023554-3. Fiction.

Tom Morrell is fourteen and his life is about to change forever. The Morrell family has farmed their land for more than one hundred years, but financial problems and poor crops have put the family and the land in jeopardy. As Tom's father, mother, and brother try to cope with their problems, their neighbors are also struggling to maintain their farms. One crisis after another affects both the community and the Morrell family, whose lives are changing rapidly.

14.48   McCrumb, Sharyn. **The Rosewood Casket.** Dutton, 1996. 303 pp. ISBN 0-525-94011-1. Fiction.

A wonderful book that honors the spirit of family and the spirit of the Appalachian region, this novel draws the reader into the story of a rosewood casket being built for a family member, and doesn't let the reader out until the mystery of the rosewood and the mountains is disclosed. The plot is one intertwined with family secrets, legends of the past, and the beautiful words and images of Appalachia.

14.49   McGuigan, Mary Ann. **Cloud Dancer.** Charles Scribner's Sons / Macmillan, 1994. 119 pp. ISBN 0-684-19632-8. Fiction.

Eileen McDonaugh is a dreaming, scheming fourteen-year-old with sad little green eyes, uncooperative brown hair, and a grim home life of poverty and hopelessness. Her parents are divorced and trapped in their own unpleasant realities. Eileen is the middle child, caught between her lovely, cynical older sister, Dierdre, and her sweet, stuttering little brother, Neal. But Eileen is gifted: she is a singer who yearns with all her heart to play the guitar. Her chance meeting with Liz, a talented musician with problems of her own, sets Eileen on a path of personal triumph with far-reaching effects on her troubled family.

14.50   Menzel, Peter. **Material World: A Global Family Portrait.** Introduction by Paul Kennedy. Text by Charles C. Mann. Photo editing by Sandra Eisert. Sierra Club Books, 1994. 255 pp. ISBN 0-87156-430-0. Nonfiction.

Created with the cooperation of the United Nations and coinciding with its Year of the Family (1994), this magnificent example of photojournalism at its best introduces statistically average families representing thirty nations worldwide. In text, pictures, and statistics, the lives of these people, with their many differences and commonalties, are presented vividly, and the concept of "global village" is made personal. MC

School Library Journal Best Adult Books for Young Adults, 1995

14.51 Metzger, Lois. **Ellen's Case.** Atheneum Books for Young Readers, 1995. 189 pp. ISBN 0-689-31934-7. Fiction.

In this sequel to *Barry's Sister*, Ellen's dedication to her brother Barry, who has cerebral palsy, continues unwaveringly. Their mother hires Jack Frazier to sue the obstetrician for damages to help care for the boy. Adamantly believing that she will always care for him herself, Ellen at first opposes the suit but abruptly reverses her position when she becomes infatuated with Frazier. The trial and her heart take over her life, initially blinding her to some pressing truths but ultimately allowing her to see things more clearly.

14.52 Mori, Kyoko. **One Bird.** Henry Holt, 1995. 242 pp. ISBN 0-8050-2983-4. Fiction.

As she did in her first hauntingly beautiful novel, *Shizuko's Daughter*, Mori here explores the themes of mother-daughter relationships, the nature of truth, and the meaning of survival. In evocative, sparse prose, the reader learns with Megumi, fifteen, how to care for injured birds—and, ultimately, how to begin to heal after experiencing the injuries to the soul that lies and deception have caused. MC

14.53 Mosher, Richard. **The Taxi Navigator.** Philomel Books, 1996. 167 pp. ISBN 0-399-23104-8. Fiction.

Although Kid Kyle is only nine, his story is a sophisticated tale of his search for the meaning of "family." As his parents, a lawyer and a banker, become increasingly distant from each other, Kid's uncle, a taxi driver, introduces him to a group of eccentrics from whom Kid learns about everything from eating crumb cake to dealing with death. ER

14.54 Mulford, Philippa Greene. **Making Room for Katherine.** Macmillan, 1994. 191 pp. ISBN 0-02-767652-8. Fiction.

Abbey's almost perfect life is changed by her father's death. Her mother moves Abbey, her twin brother Shel, and her younger sister Joyce to Connecticut to begin again. Then life is further disrupted by the unexpected arrival of their younger, but more worldly, cousin Katherine. Abbey's mother is dating a man whom she may marry, leaving Abbey to deal with the daring Katherine and her own teenage world. Humor and love become the glue which bonds this "new" family.

14.55 Murphy, Barbara Beasley. **Fly Like an Eagle.** Delacorte Press, 1994. 180 pp. ISBN 0-385-32035-3. Fiction.

Horace, "Ace," is a seventeen-year-old who longs for a girl, an acting career, and some excitement in his working-class family. Adventure begins when his father reveals his compulsion to seek his unknown roots—he was raised in an orphanage until he was adopted at the age of five! Since Ace's efforts at a summer job have failed, Ace is coerced into joining his father in a shabby Volkswagen bug on the road trip west, and learns much more than his family tree. ER MC

ALA Quick Picks for Young Adults, 1995

14.56   Myers, Walter Dean. **The Glory Field.** Scholastic, 1994. 375 pp. ISBN 0-590-45897-3. Fiction.

Walter Dean Myers traces several generations of the Lewis family by focusing on the lives of six of its members, one in each generation from 1753 to 1994. Each family member struggles with issues of racism, survival, and identity. Characters include Lizzie, who in 1864 escapes from her plantation to fight for the Union; Elijah, who in 1900 must leave home because his independent ideas counter those of the local whites; Luvenia, who in 1930 does not return home because of her desire to go to college; and Tommy, who in 1964 is pushed to integrate the state university. All generations of the Lewis family are bound together by their ownership of the Glory Field, a plot of land representing the family's heritage and survival. MC

ALA Best Books for Young Adults, 1995
Notable 1994 Children's Trade Books in the Field of Social Studies

14.57   Namioka, Lensey. **April and the Dragon Lady.** Browndeer Press / Harcourt, Brace, 1994. 214 pp. ISBN 0-15-276644-8. Fiction.

How can sixteen-year-old April Chen maintain her traditional family connections while pursuing her own goal of attending the Colorado School of Mines? Torn between family and self, April struggles with a domineering grandmother who will only accept things on her own terms. April feels compelled to drop out of the orchestra and after-school activities to care for her grandmother, and family responsibilities weigh heavily as she tries to find her "American" self. MC

14.58   Naylor, Phyllis Reynolds. **Ice.** Atheneum Books for Young Readers, 1995. 199 pp. ISBN 0-689-80005-3. Fiction.

When the tension mounts between thirteen-year-old Chrissa and her mother, Chrissa is sent to live with her grandmother. Adjusting to farm life after years in New York City proves far easier than adjusting to the knowledge Chrissa gains about her father and his secret past, but as Chrissa helps her grandmother outwit a money-hungry pair of evangelists, and as she develops self-confidence through her blossoming romance with a neighbor boy and through her work as a baby-sitter, Chrissa is able to come to terms with her family's history. ER

14.59   Nolan, Han. **Send Me down a Miracle.** Harcourt Brace, 1996. 250 pp. ISBN 0-15-200978-7. Fiction.

At fourteen, Charity figures she will follow in the footsteps of her conservative preacher father. But she becomes confused when she meets the free-spirited artist Adrienne Dabney, who announces, after a month in a sensory-deprivation experiment, that she has seen Jesus, thus causing an uproar both in the town and in Charity's heart.

14.60   O'Brien, Tim. **In the Lake of the Woods.** Penguin Books, 1994. 303 pp. ISBN 0 14 02.5094 8. Fiction.

Pursuing his goal of a career in politics, John Wade uses the mastery of illusion and mystery he has garnered from years of practicing magic to create a winning performance. His charmed life disintegrates, however, when his involvement in Vietnam's My Lai massacre is exposed along with his attempted coverup. Wade's future becomes even more bleak when his wife vanishes from their rented cabin on a remote northern Minnesota lake and local police suspect him of foul play. Adult situations and language.

ALA Notable Books for Children, 1995

14.61   Pears, Tim. **In the Place of Fallen Leaves: A Novel.** Donald I. Fine, 1995. 310 pp. ISBN 1-55611-423-0. Fiction.

Pears's first novel revolves around thirteen-year-old Alison Freemantle as her family and village struggle through the 1984 drought and teachers' strike in rural Devon, England. Against this hot, dry backdrop, Alison recounts intuitively the stories of her grandparents' lives, the dreams and strife of her mother, her two brothers, and her sister, and the tragedy of her father's mental illness. As the strike and drought lengthen into September, Alison develops a strange relationship with Jonathan, an aristocratic loner, and becomes aware of changes in herself and tears in the fabric of her family.

14.62   Pfeffer, Susan Beth. **Twice Taken.** Delacorte Press, 1994. 176 pp. ISBN 0-385-32033-7. Fiction.

Temporarily angry at her father, with whom she has lived for most of her sixteen years, Brooke hears herself described on a television show featuring stories of missing children and calls in. Much to her dismay, she discovers that her father had kidnapped her when she was a young child. Despite her protests, Brooke must go to live with her mother, stepfather, and step-siblings. Her "new" family calls her by her original name, Amy, and prohibits any contact with her father. This book probes Brooke/Amy's difficult adjustment to her new family, her new school, and the new friends she makes in the Freak-of-the-Month club that she joins at school. ER

IRA Teacher's Choice, 1996

14.63   Porte, Barbara Ann. **Something Terrible Happened: A Novel.** Orchard Books, 1994. 214 pp. ISBN 0-531-06869-2. Fiction.

> "Daughter, dear daughter,
> Don't weep for me when I'm gone,

Wherever you go, my spirit will follow,
A mother's love is that strong."

These are words from a song sung to ten-year-old Gillian by her mother, who is dying of AIDS. Gillian, whose heritage is biracial, is sent to live with her deceased father's all-white family in the South. The narrator tells Gillian's story, one of love, strength, and resilience. "Something terrible happened," but from adversity, strength of character arises. MC

ALA Best Books for Young Adults, 1995

14.64 Power, Susan. **The Grass Dancer.** G. P. Putnam's Sons, 1994. 300 pp. ISBN 0-399-13911-7. Fiction.

The mysticism of the Dakota Sioux is powerfully presented here through a myriad of contemporary characters and ancestral spirits. Teenager Charlene Thunder is reluctantly controlled by her grandmother's evil medicine. She is interested in dashing Harley Wind Soldier, who refuses to look into his own soul. Jeannette McVay, a white Easterner, visits the reservation to study the culture but falls victim to a spell which compels her to remain. These and other characters demonstrate the interconnectedness of lives, both past and present, and weave a fascinating web. MC

ALA Best Books for Young Adults, 1995
ALA Notable Books for Children, 1995
Booklist Editor's Choice, 1995

14.65 Reiss, Kathryn. **Pale Phoenix.** Harcourt Brace, 1994. 256 pp. ISBN 0-15-200030-5. Fiction.

Fifteen-year-old Miranda Browne's ride to school through snowy Massachusetts streets is chilling as Mrs. Browne narrowly misses hitting Abby, a pale and sullen girl who is crossing the street. A mysterious figure, Abby appears and disappears at school; Miranda becomes curious and follows her. A stone whistle, Abby's fear of fire, stolen food, and the sobbing only Miranda can hear combine to unfold Abby's unbelievable past and "transport" Miranda and her best friend, Dan, to Abby's "home."

14.66 Roybal, Laura. **Billy.** Houghton Mifflin, 1994. 236 pp. ISBN 0-395-67649-5. Fiction.

When he was ten, Billy Melendez was kidnapped by his biological father from a Little League game, and for six years he has managed to forget the family with whom he lived until that fateful day. He and his father, cowboys in New Mexico, are getting along just fine until Billy is taken to the police station for fighting in a barroom brawl and the police computer records change his life. He is reunited with his "parents," but has to make a painful transition, facing a new environment in which he does not fit and a family he no longer knows.

ALA Best Books for Young Adults, 1995
ALA Quick Picks for Young Adults, 1995

14.67 Shepard, Elizabeth. **H.** Penguin Books, 1995. 160 pp. ISBN 0 14 02.4389 5. Fiction.

Told entirely through letters, this novel traces a year in the life of troubled twelve-year-old Benjamin, who is autistic, mentally ill, or weird depending upon the point of view of the letter writers, who include his parents, his psychiatrist, his sister, and his camp counselors. Through these letters and those written by Benjamin to his best friend, Elliot, we view Benjamin's movement along a traumatic path toward a more normal life.

14.68 Sonnenmark, Laura A. **A Summer for Always.** Avon Flare, 1995. 150 pp. ISBN 0-380-78028-3. Fiction.

What happens when you are turning sixteen and away on a family vacation with your mother and little brother, and you meet HIM? That's what Marty has to figure out the summer of her sixteenth birthday while vacationing in Maine. But, she has one extra problem: her mom. How can she have a wonderful time with Michael and still keep the secret of her mother's alcoholism? Secrets are meant to be kept—or are they? This is one of the questions Marty must answer during that summer.

14.69 Springer, Nancy. **Looking for Jamie Bridger.** Dial Books for Young Readers, 1995. 159 pp. ISBN 0-8037-1773-3. Fiction.

Who is Jamie Bridger? This is the question that young Jamie Bridger must answer for herself. This young teen is being raised by her grandparents, and every time she asks about her parents she gets no response. Finally, after her grandfather's death, Jamie decides to unravel this mystery herself. Her quest is complicated by the deterioration of her grandmother's mental health and by the fact that no one is willing to discuss Jamie's parentage. However, Jamie triumphs, and she finds out the surprising answers to her questions. ER

14.70 Tate, Eleanora E. **A Blessing in Disguise.** Delacorte Press, 1995. N.p. ISBN 0-385-32103-1. Fiction.

Zambia is bored living with her aunt and uncle and cousin. But she thinks life will improve now that her father, Snake, has opened a night club in "do-nothing" Deacons Neck, South Carolina. Little does she know that what she will learn about her father and mother will cause almost as much pain as the bullet that rips through her body during the drug-related shootings that accompany the opening of the club. Tate explores the meaning of family and the differences between loving, liking, and accepting others as she tells the story of one hot summer in twelve-year-old Zambia's life. ER MC

14.71 Taylor, Mildred D. **The Well: David's Story.** Dial Books for Young Readers, 1995. 92 pp. ISBN 0-8037-1802-0. Fiction.

The Logan family is already well known to the millions of readers of Mildred Taylor's Newbery Medal–winning novel *Roll of Thunder, Hear My Cry* and the many other stories of the Logan family's attempts to survive in 1930s Mississippi. This easy-to-read story depicts the lives of the Logans a generation earlier, when David, the father in *Roll of Thunder*, and his strong-willed brother are young boys. David and Hammer must help their mother maintain their land during a horrible drought. Meanwhile, the Logans have the only working well in the area, and all the neighboring people, black and white, come to use their water. Problems arise when Hammer runs into trouble with the bigoted Charlie Simms, and the escalating conflict between Hammer and Charlie threatens to destroy the precarious peace created by the well. Throughout the story young David must do his best to keep his brother alive and protect his family's land. ER MC

ALA Notable Books for Children, 1996
Jane Addams Award, 1996

14.72   Thesman, Jean. **Cattail Moon.** Houghton Mifflin, 1994. 197 pp. ISBN 0-395-67409-3. Fiction.

Constant bickering with her mother forces Julia Foster to leave her yuppie life with her mom and her stepdad and move to a small town in the Cascade Mountains with her father and grandmother. Life is simpler and seems uncomplicated until the mysterious girl with the haunting voice appears to Julia. Is it a ghost, or an overactive imagination—or is there really a young girl in the cattails? This romantic mystery will hold the reader's attention as Julia learns how to make the right decisions. ER

IRA Teacher's Choice, 1996

14.73   Voigt, Cynthia. **When She Hollers.** Scholastic, 1994. 177 pp. ISBN 0-590-46714-X. Fiction.

Twenty-four hours in the life of an abused person can seem like an eternity, especially when they are replayed day in and day out. Cynthia Voigt thrusts the reader into the world of Tish, a teenage victim of sexual abuse. The harsh reality of abuse and the impact it has on its victim is frankly portrayed.

ALA Best Books for Young Adults, 1995
ALA Quick Picks for Young Adults, 1995

14.74   Watkins, Yoko Kawashima. **My Brother, My Sister, and I.** Bradbury Press, 1994. 275 pp. ISBN 0-02-792526-9. Fiction / Nonfiction.

Thirteen-year-old Yoko Kawashima tells the story of how she, her seventeen-year-old sister Ko, and her twenty-one-year-old brother Hideyo survived as refugees in post–World War II Japan. With barely enough food and money to survive, the three siblings encounter one difficulty after another, including a fire that destroys their factory-warehouse home and severely injures Ko. While Ko recovers in the hospital, Yoko and Hideyo must overcome horrible accusations. Despite her protestations, Yoko is also made to go to school, where she is terrorized for being a scholarship student. Throughout all their struggles, the Kawashimas stay together and search for their long-missing father. This book provides a fascinating look at life in post-war Japan and is a sequel to the author's earlier *So Far From the Bamboo Grove.* MC WL

ALA Best Books for Young Adults, 1995
Notable 1994 Children's Trade Books in the Field of Social Studies

14.75 Watson, Larry. **Justice.** Milkweed Editions, 1995. 226 pp. ISBN 1-57131-002-9. Fiction.

In this sequel to *Montana 1948,* the characters who fuel the earlier book's plot are more fully revealed. Teenaged Julian moves his widowed mother to Montana and struggles so successfully to build the Hayden name that by the time his two sons reach maturity that name is law. What sort of man can accomplish that? What is the impact on his family? The opening chapter contains rough scenes and language, though that is not characteristic of the rest of the book.

School Library Journal Best Books, 1995

14.76 West, Dorothy. **The Wedding.** Anchor Books / Doubleday, 1995. 240 pp. ISBN 0-385-47144-0. Fiction.

The hopes, myths, and fears of color—white against black, white mixed with black, either one using the other—converge around the momentous event of a wedding in the 1950s in the area of Martha's Vineyard populated by elite blacks and known as the Oval. *The Wedding* is a beautifully written story of race, class, and gender by an author renowned as a pivotal figure in literary circles since the Harlem Renaissance. MC

School Library Journal Best Adult Books for Young Adults, 1995

14.77 White, Ruth. **Belle Prater's Boy.** Farrar, Straus and Giroux, 1996. 196 pp. ISBN 0-374-30668-0. Fiction.

Living in a small rural community entitles the residents of the area to know everything about everyone, or so many of them believe. When Gypsy's sixth-grade cousin moves next door, Gypsy is determined to unravel the mystery of Woodrow and his mother, Belle Prater, who "up and disappeared." This quest story focuses on the closeness of family and the power of family to help one of its members through a loss.

School Library Journal Best Books, 1996

14.78 White, Ruth. **Weeping Willow.** Aerial / Farrar, Straus and Giroux, 1994. 246 pp. ISBN 0-374-48280-2. Fiction.

Ernestina "Tiny" Lambert is growing up in rural Virginia, but life is difficult in many ways, primarily because she is haunted by and taunted about her abusive family. With the support of her band director, her Aunt

Evie, and her friends, Tiny joins the ranks of survivors of abuse in this poignant story of female strength.

14.79   Willey, Margaret. **Facing the Music.** Delacorte Press, 1996. 184 pp. ISBN 0-385-32104-X. Fiction.

No one in the house can mention the death of her mother—not Lisa, not her brother Mark, not their father. Once close, they now avoid one another. Sick of always taking care of his younger sister, Mark becomes consumed with starting a band with two friends. When the other band members discover Lisa's fabulous voice, and she enthusiastically joins the group, irreversible changes occur in all their lives.

14.80   Williams, Michael. **The Genuine Half-Moon Kid.** Lodestar Books / Dutton, 1994. 199 pp. ISBN 0-525-67470-5. Fiction.

In order to escape a dysfunctional family life, seventeen-year-old Jay Watson sneaks into the fish hatchery where he works, diving into its huge tanks to swim with the tropical fish. Living with the turmoil of South Africa's changes, a mother who has too many boyfriends, and a grandmother who eats spoons, Jay welcomes the quest in search of treasure on which his grandfather's will sends him, a journey that brings Jay peace at last. Mature situations. MC WL

14.81   Williams-Garcia, Rita. **Like Sisters on the Homefront.** Lodestar Books / Dutton, 1995. 165 pp. ISBN 0-525-67465-9. Fiction.

At fourteen, Gayle spends her time hanging out with her "sisters" and mothering her baby. When she gets into trouble again, Mama sends her down South to live with her high-minded aunt and her uncle, a strict minister. Worst of all, Gayle is subjected to her straitlaced cousin Cookie, who could never be one of Gayle's "sisters." Surprisingly, the companionship of Great, the family matriarch and keeper of the family history, has a deep effect on Gayle, who begins to feel the healing power of family. MC

ALA Best Books for Young Adults, 1996
ALA Quick Picks for Young Adults, 1996
School Library Journal Best Books, 1996
Booklist Editor's Choice, 1996
Publisher's Weekly Best Books, 1996
Coretta Scott King Honor Book, 1996
Notable 1995 Children's Trade Books in the Field of Social Studies

14.82   Wittlinger, Ellen. **Noticing Paradise.** Houghton Mifflin, 1995. 184 pp. ISBN 0-395-71646-2. Fiction.

In alternating chapters, teenagers Noah and Cat describe their three-week trip to the Galapagos Islands. Traveling with his brother, Noah is bitter because his father has just left his mother; traveling with her parents, Cat is reluctant to meet new people. Noah and Cat describe their developing relationship as they struggle to solve a mystery involving rare tortoises and to help Noah deal with his parent's breakup.

14.83   Woodson, Jacqueline. **Autobiography of a Family Photo: A Novel.** Plume, 1996. 113 pp. ISBN 0-452-27098-7. Fiction.

Reminiscent of *The House on Mango Street*, this novel presents a series of memories of an unnamed African American narrator who shares her coming of age in 1970s Brooklyn. Recollections of family violence blend with more wistfully portrayed vignettes. MC

14.84   Woodson, Jacqueline. **From the Notebooks of Melanin Sun.** Blue Sky Press / Scholastic, 1995. 141 pp. ISBN 0-590-45880-9. Fiction.

In this lyrically written book, thirteen-year-old Melanin Sun tells how his beautiful relationship with his mother deteriorates. Melanin Sun, who has always been a victim of prejudice because of his very dark skin, must confront his own prejudices when his mother falls in love with a white woman. Not only must Melanin deal with his own feelings, but also with those of his friends, who also react strongly to his mother's new relationship. MC

ALA Best Books for Young Adults, 1996
Coretta Scott King Honor Book, 1996
Notable 1995 Children's Trade Books in the Field of Social Studies

14.85   Woodson, Jacqueline. **I Hadn't Meant to Tell You This.** Delacorte Press, 1994. 115 pp. ISBN 0-385-32031-0. Fiction.

Marie lives in the rich black half of town but, almost against her will, becomes friends with Lena, whom her father would call "whitetrash." When Lena reveals the cause of her basic unhappiness, that her father molests her, Marie pledges to keep the secret. Marie doesn't want her new friend to leave; their common bond, motherlessness (Lena's died, Marie's walked out) is too important. Both struggle with their respective heartaches as well as twelve-year-olds can. ER MC

ALA Best Books for Young Adults, 1995
ALA Notable Books for Children, 1995
Booklist Editor's Choice, 1995
Coretta Scott King Honor Book, 1995
Notable 1994 Children's Trade Books in the Field of Social Studies

Titles Annotated in Other Chapters Related to Family Relationships

Alvarez, Julia. *In the Time of the Butterflies*. Historical Fiction.

Artenstein, Jeffrey. *Runaways*. Diaries.

Buffie, Margaret. *Someone Else's Ghost*. Death.

Bunkley, Anita Richmond. *Black Gold*. Romance.

Carter, Alden R. *Between a Rock and a Hard Place*. Adventure.

Charbonneau, Eileen. *Honor to the Hills*. Historical Fiction.

Charbonneau, Eileen. *In the Time of the Wolves*. Historical Fiction.

Christiansen, C. B. *I See the Moon*. Choices.

Christopher, Matt. *Fighting Tackle*. Sports.

Cooney, Caroline B. *Flash Fire*. Adventure.

Cross, Gillian. *New World*. Science Fiction.

Danticat, Edwidge. *Breath, Eyes, Memory*. Choices.

Davis, Ossie. *Just like Martin*. Choices.

Desetta, Al, ed. *The Heart Knows Something Different*. Diaries.

Ducey, Jean Sparks. *The Bittersweet Time*. Historical Fiction.

Farish, Terry. *Talking in Animal*. Animals.

Fenwick, Elizabeth. *Adolescence: The Survival Guide for Parents and Teenagers*. Self-Help.

Ferris, Jean. *Signs of Life*. Death.

Fox, Paula. *The Eagle Kite*. Death.

Friedman, Carl. *Nightfather*. Holocaust.

Fromm, Pete. *Monkey Tag*. Religion.

Hahn, Mary Downing. *Look for Me by Moonlight*. Horror.

Hamilton, Virginia. *Arilla Sun Down*. Choices.

Haynes, Betsy. *Deadly Deception*. Mysteries.

Hiçyilmaz, Gaye. *The Frozen Waterfall*. Friendships.

Hodge, Merle. *For the Life of Laetitia*. School.

Hoobler, Dorothy, and Thomas Hoobler. American Family Album series. Diaries.

Howker, Janni. *The Topiary Garden*. Arts.

Hudgins, Andrew. *The Glass Hammer: A Southern Childhood*. Poetry.

James, Mary (also known as M. E. Kerr). *Frankenlouse*. School.

Jenkins, Lyll Becerra de. *So Loud a Silence*. Choices.

Karr, Kathleen. *In the Kaiser's Clutch*. Historical Fiction.

Karr, Mary. *The Liar's Club*. Autobiography.

Krisher, Trudy. *Spite Fences*. Choices.

Lakin, Patricia. *Everything You Need to Know When a Parent Doesn't Speak English*. Self-Help.

Lane, Dakota. *Johnny Voodoo*. Romance.

Lasky, Kathryn. *Beyond the Burning Time*. Historical Fiction.

Lasky, Kathryn. *Memoirs of a Bookbat*. Religion.

Lewis, Sinclair. *Dodsworth*. Classics.

Lynch, Chris. *Blood Relations*. Choices.

Lynch, Chris. *Mick*. Choices.

Marsden, John. *Letters from the Inside*. Friendships.

McGraw, Erin. *Lies of the Saints*. Short Stories.

Meyer, Carolyn. *Gideon's People*. Religion.

Myers, Christopher A., and Lynne Born Myers. *Forest of the Clouded Leopard*. Choices.

Napoli, Donna Jo. *Zel*. Myths.

Nelson, Theresa. *Earthshine*. Death.

Orlev, Uri. *Lydia, Queen of Palestine*. Holocaust.

Pausewang, Gudrun. *Fall-out*. Choices.

Petersen, P. J. *Liars*. Mysteries.

Porter, Penny. *The Keymaker: Born to Steal*. School.

Randle, Kristen D. *The Only Alien on the Planet*. Friendships.

Rinaldi, Ann. *Broken Days*. Historical Fiction.

Rinaldi, Ann. *A Stitch in Time*. Historical Fiction.

Rodowsky, Colby. *Remembering Mog*. Death.

Rodowsky, Colby. *Sydney, Invincible*. School.

Rumbaut, Hendle. *Dove Dream*. Choices.

Salisbury, Graham. *Under the Blood-Red Sun*. War.

Savage, Deborah. *To Race a Dream*. Choices.

Schwandt, Stephen. *Holding Steady*. Death.

Shoup, Barbara. *Wish You Were Here*. Friendships.

Skinner, Margaret. *Molly Flanagan and the Holy Ghost*. Religion.

Snyder, Melissa. *Souvenirs*. Death.

Sweeney, Joyce. *Shadow*. Mysteries.

Taylor, Theodore. *Sweet Friday Island*. Adventure.

Tolan, Stephanie S. *Welcome to the Ark*. Friendships.

Turner, Glennette Tilley. *Running for Our Lives*. Historical Fiction.

Villaseñor, Victor. *Walking Stars*. Autobiography.

Voigt, Cynthia. *Building Blocks*. Friendships.

Werlin, Nancy. *Are You Alone on Purpose?* Friendships.

Westall, Robert. *Gulf*. War.

Williams, Gregory Howard. *Life on the Color Line: The True Story of a White Boy Who Discovered He Was Black*. Autobiography.

Wright, Betty Ren. *Out of the Dark*. Horror.

Wright, Richard. *Rite of Passage*. Adventure.

15 Fantasy

"This world is not conclusion
A species stands beyond
Invisible; as music
But positive as sound."

Emily Dickinson

"Can Fancy's fairy hands no veil create
To hide the sad realities of fate?"

Thomas Campbell

15.1   Abbey, Lynn. **Beneath the Web.** Ace Books, 1994. 309 pp. ISBN 0-441-00084-3. Fiction.

This is a fast-paced, exciting fantasy novel! The story begins in the land of Walensor, a country held together by the Web. All things are connected to the Web by magic and deceit. But for some reason the Web is fading and dying away. Many have lost their lives as a result. The outcome hinges on a woman named Berika, who has practiced her connection to the Web secretly. What she decides to do will save or destroy the land of Walensor.

15.2   Alexander, Lloyd. **The Arkadians.** Dutton Children's Books, 1995. 272 pp. ISBN 0-525-45415-2. Fiction.

Lucian is the bean counter in the palace of the antifeminist Bear clan's warrior-king. When Lucian discovers fraud and corruption among the powerful royal soothsayers, he is forced to flee for his life. Despite his youth and inexperience, his honesty and goodness guide him through many harrowing adventures and win him the heart of Joy-in-the-Dance, a girl with great energy, wisdom, and power. Lucian's story is told in an epic style with plenty of mythologically based characters to enliven the plot. ER

15.3   Anthony, Piers, and Phillip José Farmer. **The Caterpillar's Question.** Ace Books, 1995. 264 pp. ISBN 0-441-00213-7. Fiction.

Jack responded to the ad to make some money. How difficult could it be to drive a disabled girl from one place to another? Things start becoming strange, however, when Jack finds himself attracted to Tappy, a girl of thirteen years. Even stranger is the land in which Jack and Tappy end up by traveling through a huge rock in the Green Mountain hills. Here Tappy plays an important part in a struggle for freedom and peace.

15.4 Applegate, K. A. Animorphs series. Scholastic, 1996. 185 pp. Fiction.
    The Encounter. ISBN 0-590-62979-4.
    The Invasion. ISBN 0-590-62977-8.
    The Message. ISBN 0-590-62980-8.
    The Predator. ISBN 0-590-62981-6.
    The Visitor. ISBN 0-590-62978-6.

A group of young adults who are able to "morph" into any kind of animal whose DNA they can acquire band together to use their powers in an effort to sabotage the plans of an invisible alien race determined to take over Earth. The strength of these action-packed adventure tales comes from Applegate's ability to describe for her readers how it would really feel to be a dolphin or a lizard while keeping the tension high and dealing with the classic struggle between the forces of good and evil. ER

15.5 Asprin, Robert. **Sweet Myth-Tery of Life.** Edited by Elizabeth B. Bobbitt. Ace Books, 1994. 226 pp. ISBN 0-441-00194-7. Fiction.

Lord Skeeve, president of M.Y.T.H. and purveyor of "magik," has returned from a campaign and is ensconced in the palace of Possiltum. The wealthy and powerful young wizard is supported by his "administrative assistant," Bunny; his demon partner, Aahz, and his pet dragon, Gleep. Still, his mind is heavy. The peasants demand lower taxes. His bodyguards demand that he take better care of himself. Queen Hemlock demands his hand in marriage! What's an up-and-coming sorcerer to do?

15.6 Avi. **City of Light, City of Dark.** Illustrated by Brian Floca. Orchard Books, 1995. 192 pp. ISBN 0-531-06800-5. Fiction.

The Kurbs are mysterious beings who own Manhattan but loan it to humans on the condition that a ritual search for the "Power" be conducted annually. From each generation, a woman blessed with special sight conducts the search ritual, handing down her skills to her daughter. This story, told in comic-book style, revolves around three young New Yorkers who become involved in one ritual search, a special-sighted woman, and a bad guy out to steal the power for himself. ER

Publisher's Weekly Best Book, 1993 in the original publication

15.7 Brown, Mary. **Pigs Don't Fly.** Baen, 1994. 370 pp. ISBN 0-671-87601-5. Fiction.

What chance would the runaway, illegitimate, orphaned, obese daughter of a prostitute have? How could she think she could guide a handsome knight, blinded and amnesiac after an attack by robbers, to the home that he can't even identify? Throw in a smelly mutt, a bony horse, and other impediments and you have a grand adventure with many more questions that can perhaps only be answered when pigs fly!

ALA Best Books for Young Adults, 1995

15.8 Bull, Emma P. J. F. **Finder: A Novel of the Borderlands.** Tor / Tom Doherty Associates, 1994. 317 pp. ISBN 0-312-85418-8. Fiction.

Thataway, and the lost is found. Orient's special talent for finding things drove him from the World to the Borderlands, which are touched by faerie magic, where Orient's talent is accepted and even affords him a living. He is called upon to use his gift to seek the source of a new designer drug human beings are taking that promises to transform them into elves but creates corpses instead. Danger and suspense abound, but not without humor, hope, and even love.

ALA Best Books for Young Adults, 1995

15.9 Callander, Don. **Dragon Companion.** Ace Books, 1994. 321 pp. ISBN 0-441-00115-7. Fiction.

Tom Whitehead, a librarian in twentieth-century America, is unexpectedly whisked away to a strange land filled with an Arthurian type of magic. Not only does Tom find himself appointed Librarian to the Historian of Carolna, Murdan of Overhall, but he is also chosen to be a Dragon Companion by none other than a dragon himself. Tom must use his research abilities to help him find peace for the land and love for himself within the land of Carolna.

15.10 Carmody, Isobelle. **The Gathering.** Dial Books, 1994. 279 pp. ISBN 0-8037-1716-4. Fiction.

"Do you believe in good and evil?" asks Nathaniel as he tries to sort through the eerie events of the past and present in the too-perfect community of Chestnut, where nothing is as it "should" be—a park with no playing children, horrible smells that no one notices, and a school headmaster who condones brutality among students. The question that he should ask is whether he and the others of the Circle who receive the Call can prevail. Even though the reader knows the good guys will win, it's difficult to put this book down until you know *how*.

ALA Quick Picks for Young Adults, 1995

15.11 Clayton, Jo. **Dance down the Stars.** Daw Books, 1994. 368 pp. ISBN 0-88677-617-1. Fiction.

With the help of some unusual companions, the Healer Serroi must find a way to destroy the Fletch—a force of evil with the ability to destroy her civilization. In this third volume of the Dancer Trilogy, Serroi and her friends are desperate, so desperate that they are willing to use themselves as bait so the Fletch will pay attention to them and not to their other allies, who are planning a surprise attack. In doing this, Serroi is captured. Can she escape in time to save her friends and civilization itself?

15.12 Cook, Rick. **The Wizardry Consulted.** Baen, 1995. 250 pp. ISBN 0-671-87700-3. Fiction.

In this installment of the "Wizardry" books, Wiz Zumwalt is being held captive by the Dragons, an intelligent form of life, on their own world. The ransom for the Wiz? The salvation of dragonkind.

15.13 Coville, Bruce. **Into the Land of the Unicorns.** Scholastic Hardcover, 1994. 159 pp. ISBN 0-590-45955-4. Fiction.

Young Cara Hunter has been raised by her grandmother since she was abandoned by her parents. In this first volume of the Unicorn Chronicles, they are being chased by a man who is after a jewel—an amulet worn by Cara. To escape, Cara's grandmother guides her into a leap to a magical, parallel land, the Land of Luster, where she meets an assortment of creatures, including Lightfoot the Unicorn. He helps her on a journey to find the secret of the amulet and the secret of herself. ER

ALA Quick Picks for Young Adults, 1996
IRA Teacher's Choice, 1996

15.14 DeChancie, John. **Bride of the Castle.** Ace Books, 1994. 181 pp. ISBN 0-441-00120-3. Fiction.

Crazy things happen to those living in Castle Perilous, not to mention those living on the outside. The characters of this adventure from the *Castle* series travel through time to strange dimensions, all from within the castle walls. What is even stranger is the twisted sense of humor the castle seems to have when playing with people's lives.

15.15 Duane, Diane. **So You Want to Be a Wizard?** Magic Carpet Books / Harcourt Brace, 1996. 370 pp. ISBN 0-15-201239-7. Fiction.

Nita has trouble fitting in with the other girls at school. She just doesn't have the same interests that they do. Nita finds solace in reading books, and she just may have found the answer to her problems in a book in the library entitled *So, You Want to be a Wizard*. She must decide whether the book is "an elaborate joke" or "the real thing" and then take the oath the book provides to become a wizard. ER

15.16 Emerson, Ru. **Night-Threads: The Science of Power.** Ace Books, 1995. 356 pp. ISBN 0-441-00286-2. Fiction.

Henri Dupret has been secretly smuggling the deadly drug Zero across the borders into the land of Rhadaz. It's up to his daughter Ariadne and her newlywed husband to help stop him. As a result of the drug Zero even the emperor seems to have gone crazy and almost anything that could have gone wrong has. What will it take to stop Dupret and his army-like miscreants?

15.17   Fleet, Robert C. **Last Mountain.** Ace Books, 1994. 288 pp. ISBN 0-441-00062-2. Fiction.

Nancy del Rio lives in a troubled part of Los Angeles with her grandmother. She discovers that she has an important link with the last unicorn alive. It's up to Nancy to find him and to discover her purpose in his destiny. Reality and magic combine in this story of maturity and love. MC

15.18   Frankos, Steven. **Cathedral of Thorns.** Ace Books, 1995. 323 pp. ISBN 0-441-00221-8. Fiction.

How can a teenaged farmer be expected to complete a heroic quest? That's what Aitchley Corlaiys keeps asking himself as he faces unimaginable beasts and hazards, although he knows it's partly for the love of the scullery maid Berlyn. With unusual companions such as a dwarf, a hybrid troll, a treacherous thief, a plant-man, and even a computer from a perpendicular future universe, Aitchley continues the adventures begun in *Beyond Lich Gate.*

15.19   Friedman, C. S. **When True Night Falls.** Daw Books, Inc., 1993. 617 pp. ISBN 0-88677-615-5. Fiction.

If you like fantasy and the eternal fight between good and evil, this is definitely a book for you. Damien Vryce, a warrior priest, and Gerald Tarrant, a sorcerer known as the Hunter, cross the dreaded ocean to Erna's eastern continent. At first, they are greeted warmly and welcomed. Soon, however, things change and they must flee. They become lost and must rely on magic to help save them. Their struggles to survive and conquer evil make good reading.

15.20   Friesner, Esther. **Majyk by Hook or Crook.** Ace Books, 1994. 262 pp. ISBN 0-441-00054-1. Fiction.

Earth cat Scandal and his magician, Kendar Gangle of Wingdingo, seek to end the rain of poultry in the fair city of Orbix. What lengths they have to go to will surprise you. Anything can happen to the sarcastic Scandal and his not-so-perfect magician and in this story it usually does.

15.21   Gardner, Craig Shaw. Dragon Circle series.
    Dragon Sleeping. Ace Books, 1995. 435 pp. ISBN 0-441-00260-9. Fiction.
    Dragon Waking. Ace Books, 1995. 360 pp. ISBN 0-441-00248-X. Fiction.

It is 1967, and the quiet suburban world of Chestnut Circle is thrust into a world of wizards, apelike creatures called the Anno, and the ever-present threat of a destructive dragon. Unlikely characters must take on heroic roles in order to save their own lives as well as the lives of their neighbors, who suddenly find themselves in a desperate challenge to survive. In the second book, everyone is racing to find all seven eyes of the dragon, which are reputed to be powerful protection from the destructive nature of the creature. As the dragon wakes, this vying for power seems to be of no avail—the dragon has plans of its own. Profanity and violent situations.

15.22 Gleason, Robert. **Wrath of God.** HarperPrism, 1994. 397 pp. ISBN 0-06-105311-2. Fiction.

An evil army reminiscent of the Mongol Hordes is invading a post-apocalyptic North America, and New Arizona's only hope lies in the past. The defenders are led by an eighty-five-year-old woman, her family, and three people she's chosen to bring through a hole in time: George Patton, Stonewall Jackson, and Amelia Earhart. Betsy Ross, the bald eagle, and Harry the triceratops also play key roles in the defense. Violence and torture are included.

15.23 Haber, Karen. **Woman without a Shadow.** Daw Books, Inc., 1995. 300 pp. ISBN 0-88677-627-9. Fiction.

Teenage empath (she has the ability to read minds and plant thoughts) Kayla John Reed runs away from the mining planet of Styx after her parents are killed in a cave-in and she runs afoul of the ruling family. She joins a group of space traders/smugglers, and her travels eventually bring her back into contact with the very people from whom she was running.

15.24 Hambly, Barbara. **Stranger at the Wedding.** A Del Rey Book/Ballantine Books, 1994. 341 pp. ISBN 0-345-38097-5. Fiction.

After six years at the Citadel studying to become a master wizard, Kyra learns that a marriage has been arranged for her younger sister Alix and fears great harm will be the result of the wedding. Despite her father's having denounced and disowned her because of her magical powers, Kyra returns home to save her sister's life. Can she locate the source of the curse and reverse the spell before an innocent girl is sacrificed to an unknown evil?

ALA Best Books for Young Adults, 1995

15.25 Harris, Deborah Turner. **Caledon of the Mists.** Ace Books, 1994. 402 pp. ISBN 0-441-00029-0. Fiction.

Reminiscent of an old Scottish folktale, *Caledon of the Mists* blends magic and the mysterious with reality. Duncan and his sister Mhairi seek to reclaim their rightful places on the throne of a distant land. What they fight to regain this throne is both the prejudice of men and the terror of misused power.

15.26   Harris, Deborah Turner. **The Queen of Ashes.** Ace Books, 1995. 448 pp. ISBN 0-441-00118-1. Fiction.

The story of Caledon continues as Queen Mhairi considers marriage to settle old scores with the Beringar kingdom. The lords of Caledon are restless in their desire for power in the land. They discover the queen's plans to marry an outsider and devise some plans of their own for her. Meanwhile, the Mists and their King of Bones lurk ever nearer to the queen and her new found "friend" Lady Mordance. What evil awaits Caledon and their queen? It's all tied to the Anchorstone that holds Caledon together—or does it?

15.27   Hood, Daniel. **Wizard's Heir.** Ace Books, 1995. 298 pp. ISBN 0-441-00231-5. Fiction.

Liam Rhenford's life has changed since the murder of his friend, the wizard Tarquin. He has inherited the wizard's house and is attended by the wizard's "familiar," a tiny telepathic dragon. When more murder and mayhem descend upon the tiny town of Southwark, Liam is forced to investigate. After his sleuthing unearths a mad ghost, a magical gryphon, and a guild of thieves, he begins to reconsider a witch's warning that there might be "more here than meets the eye."

15.28   Hunter, Mollie. **The Walking Stones.** Harcourt Brace, 1996. 168 pp. ISBN 0-15-200995-7. Fiction.

This fantasy of Donald and a hydroelectric company is set in a glen that is about to be flooded. One man, Bodach, wants to hold back "progress," and he uses ancient stone circles, co-walkers, and all his powers to do so.

15.29   Jacques, Brian. **The Bellmaker.** Illustrated by Allan Curless. Philomel Books, 1994. 352 pp. ISBN 0-399-22805-5. Fiction.

Seventh in the *Redwall* series, this medieval adventure revolves around the evil foxwolf Nagru's takeover of the squirrel-king Gael's castle. As small rebel forces within the kingdom form, they are unexpectedly aided by Mariel, a mousemaiden warrior from the far Redwall monastery, and her band of assorted animal warriors. Guided by a dream, Mariel's father, the Redwall Bellmaker, gathers a makeshift army to aid Gael's kingdom. The characters are richly diverse and compellingly human.

15.30   Jansson, Tove. **Moominpappa's Memoirs.** Translated by Thomas Warburton. A Sunburst Book/Farrar, Straus and Giroux, 1994. 162 pp. ISBN 0-374-45307-1. Fiction.

This is a vivid account of the life of Moominpappa, father of Moomintroll. It details his many adventures from the time he escapes from the Foundling Home to his incredible ocean voyage and his dramatic meeting with Moominmamma. If you like fantasy and imaginative writing, you'll like this story. ER WL

15.31 Jones, Diana Wynne. **The Crown of Dalemark.** Greenwillow Books, 1995. 471 pp. ISBN 0-668-13363-0. Fiction.

The Crown of Dalemark combines modern times with long ago in a story about deception, war, and friendship. Maewen finds herself wrapped up in a scheme that stretches over hundreds of years. Not only is she involved, but Maewen is the only means the Undying have to change history into what it should have been, and the final battle takes place not on a battlefield but at Maewen's very own house.

15.32 Kellogg, Marjorie B. **The Book of Earth.** Daw Books, 1995. 334 pp. ISBN 0-88677-574-4. Fiction.

Erde is the only child and daughter of a very powerful lord of the land. Already struck by tragedy twice, Erde finds herself the focus of yet another evil beneath her own roof, and her father is swept up in the fight against her. Erde's attempt to right the wrongs in her life lead her on an adventure during which she must learn to trust again, in this first volume of the Dragon Quartet.

15.33 Kindl, Patrice. **Owl in Love.** Puffin Books, 1994. 204 pp. ISBN 0-14-037129-X. Fiction.

Owl's teenage life is complicated. First, her parents are witches. Next, Owl can change into a real owl at any time. This may seem funny to some people, but not to Owl. Nor does she laugh when her "owl-self" says that her one-in-a-lifetime love is Mr. Lindstrom, her gray-haired science teacher. As Owl is drawn to him, she must try to understand why her human side is concerned about the secret boy in the woods. ER

ALA Best Books for Young Adults, 1995

15.34 Kurtz, Katherine, and Deborah Turner Harris. **Dagger Magic: A Novel of** *The Adept.* Ace Books, 1996. 375 pp. ISBN 0-441-00304-4. Fiction.

Three Scotsmen are great and enduring friends and members of "The Hunting Lodge": Sir Adam Sinclair—renowned psychiatrist, baronet, and forensic consultant; Peregrine Lovat—talented portrait artist and newlywed; and Detective Noel McLeod—chief inspector of the Lothian and Borders Police. But they are also members of "The Adept," practitioners of white magic who must step forward once again to do battle with an ancient adversary—*evil*.

15.35 Lackey, Mercedes. **The Fire Rose.** Baen, 1995. 433 pp. ISBN 0-671-87687-2. Fiction.

Rosalind Hawkins is not a typical young lady of turn-of-the-century Chicago. High-spirited and highly educated, when her father's death leaves her not only alone but unexpectedly penniless she does not hesitate to accept a mysterious job offer in San Francisco. She soon learns that her talents in medieval languages are needed by a powerful magician who is paying dearly for his hubris: he is stuck in a state of being half-wolf, half-man! Rose's strength of character and mind serve her well. There are many spells cast in this tale, not the least of which is the one Lackey casts over the reader.

15.36   Lee, Stan, editor. **The Ultimate Spider-Man.** Byron Preiss Multimedia / Boulevard Books, 1994. 347 pp. ISBN 1-57297-103-7. Fiction.

This collection of short stories, written and illustrated by some of the best in the comic-book business, are all about a favorite among comic readers everywhere: Spider-Man. Some writers attempt to reveal the beginnings of Spider-Man, while others set the usual traps for and describe the evasion tactics of the masked web-slinger.

15.37   Levy, Robert. **Clan of the Shape-Changers.** Houghton Mifflin, 1994. 183 pp. ISBN 0-395-66612-0. Fiction.

Susan is a shape-changer. She can use the power of her mind to become any living thing she wishes. But can she save the people she loves from death? When Susan, the wolf Farrun, and Jeffrey must face dangers caused by nature and the Shamans to free the King of Reune and save all those living in the Thoral Mountains, their adventures make exciting reading.

15.38   Logston, Anne. **Dagger's Point.** Ace Books, 1995. 264 pp. ISBN 0-441-00134-3. Fiction.

This novel is the thrilling continuation of the Shadow series. Shadow's niece, Jaellyn, and her friend Tanis set out on the adventure of a lifetime in search of Jaellyn's missing soul. Without her soul, Jaellyn will never be able to mature fully into the women she is supposed to be. Braving dangerous roads and forests, Jaellyn must find her true father to complete her adulthood, although there's a chance he won't be willing to help his "half-breed" daughter.

15.39   Logston, Anne. **Wild Blood.** Ace Books, 1995. 227 pp. ISBN 0-441-00243-9. Fiction.

Sixteen-year-old Ria, half-elf, half-human, embarks on a journey to find her twin brother, Valann, who lives with the elves of Heartwood, while she has been reared as a human being by the High Lord Sharl and his wife. Ria's mother had separated her children at birth in hopes that someday they would reunite the splintered alliance between elves and humans. The twins feel strange and unwanted by those with whom they live, since Valann strongly resembles the human parent while Ria is more elflike in appearance and behavior. In time, both learn to deal with personal differences and cultural misunderstandings.

15.40   MacLachlan, Patricia. **Tomorrow's Wizard.** Magic Carpet Books / Harcourt Brace, 1996. 66 pp. ISBN 0-15-201276-1. Fiction.

Tomorrow, the wizard, did not understand why his apprentice, Murdoch, did not hear the clattering of the High Wizard when he shook his tin tankard. And, frankly, this worried Tomorrow. Murdoch is able to hear the wishes of others and is even able to grant simple wishes on his own, but if he can't hear the High Wizard Murdoch's own future as a wizard is uncertain. ER

15.41 Marley, Louise. **Sing the Light.** Ace Books, 1995. 291 pp. ISBN 0-441-00272-2. Fiction.

Nevya is a planet of ice, foreboding and dangerous. Summer comes to the planet once every five years, providing a short respite from the grip of winter. It is the Cantrixes with their instruments and voices who create warmth and light for the people of Nevya. Sira is the newest and youngest Cantrix and must serve the House of Bariken. She quickly learns that it is not the planet's cold that is her worst enemy.

15.42 Matas, Carol, and Perry Nodelman. **Of Two Minds.** Simon and Schuster Books for Young Readers, 1995. 200 pp. ISBN 0-689-80138-6. Fiction.

Princess Lenora doesn't want to marry anyone, least of all her parents' choice, skinny, boring Coren. She desires adventure and resents being forbidden to use her people's gift of imagining anything into reality, while Coren refuses to engage in his people's ability to enter others' minds because he longs for a calm, stable life. This unlikely pair is suddenly catapulted into a dangerous world where only by sharing their mental powers can they save themselves.

School Library Journal Best Books of 1995

15.43 McCaffrey, Anne. **Lyon's Pride.** Ace Books, 1995. 327 pp. ISBN 0-441-00141-6. Fiction.

The story of *Rowan* continues with the children of Damia and Afra Lyon coming together to save the universe. In order to accomplish this, the siblings must combine their talents in the areas of telekinesis, telepathy, and empathy. Isthian, Laria, Rojer, and Zara Lyon fight united against the Hiver aliens to protect the world the Lyon family loves.

15.44 McCaffrey, Anne, and Jody Lynn Nye. **Treaty at Doona.** Ace Books, 1994. 342 pp. ISBN 0-441-00089-4. Fiction.

The Humans and Hrrubans have learned to live in harmony on Doona. They are even considering expanding their trading and are in the middle of a trade conference when their peace is shattered by the arrival of a huge vessel unlike any ever seen. The beings on board are the Gringgs, who say they have come in peace and wish to get acquainted. But have they really? Many of the Humans and Hrrubans are frightened by the size and power of the Gringgs. Do they come in friendship, or to take over?

15.45   Myers, Walter Dean. **Shadow of the Red Moon.** Illustrated by Christopher Myers. Scholastic Hardcover, 1995. 183 pp. ISBN 0-590-45895-7. Fiction.

This fantasy tells the story of a post-apocalyptic world in which Jon, a fifteen-year-old Okalian, must leave his home, Crystal City, because it is being attacked by the Fens, a marauding group of children. Only children fifteen years old and younger can survive outside the protection of the Crystal City. Jon joins up with other Okalians as they journey towards their Ancient Land and confront hostile Fens and other obstacles.

15.46   Napoli, Donna Jo. **The Magic Circle.** Puffin Books, 1995. 118 pp. ISBN 0-14-037439-6. Fiction.

A step beyond Hansel and Gretel, *The Magic Circle* tells the story behind the story of the wicked witch and how she came to be living in the candy house. The witch, referred to as "the Ugly One," is tricked into becoming what she is, an evil one who desires human flesh. How does the Ugly One cope with her newly cursed desire? What really happens to Hansel and Gretel?

15.47   Niles, Douglas. **A Breach in the Watershed.** Ace Books, 1995. 433 pp. ISBN 0-441-00208-0. Fiction.

For centuries the lands of the watershed were at peace. These included Dalethica, the land of life, Faerine, the land of magic, and Duloth-Trol, the land of death and decay where the Darkwater flows. Now the watershed has been breached and a poisonous evil flows forth. Only a handful of heroes remain to defend what is pure, fighting a battle of hope against a dark god who has a profound, all-consuming thirst for the destruction of the watershed.

15.48   Norton, Andre, with P. M. Griffin and Mary H. Schaub. **Flight of Vengeance.** Tor / Tom Doherty Associates, Inc., 1992. 383 pp. ISBN 0-812-50706-1. Fiction.

Three authors combine their efforts to produce the conclusion of the epic adventure Witch World: The Turning. Each author relates a separate story surrounding one singular event of great magnitude. The witches of the adventure and their quest for power have a devastating effect on the rest of the world. What the outcome of the "turning" is depends upon four survivors of the destruction.

15.49   O'Donohoe, Nick. **The Magic and the Healing.** Ace Books, 1994. 324 pp. ISBN 0-441-00053-3. Fiction.

BJ Vaughn, a young veterinary student, finds herself in the world of Crossroads, where an injured unicorn needs help. She has entered a world where the creatures of imagination live and breathe, and hurt.

Here BJ, tending to centaurs and griffins and magical cats, will discover the joy of healing and the wonder of magic. The book is a must for all readers who like the joy of suspending belief and entering the world of imagination.

15.50 O'Donohoe, Nick. **Under the Healing Sign.** Ace Books, 1995. 337 pp. ISBN 0-441-00180-7. Fiction.

BJ Vaughn practices veterinary medicine in a place called Crossroads. Crossroads is like no other place in the world; in fact, Crossroads is exactly that, a place where all roads from other worlds cross. The animals in Crossroads are a little unusual as well: griffins, centaurs, wyrs, and other types of "animals" rely on BJ's practice. An outside force threatens to destroy the peace of Crossroads and it is up to BJ and her friends to save the animals and themselves in the process.

15.51 Price, Susan. **Ghost Dance: The Czar's Black Angel.** Farrar, Straus and Giroux, 1994. 217 pp. ISBN 0-374-32537-5. Fiction.

Shingebiss is not yet a shaman, although she is the apprentice to a shaman whom she calls "Granny." When men from the Northlands come seeking her, Granny refuses to help save the land that the Czar is destroying. Shingebiss is sent away to the shaman's sister's house to continue her apprenticeship, but the Northlands dilemma weighs heavily on her heart. Shingebiss decides to take matters into her own hands and must face the terrible Czar on her own. MC

15.52 Regan, Dian Curtis. **Princess Nevermore.** Scholastic Hardcover, 1995. ISBN 0-590-45758-6. Fiction.

Be careful what you wish for! Princess Quinelle, Quinn to her friends, should have remembered the age-old adage. Young Quinn has always longed to see what life on Earth is like. When her wish becomes a reality she must face the complications of teenage life today, complete with its friendships and the love of a young man. All of these new experiences faced by Quinn create a delightful modern-day fantasy.

15.53 Rovin, Jeff. **Mortal Kombat.** Boulevard Books, 1995. 293 pp. ISBN 1-57297-059-6. Fiction.

This is the story about the characters in the controversial video game *Mortal Kombat* and their secrets. The characters Johnny Cage, Sonya Blade, and Liu Kang are fighting in the battle of their lives against a giant named Goro and the master sorcerer Shang Tsung, who want to destroy the earth. Johnny, Sonya, and Liu must obtain a strange amulet which will bring them more than fame; it will bring safety for their world.

15.54 Russell, Sean. **World without End.** Daw Books, 1994. 606 pp. ISBN 0-88677-624-4. Fiction.

This novel is the first book of the Moontide and Magic Rise series. The story features Tristam Flattery, a naturalist who has been chosen by some very influential people to carry out a task which will save the king's life. However, Tristam is kept in the dark as to what role he actually plays in the political warfare going on around him. What is the secret behind the Regis plant Tristam has been commissioned to find? What strange talents do the others believe Tristam holds? Whatever they believe, Tristam Flattery must discover before it's too late to save himself.

15.55   Salvatore, R. A. **The Dragon's Dagger.** Ace Books, 1994. 313 pp. ISBN 0-441-00078-9. Fiction.

Gary Leger returns to the land of Faerie in this sequel to *The Woods out Back*. Being part of a different world is fascinating and challenging for Gary and he enjoys every minute of the danger. His adventure includes a wicked king, a plotting witch, a destructive dragon, and some pretty unusual friends. What will Gary have to do to get the land back under control?

15.56   Salvatore, R. A. **Dragonslayer's Return.** Ace Books, 1995. 326 pp. ISBN 0-441-00228-5. Fiction.

This sequel to *The Dragon's Dagger* finds young adult Gary Leger, now in his twenties, trying to come to terms with the death of his father as he returns to the land of Faerie for further adventures. This time, his wife Diane accompanies him to the land of elves, dwarfs, leprechauns, trolls, witches, goblins, humans, and other beings.

15.57   Scarborough, Elizabeth Ann. **The Godmother.** Ace Books, 1994. 341 pp. ISBN 0-441-00269-2. Fiction.

Rose Samson is a social worker in Seattle, Washington. Little does she know that an off-the-cuff wish she made for a fairy godmother has become a reality when Felicity Fortune arrives in town. Felicity shows Rose how to hope for good again when she involves Rose in the lives of several people who seem to need Rose to survive.

15.58   Scarborough, Elizabeth Ann. **The Godmother's Apprentice.** Ace Books, 1994. 294 pp. ISBN 0-441-00252-8. Fiction.

Snohomish Quantrill becomes "the godmother's apprentice" after she reaps the benefits of having a "fairy" godmother herself. Felicity, one of the godmothers, takes Sno to Ireland with her for training. Sno learns the benefits as well as the limitations of being a fairy godmother when she has to deal with a house imp living in their home. Along with her companion Puss, the talking cat, Sno also learns some important lessons about life and love.

15.59   Sebanc, Mark. **Flight to Hollow Mountain.** William B. Eerdmans, 1996. 412 pp. ISBN 0-8028-3794-8. Fiction.

The Talamadh, a beautiful harp, has for years provided the harmony necessary to maintain peace in the realms of Middle Earth. But moral and social decay have begun; treachery is at hand. The Talamadh has been stolen, and, in the epic tradition of Tolkien, it falls to a young lad, Kalaguinn, to rescue the harp and restore serenity to the land in this first volume of *The Talamadh*.

15.60 Service, Pamela F. **Storm at the Edge of Time.** Walker and Company, 1994. 192 pp. ISBN 0-8027-8306-6. Fiction.

Three young people, related to one another but from different time periods, are recruited by an ancient wizard to defeat an evil about to envelop the world. A young Viking, a modern American middle school girl, and a half-human boy from the future must work together and through time on the Orkney Islands to recover three magical staffs and battle an impending storm of destruction.

15.61 Sherman, Josepha. **Gleaming Bright.** Walker and Company, 1994. 170 pp. ISBN 0-8027-8296-5. Fiction.

This is the story of Princess Finola, who, accompanied by an enchanted stag and a sly outlaw, Fiain, sets out on a perilous journey to retrieve a golden box called Gleaming Bright that is a granter of wishes. Gleaming Bright was a gift from the wizard Cathbad to King Donal, Finola's father, but was stolen by the envious Rhegeth, the Dark Druid, who is out to corrupt Gleaming Bright to his evil ways. With Gleaming Bright in the hands of Rhegeth, the princesses's land of Irwain is vulnerable to foreign invasion and famine. This is classic fantasy true to the genre.

15.62 Shinn, Sharon. **The Shape-Changer's Wife.** Ace Books, 1995. 200 pp. ISBN 0-441-00261-7. Fiction.

Aubrey, a young wizard, has learned all he can from old Cyril, his mentor. Wanting to perfect his art of wizardry, Aubrey travels to a far-off land to study with Glyrendon, the powerful shape-changer. There he not only discovers the art of shape-changing, but also encounters love in the person of Lilith, Glyrendon's wife. Aubrey soon has to summon all of his magical powers to fend off the wrath of the powerful shape-changer.

15.63 Shusterman, Neal. **Scorpion Shards.** Tor / Tom Doherty Associates, 1995. 240 pp. ISBN 0-812-52465-9. Fiction.

In this classic tale of the fight between good and evil, six teenagers learn that a dark force is controlling their lives, feeding on their real but not-so-nice emotions. They must find each other, experience guilt, learn about forgiveness, and, ultimately, determine how to take responsibility for their lives as they travel across the country in this tale that is part adventure, part science fiction, and part philosophical treatise.

15.64   Smith, Sherwood. **Wren's Quest.** Jane Yolen Books / Harcourt Brace, 1993. 199 pp. ISBN 0-15-200976-0. Fiction.

Wren, a magician's apprentice, sets out on a journey to find her origins and is beset by the spells of a mysterious evil force that pursues her and her companion Prince Conor Shaltar. They must resort to casting spells despite their inexperience, which causes even more trouble. All of Wren's newly acquired skills are put to the test by an experienced and unscrupulous adversary who wickedly plans to destroy her and her friends.

15.65   Stasheff, Christopher. **M'Lady Witch.** Ace Books, 1994. 247 pp. ISBN 0-441-00113-0. Fiction.

Cordelia Gallowglass and the Prince have been friends since childhood, a relationship complicated by the fact that both Cordelia and Alain are headstrong and stubborn. They must discover for themselves if marriage is in their future, and in order to accomplish this Cordelia and Alain put into motion a cat-and-mouse game of romance.

15.66   Stasheff, Christopher. **Quicksilver's Knight.** Ace Books, 1995. 281 pp. ISBN 0-441-00229-3. Fiction.

Geoffrey Gallowglass is a young man bewitched by love. He just doesn't know which woman to trust. Should he love the beautiful and brave thief called Quicksilver or the sultry and subversive Moraga, a witch who will do anything for the throne of Graymare? Everything depends on his choice.

15.67   Stewart, Sean. **Nobody's Son.** Ace Books, 1995. 273 pp. ISBN 0-441-00128-9. Fiction.

Mark is a carpenter, determined to win the gratitude of King Astin by breaking the ancient spell of Ghostwood. Quest accomplished, he looks forward to his reward and his "happily ever after." His greatest challenge, however, is still ahead. The new dukedom is an ill-fitting mantle, and the hand he has claimed in marriage, Princess Gail's, is more likely to club than to caress. Moreover, he must battle his private demon, his father's desertion, and the fact that he is "nobody's son."

15.68   Tepper, Sheri S. **The Awakeners.** Orb / Tom Doherty Associates, Inc., 1994. 491 pp. ISBN 0-312-89022-2. Fiction.

The lands of Northshore and Southshore are cleaved by a tidal river that determines the rhythm of life on the Northshore. After thousands of years, life on the Northshore has evolved into a cruel society where bird-like creatures manipulate human beings for their own use with the help of the Awakeners, specially chosen humans who perpetuate an oppressive religious discipline. Some Awakeners, however, decide to rebel, aided by Thrasne, a river boatman, and the peaceful Noor in their quest for liberty.

15.69 Varley, John, and Ricia Mainhardt, editors. **Superheroes.** Ace Books, 1995. 373 pp. ISBN 0-441-00137-8. Fiction.

Although the moods of the stories in this fantasy collection range from humorous to very serious, all the stories feature superheroes. They deal with contemporary issues such as abusive relationships, crime, responsibility, and personal integrity. Some stories contain occasional strong language.

15.70 Watt-Evans, Lawrence, and Esther M. Friesner. **Split Heirs.** Tor / Tom Doherty, 1993. 317 pp. ISBN 0-812-52029-7. Fiction.

When triplets are born to the royal household, Queen Artemisia begins plotting to save her doomed children. The "split heirs" begin lives of magic, swordsmanship, and shepherding in a crazy, mixed-up world of fantasy. This hilarious story has the reader guessing what's going to happen next while it satirizes fantasy to the fullest.

15.71 Wrede, Patricia C. **Book of Enchantments.** Jane Yolen Books / Harcourt Brace, 1996. 226 pp. ISBN 0-15-201255-9. Fiction.

If you used to love unicorns and fairy tales, or if you still enjoy magic and humor, these ten stories are for you. In one story, a singing harp made of the bones of a dead princess tell of her murder. In another tale, a young woman is able to see what choices she might make in the present and how they will affect her future. In the last story, the Frying Pan of Doom becomes the sign of a young kitchen maid's elevation to her rightful position as queen. The volume is completed with a recipe for "Quick After-Battle Triple Chocolate Cake," used by barbarian swordsmen, and kindly translated from the original for modern bakers.

15.72 Wrede, Patricia C. **Talking to Dragons.** Scholastic, 1995. 255 pp. ISBN 0-590-48475-3. Fiction.

Sixteen-year-old Daystar is sent by his mother Cimonrene into the Enchanted Forest with a mysterious sword, his good manners, and an order not to return until he can explain why he had to leave. Daystar discovers immediately that politeness is the key to survival as he rescues a fire witch from a thorny hedge simply by saying "please." This coming-of-age fantasy adventure blends magic, mystery, and humor with the hero's uncommon good sense in this fourth installment of the *Enchanted Forest Chronicles*.

15.73 Yep, Laurence. **Dragon Cauldron.** HarperTrophy / HarperCollins, 1991. 312 pp. ISBN 0-06-440398-X. Paperback. Fiction.

Dragon Cauldron is the third book in a series by Laurence Yep. The main characters are a dragon named Shimmer, a magical monkey, a repentant witch named Civet, and two argumentative humans. These five must repair the broken cauldron to save Shimmer's dying species of dragons while proving themselves loyal friends. MC

15.74   Yep, Laurence. **Dragon War.** HarperTrophy / HarperCollins, 1992. 313 pp. ISBN 0-06-440525-7. Fiction.

In this exciting conclusion to the Dragon series, Shimmer, the wizard Monkey, and Indigo must reclaim the dragon cauldron and set free the soul of Thorn, which is trapped inside it. They change into many things to trick the Boneless King and his followers. Will they, at last, elude evil and save Thorn? MC

15.75   Yolen, Jane. **Dragon's Blood.** Magic Carpet Books / Harcourt Brace, 1996. 304 pp. ISBN 9-15-200866-7. Fiction.

Bond servants in Master Sakhan's dragon barns are kept under close supervision on the dragon-raising planet of Austar IV. Jakkin Stewart was sold into bondage to these barns after his father's untimely death. Jakkin must find a way to steal a hatchling dragon in order to release himself from his bondage and become a Master himself. He plans to secretly train the dragon to fight in the pits, but not only does he plan to fight—he plans to win.

15.76   Yolen, Jane. **The Wild Hunt.** Illustrated by Francisco Mora. Harcourt Brace, 1995. 141 pp. ISBN 0-15-200211-1. Fiction.

In this story, Yolen creates two worlds that seem to be the same and yet are not. In alternating chapters, two boys, Jerold and Gerund, learn about the destructive "wild hunt." At the urging of a white cat and a clumsy dog, the two wade through deep snowy fields to confront the Great Horned King and his slavering dogs on their deathly hunt. With surprising twists, Yolen develops the themes of courage and the burdens of heroism. ER

15.77   Zambreno, Mary Frances. **Journeyman Wizard.** Jane Yolen Books / Harcourt Brace, 1994. 263 pp. ISBN 0-15-200022-4. Fiction.

In this sequel to *A Plague of Sorcerers*, seventeen-year-old Jermyn travels to Land's End, where he will complete his studies as a spellmaker with the famous sorceress Lady Jean Allons. When his mentor is murdered while working a spell with him, he is blamed for her death. Armed only with magic and assisted by the beautiful Brianne, he must overcome the powers of evil to prove his innocence and find the real killer. Fans of magic, witches, and sorcery will be spellbound by *Journeyman Wizard*.

Titles Annotated in Other Chapters Related to Fantasy

Dann, Jack, and Gardner Dozois, eds. *Dinosaurs II.* Short Stories.

Friedman, M. J. *Lois and Clark: Deadly Games.* Television.

Hague, Michael, ed. *The Book of Dragons.* Myths.

Hamilton, Laurell K. *The Laughing Corpse.* Horror.

Hite, Sid. *Answer My Prayer.* Romance.

Jennings, Paul. *Unbearable! More Bizarre Stories.* Short Stories.

Lee, Stan, ed. *The Ultimate Silver Surfer.* Short Stories.

Service, Pamela F. *Stinker's Return.* Science Fiction.

Sleator, William. *Dangerous Wishes.* Adventure.

Strauss, Victoria. *Guardian of the Hills.* Choices.

Sutcliff, Rosemary. *The Light beyond the Forest: The Quest for the Holy Grail.* Myths.

Sutcliff, Rosemary. *The Sword and the Circle: King Arthur and the Knights of the Round Table.* Myths.

Taylor, L. A. *Cat's Paw.* Adventure.

Turner, Megan Whalen. *Instead of Three Wishes.* Short Stories.

Voigt, Cynthia. *Jackaroo.* Myths.

Wangerin, Walter, Jr. *The Crying for a Vision.* Choices.

Weis, Margaret, ed. *Fantastic Alice.* Short Stories.

16 Friendships

"The basement kitchen of the brownstone house where my family lived was the usual gathering place. Once inside the warm safety of its walls the women threw off their drab coats and hats, seated themselves at the large center table, drank their cups of tea and cocoa and talked . . . endlessly, passionately, poetically and with impressive rage. No subject was beyond them."

Paule Marshall

"Best friend, my well-spring in the wilderness!"

George Eliot

16.1   Fitch, Janet. **Kicks.** Clarion Books, 1995. 251 pp. ISBN 0-395-69624-0. Fiction.

For fifteen-year-olds Laurie Greenspan and Carla Moore, this was going to be the perfect summer—beach, boys, and hanging out. Laurie is determined to learn to be more like Carla, who is wild, carefree, boy-crazed, and in charge. Although uncomfortable with the hitchhiking and shoplifting they do, Laurie still thinks that acting like Carla will make her happy. It isn't until she has to rescue her friend from a bikers' party that Laurie starts to realize it might be better just to be herself.

16.2   Gaines, Ernest J. **A Lesson before Dying.** Vintage Contemporaries / Vintage Books / Random House, 1994. 256 pp. ISBN 0-679-74166-6. Fiction.

Characterized to the jury as a "hog" by his own defense attorney, Jefferson is sentenced to be executed for a murder he didn't commit. His grandmother recruits the local black teacher, Grant Wiggins, who narrates the story, to instill some pride in Jefferson before he dies. Set in a small Louisiana Cajun community in the late 1940s, the novel explores issues of race, relationships, and heroism. MC

National Book Critics Circle Award for Fiction for original publication, 1993

16.3   Garland, Sherry. **Letters from the Mountain.** Harcourt Brace, 1996. 211 pp. ISBN 0-15-200661-3. Fiction.

The Northside Lynch Mob has sworn Taylor to secrecy after one of their stunts causes DeWayne Lockhart to slip into a coma. But guilt is tearing at Taylor, and when his Aunt Etta, to whom his mother has sent him to get him away from the gang, tells him he must write a letter every day, he begins to work out his feelings through his writing. He's helped in his movement toward maturity through lessons he soon begins to learn from the son of a dirt-poor post cutter who, nevertheless, seems richer than Taylor in many ways. ER

16.4 Goldman, E. M. **The Night Room.** Viking, 1995. 216 pp. ISBN 0-670-85838-2. Fiction.

Sometimes dreams come true, but sometimes so do nightmares. Ira thinks it a stroke of good luck to be chosen to participate in the Argus computer project, especially since one of the other six participants is Sandra Wilcox, the girl of his dreams. Ira and his friends will have the opportunity to peek eleven years into their future, to their tenth high school reunion, through a computer-generated simulation. Eager to learn what the future holds for them, Ira and his friends enter the "night room." Eagerness turns to fear as they learn that one of them will not make it to the reunion. Who will be missing from the reunion, and why? Can anyone change the dire prediction? ER

ALA Quick Picks for Young Adults, 1996

16.5 Grove, Vicki. **The Crystal Garden.** G. P. Putnam's Sons, 1995. 224 pp. ISBN 0-399-21813-0. Fiction.

Eliza and her mother are trying to make a new start in Gouge Eye, Missouri. Eliza's mother has a new boyfriend who is trying to find success in nearby Branson as a country music singer. Eliza desperately wants to make friends at her new school, but the only person who befriends her is Deirdre, a smart girl who just happens to live in a trailer home. Their friendship is tested when Eliza must make a difficult choice—to try to be with the "in crowd" or to keep a true friend.

16.6 Haseley, Dennis. **Getting Him.** Farrar, Straus and Giroux, 1994. 154 pp. ISBN 0-374-32536-7. Fiction.

Donald hates his neighbor Harold, who has caused Donald's dog to be severely injured. Along with some local boys, Donald plots to get revenge on Harold and decides that to do so he must pretend to become Harold's friend so that he can learn the boy's weak spot. During his quest, Donald learns much about being friendly to a very withdrawn, peculiar boy. The more he learns about Harold, the more blurry the line between revenge and friendship becomes for Donald, and he must ultimately decide who his real friends are.

16.7 Hiçyilmaz, Gaye. **The Frozen Waterfall.** Farrar, Straus and Giroux, 1993. 325 pp. ISBN 0-374-32482-4. Fiction.

Twelve-year-old Selda and her mother and two sisters immigrate from Turkey to Switzerland to join her father and two brothers, who have been living there for years and working at well-paying jobs not found in their homeland. At first Selda feels strange and unwanted both by members of her own family and by the other children at school, who are uncertain about the foreigner in their class. In time she learns how to deal with cultural differences and overcomes misunderstandings. ER MC

16.8   Lee, Marie G. **Saying Goodbye.** Houghton Mifflin, 1994. 219 pp. ISBN 0-395-67066-7. Fiction.

So, what's college all about? Ellen, who was a senior in *Finding My Voice,* is now a freshman at Harvard. Despite her newfound independence the presence of her sister, also a student, and the desire of her parents that she become a doctor make Ellen's life confusing. She rooms with Leecia, an African American student, meets other Korean students, takes tae kwon do against her sister's wishes, and stands up for herself when she enrolls in a creative writing class instead of a premed class. Ellen wants to be a writer, but she must first learn and accept who she is. As she makes transitions, she encounters many challenges: dealing with romance, learning to get along with new friends (including those from other cultures), adjusting to college, and accepting her Asian roots. MC

16.9   Levoy, Myron. **A Shadow like a Leopard.** HarperTrophy, 1994. 184 pp. ISBN 0-06-440458-7. Fiction.

Except for the companionship of his knife, fourteen-year-old Ramon is alone on the streets of New York City. His mother is in the hospital, his father is in jail, and Ramon is determined to get into the gang. But he also wants to be a writer. Little does he know that after he tries to rob Mr. Glaser, an old man in a wheelchair, his life will never be the same. MC

16.10   Marsden, John. **Letters from the Inside.** Houghton Mifflin, 1994. 147 pp. ISBN 395-68985-6. Fiction.

At first Tracey and Mandy seem like ordinary pen pals as they correspond about their lives, but their relationship becomes increasingly complex as they reveal more of the truth about their lives and about the intensity of the problems they are trying to face. Both are imprisoned, one literally and one in a very difficult family situation. MC WL

ALA Best Books for Young Adults, 1995
ALA Quick Picks for Young Adults, 1995
School Library Journal Best Books for 1994

16.11   Neenan, Colin. **Live a Little.** Harcourt Brace, 1996. 252 pp. ISBN 0-15-201242-7. Fiction.

Hale O'Reilly, from Neenan's earlier *In Your Dreams,* returns with his sarcastic wit and underlying sensitivity in this story of how his relationship with his best friends Zoe and Sonny lead to an explosion of emotions during their senior year of high school.

16.12   Powell, Randy. **The Whistling Toilets.** Farrar, Straus and Giroux, 1996. 243 pp. ISBN 0-374-38381-2. Fiction.

Sure, Ginny is his best friend, but now that she is coming back home after months on the tennis circuit, Stan is not sure how to act. Are his feelings for her changing in a romantic direction? There's not much chance to ponder or discuss anything, because everyone seems very concerned about Ginny's deteriorating game, and Stan is expected to be part of the solution. Can he figure himself out and help someone else at the same time?

16.13 Randle, Kristen D. **The Only Alien on the Planet.** Scholastic Hardcover, 1995. 228 pp. ISBN 0-590-46309-8. Fiction.

He never speaks, he never smiles, he is impenetrable. Torn between intrusiveness and curiosity, Ginny is determined to make contact with "The Alien," as his new classmates call him. However, as she and her friend Caulder get closer to Smitty, "The Alien," his mask becomes more sinister and they are eventually forced to examine its origins as well as the basis for their relationships with Smitty and with each other.

ALA Best Books for Young Adults, 1996
ALA Quick Picks for Young Adults, 1996

16.14 Rosenberg, Liz. **Heart and Soul.** Harcourt Brace, 1996. 213 pp. ISBN 0-15-200942-6. Fiction.

Willie Steinberg, a cellist, has dropped out of a private music and art high school in the middle of her senior year and returned home to Richmond, Virginia. Her father is always away; her mother seems to do nothing but wait for mail. Willie wants to be Beethoven but feels like no one. After a bizarre adventure with strange Malachi Gelb that ends when she helps to reconcile him with his father, Willie begins to view life differently, learning to overcome her frightening prejudice against Jews and her sometimes overwhelming depression. MC

16.15 Shoup, Barbara. **Wish You Were Here.** Hyperion Books for Children, 1994. 282 pp. ISBN 0-7868-0028-3. Fiction.

Jackson can't even admit the betrayal he feels when his best friend Brady runs away. Meanwhile, his mother is marrying a man who is as straight as his father is hip. He'll suddenly have two young sisters, school is pointless, and his friends are jerks. Tumultuous events rip senior year apart. Be prepared for realistic teen dialogue and the issues of drugs, drinking, and sex, as Jax struggles to keep his balance on the shifting sands of his life.

ALA Best Books for Young Adults, 1995

16.16 Soto, Gary. **Summer on Wheels.** Scholastic Hardcover, 1995. 163 pp. ISBN 0-590-48365-X. Fiction.

In this easy-to-read novel, Soto has written about the adventures of Hector and Mando, two young Latino boys who have summer time on their hands. For six days they bike across California, stopping at the homes of relatives along the way. The boys encounter people from all walks of life and find that their friendship grows during the bicycle trip. Spanish words are sprinkled throughout the text, giving the reader a feel for the language. ER MC

16.17 Staples, Suzanne Fisher. **Dangerous Skies.** Frances Foster Books / Farrar, Straus and Giroux, 1996. 232 pp. ISBN 0-374-31694-5. Fiction.

Whenever Buck is not needed on the farm, he can be found in remote areas of the Chesapeake Bay with his best friend Tunes, the difference in their race and gender causing them no trouble whatsoever. Buck's carefree youth and innocent years end abruptly, however, when he is forced to see the reality of the way these issues are of concern in the larger social fabric. A fatal flaw in its delicate weave causes destruction, and Buck is frustratingly powerless to stop the unraveling. MC

16.18 Tolan, Stephanie S. **Welcome to the Ark.** Morrow Junior Books, 1996. 240 pp. ISBN 0-688-13724-5. Fiction.

In an increasingly violent world, four brilliant yet troubled adolescents are brought together at a group home for mentally ill youths. Miranda, Doug, Taryn, and Elijah are unable to survive in a world that views them as freaks. Through the help of some caring therapists, the four children form a strong bond and realize that they have tremendous power if they link their minds together. They begin to want to change the world, but they must deal with the local threat of a meddling psychiatrist.

16.19 Vail, Rachel. **Ever After.** Avon Flare, 1994. 136 pp. ISBN 0-380-72465-0. Fiction.

Molly feels confused about everything and worries about the past, the present, and the future—and her worries may, in fact, be justified. Molly struggles to maintain her friendships as she also tries to figure out how to stay true to herself, a task that's especially difficult since she's never quite sure exactly who she is. She does know, though, that she's eager to not be so "vanilla" anymore, but rather to find a flavor that's truly "Molly."

16.20 Voigt, Cynthia. **Building Blocks.** Scholastic, 1994. 128 pp. ISBN 0-590-47732-3. Fiction.

Twelve-year-old Brann Connell is tired of his parents' fighting, especially the passive role his father takes. After one such fight, Brann curls up and falls asleep among the toy-block fortress his father had built, and when he awakes he finds himself transported to a different time—a time when his father is a boy and Brann is his friend. Although his stay is short, Brann begins to understand the man who is his father.

16.21 Werlin, Nancy. **Are You Alone on Purpose?** Houghton Mifflin, 1994. 204 pp. ISBN 0-395-67350-X. Fiction.

Alison Shandling and Harry Roth have only one thing in common. They hate each other. Fourteen-year-old Alison is smart and perfect, so that her parents can give Adam, her autistic twin brother, all their attention. Harry is obnoxious, athletic, and a bully. When Harry is paralyzed in an accident, Alison takes it upon herself to befriend him out of guilt. Eventually, however, she realizes that they have become true friends. MC

ALA Quick Picks for Young Adults, 1995

16.22 Yumoto, Kazumi. **The Friends.** Translated by Cathy Hirano. Farrar, Straus and Giroux, 1996. 170 pp. ISBN 0-374-32460-3. Fiction.

During the summer before they will take their school entrance exams, Kiyama, Kawabe, and Yamashita puzzle over the meaning of death—and life. The boys attempt to answer the multitude of questions they have about the subject by watching a rather decrepit old man, but they learn more than they bargain for when he begins watching them in turn. ER MC WL

Mildred L. Batchelder Award, 1997

Titles Annotated in Other Chapters Related to Friendships

Bellairs, John, and Brad Strickland. *The Drum, the Doll, and the Zombie*. Mysteries.

Bennett, Cherie. *Sunset Fire*. Romance.

Bennett, Jill. *Baa Baa Dead Sheep*. Mysteries.

Brooks, Bruce. *What Hearts*. Family.

Bunting, Eve. *Spying on Miss Muller*. School.

Butler, Octavia. *Parable of the Sower*. Adventure.

Carver, Jeffrey A. *Star Rigger's Way*. Science Fiction.

Davidson, Nicole. *Farewell Kiss*. Mysteries.

Deem, James. *3 nbs of Julian Drew*. Family.

Galloway, Les. *The Forty Fathom Bank*. Adventure.

Gelb, Alan. *My Best Friend Died*. Death.

Hesse, Karen. *Phoenix Rising*. Death.

Hewett, Lorri. *Soulfire*. Choices.

Hinojosa, Maria. *Crews*. Diaries.

Hobbs, Will. *Far North*. Adventure.

Hunter, Mollie. *The Walking Stones*. Fantasy.

Hurwin, Davida. *A Time for Dancing*. Death.

Johnson, Scott. *Overnight Sensation*. Choices.

Killingsworth, Monte. *Circle within a Circle*. Science.

Klass, Sheila Solomon. *The Next Stop: Nowhere*. Family.

Lawrence, Louise. *The Patchwork People*. Science Fiction.

Miller, G. Wayne. *Coming of Age*. School.

Miner, Jane Claypool. *Winter Love, Winter Wish*. Romance.

Monson, A. M. *The Deer Stand*. Animals.

Phillips, Ann. *A Haunted Year*. Horror.

Plummer, Louise. *The Unlikely Romance of Kate Bjorkman*. Romance.

Powell, Randy. *Is Kissing a Girl Who Smokes like Kissing an Ashtray?* Dating.

Rapp, Adam. *Missing the Piano*. School.

Ruby, Lois. *Skin Deep*. Choices.

Say, Allen. *The Ink-Keeper's Apprentice*. Arts.

Sleator, William. *Dangerous Wishes*. Adventure.

Voigt, Cynthia. *Izzy, Willy-Nilly*. Choices.

White, Richard. *Jordan Freeman Was My Friend*. War.

Woodson, Jacqueline. *I Hadn't Meant to Tell You This*. Family.

Wright, Bob. *Fast Break*. Sports.

Wurmfeld, Hope. *Baby Blues*. Choices.

17 Historical Fiction

"History fades to fable; fact becomes clouded with doubt and controversy; the inscription moulders from the tablet; the statue falls from the pedestal. Columns, arches, pyramids, what are they but heaps of sand; and their epitaphs but characters written in the dust?"

Washington Irving

17.1 Alder, Elizabeth. **The King's Shadow.** Farrar, Straus and Giroux, 1995. 259 pp. ISBN 0-374-34182-6. Fiction.

Evyn, a young Welsh serf, is brutally attacked by local bullies who leave him orphaned and mute at a feast in 1063. Although he is sold into slavery, his mistress is not harsh, and he is even taught to read and write, a skill primarily known only by monks. Evyn proves his worth, and ultimately stands beside King Harold, the brave Saxon, at the Battle of Hastings, fighting the Norman invaders led by William the Conqueror.

School Library Journal Best Books, 1995
International Reading Association Children's Books Award, 1996

17.2 Alvarez, Julia. **In the Time of the Butterflies.** Algonquin Books of Chapel Hill, 1994. 321 pp. ISBN 1-56512-038-8. Fiction.

The Caribbean nation of the Dominican Republic suffered the cruel dictatorship of General Rafael Trujillo for over thirty years of this century. It is rare for women to join a guerrilla revolt, but the four Mirabel sisters are not ordinary women. They take turns telling the story of their struggles—with parents, against government, within their own families, for freedom. It is not necessary to be female, Latina, or a revolutionary to become immersed in the lives of Las Mariposas, the Butterflies, who are based on actual people. MC WL

ALA Notable Books for Children, 1995
ALA Best Books for Young Adults, 1995

17.3 Anderson, Rachel. **Black Water.** Henry Holt, 1995. 168 pp. ISBN 0-8050-3847-7. Fiction.

Worse than the fact that there was no treatment for epilepsy in the nineteenth century, this misunderstood disease was considered a disgrace. The victim was seen as possessed or mad and unsuited for society. Somehow, Albert Edward manages to love his impoverished mother despite her desperate and deluded appeals to charlatans who claim to be able to cure him. More astonishing, with no formal education and after years of seclusion he becomes self-reliant. This story is based on the life of an actual Victorian epileptic.

School Library Journal Best Books, 1995

17.4   Binstock, R. C. **Tree of Heaven.** Soho, 1995. 212 pp. ISBN 1-56947-038-3. Fiction.

During the Japanese invasion of China in the 1930s, an unlikely story of love emerges. Orphaned, probably widowed, filthy, and starving, a plain Chinese girl is found hiding in a barnyard. Captain Kuroda, for reasons unknown even to him, rescues Li from torture and rape by his Japanese troops. Li becomes his servant and ultimately his lover in this drama of the peculiar machinations of the human mind and heart. MC

School Library Journal Best Adult Books for Young Adults, 1995

17.5   Bunting, Eve. **SOS Titanic.** Harcourt Brace, 1996. 246 pp. ISBN 0-15-200271-5. Fiction.

The story of the *Titanic,* the "unsinkable," doomed ship that hit an iceberg and sank in the frigid North Atlantic in 1912, killing as many as 1,500 people, is well known. In this book, therefore, the only question is who of the many characters will survive. Will fifteen-year-old Barry, the protagonist, be declared a child or a man—a declaration that means life or death? Will the wicked Flynns, bullies from his Irish village, make it? What about their pretty sister Pegeen? Or Mr. Scollins, the somewhat stodgy paid traveling companion for Barry, or the likable Watley, steward for the first-class passengers? The suspense is almost as chilling as the night air over the vast, dark waters of the Atlantic.

17.6   Burks, Brian. **Runs with Horses.** Harcourt Brace, 1995. 118 pp. ISBN 0-15-200264-2. Fiction.

Runs with Horses is sixteen years old and a member of a small group of Apaches. He is excited about the challenges of his training for manhood, but the year is 1886. Even though Runs with Horses and his friend Little Face go on a dangerous raid with the great warrior Geronimo, their chances to become men are cut short by whites to the north, who "numbered more than the stars." This story conveys the violence of the lives of the last free band of the Chiricahua Apaches and the broken promises of the "White Eyes" who took the Apaches' land in Arizona and moved them to a reservation in Florida. ER MC

17.7   Charbonneau, Eileen. **In the Time of the Wolves.** Tor / Tom Doherty Associates, 1994. 180 pp. ISBN 0-812-53361-5. Fiction.

Fourteen-year-old Joshua Woods yearns to continue his education at prestigious Harvard, but his father's opposition to such an idea is strong and not even his mother's support and influence help his cause. Joshua's dilemma is quickly forgotten by everyone but him in this spring of 1824, when his father's strange prediction of a "year without summer" eerily comes true. Embarrassed by his father's ancestral beliefs and customs, Joshua runs away from his family into the arms of his father's enemies where, at last, he learns the lessons of loyalty. MC

17.8 Charbonneau, Eileen. **Honor to the Hills.** Tor / Tom Doherty Associates, 1996. 192 pp. ISBN 0-312-86094-3. Fiction.

The saga of the Woods family continues beyond *The Ghosts of Stony Cove* as fifteen-year-old Lily Woods becomes involved in her family's secret mission to help slaves travel north on the Underground Railroad. The Woodses fight prejudice against African Americans, Native Americans, and Irish Americans in their beloved Catskill Mountains of New York. MC

17.9 Coombs, Karen M. **Sarah on Her Own.** Avon Flare, 1996. 212 pp. ISBN 0-380-78275-8. Fiction.

Fourteen-year-old Sarah Douglas arrives in the new colony of Virginia alone after a tortuous sea journey that claims the life of her only relative. Determined to return to England, she faces many setbacks as she tries to earn her fare. Along the way, she finds strength, courage, admiration for this new desolate land, and even love.

17.10 Cushman, Karen. **Catherine, Called Birdy.** Clarion Books, 1994. 169 pp. ISBN 0-395-68186-3. Fiction.

Karen Cushman presents a strong female character against the background of medieval England. Catherine, having been born into the family of a knight, must deal with the fact that she has less control over her destiny than the peasants working her father's land. She has no say in whom she marries, must learn to be a "lady," and is cautioned against pursuing any kind of intellectual life. During Catherine's fight against convention in this wonderfully rich book the reader is drawn across a landscape of country fairs, feasting in the great hall, cold, snowy days, warm summer days when the sheep are shorn, and a host of smells, tastes, and textures that one would encounter only in the year 1290.

Newbery Honor Book, 1995
ALA Best Books for Young Adults, 1995
ALA Notable Books for Children, 1995
Booklist Editors' Choice, 1995
School Library Journal Best Books, 1994
ALA Quick Picks for Young Adults, 1995
IRA Teacher's Choice, 1995

17.11 Cushman, Karen. **The Midwife's Apprentice.** Clarion Books, 1995. 122 pp. ISBN 0-395-69929-6. Fiction.

For a short novel, this story is rich with detail from the fourteenth century and draws a very complex main character. Alyce is a young orphan of twelve or thirteen who, at first blush, is simply taken advantage of by an older woman who is a midwife. As the midwife goes about her business, Alyce learns her trade almost by default. It is only by the end of the novel that we come to understand the reasoning behind this woman's harsh treatment of her apprentice. This revelation is only one of a series of surprises the novel holds for the reader. The plot is never predictable and the story holds an equal share of fascinating cultural history and descriptions of a young girl coming of age.

Newbery Medal, 1996
ALA Notable Books for Children, 1996
Booklist Editors' Choice, 1996
School Library Journal Best Books, 1996

17.12   D'Aguiar, Fred. **The Longest Memory: A Novel.** Pantheon Books, 1994. 138 pp. ISBN 0-679-43962-5. Fiction.

This is a powerful first-person narrative about the degradation of slavery. The narrator is an older man, nearing the end of his life, who recounts the shameful stories that haunt him, including how he witnessed his son being beaten to death. MC

17.13   Dalkey, Kara. **Little Sister.** Jane Yolen Books / Harcourt Brace, 1996. 208 pp. ISBN 0-15-201392-X. Fiction.

Mitsuko, "Little Sister," is only thirteen when, in twelfth-century Japan, her village is attacked by outlaws and her family is carried away for the warlord. Finding herself alone, she also finds the courage to travel to the netherworld of Japanese mythology in order to seek the aid of mysterious creatures there who, she hopes, will help her restore her family's honor. MC

17.14   de Trevino, Elizabeth Borton. **Leona: A Love Story.** Farrar, Straus and Giroux, 1994. 149 pp. ISBN 0-374-37089-3. Fiction.

Will Leona be forced to marry her guardian's choice, a man old enough to be her father, or will she find a way to marry her true love, a young revolutionary in Mexico's struggle for independence? Based on the true life of Mexico's Heroine of the Independence, this novel by a Newbery Medal–winning author tells the story of a strong-willed young woman who overcomes many obstacles to her own happiness and her country's freedom from Spain. MC WL

17.15   DeFord, Deborah H., and Harry S. Stout. **An Enemy among Them.** Houghton Mifflin Company, 1987. 200 pp. ISBN 0-395-70108-2. Paperback edition. Fiction.

Margaret Volpert's German American family supports the Revolution in December, 1776, but when a Hessian prisoner of war comes to live in their home, Margaret and all the Volperts must carefully examine their loyalties. Eventually, Margaret learns to judge people by their actions, not by superficial labels, in this historically based, romantic spy adventure. MC

17.16   Doherty, Berlie. **Street Child.** Orchard Books, 1994. 154 pp. ISBN 0-531-06864-1. Fiction.

"Jim Jarvis. Want to know who that is? It's me! Only thing I've got is my name. . . . " After losing his home, family, and friends, Jim may feel he has only his name, but his spirit, courage, and humanity allow him to survive as an orphan in the streets of London in the 1860s, streets whose harshness we are familiar with from the works of Charles Dickens. Based on a true story, this tale tells how Jim finally meets a caring man who establishes Britain's first schools and homes for needy street children. ER

17.17 Ducey, Jean Sparks. **The Bittersweet Time.** William B. Eerdmans, 1995. 109 pp. ISBN 0-8028-5096-0. Fiction.

As the Depression begins to take hold in the autumn of 1929 and families struggle to make ends meet, Jane finds her life being turned topsy-turvy. Her father loses his job, and now she and her sister will have to wear their too-short coats and their old stockings. How embarrassing! Jane, dreaming of becoming a writer someday, keeps track of her and her family's hardships through a daily journal. Will things ever get better for the Hartley family? ER

17.18 Garden, Nancy. **Dove and Sword: A Novel of Joan of Arc.** Farrar, Straus and Giroux, 1995. 236 pp. ISBN 0-374-34476-0. Fiction.

Gabrielle reminisces about her days with her childhood friend, Joan of Arc, as the Maid takes up arms in an effort to have the rightful heir to the French throne crowned king. From their shared days as girls in the village of Domremy to Joan's burning at the stake for heresy, Gabrielle puts herself at risk to watch over her friend. MC

17.19 Hansen, Joyce. **The Captive.** Scholastic Hardcover, 1994. 195 pp. ISBN 0-590-41625-1. Fiction.

Kofi delights in the beautiful carved flute given to him by his father, a great Ashanti chief. He is celebrating his twelfth year as his family journeys to an important clan meeting in their West African kingdom. Yet days later, Kofi finds himself aboard a "water house" (slave ship), betrayed and sold by the family slave Oppong. Kofi travels from sunny West Africa to Puritan New England, leaving behind everything except his flute. How will Kofi find the strength and the means to rebuild his life? MC

Notable 1994 Children's Trade Books in the Field of Social Studies

17.20 Holland, Isabelle. **Behind the Lines.** Scholastic Hardcover, 1994. 194 pp. ISBN 0-590-45113-8. Fiction.

Katie O'Farrell's job, essential for the support of her newly immigrated Irish family, is repeatedly jeopardized by her determined attitude against the prejudice she finds in her new home, the New York City of the 1860s. She fights against her brother, who is determined to let the rich Lacey family pay for him to go to war in place of their son, who is about to be drafted. But Katie must also come to terms with the prejudices she holds against African Americans, the English, and Protestants.

17.21   Irwin, Hadley. **Jim-Dandy.** Margaret K. McElderry Books / Macmillan, 1994. 133 pp. ISBN 0-689-50594-9. Fiction.

Caleb and his beloved horse, Jim-Dandy, find themselves in the middle of the Indian Wars with George Custer after Caleb leaves his strict stepfather's house on the Kansas plains. But the cavalry's dedication to the killing of the Cheyennes does not fit with Caleb's earlier experiences with the Indians. Choosing between staying with the military or returning to his harsh home may mean making a decision between his conscience and his love for the horse he has raised and trained since birth. ER MC

17.22   Karr, Kathleen. **In the Kaiser's Clutch.** Farrar, Straus and Giroux, 1995. 182 pp. ISBN 0-374-33638-5. Fiction.

Fitz and Nelly Dalton are starring in a series of silent movies and helping the war effort against the Germans in World War I. With their recently widowed mother, they have more than their reduced circumstances to worry about, however, because someone seems determined to hurt them. Maybe the culprit is involved in their father's mysterious death. Diabolical schemes, evil characters, and even descriptions of early chemical warfare abound in this dramatic novel. ER

17.23   Lasky, Kathryn. **Beyond the Burning Time.** The Blue Sky Press, 1994. 275 pp. ISBN 0-590-47331-X. Fiction.

Mary Chase's fear is increasing daily. Several friends of the twelve-year-old are exhibiting increasingly odd behavior, and Mary worries that they are the victims of spells cast by witches. Can it really be possible that some of the town's most respected citizens are involved in witchcraft and are hurting the young people of Salem Village? Mary and her widowed mother, struggling to run the family farm, are drawn into the events of one of the most shocking chapters of American history. Based on extensive research, Mary's story reminds us of our obligation to make moral choices and to understand the past so that "we may all join in and say 'never again.'"

ALA Best Books for Young Adults, 1995

17.24   Lasky, Kathryn. **Beyond the Divide.** Aladdin Paperbacks, 1995. 297 pp. ISBN 0-689-80163-7. Fiction.

Fourteen-year-old Meribah Simon journeys with her father from her Amish home in Pennsylvania into the American West in 1849. A rich panorama of the time is skillfully woven with the clash of cultures this reflective and self-reliant girl experiences. Included in the "Afterword" and "Author's Note" are research sources and reflections on Lasky's inspiration for this novel. MC

17.25 Lasky, Kathryn. **True North: A Novel of the Underground Railroad.** The Blue Sky Press, 1996. 267 pp. ISBN 0-590-20523-4. Fiction.

Afrika is following the North Star, fleeing from a cruel life as a slave. She is being helped by the Underground Railroad, a movement that soon recruits fourteen-year-old Lucy Bradford of Boston into its service. Well-researched and historically accurate, Lasky's story describes the intersection of the lives of these two young women when Lucy helps Afrika in her quest for true north. MC

17.26 Llorente, Pilar Molina. **The Apprentice.** Illustrated by Juan Ramón Alonso. Translated by Robin Longshaw. Farrar, Straus and Giroux, 1993. 101 pp. ISBN 0-374-30389-4. Fiction.

Thirteen-year-old Arduino's dream of becoming an apprentice painter seems to be coming true as he leaves his family's tailoring business to join the workshop of Maestro Cosimo di Forli in Florence. His difficult life as an apprentice during the Renaissance is complicated when he discovers the existence of the maestro's former apprentice secretly shackled in the attic and is framed by a co-worker. Friendship and truth are finally rewarded, and both Arduino and his new maestro, Danato, begin a bright future. WL

Mildred L. Batchelder Award, 1994

17.27 Llywelyn, Morgan. **Brian Boru: Emperor of the Irish.** Tor / Tom Doherty Associates, 1995. 156 pp. ISBN 0-312-85623-7. Fiction.

In the late 900s, Ireland is plagued by Viking invaders, the clashing cultures of paganism and early Christianity, and warring tribes within. Ten-year-old Brian Boru is the youngest son of a king from one of the lesser tribes, but by using his brawn, shrewd political sense, and compassion, he rises to become the one man who can unite all the forces to become Emperor of the Irish. ER MC

17.28 Llywelyn, Morgan. **Strongbow: The Story of Richard and Aoife.** Tor / Tom Doherty Associates, 1996. 156 pp. ISBN 0-312-86150-8. Fiction.

Changing the history of Ireland forever, Richard de Clare and Aoife capture a kingdom during the twelfth century. The historically unlikely match between the Norman knight and his fiery Irish princess wife parallels the turbulence of their time. Headstrong and independent, the two share a love as fierce as the battles they fight.

17.29 Matas, Carol. **The Burning Time.** Delacorte, 1994. 113 pp. ISBN 0-385-32097-3. Fiction.

Rose's mother Suzanne is a gifted healer in sixteenth-century France. After Rose's father dies, his brothers are outraged that he left his farm to his wife rather than follow tradition, which would have made the farm theirs. Out of greed, they accuse Suzanne of witchcraft, precipitating a lethal witch-hunt involving even Rose herself. Heroically, Rose struggles to save her mother. MC

ALA Quick Picks for Young Adults, 1995
IRA Young Adult Choices for 1996

17.30   McCaffrey, Anne. **Black Horses for the King.** Harcourt Brace, 1996. 220 pp. ISBN 1-15-227322-0. Fiction.

Galwyn Varianus knows languages and horses. He is just the kind of young man Lord Artos, later known as King Arthur, needs as he prepares to ward off the invading Saxons. Historically accurate details, such as a description of the first use of horseshoes, are interwoven into a story that includes intrigue, revenge, and compassion.

17.31   Merino, José María. **Beyond the Ancient Cities.** Translated by Helen Lane. Farrar, Straus and Giroux, 1994. 209 pp. ISBN 0-374-34307-1. Fiction.

Half-Spanish and half–Native American, Miguel learns firsthand of the ruination of the once-magnificent culture of the Native Americans by the Spanish as he and his godfather leave their homes in sixteenth-century Mexico and travel to Panama. Over land and sea, they have many adventures with exploiting explorers, other native groups, and even a pirate. MC WL

17.32   Paterson, Katherine. **Lyddie.** Puffin Books, 1995. 183 pp. ISBN 0-14-037389-6. Fiction.

Lyddie Worthen is on her own, and so when she hears about the mill jobs available in Lowell, Massachusetts, she heads there with the idea of earning enough money to reunite her family. Paterson tells the remarkable story of a strong, determined young woman, uneducated but spirited, who eventually has to choose whether to fight for better working conditions in the factories, or to stay quiet and continue to pursue her dream during America's rapid move into industrialism.

17.33   Paterson, Katherine. **Rebels of the Heavenly Kingdom.** Puffin, 1995. 229 pp. ISBN 0-14-037610-0. Fiction.

Wang Lee is only fifteen when he is kidnaped by bandits while gathering the last of his family's harvest. He is set free by beautiful Mei Lin, a soldier in the army fighting for the Heavenly Kingdom of the Great Peace. Wang Lee joins this army, but as he and Mei Lin realize the depth of their affection for each other, they both begin to wonder whether war can lead to peace, and whether they can give allegiance to a cause that asks them to deny their love. MC

17.34   Paulsen, Gary. **The Rifle.** Harcourt Brace, 1995. 105 pp. ISBN 0-15-292880-4. Fiction.

The life history of one rifle, paralleling the history of the United States, is traced by Paulsen from its creation in Philadelphia when Pennsylvania was still a colony through its service in the American Revolution.

The rifle disappears for years until it is rediscovered in 1993, found hidden in an attic. It changes hands until it reaches a fateful conclusion: by chance igniting from sparks in a fireplace, the rifle fires and kills with deadly aim and accuracy. The author gives the rifle a personality and successfully interweaves its tale with the lives of the persons who interact with it, providing minibiographies of the different persons who love guns, especially the one at the heart of this unusual novel.

Notable 1995 Children's Trade Books in the Field of Social Studies

17.35   Rinaldi, Ann. **The Blue Door.** Scholastic, 1996. 273 pp. ISBN 0-590-46051-X. Fiction.

In *The Blue Door*, the final installment of Rinaldi's Quilt Trilogy, Amanda, fourteen, is sent north from South Carolina to her mother's family. But she is a witness to a crime soon after her arrival, and, to survive, goes into hiding, disguising herself and going to work in her great-grandfather's textile mill. As she experiences the terrible working conditions in the mill, she has to decide how to confront the oldest member of her family, and how to complete the family quilt that he tore apart so long ago.

17.36   Rinaldi, Ann. **Broken Days.** Scholastic Hardcover, 1995. 270 pp. ISBN 0-590-46053-6. Fiction.

In this second book of Rinaldi's Quilt Trilogy, set against the backdrop of the War of 1812 and the Indian Wars, a second generation of the Chelmsford family deals with the secrets and psychological burdens of the previous generation. Jealousy causes young Ebie Chelmsford to attack her half-Indian cousin, who shocks staid Salem and her more proper family. Ironically, Walking Breeze teaches Ebie about honesty and courage as Ebie strives to face her "broken days"—the time set to finish a task. MC

17.37   Rinaldi, Ann. **Finishing Becca.** Gulliver Books / Harcourt Brace, 1994. 356 pp. ISBN 0-15-200879-9. Fiction.

Based on the true story of Peggy Shippen, a rich and spoiled Philadelphia girl who married Benedict Arnold, this is the fictional story of Becca, who is sent to the Shippens' to be Peggy's personal maid. Becca comes face to face with the conflicts of war—the harsh conditions her brother, a soldier with Washington, faces daily in contrast to the pampered existence led by those loyal to the Crown. In her quest to "finish Becca," she must choose sides.

17.38   Rinaldi, Ann. **Hang a Thousand Trees with Ribbons: The Story of Phillis Wheatley.** Gulliver Books / Harcourt Brace, 1996. 338 pp. ISBN 0-15-200877-2. Fiction.

Phillis Wheatley began life named Keziah but was snatched from her home in Senegal and sold into slavery in Boston in 1761. As something of an experiment, the son of the household instructed the waif, and she became America's first published black poet. The inclusion of many well-known historical figures helps establish the novel's pre–Revolutionary War setting and allows a comparison of the colonists' frustrations with those of the slaves. Despite its somewhat hurried ending, this is a satisfying tale. MC

17.39   Rinaldi, Ann. **Keep Smiling Through.** Harcourt Brace, 1996. 188 pp. ISBN 0-15-200768-7. Fiction.

Kay's life has been shaped by war—World War II has taken its toll on her childhood with its demands of rationing and sacrifice. There is also a war at home, where her selfish stepmother takes out her anger on the five Hennings children. Young Kay, who has always strived to do right, begins to learn "that you can be good and do the right thing and sometimes it goes bad for you anyway."

17.40   Rinaldi, Ann. **The Secret of Sarah Revere.** Gulliver Books / Harcourt Brace, 1995. 310 pp. ISBN 0-15-200393-2. Fiction.

The famous Revere family is full of secrets, and thirteen-year-old Sarah wants to be in on most of them. In fact, Sarah brings Rebecca, Paul's second wife and Sarah's new stepmother, in on some of his secrets. Yet Rebecca has secrets of her own, and so Sarah becomes concerned with questions such as "What matters—the truth or what people think?" As the new nation struggles to come into being, Sarah struggles with growing up and finding her own way.

17.41   Rinaldi, Ann. **A Stitch in Time.** Scholastic, 1994. 292 pp. ISBN 0-590-46055-2. Fiction.

The Revolutionary War is over, and, like the country as a whole, the Chelmsford family of Salem, Massachusetts, is experiencing both the excitement and the pain of growth, in this first volume of Rinaldi's Quilt Trilogy, which depicts the lives of three generations of a New England family. Led by the eldest sister, Hannah, the family learns some painful secrets about the past, fights against prejudice, and makes strides toward a bright future. At the center of the story is a quilt being worked on by Hannah and her two sisters, each of whom has chosen a very different life for herself.

17.42   Ruby, Lois. **Steal away Home.** Macmillan, 1994. 192 pp. ISBN 0-02-777883-5. Fiction.

What secrets an old house can hide—like 135-year-old skeletons! That's what Dana Shannon finds in the secret room of her house. In chapters that alternate between 1994 and 1856, the mystery behind the skeleton is solved, and Dana learns about life in the Kansas Territory as the struggle between proslavery and free-state forces grows in the years before the Civil War. Her co-protagonist, James Weaver, a nineteenth-century Quaker, comes to terms with his faith and his family's choice to challenge slavery by using their home as a station on the Underground Railroad. ER MC

Notable 1994 Children's Trade Book in the Field of Social Studies
IRA Teachers Choice, 1996

17.43   Stolz, Mary. **Cezanne Pinto: A Memoir.** Alfred A. Knopf, 1994. 279 pp. ISBN 0-679-84917-3. Fiction.

The slave who made up his own name and guessed his age to be twelve when he ran away is an old man now. He can remember "the quarters," his mother's being sold, the woman who taught him to read and guided him to freedom, the Canadian family by whom he was cherished, and the Texas cattle drives he was a part of. But he is still waiting, without bitterness, for true equality. Moving but not maudlin, this is a great story for readers of any ethnic group or age. MC

ALA Best Books for Young Adults, 1995

17.44   Sutcliff, Rosemary. **The Lantern Bearers.** Sunburst / Farrar, Straus and Giroux, 1994. 280 pp. ISBN 0-374-44302-5. Fiction.

As their empire declines, the Romans leave Britain. Aquila, however, decides to stay and protect his land from barbaric invaders. Over the years he will lose his family, become a slave to the Jutes, and rise among the ranks to help Britain unite under one king. Listening to the tales of the hero Odysseus, Aquila ponders his own loyalty and integrity and becomes more self-aware as a result.

Awards won by original publication:
Carnegie Medal
ALA Notable Books for Children

17.45   Sutcliff, Rosemary. **Outcast.** Illustrated by Richard Kennedy. Sunburst / Farrar, Straus and Giroux, 1995. 229 pp. ISBN 0-374-45673-9. Fiction.

Beric "was not born to be drowned," his stepfather declares after pulling the infant boy from stormy waters off the coast of England. Twice he dodges potential death at sea. In addition, he survives cruel slavery among the Romans and life as a rower in the galley of a Roman ship, and his strong personality allows him to survive with pride and integrity. The reader gets a glimpse at the empire of ancient Rome.

17.46   Sutcliff, Rosemary. **Warrior Scarlet.** Illustrated by Charles Keeping. Sunburst / Farrar, Straus and Giroux, 1994. 207 pp. ISBN 0-374-48244-6. Fiction.

Bronze Age boys become men during their three years in the Boy's House, where they learn the skills and discipline necessary to become hunters for their families and warriors for their tribe, gaining the right to wear the warrior's scarlet. Drem must meet the challenges all boys face, but he must meet these challenges in spite of his withered arm and others' doubts about his capabilities.

Awards won by original publication:
ALA Notable Book
Carnegie Medal Honor Book

17.47   Taylor, Theodore. **The Bomb.** Harcourt Brace, 1995. 195 pp. ISBN 0-15-200867-5. Fiction.

During World War II, Sorry, his family, and the other inhabitants of the small Western Pacific island of Bikini survive an invasion by the Japanese and in 1946 welcome the arrival of the U.S. Navy and the security it offers. Although most of the islanders trust the U.S. government's offer to relocate them to another atoll, so testing of the newly developed atom bomb can begin, Sorry and a few others suspect that their beautiful island is about to be ruined forever. Now fourteen-year-old Sorry must calculate the risk in standing up for his principles. *The Bomb*'s award-winning author based this fictional account on actual events he witnessed as a young naval officer. MC

ALA Best Books for Young Adults, 1996
Notable 1995 Children's Trade Books in the Field of Social Studies
Scott O'Dell Award for Historical Fiction, 1996

17.48   Temple, Frances. **The Ramsay Scallop.** Orchard Books, 1994. 310 pp. ISBN 0-531-06836-6. Fiction.

Elenor, at fourteen, feels unready to be married, but her betrothed, Thomas, is among the boys returning from the Crusades after eight years of what she imagines to be the kind of great adventures she'll never get to experience. The wise parish priest sends them on a pilgrimage to Spain, ostensibly to seek forgiveness for the sins of all the village. His ulterior motives are to heal the breach in Thomas's faith from the unholy wars and to give the youngsters time together. MC WL

ALA Best Books for Young Adults, 1995
Booklist Editors' Choice, 1995

17.49   Turner, Glennette Tilley. **Running for Our Lives.** Illustrated by Samuel Byrd. Holiday House, 1994. 193 pp. ISBN 0-8234-1121-4. Fiction.

After experiencing years of slavery and oppression in Missouri, Luther, his parents, his sister, and baby Dilly bravely escape and then reunite. Then, as "passengers" on the Underground Railroad, they must part, continuing by separate routes. Once in Canada, having reached their dream of freedom, they never give up their quest to be united as a family again. MC

17.50   Vick, Helen Hughes. **Walker's Journey Home.** Harbinger House, 1995. 182 pp. ISBN 1-57140-000-1. Fiction.

In this sequel to *Walker of Time,* fifteen-year-old Walker, a Native American who has traveled back to the 1200s, is leading his tribe through a dangerous journey over the difficult terrain of the Southwest. Nature and man conspire against them as the tribe searches for a new home on the Hopi Mesa, meeting mystery and romance along the way. MC

17.51   Walsh, Jill Paton. **Grace.** Sunburst Book / Farrar, Straus and Giroux, 1994. 256 pp. ISBN 0-374-42792-5. Fiction.

Young Grace and her father brave heavy seas to save a group of shipwrecked survivors whom Grace has spotted from her watch at their nearby lighthouse. This heroic act forever changes the solitary life that Grace and her family once lived. Newspapers spread her fame, and while artists, philanthropic societies, and sightseers idealize Grace, local villagers spread rumors that the deed was done for monetary gain. Grace struggles to keep her identity in this compelling and sensitively written story of a nineteenth-century heroine.

School Library Journal Best Book of the Year, 1991

17.52   Walter, Mildred Pitts. **Second Daughter: The Story of a Slave Girl.** Scholastic, 1996. 214 pp. ISBN 0-590-48282-3. Fiction.

America's Revolutionary War won the freedom of the colonists from the English crown, but African slaves did not win the same right even though they fought in the war. Through the eyes of outspoken Aissa, we follow the lives of a community of young slaves in New England as they begin to use the newly written Constitution and laws to win their freedom in Massachusetts, in a story inspired by an actual 1781 court case. MC

17.53   Yep, Laurence. **Hiroshima.** Scholastic, 1995. 52 pp. ISBN 0-590-20832-2. Fiction.

Twelve-year-old Sachi and her older sister are on their way to school and work in war-torn Hiroshima, Japan, on the morning of August 6, 1945; it looks as though it might be a nice day. Little do they, nor does the rest of the world, know that this is the day the history of the world will change with the dropping of the atom bomb. Based on the accounts of actual survivors, this novella paints a picture of the bombing of Hiroshima and the world after nuclear weapons have become a reality. ER MC

Notable 1995 Children's Trade Books in the Field of Social Studies

Titles Annotated in Other Chapters Related to Historical Fiction

Beatty, Patricia. *Jayhawker.* War.
Bosse, Malcolm. *The Examination.* Adventure.

Duong Thu Huong. *Paradise of the Blind*. Choices.
Elrod, P. N. *Death and the Maiden*. Horror.
Garland, Sherry. *Indio*. Adventure.
Levitin, Sonia. *Escape from Egypt*. Religion.
Merino, José María. *The Gold of Dreams*. Adventure.
Moquist, Richard. *The Franklin Mysteries*. Mysteries.
Paterson, Katherine. *Jip: His Story*. Choices.
Pausewang, Gudrun. *The Final Journey*. Holocaust.
Reuter, Bjarne. *The Boys from St. Petri*. War.
Robertson, Elizabeth W. *Weep Not for Me, Dear Mother*. Diaries.
Sauerwein, Leigh. *The Way Home*. Short Stories.
Taylor, Mildred D. *The Well: David's Story*. Family.
Temple, Frances. *Taste of Salt: A Story of Modern Haiti*. Choices.
Terris, Susan. *Nell's Quilt*. Choices.
Voigt, Cynthia. *Jackaroo*. Myths.
Watson, Larry. *Justice*. Family.
Wisler, G. Clifton. *Mr. Lincoln's Drummer*. War.

18 History, Geography, Archeology, and Anthropology

"Historians ought to be precise, faithful, and unprejudiced; and neither interest, nor fear, nor hatred, nor affection should make them swerve from the way of truth."

Miguel de Cervantes

"Read history: so learn your place in time."
Edna St. Vincent Millay

18.1 American War series. Enslow.

Kent, Deborah. **The Vietnam War: "What Are We Fighting For?"** 1994. 127 pp. ISBN 0-89490-527-9. Nonfiction.

Kent, Zachary. **World War I: "The War to End Wars."** 1994. 122 pp. ISBN 0-89490-523-6. Nonfiction.

Stein, R. Conrad. **World War II in Europe: "America Goes to War."** 1994. 127 pp. ISBN 0-89490-525-2. Nonfiction.

The straightforward chronological layout in these books, interspersed with simple maps, quotations, and photographs, adds to their value for students of these eras. Each contains chapter notes, further reading, and an index. The quantitative information and biographical anecdotes combine to present a brief but engrossing overview of America's war history. ER

18.2 Ashabranner, Brent. **A New Frontier: The Peace Corps in Eastern Europe.** Photographs by Paul Conklin. Cobblehill Books/Dutton, 1994. 101 pp. ISBN 0-525-65155-1. Nonfiction.

In straightforward fashion, Ashabranner gives a brief history of the Peace Corps, the idealism which created it, and the pragmatic successes which have sustained it for a generation. Peoples in emerging post–Cold War Europe who are trying to adapt to the technological realities of the capitalist world are depicted. Both the Peace Corps workers and native citizens of Poland, the Czech Republic, Slovakia, Bulgaria, and Romania are portrayed as welcome neighbors in the new world order. ER MC

18.3 Ashby, Ruth, and Deborah Gore Ohrn, editors. **Herstory: Women Who Changed the World.** Introduction by Gloria Steinem. Viking, 1995. 304 pp. ISBN 0-670-85434-4. Nonfiction.

Herstory is an essential reference source for research containing short articles on women divided into three broad categories: from prehistory to 1750, from 1750 to 1850, and from 1890 into today's modern global community. This informative collective biography accurately reflects women's contributions through the ages in areas including human rights, the arts and humanities, health issues, politics and government, sports, and contemporary issues. Three useful indexes catalog the articles geographically, alphabetically, and by occupation. Selected photographs are also included. MC

Notable 1995 Children's Trade Books in the Field of Social Studies

18.4   Barboza, Steven. **Door of No Return: The Legend of Gorée Island.** Cobblehill Books / Dutton, 1994. 41 pp. ISBN 0-525-65188-8. Nonfiction.

The African and African American experience is evocatively bridged in this slender yet powerful volume about the history of a slavery onloading post. Barboza packs enough thoughtful description into the text and accompanying photographs to take each reader on a vicarious three-hundred-year journey. A concluding autobiographical tie brings the search for ethnic continuity full circle. ER MC

Notable 1994 Children's Trade Books in the Field of Social Studies

18.5   Brandenburg, Jim. **Sand and Fog: Adventures in Southern Africa.** Edited by Joann Bren Guernsey. Walker, 1994. 44 pp. ISBN 0-8027-8232-9. Nonfiction.

Wildlife photographer Jim Brandenburg explores the Namib desert of Southwest Africa in search of the elusive oryx and the perfect picture. During his travels, he learns that what appears to be a barren wasteland is actually home to people and animals that exist nowhere else on the earth.

18.6   **Chronicle of the Olympics: 1896–1996.** Dorling Kindersley, 1996. 312 pp. ISBN 0-7894-0608-X. Nonfiction.

A century of Olympic game facts, factoids, photography, timelines, and records is presented here in a concise chronological package. This 312-page compendium will satisfy the needs of the sports enthusiast, the casual reader, and the person in need of a reference about Olympic sites, events, and athletes. This volume is a solid value for the library and the classroom. ER

18.7   Chicoine, Stephen, and Brent Ashabranner. **Lithuania: The Nation That Would Be Free.** Cobblehill Books / Dutton, 1995. 64 pp. ISBN 0-525-65151-9. Nonfiction.

This is an excellent resource on Lithuania in the 1990s. The bravery of its citizens in the face of Soviet might, their endurance of the daily scarcity of resources, and their determination to build a free society for future generations is clearly portrayed. Maps, statistics, demographic data, a bibliography, and colorful photographs enhance this text. ER

18.8   Clare, John D., editor. **Ancient Greece.** Gulliver Books / Harcourt Brace, 1994. 64 pp. ISBN 0-15-200516-1. Nonfiction.

Part of the Living History series, this book combines photographs, artifacts, text, and timelines in a captivating format that brings the era excitingly alive. *Ancient Greece* describes the life of a man and a woman from birth to death, and includes information on farming, sacrifices, and festivals as well as the expected coverage of Sparta, the Olympic games, and the Athenian empire. Altogether, this is a highly recommended book for those intimidated by dense text or for enthusiasts of the period. ER

Notable 1994 Children's Trade Books in the Field of Social Studies

18.9   Clare, John D., editor. **Industrial Revolution.** Gulliver Books / Harcourt Brace, 1994. 64 pp. ISBN 0-15-200514-5. Nonfiction.

This book is part of the Living History series, which combines photographs, artifacts, text, and timelines in a captivating format that brings each era excitingly alive. Each book is well designed and indexed for ease of use, with page layouts that draw attention from the illustrations to the accompanying text. The Industrial Revolution is a frequently studied era about which there is little for the high school student. The material covered in this volume provides an insight into the changes in life and work brought about during the era, and the system of wealth that resulted, which determines much of the world order today. Beginning with the feudal system, the book addresses topics such as railways, factories, education, and women in the workplace. A highly recommended addition to a library or classroom. ER

18.10   Colman, Penny. **Rosie the Riveter: Women Working on the Home Front in World War II.** Crown, 1995. 120 pp. ISBN 0-517-59790-X. Nonfiction.

Events of World War II are neatly woven into the history of women in the workplace during this brief but critical time period. New federal agencies disseminated propaganda to encourage the recruiting of female workers, attempting to counter the prejudices of employers, husbands, and society in general. The impressive accomplishments made by women during the period are well described, often in the women's own words. Their mercurial rise to financial and emotional power and sudden dismissal at war's end make fascinating reading for a wide audience. The text includes a bibliography, a chronology, an index, and many illustrations. ER

School Library Journal Best Books 1995

18.11   Colman, Penny. **Toilets, Bathtubs, Sinks, and Sewers: A History of the Bathroom.** Atheneum / Maxwell Macmillan, 1994. 70 pp. ISBN 0-689-31894-4. Nonfiction.

Through simple writing and black-and-white photographs, this book provides an overview of the history of toilets and bathing from Mesopotamia to the present, adding a fascinating perspective to our normal view of history. ER

ALA Quick Picks, 1995
ALA Best Books for Young Adults, 1995
ALA Notable Books for Children, 1995

18.12   Cooper, Michael L. **Bound for the Promised Land: The Great Black Migration.** Lodestar Books / Dutton, 1995. 85 pp. ISBN 0-525-67476-4. Nonfiction.

This slender volume offers insight into the migration of more than one million African Americans during the period between the beginning of World War I and the Great Depression. Personal, economic, and historical forces are integrated to enhance the reader's understanding of this movement, the impact of which is so tightly linked with current events. Clear writing and archival photographs enhance the book's value to students and invite the casual reader to take in the voices and life experiences it portrays. ER MC

Notable 1995 Children's Trade Books in the Field of Social Studies

18.13   Cott, Nancy F., general editor. **The Young Oxford History of Women in the United States.** Oxford University Press, 1995. Multi-volume. ISBN 0-19-508830-1 (series). Nonfiction.

This eleven-volume reference series contains clearly presented information, numerous illustrations, chronologies, suggestions for further readings, a biographical supplement, a list of museums and historic sites related to the history of American women, and an index that makes it easy to access all this information. The work spans the pre-Columbian era to the present day in chronological sequence and is written by a variety of scholars. As a reference tool, this is certain to be well used by both students and faculty.

18.14   Crawford, Peter. **Nomads of the Wind: A Natural History of Polynesia.** BBC Books / Parkwest, 1994. 264 pp. ISBN 0-563-36707-5. Nonfiction.

Glossy photographs highlight the dense text of this volume, making one long to travel to the paradise that can still be found in the Polynesian Islands. Produced to accompany a major BBC television series, this book includes the geography, history, ecology, and human rights issues of the region from antiquity to present day. MC

18.15   Exploration into . . . series. New Discovery Books, 1995. 48 pp. Nonfiction.

Asikinack, Bill, and Kate Scarborough. **Exploration into North America.** ISBN 0-02-718086-7.

Darin-Smith, Kate. **Exploration into Australia.** ISBN 0-02-718088-3.

Although written for a younger audience, this series is suitable for high school students wishing to gain an overview of the topic addressed in each volume. The texts are brief, broad in scope, and generously illustrated, and a timeline comparing concurrent events in different geographic regions, a glossary, and an index are appended to each. ER MC

18.16　Food and Feasts series. New Discovery Books, 1996. 32 pp. Nonfiction.
　　　Dawson, Imogen. **Food and Feasts in Ancient Greece.** ISBN 0-02-726329-0.
　　　Martell, Hazel Mary. **Food and Feasts with the Vikings.** ISBN 0-02-726317-7.

In each volume of the Food and Feasts series, an overall sketch of how food was obtained and prepared in the era under consideration, which foods were popular, and what social customs surrounded food and drink are presented simply and illustrated thoroughly. Recipes, a glossary, a bibliography, and an index are included in each volume, making the series a good resource. ER MC

18.17　Fremon, David K. **Japanese-American Internment in American History.** Enslow, 1996. 128 pp. ISBN 0-89490-767-0. Nonfiction.

The shameful time during U.S. history when American citizens and innocent immigrants were imprisoned because of their heritage is seldom discussed in school. Personal accounts of this deplorable situation show that the irony of fighting against persecution of Jews in Europe while violating the rights of Japanese at home did not escape the victims of this post–Pearl Harbor panic. Simply written, this book also includes a useful timetable, chapter notes, a bibliography, and an index. ER MC

18.18　Gravett, Christopher. **Castle.** Photographs by Geoff Dann. Alfred A. Knopf, 1994. 64 pp. ISBN 0-679-86000-2. Nonfiction.

Another captivating Eyewitness Book, this volume explains castle construction primarily with pictures and brief captions. The evolution of the buildings; their purposes, construction, architecture, component parts, and weapons; and the occupants and craftspeople who made them come alive are all touched upon. ER

ALA Quick Picks for Young Adults, 1995

18.19　Harris, Jacqueline L. **The Tuskegee Airmen: Black Heroes of World War II.** Dillon Press, 1996. 144 pp. ISBN 0-382-39215-9. Nonfiction.

Although African Americans have wanted to fly from the beginning of aviation history, they had to overcome racial prejudice in order to participate. Even in the midst of the terrible manpower shortages during World War II, racism excluded qualified blacks from the Air Corps. First Lady Eleanor Roosevelt pushed the Air Corps to find a way to allow blacks to serve as airmen, nonetheless, and the 99th Pursuit Squadron was established. Because the training of these young aviators took place at Tuskegee Institute in Alabama, the trainees were dubbed the Tuskegee Airmen. In spite of adverse conditions and a reluctance on the part of some to allow them to see combat, the Tuskegee Airmen demonstrated the highest levels of ability and courage. ER MC

18.20   Haskins, Jim. **The Harlem Renaissance.** The Millbrook Press, 1996. 192 pp. ISBN 1-56294-565-3. Nonfiction.

This beautifully designed book carries the reader into Harlem during its heyday and creates lively impressions of those who have shaped our culture so profoundly in this century. Cross-curricular in the best sense of the word, this trip into an era of high energy and prolific output by African Americans in the pre-Depression era is one well worth taking, both for research and just for pleasure. MC

18.21   Herb, Angela M. **Beyond the Mississippi: Early Westward Expansion of the United States.** Lodestar Books / Dutton, 1996. 138 pp. ISBN 0-525-67503-5. Nonfiction.

This book chronicles the westward expansion of the United States; such topics as the Lewis and Clark Expedition, the growth of fur trading, the Oregon Trail, the Indian Wars, the expansion into Texas, and the lure of gold in California are all addressed. The chapters are easy to read, and they are embellished with pictures, illustrations, and maps. Personal narratives are included, making this general history come alive for the reader. An index and a glossary are also included. ER

18.22   Hermes, Jules. **The Children of Morocco.** Carolrhoda Books, 1995. 48 pp. ISBN 0-87614-857-7. Nonfiction.

No television! Shopping in an open-air market instead of an air-conditioned mall! Living in the desert or in a casbah! Herding sheep! Being considered an adult at age twelve! Yes, daily life for the children of Morocco is very different from life in the United States. A brief history of Morocco and discussions of its culture and religion are included with brilliant color photographs and maps to show the unique beauty of this African land and its people. ER MC

Notable 1995 Children's Trade Books in the Field of Social Studies

18.23   Jackson, Donna M. **The Bone Detectives: How Forensic Anthropologists Solve Crimes and Uncover Mysteries of the Dead.** Little, Brown, 1996. 48 pp. ISBN 0-316-82935-8. Nonfiction.

Using scientific knowledge of human skeletons, the forensic anthropologist can tell the foods eaten and the diseases and injuries suffered in life, along with the height, age, race, and sex of a dead person. A "bone detective" who helps police and other medical experts, these specialists solve crimes and mysteries when all that is left is the skeleton. ER

School Library Journal Best Books, 1996

18.24 Kort, Michael G. **China under Communism.** The Millbrook Press, 1994. 176 pp. ISBN 1-56294-450-9. Nonfiction.

The author, a professor and coauthor of a textbook on twentieth-century China, brings the reader through four thousand years of Chinese development to present-day China. The contributions and underlying philosophies and principles of the society are presented simply, interspersed with black-and-white photographs. The chronological order provides straightforward information for students and/or teachers. A glossary, a list of recommended readings, and an index are included. MC

18.25 La Fontaine, Ray, and Mary La Fontaine. **Oswald Talked: The New Evidence in the JFK Assassination.** Pelican, 1996. 454 pp. ISBN 1-56554-029-8. Nonfiction.

Did Lee Harvey Oswald act alone in the assassination of President John F. Kennedy in 1963? Why were the records of three tramps who were arrested the day of the assassination destroyed? Did the connections between Oswald and Jack Ruby deserve examination by the Warren Commission? These questions are examined, adding new insight into the conspiracy theories that Oswald did not act alone. Mature reading.

18.26 Levinson, Nancy Smiler. **Turn of the Century: Our Nation One Hundred Years Ago.** Lodestar Books / Dutton, 1994. 127 pp. ISBN 0-525-67433-0. Nonfiction.

Concentrating on the years linking the nineteenth and twentieth centuries, Levinson has expanded topics found in history texts with maps, photographs, and reproductions of period art. She details the lives of our ancestors from each time period, drawing on film and audio recordings to capture their world in ways not available prior to this time period. This volume is a useful addition to a library, teacher resource collection, or classroom. MC

Notable 1994 Children's Trade Books in the Field of Social Studies

18.27 Madgwick, Wendy. **Citymaze! A Collection of Amazing City Mazes.** Illustrated by Dan Courtney, Nick Gibbard, Dean Entwistle, and John Fox. The Millbrook Press, 1995. 40 pp. ISBN 1-56294-561-0. Nonfiction.

Readers will enjoy this simple-looking book, which includes entertainment and information in equal parts! Double-page spreads depict major cities from aerial views. The reader is taken on a tour of highlights that include many of the world's most renowned landmarks. This book's appeal is not only what it shows but also the way it encourages the reader to continue traveling. ER

18.28 Mann, Kenny. African Kingdoms of the Past series. Dillon Press, 1996.
   Kongo, Ndongo: West Central Africa. 105 pp. ISBN 0-87518-658-0. Nonfiction.
   Monomotapa, Zulu, Basuto: Southern Africa. 105 pp. ISBN 0-87518-659-9.

This series organizes the history of African kingdoms by geographical area. In a lively style suitable for a wide audience, the author describes the riches of African lands and cultures, the rivalries of African peoples, and the invasions of Europeans as part of the larger story of the rise and fall of major kingdoms. Each book includes many illustrations, an index, a bibliography, maps, pronunciations given parenthetically within the text, and a pronunciation key. MC

18.29   Marrin, Albert. **Unconditional Surrender: U.S. Grant and the Civil War.** Atheneum / Maxwell Macmillan, 1994. 200 pp. ISBN 0-689-31837-5. Nonfiction. **Virginia's General: Robert E. Lee and the Civil War.** Atheneum / Maxwell Macmillan, 1994. 218 pp. ISBN 0-689-31838-3. Nonfiction.

Each of these works continues the author's much-awarded tradition of thorough research combined with a human portrait of American history. Biographical information surrounds the body of the book, which concentrates on the Civil War contributions made by Grant and Lee. Maps, black-and-white illustrations, notes, and suggestions for further reading also enhance the usefulness of these texts. Each is developed to be read equally for pleasure and for reference, and they are highly recommended for library, departmental, or personal collections. ER

Unconditional Surrender:
School Library Journal Best Books, 1994
ALA Best Books for Young Adults, 1995
Booklist Editors' Choice, 1995
Notable 1994 Children's Trade Books in the Field of Social Studies
IRA Teacher's Choice, 1996

Virginia's General:
ALA Best Books for Young Adults, 1996
School Library Journal Best Books, 1996
Notable 1994 Children's Trade Books in the Field of Social Studies
IRA Teacher's Choice, 1996

18.30   McCormick, Anita Louise. **Native Americans and the Reservation in American History.** Enslow, 1996. 128 pp. ISBN 0-89490-769-7. Nonfiction.

Simply written, this book provides an overview of the interaction between white settlers and Native Americans from East Coast to West, and from the first encounters to the present. Even in this brief volume, the pattern of intrusion, scorn, false treaties, and broken promises is clear. Recently, self-determination has begun to recreate tribal functions, but McCormick documents that there is much progress still to be made. ER MC

18.31   McKissack, Patricia C., and Fredrick L. McKissack. **Christmas in the Big House, Christmas in the Quarters.** Illustrated by John Thompson. Scholastic, 1994. 68 pp. ISBN 0-590-43027-0. Nonfiction.

One could guess that holiday celebrations in the homes of plantation owners would contrast sharply with those in the slave quarters. The authors create from their vast research a description of one Christmas, that of 1859, just a few years before the end of slavery. History, tradition, the Abolitionist movement, recipes, songs, and dances are interwoven to illustrate a brief, lively tapestry, one side as lovely and touching as the other. ER MC

Coretta Scott King Award, 1995
Notable 1994 Children's Trade Books in the Field of Social Studies

18.32   McKissack, Patricia C., and Fredrick L. McKissack. **Rebels against Slavery: American Slave Revolts.** Scholastic, 1996. 165 pp. ISBN 0-590-45735-7. Nonfiction.

This text describes the stories of the many people who fought against slavery from colonial times to the Civil War. The stories include Nat Turner's thirty-day slave revolt, Clinque's revolt on the slave ship *Amistad* and subsequent success in being allowed to return to Africa, and the Maroons, runaway slaves who set up their own hidden communities in the South. MC

18.33   McKissack, Patricia, and Fredrick McKissack. **Red-Tail Angels: The Story of the Tuskegee Airmen of World War II.** Walker, 1995. 136 pp. ISBN 0-8027-8292-2. Nonfiction.

The history of segregation in the United States military is told with a focus on the "experiment" held at Tuskegee, Alabama. Responding to much pressure, an all-black fighter squadron was established, but the unit was expected to fail. The belief that African Americans were inferior beings was widely held and even "documented" in official military reports. Instead, the Ninety-ninth Fighter Squadron distinguished itself throughout World War II, winning numerous commendations. The book includes many photographs of the men and their planes, an appendix, a bibliography, and an index. MC

Notable 1995 Children's Trade Books in the Field of Social Studies

18.34   McKissack, Patricia, and Fredrick McKissack. **The Royal Kingdoms of Ghana, Mali, and Songhay: Life in Medieval Africa.** Henry Holt, 1994. 142 pp. ISBN 0-8050-1670-8. Nonfiction.

Although civilizations flourished in the Western Sudan while Europe was being consumed by war and disease, most Americans know little of this rich history. The authors note which aspects of that history, whether passed down orally or from hearsay reports, may lack confirmation while presenting as full a picture as possible of the cultures of this region from somewhat limited sources. ER MC

Notable 1994 Children's Trade Books in the Field of Social Studies

18.35　Mettger, Zak. **Till Victory Is Won: Black Soldiers in the Civil War.** Lodestar Books / Dutton, 1994. 118 pp. ISBN 0-525-67412-8. Nonfiction.

Shortly after shots were fired on Fort Sumter, African Americans volunteered to fight on the side of the Union. However, it took two years and the near defeat of the Union forces before blacks were allowed to fight in a war many of them saw as a struggle to end slavery. This volume contains accounts of the formation of all-black regiments and their exploits in battle as well as the discrimination they faced and fought on and off the fields of battle. MC

18.36　Morin, Isobel V. **Days of Judgment: The World War II War Crimes Trials.** The Millbrook Press, 1995. 144 pp. ISBN 1-56294-442-8. Nonfiction.

A concise recounting of war crimes trials that occurred on both the European and the Asian fronts makes this book valuable for a high school library or departmental collection. In addition to learning about the Nuremberg Trials, the reader also learns of those brought to justice in Japan and other Asian nations. Short biographical sketches, black-and-white photographs, a bibliography, and notes contribute to the book's worth for historical and ethical studies.

18.37　Morin, Isobel V. **Impeaching the President.** The Millbrook Press, 1996. 159 pp. ISBN 1-56294-668-4. Nonfiction.

Morin has provided an in-depth study of the impeachment process as written into the U.S. Constitution by the founding fathers. The ins and outs of how the Senate and House have used impeachment against presidents Andrew Johnson, Richard Nixon, and Ronald Reagan are described, and a table of contents, source notes, a glossary, a bibliography, and an index are included.

18.38　Murphy, Jim. **The Great Fire.** Scholastic, 1995. 144 pp. ISBN 0-590-47267-4. Nonfiction.

Once again Jim Murphy provides a variety of first-person perspectives on an event in American history that will prove interesting to students of all ages. A trip to Chicago is not necessary to become drawn into the drama, fact, and legend of the Great Fire of 1871. For more than 125 years, people have associated Mrs. O'Leary's cow with this tragedy; this book clears the reputation of both the cow and her owners. A bibliography including both primary and secondary sources will be useful for study. ER

Newbery Honor Book, 1996
ALA Best Books for Young Adults, 1996
ALA Quick Picks for Young Adults, 1996
NCTE Orbis Pictus Award, 1996
School Library Journal Best Books, 1996
Booklist Editors' Choice, 1996
Publisher's Weekly Best Books, 1996
Notable 1995 Children's Trade Books in the Field of Social Studies

18.39   Newman, Richard, and Marcia Sawyer, Ph.D. **Everybody Say Freedom: Everything You Need to Know about African-American History.** Foreword by Henry Louis Gates, Jr. Plume, 1996. 318 pp. ISBN 0-452-27593-8. Nonfiction.

Ranging from 1619 to 1995, this book provides a survey of African American/United States history. Written for the student, each chapter begins with a list of questions that are then answered in a narrative, anecdotal style focusing on people, not just events. Men and women; politicians, artists, and athletes; and both the famous and the less-known are all represented. Quotations, further references, and an index are included in this helpful, interesting, and easy-to-use reference source. MC

18.40   Novas, Himilce. **Everything You Need to Know about Latino History.** Plume, 1994. 334 pp. ISBN 0-452-27100-2. Nonfiction.

A "How to Read This Book" section invites the reader to explore the contents in an interactive manner. The size, the layout, an index, and the book's question-and-answer format support this invitation to dip into lesser-known contributions of Mexicans, Puerto Ricans, Cubans, and other Latinos and their cultures. Recommended for use by faculty and students. ER MC

18.41   Platt, Richard. **In the Beginning . . . The Nearly Complete History of Almost Everything.** Illustrated by Brian Delf. Dorling Kindersley, 1995. 76 pp. ISBN 0-7894-0206-8. Nonfiction.

Timelines provide an easy way to examine history, and this book provides a series of full-page, illustrated timelines that trace the developments of a variety of aspects of everyday life, from clothing to weapons, over a wide span of years. An introduction summarizes the circumstances from as far back as thirty thousand years ago to as recently as ten years ago. Attractive illustrations and end pages make this a great addition to any collection. ER

18.42   Powledge, Fred. **Working River.** Photographs by Fred Powledge. Farrar, Straus and Giroux, 1995. 136 pp. ISBN 0-374-38527-0. Nonfiction.

The Patuxent River in Maryland offers transportation, recreation, food, and beauty. This working river's history is traced beginning in precolonial times, when the population along the river was 1,300, to the present. Now, with 490,000 people living along its banks, Powledge describes a need to protect the river from household and industrial pollution. The author also details programs being developed to enlist the help of both schoolchildren and adults in preserving the beauty of this "working river."

18.43   Rees, Bob, and Marika Sherwood. **The Black Experience: In the Caribbean and the U.S.A.** Peter Bedrick Books, 1993. 64 pp. ISBN 0-87226-117-4. Nonfiction.

Originally published in the United Kingdom, this volume presents facts about the black experience in the Caribbean and the United States in a more global context than do most U.S.-based books. This broader perspective gives it additional value in a library collection. ER MC

18.44 Smith, John David. **Black Voices from Reconstruction 1865–1877.** The Millbrook Press, 1996. 275 pp. ISBN 1-56294-583-1. Nonfiction.

The Reconstruction was a time in U.S. history during which the nation had to readjust to a different social order after the Civil War. Using original source documents, Smith creates a narrative rich with the voices of former slaves describing their experiences during this turbulent journey into the future.

18.45 Stefoff, Rebecca. **The Young Oxford Companion to Maps and Mapmaking.** Oxford University Press, 1995. 303 pp. ISBN 0-19-508042-4. Nonfiction.

Even a casual reader will quickly be absorbed by the clean layout and presentation of material in this volume. An alphabetical arrangement covers topics from Académie de Science to Zenith. This work, which includes a chronology, a list of mapmakers' groups, sites of map collections, a bibliography, and an index provides more information than the word "young" in the title implies. It would make a solid addition to a library or departmental reference collection.

18.46 Stein, R. Conrad. **The Mexican Revolution, 1910–1920.** New Discovery Books / Maxwell Macmillan, 1994. 160 pp. ISBN 0-02-786950-4. Nonfiction.

Written by an American who has lived in Mexico, this volume covers the years surrounding the Mexican Revolution. A table of contents, a chronology, biographical sketches, suggestions for further reading, an index, and period photographs add to the usefulness of this book for students of the period. The chronological approach, as it traces the impact of dominant historical figures, adds life to a span of years which still affects our relationship with our neighbor to the south but which is rarely covered in depth by the high school history curriculum. MC WL

18.47 Sullivan, George. **Slave Ship: The Story of the Henrietta Marie.** Cobblehill Books / Dutton, 1994. 77 pp. ISBN 0-525-65174-8. Nonfiction.

This engrossing chronicle combines an overview of a cruel trade in human life with the determined efforts of modern adventurers and descendants to honor the Middle Passage traversed by their ancestors. At times a detective story, combined with knowledge, perseverance, and luck, this text allows the reader to travel with members of the National Association of Black Scuba Divers as they place a memorial at the site of the shipwrecked *Henrietta Marie*. A strongly recommended title for study and independent reading. ER MC

18.48   Symynkywicz, Jeffrey B. **Germany: United Again.** Dillon Press, 1996. 135 pp. ISBN 0-87518-634-3. Nonfiction.

The changes in the politics and economics of Germany brought about by reunification are outlined briskly and clearly in this book along with their impact on other European countries and on the United States. Black-and-white historical photographs, notes, a glossary, a timeline, a bibliography, and an index are included in this volume from the Fall of Communism series. MC

18.49   Thompson, Sharon Elaine. **Death Trap: The Story of the La Brea Tar Pits.** Lerner, 1995. 72 pp. ISBN 0-8225-2851-7. Nonfiction.

Located in modern downtown Los Angeles is a forty-thousand-year-old gravesite, the last resting place of thousands of prehistoric animals and one human being. *Death Trap* takes the reader inside the La Brea Tar Pits, the asphalt pool that has captured for scientific study the ancient bones of saber-toothed cats, mastodons, and mammoths. Through text, color photographs, and illustrations, the reader will learn how the tar pits were formed, how animals were trapped in them, and what little is known about the La Brea Woman, the only human skeleton ever found. Take a journey back in time—but don't stand too close to the edge of the "hidden, black death trap." ER

18.50   Thwaite, Ann. **The Brilliant Career of Winnie-the-Pooh: The Definitive History of the Best Bear in All the World.** Dutton Children's Books, 1994. 192 pp. ISBN 0-525-45248-6. Nonfiction.

"Pooh" devotees will enjoy sharing this collection of memories and memorabilia about the world's most loved bear, his friends, his history, and the human beings who shared his space and early life. An inviting design and liberal use of illustrations encourage readers to extend their visit into upper-class British life in the early twentieth century. An interesting look at copyright ownership and an index add to the merit of a charming book.

18.51   **The Visual Dictionary of Ancient Civilizations.** Dorling Kindersley, 1994. 64 pp. ISBN 1-56458-701-0. Nonfiction.

This volume lives up to its title with clearly labeled photographs of art, artifacts, and models from civilizations long gone. Ancient life is chronologically documented by a short text that provides an introduction to each era, while timelines and an index add accessibility. This volume is recommended for library, classroom, or personal collections. ER MC

18.52   Vogel, Carole Garbuny. **The Great Midwest Flood.** Little, Brown, 1995. 32 pp. ISBN 0-316-90248-9. Nonfiction.

The flood of 1993 in the U.S. Midwest produced oozing muck, mud, mildew, warped floors, and rotten walls. Vogel describes the flood, studies the people who fought bravely but lost everything in it, and portrays the people who helped them survive. Maps, pictures, and illustrations are used to show their courage and sense of purpose. ER

18.53   Wheeler, Marjorie Spruill, editor. **One Woman, One Vote: Rediscovering the Woman Suffrage Movement.** NewSage Press, 1995. 371 pp. ISBN 0-939165-26-0. Nonfiction.

This anthology documents the struggle for a woman's right to vote in the United States. Researched and recorded by notable women, this book educates the reader about the women's suffrage movement, its victories and defeats, its methods and strategies, and its politics and history.

18.54   Wormser, Richard. **Hoboes: Wandering in America, 1870–1940.** Walker, 1994. 136 pp. ISBN 0-8027-8279-5. Nonfiction.

With the number of homeless people seen today, it is hard to imagine that, for a time, being a hobo was viewed as extremely attractive by young, adventure-seeking boys. The hobo lifestyle, its castes and hazards, and the causes of the periodic increases and eventual decline of the hobo population are chronicled here, accompanied by fitting photographs.

ALA Quick Picks for Young Adults, 1995

18.55   Zeinert, Karen. **Those Remarkable Women of the American Revolution.** The Millbrook Press, 1996. 96 pp. ISBN 1-56294-657-9. Nonfiction.

Touching upon an area of U.S. history that has been largely neglected, Zeinert examines the contributions of various women, both patriot and Loyalist, to the American Revolution, from the battlefield to the press, and shows how they challenged traditional female roles. Women from those as prominent as Abigail Adams to the poorest camp followers played a significant role in society at a time when it was considered unnatural to do so. Written in an easy narrative style, the text also includes illustrations, a timeline, a bibliography, and an index. ER

Titles Annotated in Other Chapters Related to History and Geography

Adams, Simon. *Visual Timeline of the Twentieth Century.* Reference.

Andryszewski, Tricia. *The Amazing Life of Moe Berg.* Autobiography.

Andryszewski, Tricia. *Immigration.* Political Science.

Ardley, Neil. *A Young Person's Guide to Music.* Arts.

Ayer, Eleanor H. *The United States Holocaust Museum.* Holocaust.

Beals, Melba Pattillo. *Warriors Don't Cry: A Searing Memoir of the Battle to Integrate Little Rock's Central High.* Autobiography.

Brand, Stewart. *How Buildings Learn.* Arts.

Child, John. *The Rise of Islam*. Religion.

Chronicle of America. Reference.

Cohen, Daniel. *Joseph McCarthy*. Autobiography.

Cumming, Robert. *Annotated Art*. Arts.

Devaney, John. *American Triumphs: 1945*. War.

Feder, Harriet K. *Mystery of the Kaifeng Scroll*. Mysteries.

Feelings, Tom. *The Middle Passage*. Art.

Ferber, Elizabeth. *Yasir Arafat*. Autobiography.

Franklin, Paula A. *Melting Pot or Not?* Human Rights.

Freedman, Russell. *Kids at Work*. Human Rights.

Gleason, Judith, ed. *Leaf and Bone: African Praise-Poems*. Poetry.

Granfield, Linda. *Cowboy*. Westerns.

Harris, David. *The Art of Calligraphy*. Arts.

Haskins, James. *The Scottsboro Boys*. Human Rights.

Haskins, Jim, and Joann Biondi. *From Afar to Zulu*. Reference.

Hopkins, Lee Bennett, ed. *Hand in Hand: An American History through Poetry*. Poetry.

Hyde, Margaret O. *Know about Tuberculosis*. Drugs.

Katz, William Loren. *Black Women of the Old West*. Westerns.

Kherdian, David. *The Road from Home*. Autobiography.

Lavender, David. *The Santa Fe Trail*. Westerns.

Lawlor, Veronica. *I Was Dreaming to Come to America*. Diaries.

Marrin, Albert. *The Sea King: Sir Francis Drake and His Times*. Autobiography.

Meltzer, Milton. *Cheap Raw Material*. College.

Meyer, Carolyn. *Rio Grande Stories*. Short Stories.

Miller, Brandon Marie. *Buffalo Gals: Women of the Old West*. Westerns.

Morris, Juddi. *The Harvey Girls*. Westerns.

Pious, Richard M. *The Young Oxford Companion to the Presidency of the United States*. Reference.

Platt, Richard. *Stephen Biesty's Cross-Sections: Castle*. Arts.

Sanford, William R. *Quanah Parker: Comanche Warrior*. Autobiography.

Silverman, Jerry. *Just Listen to This Song I'm Singing: African-American History through Song*. Arts.

Staples, Suzanne Fisher. *Haveli*. Adventure.

Stefoff, Rebecca. *Mao Zedong*. Autobiography.

Steiner, Barbara. *The Mummy*. Horror.

Switzer, Ellen. *The Magic of Mozart*. Arts.

Thomas, Roy Edwin, compiler. *Come Go with Me: Old-Timer Stories from the Southern Mountains*. Diaries.

Tilton, Rafael. *The Importance of Margaret Mead*. Autobiography.

Wilson, Elizabeth B. *Bibles and Bestiaries*. Arts.

19 Holocaust

"Benevolence is the distinguishing characteristic of man. As embodied in man's conduct, it is called the path of duty."

Mencius

"I am a man and nothing in man's lot can be indifferent to me."

Terence

"We owe to man higher success than food and fire. We owe man to man."

Ralph Waldo Emerson

19.1   Ayer, Eleanor H. **The United States Holocaust Memorial Museum: America Keeps the Memory Alive.** Dillon Press / Maxwell Macmillan, 1994. 79 pp. ISBN 0-87518-649-1. Nonfiction.

This descriptive account of the United States Holocaust Memorial Museum propels readers along on a parallel journey through history and the museum's exhibits. Color photographs and detailed descriptions of the building's design and displays allow readers to experience this important new structure. Along with those visiting the museum, readers are challenged to "bear witness" and gain an understanding of others. Featured biographies of Holocaust victims and survivors add authenticity and help personalize the visit for the reader. ER

19.2   Ayer, Eleanor H., with Helen Waterford and Alfons Heck. **Parallel Journeys.** Atheneum Books for Young Readers, 1995. 256 pp. ISBN 0-689-31830-8. Nonfiction.

Ayer has paralleled the true stories of Helen Waterford, a Jewish girl growing up in Frankfurt, Germany, and Alfons Heck, a German boy drawn to the Nazi regime. Helen is forced to flee and go into hiding until she is caught by the Gestapo and shipped to the Auschwitz death camp in Poland. Meanwhile, Alfons rises to power in the Hitlerjugend. Forty years later, the two meet in America and join forces to educate young people about peace and understanding. MC ER WL

ALA Best Books for Young Adults, 1996

19.3   Bachrach, Susan D. **Tell Them We Remember: The Story of the Holocaust.** Little, Brown, 1994. 109 pp. ISBN 0-316-69264-6. Nonfiction.

Drawing on the United States Holocaust Memorial Museum's vast collection of photographs, relics, maps, and video- and audiotaped histories, this book describes and documents the tragedy of the Holocaust. Excerpts from identity cards tell the stories of young people whose lives were interrupted after the Nazis came to power in Germany. Many of them did not survive, but a few lived to pass these stories on with the hope that they will not be forgotten. MC

ALA Best Books for Young Adults, 1995
ALA Notable Books for Children, 1995
ALA Quick Picks for Young Adults, 1995
Booklist Editors' Choice, 1995
Notable 1994 Children's Trade Books in the Field of Social Studies
IRA Young Adult Choice, 1996
IRA Teacher's Choice, 1995

19.4   Boas, Jacob. **We Are Witnesses: Five Diaries of Teenagers Who Died in the Holocaust.** Henry Holt, 1995. 196 pp. ISBN 0-8050-3702-0. Nonfiction.

This collection of five diaries by Jewish teenagers writing during the Holocaust transmits their horror, anger, frustration, and suffering at the hands of the Nazis. The accounts of David Rubinowicz, Yitzhak Rudashevski, Moseh Flinker, Eva Heyman, and Anne Frank chronicle the experience of the ordinary teenager caught in a horrific and senseless tragedy. The diaries are accompanied by photographs of the writers and their loved ones. MC WL

ALA Best Books for Young Adults, 1996
Notable 1995 Children's Trade Books in the Field of Social Studies

19.5   Friedman, Carl. **Nightfather.** Translated by Arnold and Erica Pomerans. Persea Books, 1994. 133 pp. ISBN 0-89255-193-3. Fiction.

In simple but lyrical language, this unforgettable book shows the effect of the Holocaust on survivors' children. The narrator's father Ephraim has "camp," but she and her brothers do not know how or why he has it. He turns everything into a story about the concentration camp. By the end of this autobiographical novel, accounts of family events are replaced with details of the death march and Ephraim's reunion with Bette, now his loving wife, who remembers. MC WL

19.6   Friedman, Ina R. **Flying against the Wind: The Story of a Young Woman Who Defied the Nazis.** Lodgepole Press, 1995. 202 pp. ISBN 1-886721-00-9. Nonfiction.

Cato, an independent, strong-willed teenager, faces the horrors of Nazi rule in World War II Germany. Disgusted with the repression of personal liberty, the destruction of arts and literature, and the inhumane treatment of the Jews, Cato joins the resistance. Cato's courage as she fights for human rights but is ultimately condemned for her efforts is proof that not all Germans were followers of Hitler. A chronology of Cato's life and a glossary of terms is included. ER MC WL

19.7   Holliday, Laurel, compiler. **Children in the Holocaust and World War II: Their Secret Diaries.** Pocket Books, 1995. 409 pp. ISBN 0-671-52054-7. Nonfiction.

Anne Frank was not the only child caught up by the horrors of the Holocaust who kept a journal. Of the many, many child diaries known, twenty-three are excerpted in this anthology. These youngsters, from ten to eighteen years old, were not in hiding; instead, they directly experienced the indignities and inhumanity of the streets, the ghettoes, and the concentration camps. There is an overwhelming sense of despair and hopelessness expressed by most of the writers, as well as the bravery of fighters and martyrs. MC WL

School Library Journal Best Adult Books for Young Adults, 1995
Booklist Editors' Choice 1996

19.8   Laird, Christa. **But Can the Phoenix Sing?** Greenwillow Books, 1995. 230 pp. ISBN 0-688-13612-5. Fiction.

Seventeen-year-old Richard is happy that his boring stepfather is away in Australia. Then Richard gets around to reading the autobiographical letter his stepfather left behind, and learns that Misha escaped from the Warsaw Ghetto at the age of fourteen and joined an intriguing group of partisan fighters. In this sequel to Laird's *Shadow of the Wall*, readers will find that the will to survive and the strength of friendship transcend time and give spirit to persecuted people throughout history. MC

ALA Best Books for Young Adults, 1996

19.9   Lipstadt, Deborah E. **Denying the Holocaust: The Growing Assault on Truth and Memory.** Plume, 1994. 278 pp. ISBN 0-452-27274-2. Nonfiction.

In 1993, a poll conducted about the Holocaust revealed that 22 percent of American adults and 20 percent of American high school students believed that it was possible that the Holocaust did not happen. This book describes a shocking, and organized, international movement that seeks to deny the Holocaust despite the tens of thousands of living witnesses and large amounts of documentation and artifacts. The author argues that this ominous attack has profound impact on history, truth, and civilization. MC WL

19.10   Nolan, Han. **If I Should Die before I Wake.** Harcourt Brace, 1994. 225 pp. ISBN 0-15-238040-X. Fiction.

Hilary is an angry teenaged neo-Nazi who is almost killed in a motorcycle crash. As she lies in a coma, she finds herself "becoming" Chana, a Polish teen living through the events of World War II. As Hilary experiences more and more of Chana's life in the ghetto, in prison, and finally in Auschwitz, her attitude toward Jews, toward her fellow neo-Nazis, and toward herself changes radically. This is a valuable book for young readers, twelve to fourteen years old, with little knowledge of the Holocaust or neo-Nazism. MC

19.11   Orlev, Uri. **Lydia, Queen of Palestine.** Translated by Hillel Halkin. Puffin Books, 1995. 168 pp. ISBN 0-14-037089-7. Fiction.

War brings out the best and the worst in Lydia, an only child caught in the midst of World War II and at the same time the war between her parents, who are separating. Lydia's mother, fearing Lydia will become another one of Hitler's victims on his march toward Romania, arranges for her to go to a kibbutz in Palestine. Lydia arrives at the kibbutz safely and then assumes her position as "queen of Palestine." She manages to survive the war as well as her parents' divorce and subsequent new relationships, and they, in turn, survive her. ER MC WL

19.12 Orlev, Uri. **The Man from the Other Side.** Translated by Hillel Halkin. Puffin Books, 1995. 186 pp. ISBN 0-14-037088-9. Fiction.

Marek is a fourteen-year-old boy living in Warsaw during World War II. Although he lives not far from the Jewish ghetto, he doesn't think much about the horrors being experienced by the Jews inside until he begins to accompany his stepfather on secret trips into the ghetto to sell food to the Jews. Marek's understanding of the world begins to grow, and he learns the secrets of his own birth and his mother's first marriage. When his maturing awareness leads him to help a fleeing Jew, Marek is thrust into the middle of the Warsaw Ghetto uprising. Told in the form of a fictional first-person narrative, this is a true story. MC WL

Awards won by original publication, 1989:
National Jewish Book Award
Mildred L. Batchelder Award
ALA Notable Book
ALA Best Book for Young Adults
Notable Children's Trade Book in the Field of Social Studies

19.13 Pausewang, Gudrun. **The Final Journey.** Translated by Patricia Crampton. Viking, 1996. 155 pp. ISBN 0-670-86456-0. Fiction.

Alice and her grandfather are all that remain of her Jewish family as they are herded onto a railway cattle car in Germany. It is only during this journey, lasting but a few days, that Alice learns the horrors of their circumstances, the truth from which she has been thoroughly shielded for years. The trip to Auschwitz suddenly exposes her to the gamut of human experience, providing a crash course in reality for the reader as well, in this superb translation from the original German text. MC WL

19.14 Ray, Karen. **To Cross a Line.** Orchard Books, 1994. 154 pp. ISBN 0-531-06831-5. Fiction.

Karen Ray's novel is based on the true story of her father-in-law's escape from Nazi Germany in 1938. Seventeen-year-old Egon Katz, driving illegally on the streets of Bremen, is in an accident with a Nazi official. To avoid arrest, Egon sets out on a harrowing journey across Germany to freedom in Denmark. This is an exciting adventure that traces the physical and emotional journey of a young man from danger to freedom and from youth to adulthood. MC

19.15 Rochman, Hazel, and Darlene Z. McCampbell, editors. **Bearing Witness: Stories of the Holocaust.** Orchard Books, 1995. 135 pp. 0-531-09488-X. Fiction / Nonfiction.

This widely varied collection of accounts, reflections, and fiction inspired by the suffering inflicted during the Holocaust is haunting and disturbing. The horror of the deaths of loved ones, the dehumanization of prisoners, the long-term effects of persecution, and the guilt of survival are carefully explored by writers such as Elie Wiesel, Ida Vos, Erika Mumford, Dorothy Rabinowitz, and Cynthia Ozick. Included are also gripping selections from the documentary *Shoah*, by Claude Lanzmann, and two episodes from Art Spiegelman's comic *Maus II: A Survivor's Tale*. MC WL

ALA Best Books for Young Adults, 1996

19.16 Rosenberg, Maxine. **Hiding to Survive: Stories of Jewish Children Rescued from the Holocaust.** Clarion Books, 1994. 159 pp. ISBN 0-395-65014-3. Nonfiction.

Fourteen Jewish adults relive their memories of their childhood struggle to survive the Holocaust. Each story focuses on the extreme measures Jewish parents had to take in order to protect their children from Hitler's mass killings of Jewish people. Every story is filled with details the adults have had etched on their minds from a horrible time when their lives were governed by hatred and persecution. MC

ALA Quick Picks for Young Adults, 1995 (Cited as ALA Recommended Books for Reluctant Young Adults Readers)
IRA Teacher's Choice, 1995

19.17 Świebocka, Teresa, editor. English edition by Jonathan Webber and Connie Wilsack. **Auschwitz: A History in Photographs.** Indiana University Press, 1993. 295 pp. ISBN 0-253-35581-8. Nonfiction.

This is a powerful and painful book. With more than three hundred photographs from the archives of the Auschwitz Museum and accompanying text, this book tells the story of the nightmarish daily occurrences of the Auschwitz concentration camp. From these pages, events teach us as well as compel us not to forget the dehumanization and murder of more than a million Jews, Poles, homosexuals, "gypsies," and other peoples deemed undesirable by the Third Reich. The afterword, "Personal Reflections on Auschwitz Today," provides some suggestions on how we can understand today the horrors that took place in Auschwitz fifty years ago. MC WL

19.18 van der Rol, Ruud, and Rian Verhoeven, in association with the Anne Frank House. **Anne Frank: Beyond the Diary: A Photographic Remembrance.** With an introduction by Anna Quindlen. Translated by Tony Langham and Plym Peters. Puffin Books, 1995. 110 pp. ISBN 0-14-036926-0. Nonfiction.

Written by staff members of the Anne Frank House in Amsterdam, this book details the life of Anne Frank and features one hundred never-before-published photographs. The text and photographs provide fascinating information about Anne Frank's life before, during, and after her now-famous days of hiding and diary-writing during the Holocaust. MC WL

Titles Annotated in Other Chapters Related to Holocaust

Heyes, Eileen. *Adolf Hitler*. Autobiography.

20 Horror

*"An' the gobble-uns 'at gits you
Ef you Don't Watch Out."*
    James Whitcomb Riley

*"What are these,
So wither'd, and so wild in their attire;
That look not like the inhabitants o' this earth
And yet are on it?"*
    William Shakespeare

20.1 Adams, Carmen. **The Claw.** Scholastic, 1995. 177 pp. ISBN 0-590-60369-8. Fiction.

Senior Kelly Reade has wanted a zoo internship for a long time. The fact that her best friend Rachel also gets an appointment makes this a summer to remember. Then, the phone calls start—phone calls threatening death. When death notes appear and cages come mysteriously unlocked, Kelly and Rachel must search to find the person who "holds the key" to the zoo mystery. ER MC

20.2 Athkins, D. E. **The Bride.** Scholastic, 1996. 159 pp. ISBN 0-590-25490-1. Fiction.

Jamie is excited to be a bridesmaid in her cousin Blaine's wedding. Remembered for her bad tricks, Blaine is now a famous model who is marrying a rich older man whose family is not happy about the wedding. Then frightening things begin to happen: a ghostly bride appears; dead doves fall from a canopy and smoke fills the ballroom during rehearsal; Jamie and the groom are locked in a burning sauna; and a rival model crashes in a flaming car. Is the mansion really haunted or are these publicity stunts? It seems there may be a dark secret that someone wants to force another to reveal. ER

20.3 Blaylock, James P. **All the Bells on Earth.** Ace Books, 1995. 376 pp. ISBN 0-441-00247-1. Fiction.

This story of the supernatural and the battle between good and evil unfolds in the ordinary setting of modern-day Orange, California. "Everyman" Walt Stebbins uncovers a plot by three locals who have sold their souls to the devil; two have already died horrible deaths and the third is using magic to try to escape from the deal. Occasional strong language.

20.4 Cargill, Linda. **The Surfer.** Scholastic, 1995. 193 pp. ISBN 0-590-22215-5. Fiction.

It should be a great Virginia Beach summer for high school swimmer Jessie Rogers. But Jessie has problems with her mom, with her boyfriend, and most of all with her self-confidence. Plagued by dreams of drowning, Jessie considers quitting the swim team. When she witnesses the drowning of a surfer, Jessie feels a double pain when people question what she really saw. Did she imagine the drowning? She must find out. ER

20.5   Cascone, A. G. **If He Hollers.** Avon Flare Books, 1995. 182 pp. ISBN 0-380-77753-3. Fiction.

This tale of kidnapping and murder takes the reader into the mind of the killer. Mary Ellen "Mel" Taylor witnessed the kidnapping of her seven-year-old friend Bobby as they played in a nearby woods, and ten years has not removed the memory from Mel's mind. Now the eyes in the woods have returned and Mel is their target. Will she avoid them and save herself? Will she tell the police what she didn't tell them ten years ago? Mel faces some difficult decisions. ER

20.6   Cooney, Caroline B. **Emergency Room.** Scholastic, 1994. 213 pp. ISBN 0-590-45740-3. Fiction.

Here is a fast-paced novel about two college students who volunteer to work in a hospital in order to learn all they can. Both Diana and Seth want careers in medicine, and they think they are prepared for anything. Working in the emergency room, however, teaches them just how unprepared they are. In one evening they witness a girl from their college dying from gunshot wounds because she was caught in crossfire, a boy dying after a horrifying motorcycle accident, and a baby being kidnapped from the hospital. Their strength is tested again and again.

20.7   Cooney, Caroline B. **Twins.** Scholastic, 1994. 183 pp. ISBN 0-590-47478-2. Fiction.

Mary Lee and Madrigal are identical twins, raised almost as one person. When Mary Lee is suddenly sent away to school, she must cope with the loss of part of her identity. She then realizes that she is totally dependent on Madrigal, whereas Madrigal seems to have "adjusted" very well. In her confusion, Mary Lee yearns to be her sister—but when that opportunity unexpectedly presents itself, Mary Lee finds out secrets that even an identical twin would not want to know. ER

20.8   Cusick, Richie Tankersley. **Silent Stalker.** Archway Paperback/Pocket Books, 1993. 214 pp. ISBN 0-671-79402-7 Fiction.

While spending the summer with her writer-father investigating a gloomy castle and medieval fair, Jenny Logan becomes prey for demented twin brothers and their equally bizarre cousin. Malcolm, Derrick, and Wil are spending time in the castle with Sir John, but they are not there for the fair. To save her own life and the lives of other innocent people, including her father, Jenny must uncover the dark secrets that the three young men hide so carefully in the rotting underground passageways of the castle.

20.9   Ellis, Carol. **The Body.** Scholastic, 1995. 195 pp. ISBN 0-590-48156-8. Fiction.

Melanie Jacobs, the new girl in town, takes a job as a reader for fellow senior Lisa Randolph, who has been tragically paralyzed in an accident. It doesn't take long for Melanie to see that there is something weird about Lisa's circumstances, her family, and some of her friends. When Lisa attempts to "talk" to Melanie through the pages of *Little Women,* Melanie tries to find the answers concerning Lisa's accident and the strange behavior of her friends. ER

20.10   Ellis, Carol. **Silent Witness.** Scholastic, 1994. 195 pp. ISBN 0-590-47101-5. Fiction.

Shortly after her friend Allen dies, Lucy realizes that something is very wrong. Odd phone calls, a ransacked locker, and a constant feeling of being watched bring her to the edge of terror. What does all of this have to do with the strange behavior of her new boyfriend? And why did it start immediately after Allen's mother asked Lucy to give some of his belongings to his friends? What did Allen leave behind that could cause someone to try to kill Lucy?

20.11   Ellis, Carol. **The Stalker.** Scholastic, 1996. 183 pp. ISBN 0-590-25520-7. Fiction.

Janna is a talented dancer and seems to be living out her dream of having adoring fans. At eighteen, she is traveling with a theater company performing *Grease,* but terrible things begin to happen after someone throws a rose and a strange message at her feet. As events become more frightening and the notes more threatening, Janna begins to suspect that her ex-boyfriend may be involved. Or maybe it is the fan who seems so obsessed—or is it someone in the company who is jealous? Is her life really in danger? ER

20.12   Elrod, P. N. **Death and the Maiden.** Ace Books, 1994. 244 pp. ISBN 0-441-00071-1. Fiction.

Imagine living your life as a vampire. Imagine being able to fly or to heal yourself if you are injured. Now imagine doing these things during the American Revolution while living on a large estate with your entire family and your servants. Superstitions run strong and you spend your time knowing that if you are caught, terrible things will happen to those you love. Yet you must risk being caught because you must have blood to live. This is the life of Jonathan Barrett.

20.13   Finnis, A., editor. **Bone Meal: Seven More Tales of Terror.** Scholastic, 1995. 243 pp. ISBN 0-590-50982-9. Fiction.

For those with a taste for terror, this anthology may titillate the appetite—or cause severe stomach upset! These seven unrelated stories have a common thread: uncommonly horrifying events.

20.14 Finnis, A., editor. **The Cat-Dogs.** Scholastic, 1995. 209 pp. ISBN 0-590-22292-9. Fiction.

Not for the faint (or warm!) of heart, these "tales of terror" live up to their name. Don't look for happy endings here! Each of these six stories is set in England, and written by a British author, but few of the foreign references or expressions present any difficulty.

20.15 Gorman, Carol. **Back from the Dead.** Avon Flare Books, 1995. 168 pp. ISBN 0-380-77433-X. Fiction.

Teenager Julia Bliss never wanted to move to her cousin Nikki's house. The girls have little in common, and Nikki's friends, the party animals of the school, take an instant dislike to Julia. When a hiking trip is marred by arson and a possible murder, Julia finds herself in a guilt-by-association trap. As she tries to solve this problem, mysterious phone calls begin. Julia now must clear up the mystery herself. ER

20.16 Hahn, Mary Downing. **Look for Me by Moonlight.** Clarion, 1995. 198 pp. ISBN 0-395-69843-X. Fiction.

Cynda visits her father and her pregnant stepmother at a remote and supposedly haunted inn her father runs in Maine. Feeling distanced from her father and his life, Cynda soon is captivated by the words and ways of a mysterious guest. She falls under Vincent's spell and becomes part of the horror and mystery of the old inn in this first-rate story of suspense.

ALA Quick Picks for Young Adults, 1996.

20.17 Hamilton, Laurell K. **The Laughing Corpse.** Ace Books, 1994. 293 pp. ISBN 0-441-00091-6. Fiction.

Anita Blake is an animator for Animators, Inc., whose job is resurrecting zombies. When her company is asked to resurrect a zombie almost three hundred years old, Anita refuses. To resurrect a zombie, a sacrifice must be made, and the older the zombie, the greater the sacrifice. To resurrect one that old would require a human sacrifice. But someone else does the resurrection and now Anita and her boss must track down and stop this rogue animator before they become sacrifices themselves.

20.18 Harrell, Janice. **The Secret Diaries, Volume I: Temptation.** Scholastic, 1994. 105 pp. ISBN 0-590-47692-0. Fiction.

Have you ever been "the new kid" in school? In her senior year Joanna moves with her father and must attend a new school. She decides that she wants to be part of one select group. There's Casey, the computer whiz; Tessa and Stephen, the couple who could be twins; and Penn, the golden boy who drives a Corvette. What dark secrets do they hide? And just who was Laurie Jenkins, the fifth member of the group, the girl who disappeared? Answering these questions could put Joanna's life in danger.

20.19 Harrell, Janice. **The Secret Diaries, Volume II: Betrayal.** Scholastic, 1994. 294 pp. ISBN 0-590-47712-9. Fiction.

Joanna's new friends are in terrible trouble. It turns out that a girl who was missing hadn't run away as everyone had thought. Her body is found—right where the friends Stephen, Tessa, and Penn placed it after Stephen pushed her off Lookout Cliff. How do the friends handle this new development? How do they keep unstable Casey from telling the police everything? By killing him with kindness, or by just killing him? And how does Joanna handle her new relationship with Penn, who may be an accomplice to murder?

20.20 Hoh, Diane. Nightmare Hall series. Scholastic. Fiction.
   The Biker. 1995. 244 pp. ISBN 0-590-25080-9.
   Book of Horrors. 1994. 244 pp. ISBN 0-590-48358-7.
   The Coffin. 1995. 237 pp. ISBN 0-590-20297-9.
   Dark Moon. 1995. 211 pp. ISBN 0-590-25078-7.
   Deadly Visions. 1995. 208 pp. ISBN 0-590-20298-7.
   The Dummy. 1995. 229 pp. ISBN 0-590-56868-X.
   The Initiation. 1994. 189 pp. ISBN 0-590-48322-6.
   Kidnapped. 1995. 245 pp. ISBN 0-590-56867-1.
   Last Breath. 1994. 243 pp. ISBN 0-590-48648-9.
   Revenge. 1995. 214 pp. ISBN 0-590-25082-5.
   Student Body. 1995. 213 pp. ISBN 0-590-20299-5.
   Truth or Die. 1994. 163 pp. ISBN 0-590-48353-6.
   The Voice in the Mirror. 1995. 227 pp. ISBN 0-590-56869-8.

Have you ever worried that your life was too ordinary? Too boring? Well, the students at Salem University don't have that problem. Hidden in the shadows, shrouded in silence, sits Nightmare Hall, given that name by the students because of the terrors that happen there. Deadly images appear in pictures. A fire rages out of control, killing teens. A girl gets locked in a coffin, a motorcyclist is terrorizing people, and a Ferris wheel spins out of control. These are a few of the horrors that await you in books in the Nightmare Hall series. Don't read them when you're alone in the house! ER

20.21 Hoh, Diane. **Prom Date.** Scholastic, 1996. 341 pp. ISBN 0-590-54429-2. Fiction.

Margaret and her friends have never been a part of the "Pops," the popular group at her high school. She and her friends aren't even going to their senior prom. Margaret's mother, however, runs the well-known Quartet, a popular fashion shop where the "Pops" get their prom gowns, so Margaret has to treat the other girls well even if that treatment isn't returned. The mystery begins as one by one girls with dates to the prom begin to be murdered by someone who is jealous of them. Which girl is the murderer and which girl will be the next victim?

20.22   Lerangis, Peter. **The Yearbook.** Scholastic, 1994. 229 pp. ISBN 0-590-46678-X. Fiction.

David signs up to work on the yearbook to be closer to Ariana. He doesn't realize that he's even closer to death. Warnings appear on the pages of the yearbook proofs under certain pictures, warnings of the impending deaths of those students. When several of those students actually die or disappear, David and Ariana must risk their own lives to stop the killings. Will they succeed?

20.23   Littke, Lael. **The Watcher.** Scholastic, 1994. 200 pp. ISBN 0-590-47088-4. Fiction.

Do you have a favorite soap opera or television show? How about a favorite character, someone whose life seems more glamorous and exciting than your own? Imagine if all the things that happen to your favorite character started happening to you. They do to Catherine Belmont. She meets a new boy, Travis Cavenaugh, and shortly thereafter things get strange. All the things happening to her favorite soap heroine, Cassandra Bly, begin happening to Catherine, for real. This might not be so bad except that someone is trying to kill Cassandra!

20.24   Main, Mary. **Tower of Evil.** WestWind / Troll Associates, 1994. 174 pp. ISBN 0-8167-3533-6. Fiction.

While Tory Madison learns to live with the tragic loss of her parents, her aunt's home on the California coast has offered peace and healing. But when she meets rock star Dag Ashton and his young daughter Elissa, Tory's sensitive nature sends up warning flares. There is something strange and hidden in Elissa's eyes. Tory attempts to solve the Ashton mystery. Within it, she finds an ancient secret that revolves around one person—Tory Madison! ER

20.25   Matthews, Penny, compiler. **Hair-Raising: Ten Horror Stories.** Scholastic, 1995. 141 pp. ISBN 0-590-48403-6. Fiction.

Almost more interesting than the stories themselves are the afterwords by each author in this ten-story anthology. The authors explain *why* they feel their story is a horror story and often reveal the experience that led to the story, most of which are tales of characters questioning their perceptions. As one author says, "Horror is what happens when you can't trust your own senses. . . . Mine is a horror of things that lurk . . . things *not human*. . . . Good horror stories should make you shudder and pause for reflection." ER

20.26   McFann, Jane. **Be Mine.** Scholastic, 1994. 244 pp. ISBN 0-590-46690-9. Fiction.

Bethany and Starling are only weeks from graduation when someone begins stalking Bethany. The stalker puts hearts on Bethany's locker and on her kitchen door, places one perfect rose inside her locker, and sends a dozen roses to her home. Bethany thinks it's romantic and hopes Starling is responsible until she starts receiving notes and then is kidnapped while wearing nothing but an oversized tee shirt. What is she supposed to do?

20.27   McFann, Jane. **Hide and Seek.** Scholastic, 1995. 201 pp. ISBN 0-590-60387-6. Fiction.

Lissa's world is a world of secrets. Growing up with her conceited father, who openly despises her, and her mother, who excuses her father's behavior, Lissa has learned to keep her feelings to herself. As her loneliness builds and her depression mounts, Lissa is haunted by one question: What did she do to make her father hate her so? Lissa seeks the answer in this realistically frightening tale of mental and verbal abuse. ER

20.28   Moore, Elizabeth. **Dark Moon II: Dreams of Revenge.** Scholastic, 1995. 167 pp. ISBN 0-590-25510-X. Fiction.

Jeffrey Thomas thought he loved Barbara until the mysterious Rebecca appeared. Now Barbara is dead, and his obsession with Rebecca grows even stronger. But who is she? Where did she come from? Why does she taunt and tease him? It occurs to Jeffrey that she may have had something to do with Barbara's death. Ghosts of the past blend with the present in this tale with allusions to the famous Salem witch trials. ER

20.29   Morse, Eric. **Friday the Thirteenth: Road Trip.** Berkley Books, 1994. 187 pp. ISBN 0-425-14383-X. Fiction.

The football game ends with a dramatic win for the Carville Hornets, and the coach names three MVPs who will be allowed to ride home with him in his van instead of on the team bus. Each MVP gets to name a cheerleader to ride with him. Finally the coach, three players, three cheerleaders, and the team mascot are in the van and heading home. But most of them won't make it. You see, Jason's back, hockey mask and all, and he's looking for new victims.

20.30   Parker, Daniel. **Dance of Death.** HarperCollins, 1996. 199 pp. ISBN 0-06-106318-5. Fiction.

Third in the Dark Hearts series, this horror story picks up the tale of teenager Allie, who has mysterious powers and has just witnessed the brutal murder of her aunt as part of a New Orleans clan's attempts to stop anyone who opposes it. Allie, along with her boyfriend Jean-Paul, must fight against the evil Isnard (Jean-Paul's twin), who is determined to kill his brother and then to use Allie and her powers to completely dominate his clan. ER

20.31   Pedersen, Ted. **True Fright: Buried Alive! and Other True Stories Scarier than Fiction.** Tor / Tom Doherty Associates, 1996. 144 pp. ISBN 0-812-54396-3. Nonfiction.

Imagine being buried alive, facing a destructive hurricane, outrunning a raging forest fire, or having a date with a ghost. These are just some of the situations that confront the characters in this collection of fifteen true or believed-to-be true stories. Be prepared to be frightened, amazed, or thrilled by these tales of the extraordinary.

20.32   Peel, John. **The Tale of the Sinister Statues.** Minstrel / Pocket Books, 1995. 119 pp. ISBN 0-671-52545-X. Fiction.

Something weird is going on at the local museum Dustin loves to visit, in this novel from the Are You Afraid of the Dark? series. Old statues are disappearing and new statues are appearing, just as two of Dustin's classmates also disappear. As Dustin and his sister Brianne desperately try to find the missing students, they come face to face with an ancient evil. ER

20.33   Peel, John. **Talons.** Archway / Pocket Books, 1993. 196 pp. ISBN 0-671-79405-1. Fiction.

Kari Temple finds Viking bones wrapped with a metal chain in the cellar of her friend Ryan's mother's store. Who was the man and how did he die? They notify Dr. Grant, who teaches at Boston University. What they uncover is more evil than any of them can believe. What is this creature that preys and kills and how can they stop it?

20.34   Phillips, Ann. **A Haunted Year.** Macmillan, 1994. 175 pp. ISBN 0-02-774605-4. Fiction.

Florence is bored. It is a Sunday afternoon during school vacation, and there isn't much for a girl to do in 1910 in England. While looking through an old album, she finds a photograph of a twelve-year-old boy and begins to ask questions. She is told that it is her dead cousin, George, but no more. Florence decides to call George, and he comes, ready to play, and fills her days. The problem starts when George comes even when he isn't called, and then doesn't go away. How will Florence solve her problem?

20.35   Piazza, Linda. **Evil in the Attic.** Avon Flare Books, 1995. 156 pp. ISBN 0-380-77576-X. Fiction.

For a teenager, Jackie Sheen has a lot to handle. Her recently divorced mother has begun to have visions. Her rented house has burned down. If that weren't enough, their new landlord is plagued by some ghostly force, which Jackie feels in the attic. She sees it possess the landlord's daughter, and an old music book appears to be the key. But why? How? As the force gets stronger, Jackie alone must confront it. ER

20.36   Pierce, Richard. **Frankenstein's Children, Book One: The Creation.** Berkley Books, 1994. 200 pp. ISBN 0-425-14361-9. Fiction.

Sara Watkins thought she and Josh would love each other and be together forever. Then, for no reason that anyone could figure out, Josh killed himself. Sara and her friends tempt fate to find a way to bring him back to life. They become modern Frankensteins—with the same horrifying results.

20.37   Pike, Christopher. **The Last Vampire.** Archway / Pocket Books, 1994. 193 pp. ISBN 0-671-87264-8. Fiction.

Alisa Perne, bright and attractive, looks to be about eighteen years old, but then she has looked that way for about five thousand years. She believes herself to be the last vampire, but discovers she is still pursued by her creator, Yaksha, the original vampire and evil incarnate. Can her centuries of experience help her outwit him? Will her love for mortal Ray Riles save or condemn her? Fans of Pike's numerous other titles will enjoy this one, and the sequel is already available.

ALA Quick Picks for Young Adults, 1995

20.38   **Ray Bradbury Chronicles: Volume 7.** Illustrated by Steve Baskerville, Del Barras, John Carnell, Lars Hokanson, Howard Simpson, Anthony Williams, and Wally Wood. Nantier, Beall, Minoustchine Publishing, 1994. N.p. ISBN 1-56163-112-4. Fiction.

These comic-book versions of five Ray Bradbury stories, endorsed by the author himself, are illustrated by five different artists with varied drawing styles. These adaptations remain quite true to the original stories, and fans of Bradbury's works or of "graphic novels" will find these to be good examples of both. ER

ALA Quick Picks for Young Adults, 1995

20.39   Rees, Celia. **Every Step You Take.** Pan Original, 1993. 181 pp. ISBN 0-330-32844-1. Fiction.

Chris O'Neill goes on the Outdoor Pursuits because her best friend Anna wants her there. Neither girl realizes how traumatic this trip will be. There's a killer on the loose, and the police think he's headed for the same house where Chris's group will be staying. And then there's Andy, the boy Chris agrees to date. Just how obsessive is his need for her? And how far will he go to make her his?

20.40   Ryp, Wolff. **Midnight Secrets, Volume 2: The Thrill.** WestWind / Troll Associates, 1994. 214 pp. ISBN 0-8167-3543-3. Fiction.

Kendra's mother warns her to always expect the unexpected, and Kendra certainly understands that. She is being visited at night by Revell, a spirit who describes psychic powers available to Kendra and warns her that they may be beyond her control. When Ariane, a distant relative, unexpectedly visits Kendra, accidents begin to happen. Ariane seems to know about Kendra's power and her nightly visitor, and Kendra must find out the secret of Revell, Ariane, and herself. ER

20.41 Scott, Michael. **October Moon.** Holiday House, 1994. 158 pp. ISBN 0-8234-1110-9. Fiction.

Rachel Stone had always heard her father yearn for a horse farm in Ireland. Now he has his wish and the family decides to vacation there. However, it seems that someone—or something—has other ideas. First, there's a series of fires. Then the accidents get worse and seem to be directed at Rachel. Rachel suspects the stable girl and her brother, but when she learns what they really are, she has very little time to save her parents or herself.

ALA Quick Picks for Young Adults, 1995

20.42 Serling, Carol, editor. **Return to the Twilight Zone.** Daw Books, 1994. 336 pp. ISBN 0-88677-576-0. Fiction.

Imaginative stories with unique twists are characteristic of this volume, including tales by such authors as Pamela Sargent, Charles Grant, and Jack Dann. From a kaleidoscope that can repattern the life of anyone who looks through it to a television set that is about to tune in to the future, these tales capture the magic, mystery, humor, and horror that are distinctive of the "Twilight Zone."

20.43 Smith, L. J. **The Forbidden Game, Volume 1: The Hunter.** Archway Paperbacks / Pocket Books, 1994. 228 pp. ISBN 0-671-87451-9. Fiction.

Jenny buys a game in a plain white box, a most unusual game in which each player must face his or her worst nightmare to win. Jenny and her friends face the game bravely, but the Shadow Man, creator of the game, has other ideas for them. He is evil and darkness and he wants Jenny for her goodness and light. He will have her if he wins the game, and he doesn't play fairly.

20.44 Smith, L. J. **The Strange Power.** Archway / Pocket Books, 1994. 230 pp. ISBN 0-671-87454-3. Fiction.

High school senior Kaitlyn Fairchild has looked forward to this opportunity. Branded a "witch" back in Ohio because of her psychic predictions, Kaitlyn becomes a member of a telepathic group of young people at a California research institute, but the experiments are not what they were advertised to be. Mind control and "brain stealing" begin to dominate the sessions, and Kaitlyn is forced to find a dangerous means of escape, in this volume from the Dark Visions series. ER

20.45   Smith, Sinclair. **Amnesia.** Scholastic, 1996. 160 pp. ISBN 0-590-50952-7. Fiction.

Alicia awakens in a hospital bed unable to recognize her own mirrored image. Her sister, Marta, appears and offers bits and pieces of information about the accident that took their parents and robbed Alicia of her memory. Uneasily, Alicia returns to their home under Marta's watchful eye. Not even her own room jars her memory; instead, she begins feeling that the surroundings have always been totally unfamiliar. Why is Marta trying so hard to isolate her from her friends, her school, and any contact with the outside world? ER

20.46   Smith, Sinclair. **Second Sight.** Scholastic, 1996. 166 pp. ISBN 0-590-60287-X. Fiction.

A few weeks ago, Grayson was blind; now she's seeing horrible murders. Is her new psychic ability the result of her recent surgery? Can she interpret her visions in time to save the victims? She is in a race to find the murderer before she becomes a casualty herself.

20.47   Steiner, Barbara. The Dark Chronicles series. Avon Flare Books, 1995. Fiction.
          The Calling. 200 pp. ISBN 0-380-77994-3.
          The Dance. 229 pp. ISBN 0-380-77441-0.
          The Gallery. 170 pp. ISBN 0-380-77689-8.

The thread in this series is the allure of the performing arts, especially dance. In *The Dance*, Melanie has two motivations for struggling to join Madame Leona's ballet group. One is to become a professional dancer; the other is to investigate the death of Paulie McMasters, who mysteriously died after becoming one of Leona's lead performers. In *The Calling*, Miki O'Ryan, who mysteriously lost her occult-obsessed father years before, becomes obsessed herself with a very odd dance troupe. This group's "night performances" blur Miki's vision of fantasy and reality. Finally, in *The Gallery*, Ladonna Martindale, a gifted young artist, finds herself drawn into the world of antique arts in the basement of the Arts Center. When a voice begins calling her to join the paintings, she faces a very difficult decision. ER

20.48   Steiner, Barbara. **The Mummy.** Scholastic, 1995. 210 pp. ISBN 0-590-20353-3. Fiction.

Lana Richardson, an archeology major, looks forward to working on a touring Egyptian mummy exhibit. Her great opportunity quickly turns into a nightmare when the mummy of an ancient prince begins "talking" to her. Dreams of past lives begin to haunt her, but she cannot explain their meaning. When she is attacked at the museum during a robbery and then becomes a suspect, she is forced to try to solve both mysteries. ER

20.49   Stine, R. L. **Call Waiting.** Scholastic, 1994. 167 pp. ISBN 0-590-47480-4. Fiction.

Karen is afraid she is losing her boyfriend Ethan to another girl. He breaks dates, telling her he has to work, but she learns he quit his job some weeks ago. So Karen claims she has call waiting and is receiving threatening calls when Ethan is already on the phone with her. Ethan falls for this until Karen's mother learns what Karen is doing and tells Ethan, in front of Karen, that they don't have call waiting! Suddenly everyone is suspicious of what Karen says and no one believes her when the threatening calls really begin. Will she have to die to prove she was telling the truth?

20.50   Stine, R. L. **College Weekend.** Parachute Press / Archway / Pocket Books, 1995. 147 pp. ISBN 0-671-86840-3. Fiction.

Tina Rivers is so excited about visiting Patterson College with her boyfriend that she doesn't even mind that her cousin Holly is coming along. The only problem is that her boyfriend is missing. And then Holly disappears too! What is going on? And just what does Christopher, her boyfriend's roommate, know about the mysteries? Readers will keep turning pages to discover just how much danger Tina herself is in. This is just one of many exciting titles in the Fear Street series.

20.51   Stine, R. L. **Halloween Night II.** Scholastic, 1994. 178 pp. ISBN 0-590-47482-0. Fiction.

Halloween is not an easy holiday for Brenda Morgan. Last year she was stabbed by her best friend. This year she has found out that her boyfriend, Jake, is dating her own cousin, Halley. Now, Halloween itself may be canceled because a maniac is on the loose. As she prepares a Halloween video for school, Brenda decides to play a Halloween prank on Jake and Halley. But Brenda finds out that sometimes things don't go as planned. Violent situations.

20.52   Stine, R. L. **I Saw You That Night.** Scholastic, 1994. 179 pp. ISBN 0-590-47481-2. Fiction.

Roxie Nelson has a crush on Lee Blume, a new boy at school. The crush turns to terror, however, when Roxie, on a bet, hides in Lee's house one night and overhears a violent struggle. A body is found and Roxie fears that Lee has a hidden personality. Matters get even more complicated when, after getting threats, Roxie struggles to find out the killer's identity, while trying not to become the next victim. ER

20.53   Stine, R. L. **Indiana Jones and the Curse of Horror Island.** Illustrated
by David B. Mattingly. Ballantine Books, 1994. 118 pp. ISBN 0-345-33605-
4. Fiction.

Have you been looking for a book that is really different? This one may
be for you. It is an interactive book; the reader chooses the plot as he or
she reads the story. Whenever there's a choice to be made by the characters in the story, the reader is given two choices and a page to turn to
for each. This interesting format means one can read the book again and
again, and it will be different each time. The book is great fun, and it
has six different endings!

20.54   Stine, R. L. **Wrong Number 2.** Parachute Press / Archway / Pocket
Books, 1995. 165 pp. ISBN 0-671-78607-5. Fiction.

In this sequel to *The Wrong Number,* Jade and Deena receive threatening phone calls and messages, and someone begins to follow them. They
then learn that the man who tried to kill them after they found evidence
that he murdered his wife may be getting out of prison on a technical-
ity. Once again, the two teenage girls find themselves struggling to survive as they try to solve the mystery of who's trying to scare them. ER

20.55   Westall, Robert. **The Stones of Muncaster Cathedral.** Sunburst / Farrar,
Straus and Giroux, 1994. 97 pp. ISBN 0-374-47119-3. Fiction.

Can an old stone gargoyle come to life? Can part of a cathedral be evil?
Or is there something even more sinister going on high up on the southwest corner of Muncaster Cathedral? Joe Clarke is a steeplejack who
accepts the contract to clean and repair the southwest corner of the roof.
While he and his crew are hard at work they discover a secret which
can and does kill. Can they stop this horror?

20.56   Windsor, Patricia. **The Blooding.** Scholastic, 1996. 281 pp. ISBN 0-590-
43309-1. Fiction.

Maris decides to accept a summer job as an *au pair* in England in an effort to prove herself to her mother. But when Barb Forrest, Maris's em-
ployer, is killed, the peaceful existence Maris has been enjoying falls to
pieces. Then Maris discovers the secret that Derek, Barb's husband, has
been keeping; she learns about his "transformations." She also realizes
that Derek plans on "blooding" her, and although she fears the loneliness such a transformation will mean, she is also proud that now her
mother will no longer be able to undermine her sense of self.

20.57   Wright, Betty Ren. **Out of the Dark.** Scholastic, 1995. 149 pp. ISBN 0-
590-43598-1. Fiction.

When Jessica's parents lose their jobs, they move from St. Louis to Wisconsin to stay in her grandmother's vacant house. Jessica begins having nightmares in which a ghostly woman in a blue dress is terrorizing

her, nightmares that soon become reality. With the help of her physically handicapped neighbor and some old diaries of her grandmother's, Jessica tries to find out who the ghost woman really is and why the ghost wants to hurt her. ER

20.58 Wright, T. M. **Little Boy Lost.** Tor / Tom Doherty Associates Book, 1995. 247 pp. ISBN 0-812-55069-2. Fiction.

Young C. J. Gale could always "see things." His intuitive powers would take him to a dream world of beauty. When his mother is murdered, however, C. J. begins to feel lost, and when his father marries the mysterious Marie C. J.'s visions turn to horror. But Marie suddenly disappears, and now that his stepbrother has done the same C. J. must fight to keep his father from that other "dream world." Mild profanity.

Titles Annotated in Other Chapters Related to Horror

Carmody, Isobelle. *The Gathering*. Fantasy.

Cooney, Caroline B. *Night School*. School.

Cramer, Alexander. *A Night in Moonbeam County*. Short Stories.

King, Stephen. *Nightmares and Dreamscapes*. Short Stories.

Macdonald, Caroline. *Hostilities: Nine Bizarre Stories*. Short Stories.

Resnick, Mike, Martin H. Greenberg, and Loren D. Estleman, eds. *Deals with the Devil*. Short Stories.

Stanley, G. E. *Happy Deathday to You and Other Stories to Give You Nightmares*. Short Stories.

Stoker, Bram. *Dracula*. Classics.

Westall, Robert. *Shades of Darkness*. Short Stories.

Whitcher, Susan. *Real Mummies Don't Bleed*. Short Stories.

Young, Richard, and Judy Dockrey Young, eds. *Ozark Ghost Stories*. Short Stories.

Zweifel, Karyn. *Southern Vampires*. Short Stories.

21 Human Rights

"Until justice is blind to color, until education is unaware of race, until opportunity is unconcerned with the color of men's skin, emancipation will be a proclamation but not a fact."

Lyndon B. Johnson

"You could smell gunfire everywhere. Children were dying in the streets, and as they were dying, the others marched forward, facing guns. . . . But the determination, the thirst for freedom in the children's hearts was such that they were prepared to face those machine guns with stones. This is what happens when you hunger for freedom, when you want to break those chains of oppression."

Winnie Mandela

21.1 Archer, Jules. **Rage in the Streets: Mob Violence in America.** Illustrated by Lydia J. Hess. Browndeer Press / Harcourt Brace, 1994. 163 pp. ISBN 0-15-277691-5. Nonfiction.

Mob violence has been a phenomenon in this country since its inception. The author examines the history of mob violence in light of such questions as: Why does it happen? What causes normally peaceful people to act as a violent force? What happens when those in authority sanction violence by the police or the military?

Notable 1994 Children's Trade Books in the Field of Social Studies

21.2 Carter, Jimmy. **Talking Peace: A Vision for the Next Generation.** Dutton Children's Books, 1995. 195 pp. ISBN 0-525-45517-5. Nonfiction.

Talking Peace is a call for peace throughout all aspects of life on both the individual and world levels. This book promotes peace from the presidency to the classroom by offering vignettes from Jimmy Carter's own life about his struggles to create a more tolerant world, both as president and private citizen. Examples of how to negotiate and maintain peace are offered.

Notable 1995 Children's Trade Books in the Field of Social Studies

21.3 Dolan, Edward F. **Your Privacy: Protecting It in a Nosy World.** Cobblehill Books/Dutton, 1995. 119 pp. ISBN 0-525-65187-X. Nonfiction.

The electronic age of information-gathering and sharing is threatening individuals' rights to privacy, according to the author of this book. Personal information about citizens is being collected and shared through computer databases for both legal and illegal purposes. The law and the Constitution are designed to protect one's rights to privacy, but technology is stretching the limits of that right. A "What You Can Do" section lists ways each individual can help protect every citizen's right to privacy.

21.4   Dunbar, Robert E. **Homosexuality.** Enslow, 1995. 104 pp. ISBN 0-89490-665-8. Nonfiction.

For generations, homosexuality has only been whispered about, provoking fear and misunderstanding. This book, part of the series called Issues in Focus, presents current scientific research on the causes of homosexuality, legal issues surrounding the gay rights movement, and the views of gays and lesbians as well as those who oppose them. A bibliography is included. ER

21.5   Duvall, Lynn. **Respecting Our Differences: A Guide to Getting Along in a Changing World.** Edited by Pamela Espeland. Free Spirit, 1994. 199 pp. ISBN 0-915793-72-5. Nonfiction.

Based on the ideas that prejudice comes from fear, fear is caused by ignorance, and knowledge can overcome fear, Duvall uses thought-provoking questions, interesting personal stories, and entertaining group activities to make learning about individual differences fun. Learning erases fear and prejudice, promotes tolerance, and benefits the individual, the larger society, and the world. A resource list and bibliography are included in this volume from the Multicultural Issues series. MC

Notable 1994 Children's Trade Books in the Field of Social Studies

21.6   Franklin, Paula A. **Melting Pot or Not? Debating Cultural Identity.** Enslow, 1995. 112 pp. ISBN 0-89490-644-5. Nonfiction.

Clear prose and eye-catching photographs direct attention to this timely topic. Students needing a brief overview of the "melting pot" concept will find a glossary and leads to other resources, along with chapters covering the sweep of United States history and the way it appears from the perspectives of various ethnic groups. ER MC

21.7   Freedman, Russell. **Kids at Work: Lewis Hine and the Crusade against Child Labor.** Photography by Lewis Hine. Clarion Books, 1994. 104 pp. ISBN 0-395-58703-4. Nonfiction.

The history of child labor abuses in the early part of the twentieth century is depicted with startling clarity through the photographs of schoolteacher and social reformer Lewis Hine. The text tells the story of Hine's life and his successes in changing child labor laws, while his fifty-seven photographs of children at work reveal the pain and hopelessness of their lives, which caused the courts to grant human rights to America's children.

ALA Best Books for Young Adults, 1995
School Library Journal Best Books, 1995

Publisher's Weekly Best Books, 1995
NCTE Orbis Pictus Honor Book, 1995
Notable 1994 Children's Trade Books in the Field of Social Studies
IRA Teacher's Choice, 1996

21.8   Gay, Kathlyn. **Rights and Respect: What You Need to Know about Gender Bias and Sexual Harassment.** The Millbrook Press, 1995. 128 pp. ISBN 1-56294-493-2. Nonfiction.

Using real-life examples, Gay examines sexual harassment from historical, legal, and personal perspectives. What conduct constitutes sexual harassment, the legal rights of victims, and the effect of harassment on both the accuser and the accused are detailed in an effort to clarify a complex and emotional social issue. Many schools and businesses are attacking the problem by offering programs that increase awareness and sensitivity. A resource guide for help and information is included.

21.9   Gillam, Scott. **Discrimination: Prejudice in Action.** Enslow,1995. 128 pp. ISBN 0-89490-643-7. Nonfiction.

Discrimination means treating people differently because of their unique traits. This informational book from the Multicultural Issues series includes specific examples of actions taken against individuals because of prejudice about gender, mental or physical disability, race, sexual orientation, or age. Each chapter focuses on one area of discrimination and includes questions to consider, information about legal actions, and suggestions for ways to combat discrimination. A discussion about the future is followed by addresses of resources and a glossary. ER MC

21.10   Gottfried, Ted. **Privacy: Individual Right v. Social Needs.** The Millbrook Press, 1994. 112 pp. ISBN 1-56294-403-7. Nonfiction.

Who protects our right to privacy? What areas of our lives can we reasonably expect to keep private? Violations of citizens' privacy occur daily through the actions of the media and law enforcement agencies, through searches and drug testing, through disclosures of confidential medical information, and in computer-generated dossiers. Gottfried attempts to define the complex nature of privacy, its legal, moral, and ethical aspects, and how it is protected through U.S. courts. Arguments by those who are adamant to protect this right and by those who believe that the welfare of the larger society must sometimes take precedence are explored though discussions of hot issues such as abortion and AIDS.

21.11   Guernsey, JoAnn Bren. **Sexual Harassment: A Question of Power.** Lerner, 1995. 95 pp. ISBN 0-8225-2608-5. Nonfiction.

From the schoolroom to the courtroom, from the workplace to the military, Guernsey looks at sexual harassment and its effect on society and individuals. Presenting this complex issue in an unbiased way, Guernsey cites case histories that reflect how society and the courts define sexual harassment, what actions victims can take, and what progress is being made in reducing its incidence.

21.12   Haskins, James. **The Scottsboro Boys.** Henry Holt, 1994. 118 pp. ISBN 0-8050-2206-6. Nonfiction.

What started out as a hobo train ride turned into a nightmare for nine black youths in Scottsboro, Alabama, in 1931. They were charged with the rape of two white girls, found guilty, and sentenced to death. *The Scottsboro Boys* describes their plight and also shows the prejudiced attitude of Southern judges, lawyers, and juries at the time and the horrible conditions of Alabama jails. The book also details the struggle between the NAACP and a Communist Party organization to defend the Scottsboro boys, a tension which continued for several years. MC

21.13   Meyer, Carolyn. **Drummers of Jericho.** Harcourt Brace, 1995. 308 pp. ISBN 0-15-200441-6. Fiction.

Moving from Denver to Jericho to spend her freshman year of high school with her father, Pazit Trujillo, a fourteen-year-old Jewish girl, discovers how difficult it is to adjust to life in the overwhelmingly "Christian" town. Not only is she an outsider because she is new in town, she is also shunned when she refuses to march in the formation of a cross for the band's big performance. But with the help of her parents, the ACLU, and her only friend, Billy, Pazit decides to stand up for her civil rights and fight for her religious freedom. MC

21.14   Newman, Gerald, and Eleanor Newman Layfield. **Racism: Divided by Color.** Enslow, 1995. 112 pp. ISBN 0-89490-641-0. Nonfiction.

Racism in America is embedded in our history, and our society suffers from its effects today. True-life examples are used to examine the causes of racism and the effects racism has on individuals and society, and practical ways concerned citizens can use to identify and work to erase the problem are given. Part of the Multicultural Issues series. MC

21.15   Sawyer, Kem Knapp. **Refugees: Seeking a Safe Haven.** Enslow, 1995. 128 pp. ISBN 0-89490-663-1. Nonfiction.

Imagine having to leave your home with only the clothes on your back and the few things you could carry. That is what millions of people are forced to do each year as the result of religious and political conflicts and economic problems in countries around the world. Learn why they must flee, the problems they encounter as refugees, and what the world community is doing to help them. A bibliography and a source list of agencies that help refugees are included. Part of the Multicultural Issues series. MC

21.16   Sherrow, Victoria. **The U.S. Health Care Crisis: The Fight over Access, Quality, and Cost.** The Millbrook Press, 1994. 128 pp. ISBN 1-56294-364-2. Nonfiction.

More than thirty-seven million Americans are without health care insurance. For those fortunate enough to have insurance, high premiums do not always ensure proper coverage or care. The cost of the American health care system, desperately in need of improvement, is astronomical for all concerned—individuals, businesses, and government. *The U.S. Health Care Crisis* traces the evolution of the current system and examines various proposed solutions, including President Clinton's plan. Key elements any new system would need to address such as costs, benefits, Medicaid, Medicare, managed care, and malpractice reform are discussed as well as issues of government involvement, provider choices, personal responsibilities, and monetary sources.

21.17   Sidel, Ruth. **Battling Bias: The Struggle for Identity and Community on College Campuses.** Viking, 1994. 290 pp. ISBN 0-670-84112-9. Nonfiction.

Battling Bias explores, through firsthand accounts, how the attitudes and values of society shape the student body makeup of U.S. college campuses and affect the attitudes and actions found there. Society's class structures and grossly unequal primary and secondary school systems play an important role in college admissions, while such issues as immigration, racism, sexism, anti-Semitism, and homophobia follow students into their new environment. There is little chance of true multiculturalism and acceptance inside the college community while the problems noted still permeate society in general, and students share here their experiences of activism, insecurity, fear, embarrassment, pain, isolation, and loneliness. There is, however, a thread of hope as students attribute their intellectual and emotional growth to their campus experiences and involvement. MC

21.18   Terkel, Susan Neiburg. **People Power: A Look at Nonviolent Action and Defense.** Lodestar Books / Dutton, 1996. 138 pp. ISBN 0-525-67434-9. Nonfiction.

An individual person, a small group, or a large crowd—each has the ability to make a difference in the world through peaceful means. *People Power* offers a way to deal with conflict without using violence. This comprehensive book includes straightforward discussions about the principles of nonviolence as well as methods and training for nonviolent actions. It is an excellent read for thought-provoking discussions on alternatives to violence in our society.

21.19   Zeinert, Karen. **Free Speech: From Newspapers to Music Lyrics.** Enslow, 1995. 128 pp. ISBN 0-89490-634-8. Nonfiction.

Music and movies that offend some people, speeches that cause others to riot, news reports that leave nothing to the imagination, books that go against the grain—are such expressions protected under the First Amendment or are they overstepping the bounds? Trace the controversial history of free speech and explore some of the challenges that have tested it, from flag burnings to drug tests. Presenting only the facts and leaving judgments to the reader, *Free Speech* examines the ongoing debate between those who wish to stretch the limits and those who wish to set them.

Titles Annotated in Other Chapters Related to Human Rights

Able, Deborah. *Hate Groups*. Political Science.

Beals, Melba Pattillo. *Warriors Don't Cry: A Searing Memoir of the Battle to Integrate Little Rock's Central High*. Autobiography.

Cox, Vic. *The Challenge of Immigration*. Political Science.

Fireside, Harvey, and Sarah Betsy Fuller. *Brown v. Board of Education: Equal Schooling for All*. Political Science.

Fremon, David K. *Japanese-American Internment in American History*. History.

Herda, D. J. *Furman v. Georgia: The Death Penalty Case*. Political Science.

Herda, D. J. *New York Times v. United States: National Security and Censorship*. Political Science.

Herda, D. J. *Roe v. Wade: The Abortion Question*. Political Science.

Hoig, Stan. *Sequoyah: The Cherokee Genius*. Autobiography.

Kort, Michael G. *China under Communism*. History.

Kuklin, Susan. *Irrepressible Spirit: Conversations with Human Rights Activists*. Diaries.

LeVert, Marianne. *The Welfare System: Help or Hindrance to the Poor?* Political Science.

McCall, Nathan. *Makes Me Wanna Holler: A Young Black Man in America*. Autobiography.

Meltzer, Milton. *Cheap Raw Material*. College.

Old, Wendie. *Marian Wright Edelman: Fighting for Children's Rights*. Autobiography.

Ousseimi, Maria. *Caught in the Crossfire: Growing Up in a War Zone*. War.

Rappaport, Doreen. *The Sacco-Vanzetti Trial*. Political Science.

Rappaport, Doreen. *Tinker vs. Des Moines: Student Rights on Trial*. Political Science.

Riley, Gail Blasser. *Miranda v. Arizona: Rights of the Accused*. Political Science.

Sherrow, Victoria. *Gideon v. Wainwright: Free Legal Counsel*. Political Science.

Stefoff, Rebecca. *Nelson Mandela: Hero for Democracy*. Autobiography.

Symynkywicz, Jeffrey. *Václav Havel and the Velvet Revolution*. Autobiography.

Velásquez, Gloria. *Juanita Fights the School Board*. School.

A World in Our Hands: Written, Illustrated, and Edited by Young People of the World in Honor of the Fiftieth Anniversary of the United Nations. Diaries.

22 Humor and Satire

"The essence of humor is sensibility; warm tender fellow feeling with all forms of existence."

Thomas Carlyle

"Everything is funny as long as it happens to somebody else."

Will Rogers

22.1   Barreca, Regina, editor. **The Penguin Book of Women's Humor.** Penguin, 1996. 658 pp. ISBN 0-14-017294-7. Fiction / Nonfiction.

This wide-ranging anthology spans the diversity of women's humor, from the satire and social commentary of Jane Austen, Erma Bombeck, and Paula Poundstone to the dry wit of Nora Ephron and Shirley Jackson. The collection is alphabetized by author and indexed by topics such as anger, domesticity, homosexuality, marriage and divorce, money, and ethnicity. Selections from over two hundred authors celebrate women's humor through storytelling, poetry, cartoons, letters, speeches, novel excerpts, and one-liners.

22.2   Brooks, Charles, editor. **Best Editorial Cartoons of the Year: 1994 Edition.** Pelican, 1994. 191 pp. ISBN 1-56554-011-5. Fiction. **Best Editorial Cartoons of the Year: 1995 Edition.** Pelican, 1995. 206 pp. ISBN 1-56554-117-0. Fiction.

Do you want to review significant events of 1993 and 1994 and have fun at the same time? Try the twenty-second and twenty-third editions of *Best Editorial Cartoons.* More than 190 cartoonists from the United States and Canada are included, as well as all the cartoons that have won major awards for excellence. Families, schools, the environment, politics: every institution is creatively lambasted. The cartoons are categorized by topic, and a brief synopsis covers the year's highlights. You'll laugh and you'll see the world through new eyes.

22.3   DeBartolo, Dick. **Good Days and Mad: A ~~Historical~~ Hysterical Tour behind the Scenes at *Mad* Magazine.** Thunder's Mouth Press, 1994. 306 pp. ISBN 1-56025-077-1. Nonfiction.

This tribute to the recently deceased founder and forty-year publisher of *Mad* magazine, Bill Gaines, reads more like a current issue and contains many hilarious pieces of artwork from past issues of the magazine. The humor that made *Mad* famous (notorious?) is blended with anecdotes that show Gaines and his "usual gang of idiots" to be as offbeat as readers would expect. The author has been a *Mad* writer for over twenty-five years. Calling all *Mad* fans!

School Library Journal Best Books, 1995 (Adult Books for Young Adults)

22.4 Elfman, Eric. **Almanac of the Gross, Disgusting, and Totally Repulsive: A Compendium of Fulsome Facts.** Illustrated by Ginny Pruitt. KidBacks / Random House, 1994. 80 pp. 0-679-85805-9. Nonfiction.

This is one book that delivers exactly what the title promises! The squeamish shouldn't even read the back cover. Arranged into categories (Gross Guts, Nauseating Nature, The Gagging Gourmet, Offensive Entertainment, and Hideous History) and clearly explained, the facts in this collection are also rated according to their degree of grossness, based on a scale of from one to three barf bags. Brief, but truly revolting, the volume even includes an index. ER

ALA Quick Picks for Young Adults, 1995

22.5 Gamble, Ed. **You Get Two for the Price of One!** Forewords by George Bush and Gerald Ford. Pelican, 1995. 160 pp. ISBN 1-56554-128-6. Nonfiction.

Ed Gamble, syndicated cartoonist for the *Florida Times-Union,* offers his recent cartoons dating back to 1992 in a collection that tackles the presidents and their first ladies, health care, foreign policy, abortion, school prayer, and O. J. Simpson! It is arranged without introduction, according to general topic areas. ER

22.6 Groom, Winston. **Gump and Co..** Pocket Books, 1996. 242 pp. ISBN 0-671-52264-7. Fiction.

The further adventures and misadventures of Forrest Gump are chronicled in this first-person, Huck Finn–style narrative, which takes the reader through the 1980s and 1990s. Forrest meets such well-known people as Oliver North, Jim Baker, Ronald Reagan, and a number of other personalities as he bumbles his way through the Iran-contra scandal, the Gulf War, and the fall of the Berlin Wall. Strong language.

22.7 Handelsman, Walt. **Political Gumbo: A Collection of Editorial Cartoons.** Pelican, 1994. 160 pp. ISBN 1-56554-054-9. Fiction.

Enjoying a tour of the Nixon Library, a middle-aged woman comments to her husband, "How realistic! My tour tape has an 18$\frac{1}{2}$ minute gap in it!" Walt Handelsman nails the economy, the environment, crime . . . and of course politics and politicians, with deadly accuracy and unforgettable imagery. The work of this brilliant cartoonist will keep you laughing throughout!

22.8 Keller, Beverly. **The Amazon Papers.** Browndeer Press / Harcourt Brace, 1996. 150 pp. ISBN 0-15-201345-8. Fiction.

At sixteen, Iris is every parent's dream child; she is never in trouble, she makes straight A's, and she is a star athlete. But when her mother goes away and Iris manages to crash her mom's car, she makes matters worse by engaging in a bizarre scheme to earn money for the repairs. At the same time, she discovers that she is the object of the attentions of two motorcycle riders; at least one of whom, Byron, turns out to be as full of surprises as she is.

22.9   Locher, Dick. **The Daze of Whine and Neurosis.** Foreword by Jack Fuller. Pelican, 1995. 160 pp. ISBN 1-56554-156-1. Nonfiction.

This collection features recent (1992–93) efforts by *Chicago Tribune* editorial cartoonist Dick Locher. Winner of the 1983 Pulitzer Prize for cartooning, Locher proves that his pen is mightier than the sword by aiming at an array of topical targets including politics, race relations, abortion, taxes, and sex education. Most provoke a ticklish and uncomfortable amusement that his editor calls "the laughter of truth."

22.10   Peters, Mike. **Grimmy: The Postman Always Screams Twice!** Tor Books / Tom Doherty Associates, 1996. 128 pp. ISBN 0-312-86103-6.

This all-new collection of the popular comic strip "Mother Goose and Grimm" includes a sixteen-page full-color "Best of the Sunday Comics" section. Funny stuff! ER

22.11   Petras, Ross, and Kathryn Petras, editors. **The 776 Even Stupider Things Ever Said.** HarperPerennial / HarperCollins, 1994. 229 pp. ISBN 0-06-095059-5. Nonfiction.

This collection of bloopers includes typos, Spoonerisms, unfortunate syntax, misused words, improper translations, and simple accidents of speech, including some that are quite crass or lewd. All are claimed to be actual quotations with their sources duly attributed. The ostensible categorization is actually part of the humor, so it is unlikely to be a practical reference source for quotations. ER

ALA Quick Picks for Young Adults, 1995

22.12   Petras, Ross, and Kathryn Petras, editors. **The 776 Nastiest Things Ever Said.** HarperPerennial / HarperCollins, 1995. 224 pp. ISBN 0-06-095060-9. Nonfiction.

For those with a pronounced mean streak, this collection of vicious putdowns of prominent personalities by others of the same rank will bring a perverse delight. ER

22.13   Townsend, Sue. **Adrian Mole: The Lost Years.** Soho, 1994. 309 pp. ISBN 1-56947-015-4. Fiction.

Adrian is back! If you haven't read the hysterically funny novel *Diary of Adrian Mole, Age 13 3/4,* do it now. And if you have, you'll find the same funny, frustratingly dense eternal adolescent, also known as "England's Foremost Nerd." Believe it or not, after innumerable adventures, amorous and otherwise, Adrian finally (at the age of twenty-four) achieves some degree of maturity, and his journal entries on his way there will keep you entertained.

22.14 Walker, Barbara K., compiler. **Laughing Together: Giggles and Grins from around the Globe.** Illustrated by Simms Taback. Free Spirit Publishing in cooperation with the U.S. Committee for UNICEF, 1992. 108 pp. ISBN 0-915793-37-7. Fiction.

"What's the quickest way to make a friend of someone? Find something you can laugh at together." This book will make friends for you from Kuwait to Latvia. Did you know that the egg is the subject of more jokes around the world than any other item? If you've got something goofy in mind, you can find a silly counterpart from any of dozens of different countries. Each joke is written in its original language as well as in English, and embellished with engaging illustrations. MC WL

22.15 Wynne-Jones, Tim. **Some of the Kinder Planets: Stories by Tim Wynne-Jones.** Orchard Books, 1995. 130 pp. ISBN 0-531-09451-0. Fiction.

Aliens dressed in red flannel p.j.'s abduct a poor country boy; a pomegranate saves Harriet's solar system project; a boy with a winning smile and the intestinal equivalent of a battlefield pastes little papers all over his torso; Cluny publishes a 'zine for people with weird ("unusual") names. These captivating stories demonstrate that friendship doesn't have to be sentimental, that even school principals have a sense of humor, and that personalities of the wacky type are endearing. MC

Governor General's Award for Children in Canada on original publication, 1993

Titles Annotated in Other Chapters Related to Humor and Satire

Asprin, Robert. *Sweet Myth-tery of Life*. Fantasy.

Conford, Ellen. *I Love You, I Hate You, Get Lost*. Short Stories.

DeChancie, John. *Bride of the Castle*. Fantasy.

Friesner, Esther. *Majyk by Hook or Crook*. Fantasy.

Juster, Norton. *Otter Nonsense*. Language.

Kimmel, Eric A., retold by. *The Adventures of Hershel of Ostropol*. Myths.

Manes, Stephen. *An Almost Perfect Game*. Sports.

Regan, Dian Curtis. *Princess Nevermore*. Fantasy.

Vande Velde, Vivian. *Tales from the Brothers Grimm and the Sisters Weird*. Myths.

Watt-Evans, Lawrence, and Esther M. Friesner. *Split Heirs*. Fantasy.

23 Language and Languages

"Once a word has been allowed to escape, it cannot be recalled."

Horace

"A sharp tongue is the only edged tool that grows keener with constant use."

Washington Irving

23.1 Agee, Jon. **Go Hang a Salami! I'm a Lasagna Hog! and Other Palindromes.** Sunburst / Farrar, Straus and Giroux, 1994. N.p. ISBN 0-374-33473-0. Nonfiction.

What's a palindrome? A word or sentence that says the same thing whether it's read forward or backward. Many people are familiar with the simple ones: "Madam, I'm Adam"; or "Able was I ere I saw Elba." But Jon Agee's palindromes go way beyond Adam and Elba, with drawings to illustrate such gems as "I, Madam, I made a radio! So I dared! Am I mad? Am I?" and "Tina! Emil! I mean it!" An enjoyable introduction to one of language's goofier games. ER

23.2 Agee, Jon. **So Many Dynamos! and Other Palindromes.** Farrar, Straus and Giroux, 1994. N.p. ISBN 0-374-22473-0. Fiction.

A follow-up volume to Agee's *Go Hang a Salami! I'm a Lasagna Hog!*, this collection of sixty palindromes ranges from the quirky ("straw warts," "snot or protons?") to the slightly off-color ("emu fume"—the illustration says it all). Elementary and middle school students would love some of these and the black-and-white illustrations, much to their teachers' chagrin. ER

ALA Quick Picks for Young Adults, 1995

23.3 Gobetti, Daniela, Robert A. Hall Jr., Frances Adkins Hall, and Susan Z. Garau. **2001 Italian and English Idioms.** 2nd ed. Barron's, 1996. 797 pp. ISBN 0-8120-9030-6. Nonfiction.

Here is another edition of this popular idiomatic guide to idioms. It is completely bilingual, with separate English-to-Italian and Italian-to-English sections, each section with its own index, all entries alphabetically arranged by keyword, each definition showing the phrase used in a sentence, and the sentence translated. Although a bit bulky for travelers, this book would be useful for instructors and students of the language.

23.4   Juster, Norton. **Otter Nonsense.** Illustrated by Michael Witte. Books of Wonder / Morrow Junior Books, 1994. N.p. ISBN 0-688-12282-5. Nonfiction.

Otter Nonsense is an enjoyable little (both in length and in page size) book of puns involving a variety of animals. Juster's puns are funny, and Witte's new watercolor and pen-and-ink drawings twist themselves into all manner of forms in order to illustrate such ideas as "pupulation explosion," "apetite," and "larks and bagels." ER

ALA Quick Picks for Young Adults, 1995

23.5   Kendris, Christopher, Ph.D. **501 Spanish Verbs.** 4th ed. Barron's, 1996. ISBN 0-8120-9282-1. Nonfiction.

The verbs in this very useful volume are alphabetically arranged and fully conjugated in all tenses, and this edition includes two new features: (1) verb drills and tests with the answers explained, and (2) definitions of basic grammatical terms with examples.

23.6   Kincher, Jonni. **The First Honest Book about Lies.** Free Spirit, 1992. 170 pp. ISBN 0-915793-43-1. Nonfiction.

Through the use of anecdotes, newspaper factoids, advertising, mind puzzles, tricks, and games, Kincher has created a book that will "help you become a wiser consumer, a more thoughtful and responsible citizen, and a better friend to yourself and others. It can give you a clearer picture of your personal standards for honesty and truth." And it's fun, too! ER

23.7   Lang, Paul. **The English Language Debate: One Nation, One Language.** Enslow, 1995. 112 pp. ISBN 0-89490-642-9. Nonfiction.

This thought-provoking book presents the historical and current overview of the problem: Is English the "official" language of America? Can its status be legislated? How far must the government be expected to go in accommodating the needs of non-English-speaking immigrants? This book is aimed at young readers, using examples of teenagers who have overcome the language barrier in becoming "Americans," as well as the opinions of language experts, sociologists, and legislators. Part of the Multicultural Issues series. ER MC

23.8   Milne, A. A. (inspired by). **Pooh's Little Instruction Book.** Illustrated by Ernest H. Shepard. Dutton Books, 1995. N.p. ISBN 0-525-45366-0. Fiction.

This is a very small book that could be subtitled "Everything I Need to Know I Learned from Pooh." Most of the epigrams culled from the Pooh books are positive little thoughts: "Brains first and then hard work" or "Nobody can be un-cheered with a balloon," but there are some "up-with-dumb" Poohish thoughts like "Spelling isn't everything. There are days when spelling Tuesday simply doesn't count," or "Those who are clever, who have Brains, never understand anything." ER

23.9   Nash, Helen. **Challenging Cryptograms.** Sterling, 1994. 128 pp. ISBN 0-8069-0594-8. Nonfiction.

Cryptograms are entertaining and challenging for students who like to solve puzzles and enjoy language. This collection of four hundred famous and not-so-famous quotations on topics ranging from television to politics, from dieting to philosophy, are written as cryptograms. The author suggests ways of solving the puzzles, as well as giving two clues for each puzzle and the solution for each. In addition to offering practice with language, the volume is also a treasure trove of insightful and often funny quotations about most aspects of modern life.

Titles Annotated in Other Chapters Related to Language and Languages

Petras, Ross, and Kathryn Petras, eds. *The 776 Even Stupider Things Ever Said.* Humor.

Petras, Ross, and Kathryn Petras, eds. *The 776 Nastiest Things Ever Said.* Humor.

24 Mysteries, Spies, and Crime

"As for the people who say murder stories incite to murder, one is tempted merely to the reckless reply that their criticisms of murder stories really might."

G. K. Chesterton

"Murder will out, cirtain, it will not fail."
Geoffrey Chaucer

24.1 ab Hugh, Dafydd. **The Pit.** HarperPaperbacks, 1996. 234 pp. ISBN 0-06-106291-X. Fiction.

In this third book of the Swept Away series, Jeanette kills a fellow teenager in self-defense—or was she wrong in her perceptions and so simply committed murder? She is determined to lay her guilt to rest by proving to herself that she was right. The search leads to terror and beyond in this fast-moving suspense novel. ER

24.2 Anderson, Kevin J., and Doug Beason. **Virtual Destruction.** Ace Books, 1996. 327 pp. ISBN 0-441-00308-7. Fiction.

This story is mostly a murder mystery, with a touch of science fiction. When a famous, controversial scientist is found dead, FBI agent Craig Kreident is assigned to investigate, and he finds a web of intrigue surrounding the dead man's virtual reality project. As for the conclusion, expect the unexpected!

24.3 Asimov, Janet. **Murder at the Galactic Writers' Society.** Daw Books, 1995. 316 pp. ISBN 0-88677-644-9. Fiction.

A newly activated android, Arda, and an Erthumoi writer from Earth encounter murder and treachery as they host a reception for the Galactic Writers' Society in this second volume in the *Isaac's Universe* series. Arda, accompanying newlywed Crotonites Princess Vush and Kolix on their honeymoon as a bodyguard and at the same time as a secret agent for the Terran Federal Bureau of Investigation, must solve the mystery of the murder and the disappearance of the irreplaceable ruulogem jewel. As an android, Arda has the same rights and responsibilities as do humans and the other races, yet she constantly battles both human and alien prejudice against her origins.

24.4 Barcus, Audrey. **Dangerous Secrets.** Avon Flare, 1996. 183 pp. ISBN 0-380-78207-3. Fiction.

Erika has to live with her mom and her stepfather and stepsister while her journalist father is on assignment in the Middle East. Her stepfather, a police officer, is investigating the suicide of a boy from Erika's school who had given her an envelope to keep safe just the day before. Mysterious teenage suicides, a pornography ring, and suspicious goings-on at school enmesh Erika in a web of intrigue.

24.5 Beere, Peter. **Kiss of Death.** Illustrated by David Wyatt. Scholastic, 1994. 174 pp. 0-590-20372-X. Fiction.

Eleanor, Sadie's new stepsister, accuses Sadie of possessing "the kiss of death" because all that has been important in Sadie's life has been taken from her. Mysteriously, Sadie's enemies begin to disappear, too. Does Sadie truly have "the kiss of death," or is an avenging angel eliminating her enemies?

24.6 Bellairs, John. Completed by Brad Strickland. **The Drum, the Doll, and the Zombie.** Dial Books for Young Readers, 1994. 153 pp. ISBN 0-8037-1462-9. Fiction.

At a party for Dr. Coote, a specialist in the folklore of magic at the University of New Hampshire, Johnny Dixon, Fergie Ferguson, and Professor Childermass laugh at Dr. Coote's souvenir drum from his trip to New Orleans. That is, until they try it out. Next thing they know, the four are embroiled in a voodoo mystery, fighting the terrifying Priests of the Midnight Blood, and trying to save their lives. ER

24.7 Bennett, Jill. **Baa Baa Dead Sheep.** Scholastic, 1993. 219 pp. ISBN 0-590-48507-5. Fiction.

Beth Green and the SAPS are preparing to perform their latest play, "Bella," a murder mystery, when the Tree Theatre's caretaker is murdered. Beth finds that she suspects everyone and can no longer trust even her best friend. The Tree Theatre becomes a dangerous place for Beth as she and the other members of the theater company attempt to put on their play despite murder and unexplained accidents, in this volume from the Point Crime series.

24.8 Bingley, Margaret. **A Dramatic Death.** Scholastic, 1994. 201 pp. 0-590-20371-1. Fiction.

In this volume from the Point Crime series, a group of young people performing a play struggle with their relationships as rehearsals turn into frightening, real-life drama, complete with terrifying accidents and eventually death. Unbelievably, one of their group is a cold-blooded killer!

24.9 Byars, Betsy. **The Dark Stairs: A Herculeah Jones Mystery.** Viking, 1994. 130 pp. ISBN 0-670-85487-5. Fiction.

An unquenchable curiosity is one of would-be sleuth Herculeah Jones's best assets. It can also land her in dangerous and frightening situations. The only child of Chico Jones, a police detective, and Mim Jones, a private investigator, Herculeah seems inevitably drawn to solving mysteries. In *The Dark Stairs*, Herculeah and her friend, Meat, get more danger and intrigue than they bargain for when they attempt to piece together a mystery involving a creepy old house nicknamed "Dead Oaks," a huge and sinister man with "million-year-old-breath," and a missing body. ER

24.10   Carris, Joan. **Beware the Ravens, Aunt Morbelia.** Little, Brown, 1995. 141 pp. ISBN 0-316-12961-5. Fiction.

A trip to England and the family estate of Harrowood by irrepressible Aunt Morbelia, her great-nephew Todd, and his best friend Jeff turns into a spine-tingling adventure when the trio are spooked by ominous, haunting moans, intrigued by a puzzling journal, and followed by an eccentric variety of overly curious strangers. ER

24.11   Cascone, A. G. **In a Crooked Little House.** WestWind / Troll Associates, 1994. 236 pp. ISBN 0-8167-3532-8. Fiction.

Students, teachers, and alumni of the boarding school Huntington Prep are entangled in a web of intrigue, suspicion, and danger in this psychological thriller. Beautiful and unsuspecting Casey is stalked by a crazed killer who knows her every move. She and her schoolmates are in danger every minute. ER

24.12   Charyn, Jerome, editor. **The New Mystery: The International Association of Crime Writers' Essential Crime Writing of the Late Twentieth Century.** Byron Preiss / Plume, 1994. 387 pp. ISBN 0-452-27133-9. Fiction.

The International Association of Crime Writers was formed in 1987 to support the genre of crime and mystery writing as it is written in a variety of cultures. This anthology reflects how mystery writing has come of age around the world by presenting authors whose commentary on modern urban life chills the reader's blood. MC WL

24.13   Clark, Mary Higgins, editor. **Bad Behavior.** Gulliver Books / Harcourt Brace, 1995. 306 pp. ISBN 0-15-200179-4. Fiction.

The International Association of Crime Writers presents a collection of crime and suspense stories both new and classic. Voodoo revenge, the lure of high-priced basketball shoes, the desperation of homelessness, a child with no past, and a deadly werewolf game are the subjects of intrigue by authors such as P. D. James, Thomas Adcock, Joyce Carol Oates, Mauricio-José Schwarz, Eric Weiner, and Sara Paretsky. MC

24.14   Cooney, Linda A. **Samantha Crane on the Run.** HarperPaperbacks, 1996. 234 pp. ISBN 0-06-106409-2. Fiction.

Fans of R. L. Stine and Christopher Pike can now enjoy a new series in their favorite genre. Samantha is bright and pretty but far too independent to hang with the popular crowd of slavish followers—instead Sam prefers helping at a local youth center. When a girl from the center is murdered, the case is assigned to Sam's mother, a rookie cop, and they are both drawn into the tragedy more personally than they ever could have predicted. ER (Other books in the series are *Samantha Crane Crossing the Line*, 218 pp., ISBN 0-06-106410-6, and *Samantha Crane on Her Own*, 264 pp., ISBN 0-06-106412-2.)

24.15   Coville, Bruce. **The A.I. Gang: Operation Sherlock.** Minstrel / Pocket Books, 1995. 211 pp. ISBN 0-671-89249-5. Fiction.

Five brilliant kids from different parts of the U.S. are brought together on a small South Pacific island when their scientist parents are recruited for a project to develop an artificial intelligence. The kids use their own intelligence and talents to discover and frustrate the schemes of both a fanatic opposed to the project and a spy. ER

24.16   Davidson, Nicole. **Farewell Kiss.** Avon Flare, 1995. 196 pp. ISBN 0-380-72246-1. Fiction.

The third volume in the Final Cruise Trilogy finds Carol Walters searching for the truth behind the mysterious killings in *First Kiss* and *Kiss of Death*. Carol is afraid that someone, maybe a friend or even someone closer, wants her dead because she knows too much.

24.17   Elster, Charles Harrington, and Joseph Elliot. **Tooth and Nail: A Novel Approach to the New SAT.** Harcourt Brace, 1994. 283 pp. ISBN 0-15-601382-7. Fiction.

Caitlin Ciccone was in for more than a college education when she arrived at Holyfield. She became part of the mystery surrounding the secret society of Tooth and Nail. This volume is a mystery and more. It contains most of the words found in the Scholastic Aptitude Test, printed in boldface type for easy reference, as well as practice exercises for analogies, sentence completions, and reading comprehension and a glossary.

24.18   Emert, Phyllis Raybin. **Mysteries of Bizarre Animals and Freaks of Nature.** Illustrated by JAEL. Tor / Tom Doherty Associates, 1994. 115 pp. ISBN 0-812-53630-4. Nonfiction.

Did you know that there is a horse that can predict the future? Are you fascinated by real vampire bats? Do sea serpents, electric eels, and maneating plants sound intriguing? Would you like to read about Sparky, the yellow Lab who saved his owner's life? Then you will enjoy this collection of short tales from the Strange Unsolved Mysteries series. ER

24.19 Emert, Phyllis Raybin. **Mysteries of the Mind and the Senses.** Illustrated by JAEL. Tor / Tom Doherty Associates, 1995. 120 pp. ISBN 0-812-53633-9. Nonfiction.

Authentic and chilling accounts of premonitions of disaster, of persons with the ability to read the history of inanimate objects, of nightmares that warn of impending danger, and of places haunted by incidents from the past are collected in this volume from the Strange Unsolved Mysteries series.

24.20 Emert, Phyllis Raybin. **Mysteries of Space and the Universe.** Illustrated by JAEL. Tor / Tom Doherty Associates, 1994. 116 pp. ISBN 0-812-53631-2. Nonfiction.

From the series Strange Unsolved Mysteries comes *Mysteries of Space and the Universe.* If you are curious about the speed of light, the future of the sun, UFOs, tunnels of blackness, Planet X, life on Mars, and red glowing disks, you will enjoy these twenty exciting stories. A handy glossary and black-and-white sketches accompany the collection. ER

24.21 Emert, Phyllis Raybin. **Mysteries of Strange Appearances from Beyond.** Illustrated by JAEL. Tor / Tom Doherty Associates, 1995. 117 pp. ISBN 0-812-53632-0. Nonfiction.

A compilation of inexplicable events that have been documented by eyewitnesses make up this book, part of the Strange Unsolved Mysteries series. Phantom carriage noises, encounters with travelers from another century, ghost lights, and restless spirits are reported by those who have actually experienced these fantastic phenomena. ER

24.22 Feder, Harriet K. **Mystery of the Kaifeng Scroll: A Vivi Hartman Adventure.** Lerner, 1995. 138 pp. ISBN 0-8225-0739-0. Fiction.

Another Vivi Hartman adventure finds Vivi traveling to Turkey to visit her mother, who she finds on her arrival is missing. Vivi reluctantly accompanies an Arab student of her mother's into the Turkish countryside to solve the mystery of an ancient Chinese scroll and her mother's disappearance. MC

24.23 Fisher, Nancy. **Side Effects.** Signet, 1994. 383 pp. ISBN 0-451-18130-1. Fiction.

The desire for everlasting youth has never been more apparent than in today's world. *Side Effects,* a medical suspense novel, explores this theme as it tells the story of a remarkable drug that has the power to bring back lost youth. A brilliant young doctor, Kate Martin, buys into the Genelife miracle, even using it herself, before she begins to suspect that there is a dark and evil truth behind the initial promise and success of the miraculous drug. Kate's determination to learn the truth about Genelife draws her into a web of international intrigue, shocking revelations, and great danger.

24.24   Forrest, Elizabeth. **Death Watch.** Daw Books, 1995. 451 pp. ISBN 0-88677-648-1. Fiction.

The legacy of a deadly serial killer who escaped from prison haunts reporter Carter Wyndall, who unwittingly gave the killer a reprieve. While a fiendishly abusive husband stalks the beautiful and vulnerable Mackenzie Smith, Carter, by chance, encounters Mackenzie as she lies hurt in an emergency room. Carter helps Mackenzie fight for inner peace against forces both real and imagined that are attempting to possess her mind through virtual reality.

24.25   Gaarder, Jostein. **Sophie's World: A Novel about the History of Philosophy.** Translated by Paulette Møller. Farrar, Straus and Giroux, 1994. 394 pp. ISBN 0-374-26642-5. Fiction.

Written by a teacher of philosophy, this book is an intricate and artful examination of philosophy set in a novel about a gifted young girl named Sophie Amundsen. Sophie is presented with an unusual mystery, as well as the opportunity to learn about Western philosophy under the tutelage of a curious teacher. And it is her growing knowledge that leads Sophie to the answers she seeks. This challenging and unique novel has been a bestseller in Scandinavia and Germany. MC WL

School Library Journal Best Books, 1995 (Adult Books for Young Adults)

24.26   Hamley, Dennis. **Death Penalty.** Scholastic, 1994. 214 pp. ISBN 0-590-20356-8. Fiction.

The Radwick Rangers football team is on its way to the premier position in British soccer when team members begin to turn up savagely murdered. Revenge, illegal betting, and game fixing combine to threaten the lives of players and their chances at football fame, in this book from the Point Crime series.

24.27   Haynes, Betsy. **Deadly Deception.** Delacorte Press, 1994. 212 pp. ISBN 0-385-32067-1. Fiction.

Rich in creature comforts but neglected by her wealthy, ambitious parents, seventeen-year-old Ashlyn Brennan has just begun to form a good friendship with Mrs. Rothlis, her high school guidance counselor. But Mrs. Rothlis is soon found murdered, and Ashlyn's troubled boyfriend, Drew, is charged with the crime. In her desperate efforts to help Drew, Ashlyn pieces together not only the solution to her friend's murder, but also some sinister truths about her own identity.

ALA Quick Picks for Young Adults, 1995
IRA Teacher's Choice, 1996

24.28   King, Laurie R. **The Beekeeper's Apprentice: Or, on the Segregation of the Queen.** St. Martin's Press, 1994. 347 pp. ISBN 0-312-10423-5. Fiction.

Because her intellect is equal to his, Mary Russell dares to speak to the aging but still esteemed Sherlock Holmes when she recognizes him during a chance encounter. At fifteen, Mary is about to enter Oxford University, but her passion for close observation turns her into a student of detection as well. Will her pompous mentor accept a mere girl as a partner? Can she become worthy of his confidence? This tale moves along rapidly and offers much more than standard crime fiction fare as it explores the relationship of the two sleuths.

ALA Best Books for Young Adults, 1995

24.29   Kuraoka, Hannah. **Missing!** Avon Flare, 1995. 147 pp. ISBN 0-380-77374-0. Fiction.

Junior Kelly Donovan is known among her family members as quite the amateur detective. Since her family is constantly moving, Kelly looks at puzzles and mysteries as diversions. But this latest move to Seattle has brought a most serious crime to Kelly's door, or so she thinks. Seattle is being tormented by a baby-kidnapper, and based on what Kelly has seen he may live right next door! But will anyone believe her? Kelly sets out to prove her theory. ER MC

24.30   L'Engle, Madeleine. **Troubling a Star.** Farrar, Straus and Giroux, 1994. 296 pp. ISBN 0-374-37783-9. Fiction.

When Vicky returns to Thornhill, Connecticut, after an exciting year in New York City, she struggles to fit back into her old life and reestablish her friendship with Adam. Just as she is settling into a routine, Vicky meets Serena, Adam's great-aunt. Serena gives her a ticket to Antarctica where Adam will be working, and the mystery begins. Vicky never imagined she would become tangled up in a plot involving nuclear waste, drugs, and family secrets.

24.31   Lerangis, Peter. **Driver's Dead.** Scholastic, 1994. 217 pp. ISBN 0-590-46677-1. Fiction.

At sixteen, Kirsten Wilkes wants to drive, but she has hit a tree with her father's car, and she cannot seem to do anything right in Driver's Education. Then Rob, a slightly dangerous loner who just happens to be a good driver, offers to give her lessons. All the while, Kirsten is haunted by the suicide of Nguyen Trang, who used to sleep in the bedroom that is now Kirsten's in her family's new home. Kirsten is compelled by Trang's restless spirit to solve the mystery of Trang's death on her way to getting her license.

24.32   Moquist, Richard. **The Franklin Mysteries.** Northwest, 1994. 197 pp. ISBN 1-56901-145-1. Fiction.

Constable Wendell Franklin finds it expedient to enlist the aid of his eccentric uncle Benjamin Franklin, who as a master puzzle solver assists him in unraveling some of the more bizarre mysteries and crimes committed on the streets of Philadelphia in the 1780s.

24.33   Murphy, T. M. The Belltown Mysteries. Silver Burdett Press.
        The Secrets of Belltown. 1996. 170 pp. ISBN 0-382-39115-2.
        The Secrets of Cranberry Beach. 1997. 148 pp. ISBN 0-382-39303-1.
        Fiction.

These fast-paced mysteries feature teen detective Orville Jacques, a sophomore supersleuth devoted to his friends and to the discovery of the truth about various murders and other foul deeds. ER

24.34   Nixon, Joan Lowery. **Shadowmaker.** Delacorte Press, 1994. 197 pp. ISBN 0-385-32030-2. Fiction.

Leaving a happy, comfortable city life for a new existence in a small provincial town is hard enough on a teenager. But in her move from Houston to Kluney, Texas, tenth grader Katie Gillian finds herself enmeshed in a tangled net of fear, intimidation, and murder. Katie and her crusading newspaper columnist mother confront the dark secrets hidden beneath the wholesome veneer of this coastal town, taking on everyone from the sheriff to the powerful owners of a local oceanside cottage. Katie, a shy, sensitive dancer, learns to draw on her inner strength to combat the forces of evil in her world.

24.35   Pageler, Elaine. Riddle Street Mystery series. High Noon Books, 1994. 44 pp. Fiction.
        The Book Party Mystery. ISBN 0-87879-988-5.
        The Haunted House Mystery. ISBN 0-87879-986-9.
        The Market Stake Out Mystery. ISBN 0-87879-984-2.
        The Radio Station Mystery. ISBN 0-87879-987-7.
        The Wrong Robber Mystery. ISBN 0-87879-985-0.

Meg Green and Brad Jones work for the *City News.* These two amateur detectives, known as the Riddle Team, work along with police sergeant Ward to solve the crimes that occur on Riddle Street. A devious drug dealer, jewelry thieves, deft-handed robbers, and a bogus ghost riddle the adventures of these two supersleuths. ER

24.36   Petersen, P. J. **Liars.** Aladdin Paperbacks, 1995. 171 pp. ISBN 0-689-80130-0. Fiction.

Sam Thompson and his friend, Marty McNabb, rue the fact that they live in boring Alder Creek, a remote California town. Soon, however, Sam discovers that he has the ancient power to sense underground water using a forked stick, and the expansion of this new power even gives him an uncanny ability to determine when people are lying. When the cabin of his prospector friend is set on fire, Sam encounters many people hiding the truth from him, even his own father. MC

24.37 Posner, Richard. **Terror Runs Deep.** Archway Paperbacks / Pocket Books, 1995. 213 pp. ISBN 0-671-88745-9. Fiction.

A letter arrives for Meg Chapin offering her a summer job working for "Uncle Jack," her father's friend, on the barrier island she knew as a child. Compelled by some unidentifiable longing, Meg takes the job. After she almost drowns, a nightmare of events forces Meg to confront her terrifying past and her "Uncle Jack" in search of the truth about her mother's death.

24.38 Resnick, Mike, and Martin H. Greenberg, editors. **Sherlock Holmes in Orbit.** Daw Books, 1995. 374 pp. ISBN 0-88677-636-8. Fiction.

Sherlock Holmes lives! In the twentieth century, the nineteenth century, the future, and even the spirit world, Holmes's adventures continue to be chronicled by Dr. Watson or a close facsimile thereof. In this anthology authorized by Dame Jean Conan Doyle, Holmes detects not only from his Baker Street address but also from America, through the looking glass, in Siberia, in outer space, in the spirit world, and ultimately in cyberspace.

24.39 Rose, Malcolm. **Concrete Evidence.** Scholastic, 1995. 214 pp. 0-590-20358-4. Fiction.

Evan, Kelly, and Sarah discover their mother's body in the rubble of a collapsed wall in their garden. Someone has killed her, and despite the prospect of facing the same fate they are determined to find out who, in this exciting volume from the Point Crime series.

24.40 Schwandt, Stephen. **The Last Goodie: A Novel.** Free Spirit, 1995. 188 pp. ISBN 0-915793-79-2. Fiction.

When Marty Oliver was five, his babysitter, seventeen-year-old Stacy Davis, was kidnapped and never found. Now seventeen himself and Southwestern High's track star, just as Stacy had been, Marty is haunted by memories of that fateful night. He can't get over the feeling that somehow what Stacy screamed at her abductor holds the key to her disappearance. Marty, while searching for the answer to this haunting question, must also pursue questions about his own identity and involvement in the mystery.

24.41 Sweeney, Joyce. **Shadow.** Delacorte Press, 1994. 216 pp. ISBN 0-385-32051-5. Fiction.

Sarah Shaheen is caught in a frightening web of death and violence. The eighth grader's beloved cat, Shadow, has died, but Sarah feels certain that Shadow is with her still. Shadow visits Sarah in dreams as well as in reality, and the only person who understands this secret is the family housekeeper, Cissy. Sarah also is dealing with the horrific violence between her two competitive brothers, Patrick and Brian. The young girl's attempts to sort out the meaning of Shadow's continued presence in her life and the psychic messages she receives help Sarah to appreciate her newfound powers and to believe in her ability to use them to good ends.

ALA Best Books for Young Adults, 1995
ALA Quick Picks for Young Adults, 1995

24.42 Westall, Robert. **A Place to Hide.** Scholastic, 1994. 199 pp. ISBN 0-590-47748-X. Fiction.

Lucy knows that her father's strange behavior can be attributed to the recent death of her mother. That is, until her mother's Rembrandt etching disappears and her father hands her a suitcase filled with money and tells her to run away, change her name, and make sure that no one will ever find her. Lucy follows the instructions and learns to adapt, until she realizes she's being watched. ER

Titles Annotated in Other Chapters Related to Mysteries, Spies, and Crime

Anthony, Patricia. *Brother Termite*. Science Fiction.

Baird, Wilhelmina. *Clipjoint*. Science Fiction.

Cooney, Caroline B. *Unforgettable*. Romance.

Garland, Sherry. *Cabin 102*. Choices.

Glenn, Mel. *Who Killed Mr. Chippendale?* School.

Graf, L. A. *Traitor Winds*. Science Fiction.

Haddix, Margaret Peterson. *Running Out of Time*. Choices.

Hood, Daniel. *Wizard's Heir*. Fantasy.

Kurtz, Katherine, and Deborah Turner Harris. *Dagger Magic*. Fantasy.

Nye, Jody Lynn. *Medicine Show*. Science Fiction.

Piazza, Linda. *Evil in the Attic*. Horror.

Ransom, Bill. *ViraVax*. Science Fiction.

Reiss, Kathryn. *Pale Phoenix*. Family.

Robinson, Spider, and Jeanne Robinson. *Starmind*. Science Fiction.

Ruby, Lois. *Steal away Home*. Historical Fiction.

Sawyer, Robert J. *End of an Era*. Science Fiction.

Springer, Nancy. *Toughing It*. Death.

Steele, Allen. *The Jericho Iteration*. Science Fiction.

Steele, Allen. *The Tranquillity Alternative*. Science Fiction.

Zambreno, Mary Frances. *Journeyman Wizard*. Fantasy.

25 Myths, Legends, and Folklore

"For with their high, clear song, the Sirens bewitch him."

Homer

"Any mythology is saner than this materialism and immeasurably less difficult to believe."

G. K. Chesterton

25.1 Adler, Bill, Jr. **Tell Me a Fairy Tale: A Parent's Guide to Telling Magical and Mythical Stories.** Plume, 1995. 173 pp. ISBN 0-452-27174-6. Nonfiction.

Adler's book is fun to read even if you're not a parent or planning to tell fairy tales to anyone! Sixty-four tales, both classics and lesser-known stories from other cultures, are briefly told, along with summaries, character sketches, plot outlines, and suggestions for making each story longer or shorter, less sexist or horrifying, or more personalized or contemporary. This guide for storytellers would be useful to teachers or students in child development, literature, or social studies classes, as well as to parents, babysitters, or older siblings. MC WL

25.2 Ballinger, Erich. **Monster Manual: A Complete Guide to Your Favorite Creatures.** Lerner, 1994. 140 pp. ISBN 0-8225-0722-6. Nonfiction.

More monsters than the mind can manage appear in this encyclopedic book. The famous and not-so-famous creatures of this and other worlds pictured and discussed in these pages will have you locking the doors and checking under your bed at night. This is a good, basic source of information.

25.3 Barnes-Murphy, Frances (retold by). **The Fables of Aesop.** Collected and illustrated by Rowan Barnes-Murphy. Lothrop, Lee and Shepard, 1994. 92 pp. ISBN 0-688-07051-5. Nonfiction.

Aesop's fables? Aren't those the animal stories with "And the moral of the story is . . . " tacked onto the end? This collection is different. Over one hundred stories—some familiar, some not—are included, with either a pen-and-ink drawing or a full-color picture. And the morals are *not* included! See if you can figure them out for yourself. The editor does, however, provide an informative introduction to Aesop and his fables. ER WL

25.4   Barron, T. A. **The Lost Years of Merlin.** Philomel Books, 1996. 326 pp. ISBN 0-399-23018-1. Fiction.

Before there was King Arthur, there was Merlin. What were the origins of the great enchanter? In this first part of a planned trilogy, the boy Merlin is struggling to find his homeland and understand his magical gift, which he considers a curse. Despite our knowledge that he will survive his quest, the outcome and its cost maintain the reader's interest in this well-told tale, and leave him or her looking forward to the next two volumes. ER

25.5   Bennett, Martin (retold by). **West African Trickster Tales.** Oxford University Press, 1994. 130 pp. ISBN 0-19-274172-1. Fiction.

The trickster, a common character in many myths and folktales, is the star in these comical stories from West Africa. Here Tortoise and the ever-popular Ananse the spider are repeatedly foiled by their own tricks and greed, which are always discovered and punished. Good is always rewarded in these tales, and human foibles humorously exposed. ER MC WL

25.6   Bruchac, Joseph (told by). **Flying with the Eagle, Racing the Great Bear: Stories from Native North America.** BridgeWater Books, 1993. 128 pp. ISBN 0-8167-3026-1. Fiction.

This book is a collection of sixteen short stories from Native North America told by a professional storyteller drawing on his own Native American heritage. Each of the four sections of the book focuses on a Native American boy's rite of passage into manhood as well as on his relationship to nature. MC

25.7   Bruchac, Joseph, and Gayle Ross (told by). **The Girl Who Married the Moon: Stories from Native North America.** BridgeWater Books, 1994. 127 pp. ISBN 0-8167-3480-1. Fiction.

Celebrating a girl's passage into womanhood with ceremony and story, these tales from Native North America demonstrate the courage, intelligence, and strength women need to face adulthood. These are not the often downtrodden women of popular culture, but women who are the equals of the men they work with to sustain their native cultures. MC

Notable 1994 Children's Trade Books in the Field of Social Studies

25.8   Cohen, Barbara, and Bahija Lovejoy. **Seven Daughters and Seven Sons.** Beech Tree Paperback Books, 1994. 220 pp. ISBN 0-688-13563-3. Fiction.

Buran is one of seven daughters in her Arab family's household. In a time when women are believed to be a curse, Buran must do something to ease her father's financial situation. Buran disguises herself as a boy and sets off to seek her fortune in a man's world. Her story combines a woman's struggle and ingenuity with romance and revenge. MC WL

25.9   Cohen, Daniel. **Real Vampires.** Cobblehill Books, 1995. 111 pp. ISBN 0-525-65189-6. Fiction.

This book is a collection of accounts of supposedly "real" vampire encounters. Each short story describes a type of vampire believed to actually exist. The stories are drawn from many countries throughout the world, including China, Hungary, and other intriguing places. The author desires those interested to read for themselves and decide what they believe: Are vampires real??

25.10   Craft, M. Charlotte (told by). **Cupid and Psyche.** Illustrated by K. Y. Craft. Morrow Junior Books, 1996. 37 pp. ISBN 0-688-13163-8. Fiction.

One of the greatest love stories of all time is retold with exquisite illustrations that capture the dark and light moods of this well-known story and its celebration of beauty, bravery, and love. ER WL

25.11   Creeden, Sharon. **Fair Is Fair: World Folktales of Justice.** August House, 1994. 181 pp. ISBN 0-87483-400-7. Fiction.

Our concern with fairness transcends time and culture, as is evident in these thirty traditional stories from many countries. Notes about our legal system help readers see how modern legal issues, such as liability law, child custody disputes, and animal rights, can be related to both famous and lesser-known ancient tales. MC WL

25.12   Eliot, Alexander. **The Global Myths: Exploring Primitive, Pagan, Sacred, and Scientific Mythologies.** Truman Talley Books / Meridan, 1994. 283 pp. ISBN 0-452-01116-7. Nonfiction.

"In a time of individual and societal troubles, when there is less certainty about familiar guideposts, we may do well to reach back for the timeless wisdom of ancient stories. Every large event, personal or shared, takes us into unfamiliar territory. Mythology helps us to face the best moments and the worst." In this retelling and study of myths generated in both ancient and contemporary cultures from around the world, Eliot demonstrates the power of myth to break down barriers of time, space, and culture and to enrich our lives. MC WL

25.13   Garner, James Finn. **Politically Correct Bedtime Stories.** Macmillan, 1994. 79 pp. ISBN 0-02-542730-X. Fiction.

"There once lived an economically disadvantaged tinker and his wife. His lack of material accomplishment is not meant to imply that all tinkers are economically marginalized, or that if they are, they deserve to be so." Recognize the story these sentences introduce? *Rapunzel!* In Finn's politically correct versions of fairy tale classics, the discriminatory, sexist, or culturally biased elements have been changed in order to liberate witches, goblins, and fairies from their demeaning stereotypes and to retell the stories in ways more in keeping with our current society. The tongue-in-cheek humor and the play on the traditional language of fairy tales make for lively and thought-provoking reading.

25.14   Gay, Kathlyn. **Keep the Buttered Side Up: Food Superstitions around the World.** Illustrated by Debbie Palen. Walker, 1995. 95 pp. ISBN 0-8027-8228-0. Nonfiction.

Thirteen chapters tell the reader about superstitions from around the world. From age-old remedies to what's lucky to eat each month of the year, this book offers a wealth of information about how various cultures try to forestall fate. Also included are interesting, little-known facts, such as how much pizza Americans consume each year. MC

25.15   Goodrich, Norma Lorre. **Ancient Myths.** Meridian, 1994. 251 pp. ISBN 0-452-01129-9. Fiction.

These prose retellings of the ancient stories of several cultures (Sumer; Egypt; Crete and Greece; Troy; Persia, Iran, and Afghanistan; India; and Rome) are not for beginners. Introductions, charts, maps, and a thorough index provide valuable aids for the reader who wants to extend his or her knowledge of world mythology. MC WL

25.16   Grant, Alan. **Batman: Knightfall and Beyond.** Illustrations by Graham Nolan and Scott Hanna. Bantam Books, 1994. 158 pp. ISBN 0-553-48187-8. Fiction.

Batman has actually been defeated. When Bruce Wayne outlives his prime and is beaten by a fierce opponent known as Bane, Bruce realizes that Gotham City must have the protection of a new Batman and appoints Jean-Paul Valley to the role. But Jean-Paul finds the thin line between serving justice and committing cold-blooded murder too difficult to distinguish. With his improved Batman suit, he can defeat the most challenging opponents. What happens when Batman turns bad? Perhaps it is only the one true Batman who can bring back justice. What will Bruce Wayne do?

25.17   Green, Roger Lancelyn. **Tales of the Greek Heroes: Retold from the Ancient Authors.** Puffin Books, 1994. 274 pp. ISBN 0-14-036683-0. Fiction.

Green's passion for Greece and its mythology and his gift as a storyteller combine in this volume to create retellings of the myths of ancient Greece that are remarkable for their clarity. From the descriptions of the coming of the immortals to those of the fall of Troy Green's craft invites the reader to experience the values and perceptions of the ancient Greeks, helping the modern reader better understand this civilization that continues to affect our lives today. MC WL

25.18   Hague, Michael, editor. **The Book of Dragons.** Illustrated by Michael Hague. William Morrow, 1995. 146 pp. ISBN 0-688-10879-21. Fiction.

Dragon lovers beware! Short stories and poetry from many cultures and several well-known authors (C. S. Lewis, Kenneth Grahame, and J. R. R. Tolkien among them) retell the sagas of dragons both fierce and kind. Fire breathers guarding untold wealth, beautiful damsels, and brave heroes travel around time and over continents in this richly illustrated collection of tales. ER MC WL

25.19 Hildebrandt, Greg. **Greg Hildebrandt's Book of Three-Dimensional Dragons.** Illustrated by Greg Hildebrandt. Compass Productions, 1994. 10 pp. ISBN 0-316-15240-4. Nonfiction.

Warning: This is a pop-up book. But readers of any age will find the five classic dragons discussed and illustrated with magnificently intricate, three-dimensional cutouts fascinating. Introducing evil dragons from all over the world as well as friendlier dragons from China, Hildebrandt's text will whet your appetite for more information about these extraordinary monsters. ER

25.20 Kimmel, Eric A. (retold by). **The Adventures of Hershel of Ostropol.** Illustrated by Trina Schart Hyman. Holiday House, 1995. 64 pp. ISBN 0-8234-1210-5.

Based on a real person who lived in the early nineteenth century, Hershel is a lively character in Jewish folklore. The trickery he uses to get food for his long-suffering wife Yente and their family pits him against his best friend, his miserly Uncle Zalman, and sometimes even against the kindly Rabbi Israel. But like tricksters from other cultures—Coyote, Ananse, and B'rer Rabbit, for example—Hershel of Ostropol can hardly be blamed for just trying to get by in a harsh world. ER MC WL

25.21 Martin, Rafe. **Mysterious Tales of Japan.** Illustrated by Tatsuro Kiuchi. G. P. Putnam's Sons, 1996. 74 pp. ISBN 0-399-22677-X.

For many years, author and storyteller Rafe Martin has been a student of Japanese culture. Here, he presents his own retellings of classic folk- and fairytales of Japan, evoking the mystery and the classic understated elegance of the Japanese style. The stories vary in tone, from the gentle to the eerie, and Martin provides insight, in his foreword, into the ways in which the tales reflect the diverse influences of Japan's Buddhist and Shinto heritages as well as of the Noh theater. ER MC WL

25.22 Napoli, Donna Jo. **Zel.** Dutton Children's Books, 1996. 227 pp. ISBN 0-525-45612-0. Fiction.

The fairytale of Rapunzel becomes even more enchanting when the characters' psychological motivations are explored. The characters in Napoli's novel are fully fleshed out and each commands some degree of sympathy: Mother with her desperate longing for a child, willing to make any sacrifice; malleable Rapunzel, uncommonly sensitive; and the nobleman whose love for Zel threatens the elaborate scheme Mother has designed for her beloved daughter. As the complexity reveals itself in alternating points of view, the tale is elevated from the silly to the sublime.

School Library Journal Best Books, 1996

25.23   Picard, Barbara Leonie (retold by). **Tales of the Norse Gods.** Illustrated by Joan Kiddell-Monroe. Oxford University Press, 1994. 152 pp. ISBN 0-19-274167-5. Fiction.

Vikings learned to pass long winter nights by telling tales of daring gods who were constantly battling giants and harsh living conditions. These tales, which span all of time from the creation of the universe to its ultimate destruction, stress the Norse values of bravery, winning in battle, and the love of a good trick. A handy pronunciation guide and a list of gods mentioned make this a valuable resource to both beginning and experienced students of Norse mythology. MC WL

25.24   Riordan, James (retold by). **Korean Folk-tales.** Oxford University Press, 1994. 133 pp. ISBN 0-19-274160-8. Fiction.

These traditional Korean tales tell of the beginnings of Korea, the values of this ancient culture, and the sacrifices of its people, through fantastic events and characters. Whether sad or happy or humorous or romantic, these stories introduce the reader to the Land of the Morning Calm. MC WL

25.25   Spariosu, Mihail I., and Benedek Dezsö. **Ghosts, Vampires, and Werewolves: Eerie Tales from Transylvania.** Illustrated by Laszlo Kubinyi. Orchard Books, 1994. 103 pp. ISBN 0-531-06860-9. Fiction / Nonfiction.

Frightening tales of young men turning into wolves; sad tales of lost loves; bitter tales of wicked parents—all these come to life as the authors retell stories they've heard in their homeland, the ever-mysterious Transylvania, where good does not always win out over evil. The appendix, which explains the beliefs and customs of this little-known region, is as interesting as the stories themselves. ER MC WL

25.26   Sutcliff, Rosemary. **The Light beyond the Forest: The Quest for the Holy Grail.** Puffin Books, 1994. 144 pp. ISBN 0-14-037150-8. Fiction.

King Arthur and his knights of the Round Table search for the Holy Grail, which can be captured by only one person—the world's most perfect knight. Lancelot, Galahad, and the other knights face their most difficult quest in this second volume of Sutcliff's trilogy.

25.27   Sutcliff, Rosemary. **The Road to Camlann.** Puffin Books, 1994. 143 pp. ISBN 0-14-037147-8. Fiction.

The famous Round Table and the fair rule it has come to represent face destruction at the hands of Mordred, Arthur's illegitimate son. While evil may appear to have won, Arthur is sure to return "in time of Britain's sorest need," in this concluding novel of Sutcliff's trilogy.

25.28 Sutcliff, Rosemary. **The Sword and the Circle: King Arthur and the Knights of the Round Table.** Puffin Books, 1994. 261 pp. ISBN 0-14-037149-4. Fiction.

King Arthur and his knights of the Round Table experience many thrilling adventures in this first of three novels retelling the familiar tale. The stories of Merlin, Lancelot, Gawain and the Green Knight, Tristan and Iseult, and Gawain and the Loathely Lady are just some of the tales of quest and romance woven together as Arthur and his knights come into power.

25.29 Tomlinson, Theresa. **The Forestwife.** Orchard Books, 1995. 166 pp. ISBN 0-531-09450-2. Fiction.

Everyone knows the legend of Robin Hood and his band of men. But until now, no one has told Maid Marian's side of the story. Of similar backgrounds and guiding philosophies, Marian and Robin are anything but attracted to one another when they first meet. Destiny prevails, however, and the two eventually begin to share their lives of good deeds. This thoroughly modern Marian keeps her own, very strong identity and career. ER

ALA Notable Books for Children, 1996
Booklist Editors' Choice, 1996

25.30 Vande Velde, Vivian. **Tales from the Brothers Grimm and the Sisters Weird.** Jane Yolen Books / Harcourt Brace, 1995. 128 pp. ISBN 0-15-200220-0.

Hansel and Gretel as murderers? Jack a drunk? Red Riding Hood despised by everyone, including her granny? Imagine the world of classic fairy tales turned upside down, and you've got the thirteen twisted stories and poems in this slim volume. It's like *The Stinky Cheese Man* for more mature audiences or the Brothers Grimm writing for *Mad.* However you describe it, this is a fun—but warped—read! ER

25.31 Voigt, Cynthia. **Jackaroo.** Scholastic, 1995. 291 pp. ISBN 0-590-48595-4.

Gwyn's harsh life as the innkeeper's daughter leaves her no time for foolish legends from the past about Jackaroo, the masked outlaw who aids those in need. Not until she is stranded with the weak, spoiled, and despised Lordling does Gwyn make a shocking discovery that leads her to question her previously held beliefs about the Lords, her friends and family, herself, and even Jackaroo.

25.32 Walker, Paul Robert. **Giants! Stories from around the World.** Illustrated by James Bernardin. Harcourt Brace, 1995. 69 pp. ISBN 0-15-200883-7.

Giants from around the world and across time come alive in this collection of stories. Famous figures like Goliath, the cyclops Polyphemus, and the giant that threatened Jack on his beanstalk stand side by side with giants from a variety of other cultures including Native American, Hawaiian, and South African. Helpful author's notes on each story's origins, colorful illustrations, and an informative bibliography make this book a good reference source as well as enjoyable reading. ER MC WL

25.33 Wilde, Oscar. **The Fairy Tales of Oscar Wilde.** Edited with an introduction by Neil Philip. Illustrated by Isabelle Brent. Viking, 1994. 141 pp. ISBN 0-670-85585-5. Fiction.

These nine gorgeously illustrated fairy tales are not for children. They are for mature readers who want poignant stories of love and friendship in tales like "The Happy Prince" and "The Selfish Giant." The introduction gives a glimpse of Wilde's simultaneously celebrated and tortured life and a hint of why his fairy tales are as sad as they are.

Titles Annotated in Other Chapters Related to Myths, Legends, and Folklore

Avila, Alfred. *Mexican Ghost Tales of the Southwest*. Short Stories.

Brainard, Cecilia Manguerra. *When the Rainbow Goddess Wept*. War.

Charbonneau, Eileen. *The Ghosts of Stony Clove*. Romance.

Dalkey, Kara. *Little Sister*. Historical Fiction.

Gatti, Anne, ed. *Tales from the African Plains*. Short Stories.

Green, Roger Lancelyn. *King Arthur and His Knights of the Round Table*. Classics.

Hartwell, David G., ed. *The Screaming Skull and Other Great American Ghost Stories*. Short Stories.

Harvey, Karen D., ed. *American Indian Voices*. Poetry.

Hobbs, Will. *Kokopelli's Flute*. Adventure.

Llywelyn, Morgan. *Brian Boru: Emperor of the Irish*. Historical Fiction.

Llywelyn, Morgan. *Strongbow: Story of Richard and Aoife*. Historical Fiction.

Lyons, Mary E., ed. *Raw Head, Bloody Bones: African-American Tales of the Supernatural*. Short Stories.

McClung, Jean. *Mischief and Mercy: Tales of the Saints*. Religion.

Pepper, Dennis. *The Oxford Book of Animal Stories*. Animals.

Power, Susan. *The Grass Dancer*. Family.

Rostkowski, Margaret I. *Moon Dancer*. Choices.

Sherman, Josepha, ed. *Orphans of the Night*. Short Stories.

Zweifel, Karyn. *Covered Bridge Ghost Stories*. Short Stories.

26 Poetry and Drama

"Reading it, however, with a perfect contempt for it one discovers in it after all, a place for the genuine."

Marianne Moore

"It is the poet's privilege to help man endure by lifting his heart."

William Faulkner

26.1   Adoff, Arnold, editor. **My Black Me: A Beginning Book of Black Poetry.** Puffin Books, 1995. 84 pp. ISBN 0-14-037443-4.

From Lucille Clifton and Langston Hughes to Nikki Giovanni and other contemporary poets, Adoff has anthologized the voices of African American poets as they celebrate their heritage, their history, and their future. ER MC

26.2   Adoff, Arnold. **Slow Dance Heart Break Blues.** With artwork by William Cotton. Lothrop, Lee and Shepard, 1995. N.p. ISBN 0-688-10569-6.

The aching sweetness and joy of first love, the devastating end of a relationship, the tingly feeling of being in close proximity to "definitive heart throb" Stanley, as well as the hunger for heroes, the cynicism that comes from seeing "the same old car . . . rolling up and down our neighborhood street" no matter how many drug busts the police have carried out—Adoff captures all these emotions and more in this slim volume of poetry enhanced by Cotton's black-and-white artwork. Wild rhythms, the music of the street and the heart, echo through these pages, whether Adoff is describing a whole-wheat pizza or a first kiss. ER

ALA Best Books for Young Adults, 1996

26.3   Antush, John V., editor. **Nuestro New York: An Anthology of Puerto Rican Plays.** Mentor, 1994. 566 pp. ISBN 0-451-62868-3.

This collection of eleven plays by and about Puerto Ricans explores issues faced by the Puerto Rican community in America. Contemporary themes such as interracial dating, AIDS, literacy, immigration, homosexuality, and urban violence emerge in the works, written between 1950 and 1992. At the same time, these plays feature young protagonists whom we watch fall in love, face the loss of loved ones, and grow through these experiences. Some of these plays are very realistic and some explore modern issues through Latin American surrealism. MC

26.4   Bagert, Brod, editor. **Poetry for Young People: Edgar Allan Poe.** Illustrated by Carolynn Cobleigh. Sterling, 1995. 48 pp. ISBN 0-8069-0820-3.

Journey through the suspenseful and sometimes gory world of Edgar Allan Poe in this collection of poetry and prose made modern with colorful and spooky illustrations. Poetic passages from Poe's most famous short stories, such as "The Tell-Tale Heart," "The Cask of Amontillado," and "The Pit and the Pendulum," follow such classic poems as "The Raven," "Annabel Lee," and "The Bells." Helpful commentary and definitions make this collection exciting and accessible to all readers. ER

26.5   Beatty, Paul. **Joker, Joker, Deuce.** Penguin Books, 1994. 108 pp. ISBN 0 14 05.8723 3.

Paul Beatty's modern, unorthodox poetry is reminiscent of e.e. cummings and the Beat poets, especially Lawrence Ferlinghetti. His expression of contemporary African American experience is laden with strong street language and allusions to notables, both historical and current. MC

ALA Quick Picks for Young Adults, 1995

26.6   Begay, Shonto. **Navajo: Visions and Voices across the Mesa.** Scholastic, 1995. 48 pp. ISBN 0-590-46153-2.

This collection combines twenty paintings by Shonto Begay with his original poetry. Begay conveys the richness of his Navajo tradition through memories of childhood and family. He also captures the struggle between the Navajo's reverence for the land and the surrounding culture's view of the land as a resource. ER MC

ALA Best Books for Young Adults, 1996
ALA Notable Books for Children, 1996
Notable 1995 Children's Trade Books in the Field of Social Studies

26.7   Bolin, Frances Schoonmaker, editor. **Poetry for Young People : Carl Sandburg.** Illustrated by Steven Arcella. Sterling, 1995. 48 pp. ISBN 0-8069-0818-1.

Experience the wanderings of a true hobo through the poetry of Carl Sandburg in this beautifully illustrated collection. More than thirty poems are accompanied by full-color drawings and interesting commentary and definitions. Sandburg was a true free spirit and his poems reflect his well-traveled life. He addresses the plight of the homeless in "Old Woman" and the concerns of Native Americans in "Buffalo Dusk," as well as the pleasures of nature and the playfulness found in language and sounds. ER

26.8   Carlson, Lori M., editor. **Cool Salsa: Bilingual Poems on Growing Up Latino in the United States.** Introduction by Oscar Hijuelos. Henry Holt, 1994. 123 pp. ISBN 0-8050-3135-9.

In "Where You From?" poet Gina Valdés says, "Soy de aquí / y soy de alla / from here / and from there / born in L.A." She captures the double lives reflected in these poems about growing up Latino in America. All of the poems are presented in their original language and in translation. The collection includes works by Sandra Cisneros, Gary Soto, Martín Espada, Ed J. Vega, and many more. The poems are especially geared to the teenage experience. ER MC

ALA Best Books for Young Adults, 1995
ALA Quick Picks for Young Adults, 1995
Notable 1994 Children's Trade Books in the Field of Social Studies

26.9   Dickinson, Emily. **Poems for Youth.** Edited by Alfred Leete Hampson. Illustrated by Thomas B. Allen. Foreword by May Lamberton Becker. Little, Brown, 1996. 111 pp. ISBN 0-316-18435-7.

Here are seventy-eight poems written by Emily Dickinson which will appeal to young readers. Many of these poems are poems of friendship which Dickinson originally wrote for her nephews and niece. Included are many well-known pieces such as "I'm nobody!" and "There is no frigate," as well as other poems which speak to nature and the cycles of time, enhanced by black-and-white drawings. ER

26.10   Doty, Mark. **Atlantis: Poems.** HarperPerennial / HarperCollins, 1995. 103 pp. ISBN 0-06-095106-0.

With luminous imagery rooted in nature and the earth, Doty writes about fate, tragedy, and beauty. His poems document the AIDS plague and the deaths of loved ones from the disease. In "Four Cut Sunflowers, One Upside Down," he writes

> They are a nocturne
> in argent and gold, and they burn
> with the ferocity
> of dying (which is to say, the luminosity
> of what's living *hardest).*

26.11   Eady, Cornelius. **You Don't Miss Your Water: Poems.** Henry Holt, 1995. 33 pp. ISBN 0-8050-3668-7.

In Eady's fourth book of poetry, he chronicles his complex relationship with his father as he sits at the dying man's bedside. The twenty-one poems tell the story of a difficult man, a son who has never lived up to his dad's expectations, a rebellious daughter, and a mother who was always disappointed. Titles include "Papa Was a Rolling Stone," "I Ain't Got No Home," and "The Way You Do the Things You Do." ER MC

26.12   Fletcher, Ralph. **I Am Wings: Poems about Love.** Photography by Joe Baker. Bradbury Press, 1994. 48 pp. ISBN 0-02-735395-8.

These thirty-three poems capture the experiences of falling in and out of love. With titles such as "Phone Call," "Crush Blush," and "Changing Channels," the poems evoke the exciting, humorous, and painful emotions of love. Written in the first person, these poems place the reader smack in the middle of what it means to be young and in love for the first time: to have a crush, to see fireworks during the first kiss, and to experience the pain of breaking up. ER

ALA Quick Picks for Young Adults, 1995
School Library Journal Best Books, 1994
IRA Teacher's Choice 1995

26.13   Giovanni, Nikki, editor. **Grand Mothers: Poems, Reminiscences, and Short Stories about the Keepers of Our Traditions.** Henry Holt, 1994. 168 pp. ISBN 0-8050-2766-1.

Nikki Giovanni writes in her introduction: "So this isn't a balanced book nor a sociological book nor a look at grandmothers through the ages. It's just a book that makes me miss the only person I know for sure whose love I did not have to earn." In this collection of poems and stories, Gwendolyn Brooks, Maxine Hong Kingston, Kyoko Mori, and Gloria Naylor celebrate their memories of their grandmothers. MC WL

Notable 1994 Children's Trade Books in the Field of Social Studies

26.14   Glaser, Isabel Joshlin, editor. **Dreams of Glory: Poems Starring Girls.** Illustrated by Pat Lowry Collins. Atheneum Books for Young Readers, 1995. 47 pp. ISBN 0-689-31891-X.

> I
> will
> remember
> with my breath
> to make a mountain . . .
>
> May Swenson

This illustrated collection of poetry focuses on girls' experiences. It contains poems by Nikki Giovanni, Gertrude Stein, Cynthia Rylant, and many others. The poetry touches on issues that are relevant to teenage girls such as self-esteem, friendship, and achievement. ER MC

26.15   Gleason, Judith, editor. **Leaf and Bone: African Praise-Poems.** Illustrated by Stéphan Daigle. Penguin Books, 1994. 241 pp. ISBN 0 14 05.8722 5.

The praise-poem is the most popular form of African story. It is composed to name children, to mark coming of age, to praise gods, and to introduce oneself. These poems come from regions from Southern Africa to the Sahara and are about everything from kings to truck drivers to bicycles to rain. The anthology is organized into sections such as "Lamentations of Women," "Animal Praises," "Pride of Hunters," and "Presence of Spirits." Informative commentaries accompany each section. MC WL

26.16 Gordon, Ruth, editor. **Pierced by a Ray of Sun: Poems about the Times We Feel Alone.** HarperCollins, 1995. 105 pp. ISBN 0-06-023613-2.

Poems such as "When I Hear Your Name" by Gloria Fuentes, "Elegy for John, My Student Dead of AIDS," by Robert Cording, and "I Am a Rock," by Paul Simon, fill this volume of work that speaks to the universal feelings of loneliness, alienation, and being different. The collection testifies to the fact that working through loneliness defies time and place—poets from all over the world at all different times in history share their experiences with loneliness here. ER MC WL

ALA Best Books for Young Adults, 1996
Booklist Editors' Choice, 1996

26.17 Harjo, Joy. **The Woman Who Fell from the Sky: Poems.** W. W. Norton, 1994. 68 pp. ISBN 0-393-31362-X.

"Stories and songs are like humans who when they laugh are indestructible"—"A Postcolonial Tale."

In her fourth volume of poetry, Joy Harjo weaves storytelling, prayer, and song. Her poems are witness to Native American tradition, modern American culture, human spirit, and the earth. Titles include "Promise of Blue Horses," "Insomnia and the Seven Steps to Grace," and "The Other Side of Yellow to Blue." ER MC

26.18 Harvey, Karen D., editor. Lisa D. Harjo, consultant. **American Indian Voices.** The Millbrook Press, 1995. 144 pp. ISBN 1-56294-382-0. Fiction.

This collection of myths, legends, poems, essays, and songs tells the story of the Native Americans: the development of a rich and spiritual culture and then the near destruction of this culture by European settlers. The themes of beliefs, traditions, change, and survival connect the works in the anthology. In the beginning of the book, Russell Boham writes, "I choose not beauty nor anger, but truth." MC

26.19 Hopkins, Lee Bennett, editor. **Hand in Hand: An American History through Poetry.** Illustrated by Peter M. Fiore. Simon and Schuster, 1994. 144 pp. ISBN 0-671-73315-X.

"But still unstoried, artless, unenhanced, / Such as she was, such as she would become," Robert Frost describes America in "The Gift Outright." This collection of poems and traditional lyrics about the United States is organized by eras and ideas and charts our country's origins from the early 1600s. It includes works by Walt Whitman, Lawrence Ferlinghetti, Lucille Clifton, Gwendolyn Brooks, and Langston Hughes, as well as traditional rhymes. ER

Notable 1994 Children's Trade Books in the Field of Social Studies

26.20   Hudgins, Andrew. **The Glass Hammer: A Southern Childhood.**
          Houghton Mifflin, 1994. 97 pp. ISBN 0-395-70010-8.

          This collection of contemporary poems tells detailed stories of a boy's
          growing up in Texas and Alabama. Themes include family, race rela-
          tions, and church. The characters are realistic and bring out the per-
          plexed and perplexing emotions of the boy.

          ALA Quick Picks for Young Adults, 1995

26.21   Hughes, Langston. **The Block: Poems.** Edited by Lowery S. Sims and
          Daisy Murray Voight. Introduction by Bill Cosby. Metropolitan Museum
          of Art / Viking, 1995. 32 pp. ISBN 0-670-86501-X.

          Bearden's six-panel collage, *The Block,* celebrates the streets of Harlem
          which inspired him. In this book, it is paired with the poems of his con-
          temporary, Langston Hughes. In the introduction, Bill Cosby writes,
          "The homes above the storefront church, the barbershop, encounters on
          the sidewalk, views through windows, all of the scenes and activities
          that we associate with urban life are a vital part" of the book. ER MC

          ALA Best Books for Young Adults, 1996

26.22   **InsectAsides: Great Poets on Man's Pest Friend.** Linocuts by Martha
          Paulos. Viking Studio Books, 1994. 55 pp. ISBN 0-670-85567-7.

          Whether you're insect-obsessed or you like witty and colorful linocuts
          or you enjoy a good poem, you will get a kick out of *InsectAsides*. In
          "Fleas Interest Me So Much," Pablo Neruda confesses, "Let them gal-
          lop on my skin, / divulge their emotions, / amuse themselves with my
          blood, / but someone should introduce them to me. / I want to know
          them closely, / I want to know what to rely on." ER

26.23   Kherdian, David, editor. **Beat Voices: An Anthology of Beat Poetry.**
          Henry Holt, 1995. 144 pp. ISBN 0-8050-3315-7.

          Hailing from all points from New York to San Francisco, beat poets and
          writers such as Allen Ginsberg, Diane di Prima, Jack Kerouac, LeRoi
          Jones, Lew Welch, and Gregory Corso write with the passion, vision,
          and hope that are still relevant today; their poems fill the pages of this
          volume, providing a useful introduction to the themes and vision of the
          Beat Generation. MC

26.24   MacLeod, Joan. **The Hope Slide; Little Sister.** Coach House Press, 1994.
          118 pp. ISBN 0-88910-463-8.

          This text consists of two one-act plays. The first, *The Hope Slide,* is a one-
          woman show in which the actor-protagonist travels back in time to the
          lives of a rebellious Canadian group, the Doukhobors, to her rebellious
          adolescence, and to the present, where she tries to grasp the meaning
          of modern life. The second play, *Little Sister,* shows five teenagers, three

girls and two boys, grappling with their images of themselves as they confront one teenager's severe eating disorder.

26.25 Mancini, Salvatore. **On the Edge of Magic.** Chronicle Books, 1996. 96 pp. ISBN 0-8118-1167-0.

Exciting black-and-white photographs of petroglyphs and rock art accompanied by prayers, poems, and songs of Native Americans grace the pages of this volume. The photographs and text are only loosely related, but each complements the spirituality of the other. MC

26.26 Marcus, Leonard S., editor. **Lifelines: A Poetry Anthology Patterned on the Stages of Life.** Dutton Children's Books, 1994. 116 pp. ISBN 0-525-45164-1.

Divided into the four sections "Small Traveler," "I Am Old Enough," "On Such a Hill," and "In the End We Are All Light," this anthology includes eighty poems that give voice to the human experience from birth to death. The diverse collection includes poetry by William Blake, E. B. White, Elizabeth Bishop, Audre Lorde, Gwendolyn Brooks, Yehuda Amichai, Maya Angelou, Mark Strand, and William Shakespeare. ER MC

Notable 1994 Children's Trade Books in the Field of Social Studies

26.27 Miller, Arthur. **The Crucible.** Introduction by Christopher Bigsby. Penguin, 1995. 143 pp. ISBN 0 14 01.8964 5.

Written in 1953, *The Crucible* tells the story of a young girl who accuses Elizabeth Proctor of being a witch in seventeenth-century Salem, Massachusetts. The play reveals a dark side of human nature as the people in the community eagerly prosecute the accused. Miller wrote, "I believe that the reader will discover here the essential nature of one of the strangest and most awful chapters in human history."

26.28 Panzer, Nora, editor. **Celebrate America in Poetry and Art: Paintings, Sculpture, Drawings, Photographs, and Other Works of Art from the National Museum of American Art, Smithsonian Institution.** Hyperion Books for Children in association with the National Museum of American Art, Smithsonian Institution, 1994. 96 pp. ISBN 1-56282-665-4.

This beautiful and inspiring collection features fine art and poetry of one hundred noted Americans of diverse ethnic backgrounds. The effect is a brilliant tapestry of America and its peoples—in triumph and disappointment, patriotism and dissent, pride and shame, joy and grief. It is suitable for a broad age range, and includes biographical information about the writers and artists. MC

ALA Best Books for Young Adults, 1995
School Library Journal Best Books, 1994
Notable 1994 Children's Trade Books in the Field of Social Studies

26.29   Philip, Neil, editor. **Earth Always Endures: Native American Poems.**
Photographs and illustrations by Edward S. Curtis. Viking, 1996. 93 pp.
ISBN 0-670-86873-6.

The poetry, prayers, and songs of diverse Native American peoples,
from the Chippewa to the Zuni, are beautifully enhanced with the photographs of Edward Curtis, 1868–1952, who took over forty thousand
pictures of Native Americans in an attempt to help preserve their cultures from the pressures of assimilation. MC

26.30   Philip, Neil, editor. **Singing America.** Illustrated by Michael McCurdy.
Viking, 1995. 160 pp. ISBN 0-670-86150-2.

Editor Neil Philip has collected poems of varied tones and forms—from
traditional verse by Walt Whitman, to songs of the Pueblo and Sioux
peoples, to African American spirituals, to modern voices such as that
of Robert Creeley—that together make up a tapestry reflecting the diversity of the American experience as witnessed by poets who use their
personal languages to describe their responses to America. MC

Notable 1995 Children's Trade Books in the Field of Social Studies

26.31   Philip, Neil, editor. **Songs Are Thoughts: Poems of the Inuit.** Illustrated
by Maryclare Foa. Orchard Books, 1995. 23 pp. ISBN 0-531-06893-5.

"Songs are thoughts, sung out with the breath when people are moved
by great forces and ordinary speech no longer suffices." Poet Orpingalik
captures the spirit of the lyrical and powerful poems that fill this collection, written by Inuit poets of North America and Greenland. Each
poem is accompanied by a colorful oil painting by Foa. ER MC WL

26.32   Rohrer, Matthew. **A Hummock in the Malookas: Poems.** W. W. Norton,
1995. 74 pp. ISBN 0-393-03798-3. Nonfiction.

Matthew Rohrer, an M.F.A. graduate of the Iowa Writers' Workshop,
writes, "The poems came out of a two-year period in Iowa during the
massive flooding and while I was a night janitor in the Van Allen astronomy building. I had a lot of time to think of the very small things,
like my mop, and how hard it worked for me." Rohrer's world is one
in which a luminous fork wants to visit the Cadillac sculpture garden
and the violin in a pawnshop promises not to laugh at the gun's joke.
ER

1994 National Poetry Series Winner.

26.33   Rylant, Cynthia. **Something Permanent.** Photography by Walker Evans.
Harcourt Brace, 1994. 61 pp. ISBN 0-15-277090-9.

Both poetry and photographs starkly tell the story of children and
adults who lived through the Great Depression. As the first poem in the
collection, "Photographs," reads, each poem gives you "some sort of
feeling / of just being . . . . " With titles such as "Bed," "House," and

"Window," these poems convey a real feeling of "something permanent." Each poem is accompanied by a crisp black-and-white glimpse
of a particular, yet universal, moment of Americana. ER

ALA Best Books for Young Adults, 1995
ALA Quick Picks for Young Adults, 1995
Booklist Editors' Choice, 1995

26.34   Schiff, Ellen, editor. **Awake and Singing: Seven Classical Plays from
the American Jewish Repertoire.** Mentor, 1995. 636 pp. ISBN 0-451-
62869-1.

This collection of plays touches on such universal themes as family,
generation gaps, immigration, and the struggle for the American dream.
The seven classic plays in this anthology cover a variety of topics and
styles characteristic of the American Jewish repertoire from 1920 to 1960.
Included are works by Aaron Hoffman, Elmer Rice, Clifford Odets,
Sylvia Regan, Arthur Laurents, S. N. Behrman, and Paddy Chayefsky.
MC

26.35   Schiff, Ellen, editor. **Fruitful and Multiplying: Nine Contemporary
Plays from the American Jewish Repertoire.** Mentor, 1996. 522 pp. ISBN
0-451-62870-5.

Included in this anthology are plays from Emily Mann, Herb Gardner,
Jeffrey Sweet, Pulitzer Prize–winner David Mamet, and many other contemporary American Jewish playwrights. This collection explores the
themes of family, religion, homosexuality, and more. In the introduction, Schiff includes comments from the playwrights that offer insights
into their work. MC

26.36   Soto, Gary. **Canto Familiar.** Harcourt Brace, 1995. 79 pp. ISBN 0-15-
200067-4.

Canto Familiar contains twenty-five poems which are written from Soto's
Mexican American cultural perspective but which speak to everyone.
The titles include "Left Shoe on the Right Foot," "Doing Dishes," and
"My Teacher in the Market." Annika Nelson's colorful prints make this
an appealing addition to anyone's poetry collection. As Soto writes in
"Eating while Reading," "What is better than / This sweet dance / On
the tongue, / And this book / That pulls you in?"—a lovely descrip-
tion for a lovely book. MC

26.37   Stafford, William. **Learning to Live in the World: Earth Poems.** Selected
by Jerry Watson and Laura Apol Obbink. Harcourt Brace, 1994. 80 pp.
ISBN 0-15-200208-1.

Stafford's fifty poems share the themes of nature, harmony, and preserv-
ing the earth. The collection is divided into five sections: "The World
Speaks Everything to Us," "Even Far Things Are Real," "It Might Go
Wild, Any Time," "I See Darkness; It Comes Near" and "You Live by

the Light You Find." The poetry affirms the connection between people and the earth. "That's what the silence meant: you're not alone. / The whole wide world pours down." ER

26.38   Wood, Nancy. **Dancing Moons.** Illustrated by Frank Howell. Doubleday Books for Young Readers, 1995. 80 pp. ISBN 0-385-32169-4.

Wood offers a serene collection of poetry and paintings in the spirit of the Native Americans of the Southwest. Ordered according to "The Twelve Great Paths of the Moon," known to the Pueblos and identified as the months of the year, they interpret not only seasons but the journey through time that is shared by everyone. MC

26.39   Worth, Valerie. **All the Small Poems and Fourteen More.** Illustrated by Natalie Babbitt. Farrar, Straus and Giroux, 1994. 194 pp. ISBN 0-374-30211-1.

Worth and Babbitt combine the original ninety-nine poems and pictures from their books *Small Poems, More Small Poems, Still More Small Poems,* and *Small Poems Again* with fourteen new small poems and pictures. New poems include "key," "string," "garage sale," and "book." If you're a fan of Worth's poetry or you just enjoy little poems about everyday things, you will want to check out this hardcover edition. ER

26.40   Yolen, Jane. **Here There Be Unicorns.** Illustrated by David Wilgus. Harcourt Brace, 1994. 115 pp. ISBN 0-15-209902-6.

From medieval to modern settings, Yolen's poetry and short stories accompanied by black-and-white drawings weave wondrous tales of unicorns. You will even learn how to capture a unicorn. That is, if you believe. "Does it matter no one believes us, / rejecting the substance, / accepting the shadow?" Yolen asks in her poem "Fossils." This is a good companion to Yolen's previous collection *Here There Be Dragons.* ER

Titles Annotated in Other Chapters Related to Poetry and Drama

Beneduce, Ann Keay (retold by). *William Shakespeare:* The Tempest. Classics.

Fiene, Pat, ed. *Expressions: Stories and Poems, Vol. 2.* Short Stories.

Kerr, Katharine, and Martin H. Greenberg, eds. *Weird Tales from Shakespeare.* Short Stories.

Lamb, Charles, and Mary Lamb. *Tales from Shakespeare.* Classics.

Ovid. *The Poems of Exile.* Classics.

Reef, Catherine. *Walt Whitman.* Autobiography.

Ross, Stewart. *Shakespeare and Macbeth.* Autobiography.

Tarpley, Natasha, ed. *Testimony: Young African-Americans on Self-Discovery and Black Identity.* Diaries.

27 Political Science and the Law

"Politics is the art of looking for trouble, finding it everywhere, diagnosing it incorrectly, and applying the wrong remedies."

Groucho Marx

"No power should be above the law."

Cicero

27.1   Aaseng, Nathan. **The O. J. Simpson Trial: What It Shows Us about Our Legal System.** Walker, 1996. 110 pp. ISBN 0-8027-8404-6. Nonfiction.

The highly publicized status of the O. J. Simpson murder trial makes it a convenient vehicle for explaining the steps in the legal process. Controversial topics related to this trial, such as media coverage and racial aspects, are discussed as they apply to the system at large. Basic words such as "acquit" are defined in both the text and the glossary, and the book provides a solid understanding of the legal system in general. ER

27.2   Able, Deborah. **Hate Groups.** Enslow, 1995. 104 pp. ISBN 0-89490-627-5. Nonfiction.

Filled with real examples of hate crimes committed by organized hate groups such as the Ku Klux Klan, skinheads, and Identity Christians, this book attempts to answer tough questions like: Why do people hate? What makes teenagers join hate groups? How are people moved to act violently against others because of differences in race, religion, gender, or sexual orientation? Also explored in this Issues in Focus book are contemporary issues surrounding hate lyrics in music and legislation making rape a hate crime. ER MC

27.3   Andryszewski, Tricia. **Immigration: Newcomers and Their Impact on the United States.** The Millbrook Press, 1995. 112 pp. ISBN 1-56294-499-1. Nonfiction.

The U.S. Census Bureau has been systematically keeping immigration records since 1819, and, as this author points out, all documents suggest that immigrants have had a positive effect on the United States. Controversy surrounding immigration to the United States has nonetheless persisted for two centuries. This book from the Issue and Debate series gives a clear overview of immigration today, as well as a historical perspective on the impact it has had on the United States. ER MC

27.4   Black, Christine M. **The Pursuit of the Presidency: '92 and Beyond.**
        Oryx Press, 1994. 201 pp. ISBN 0-89774-845-X. Nonfiction.

This in-depth analysis of the 1992 campaign for the U.S. presidency
chronicles the political fortunes of Bill Clinton, George Bush, Ross Perot,
and the rest who aspired to this nation's highest office. Black's book
includes a history and exposition of the political process in the context
of this election, revealing the strategies of the political hopefuls and
analyzing their success or failure.

27.5   Cox, Vic. **The Challenge of Immigration.** Enslow, 1995. 128 pp. ISBN
        0-89490-628-3. Nonfiction.

Many Americans feel pride in their immigrant ancestry and in the lives
that their relatives created. However, today the issue of immigration is
a hot one about which Americans have various feelings. From the series Multicultural Issues, Vic Cox presents an overview of the history
of immigration and the challenges faced by immigrants today. Finally,
he urges that "we need to probe our values and hopes, to define our
personal vision of what America is all about." ER MC

27.6   Fireside, Harvey, and Sarah Betsy Fuller. **Brown v. Board of Education:
        Equal Schooling for All.** Enslow, 1994. ISBN 0-89490-469-8. Nonfiction.

The authors examine the history as well as the impact of school segregation in this volume from the Landmark Supreme Court Cases series.
They relate the story of Linda Brown and many other African Americans who were refused admittance to their neighborhood schools. Questions that will stimulate critical thinking about this decision are posed.
ER MC

27.7   Haas, Carol. **Engel v. Vitale: Separation of Church and State.** Enslow,
        1994. 128 pp. ISBN 0-89490-461-2. Nonfiction.

On June 25, 1962, the United States Supreme Court ruled prayer in public schools unconstitutional. In this volume from the Landmark Supreme
Court Cases series Haas looks at the history of this decision, and the
ideas and arguments of the people behind it in the context of the constitutional question of separation of church and state. ER

27.8   Herda, D. J. **Furman v. Georgia: The Death Penalty Case.** Enslow, 1994.
        99 pp. ISBN 0-89490-489-2. Nonfiction.

In 1967 a twenty-six-year-old black man accidentally shot a father of five
young children and was sentenced to death. By tracing the history of
capital punishment in the United States, the author provides a background to the steps in the appeals process that led to the U.S. Supreme
Court's decision to find that capital punishment as it was practiced in
the U.S. was cruel and unusual punishment. Another in the Landmark
Supreme Court Cases series. MC

27.9 Herda, D. J. *New York Times* v. United States: National Security and Censorship. Enslow, 1994. 104 pp. ISBN 0-89490-490-6. Nonfiction.

Does the United States government have the right to suppress free speech in the interest of national security? This addition to the Landmark Supreme Court Cases series begins with the United States government's attempt to keep embarrassing information out of the newspapers during the Vietnam War, returns to the Constitution for a definition of free speech, and discusses the continued debates between those who believe in the public's right to uncensored information and those who emphasize the government's responsibility to protect its people.

27.10 Herda, D. J. **Roe v. Wade: The Abortion Question.** Enslow, 1994. 104 pp. ISBN 0-89490-459-0. Nonfiction.

While the abortion rights question makes headlines today, this book, another in the Landmark Supreme Court Cases series, looks at the people who were involved in the landmark 1973 decision, the constitutional basis for the decision, and the effects it has had on women and society. A balanced representation of the facts is presented, and definitions of legal terms are included. ER

Notable 1994 Children's Trade Books in the Field of Social Studies

27.11 Hjelmeland, Andy. **Prisons: Inside the Big House.** Lerner, 1996. 112 pp. ISBN 0-8225-2607-7. Nonfiction.

In this volume from the Pro/Con series, all sides of prison issues are presented. With easy-to-read charts and graphs, comparisons of crime rates, prison populations, prison costs, and alternative methods of punishment, the book allows the reader to develop informed opinions on this social problem that is becoming larger and more complex each year. Legal terms are defined to aid the reader in understanding the social and legal aspects of crime both in this book and in today's news.

27.12 Hyde, Margaret O. **Gambling: Winners and Losers.** The Millbrook Press, 1995. 96 pp. ISBN 1-56294-532-7. Nonfiction.

Hyde discusses the pros and cons of gambling, and she provides a brief history of the subject. Other topics addressed include legal vs. illegal gambling, government control of gambling, compulsive gambling, and young gamblers. A "Suggestions for Further Reading" section and a glossary of gambling terms add to the volume's usefulness. ER

27.13 Hyde, Margaret O. **Kids in and out of Trouble.** Cobblehill Books, 1995. 104 pp. ISBN 0-525-65149-7. Nonfiction.

Teen crime is increasing at an alarming rate. This book examines the reasons kids get into trouble, the crimes they commit, and the workings of the juvenile justice system. Graphic case studies illustrate this growing problem, and a list of programs and solutions that teens can use to help reverse this trend is offered. A glossary of terms and a bibliography are included.

27.14   Kronenwetter, Michael. **The Peace Commandos: Nonviolent Heroes in the Struggle against War and Injustice.** Timestop / New Discovery Books, 1994. ISBN 0-02-751051-4. Nonfiction.

This is an account of the peacemakers in American society, including such figures as Henry David Thoreau, Dorothy Day, and Martin Luther King Jr., as well as those who have influenced them. Tracing the history of the peace movement in America, the author explains the philosophy of peace and how pacifists have endured in the face of war, and offers alternative ways of attaining peace.

27.15   Kronenwetter, Michael. **Political Parties of the United States.** Enslow Publishers, 1996. 128 pp. ISBN 0-89490-537-6. Nonfiction.

Those with an interest in politics will find this objective look at the Democratic, Republican, and third parties useful. Information as to the history, roles, current status, and future of the political system of the United States is presented to help the reader develop an informed opinion about participating in the political process. The volume, part of the Government in Action series, includes a glossary, chapter notes, an index, and a number of black-and-white photographs. ER

27.16   Landau, Elaine. **Your Legal Rights: From Custody Battles to School Searches, the Headline-Making Cases That Affect Your Life.** Walker, 1995. 84 pp. ISBN 0-8027-8359-7. Nonfiction.

Society has progressed from condoning infanticide to exploiting child labor to ruling in favor of a boy's suit to divorce his mother and choose his own parents. Despite this improvement in the treatment of children, the author points out that serious challenges related to the rights of children are still to be met both in the United States and abroad. Appendices include some clarification of the rights of minors and a list of organizations concerned with the welfare of children.

27.17   LeVert, Marianne. **The Welfare System: Help or Hindrance to the Poor?** The Millbrook Press, 1995. 112 pp. ISBN 1-56294-455-X. Nonfiction.

While the subject of welfare reform is an explosive issue today, readers come to understand all sides of the debate, the history of welfare, and the future possible directions in *The Welfare System*. LeVert presents the views of diverse people on welfare, as well as of both liberal and conservative thinkers. Black-and-white photographs, a glossary, and an index accompany this contemporary examination from the Issue and Debate series. ER

27.18 Oliver, Marilyn Tower. **Gangs: Trouble in the Streets.** Enslow, 1995. 128 pp. ISBN 0-89490-492-2. Nonfiction.

We've all read about gangs in newspapers and magazines and we've seen results of their feuding on TV news programs. The physical harm and emotional turmoil that are products of a gang environment cut across race, age, and nationality, visit small towns and large cities, and claim victims both inside and outside their own membership. In this volume from the Issues in Focus series, Oliver explains the history of gangs in the United States and the reasons their numbers are growing, and examines gang life from recruitment to distribution of jobs. An extensive bibliography, as well as a glossary and suggestions for further reading (both fiction and nonfiction), are included in this informative yet easy-to-read overview. ER MC

27.19 Rappaport, Doreen. **The Sacco-Vanzetti Trial.** HarperTrophy / HarperCollins, 1994. 175 pp. ISBN 0-06-446113-0. Nonfiction.

On August 22, 1927, Nicola Sacco and Bartolomeo Vanzetti were electrocuted after seven years of a trial and subsequent appeals of their first-degree murder conviction. The reader is asked to be the judge and the jury in deciding the fate of these two political radicals and immigrants, and to consider whether or not their prosecution resulted from their political beliefs and their immigrant status. Part of the Be the Judge / Be the Jury series. MC

27.20 Rappaport, Doreen. **Tinker vs. Des Moines: Student Rights on Trial.** HarperTrophy / HarperCollins, 1994. 153 pp. ISBN 0-06-446114-9. Nonfiction.

In 1965, in the Des Moines school district, twelve students wore black armbands to school to mourn the dead of both sides in the Vietnam War. Anticipating disruption in the schools, the Des Moines school board banned the wearing of armbands and suspended those students who wore them to school. Believing that their right to free speech had been violated, the students sued the school board. Rappaport asks the reader to be the judge and the jury as this case moves through the judicial process, in another volume in the Be the Judge / Be the Jury series. ER

27.21 Riley, Gail Blasser. **Miranda v. Arizona: Rights of the Accused.** Enslow, 1994. 128 pp. ISBN 0-89490-504-X. Nonfiction.

"You have the right to remain silent . . . " Learn the origin of the Miranda warning, the constitutional basis for it, and details of the famous case that led to the requirement that criminal suspects be advised of their rights when arrested, in this addition to the Landmark Supreme Court Cases series. Situations are given that allow the reader to determine whether the civil rights of an accused person were violated, and a glossary of legal terms is included.

27.22   Sherrow, Victoria. **Censorship in Schools.** Enslow, 1996. 128 pp. ISBN 0-89490-728-X. Nonfiction.

Where do a student's First Amendment rights end, and who draws the line? Discussions of censorship of library books, textbooks, school newspapers, courses, teachers, dress, and the Internet are set in historical context with references to famous court cases. An index, chapter notes, a bibliography, and addresses of organizations devoted to preserving freedom of expression are included, making this volume in the Issues in Focus series an easy-to-read, useful introduction to the topic.

27.23   Sherrow, Victoria. **Gideon v. Wainwright: Free Legal Counsel.** Enslow, 1995. 104 pp. ISBN 0-89490-507-4. Nonfiction.

Part of the Landmark Supreme Court Cases series, this book deals with the right of an accused person to receive free legal counsel. The history of the case, the historical context of the issue, discussion questions, a glossary, chapter notes, and an index are included. This case, heard and decided in 1963, is placed in the context of other prisoner rights cases. Students' research in several disciplines could benefit from the availability of this series.

27.24   Stevens, Leonard A. **The Case of Roe v. Wade.** G. P. Putnam's Sons, 1996. 188 pp. ISBN 0-399-22812-8. Nonfiction.

The history of the landmark Supreme Court decision that legalized abortion in 1973 began with state laws enacted over a hundred years earlier. Changing social pressures, from early anti-vice zealots to Margaret Sanger's campaigns for birth control to recent attacks on abortion clinics, are chronicled, as well as the actual case of *Roe v. Wade*. Although focusing on pro-choice advocates, this book provides a valuable overview of women's progress toward reproductive rights, and includes a bibliography, a glossary, appendices, and an index.

Titles Annotated in Other Chapters Related to Politics and the Law

Archer, Jules. *Rage in the Streets: Mob Violence in America*. Human Rights.

Blue, Rose, and Corinne J. Naden. *People of Peace*. Autobiography.

Bredeson, Carmen. *Henry Cisneros*. Autobiography.

Bredeson, Carmen. *Ross Perot*. Autobiography.

Brooks, Charles, ed. *Best Editorial Cartoons of the Year. 1994 Edition*. Humor.

Brooks, Charles, ed. *Best Editorial Cartoons of the Year. 1995 Edition*. Humor.

Carter, Jimmy. *Talking Peace*. Human Rights.

Castañeda, Omar S. *Imagining Isabel*. Choices.

Creeden, Sharon. *Fair Is Fair: World Folktales of Justice*. Myths.

Davidson, Sue. *A Heart in Politics: Jeannette Rankin and Patsy T. Mink*. Autobiography.

Dickinson, Peter. *Shadow of a Hero*. Choices.

Dolan, Edward F. *Your Privacy*. Human Rights.

Gay, Kathlyn. *Rights and Respect: What You Need to Know about Gender Bias and Sexual Harassment*. Human Rights.

Gottfried, Ted. *Privacy*. Human Rights.

Handelsman, Walt. *Political Gumbo: A Collection of Editorial Cartoons*. Humor.

Judson, Karen. *Computer Crime*. Computers.

Lang, Paul. *The English Language Debate*. Language.

Morris, Jeffrey. *The Jefferson Way*. Autobiography.

Morris, Jeffrey. *The Washington Way*. Autobiography.

Morris, Jeffrey. *The Truman Way*. Autobiography.

Patrick, John J. *The Young Oxford Companion to the Supreme Court of the United States*. Reference.

Sherrow, Victoria. *The U.S. Health Care Crisis*. Human Rights.

Sidel, Ruth. *Battling Bias*. Human Rights.

Siegel, Dorothy Schainman. *Ann Richards*. Autobiography.

Stacey, T. J. *Hillary Rodham Clinton*. Autobiography.

Symynkywicz, Jeffrey B. *Germany: United Again*. History.

Underhill, Lois Beachy. *The Woman Who Ran for President: The Many Lives of Victoria Woodhull*. Autobiography.

Warren, James A. *Cold War*. War.

Zeinert, Karen. *Free Speech*. Human Rights.

28 Recreation, Travel, and Leisure Time Activities

"Is not life a hundred times too short for us to bore ourselves?"
Friedrich Nietzsche

"Mingle your cares with pleasure now and then."
Dionysius Cato

28.1　Besmehn, Bobby. **Juggling Step-by-Step.** Sterling / Chapelle, 1994. 79 pp. ISBN 0-8069-0814-9. Nonfiction.

Want to perfect your yo yos, fakes, or columns? Perhaps your cascades need work or your shower isn't what you want it to be. This is the book for you and anyone else anxious to become an expert juggler. Great color photographs demonstrating each step from beginning to more complex moves and clear, concise directions from a professional juggler will have you amazing your friends with your dexterity. Keep your eye on the ball . . . and the club . . . and the bean bag!

28.2　Camp, Jeffery. **Paint: A Manual of Pictorial Thought and Practical Advice.** Dorling Kindersley, 1996. 272 pp. ISBN 0-7894-0633-0. Nonfiction.

This manual includes hints, tips, and secrets for teaching painting and covers a wide range of topics including the use of color and images, as well as works by well-known artists. The key to learning to paint, according to Camp, is copying great painters, and he shows how such a technique will help the student learn how to paint naturally. Each chapter is concise and illustrated with numerous examples, making this a valuable tool for the would-be artist.

28.3　CasaBianca, Louis. **First-Time Europe: A Rough Guide Special.** Illustrated by Jerry Swaffield. Rough Guides, 1996. 224 pp. ISBN 1-85828-210-1. Nonfiction.

Every year thousands of people travel to Europe for the first time. Plenty of excellent guide books are available for every conceivable region of Europe, but only careful planning can help the first-time traveler avoid common mistakes and frustrations, save time and money, and generally get the most out of the trip. The author offers thorough commonsense advice on all aspects of planning a trip to Europe: passports; transportation to, within, and between countries; and budgeting, luggage, food, lodging, clothing, security, communications, currency, and safety.

Maps, major rail routes, and the addresses and phone numbers of national tourist offices, airlines, discount flight agents, travel book and map stores, and travel equipment suppliers are provided, along with international telephone codes and basic words and phrases for survival in twenty-one languages.

28.4 **The Complete Book of Sewing.** Dorling Kindersley, 1996. 320 pp. ISBN 0-7894-0419-2. Nonfiction.

Whether you have sewn for years or are just starting out, this is the manual for you. It covers every technique involved in sewing and making clothes, and helps the experienced stitcher to reinforce skills. Each technique is illustrated step-by-step with color photographs for easy understanding, which, along with a glossary, an index, and highlighted "tip boxes," makes this a valuable addition to anyone's reference shelf.

28.5 Frank, Ben G. **A Travel Guide to Jewish Europe.** 2nd ed. Pelican, 1996. 600 pp. ISBN 1-56554-037-9. Nonfiction.

This text takes readers through historic Jewish Europe country by country. Within each country description, Frank lists kosher restaurants and cafés, synagogues, museums, and other cultural heritage sites, all arranged by city. MC

28.6 Friedhoffer, Bob. **The Magic Show: A Guide for Young Magicians.** Illustrated by Linda Eisenberg. The Millbrook Press, 1994. 64 pp. ISBN 1-56294-355-3. Nonfiction.

If you want to learn to perform simple magic tricks, this is the book for you. Eighteen tricks are explained step-by-step including the effect you want to achieve, the props needed, and how to perform the set-up, routine, and patter. Easy-to-follow illustrations are included for each trick. A glossary, a booklist, and lists of magic magazines, magic clubs, and suppliers of magic equipment are included as a resource.

28.7 Gardner, Robert. **Crime Lab 101: Experimenting with Crime Detection.** Walker, 1994. 96 pp. ISBN 0-8027-7420- 2. Nonfiction.

Would you like to be a criminalist, someone who uses scientific techniques to investigate crimes? The twenty-five activities in this book will let you practice. Find out how to analyze fingerprints, blood types, hair, fibers, and lip prints to solve crimes. Learn how to crack secret codes and match handwriting. ER

28.8 Gordon, Malcolm. **Outback Australia at Cost: A Traveller's Guide to the Northern Territory and Kimberley.** Little Hills Press, 1994. 576 pp. ISBN 1-86315-046-3. Nonfiction.

From lonely road houses in outlying settlements to the cities of Darwin and Alice Springs, Gordon provides a comprehensive guide for the traveler interested in experiencing Australia's "outback." Tips are provided on where to stay, where to eat, what to pack given the landscape and climate, where to drive, what national parks and other landmarks to visit, and where to shop.

28.9   Joyce, Katherine. **Astounding Optical Illusions.** Sterling, 1994. 96 pp. ISBN 0-8069-0431-3. Nonfiction.

This is a book of tricks for the eye and for the mind, designed to help the reader have fun while learning about illusions and how they work. There are optical illusion designs, hidden pictures, and shadow illustrations for the reader to try solving, as well as chapters on illusion tricks, illusion magic, and tactile illusions which the reader is challenged to perform with experiments. It is a book for anyone interested in how we see and what it is we think we see, and would be excellent in the classroom for the study of perception. ER

28.10   Krizmanic, Judy. **A Teen's Guide to Going Vegetarian.** Illustrated by Matthew Wawiorka. Foreword by T. Colin Campbell. Viking, 1994. 218 pp. ISBN 0-670-85114-0. Nonfiction.

Krizmanic has provided a useful reference for anyone interested in vegetarianism. Chapters on how to ensure a healthy, balanced diet, how to snack, what to say to friends who don't quite understand the concept, and how to "come out" to parents, among others, make for an informative text that is easy to read either as an introduction to a different lifestyle or as a companion piece for those who have already chosen to go vegetarian.

28.11   Martin, Wendy, editor. **Colonial American Travel Narratives.** Penguin, 1994. 352 pp. ISBN 0 14 03.9088 X. Nonfiction.

The common focus of these four narratives is travel. Mary Rowlandson's 1677 captivity narrative, Sarah Kemble Knight's 1704 travel journal, William Byrd's 1728 surveyor's diary, and Alexander Hamilton's 1744 travel narrative encompass a geographically diverse area from Maine to North Carolina, and they mark the chronological shift from colonist as outsider to colonist as resident. These texts are a useful primary resource for the advanced reader interested in eighteenth-century life.

28.12   McGill, Ormand. **Mind Magic: Tricks for Reading Minds.** Illustrated by Anne Canevari Green. The Millbrook Press, 1995. 64 pp. ISBN 1-56294-465-7. Nonfiction.

Impress your friends with these ten magical mind-reading tricks from a world-acclaimed magician. They will believe that you can read minds, see hidden objects, and predict the future with tricks such as "Open Sesame!" "Dead or Alive?" and "Modus Operandi: ESP." With helpful and entertaining illustrations accompanying the simple instructions, you will master the tricks with a little rehearsal. But remember, keep the secrets to yourself! ER

28.13 McManners, Hugh. **The Backpacker's Handbook.** Dorling Kindersley, 1995. 160 pp. ISBN 1-56458-852-1. Nonfiction.

McManners describes all the beginning backpacker needs to know to get started. He provides advice on every aspect of backpacking, from choosing equipment and developing orienteering skills to testing wild flowers for edibility and purifying water. Richly illustrated with photographs and step-by-step instructions, this book belongs in the backpack of anyone adventuring into the wild for hiking and camping excitement.

28.14 McManners, Hugh. **The Complete Wilderness Training Book.** Dorling Kindersley, 1994. 192 pp. ISBN 1-56458-488-7. Nonfiction.

You are hopelessly lost in the woods and without a compass. What do you do? This book presents at least six ways to find direction without a compass, and that is just an example of the hundreds of useful outdoor survival skills presented. This book pretty nearly lives up to its title as a "complete" overview of field skills. High-quality photographs and diagrams on every page aid understanding, as does a glossary of terms.

ALA Quick Picks for Young Adults, 1995

28.15 Munson, Robert S. **Favorite Hobbies and Pastimes: A Sourcebook of Leisure Pursuits.** American Library Association, 1994. 366 pp. ISBN 0-8389-0638-9. Nonfiction.

If you're searching for a new hobby, look no further. This reference book about more than ninety hobbies, crafts, and pastimes includes a brief but informative description and history of each entry, a bibliography, lists of equipment and supplies needed, and information regarding related associations. Interests range from astronomy to baseball, coin collecting to ice hockey, wrestling to model cars and planes, needle arts to water skiing. Very useful for further research is the library classification of subjects, including both Library of Congress and Dewey Decimal System call numbers. An excellent reference, this sourcebook of hobbies and crafts will inspire new interests and provide additional information for established pursuits.

28.16 Owens, Thomas S. **Collecting Baseball Memorabilia.** The Millbrook Press, 1996. 96 pp. ISBN 1-56294-579-3. Nonfiction.

Collecting Baseball Memorabilia explains how to get started in this hobby. It tells the reader where to find treasures and how to write for free items. Pictures are provided to show how newspapers, programs, schedules, products, cards, and autographs can be collected and displayed. Addresses, a glossary, and an index are also included.

28.17   Reid, Lori. **The Art of Hand Reading.** Dorling Kindersley, 1996. 120 pp. ISBN 0-7894-1060-5. Nonfiction.

The mysteries of palmistry are revealed in greater detail than most people realize exists. Although practicing hand reading undoubtedly improves one's technique and expertise on its own, the basics of how to read the entire hand are as clearly described and generously illustrated as would be expected from a Dorling Kindersley publication. Have fun interpreting the shape, lines, mounts, nails, patterns, and fingerprints on the hands of friends and family!

28.18   Rutledge, Len. **Maverick Guide to Malaysia and Singapore.** Pelican, 1994. 474 pp. ISBN 0-88289-990-2. Nonfiction.

This book is a resource guide for those interested in reading about Malaysia and Singapore before traveling or for general interest. The book includes a wealth of information for the traveler in chapters on transportation, culture, dining, sightseeing, sports, shopping, and related areas of interest. There are also sections on the geography, history, and people of these two countries. MC

28.19   Ryan, Steve. **Test Your Math IQ.** Sterling, 1994. 96 pp. ISBN 0-8069-0724-X. Nonfiction.

If you like math puzzles, this is your book, with seventy-eight different activities to keep you busy. Some use simple addition, subtraction, multiplication, and division, while others require more difficult manipulations. Start with the easier one-pencil selections and work your way up to the three-pencil mind benders. Solutions for all the puzzles are included.

28.20   Scott, Peter W. **The Complete Aquarium.** Photography by Jane Burton and Kim Taylor. Dorling Kindersley, 1995. 192 pp. ISBN 0-7894-0013-8. Nonfiction.

A collection of beautiful photographs and a well-organized and comprehensive text make this volume an excellent reference guide for the aquarium hobbyist. Sixteen tank set-ups, intended to re-create natural aquatic environments, are presented and explained in detail. Whether your interest is in an Amazon rain forest stream, an East African rocky lake, or a British rock pool, information on water management, filtration, heating, lighting, plants, food, breeding, equipment, and health care is provided in text, photographs, and charts. A glossary, an index with generous cross-referencing, and appendices discussing water chemistry and biological filtration are included.

28.21   Townsend, Charles Berry. **World's Most Amazing Puzzles.** Sterling, 1994. 128 pp. ISBN 0-8069-8761-8. Nonfiction.

This is the seventh book in a series designed to preserve outstanding puzzles that have perplexed and astounded thinking people through the years. Here, for example, is the "Ghost" puzzle. The Ghost asks, "How dare you disturb my resting place! Answer this question quickly, or join me for eternity. What is that from which you may take away the whole and yet have some left?" These kinds of questions and visual puzzles tax readers to use their analytical skills. The book is a goldmine for teachers looking for problems to challenge the logical and critical thinking of their students or for students seeking to challenge one another. By the way, the answer to the Ghost's question is "wholesome"— take away the "whole" and you are left with "some"! ER

28.22   Turner, Don. **Maverick Guide to Bali and Java.** 2nd ed. Pelican, 1995. 310 pp. ISBN 1-56554-052-2. Nonfiction.

You wouldn't want to travel to Bali or Java without this guide. It is full of details about the small, beautiful Indonesian island of Bali and its neighbor, Java. The first four chapters tell about how to get to the islands, and about the Balinese and Javanese peoples and their land, language, food, arts, and cultural expectations. Each of the last six chapters, divided by regions of Bali and Java, includes sections about transportation, lodging, dining, sightseeing, sports, shopping, and entertainment. Maps and a detailed index are also included. MC

28.23   Willis, Norman D. **Amazing Logic Puzzles.** Illustrated by Jim Sharpe. Sterling, 1994. 128 pp. ISBN 0-8069-0564-6. Nonfiction.

These are brand-new logic puzzles that take the reader to the magical worlds of Sir Hector the Dragon Fighter, the Black Knight, and Mordin the Sorcerer. What is presented are stimulating encounters with deductive thinking. There are six types of logic problems presented, dealing with hypothesis, with who did it, with letters for digits, with standards for veracity, with arrangements in order, and with fragments of information. After each problem there are clues, and at the end there are solutions. This could well be a must book for developing critical thinking skills.

Titles Annotated in Other Chapters Related to Recreation, Travel, and Leisure Time Activities

Ballantine, Richard, and Richard Grant. *Richards' Bicycle Repair Manual.* Airplanes.

Camp, Jeffery. *Draw: How to Master the Art.* Arts.

Chapman, Richard. *The Complete Guitarist.* Arts.

Crawford, Peter. *Nomads of the Wind: A Natural History of Polynesia.* History.

Evans, Jeremy. *Adventurers: Skateboarding.* Sports.

Evans, Jeremy. *Adventurers: Surfing.* Sports.

Holbrook, Mike. *Adventurers: Snorkeling.* Sports.

Horton, James. *An Introduction to Drawing.* Arts.

Nash, Helen. *Challenging Cryptograms.* Language.

Paulsen, Gary. *Father Water, Mother Woods*. Diaries.
Pellowski, Michael Morgan. *The Art of Making Comic Books*. Arts.
Smith, Ray. *An Introduction to Perspective*. Arts.
Smith, Ray. *Oil Painting Portraits*. Arts.

29 Reference

"He who knows only his side of the case knows little of that."
John Stuart Mill

"The better part of every man's education is that which he gives himself."
James Russell Lowell

29.1 Adams, Simon. **Visual Timeline of the Twentieth Century.** Dorling Kindersley, 1996. 48 pp. ISBN 0-7894-0997-6. Nonfiction.

Adams has captured and organized in a visual format the continually chaotic history of this century. Images of key people, of key events, and of key places in the world's ongoing struggle for peaceful co-existence leap off the page to show the reader what was happening and when all over the globe.

29.2 Andryszewski, Tricia. **Abortion: Rights, Options, and Choices.** The Millbrook Press, 1996. 112 pp. ISBN 1-56294-573-4. Nonfiction.

Abortion is one of today's most controversial issues. Almost everyone has a strong opinion on the subject. This book offers an objective perspective on the legal, medical, and moral aspects of the abortion debate. The before and after *Roe v. Wade* environments and the pro-choice and anti-abortion points of view receive equal time. This reference text, part of the Issue and Debate series, provides a good overview of the issue.

29.3 Ardley, Neil. **Dictionary of Science.** Dorling Kindersley, 1994. 192 pp. ISBN 1-56458-349-X. Nonfiction.

The *Dictionary of Science* is a listing of two thousand key words arranged thematically. The book is divided into chapters, including a guide to help users, a list of abbreviations, a short biography of 150 scientists, and a complete index. "See also" references are used to guide readers to related information. Diagrams, illustrations, and charts are also included to explain concepts and phrases.

29.4 Ash, Russell. **Incredible Comparisons.** Dorling Kindersley, 1996. 63 pp. ISBN 0-7894-1009-5. Nonfiction.

This fascinating reference book visually and textually compares subjects in an effort to clarify relationships. For example, a drowning Statue of Liberty graphically illustrates what would happen if all the ice in the world were to melt, and the picture of a hailstone next to a tenpin bowling ball captures the size of the enormous hail that once fell on Coffeyville, Kansas. This book will provide the reader with hours of "You've got to be kidding!" fun. ER

29.5   Ash, Russell. **The Top Ten of Everything 1996.** Dorling Kindersley, 1995. 281 pp. ISBN 0-7894-0196-7. **The Top Ten of Everything.** Dorling Kindersley, 1994. 288 pp. ISBN 1-56458-703-7. Nonfiction.

Hundreds of amazing facts about the superlatives in thirteen major categories are crammed into these books, which provide the answers to many questions. Curious readers will easily find information about the world's highest-earning entertainers, most Grand Slam titles, largest polished gems, longest suspension bridges, most expensive musical instruments, and much more. Hard facts and trivia both make these very visual books informative and entertaining. ER

ALA Quick Picks for Young Adults, 1995

29.6   Beetz, Kirk H., editor. **Beacham's Guide to Literature for Young Adults, Volumes 6–8.** Walton Beacham, 1994. 1673 pp. (combined). ISBN 0-933833-32-6. Nonfiction.

This multi-volume set expands upon the original five volumes of *Beacham's Guide to Literature for Young Adults* by presenting analytical essays, author information, and study guide material for 225 works of fiction and nonfiction published since 1980. The titles included vary in terms of their reading difficulty and the maturity required to handle their subject matter; thus every reader should be able to find something. It is a useful source of information for librarians, teachers, and readers who want to know more about a favorite author or who are doing research for a paper. Volume 8 includes a cumulative index for the entire series, and each volume includes an appendix of titles grouped by themes and a glossary of literary terms.

29.7   Busenberg, Bonnie. **Vanilla, Chocolate, and Strawberry: The Story of Your Favorite Flavors.** Lerner, 1994. 112 pp. ISBN 0-8225-1573-3. Nonfiction.

Did you know that the flavors vanilla, chocolate, and strawberry have been enjoyed for more than five hundred years? This book details the discovery, myths, growing areas, and uses of the flavors. Photographs, illustrations, charts, maps, and recipes make the flavors vanilla, chocolate, and strawberry interesting as well as delicious. ER

ALA Quick Picks for Young Adults, 1995

29.8   Cart, Michael. **From Romance to Realism: Fifty Years of Growth and Change in Young Adult Literature.** HarperCollins, 1996. 312 pp. ISBN 0-06-024289-2. Nonfiction.

Beginning with definitions of adolescence and of young adult literature (YAL), Cart traces YAL from the 1940s to the present, looking closely at early and recent romance novels. He distinguishes realism from problem novels, discusses significant authors in each decade, takes a look at YA classics, and examines the influence of popular culture and marketing trends. He believes YAL, which must not be silenced, needs to address the real lives of young people with artistic relevance. With its extensive index and bibliography, this thought-provoking book will be useful to teachers and also interesting to high school readers.

29.9   Cart, Michael. **What's So Funny? Wit and Humor in American Children's Literature.** HarperCollins, 1995. 223 pp. ISBN 0-06-024453-4. Nonfiction.

Cart outlines the factors involved in writing humorous children's books, studying talking-animal fantasies, hyperbole, and tall-tale humor, and domestic / family comedy since 1920. He argues that although funny books often fail to receive critical acclaim, they are deserving of the same level of recognition for their craft as more serious literature receives. He studies the talents of writers from Sid Fleishman to Beverly Cleary in his efforts to describe what it is that makes a reader laugh out loud at a book.

29.10   Carter, Betty. **Best Books for Young Adults: The Selections, the History, the Romance.** American Library Association, 1994. 214 pp. ISBN 0-8389-3439-0. Nonfiction.

This single volume contains all the "Best" selections since the founding of the American Library Association's "Best Books for Young Adults" in 1966. Carter's introduction provides an overview of the significance of the list and of reading trends of young adults, and also includes biographical essays and selected letters from the authors. Teachers, parents, librarians, and young readers searching for the best books available will find this volume a gold mine of information, and very reader-friendly thanks to its index and list of works cited.

29.11   Challoner, Jack. **The Visual Dictionary of Physics.** Art editor Simon Murrell. Dorling Kindersley, 1995. 64 pp. ISBN 0-7894-0239-4. Nonfiction.

Challoner has created an eye-catching quick reference to the world of physics and scientific processes, including overviews of matter, energy, physical forces, motion, simple machines, electricity, magnetism, light, atoms, and nuclear and particle physics. The language and visual connections require a fair amount of abstract synthesis on the part of the reader, but provide a useful, if not simple, introduction to these topics.

29.12   **Chronicle of America.** Dorling Kindersley, 1995. 1008 pp. ISBN 0-7894-0124-X. Nonfiction.

This entry in the successful Chronicle series looks at the history of the United States. Timelines, newspaper-style articles, and artifact illustrations cover the pre-Columbian period to President Clinton's administration in chronological sequence. Information on states, a chart showing the layout of the federal government, and a fifty-five-page index make this a good value for library and classroom use.

29.13   Clayman, Charles, editor. **The Human Body: An Illustrated Guide to Its Structure, Function, and Disorders.** Dorling Kindersley, 1995. 240 pp. ISBN 1-56458-992-7. Nonfiction.

This beautifully illustrated volume uses medical drawings as well as MRI, contrast X-ray, microscopy, and CT scanning images to introduce the reader to the wonders of the human body and how it works. More than a thousand images are used along with clear, concise text to explain such processes as digestion and muscle contraction. The causes, symptoms, diagnosis, and treatment of a number of diseases and disorders are also investigated. An extensive glossary and an index make this an excellent reference source.

29.14   Clute, John. **Science Fiction: The Illustrated Encyclopedia.** Dorling Kindersley, 1995. 312 pp. ISBN 0-7894-0185-1. Nonfiction.

A history of science fiction and fantasy is presented here through brief descriptions and timelines that help place specific works and trends in these fields into their historical context. Science fiction films, television, books, magazines, illustrations, and authors from the nineteenth century through 1994 are listed and discussed. Included, too, are numerous color illustrations and photographs and a list of science fiction classics, each with a short explanation.

ALA Best Books for Young Adults, 1996

29.15   **The DK Geography of the World.** Dorling Kindersley, 1996. 304 pp. ISBN 0-7894-1004-4. Nonfiction.

In this stunning atlas each country of the world is described in overview. Each entry includes information about the country's physical geography, its people, and its important features, as well as a description of the role of the country in today's global village. Maps, flags, and "fact boxes" about such topics as the country's currency or literacy rate are also included.

29.16   **The Dorling Kindersley Visual Encyclopedia.** Dorling Kindersley, 1995. 424 pp. ISBN 1-56458-985-4. Nonfiction.

Feast your eyes on over four hundred pages of information on eleven general fields of knowledge including geography, sports, science and technology, and beliefs, customs, and societies. Pages are packed with photographs, diagrams, charts, and information ranging from the serious to the ridiculous. A user-friendly index is also provided.

29.17   **The Eyewitness Atlas of the World.** Dorling Kindersley, 1994. 160 pp. ISBN 1-56458-297-3. Nonfiction.

This handsome atlas begins by describing Earth in general, providing an overview of its structure, climates, vegetation, people, and the world today. The process of making the atlas is described next. Then, each continent is presented and the countries of that continent follow, each shown in wonderfully detailed large-scale maps including rivers, mountains, lakes, roads, and major cities. The visual appeal of the atlas is enhanced through over a thousand photographs, diagrams, and other visuals designed to help the user better appreciate the nature of each region of the world. This easy-to-use, visually stimulating, and informative text provides an up-to-date, state-of-the-art view of the world.

29.18 Farndon, John. **Dictionary of the Earth.** Dorling Kindersley, 1994. 192 pp. ISBN 1-56458-709-8. Nonfiction.

Earth scientist Farndon has collected over two thousand key terms relating to geography, geology, meteorology, and ecology, for which he has provided easy-to-understand definitions organized thematically. The accompanying visuals in full color, as well as the cross-references and the index, make this a handy, user-friendly reference tool for anyone interested in our planet and its workings.

Notable 1995 Children's Trade Books in the Field of Social Studies

29.19 Freedman, Michael. **Culturescope: The Princeton Review Guide to an Informed Mind.** High school ed. Random House, 1995. 500 pp. ISBN 0-679-75366-4. Nonfiction.

Fostering cultural literacy for high school students is at the heart of this publication. Topics include history, geography, science and technology, religion, literature, art, and music. The book begins with a multiple-choice cultural literacy quiz. Additional quiz questions are included throughout the book, which also contains photographs, maps, charts, and illustrations.

29.20 Freedman, Michael. **The Princeton Review Student Advantage Guide to Summer, 1996 Edition.** Random House, 1995. 205 pp. ISBN 0-679-76470-4. Nonfiction.

Essentially, this is a guide of activities for high school and college students to consider investigating as they plan their summer activities. The book covers camps, travel, internships, volunteer and academic programs, and jobs. Sources of additional information, with addresses and phone numbers, are also included, along with sections on useful videos, music, and books.

29.21 Glover, Denise M., editor. **Voices of the Spirit: Sources for Interpreting the African-American Experience.** American Library Association, 1995. 211 pp. ISBN 0-8389-0639-7. Nonfiction.

Using oral histories, the written word, and images to portray the African American experience, Glover provides information to better prepare her readers for living in a multiethnic society. She annotates sources from 1883 to the present that serve to highlight the courage, self-respect, and heroism of African Americans, and the picture that emerges serves to break down stereotypes and ethnic boundaries. MC

29.22   Griffin-Pierce, Trudy. **The Encyclopedia of Native America.** Viking, 1995. 192 pp. ISBN 0-670-85104-3. Nonfiction.

The author, of Catawban ancestry, presents Native American history from their perspective, through their words, and with their photographs. The reader visits the Iroquois, Algonquians, Choctaw, and Apache peoples and meets the real Pocahontas and dozens of other Native Americans who have contributed to this rich history. Paintings and maps help guide the reader through their stories, as one explores the military tactics, arts and crafts, pastimes and games, politics, and religions of the earliest Americans. Seven cultural and geographical areas are presented, each described in detail. Lists of resources and recommendations for further reading are included. MC

29.23   Harris, Laurie Lanzen, editor. **Biography Today: Profiles of People of Interest to Young Readers.** Omnigraphics, 1994. 342 pp. ISBN 1-55888-345-2. Nonfiction.

This biographical dictionary provides information about the entertainers, athletes, writers, illustrators, cartoonists, and political leaders who are, according to librarians, of most interest to young adult readers. Each of the forty-two biographical sketches includes a photograph, career highlights, honors and awards, and other personal information. The use of bold headings allows a reader to easily scan an entry for desired information. Obituaries are also included where appropriate, providing an overview of an individual's entire career. Figures included range from Lois Duncan, young adult author, to Denzel Washington, actor, to Rudolf Nureyev, ballet dancer, to Hillary Clinton, first lady. An appendix of updates for individuals profiled in the 1991 edition, a name index, and a general index add to the volume's appeal and usefulness.

29.24   Haskins, Jim, and Joann Biondi. **From Afar to Zulu: A Dictionary of African Cultures.** Walker, 1995. 212 pp. ISBN 0-8027-8290-6. Nonfiction.

Anyone interested in knowing more about Africa's diverse cultures will appreciate this useful reference. Supplemented with many black-and-white photographs, the text provides information on thirty of Africa's most populous cultures. Each entry includes demographic information, a map of the region, an overview of the customs and beliefs that distinguish the culture from others, and notes about both historical and recent developments within the culture. Some of Africa's vanished cultures, such as those of the kingdoms of Mali and Ghana, are also discussed. ER MC WL

29.25   Kidron, Michael, and Ronald Segal. **The State of the World Atlas.** New rev. 5ᵗʰ ed. Penguin, 1995. 160 pp. ISBN 0-14-025204-5. Nonfiction.

This set of fifty maps provides a unique reference source. Subjects such as global warming, urban populations, life expectancy, illiteracy rates, and plagues are covered in a view of the world useful for study and research. Students will find this atlas extremely helpful for any report dealing with any current event as it includes notes, sources, and an index.

29.26 Kimeldorf, Martin. Edited by Pamela Espeland. **Creating Portfolios for Success in School, Work, and Life.** Free Spirit, 1994. 85 pp. ISBN 0-915793-73-3. Nonfiction.

In jargon-free prose and in an easy-to-use format, Kimeldorf describes four basic types of portfolios (student, project, expert and professional, and personal), provides exercises designed to help the portfolio maker begin the creation process; continues with exercises and advice on issues such as organization, writing descriptions, and enriching them; outlines ways to organize portfolios; and concludes with information about the nuts and bolts of presenting a portfolio and fielding questions. A teacher's guide is also available to help teachers who are guiding students through the portfolio process.

29.27 Levine, Michael. **The Kid's Address Book: Over 2,000 Addresses of Celebrities, Athletes, Entertainers, and More . . . Just for Kids!** Perigee / Berkley, 1994. 219 pp. ISBN 0-399-51875-4. Nonfiction.

Here is a book sure to catch the interest of anyone who reads. This book contains over two thousand addresses of celebrities, entertainers, and athletes. In addition, there is a section listing the addresses of the offices of heads of state all around the world. This is a great resource for students and teachers. ER

29.28 Lukens, Rebecca J. **A Critical Handbook of Children's Literature.** 5th ed. HarperCollins College Publishers, 1995. 352 pp. ISBN 0-673-46937-9. Nonfiction.

In this easy-to-use handbook, Lukens proves that books for children can be valuable works of art worthy of critical analysis and study. She provides an overview of the essential literary elements, describing how these concepts can be used in evaluating books for children, and discusses the distinguishing features of specific genres such as picture books, informational books, poetry anthologies, fantasy, formula fiction, myths, folktales, and legends.

29.29 Melton, H. Keith. **The Ultimate Spy Book.** Dorling Kindersley, 1996. 176 pp. ISBN 0-7894-0443-5. Nonfiction.

Famous spy operations, equipment, and techniques are detailed in this publication, which includes numerous color and black-and-white photographs as well as illustrations, charts, and pictures. Basically covering the period between the American Civil War and the Cold War, the book deals with topics such as the people involved in spying, their exploits, and the risks and rewards they experienced. A glossary of terms is included.

29.30   Monroe, Judy. **Phobias: Everything You Wanted to Know, but Were Afraid to Ask.** Enslow, 1996. 112 pp. ISBN 0-89490-723-9. Nonfiction.

Phobias can be specific, such as a fear of flying or a fear of open spaces, or they can be social, such as a fear of public speaking. In this volume from the Issues in Focus series Monroe discusses the history of phobias, provides a brief summary of each, and outlines causes and treatments. A list of places to tap for further information and help in dealing with various phobias and anxiety disorders is also provided. ER

29.31   **1001 Questions and Answers.** Dorling Kindersley, 1995. 64 pp. ISBN 0-7894-0205-X. Nonfiction.

For use in a large or small group setting, the publishers have created an entertaining way to study a large group of topics. Each page is filled with easy-to-understand questions and colorful photographs, and an answer key is provided at the back of the book. The topics range from ancient Egypt, Greece, and Rome to movies, television, and theater. All ages will enjoy testing their knowledge against the questions. An index is included for easy cross-reference.

29.32   Patrick, John J. **The Young Oxford Companion to the Supreme Court of the United States.** Oxford University Press, 1994. 367 pp. ISBN 0-19-507877-2. Nonfiction.

The articles in this encyclopedia allow the reader to find information about the U.S. Supreme Court by word, idea, or name. In general, the entries are organized by topic, including biographies, decisions of the court, and core concepts such as constitutionalism and due process. For anyone interested in learning more about the law and its relationship to the concept of liberty on which the United States rests, this volume will be a great resource.

29.33   Pickford, Nigel. **The Atlas of Shipwrecks and Treasures.** Dorling Kindersley, 1994. 200 pp. ISBN 1-56458-599-9. Nonfiction.

Over fourteen hundred shipwrecks through the ages, with their precious cargoes of bronze, gold, finely crafted jewelry, and porcelain are described here with pictures as well as paintings from the appropriate era. Forty of the most famous shipwrecks are chronicled in detail, with a profile for each of the extraordinary attempts made to reclaim its archeological treasures. Maps of the world's oceans and seas, showing the locations of the wrecks, are also offered.

29.34   Pious, Richard M. **The Young Oxford Companion to the Presidency of the United States.** Oxford University Press, 1994. 304 pp. ISBN 0-19-507799-7. Nonfiction.

Arranged alphabetically, the articles in this volume cover words, concepts, and names related to the presidency of the United States. Articles

about people such as presidents, vice presidents, and selected first ladies include biographical overviews and commentaries on career highlights. Terms such as "brains trust" or "patronage Presidential" are followed by definitions and historical examples. Every entry concludes
with cross-references and a further reading list. This book is one in a
series including *The Young Oxford Companion to the Congress of the United
States* and *The Young Oxford Companion to the Supreme Court of the United
States.*

Notable 1994 Children's Trade Books in the Field of Social Studies

29.35   Platt, Richard. **Stephen Biesty's Incredible Explosions.** Illustrated by
Stephen Biesty. Dorling Kindersley, 1996. 32 pp. ISBN 0-7894-1024-9.
Nonfiction.

Colorful and lively, this book rivals the visual dictionaries, cross-sections, and "how things work" books for popular appeal, although it is
more suited for entertaining browsing than for actual research. Topics
illustrated, with abundant captions, include an old steam tractor, a fire
in a high-rise, a space station, an airport, a windmill, a city, an Antarctic base, a movie studio, Venice, Tower Bridge, the human body, and
the Grand Canyon. ER

29.36   Pockets series. Dorling Kindersley, 1995. 128 pp. Nonfiction.
Brewer, Sarah. **Body Facts.** ISBN 0-7894-1018-4.
Costello, Darby, and Lindsay Radermacher. **Astrology.** ISBN 0-7894-
1019-2.
Eden, Philip, and Clint Twist. **Weather Facts.** ISBN 0-7894-0218-1.
Labi, Esther. **World Atlas.** ISBN 0-7894-0215-7.

The Pockets series provides easy-to-use collections of facts about diverse
topics. Each title is organized by topic and includes a "How to Use This
Book" section, a guide to the well-drawn visuals, and an index. Every
pair of pages provides an overview of a different aspect of the topic,
making these tiny books a quick and enjoyable reference for the busy
scholar. ER

29.37   Reed, Arthea J. S. **Comics to Classics: A Guide to Books for Teens and
Preteens.** Penguin Books, 1994. 238 pp. ISBN 0-14-023712-7. Nonfiction.

This informative handbook is written for parents to help them connect
with young adults in the area of reading. It discusses the psychological
makeup of the adolescent reader and offers guidelines about how to help
the adolescent select worthwhile reading material with pertinent topics such as "What to Look for in Good Multicultural Literature" and
"Characteristics of Good Science Fiction for Young Adults." It also provides hints about how to discuss literature with an adolescent reader.
An annotated list of classic and contemporary books with codes indi-
cating appropriateness for age, gender, and reading level is included.

29.38   Rees, Dafydd, and Luke Crampton. **Encyclopedia of Rock Stars.**
         Dorling Kindersley, 1996. 951 pp. ISBN 0-7894-1263-2. Nonfiction.

         This volume contains everything anyone would want to know about
         every rock star from the 1950s to the present, including information
         about each artist's family, early years, hit recordings, major musical
         events, musical influences, and biographical information. Not a book
         to be read from cover to cover, it is a comprehensive reference book for
         rock music enthusiasts. MC

29.39   Schon, Isabel, editor. **Contemporary Spanish-Speaking Writers and Il-
         lustrators for Children and Young Adults: A Biographical Dictionary.**
         Translated by Jason Douglas White. Greenwood Press, 1994. 248 pp.
         ISBN 0-313-29027-X. Nonfiction.

         Biographical information is given on more than two hundred contem-
         porary Spanish-speaking writers and illustrators for children and young
         adults from Mexico, Spain, the United States, and the countries of Cen-
         tral and South America. Entries include personal data, address and ca-
         reer information, memberships in professional organizations, awards
         and honors, bibliographic information, sidelights, and critical sources.
         An appendix lists authors and illustrators by country of origin, and an
         index is also included. MC WL

29.40   Smith, Karen Patricia, editor. **African-American Voices in Young Adult
         Literature: Tradition, Transition, Transformation.** Scarecrow Press,
         1994. 405 pp. ISBN 0-8108-2907-X. Nonfiction.

         This collection of essays provides a detailed overview of the African
         American presence in young adult literature. Contributors analyze such
         diverse topics as how a white feminist reads African American female
         poets, how mother-daughter relationships are presented in African
         American young adult fiction, how periodicals for adolescent African
         Americans are a neglected resource, and how online databases could
         be used to disseminate information about contemporary African Ameri-
         can young adult literature. The breadth of topics explored and the depth
         of the analyses make this a valuable resource for researchers interested
         in the importance of African American contributors to the field of young
         adult literature. MC

29.41   Smith, Miranda. **Living Earth.** Dorling Kindersley, 1996. 192 pp. ISBN
         0-7894-0644-6. Nonfiction.

         Typical of the Eyewitness series, this lavishly illustrated volume makes
         very good browsing, while the extensive index enables it to serve as a
         reference source as well. The limited use of text will enhance the book's
         appeal to visual learners. ER

29.42   Spencer, Pam, editor. **What Do Young Adults Read Next? A Reader's Guide to Fiction for Young Adults.** Gale Research, 1994. 816 pp. ISBN 0-8103-8887-1. Nonfiction.

This "readers' advisory tool" is designed to help any young adult reader find titles that reflect his or her interests. Each of the 1,509 entries, which are organized alphabetically by author, includes the book's title, age range, subjects, characters, setting, brief plot overview, reviewing sources, awards, other books by the same author, and other books the reader might like introduced with one-sentence synopses. Other useful features include the indexes (series, awards, time periods, geographic areas, subjects, character names, character descriptions, appropriate readers' ages, authors, and titles), and an introductory essay about the field of young adult literature from 1988 to 1992.

29.43   Sullivan, Helen, and Linda Sernoff. **Research Reports: A Guide for Middle and High School Students.** The Millbrook Press, 1996. 121 pp. ISBN 1-56294-694-3. Nonfiction.

This is a welcome "how-to" book on writing research reports. Online research, word processors, and CD-Rom references are included. The visual format, step-by-step procedures, and good examples add to the text's value.

29.44   van Rose, Susanna. **The Earth Atlas.** Illustrated by Richard Bonson. Dorling Kindersley, 1994. 64 pp. ISBN 1-56458-626-X. Nonfiction.

Have you ever wondered how the earth formed from a cloud of gas and dust? Do you know why geysers gush and earthquakes shake? Can you describe what is inside a volcano or under a glacier? The answers to these questions and more can be found in *The Earth Atlas*, a visual guide to the forces that have shaped our planet. Colorful graphics, photographs, and a very thorough index makes this a fun volume to browse and from which to learn more about our planetary home. ER

Notable 1994 Children's Trade Books in the Field of Social Studies

29.45   **The Visual Dictionary of Prehistoric Life.** Dorling Kindersley, 1995. 64 pp. ISBN 1-56458-859-9. Nonfiction.

The beautiful illustrations and photographs of the Eyewitness Visual Dictionary series and the clear, concise text make it enjoyable for all readers to use. Ships, animals, plants, military uniforms, ancient civilizations, and the earth are only some of the things explained and shown in great detail. An extensive index and detailed labeling of illustrations and photographs give readers access to the particular terms associated with each topic. This series is a wealth of information and a pleasure to explore.

29.46   Wittels, Harriet, and Joan Greisman. **The Clear and Simple Thesaurus Dictionary.** Edited and with an introduction by William Morris. Grosset and Dunlap, 1996. 319 pp. ISBN 0-448-41555-0. Nonfiction.

Originally titled *The Young People's Thesaurus Dictionary*, this revised edition lives up to its new name. The print is large and well-spaced, antonyms are clearly distinguished by gray type, and the size of the volume is easily manageable. All of these features make it a particularly useful item for those intimidated by more elaborate resources.

29.47   Wolfson, Evelyn. **From Abenaki to Zuni: A Dictionary of Native American Tribes.** Illustrations by William Sauts Bock. Walker, 1995. 215 pp. ISBN 0-8027-7445-8. Nonfiction.

Wolfson provides information on sixty-eight of the largest Native American tribes of North America. In an easy-to-use format, she describes their history and culture including details of what they wore, what they ate, how they traveled, and where their descendants live today. ER MC

Titles Annotated in Other Chapters Related to Reference

The Art Book. Arts.

Ballinger, Erich. *Detective Dictionary*. College.

Ballinger, Erich. *Monster Manual*. Myths.

Cheney, Glenn Alan. *Teens with Physical Disabilities*. Self-Help.

Couper, Heather, and Nigel Henbert. *Black Holes*. Science.

Elster, Charles Harrington, and Joseph Elliot. *Tooth and Nail: A Novel Approach to the New SAT*. Mysteries.

Flynn, Tom, and Karen Lound. *AIDS: Examining the Crisis*. Drugs.

Gardner, Robert. *Crime Lab 101*. Recreation.

Hopkins, Lee Bennett. *Pauses: Autobiographical Reflections of 101 Creators of Children's Books*. Autobiography.

Hyde, Margaret O. *Gambling: Winners and Losers*. Political Science.

Kent, Sarah. *Composition*. Arts.

Lloyd, Elizabeth Jane. *Watercolor Still Life*. Arts.

Mullen, Chris, with Brian Coleman. *The Young Basketball Player*. Sports.

Munson, Robert S. *Favorite Hobbies and Pastimes*. Recreation.

Novas, Himilce. *Everything You Need to Know About Latino History*. History.

Opie, Mary-Jane. *Sculpture*. Arts.

Parker, Steve. *Natural World*. Animals.

Platt, Richard. *Smithsonian Visual Timeline of Inventions*. Science.

Slap, Gail B., and Martha M. Jablow. *Teenage Health Care*. Drugs.

Stefoff, Rebecca. *The Young Oxford Companion to Maps and Mapmaking*. History.

The Sports Illustrated 1995 Sports Almanac. Sports.

Tyning, Thomas F. *A Guide to Amphibians and Reptiles*. Animals.
The Visual Dictionary of Ancient Civilizations. History.
The Visual Dictionary of the Skeleton. Science.
Wilson, Anthony. *Dorling Kindersley Visual Timeline of Transportation*. Airplanes.
Wilson, Hugo. *The Encyclopedia of the Motorcycle*. Airplanes.

30 Religion, Cults, and Inspiration

"Nobody can deny but religion is a comfort to the distressed, a cordial to the sick, and sometimes a restraint on the wicked; therefore, whoever would laugh or argue it out of the world without giving some equivalent for it, ought to be treated as a common enemy."

Mary Wortley Montague

"There are, on the way to Rainy Mountain, many landmarks, many journeys in one. From the beginning the migration of the Kiowas was an expression of the human spirit, and that expression is most truly made in terms of wonder and delight."

N. Scott Momaday

"Nature has created us with the capacity to know God, to experience God, . . . "

Alice Walker

30.1   Bennett, William J., editor. **The Book of Virtues for Young People: A Treasury of Great Moral Stories.** Silver Burdett Press, 1996. 378 pp. ISBN 0-382-24923-2. Fiction.

Learn about self-discipline from George Washington and the fables of Aesop; about compassion from the Civil War experiences of Clara Barton and from a master teller of folklore, Leo Tolstoy; and about courage from Anne Frank, the biblical David, and Rosa Parks. These are some of the stories, myths, and poetry included in this volume that continue to be treasured for their wisdom and truth about human possibilities. MC

30.2   Biffi, Inos. **An Introduction to the Liturgical Year.** Illustrated by Franco Vignazia. William B. Eerdmans Publishing, 1995. 100 pp. ISBN 0-8028-5103-7. Nonfiction.

This New Testament–based book discusses the life of Jesus though the Christian celebrations of the liturgical year. The entire liturgical year is explained including Advent, Christmas, Lent, and Easter. Colorful illustrations accompany the text. The introduction states that this book will be helpful to readers interested in Christian beliefs, and to those considering converting to the Christian faith. ER

30.3   Child, John. **The Rise of Islam.** Peter Bedrick Books, 1995. 64 pp. ISBN 0-87226-116-6. Nonfiction.

There are one billion Muslims in the world today. This book tells about Islam, their religion, and about Muhammad, their leader. It includes information about their world and ideas: Arabs, Baghdad, the roles of men and women, Islamic art, medicine, schools, the Crusades, and the rise and fall of the Ottoman Empire. Features include pictures and illustrations, accompanying information written in paragraph format but organized like an outline, with sources named for each point and keywords in bold print. ER MC

30.4   Cohen, Daniel. **Cults.** The Millbrook Press, 1994. 135 pp. ISBN 1-56294-324-3. Nonfiction.

Cults are not as popular as their founders would have the public believe, according to this author. In fact, dropout rates are high, although people who are lonely, poor, and without families are frequently attracted to the camaraderie of cults. Cult leaders claim to be divinely inspired messengers of God, but they do not teach the truth. Instead, men like David Koresh and Jim Jones prey on innocent people during times of crisis; some even claim to be the Messiah. MC

30.5   **Dangerous Journey.** Candle Books / Eerdmans, 1994. 126 pp. ISBN 0-8028-3619-4. Fiction.

The story of John Bunyan's *Pilgrim's Progress* is presented in this lushly illustrated version of the classic allegory. *Dangerous Journey* chronicles the challenges and trials that Christian and later his wife and children encounter while searching for Paradise, as well as the escape from the doomed City of Destruction.

30.6   Fromm, Pete. **Monkey Tag.** Scholastic Hardcover, 1994. 336 pp. ISBN 0-590-46525-2. Fiction.

What begins as an adventurous and forbidden game of tag underneath the football stadium's bleachers ends in paralysis for twelve-year-old twin Thad. While Thad struggles to recover from his physical injuries, his twin brother Eli struggles with injuries of his own. Blaming himself and God for the accident, Eli wrestles with his Roman Catholic faith and wonders how God could have let this happen. ER

30.7   Gellman, Rabbi Marc, and Monsignor Thomas Hartman. **How Do You Spell God? Answers to the Big Questions from Around the World.** Illustrated by Jos. A. Smith. Morrow Junior Books, 1995. 206 pp. ISBN 0-688-13041-0. Nonfiction.

Gellman and Hartman, the "God Squad" of national cable TV, combine humor with a clear sensitivity to the difficulties inherent in discussing "big questions." In this volume, they describe how each of the major religions of the world answer tough queries, from "What happens after death?" to "Why do good people have to experience bad events?" As a result of their original organizational structure, readers emerge with a clear sense of what commonalities are shared by the world's religions, why they are, even so, quite different, and why we should all try to understand one another's beliefs. MC

30.8   Goldin, Barbara Diamond. **Bat Mitzvah: A Jewish Girl's Coming of Age.** Viking, 1995. 146 pp. ISBN 0-670-86034-4. Nonfiction.

This text explores the history and tradition behind the bat mitzvah, the ceremony in which a Jewish girl marks her transition into adulthood. The first section of the book examines the lives of many impressive Jewish women, biblical and historical, whose lives demonstrated Jewish women's independent spirit long before the first official bat mitzvah was performed in the 1920s. The second section of the book describes the different religious components of an actual bat mitzvah and concludes with thoughts about the implications of the ceremony for Jewish women's future lives. MC

30.9   Herman, Charlotte. **What Happened to Heather Hopkowitz?** The Jewish Publication Society, 1994. 186 pp. ISBN 0-8276-0520-X. Fiction.

Friday nights were for bowling, and cheeseburgers were the favorite food of fourteen-year-old Heather until her parents leave her for a month with an Orthodox Jewish family. Heather begins to appreciate and connect with a tradition of faith that her parents haven't practiced in their home. The challenge of confronting her parents and her friends with her new knowledge forces Heather to confirm what she believes and who she is. ER MC

30.10   Jordan, Michael. **I Can't Accept Not Trying: Michael Jordan on the Pursuit of Excellence.** Photographs by Sandro Miller. HarperSanFrancisco / HarperCollins, 1994. 36 pp. ISBN 0-06-251190-4. Nonfiction.

Extremely brief and straightforward, this book provides a statement of basketball great Michael Jordan's philosophy of achievement. Fans will find it inspirational. ER MC

ALA Quick Picks for Young Adults, 1995

30.11   Kimmel, Eric A. **Bar Mitzvah: A Jewish Boy's Coming of Age.** Illustrated by Erika Weihs. Viking, 1995. 133 pp. ISBN 0-670-85540-5. Nonfiction.

What does it mean for a Jewish boy to become bar mitzvah? This book details the yearlong study and preparation required as well as the big day itself by explaining, comparing, and contrasting the bar mitzvah to coming-of-age ceremonies in other cultures. Rich personal reminiscences from men of many ages help Jews and non-Jews understand the many rituals that allow a Jewish boy to become a man, or "one who has the obligation of fulfilling commandments." MC

30.12   Lasky, Kathryn. **Memoirs of a Bookbat.** Harcourt Brace, 1994. 215 pp. ISBN 0-15-215727-1. Fiction.

Harper Jessup is a young woman of fourteen who loves books and loves to read, but who has a problem. Her mother and father, who have kept the family on the move across America, want the best for her, and for the schools and communities they visit, but have become what Harper calls "migrants for God." Her parents are engaged in the public promotion of censorship, and Harper realizes that their quest for control of how and what people should think has become a quest to control her choices and decisions. This is a book with a strong young woman as the central character, and it deals with two difficult subjects, censorship and religious values in a family. It is an excellent book dealing with values clarification for mature readers.

30.13   Levitin, Sonia. **Escape from Egypt.** Little, Brown, 1994. 267 pp. ISBN 0-316-52273-2. Fiction.

Jesse, a Hebrew slave, and Jennat, half-Egyptian and half-Syrian, live in two very different worlds. Jennat is the servant of a rich Egyptian mistress and Jesse is from the tribe of Israelites who follow Moses and believe in God. While Jesse's mother is an ardent believer, his father's only concern is survival and he attempts to curry favor with the rich and powerful Egyptians. When Jesse and Jennat become attracted to each other despite their differences, his parents are adamantly opposed. As Jennat becomes more devoted to Jesse and fascinated by the Israelites' beliefs, both young people are embroiled in the Exodus and wanderings in the wilderness and in conflicts among the believers. MC

ALA Best Books for Young Adults, 1995
Booklist Editors' Choice, 1995

30.14   Maxwell, Will N., editor. **The Country Music Guide to Life.** Signet / Penguin Books, 1994. 147 pp. ISBN 0-451-17955-2. Nonfiction.

Words of wisdom and plain speaking from the outspoken stars of country music are compiled in this collection of confessions and advice that reveals the honesty and sensitivity of America's country musicians and their music. Included for the aficionado of country is a country music I.Q. test that challenges the reader's expertise.

30.15   McClung, Jean. **Mischief and Mercy: Tales of the Saints.** Tricycle Press, 1993. 212 pp. ISBN 1-883672-02-3. Nonfiction.

Thirteen whimsical, humorous stories about saints—Mary Magdalene, Jesus, St. Nicholas, and others—are told here. Why do we associate the hearts and flowers of Valentine's Day with St. Valentine, a spoiled Roman lord, or Francis of Assisi with a love of animals? Did you know St. Nicholas moved to the North Pole to become Santa Claus because of his bad temper? There are many more little-known gems about saints and near-saints in *Mischief and Mercy*. Catholic Digest Book Club Selection. Some violence and sexual references.

30.16   Medieval Wisdom series. Chronicle Books, 1994. Nonfiction.
      Alchemy: The Art of Knowing. ISBN 0-8118-0473-9.
      Chivalry: The Path of Love. 0-8118-0464-X.
      Mysticism: The Experience of the Divine. 0-8118-0484-4.

If an interest in medieval alchemy, chivalry, and mysticism has been on hold for lack of information, this set of little books is just the answer. Beautifully illustrated with colored plates, each volume provides an enlightening introduction to the subject and presents a clear, concise, and thorough explanation of the practices so valued during the Middle Ages. Many of the names of the period may be familiar, but their impact on alchemy, chivalry, or mysticism may be entirely new.

30.17   Meyer, Carolyn. **Gideon's People.** Gulliver / Harcourt Brace, 1996. 297 pp. ISBN 0-15-200303-7. Fiction.

In the summer of 1911, Isaac Litvak finds himself in an Amish household after a wagon accident. As he tries to understand their customs, very different from his own Orthodox Jewish traditions, Isaac is solicited by Annie to help her prevent her brother, Gideon, from running away from the community. As they wrestle with their rebellious impulses and struggle to define themselves outside their narrowly conceived heritages, Isaac and Gideon learn just how much they have in common. MC

30.18   Morpurgo, Michael. **The War of Jenkins' Ear.** Philomel Books, 1995. 171 pp. ISBN 0-399-22735-0. Fiction.

Toby is miserable at Redlands, a boarding school. Then he meets two people who both fascinate him: Wanda, a pretty young kitchen worker, and a new boy, Christopher, who is mystically calm and self-assured. The antagonism between the school's privileged class and the local boys is reminiscent of *The Outsiders,* and the interaction among the Redlands boys brings *The Chocolate War* to mind. Above it all is Christopher, who believes he is Jesus and chooses Toby to be his first disciple. ER

School Library Journal Best of 1995
Booklist's "Top of the List," 1995

30.19   Napoli, Donna Jo. **Song of the Magdalene.** Scholastic, 1996. 241 pp. ISBN 0-590-93705-7. Fiction.

Miriam is considered "unclean" in ancient Israel; having seizures makes her an outcast from her society. She finds a friend, nonetheless, in Abraham, who teaches her to read holy texts and to sing. But this relationship leads to Miriam's exile—and, with nothing left to lose, Miriam seeks out a miraculous healer in Galilee, under whose tutelage she becomes the woman known throughout history as Mary Magdalene. MC

30.20 Paterson, Katherine. **Who Am I?** William B. Eerdmans, 1994. 88 pp. ISBN 0-8028-5072-3. Nonfiction.

At various points in our lives, we all wonder about some of the same difficult questions: Who am I? Where do I belong? Where is God? In this updated version of a book she wrote in 1966, Paterson uses personal stories in five short chapters as she discusses her answers to these questions. Her honesty and compassion make this a good read for all ages, especially with her suggestions for getting along with different kinds of families. ER

30.21 Skinner, Margaret. **Molly Flanagan and the Holy Ghost.** Algonquin Books of Chapel Hill, 1995. 242 pp. ISBN 1-56512-026-4. Fiction.

Twelve-year-old Molly Flanagan continually battles for her rightful place and personal independence in a 1950s Memphis family dominated by two grandmothers—one Roman Catholic and the other Southern Baptist. The two are locked in a struggle, waging war over Molly's immortal soul. Free-spirited Molly, however, has ideas of her own and surprises for everyone. This heartwarming story allows the reader to see the adult world surrounding Molly through the eyes of a very insightful young girl.

30.22 Spencer, William. **Islamic Fundamentalism in the Modern World.** The Millbrook Press, 1995. 88 pp. ISBN 1-56294-435-5. Nonfiction.

Islamic fundamentalism is associated with the government of the late Ayatollah Khomeini in Iran, death threats to British writer Salman Rushdie, and the bombing of the World Trade Center in New York City, a violent, terrorist act. By examining the origins, beliefs, and historical development of the Islamic religion, the author helps young readers begin to gain another perspective on Islamic fundamentalism. MC

30.23 Wallace, Martin. **Celtic Saints.** Illustrated by Ann MacDuff. Chronicle Books, 1995. 60 pp. ISBN 0-8118-1178-6. Nonfiction.

One in a series of little Irish books, this tiny volume tells the story of twenty-one Celtic saints, including St. Patrick of Ireland. Historical facts and myths have been combined in the legends of these amazing people, such as Brigid of Kildare, David of Wales, and Brendan the Navigator, whose second sea voyage to locate the Promised Land may have resulted in the earliest discovery of America. Beautiful illustrations accompany each brief account. This book could be paired with *Catherine, Called Birdie,* in which Catherine names the feast days of various saints at the beginning of her diary entries.

30.24   Williams, John Tyerman. **Pooh and the Philosophers: In Which It Is Shown that All of Western Philosophy Is Merely a Preamble to Winnie-the-Pooh.** Illustrated by Ernest H. Shepard. Dutton, 1995. 212 pp. ISBN 0-525-45520-5. Nonfiction.

Similar to *The Tao of Pooh,* this facetious critique shows how Winnie-the-Pooh consistently illustrates the thoughts of the great Western philosophers more clearly than those who originated the ideas. This book will best be appreciated by those with at least a passing knowledge of the philosophical principles discussed.

30.25   Wormser, Richard. **American Islam: Growing Up Muslim in America.** Walker, 1994. 122 pp. ISBN 0-8027-8343-0. Nonfiction.

Bridging their religious and cultural traditions and American society, young Muslims are challenged with family, school, and relationships. Beginning with a brief history and the major tenets of Islam, the author explores the rise of Islam in the African American community, including the Nation of Islam and the role of Louis Farrakhan as well as mainstream Islam. This book helps replace many of the negative stereotypes with positive thoughts and feelings of young American Muslims. MC

Titles Annotated in Other Chapters Related to Religion, Cults, and Inspiration

Achebe, Chinua. *Things Fall Apart.* Classics.

Barr, Roger. *The Importance of Malcolm X.* Autobiography.

Brown, Kevin. *Malcolm X: His Life and Legacy.* Autobiography.

Casey, Maude. *Over the Water.* Family.

Cohen, Barbara. *David.* Autobiography.

Foreman, Lelia Rose. *Shatterworld.* Science Fiction.

Gaardner, Jostein. *Sophie's World.* Mysteries.

Haas, Carol. *Engel v. Vitale: Separation of Church and State.* Political Science.

MacDonald, Fiona. *A Sixteenth Century Mosque.* Arts.

Meyer, Carolyn. *Drummers of Jericho.* Human Rights.

Nolan, Han. *Send Me down a Miracle.* Family.

Paterson, Katherine. *A Midnight Clear.* Short Stories.

Rodowsky, Colby. *Lucy Peale.* Romance.

Schmidt, Gary D. (retold by). *John Bunyan:* Pilgrim's Progress. Classics.

31 Romance

"The worst of having a romance of any kind is that it leaves one so unromantic."

Oscar Wilde

"If you are afraid of loneliness, don't marry."
Anton Chekhov

*"If I had loved you less or played you slyly
I might have held you for a summer more."*
Edna St. Vincent Millay

31.1 Applegate, Katherine. **Summer: July's Promise.** Archway Paperbacks / Pocket Books, 1995. 230 pp. ISBN 0-671-51031-2. Fiction.

Seventeen-year-old Summer left Bloomington, Minnesota, to spend the summer at her cousin's house in Crab Claw Key, Florida. When she is not working as a waitress, Summer spends time making friends, learning to skindive, and avoiding trouble. She also tries to figure out who the three guys are in the tarot cards. One will seem perfect, one will be a total mystery, and the other one will be dangerous. ER

31.2 Applegate, Katherine, Ellen Conford, Alane Ferguson, and Lee Wardlaw. **See You in September.** Avon Flare Books, 1995. 161 pp. ISBN 0-380-78088-7. Fiction.

Four popular romance writers' works are gathered around the themes of summer love and going back to school. Teens learn the comfort of connecting with a "soulmate" and the agony of lost love, shown not to be solely one generation's pain. Notes from the authors after each piece, typical of their respective styles, personalize the stories. ER

31.3 Baker, Jennifer, creator. Last Summer, First Love series. Fiction. Scholastic Inc., 1994.

Baker, Carin Greenberg. **A Time to Love.** 232 pp. ISBN 0-590-48323-4. **Good-bye to Love.** 235 pp. ISBN 0-590-48324-2.

A Time to Love and its sequel, *Good-bye to Love,* feature a romance between small town resident Hoppy Paige and Chris Franklin, the son of a wealthy resort owner. While the couple is able to overcome family objections to their dating, they are faced with a more serious challenge: Holly is diagnosed with the incurable disease lupus. This debilitating disease changes everything for Holly, but Chris is determined to give her a chance at life and love. In the sequel, Chris and Holly run away from home to escape their parents' objections to their relationship. Initially, the couple has a wonderful time while their family members frantically try to discover their whereabouts. Eventually, however, the reality of Holly's medical condition intrudes, and they return home with Holly desperately ill. While romance is the focus of these two books, the theme of young adults coping with illness is an important subplot.

31.4   Baker, Jennifer. **The Rose: A Novel Based on *Beauty and the Beast*.** Scholastic, 1996. 185 pp. ISBN 0-590-25948-2. Fiction.

The Rose is a modern rendition of the fairy tale "Beauty and the Beast." Peter Crowley, the beast, was placed under a spell long ago, and in order to escape his sentence he must earn the love of another. Bonnie Oliviera, the beauty, is his last hope. This novel deals with the theme of the power of true love and beauty that is more than skin-deep.

31.5   Bennett, Cherie. **Sunset Fire.** Berkley / Splash, 1994. 211 pp. ISBN 0-425-14360-0. Fiction.

In the twenty-third book of the Sunset Island series, Emma, Carrie, and Samantha take summer jobs away from home. Since Emma has called off her marriage to Kurt, his appearance on the island causes tension between them and painful memories. Can they let bygones be bygones and try to work it out? Will Emma's friendship with Samantha be destroyed because she's good friends with Pres? Sam thinks something romantic is going on between Emma and Pres, but she wouldn't steal her best friend's boyfriend—would she? It's a red-hot summer in *Sunset Fire* and someone's about to get burned!

31.6   Bennett, Cherie. **Teen Angels #3: Angel Kisses.** Avon Flare Books, 1996. 148 pp. ISBN 0-380-78249-9. Fiction.

Melody is the last of three angel friends to have her first "Earth assignment": She and her friends died untimely deaths with lessons still to learn, so to accomplish their education, they must each perform "assignments" on Earth. Usually the angel has a tough case in the form of an earthling gone, or going, wrong, and Melody's case is no exception. She must save a snobby, self-righteous rich girl from destroying herself and anyone who stands in her way.

31.7   Bezzant, Pat. **Angie.** Fawcett Juniper, 1994. 170 pp. ISBN 0-449-70440-8. Fiction.

Sixteen-year-old Angie is learning-disabled, but she is the oldest of three sisters with two loving parents and has a good attitude about her differences. She attends a school where she is mainstreamed in regular classes. However, even Angie is surprised when the cutest, smartest, and most popular boy at school becomes interested in her. Before long, the two are very close and Angie finds herself sharing her deepest feelings with Steven. She begins to wonder why he talks so little about himself. Could he have an ulterior motive for dating Angie?

31.8 Bunkley, Anita Richmond. **Black Gold.** Signet, 1995. 448 pp. ISBN 0-451-17973-0. Fiction.

Proud, beautiful Leela Wilder has finally found happiness, after being orphaned as a child, when she marries rich landowner T. J. Wilder. Their time together, however, is fraught with problems of prejudice, family, greed, and ambition in oil-rich Texas. When T. J. dies unexpectedly, Leela must raise their young son and work the 340-acre farm alone until she meets Victor Beaufort, the only black wildcatter in Texas. Victor discovers oil on Leela's land and Leela discovers Victor. MC

31.9 Chandler, Elizabeth. **Kissed by an Angel.** Archway Paperbacks / Pocket Books, 1995. 230 pp. ISBN 0-671-89145-6. Fiction.

Ivy wants nothing to do with Tristan. She isn't the sort of girl to be impressed with the star of the swimming team, nor does she have the time for his attention-getting measures. Ivy is more concerned about her belief in angels and how those angels are going to help her through her mother's marriage. When Ivy finds Tristan in the kitchen pantry during her mother's wedding, her resolve to resist Tristan becomes even more firm—or does it?

31.10 Charbonneau, Eileen. **The Ghosts of Stony Clove.** Tor / Tom Doherty Associates, 1995. 164 pp. ISBN 0-812-55186-9. Fiction.

Ginny's hair-raising tale of a haunted mansion and its lone inhabitant, Squire Sutherland, raises modern issues—child abuse and prejudice—against the backdrop of the early 1800s in the mountains of New York State. Ginny and her friend, Asher Wood, set off to find some adventure and discover more than they bargained for. Legends, ghosts, murder, and romance weave an interesting novel. ER

31.11 Conford, Ellen, Ellen Leroe, Jane McFann, and Jean Thesman. **A Night to Remember.** Avon Flare Books, 1995. 152 pp. ISBN 0-380-78038-0. Fiction.

This collection of short stories by such well-known authors as Ellen Conford, Ellen Leroe, Jane McFann, and Jean Thesman all revolve around the most important night of the school year: prom night. The stories describe pre-prom disasters, the trauma of finding the perfect date, and dreams coming true on prom night . . . a magical "night to remember."

31.12 Cooney, Caroline B. **Unforgettable.** Scholastic, 1994. 280 pp. ISBN 0-590-47877-X. Fiction.

When Hope's dad finds her surrounded by strangers on a Boston street, she insists she has lost her memory. She claims not to know him, nor does she seem to recognize the luxurious hotel suite and lavish surroundings he calls home. Mitch, the young man who befriends Hope before her father appears, cannot forget her, and keeps looking for her until he finds her. Soon, Hope and Mitch are involved in a dangerous adventure involving international crime and experienced con artists. Before the weekend is over, Hope learns some astonishing things about her true identity.

31.13   Gill, Janet E. **When Darkness Calls.** Avon Flare Books, 1996. 150 pp. ISBN 0-380-78283-9. Fiction.

Moving to a new neighborhood after the death of her father, Ellie finds it difficult to make new friends at Tyler High School. She was a popular, active student at her former school, and she is determined to make her mark at Tyler. Peter Drake, a handsome student, promises to fulfill all of Ellie's dreams. She soon learns, however, that Peter's abilities are tinged with evil, and her whole sense of right and wrong is challenged.

31.14   Hite, Sid. **Answer My Prayer.** Henry Holt, 1995. 182 pp. ISBN 0-8050-3406-4. Fiction.

In the fantasy land of Korasan, jeefwood trees are the main source of income for the artisan guilds. All of this is about to change because of the economic greed of another country, but Lydia and an angel find the courage to sail to another land and save the day. Romance also is found under a jeefwood tree.

31.15   Kaye, Marilyn. **Dream Lover.** Westwind / Troll, 1995. 222 pp. ISBN 0-8167-3593-X. Fiction.

Juliet is a young woman with her life all planned. She knows what she wants to study in college, and how to achieve her goals. She has an equally sensible boyfriend and her life is moving along just as she had anticipated. Then a mysterious young man enters her life who appears to be the embodiment of a dead rock star. Despite Juliet's attempt to resist his influence, she finds herself caught up in a whirlwind while her previous plans seem to be forgotten. She is well aware of what happened to the first Luke Dennison, and she fears the new Luke is on the same self-destructive path, and is taking her along for the ride.

31.16   Lane, Dakota. **Johnny Voodoo.** Delacorte Press, 1996. 199 pp. ISBN 0-385-32230-5. Fiction.

Who is Johnny Voodoo? Deirdre, unhappy and lonely ever since her father uprooted the family from Manhattan following the death of her mother, is never quite sure. But she does know that his presence in her new Louisiana life is its one bright spot, and from him Deirdre and the readers of this first novel will learn a great deal about love and about honoring oneself.

31.17   Malcolm, Jahnna N., and Laura Young. **Rebel Angels: Winging It.** HarperPaperbacks / HarperCollins, 1996. 162 pp. ISBN 0-06-106438-6. Fiction.

Peter and Serafina, angels-in-training, become involved with Jennifer, who runs a soup kitchen in Seattle, as well as with Erin, who disappeared from that shelter. Together they untangle a series of mysteries related to the happenings at the shelter, raising questions in the process about whether Jennifer's means can possibly justify her ends. ER

31.18   McDaniel, Lurlene. **Saving Jessica.** Bantam Books, 1996. 191 pp. ISBN 0-553-56721-7. Fiction.

Jessica and Jeremy are a good match in more ways than one. His desire to donate one of his healthy kidneys to save Jessica from fatal kidney failure or a lifetime of restricted diet and frequent dialysis comes from their deep love. However, his parents have already lost one son, and aren't ready to risk their only other one. Just who has the right to say what Jeremy does with his body becomes an issue for this troubled family and the courts.

31.19   Miner, Jane Claypool. **Winter Love, Winter Wishes.** Scholastic, 1994. 371 pp. ISBN 0-590-48152-5. Fiction.

Brittany and Willow are excited about their mother's plan to turn their home into a boarding house for college students. They are not excited, however, about having Anna, their old-fashioned six-foot-tall cousin from a small farming community, move in with them and go to their high school. But the girls learn over time to respect one another's differences, and that Prince Charming is not always who you think.

31.20   Musson, Jean. **Silk Domino.** Robert Hale / Parkwest, 1993. 159 pp. ISBN 0-7090-4924-2. Fiction.

A tragic car accident kills her mother and leaves Melissa blind and the inheritor of the costume business they both loved. Just as Melissa is struggling to adjust, her old lover, Michael, returns to her life. Michael's appearance seems to bring in its wake several strange occurrences, including one that nearly costs Melissa her life.

31.21   Narayan, Kirin. **Love, Stars, and All That.** Pocket Books, 1994. 311 pp. ISBN 0-671-79395-0. Fiction.

Gita is an attractive young Indian woman pursuing graduate studies at the University of California at Berkeley. Despite her immersion in Western culture, she has strong memories of her life in India. There is increasing pressure on Gita to find her perfect mate, and for a time she tries to do just that—with less-than-perfect results. Finally, she determines to remain true to herself even when the two cultures that influence her seem to be on a collision course. MC

31.22   Neenan, Colin. **In Your Dreams.** Harcourt Brace, 1995. 246 pp. ISBN 0-15-200885-3. Fiction.

Hale O'Reilly is fifteen years old and has never been kissed, which doesn't really bother him until he falls in love—with his older brother's girlfriend. Despite his quick wit and gift for words, his life suddenly becomes complicated and very frustrating as he tries to deal with his feelings of love without being discovered by his brother. ER

31.23   Plummer, Louise. **The Unlikely Romance of Kate Bjorkman.** Delacorte Press, 1995. 183 pp. ISBN 0-385-32049-3. Fiction.

Kate is bright and level-headed, too tall and bookish to see herself as alluring, but interested enough to read the romance novels that her glamorous, manipulative friend Ashley presses upon her along with advice on beauty and flirting. Kate decides to write her own realistic novel chronicling her first—and forever?—romance with her older brother's college friend, Richard. So *this* is what Ashley has been jabbering about! ER

School Library Journal Best of 1995

31.24   Rees, Elizabeth M. **Plainsong for Caitlin.** Avon Flare Books, 1996. 163 pp. ISBN 0-380-78216-2. Fiction.

Caitlin and her sister Rebecca start west to begin a new life when Rebecca becomes a mail order bride. They find the adventure of a lifetime and much more, such as drought, storms, plagues of grasshoppers, and, ultimately, death for one of them.

31.25   Ripslinger, Jon. **Triangle.** Harcourt Brace, 1994. 277 pp. ISBN 0-15-200048-8. Fiction.

The old saying "Two's company, three's a crowd" is true for Joy, Jeremy, and Darin. Best friends since elementary school, the threesome find everything changing when Joy and Jeremy become romantically involved, unaware that Darin is secretly in love with Joy. A tragic accident, a secret relationship, and an unexpected pregnancy put a strain on the three friends, which results in painful decisions about their lives and shatters friendships. Mature themes and situations.

31.26   Rodowsky, Colby. **Lucy Peale.** Aerial Fiction / Farrar, Straus and Giroux, 1994. 167 pp. ISBN 0-374-44659-8. Fiction.

It didn't take long for Preacher Peale to figure out that his teenage daughter Lucy was pregnant. When he decided to make her the object of his sermon at his camp meeting, however, Lucy took off. Her attempts to find work are unsuccessful and she finds herself broke and alone until she meets Jake. Kind, sensitive Jake is unlike anyone else Lucy has ever known. He takes care of Lucy as her pregnancy progresses and introduces her to his warm, loving family. Despite the differences in their backgrounds, it looks as if they will make it until Lucy realizes what Jake is giving up to have her in his life.

31.27 Smith, Nancy Covert. **Apple Valley: Destiny.** Avon Flare Books, 1995. 150 pp. ISBN 0-380-78091-7. Fiction.

This is the fourth book in a series featuring DeLanna and Andrew Tabor. After they marry, the young couple set out from the bustling Philadelphia of the 1860s for a new life in an untamed Ohio. DeLanna misses her family and many of the comforts of her old home, while Andrew, who comes from a much poorer family, sees each day as a challenge and as an opportunity to build something of his own. Despite the difficulties of their lives, DeLanna and Andrew create a home, make friends, and finally begin a family of their own.

31.28 Tamar, Erika. **The Things I Did Last Summer.** Harcourt Brace, 1994. 294 pp. ISBN 0-15-282490-1. Fiction.

Seventeen-year-old Andy Szabo spends an eventful and unexpected summer in Bay Island Beach experiencing his first romantic relationship while working as a reporter for the local newspaper and babysitting for his pregnant stepmother. When he meets twenty-year-old Susan, an *au pair* for the reclusive Carlyles, he is captivated. The two begin meeting in secret although he doesn't know why. By the end of the summer, Andy learns the painful reason Susan had been so secretive . . . she is married.

31.29 Webster, Jean. **Daddy-Long-Legs.** Illustrations by the author. Puffin Books, 1995. 185 pp. ISBN 0-14-037455-8. Fiction.

Raised in an orphanage and brimming with pride, Judy Abbott is surprised at the unexpected offer from an anonymous trustee to enter an unknown world and attend an exclusive New England college for women. Alone and insecure, Judy chooses to confide her secrets to her benefactor by writing a series of letters during her four years at college. Through the letters, the reader witnesses the many changes in Judy's life that the generosity of Daddy-Long-Legs makes possible. ER

31.30 Wyss, Thelma Hatch. **A Stranger Here.** HarperTrophy / HarperCollins, 1996. 132 pp. ISBN 0-06-447098-9. Fiction.

When Jada Sinclair finds herself helping out her Aunt May and Uncle Mac on their Idaho farm for the whole summer, she makes up her mind to make the best of it. The situation becomes interesting as Jada discovers the spirit of Starr Freeman, a man who died on the same day Jada was born in 1960. The relationship between Jada and Starr grows as they spend time together when Jada isn't working. Jada must find a way to discover Starr's intent for returning to this life; she hopes his future plans include her. ER

Titles Annotated in Other Chapters Related to Romance

Alcott, Louisa May. *Rose in Bloom*. Classics.

Bonner, Cindy. *Looking after Lily*. Westerns.

Brandon, Jacqueline. *Perfect Solution*. School.

Brontë, Charlotte. *Jane Eyre*. Classics.

Cardillo, Joe. *Pulse*. Science.

Cohen, Barbara, and Bahija Lovejoy. *Seven Daughters and Seven Sons*. Myths.

Ferris, Jean. *Invincible Summer*. Death.

Feuer, Elizabeth. *Paper Doll*. Arts.

Hill, Elizabeth Starr. *Curtain Going Up!* Television.

Hoh, Diane. *Prom Date*. Horror.

Kindl, Patrice. *Owl in Love*. Fantasy.

L'Engle, Madeleine. *Troubling a Star*. Mysteries.

Landolphi, Suzi. *Hot, Sexy and Safer*. Drugs.

Lawrence, D. H. *Women in Love*. Classics.

Neenan, Colin. *Live a Little*. Friendships.

Qualey, Marsha. *Come in from the Cold*. War.

Shusterman, Neal. *Dissidents*. Adventure.

Stasheff, Christopher. *M'Lady Witch*. Fantasy.

Stasheff, Christopher. *Quicksilver's Knight*. Fantasy.

Tomlinson, Theresa. *The Forestwife*. Myths.

Wittlinger, Ellen. *Noticing Paradise*. Family.

32 School

"The common school is the greatest invention ever made by man."
Horace Mann

"Education consists mainly in what we have unlearned."
Mark Twain

32.1 Asher, Sandy. **A Senior Class Yearbook: Out of Here.** Puffin Books, 1995. 148 pp. ISBN 0-14-037441-8. Fiction.

For some students in the eighty-eighth graduating class of Oakview High, their senior year represents the last tortuous restriction before they are free. For others, it means a last chance to prove themselves. All the flavors of adolescence—"brain," "loser," "athlete," "loner," "homecoming queen"—intersect in this small academic community, sometimes subtly, sometimes dramatically. As the lives of these young people intertwine, each individual comes to realize that, for better or worse, high school is an unforgettable experience.

32.2 Banfield, Susan. **Ethnic Conflicts in Schools.** Enslow, 1995. 104 pp. ISBN 0-89490-640-2. Nonfiction.

Beginning with factors that contribute to ethnic conflicts, this book, part of the Multicultural Issues series, includes information about what schools and students are doing to turn cultural diversity into positive learning experiences. From immigration in the early 1900s and school desegregation in the 1950s to recent situations of racial harassment, conflicts often result from misunderstanding about cultural traditions. Various situations are discussed, from name-calling to more physical acts of violence. Of particular interest are conflict resolution programs in Miami, Florida, and Newton, Massachusetts. A glossary and an index are included. MC

Notable 1995 Children's Trade Books in the Field of Social Studies

32.3 Brandon, Jacqueline. **Perfect Solution.** Robert Hale/Parkwest, 1993. 157 pp. ISBN 0-7090-4894-7. Fiction.

Tanya Chardwell, a math teacher, has an unsuccessful appointment with the widower father of a challenging pupil, Dominic Anderson. Later, she accepts a holiday tutoring job on a Greek island only to find out that she will be working with her former student, Dominic. To make matters worse, Tanya becomes attracted to the handsome and demanding Mr. Anderson. In the end, the two come up with the perfect solution to their problems, in this Rainbow Romance.

32.4   Bunting, Eve. **Spying on Miss Müller.** Clarion Books, 1995. 179 pp. ISBN 0-395-69172-9. Fiction.

Jessie resides in a boarding school in Belfast during World War II. After learning that her favorite German teacher is part German herself, Jessie worries that her teacher may also be a spy. Jessie and her friends set out to determine one way or another whether Miss Müller is a Nazi agent. In addition, Jessie is also trying to cope with her father's drinking problem and worrying about her favorite cousin, who is in the army fighting Germans in France.

32.5   Cooney, Caroline B. **Driver's Ed.** Delacorte Press, 1994. 184 pp. ISBN 0-385-32087-6. Fiction.

Neither Remy Marland nor Morgan Campbell can wait to turn sixteen and get a driver's license. Remy likes to drive and admire Morgan in the back seat. Morgan thinks about driving and girls, especially Remy. Who would have thought that on their date Morgan and Remy would pull a stunt that would affect so many people for the rest of their lives? As a result, everyone learns that driver's education is a life-or-death course in school.

ALA Best Books for Young Adults, 1995
ALA Quick Picks for Young Adults, 1995
Booklist Editors' Choice, 1995
IRA Teacher's Choice Award, 1996

32.6   Cooney, Caroline B. **Night School.** Scholastic, 1995. 187 pp. ISBN 0-590-47878-8. Fiction.

A strange combination of students sign up for a night-school class: the perfect Andrew; Mariah, who constantly dreams about him; Ned, who is struggling to be normal; and Autumn, who wants to be an individual. Their chilling experiences raise many questions: Who is the dark, mysterious instructor forcing them to scare people? Why can't they stop? Will Mariah's timid brother Bevin be saved? The teens learn about the choice between kindness and cruelty. ER

32.7   Dexter, Catherine. **Alien Game.** Morrow Junior Books, 1995. 204 pp. ISBN 0-688-11332-X. Fiction.

When Christina arrives at Oak Hill School she impresses her new peers with her skill at playing "Elimination," a tagging game in which participants are "eliminated" one by one. Zoe Brooks watches Christina and her victims, who seem to be increasingly under her spell, to an extent that those who refuse to play find themselves attacked. Zoe realizes someone has to stop Christina before Christina goes too far. ER

32.8   Glenn, Mel. **Who Killed Mr. Chippendale? A Mystery in Poems.** Lodestar Books, 1996. 100 pp. ISBN 0-525-67530-2. Fiction.

Told entirely in free verse poems, this book describes the reactions of students, colleagues, and others when a teacher at Tower High School is shot to death as the school day begins. Comments about Robert Chippendale, views about what school is and is not for various people, and the concerns and characteristics of young people come through in each individual's thoughts. ER MC

32.9   Hayes, Daniel. **Flyers.** Simon and Schuster Books for Young Readers, 1996. 203 pp. ISBN 0-689-80372-9. Fiction.

While Gabe and his friends are filming a horror movie as a school project, they become curious about odd happenings in the neighborhood. As Gabe investigates an empty house, his father's melancholy, and the disappearance of food and clothing from his own home, he learns that the mysteries run deeper than he first suspected.

32.10   Hodge, Merle. **For the Life of Laetitia.** Aerial / Farrar, Straus and Giroux, 1995. 214 pp. ISBN 0-374-42444-6. Fiction.

"Lacey" is the first in her extended family to qualify for secondary school. She must leave her grandmother, and her happy village home in Sooklal Trace, and live in La Puerta with her strange, distant father, oppressed stepmother, and small stepbrother. At school she encounters prejudiced teachers, becomes friends with poor Anjanese, makes good grades, and gets in trouble, too. *Laetitia* would work well with *Imagining Isabel*, a book set in Guatemala. MC WL

32.11   James, Mary (also known as M. E. Kerr). **Frankenlouse.** Scholastic Hardcover, 1994. 184 pp. ISBN 0-590-46528-7. Fiction.

Nick Reber wants to be a cartoonist. He draws cartoons, with book lice representing people in his life, to escape into his own world and evade his father's control. His father, however, wants Nick to stay in the military after his schooling at Blister Academy. Nick also becomes involved with his friends and their troubled relationships with their parents as he tries to sort out his own life.

32.12   Karas, Phyllis. **The Hate Crime.** Avon Flare Books, 1995. 183 pp. ISBN 0-380-78214-6. Fiction.

Zack's father, the district attorney, has a difficult case that ends up disturbing Zack's lacrosse games and his relationships with his wonderful new girlfriend Rachael and his best friend Ricky. Zack ultimately learns a lot about the Holocaust, its effects on survivor's children, and the existence of vicious hatreds. This story was clearly written to make a point about the horrible injustices and frightening consequences of anti-Semitism. MC

32.13   McCants, William D. **Much Ado about Prom Night.** Browndeer Press / Harcourt Brace, 1995. 232 pp. ISBN 0-15-200083-6. Fiction.

Becca Singleton is a peer counselor at Luna Point High in southern California who is also an honor student and surfer. She is great at giving advice, but her own life is in shambles. She has an unfaithful boyfriend, her younger brother is into shaving his head and wearing leather jackets, and she has just found out that she has been put at the bottom of Eddy Baldwin's prom-date list. Becca is depressed and down and out, but she does not stay that way for long!

ALA Best Books for Young Adults, 1996
ALA Quick Picks for Young Adults, 1996

32.14   McClain, Ellen Jaffe. **No Big Deal.** Lodestar Books, 1994. 187 pp. ISBN 0-525-67483-7. Fiction.

After hearing rumors that her favorite teacher is gay, Janice learns that Mr. P.'s car has been vandalized and that the people of West River want him fired. She knows the pain of being different—for years she has been the object of ridicule because of her weight—and decides to take a stand. Janice places herself in opposition to many students and parents to let West River know that being homosexual does not prevent Mr. P. from being a fantastic teacher.

32.15   Miller, G. Wayne. **Coming of Age: The True Adventure of Two American Teens.** Random House, 1995. 253 pp. ISBN 0-679-42326-5. Nonfiction.

What's it like to grow up in the nineties in a small town away from urban violence? This true story about Dave, his family, favorite teachers, girlfriend, and underground newspaper provides one answer. Funny, intelligent Dave hopes to get into a good college (but not to study science), make the basketball team, and be the class clown. This entertaining and informative book ends with the author's conclusion that it is more difficult to grow up today, but the fundamental issues of adolescence remain unchanged.

32.16   Neufeld, John. **A Small Civil War.** Aladdin Paperbacks, 1996. 216 pp. ISBN 0-689-80771-6. Fiction.

Georgia Van Buren is incensed when Fairchild Brady decides that *The Grapes of Wrath* should not be read by tenth-grade classes at Owanka High. Georgia, thirteen, leaps to the defense of the book, while her older sister, Ava, tries to report objectively on the situation for the high school paper, efforts that are made difficult by the fact that Ava's boyfriend is Brady's son. The situation ultimately results in violence and both sisters find themselves embroiled in a battle that forces them to change their perceptions of themselves, their family, and their town.

32.17   Porter, Penny. **The Keymaker: Born to Steal.** Harbinger House, 1994. 153 pp. ISBN 0-943173-99-X. Fiction.

High school senior Jimmy Cooper is a good locksmith as well as a thief. After making friends with the school janitor, Nick, Jimmy is able to make duplicate keys to various doors in the school. When the school is robbed of valuable equipment, the janitor is wrongly accused, and Jimmy must make difficult choices that affect many lives—most important, his own.

32.18   Rapp, Adam. **Missing the Piano.** Viking, 1994. 198 pp. ISBN 0-670-85340-2. Fiction.

When his sister gets the part of Cosette in the road show of *Les Misérables*, Mike's mother must accompany her, so Mike becomes his father's responsibility. At his new wife's suggestion, Mr. Tegroff sends Mike to a military boarding school. Mike's disappointment at not being able to try out for his high school basketball team and his father's detached attitude exacerbate the difficulty he has in adjusting to an intimidating military environment. Basketball provides Mike comfort while he copes with brutal hazing, loneliness, and bigotry. MC

ALA Best Books for Young Adults, 1995
ALA Quick Picks for Young Adults, 1995
IRA Teacher's Choice Award, 1996

32.19   Rodowsky, Colby. **Sydney, Invincible.** Farrar, Straus and Giroux, 1995. 144 pp. ISBN 0-374-37365-5. Fiction.

This will be Sydney's year. She has a boyfriend, a newlywed mother who is very happy, and a new creative writing teacher. Then her boyfriend's parents divorce, her mother becomes pregnant, and creative writing becomes journalism, which Sydney hates. Drawing upon her inner strengths, Sydney manages to overcome these crises with a sense of humor and spirit which makes her invincible.

32.20   Velásquez, Gloria. **Juanita Fights the School Board.** Piñata Books, 1994. 149 pp. ISBN 1-55885-115-1. Fiction.

Juanita, one of six children of Mexican immigrants, lives in a town that is home to few other Mexicans or African Americans. She wants to stay in school and graduate but is expelled for fighting with Sheena, who made racial remarks about the Chávez family. A counselor, Ms. Martínez, helps Juanita learn to control her temper, and Sam, a white lawyer, donates his time to help Juanita try to convince the school board to let her return to school. ER MC

Titles Annotated in Other Chapters Related to School

Alcott, Louisa May. *Little Men*. Classics.

Barcus, Audrey. *Dangerous Secrets*. Mysteries.

Bennett, Cherie. *Teen Angels #3: Angel Kisses*. Romance.

Boga, Steve. *The Lunch Bowl*. Sports.

Boga, Steve. *Side Kick*. Sports.

Boyd, Candy Dawson. *Fall Secrets*. Arts.

Cascone, A. G. *In a Crooked Little House*. Mysteries.

Cooney, Linda A. *Samantha Crane on the Run*. Mysteries.

Cruise, Beth. *Computer Confusion*. Computers.

Draper, Sharon M. *Tears of a Tiger*. Death.

Dygard, Thomas J. *Game Plan*. Sports.

Dygard, Thomas J. *The Rebounder*. Sports.

Dygard, Thomas J. *Running Wild*. Sports.

Fiedler, Lisa. *Curtis Piperfield's Biggest Fan*. Dating.

Garden, Nancy. *Good Moon Rising*. Dating.

Goldman, E. M. *The Night Room*. Friendships.

Gorman, Carol. *Back from the Dead*. Horror.

Green, Henry. *Pack My Bag*. Autobiography.

Grove, Vicki. *The Crystal Garden*. Friendships.

Hoh, Diane. Nightmare Hall series. Horror.

Johnston, Norma. *The Image Game*. Dating.

Lerangis, Peter. *Driver's Dead*. Mysteries.

Lerangis, Peter. *The Yearbook*. Horror.

Morse, Eric. *Friday the Thirteenth: Road Trip*. Horror.

Murrow, Liza Ketchum. *Twelve Days in August*. Sports.

Reynolds, Marilyn. *Beyond Dreams*. Short Stories.

Ripslinger, Jon. *Triangle*. Romance.

Schwandt, Stephen. *The Last Goodie*. Mysteries.

Sherrow, Victoria. *Censorship in Schools*. Political Science.

Spinelli, Jerry. *Jason and Marceline*. Dating.

Stine, R. L. *College Weekend*. Horror.

Westall, Robert. *Falling into Glory*. Dating.

Wright, Bob. *Strike Zone*. Sports.

33 Science and the Environment

"This earth is the honey of all beings; all beings the honey of this earth."

Upanishads

"If you want truly to understand something, try to change it."

Kurt Lewin

33.1   Aaseng, Nathan. **Jobs vs. the Environment: Can We Save Both?** Enslow, 1994. 112 pp. ISBN 0-89490-574-0. Nonfiction.

Does the United States have the right to tell Brazil not to cut down their forests when the United States has done the same thing? Are spotted owls more important than loggers' jobs? This book explores the debate between saving jobs today versus saving the world for tomorrow. Past, present, and future concerns are discussed in depth and alternatives to save both jobs and the environment are presented for consideration, in this volume from the Issues in Focus series.

33.2   Ackerman, Jennifer. **Notes from the Shore.** Illustrated by Karin Grosz. Penguin Books, 1996. 190 pp. ISBN 0-14-01-7788-4. Nonfiction.

Ackerman provides a close look at life by the shore of the Delaware Bay. Replete with observations on the curious and the common, each chapter is part botany, part biology, part zoology, part ecology, part history, part archeology—yet the whole is as captivating as beautiful literature. Those who discover this book have indeed found a treasure.

33.3   Andryszewski, Tricia. **The Environment and the Economy: Planting the Seeds for Tomorrow's Growth.** The Millbrook Press, 1995. 112 pp. ISBN 1-56294-524-6. Nonfiction.

The author sets forth objectively the history of the environment of the United States and the various presidents, events, and political projects, such as Theodore Roosevelt, the Dust Bowl, and the Tennessee Valley Authority, which have led to the current state of the environment. This text, part of the Issue and Debate series, is a good beginning for a deeper look into the economic and social impact of environmental policies. Many sides of the issue, including the radical, are presented to help readers decide on their own positions. Specific industries are highlighted for in-depth study. The text includes an index, black-and-white photographs, and a list of environmental organizations to contact for more information.

33.4   Andryszewski, Tricia. **What to Do about Nuclear Waste.** The Millbrook Press, 1995. 128 pp. ISBN 1-56294-577-7. Nonfiction.

Nuclear waste is an immense problem for the United States and the world. This book explores in detail the history of nuclear energy in the United States from World War II to the present. Issues analyzed include the waste generated by nuclear power generation and nuclear weapons testing, their ramifications for the environment, and the health of the people exposed to testing. While the book does not provide the definitive answer to what to do about nuclear waste, it does lay out the problem in detail to generate discussion and is supplemented with useful notes, a glossary, a bibliography, and black-and-white photographs.

33.5   Barrow, Lloyd H. **Adventures with Rocks and Minerals, Book II: Geology Experiments for Young People.** Enslow, 1995. 96 pp. ISBN 0-89490-624-0. Nonfiction.

These geology experiments all use easily obtained, everyday materials and the procedures are meticulously explained, making them suitable for young scientists to perform at home. The discussion portion of each experiment clarifies the principle demonstrated. The principles are progressively more advanced, covering such topics as rock formation, erosion, and plate tectonics, but the experiments themselves remain simple to perform. This volume, part of the Adventures with Science series, would be suitable for science fair projects, teachers' demonstrations, or anyone with an interest in geology or earth science. ER

33.6   Bridgman, Roger. **Technology.** Dorling Kindersley, 1995. 64 pp. ISBN 1-56458-883-1. Nonfiction.

Part of the Eyewitness Science series, this work explains the many technologies that enhance our lives today. Beginning with mankind's earliest efforts, the author surveys most basic technologies, including those used in agriculture, manufacturing, communications, and medicine. He clarifies and expands on each technological process using a combination of narrative text, definition, demonstration, color illustrations, and vivid photographs. The result is an engaging tour of human machinations, from pottery to plastic, from leeches to lasers. ER

33.7   Butterfield, Moira. **Look Inside Cross-Sections: Space.** Illustrated by Nick Lipscombe and Gary Biggin. Dorling Kindersley, 1994. 32 pp. ISBN 1-56458-682-0. Nonfiction.

Want to look inside the Hubble Telescope or learn what equipment you need to walk in space? Clear and concise illustrations and explanations about these and more space topics are found in this easy-to-read book. Notable people are introduced, events are highlighted, and equipment is detailed, giving the reader a solid introduction to such spacecraft as Skylab, Voyager, and the Apollo series. A space timeline and a glossary add interest and organization. This book is part of the Look Inside Cross-Section series. ER

ALA Best Books for Young Adults, 1995

33.8   Butterfield, Moira. **Richard Orr's Nature Cross-Sections.** Illustrated by Richard Orr. Dorling Kindersley, 1995. 30 pp. ISBN 0-7894-0147-9. Nonfiction.

The natural world is presented in cross-sections in this colorfully illustrated and informative book. Animal homes and habitats including the beaver lodge, beehive, rainforest, ocean, and others are described in detail. Double-page artwork and two stunning gatefolds make this book a must for anyone interested in the natural world. It includes an index for easy reference. ER

33.9   Cardillo, Joe. **Pulse.** Dutton Children's Books, 1996. 201 pp. ISBN 0-525-45396-2. Fiction.

When seventeen-year-old Jason and his girlfriend Kris decide to found Pulse, an environmental group dedicated to saving the Pine-haven wilderness area from the greediness of city hall, they discover that their determination will prove to have fatal consequences.

33.10   Cole, Michael D. Countdown to Space series. Enslow, 1995. 48 pp. Nonfiction.
Apollo 11: First Moon Landing. ISBN 0-89490-539-2.
Apollo 13: Space Emergency. ISBN 0-89490-542-2.
Challenger: America's Space Tragedy. ISBN 0-89490-544-9.
Columbia: First Flight of the Space Shuttle. ISBN 0-89490-543-0.
Friendship 7: First American in Orbit. ISBN 0-89490-540-6.
Vostok 1: First Human in Space. ISBN 0-89490-541-4.

This series chronicles major events in the space race from the first Soviet cosmonaut to orbit the earth, Yuri Gagarin, to the space shuttle flights, including the *Challenger* disaster. Each text includes black-and-white photographs and a glossary of scientific terms. ER MC

33.11   Cornelius, Geoffrey, and Paul Devereux. **The Secret Language of the Stars and Planets: A Visual Key to the Heavens.** Chronicle Books, 1996. 176 pp. ISBN 0-8118-1200-6. Nonfiction.

In short, easy chapters, the authors provide a detailed reference source for information on the stars and planets. Information is pulled from astronomy, astrology, archeology, mysticism, and ancient beliefs. Each chapter provides appropriate maps, drawings, and photographs. The planets, constellations, pyramids, and other wonders are included for the reader's interest. Unusual observations, such as that the Milky Way mirrors closely the River Nile, bring ancient stories and science together.

With an index, a glossary, and a bibliography, the authors have created a reference tool to use in numerous subjects.

33.12   Couper, Heather, and Nigel Henbest. **Black Holes.** Illustrated by Luciano Corbella. Dorling Kindersley, 1996. 45 pp. ISBN 0-7894-0451-6. Nonfiction.

The mystery of black holes is put to rest in this information-packed book. Every inch of the large 9" x 11" pages is filled with colorful depictions of the world of black holes and accompanying textual information. The authors also postulate what it would be like if one were to "fall into" a black hole, and they entertain the theoretical possibility of wormholes and time travel. Besides the amateur scientist, the science fiction reader or writer will also find this book fascinating.

33.13   Getting Started In Science series. Enslow, 1995. Nonfiction.
Gardner, Robert, and David Webster. **Experiments with Balloons.** 104 pp. ISBN 0-89490-669-0.
Gardner, Robert. **Experiments with Bubbles.** 104 pp. ISBN 0-89490-666-6.
Gardner, Robert. **Experiments with Lights and Mirrors.** 112 pp. ISBN 0-89490-668-2.
Gardner, Robert. **Experiments with Motion.** 112 pp. ISBN 0-89490-667-4.

These books, part of the Getting Started in Science series, are excellent resources for those interested in science. Easy-to-do experiments are presented, complete with the scientific principles they illustrate, step-by-step instructions, and detailed illustrations. You will learn how science works because you will be investigating the world as scientists do. When studied in this way, science is fun! ER

33.14   Gardner, Robert. **Science Projects about Electricity and Magnets.** Enslow, 1994. 128 pp. ISBN 0-89490-530-9. Nonfiction.

Like its companion books, this text describes several science projects students can create at home using simple materials, this time to learn about electricity and magnets. Many of these projects are perfect science fair projects. Projects described include how to make a light bulb, a fuse, a battery, a simple electric motor, a magnetic compass, and a working flashlight. Each project includes an ingredient chart and diagrams. ER

33.15   Gardner, Robert. **Science Projects about Light.** Enslow, 1994. 128 pp. ISBN 0-89490-529-5. Nonfiction.

This book enables readers to discover different ways of understanding and using light. Each chapter outlines different experiments and projects students can conduct at home using safe, simple materials. Projects focus on the paths of light, changing light paths, working with light and color, and much more. Many of these projects are perfect for science fair projects. Each experiment and project is accompanied by an ingredient chart and diagrams. ER

33.16   Gardner, Robert, and Eric Kemer. **Science Projects about Temperature and Heat.** Enslow, 1994. 128 pp. ISBN 0-89490-534-1. Nonfiction.

This easy-to-follow book describes several science projects, supplemented with interesting information about temperature and heat, that students can create at home using simple materials. Many of these projects are perfect science fair projects. Projects described include how to build liquid and air expansion thermometers, how to create heat by shaking, and how to melt ice. The book includes simple directions, easy-to-read diagrams, and ingredient charts. ER

33.17   Gardner, Robert, and David Webster. **Science Projects about Weather.** Enslow, 1994. 128 pp. ISBN 0-89490-533-3. Nonfiction.

Simple, clear black-and-white illustrations accompany basic weather experiments. The sequential directions outline an experiment performable by most students working independently. Suggestions for science fair projects, safety tips, and lists of suppliers of materials are welcome additions for librarians, teachers, parents, and students. ER

33.18   Gribbin, John, and Mary Gribbin. **Time and Space.** Dorling Kindersley, 1994. 64 pp. ISBN 1-56458-619-7. Nonfiction.

Anyone interested in black holes, "God's dice," the time/space continuum, and even time machines will enjoy this easy-to-read volume in the Eyewitness Science series. The Gribbins manage to make concepts such as the theory of relativity, the ultimate speed limit, Schrodinger's cat, and the twin paradox understandable for all readers. The text is amply illustrated and complemented with color photographs, and browsing is made easy by the fact that each topic is presented in the space of only two pages.

33.19   Hughes, Ted. **The Iron Woman.** Engravings by Barry Moser. Dial Books, 1995. 109 pp. ISBN 0-8037-1796-2. Fiction.

In this short novel, Lucy is the first human being to meet Iron Woman, a giant who arises out of the sludge of a swamp polluted by a local factory. Iron Woman has come to destroy the people at the factory, who are destroying the land. Lucy, whose father works at the factory, tries to stop Iron Woman's destructive intent and, at the same time, tries to stop the factory from polluting the countryside. To do so, Lucy calls upon the help of a young boy, Hogarth, who brings with him Iron Man, another giant. They do not succeed until all the men in England over eighteen are turned into giant fish. ER

33.20   Kettelkamp, Larry. **ETs and UFOs: Are They Real?** Morrow Junior Books, 1996. 83 pp. ISBN 0-688-12868-8. Nonfiction.

Some of the most famous reports of UFO sightings and alien abductions are discussed from the viewpoint that the witnesses are reliable and a coverup of some kind occurred in each case to keep the general public unaware of the realities involved. Those readers interested in such phenomena will surely enjoy this book, but skeptics are not likely to be convinced. ER

33.21   Laughlin, Robin Kittrell. **Backyard Bugs.** Photographs by Robin Kittrell Laughlin. Foreword by Sue Hubbell. Chronicle Books, 1996. 76 pp. ISBN 0-8118-0907-2. Nonfiction.

This beautiful little book includes photographs and a short, humorous tale about each of forty different creatures. The author's work shows her appreciation of the little things that run the world, from beetles and spiders to butterflies. Her photographs show amazing details, startling colors, and even facial expressions. In addition to amusing literary quotations, the scientific and common name of each bug accompanies the text. There is a separate section with background information about the bug families, and a glossary.

33.22   Lippincott, Kristen. **Astronomy.** Dorling Kindersley, 1994. 64 pp. ISBN 1-56458-680-4. Nonfiction.

What do Napier's bones, nineteenth-century spectroscopes, Persian astrolabes, and a refracting telescope have in common? They are all tools used at different points in history for viewing the stars. This volume in the Eyewitness Science series provides an overview of the major technological breakthroughs in the field, as well as of the major contributions of the various intellectual giants who have turned their eyes skyward throughout history. Each planet is photographed, illustrated, and described, and other elements of the solar system are similarly treated in this colorful, easy-to-read text. ER

33.23   Mebane, Robert C., and Thomas R. Rybolt. **Adventures with Atoms and Molecules, Book 5: Chemistry Experiments for Young People.** Enslow, 1995. 96 pp. ISBN 0-89490-606-2. Nonfiction.

Can an onion bring tears to your eyes? Does the top or the bottom of a wet paper towel dry more quickly? How do you build an atomic bomb? Okay, they don't show you how to build a bomb, but thirty other chemistry experiments are presented in this book from the Adventures with Science series, complete with illustrated step-by-step instructions as well as observation and discussion notes. These experiments present basic principles of chemistry in a way that shows that learning about science can be fun. ER

33.24 Patent, Dorothy Hinshaw. **The Vanishing Feast: How Dwindling Genetic Diversity Threatens the World's Food Supply.** Gulliver Green / Harcourt Brace, 1994. 224 pp. ISBN 0-15-292867-7. Nonfiction.

What is biodiversity? As we near the twenty-first century with a rapidly growing population that needs food and nourishment, this is a question that we need to explore. *The Vanishing Feast* explains how many of today's plant species are in danger of extinction within the next fifty years. What can we do, or are we too late? With the right kind of education and protection, argues the author, we can preserve our precious plant and animal kingdoms.

33.25 Platt, Richard. **Smithsonian Visual Timeline of Inventions.** Dorling Kindersley, 1994. 64 pp. ISBN 1-56458-675-8. Nonfiction.

This text, as its name suggests, is a visual timeline with brief descriptions and illustrations of inventions throughout history. The book is broken into five chronological chapters, starting with 600,000 B.C. and continuing to the present day. Invention themes are also discussed including the first inventions, printing and the spread of ideas, steam power and the industrial revolution, electric power and the modern world, and transistors and the information age. The book is a perfect reference text for any classroom. ER

Notable 1994 Children's Trade Books in the Field of Social Studies

33.26 Plotkin, Mark J. **Tales of a Shaman's Apprentice: An Ethnologist Searches for New Medicines in the Amazon Rain Forest.** Penguin Books, 1994. 328 pp. ISBN 0-14-012991-X. Nonfiction.

Mark Plotkin apprenticed himself to several shamans in the Amazon rainforest in order to learn the medicinal properties of the plants they used to treat anything from parasite infestation, gonorrhea, and kidney stones to the common cold. He pleads for preservation of the native cultures of the rainforest, hoping to save the shamans' knowledge of the curative powers of plants from extinction. Caution: There is a section in this book dealing with experimentation with hallucinogenic drugs which may make this book inappropriate for high school students. MC

33.27 Souza, D. M. **Space Sailing.** Lerner, 1994. 61 pp. ISBN 0-8225-2850-9. Nonfiction.

You are part of the technical crew preparing for a mission to Mars. You carefully check all the instruments, confirming that all is ready to go. You now check the most important part of the spacecraft, the sails. Sails? Such a scenario is not as outrageous as you might think. The use of sails is being explored as a possible mode of interplanetary transportation. *Space Sailing* traces the origin of this unique experiment and details the design, building, and maintenance of the components. Numerous illustrations and a brief glossary help the reader understand and visualize this new means of space travel.

33.28   **Visual Dictionary of the Skeleton.** Dorling Kindersley, 1995. ISBN 0-7894-0135-5. Nonfiction.

Human, animal, and plant skeletons are set forth with illustrations and pictures in order to provide a complete visual reference tool for interested learners, who can now explore skeletons from the inside out, learning about structures and functions of all types of animal and plant skeletons. Informative explanations are included as well as an index for cross reference. This volume, part of the Eyewitness Visual Dictionary series, is a high-quality tool that is user-friendly and will be consulted much over the years. ER

33.29   Vogel, Shawna. **Naked Earth: The New Geophysics.** Dutton, 1995. 218 pp. ISBN 0-525-93771-4. Nonfiction.

Vogel's book reveals the interior mysteries of our planet. The author describes how contemporary geophysical researchers are exploding older theories about the center of the planet through amazing new technologies, and she explains, in plain English, current views on the nature of the earth's core.

33.30   Woods, Michael. **Science on Ice: Research in the Antarctic.** The Millbrook Press, 1995. 83 pp. ISBN 1-56294-498-3. Nonfiction.

This book introduces readers to the least-known continent in the world—Antarctica. Through pictures and text, the book describes Antarctica's unique terrain, geography, and weather, as well as the many important ways research conducted on Antarctica is helping scientific understanding of the world's environment, evolution, and astronomy. The book also explains how Antarctica is "Mars on Earth," and how scientists planning trips to Mars are able to use Antarctica as a practice area because it closely resembles Martian terrain and weather.

Titles Annotated in Other Chapters Related to Science and the Environment

Anderson, Margaret J. *Charles Darwin: Naturalist.* Autobiography.

Ardley, Neil. *Dictionary of Science.* Reference.

Ash, Russell. *Incredible Comparisons.* Reference.

Baldwin, Joyce. *DNA Pioneer: James Watson and the Double Helix.* Autobiography.

Brynie, Faith Hickman. *Genetics and Human Health.* Drugs.

Challoner, Jack. *The Visual Dictionary of Physics.* Reference.

Colman, Penny. *Toilets, Bathtubs, Sinks, and Sewers: A History of the Bathroom.* History.

Darling, David. *Computers of the Future*. Computers.

Day, Nancy. *Animal Experimentation: Cruelty or Science?* Animals.

Emert, Phyllis Raybin. *Mysteries of Space and the Universe*. Mysteries.

Goldenstern, Joyce. *Albert Einstein*. Autobiography.

Hewetson, Sarah. *Eye Magic: Fantastical Optical Illusions*. Arts.

Himrich, Brenda L., and Stew Thornley. *Electrifying Medicine*. Drugs.

Hyde, Margaret O., and Elizabeth H. Forsyth. *Know about AIDS*. Drugs.

Jackson, Donna M. *The Bone Detectives: How Forensic Anthropologists Solve Crimes and Uncover Mysteries of the Dead*. History.

Keene, Ann T. *Earthkeepers*. Autobiography.

Killingsworth, Monte. *Circle within a Circle*. Choices.

Klass, David. *California Blue*. Choices.

Koebner, Linda. *Zoo Book*. Animals.

McPherson, Stephanie Sammartino. *Ordinary Genius: The Story of Albert Einstein*. Autobiography.

Nichols, Michael. *The Great Apes*. Animals.

Parker, Steve. *Medicine*. Drugs.

Poynter, Margaret. *Marie Curie: Discoverer of Radium*. Autobiography.

Preston, Richard. *The Hot Zone*. Drugs.

Smith, Miranda. *Living Earth*. Reference.

Sobel, Dava. *Longitude: The True Story of a Lone Genius Who Solved the Greatest Scientific Problem of His Time*. Autobiography.

Stafford, William. *Learning to Live in the World*. Poetry.

Streissguth, Tom. *Rocket Man: The Story of Robert Goddard*. Autobiography.

Swanson, Diane. *Safari beneath the Sea*. Animals.

Tattersall, Ian. *Primates: Lemurs, Monkeys, and You*. Animals.

Thompson, Sharon Elaine. *Death Trap: The Story of the La Brea Tar Pits*. History.

34 Science Fiction

"Men love to wonder, and that is the seed of our science."
Ralph Waldo Emerson

"If the world were good for nothing else, it is a fine subject for speculation."
William Hazlitt

"Miracles do not happen."
Matthew Arnold

34.1 Aiken, Joan. **Cold Shoulder Road.** Delacorte Press, 1995. 283 pp. ISBN 0-385-32182-1. Fiction.

In the newest addition to the Wolves of Willoughby Chase chronicles, Is and her cousin Arun are returning home, having freed children enslaved in northern mines. When they get to Folkestone, home to Arun, they discover that his mother has vanished. Their attempts to find her bring them into contact with members of a mysterious, silent sect of violent smugglers called the Merry Gentry.

34.2 Allen, Roger MacBride. **The Shattered Sphere.** Tor / Tom Doherty Associates, 1994. 412 pp. ISBN 0-312-85734-9. Fiction.

This, the second book in the Hunted Earth series, begins where the first, *The Ring of Charon* (1990), concludes. Earth had been abducted from the solar system by the Charonians and placed in a distant system. Scientists on Earth as well as those left behind in the solar system search for a way to free the planet. As it turns out, the Charonians' archenemy, the Adversary, is the key. The book contains some complicated scientific ideas, and presents strong female characters.

34.3 Anderson, Poul. **Harvest of Stars.** Tor / Tom Doherty Associates, 1994. 531 pp. ISBN 0-812-51946-9. Fiction.

Gutsy Kyra Davis, space pilot for the Fireball Corporation, rescues the preserved intelligence of her company's deceased founder, Anson Gutherie, from the clutches of the totalitarian government of North America. Together they enlist the aid of a myriad of rebels that can no longer tolerate the oppression of a government which desires to dominate the solar system. Ultimately, they lead a cadre of pioneers to a new star system in search of their destiny.

34.4 Anthony, Patricia. **Brother Termite.** Ace Books, 1995. 261 pp. ISBN 0-441-00187-4. Fiction.

Aliens have been active in American affairs since the Eisenhower years, first secretly but now openly. An alien is even now the White House Chief of Staff, the real power behind a popular but alien-controlled president. The story unfolds as a political thriller, with aliens and humans conspiring against one another in plots that could lead to mutual extinction. Some strong language.

34.5   Anthony, Piers, and Roberto Fuentes. **Dead Morn.** Ace Books, 1994. 340 pp. ISBN 0-441-00052-5. Fiction.

Yellow Six 048197 lives in an underground caste society known as Fidelia in the twenty-fifth century, where love between members of different castes is illegal. Because he breaks this law and is caught, he is forced by the leaders of the post–nuclear war state to travel back in time to twentieth-century Cuba to effect some social engineering for his own time. Fidel Castro and Che Guevara play roles in his adventure. There are several sexual situations and strong language throughout the book.

34.6   Baird, Wilhelmina. **Clipjoint.** Ace Books, 1994. 325 pp. ISBN 0-441-00090-8. Fiction.

In this sequel to *Crashcourse,* the two surviving main characters, Cass and Moke, investigate the possible reappearance of their friend Dosh, who died during the filming of a cyber-drama two years ago. The first-person narration is an updated version of a 1940s smart-aleck detective dialogue, providing some humor, but also making some aspects of the plot difficult to follow. Adult situations, strong language, violence.

34.7   Benford, Gregory, Hal Colebatch, Mark O. Martin, and Paul Chafe. Created by Larry Niven. **Man-Kzin Wars VII.** Baen Books, 1995. 345 pp. ISBN 0-671-87670-8. Fiction.

Part of a larger series, the stories in this volume are linked by humankind's struggles with aliens known as the Kzin. This volume includes three long short stories, or novelettes: "The Colonel's Tiger," "A Darker Geometry," and "Prisoner of War."

34.8   Card, Orson Scott, and Kathryn H. Kidd. **Lovelock.** Tor / Tom Doherty Associates, 1994. 283 pp. ISBN 0-312-85732-2. Fiction.

Lovelock, a mentally enhanced monkey whose role is to witness and record the daily activities of a famous scientist, tells the story of his space voyage aboard the colony ship *Ark* in this satirical novel. In this future time, all important people are assigned a "witness," which can be a monkey, pig, bird, or other animal. Lovelock is more human than anyone realizes, as he rebels from his assigned place in life by breaking through his conditioning. Part of the Mayflower Trilogy series, the book contains adult situations.

34.9   Carver, Jeffrey A. **Star Rigger's Way.** Tor / Tom Doherty Associates, 1994. 217 pp. ISBN 0-812-53444-1. Fiction.

After his starship crewmates are killed, Star Rigger Gev Carlyle must cooperate with an outcast catlike alien, Cephean, for survival. They succeed in merging their minds in order to bring the ship into port. Further adventures occur as the two search the universe for a previous starship team with which Gev served; meanwhile, the friendship and understanding between Gev and Cephean grows. This is the first book of the Star Rigger Universe series; it contains descriptive sexual content.

34.10   Christopher, John. **A Dusk of Demons.** Macmillan, 1994. 175 pp. ISBN 0-02-718425-0. Fiction.

Upon the death of the Master, Ben learns he is the Master's son and heir–and the new Master of Old Isle. But Ben does not know what power he has or how to use it against the demons when they come. They burn down the house and threaten the lives of those who live on Old Isle. Ben escapes from the demons several times before being caught. What is their story? What do they want?

34.11   Claremont, Chris. **Sundowner.** Ace Books, 1994. 346 pp. ISBN 0-441-00070-3. Fiction.

In this third book of the Nicole Shea adventures, the futuristic story revolves around the first human/alien (Halyan't'a) spaceflight project, which faces violent opposition from some segments of both societies. Nicole is the key participant in the project, but she's unaware of a secret genetic engineering experiment using her as a guinea pig giving her Halyan't'a traits, in a plot complicated with some difficult concepts. Some strong language.

34.12   Crispin, A. C., and Kathleen O'Malley. **Silent Songs.** Ace Books, 1994. 295 pp. ISBN 0-441-00061-4. Fiction.

As the Interrelator on the planet Trinity, Tesa has spent the last year establishing a relationship with the Grus, the aliens who live there. In fact, the leader has renamed her Good-Eyes and made her part of his family. She is looking forward to the arrival of several new scientists. When they arrive, her young friend Jib establishes a telepathic link with the Singers, the aquatic species who inhabit the River and who were formerly feared by the Grus. Suddenly, all their lives are threatened by an invasion by the Anurans, amphibious beings from a distant world whose intentions are most hostile. Can Tesa, Jib, and the other scientists save the two native species from extinction? Book 5 of the StarBridge series.

34.13   Cross, Gillian. **New World.** Holiday House, 1994. 171 pp. ISBN 0-8234-1166-4. Fiction.

Miriam and Stuart, two teenagers hired by a game company, test their skills in playing a virtual reality game before it is available on the market. Both young people find themselves vying for positions in the game's strange world. They just cannot stay away. But things begin to go awry when the game seems to prey upon the teenagers' deepest fears. Who could have known of Stuart's fear of spiders or Miriam's dreams of the eyes?

34.14   DeChancie, John. **Living with Aliens.** Ace Books, 1995. 183 pp. ISBN 0-441-00204-8. Fiction.

Thirteen-year-old Drew Hayes narrates the story of two outcast space aliens who come to live with his Ohio family. The aliens enjoy "getting stupid" and "flarning" around in their shrinkable/expandable flying saucer. Drew begins telling the story in a rambling style, full of misspellings and grammatical errors, but his narration grows in sophistication as his appreciation of reading and writing progresses.

34.15   Doyle, Debra, and James D. Macdonald. **By Honor Betray'd.** Tor / Tom Doherty Associates, 1994. 407 pp. ISBN 0-812-51706-7. Fiction.

This third novel in the Mageworld Trilogy finds Beka Rosselin-Metadi, the Domina of the destroyed planet Lost Entibor, and her family and allies outlaws after their defeat at the hands of the Magelords. Despite treachery and betrayal, Beka survives and is joined by her brothers: Ari, huge, powerful, and faithful, and Owen, whose adept powers along with those of his brother's bride, Liannat, aid Beka in the galaxy's ultimate battle with the Magelords for survival.

34.16   Drake, David. **Igniting the Reaches.** Ace Books, 1994. 260 pp. ISBN 0-441-00179-3. Fiction.

A millennium has passed since the human empire's collapse, and the scattered remnants of humankind are once again traveling to distant worlds. Earth and Venus have become rivals much the same way that England and Spain were during the sixteenth century, and this story of trader-pirates from Venus is reminiscent of tales of English "Sea Dogs" of old. Strong language.

34.17   Drake, David. **Through the Breach.** Ace Books, 1995. 327 pp. ISBN 0-441-00171-8. Fiction.

Human space pirates from Venus continue to plunder the colonies and trading ships of Earth's tyrannical Federation government in this sequel to *Igniting the Reaches*. There's plenty of battle action to keep the reader turning the pages. Strong language.

34.18   Ecklar, Julia. **Regenesis.** Ace Books, 1995. 269 pp. ISBN 0-441-00189-0. Fiction.

Long ago and light years away, there was a story about a man named Noah who saved from extinction two of every kind of animal by leading them onto his boat, the Ark. Now, Noah's Ark is the name of a project whose mission is the same, to save the animals. Once again, the earth has become an unsafe and unfriendly place, but this time the human beings and beasts cannot remain on the planet. New homes must be found somewhere in the galaxy. Enter a world of robots, prelates, and cop shops. Travel to a time when human beings as we know them are regarded as aliens. Read about a time in the history of our world that is imaginary or fast approaching.

34.19   Etheridge, Rutledge. **The First Duelist.** Ace Books, 1994. 280 pp. ISBN 0-441-00063-0. Fiction.

Twenty-second-century humankind has fallen under the rule of a corrupt, self-serving, short-sighted government that Simon Barrow is dedicated to change. The story follows Simon from a sixteen-year-old wrongly convicted of a crime and sentenced to a prison asteroid to an adult leader. During his time on the prison asteroid, Simon proves his intelligence and prowess as a warrior, making connections with people who will play an important role in his, and humankind's, future. Their escape has its effects on all of society.

34.20   Farmer, Nancy. **The Ear, the Eye and the Arm.** Orchard Books, 1994. 311 pp. ISBN 0-531-06829-3. Fiction.

Harare, Zimbabwe, in 2194 is a society combining ancient tribal beliefs and customs with flying limousines, robot motorcycles and maids, and synth-food made from bacteria. The sheltered children of General Amadeus Matsika, the national security chief, find themselves in great danger when they venture into this world on an innocent scout trip. Kidnapped by bizarre enemies of their powerful father, Tendai, Rita and Kuda demonstrate timeless courage and resourcefulness. Many details of Zimbabwean history and culture are woven into this story of suspense, and a thorough glossary and an appendix enhance the novel. MC

ALA Best Books for Young Adults, 1995
ALA Notable Books for Children, 1995
Newbery Honor Book, 1995

34.21   Foreman, Lelia Rose. **Shatterworld.** William B. Eerdmans, 1995. 162 pp. ISBN 0-8028-5097-9. Fiction.

Rejoice is a typical almost-thirteen-year-old. She's impatient with her parents, intolerant of her brother, and eager to pursue her interest in astronomy. Yet everything else in Rejoice's life is far from normal. Her parents are members of a religious community who fled upheaval and violence on Earth, settling on a planet a thousand light years from home where six-legged, six-tentacled hexacrabs dwell. Here, new crises test their faith and threaten the lives of every creature on the planet.

34.22   Galanter, Dave, and Greg Brodeur. **Foreign Foes.** Pocket Books, 1994. 274 pp. ISBN 0-671-88414-X. Fiction.

In this thirty-first book of the Star Trek: The Next Generation series, the crew of the starship *Enterprise* plays host to a peace conference between the warring Klingons and Hidrans. The Hidran ambassador mysteriously dies, but kills a Klingon delegate before meeting his fate. Lt. Worf, the security officer of the *Enterprise* and himself a Klingon, is accused of killing the ambassador. With the peace process unraveling, certain individuals begin to act strangely. The story moves toward solving not only the murder mystery, but a medical one as well.

34.23   Gilden, Mel. **The Pumpkins of Time.** Browndeer Press / Harcourt Brace, 1994. 224 pp. ISBN 0-15-276603-0. Fiction.

A space-traveling pickup truck, time-traveling pumpkins, a squidlike alien, dandelion mush, two fourteen-year-olds, and an antique comic book collection combine in this adventure about rescuing the earth. And don't forget a mysterious cat, H. G. Wells, who has a significant role in this easy-to-read tale. ER

34.24   Graf, L. A. **Traitor Winds.** Pocket Books, 1994. 275 pp. ISBN 0-671-86913-2. Fiction.

In this seventieth book based on the original Star Trek series, the earth-bound former bridge crew of the starship *Enterprise* struggles to unravel a conspiracy that implicates two of them in a treasonous plot. Sulu, Chekov, and Uhura are the main characters in the story, which unfolds in locations such as Baltimore, Annapolis, Assateague Island, San Francisco, and White Sands, as well as on board the earth-orbit-docked *Enterprise*. Admiral Kirk, Mr. Scott, and Dr. McCoy also play important roles in the drama.

34.25   Haldeman, Jack C. II, and Jack Dann. **High Steel.** Tor / Tom Doherty Associates, 1993. ISBN 0-812-51433-5. Fiction.

It's two centuries into the future, in an age in which giant corporations have as much power as nations. Native American John Stranger is drafted by one of these corporations to perform dangerous construction work in space. His unique abilities lead to his being used as a pawn in corporate research and power struggles, but from his dreams, John learns he has powers of his own handed down by his people. Strong language and some graphic, adult situations. MC

34.26   Heinlein, Robert A. **Podkayne of Mars.** Baen Books, 1995. 282 pp. ISBN 0-671-87671-6. Fiction.

Podkayne Fries, whose goal in life is to become the first female starship captain, and her eleven-year-old younger brother travel from their home planet of Mars to Venus to meet an uncle who will cast an important vote at the Three Planets Conference, a vote that others will wish to control. This volume also contains a series of essays by readers of this story discussing the main character's fate.

34.27   Kagan, David. **Sunstroke.** Ace Books, 1995. 308 pp. ISBN 0-441-00256-0. Fiction.

An American satellite designed to convert the sun's energy into microwaves and beam them back to Earth for power is mysteriously attacked and damaged, causing it to unleash a death ray on the planet. A political coverup hampers efforts to bring the situation under control, as a nuclear war and polar meltdown loom. Occasional strong language.

34.28   Knight, Damon. **Why Do Birds.** Orb / Tom Doherty Associates, 1994. 272 pp. ISBN 0-312-89009-5. Fiction.

A nondescript man dressed in a 1930s-vintage brown suit and wearing a fedora is released from a mental hospital in the early twenty-first century. This man, Ed Stone, wears a ring that causes people to believe his fantastic story and do his bidding. Ed Stone had been kidnapped from the 1930s by aliens that have commissioned him to gather together the world's populations and put them in a box in order to save them from earth's inevitable destruction.

34.29   Kress, Nancy. **Beggars and Choosers.** Tor / Tom Doherty Associates, 1994. 316 pp. ISBN 0-312-85749-7. Fiction.

Twenty-second-century genetic engineering has created new castes: the donkeys, enhanced in the womb however their parents choose or can afford, and Livers, peasants whose socioeconomic status precludes such modifications. The nonproductive Livers are nonetheless totally provided for by the donkey government and are trained to see themselves as aristocrats. Intellectually superior to donkeys, however, are the exiled Sleepless, who are now being superseded by their offspring, the SuperSleepless. The struggle: Who should control technology as it develops beyond nearly everyone's comprehension?

School Library Journal Best Adult Books for Young Adults, 1995

34.30   Lawrence, Louise. **The Patchwork People.** Clarion Books, 1994. 230 pp. ISBN 0-395-67892-7. Fiction.

First impressions can be quite misleading, even in this futuristic society. Helena was brought up with money and the best of everything. Hugh had to struggle to survive. They would never have expected to become friends, let alone come to care so deeply about each other. However, society and Helena's family seem determined to keep them apart. Will they ever find a way to be together? The Patchwork people give Helena and Hugh the hope they need and the realization that only *they* can control their destiny.

34.31 McDevitt, Jack. **The Engines of God.** Ace Books, 1995. 419 pp. ISBN 0-441-00284-6. Fiction.

Centuries into the future, human explorers begin discovering ancient monuments on distant worlds. Archeologists visit the various monuments and abandoned city sites to gather clues about their makers, as Earth's own future becomes increasingly uncertain. Pilot Priscilla Hutchins (Hutch) is the central character in this story of adventure and mystery. All questions are not answered by the book's end, and a sequel is strongly implied.

34.32 Norton, Andre, and P. M. Griffin. **Firehand.** Tor / Tom Doherty Associates, 1994. 220 pp. ISBN 0-312-85313-0. Fiction.

Ross Murdoch, previously a criminal, is recruited by the Project's leader, Gordon Ashe. These two men must combine their efforts to save all civilizations from the Baldies. The Baldies are out to destroy all races through time travel, and Murdoch and Ashe must go back in time to prevent the destruction of Earth. They need Firehand to accomplish this mission. Will this legend be enough? Violence.

34.33 Nye, Jody Lynn. **Medicine Show.** Ace Books, 1994. 261 pp. ISBN 0-441-00085-1. Fiction.

In this sequel to *Taylor's Ark,* the Taylor family is being hounded by bounty hunters recruited by a powerful man they helped put in prison. The Taylors, along with the crew of their spacecraft and assorted animals, land on Poxt, a distant planet where a strange aging disease is attacking the small human colony as well as another intelligent lifeform, ottles, a cross between otters and turtles. Main character Dr. Shona Taylor works to solve the medical mystery and to protect her family.

34.34 Osborne, Cary. **Iroshi.** Ace Books, 1995. 216 pp. ISBN 0-441-00130-0. Fiction.

In the distant future, humankind has reached the stars and lives scattered across the universe under chaotic conditions. Enter Laicy Campbell, who becomes known as "Iroshi" following her intense martial arts training. Iroshi leaves Earth to seek her destiny, only to find that she must return there to fulfill it. Her powers lie not only in her capacity for violence, but in communicating with soul spirits through her special mind powers as well.

34.35 Pohl, Frederik. **The Voices of Heaven.** Tor / Tom Doherty Associates, 1994. 347 pp. ISBN 0-312-85643-1. Fiction.

Antimatter technician Barry Di Hoa is shanghaied from his home on the moon and sent to Pava, a colony planet many light years away where the human population struggles to survive shortages as well as religious zealotry. The narration follows in first person, after an alien interrogator asks Barry a few questions to begin each chapter. As Barry admits during his story, he's also the victim of a mental disorder that occasionally clouds his judgment. Though there is a good deal of subtle humor, there is also occasional strong language in this novel.

34.36   Ransom, Bill. **Burn.** Ace Books, 1995. 315 pp. ISBN 0-441-00246-3. Fiction.

In this sequel to *ViraVax*, a religious sect looses a deadly virus on the world. A pair of cloned teens, manufactured by the sect, work to solve the mystery of the virus and to save humanity from a situation occurring in the near future. Some adult content.

34.37   Ransom, Bill. **ViraVax.** Ace Books, 1994. 307 pp. ISBN 0-441-00083-5. Fiction.

It's the year 2015 in Costa Brava, a recently formed Central American nation which hosts a mysterious private lab complex run by religious zealots, the Children of God. A U.S. military officer with ties to the lab, his teenage son, and the teenage daughter of a deceased lab scientist fight to learn the awful secrets of the complex, secrets that could hold global consequences as well as very personal ones for each of them. The story contains some complicated concepts including explanations of genetic engineering as well as some adult content.

34.38   Reed, Robert. **Beyond the Veil of Stars.** Tor / Tom Doherty Associates, 1994. 318 pp. ISBN 0-312-85730-6. Fiction.

Even as an adolescent, Cornell has an unusual life assisting his father in studying possible alien landing sites in the Midwest. As he grows into adulthood, Cornell is selected for a secret government program to explore new worlds in search of intelligent life, but the explorers must alter their own physical forms to adapt to the worlds they visit. Eventually, Cornell discovers that aliens have been living among humans by using the same means through which he explores other worlds.

34.39   Robinson, Spider. **The Callahan Touch.** Ace Books, 1995. 221 pp. ISBN 0-441-00133-5. Fiction.

Jake Stonebender tells the story of his newly opened tavern, Mary's Place, in this continuation of the Callahan novels. Patrons include time travelers, both human and nonhuman, and most of the novel revolves around their often humorous conversations with one another. Strong language.

34.40   Robinson, Spider, and Jeanne Robinson. **Starmind.** Ace Books, 1995. 292 pp. ISBN 0-441-00209-9. Fiction.

Contrary to the usual violent, war-torn depiction of human space travel and habitation, perhaps an enlightened, egalitarian future awaits. For

Rhea, however, her earth ties remain strong, creating strife when her husband wishes to move the family to space for a career-capping job. Worse, powerful terrorists on Earth threaten the Starmind that has brought peace and prosperity to the universe. A myriad of motivations, relationships, and possibilities are explored, not without violence, in this last installment of a trilogy.

34.41   Sawyer, Robert J. **End of an Era.** Ace Books, 1994. 222 pp. ISBN 0-441-00114-9. Fiction.

Two Canadian scientists from the year 2013 embark on humankind's first time travel mission sixty-five million years into the past to study dinosaurs and their extinction. They discover intelligent Martian virus lifeforms controlling earth and its creatures, and they battle with the viruses to keep them from traveling forward in time to the present. Time travel and its implications, including divergent time strands, are explored.

34.42   Scott, Michael. **Gemini Game.** Holiday House, 1994. 159 pp. ISBN 0-8234-1092-7. Fiction.

Fifteen-year-old twins Liz and B. J. O'Connor are well known and highly regarded in their profession as "game makers." In the twenty-first-century world of virtual reality computer games, their skills have brought them much fame and wealth. Not everyone, however, is hoping for their continued success. Someone has tampered with their most popular game, "Night's Castle," and now twelve players have fallen into comas as a result. As fugitives from the police and with accusations flying all around them, Liz and B. J. must play their own game and risk becoming victims to learn what has gone wrong and who wants them off the playing field. ER

34.43   Service, Pamela F. **Stinker's Return.** Fawcett Juniper, 1993. 88 pp. ISBN 0-449-70438-6. Fiction.

Stinker, an alien known also as Tsyng Yr who has taken on the form of a skunk, must redeem himself and avoid interplanetary war by enlisting the aid of his former compatriots Karen and Jonathan. These teenagers take on museum security, NASA, and the president in an attempt to help their outer-space friend.

34.44   Shelley, Rick. **The Buchanan Campaign.** Ace Books, 1995. 375 pp. ISBN 0-441-00292-7. Fiction.

The out-of-the-way planet of Buchanan becomes a futuristic battleground between the two powers of the universe, the Federation and the Second Commonwealth. The characters are reminiscent of those in World War II bravado films, doing their duty for king and country, as the Commonwealth, a Britain-like society, faces a militaristic federation.

34.45   Sleator, William. **Interstellar Pig.** Puffin Books, 1995. 197 pp. ISBN 0-14-037595-3. Fiction.

In the beginning, Barney's vacation seems fairly routine. Then an exotic trio moves into the cottage next door. Barney finds their interest in him flattering, and he finds the board game they constantly play, "Interstellar Pig," almost addicting. But then he becomes suspicious. Who are his neighbors, really? Why are they so interested in Barney and his house? And, most important, what are the consequences of losing at the game? With an off-the-wall sense of humor and a well-honed instinct for plotting, Sleator pulls the reader into Barney's summer adventure.

Awards won by original publication, 1984:
ALA Notable Book
ALA Best Books for Young Adults

34.46   Sleator, William. **The Night the Heads Came.** Dutton Children's Books, 1996. 154 pp. ISBN 0-525-45463-2. Fiction.

Leo, sixteen, is driving his best friend, Tim, to catch a bus to New York for a secret interview about his artwork when some force stops the car. Strange creatures capture them and take their blood before releasing Leo. Where is Tim and why do the Others want his drawings? How can Leo explain heads and bodies that are separated? Leo's parents try to support him as he talks to the police and to Tim's mean father. When a changed Tim returns with a portfolio full of grotesque pictures, Leo realizes that their memories have been altered and some strange force is changing people's personalities.

34.47   Stearns, Michael, editor. **A Starfarer's Dozen: Stories of Things to Come.** Illustrated by Michael Hussar. Jane Yolen Books / Harcourt Brace, 1995. 218 pp. ISBN 0-15-299871-3. Fiction.

Over a dozen short stories of adventure, fantasy, terror, tragedy, and humor exploring the possibilities of things to come for the young starfarers of the future lie in wait for the reader in this collection.

34.48   Steele, Allen. **The Jericho Iteration.** Ace Books, 1994. 279 pp. ISBN 0-441-00097-5. Fiction.

In the not-too-distant future, 2013, a major earthquake has laid waste much of St. Louis, resulting in a paramilitary federal agency's taking control of the area and governing it in the manner of a Central American dictatorship. A newspaper reporter, Gerry Rosen, with his own personal demons, stumbles upon a story involving an artificial intelligence accidentally set free through computers and a planned coup d'etat. Strong language.

34.49   Steele, Allen. **The Tranquillity Alternative.** Ace Books, 1996. 306 pp. ISBN 0-441-00299-4. Fiction.

History is re-envisioned in this modern-day story about an expedition to the moon to dismantle a nuclear missile site. For example, the space program has been in existence since World War II, Robert Kennedy, not John, has been president, and Michael Jackson is a civil rights leader. Foreign intrigue, complete with hidden terrorists, interferes with the mission plan as the reader starts to become aware of who is really who. Strong language.

34.50   Vornholt, John. **Star Trek Generations.** Minstrel Books / Pocket Books, 1994. 115 pp. ISBN 0-671-51901-8. Fiction.

Based on the film of the same title, the story begins with the disappearance of the retired Captain Kirk during a space rescue attempt. Seventy-eight years later, Captain Picard and the crew of the starship *Enterprise* face a mad scientist and an energy source known as a nexus which can alter time and reality. Through the nexus, Picard meets Kirk, and together they face the madman.

34.51   Weber, David. Honor Harrington series. Baen. 367-442 pp. (varies).
         Flag in Exile. 1995. ISBN 0-671-87681-3.
         Field of Dishonor. 1994. ISBN 0-671-87624-4.
         The Short Victorious War. 1994. ISBN 0-671-87596-5.

In the latest of the series, *Flag in Exile,* the tendency of Honor Harrington, space captain and toughest woman in any galaxy, to make enemies continues. Her primary concern is doing her duty; she worries little about the impact on those with fewer scruples, many of whom have formidable power. This series is heavily laden with technical language and the mechanics of the crafts and battles, appealing to those who like the "science" in their science fiction.

34.52   Wilson, Robert Charles. **Mysterium.** Spectra / Bantam, 1994. 309 pp. ISBN 0-553-56953-8. Fiction.

An incredibly gifted Nobel Prize–winning physicist, Alan Stern, joins a secret government project only to pursue his real obsession: the possibility of parallel worlds attainable through atomic manipulation. An error in the research, however, jolts a whole Michigan town into an alien, hostile reality where its presence is decidedly unwelcome. The few residents who can guess at the cause must grapple with how to escape the nightmare. To flee from it or to enter deeper into the unknown?
ALA Best Books for Young Adults, 1995

Titles Annotated in Other Chapters Related to Science Fiction

Asimov, Janet. *Murder at the Galactic Writers' Society.* Mysteries.
Clute, John. *Science Fiction: The Illustrated Encyclopedia.* Reference.

Forrest, Elizabeth. *Death Watch*. Mysteries.

Gibson, William. *Johnny Mnemonic*. Television.

Gleason, Robert. *Wrath of God*. Fantasy.

Mikaelsen, Ben. *Countdown*. Adventure.

Pedersen, Ted, and Mel Gilden. *Cybersurfers: Cybercops and Flame Wars*. Computers.

Pedersen, Ted, and Mel Gilden. *Cybersurfers: Ghost on the Net*. Computers.

Preiss, Byron, ed. *Ray Bradbury Chronicles, Vol. 7*. Horror.

Verne, Jules. *Journey to the Center of the Earth*. Classics.

Vick, Helen Hughes. *Walker's Journey Home*. Historical Fiction.

35 Self-Help

"It is vain to ask of the gods what a man is capable of supplying for himself."

Epicurus

"Nevertheless, live,
Conduct your living in the noise and whip of the whirlwind."

Gwendolyn Brooks

35.1   Cheney, Glenn Alan. **Teens with Physical Disabilities: Real-Life Stories of Meeting the Challenges.** Enslow, 1995. 112 pp. ISBN 0-89490-625-9. Nonfiction.

Acceptance by peers is a strong driving force during the teenage years, yet physical disabilities sometimes make acceptance both more desirable and more difficult. Presented in this collection of stories, part of the Issues in Focus series, are the thoughts and actions of eight teens, each facing a physical limitation. From the boy paralyzed by crossfire during a drug deal to the deaf and nearly blind girl, we meet extraordinary strength and maddening frustrations, touching compassion and unbelievable rudeness. In this slim volume, many questions are answered and many more arise regarding senseless acts of violence and cruel turns of fate. A list of resources and a good bibliography set the stage for further investigation.

ALA Quick Picks for Young Adults, 1996

35.2   Espeland, Pamela, and Rosemary Wallner. **Making the Most of Today: Daily Readings for Young People on Self-Awareness, Creativity, and Self-Esteem.** Free Spirit, 1991. 382 pp. ISBN 0-915793-33-4. Nonfiction.

Looking for words of encouragement or of inspiration? The quotations and inspirational meditations in *Making the Most of Today* provide a positive start to your day or encouragement when things aren't going quite the way you would expect. Many well-known persons, Bill Cosby, Nikki Giovanni, and Billy Joel among them, offer their favorite quotations and suggestions and encourage and promote positive self-awareness. They also offer problem-solving ideas and personal inspiration.

35.3   Fenwick, Elizabeth, and Dr. Tony Smith. **Adolescence: The Survival Guide for Parents and Teenagers.** Photographs by Barnabas Kindersley. Dorling Kindersley, 1994. 286 pp. ISBN 1-56458-330-9. Nonfiction.

This reference book will help both parents and teens "get through" adolescence. The four-part book takes readers from physical development through illness and health. The white pages are mainly for parents while the blue are for teens. Gray-tinted boxes, listed in their own table of contents for easy reference, highlight special concerns for parents. Case histories include conversations from both groups.

35.4   Goldman, Jane. **Streetsmarts: A Teenager's Safety Guide.** Barron's, 1996. 141 pp. ISBN 0-8120-9762-9. Nonfiction.

From tips on building confidence to chapters on topics as diverse as how to use body language as self-defense and what sources to contact when you need help in a hurry, Goldman's guide provides useful advice for staying safe on the streets, on a date, and on public transportation. ER

35.5   Hicks, John. **Dating Violence: True Stories of Hurt and Hope.** The Millbrook Press, 1996. 112 pp. ISBN 1-56294-654-4. Nonfiction.

Hicks explores emotional and psychological abuse, which sometimes characterizes relationships, through interviews with both abusers and victims. The true stories of these young people tell how the abusive relationships began, developed, and ended. The author explores the cycle of violence, characteristics of unhealthy relationships, the need for honest communication, and conflict resolution techniques as alternatives to violence, in hopes that anyone involved in an abusive situation will understand the warning signs and have the courage to take steps to alter the nature of the relationship.

35.6   Hipp, Earl. **Fighting Invisible Tigers: A Stress Management Guide for Teens.** Illustrated by Michael Fleishman. Free Spirit, 1995. 153 pp. ISBN 0-915793-80-6. Nonfiction.

If you just can't cope, this book is for you. Through quotations from teens, questionnaires, and humorous anecdotes, the physical and mental effects of teen stress are examined. Follow the easy methods for developing coping skills, starting life-style changes, and creating a strong self image, and you will conquer stress and take charge of your life simply and effectively.

35.7   Johnson, Anne Akers. **Hair: A Book of Braiding and Styles.** Klutz Press, 1995. N.p. ISBN 1-57054-018-7. Nonfiction.

The tricks to pulling hair into quiffs, braided chignons, ponytail wraps, inside-out French braids, and many more interesting styles are explained with easy-to-follow directions illustrated by colorful, glossy photographs. The book comes with three scrunchies for use in elegant and less formal settings. ER

35.8   Karnes, Frances A., and Suzanne M. Bean. **Leadership for Students: A Practical Guide for Ages 8–18.** Prufrock Press, 1995. 180 pp. ISBN 1-882664-12-4. Nonfiction.

Effective leadership is a marketable skill. Frances Karnes and Suzanne Bean have created a practical handbook which promotes effective, constructive leadership skills for young adults. This is an outstanding resource for both students and teachers. ER

35.9   Kincher, Jonni. **Psychology for Kids II: Forty Fun Experiments That Help You Learn about Others.** Edited by Pamela Espeland. Free Spirit, 1995. 160 pp. ISBN 0-915793-83-0. Nonfiction.

Following the success of *Psychology for Kids,* Kincher has once again described, in an easy-to-follow format, instructions for forty experiments categorized into chapters such as "Attitudes and Beliefs," "Gender Differences," and "Memory and Learning," for young scientists eager to interact with and learn more about the people in their world. The directions include information about materials, the nature and number of the subjects needed ("as many people as you want to test" or two groups of people with the same number in each group), and data collection procedures. By engaging in practical investigations, students will practice observation skills, learn the scientific method, develop an appreciation for the strengths and limitations of experimental psychology, and have a forum for talking with others about difficult subjects.

35.10   Lakin, Patricia. **Everything You Need to Know When a Parent Doesn't Speak English.** Rosen, 1994. 64 pp. ISBN 0-8239-1691-X. Nonfiction.

Everyone wants to fit in and feel a sense of belonging. Coming from another country may seem exotic, but special stresses fall on children of non-English-speaking parents. This book, a new volume in the well-known Need to Know Library series, is very reassuring that in this land of immigrants "you are not alone." Adolescents of various backgrounds describe their situations, responses, and methods of coping. Names and addresses of groups that offer help are listed at the back. ER

ALA Quick Picks for Young Adults, 1995

35.11   Landau, Elaine. **The Beauty Trap.** Open Door / New Discovery Books / Maxwell Macmillan, 1994. 128 pp. ISBN 0-02-751389-0. Nonfiction.

As a female, would you prefer to be drop-dead gorgeous or the class genius? Most teenage girls would choose the former. Landau presents a well-researched treatise, complete with endnotes and personal anecdotes, on society's expectations that women be beautiful. She exposes the pressures the media exerts on females to possess the perfect body, often leading to physical problems such as bulimia and the aftermath of breast surgery, as well as what becomes of women when beauty wanes during middle age.

35.12   Lewin, Elizabeth, and Bernard Ryan, Jr. **Simple Ways to Help Your Kids Become Dollar-Smart.** Walker, 1994. 92 pp. ISBN 0-8027-7429-6. Nonfiction.

Money. Tension arises between parents and their children of all ages when the word is spoken. But Lewin and Ryan's premise is that it need not be a taboo subject. In straightforward prose, they offer tips on creating and using a spending plan, dealing with the allowance issue, saving money, establishing credit, and other topics related to developing money sense.

35.13   Lewis, Barbara A. **The Kid's Guide to Service Projects: Over Five Hundred Service Ideas for Young People Who Want to Make a Difference.** Edited by Pamela Espeland. Free Spirit, 1995. 169 pp. ISBN 0-915793-82-2. Nonfiction.

Begin by scanning the contents and discover more that five hundred ideas for service for young people related to the environment, politics, senior citizens or the homeless, safety, and crime. Once an area is chosen, follow the "Ten Steps to Successful Service Projects" and learn how to get started, how to get resources, and how to evaluate the experience. This book provides step-by-step directions and resources that make service projects possible and successful with young people. ER

35.14   Mather, Cynthia L., with Kristina E. Debye. **How Long Does It Hurt? A Guide to Recovering from Incest and Sexual Abuse for Teenagers, Their Friends, and Their Families.** Illustrated by Judy Wood. Foreword by Eliana Gil. Jossey-Bass, 1994. 265 pp. ISBN 1-55542-674-3. Nonfiction.

Many of the attitudes, worries, and fears of victims of sexual abuse are addressed in this volume in a supportive and encouraging manner. The author herself was sexually abused by her biological father, and she speaks of both males and females as potential victims or abusers. There are also chapters on legal issues, how to be a friend to a victim, and where to get help.

ALA Quick Picks for Young Adults, 1995

35.15   Packer, Alex J. **Bringing Up Parents: The Teenager's Handbook.** Edited by Pamela Espeland. Illustrated by Harry Pulver, Jr. Free Spirit, 1992. 264 pp. ISBN 0-915793-48-2. Nonfiction.

At some point, most teenagers experience conflict with their parents or other significant adults in their lives. Packer has provided strategies for both teenagers and parents to use to avoid and resolve conflicts. Issues such as personal space, curfews, interaction style, freedom and responsibility, compromise, apologies, and even trust funds are addressed in a humorous but down-to-earth fashion. The overall message Packer sends is that both parents and teenagers have to learn to respond to one another and to interact in ways that demonstrate acceptance and tolerance of the different views they bring to bear on points of tension, in order to avoid nagging, scolding, and attacking in the family.

35.16   Wiseman, Rosalind. **Defending Ourselves: A Guide to Prevention, Self-Defense, and Recovery from Rape.** The Noonday Press / Farrar, Straus and Giroux, 1994. 216 pp. ISBN 0-374-52415-7. Nonfiction.

As the women in this book tell their stories, some of date rape, others of assault, their personal experiences draw the reader into the world of abuse and terror, hospitals and police, fear and self-defense. Working through her own battles with an abusive partner, the author presents physical and emotional self-defense skills for women, advice about how to deal with police, counselors, and the courts following an assault, and support for family members also affected by the trauma. Important reading for both women and men, **Defending Ourselves** strives to increase physical and emotional safety for women and emotional healing for all involved.

35.17 Wood, Heather. **101 Marvelous Money-Making Ideas for Kids.** Tor / Tom Doherty Associates, 1995. 147 pp. ISBN 0-812-52060-2. Nonfiction.

Who couldn't use some extra cash? This book will be a valuable resource for anyone wanting to turn his or her talents into a money-making enterprise. With information on topics from how to look for a job, how to take care of a personal business, and how to do market research, as well as on hundreds of activities from traditional standbys such as babysitting to less well-known options such as internships, Wood's practical, easy-to-follow text will be a useful guide. ER

Titles Annotated in Other Chapters Related to Self-help

Armstrong, William H. *Study Is Hard Work*. College.

Cummings, Rhoda Woods, and Gary L. Fisher. *The School Survival Guide for Kids with LD (Learning Differences)*. College.

Fry, Virginia Lynn. *Part of Me Died, Too: Stories of Creative Survival among Bereaved Children and Teenagers*. Death.

Hawksley, Lucinda, and Ian Whitelaw, editors. *101 Essential Tips: Yoga*. Drugs.

Kimeldorf, Martin. *Creating Portfolios for Success in School, Work, and Life*. Reference.

Levine, Beth. *Divorce: Young People Caught in the Middle*. Family.

Lewin, Elizabeth, and Bernard Ryan, Jr.. *Simple Ways to Help Your Kids Become Dollar-Smart*. Self-Help.

McCutcheon, Randall. *Can You Find It? Twenty-five Library Scavenger Hunts to Sharpen Your Research Skills*. College.

Nelson, Richard E., and Judith C. Galas. *The Power to Prevent Suicide: A Guide for Teens Helping Teens*. Death.

Pollack, Rachel, and Cheryl Schwartz. *The Journey Out: A Guide for and about Lesbian, Gay, and Bisexual Teens*. Dating.

Pope, Loren. *Colleges That Change Lives: Forty Schools You Should Know about Even if You're Not a Straight-A Student*. College.

Schumm, Jeanne Shay, and Marguerite Radencich. *School Power: Strategies for Succeeding in School*. College.

36 Short Stories

"My stories run up and bite me on the leg. I respond by writing down everything that goes on during the bite. When I finish, the idea lets go and runs off."

Ray Bradbury

"A lie hides the truth. A story tries to find it."

Paula Fox

36.1   Avila, Alfred. **Mexican Ghost Tales of the Southwest.** Illustrated by Alfred Avila. Compiled by Kat Avila. Piñata Books, 1994. 172 pp. ISBN 1-55885-107-0. Fiction.

Kat Avila has compiled ghost stories, handed down from her father, into a collection of haunting tales. Each story is illustrated by Alfred Avila himself, enabling the reader to envision the horror set forth in the dialogue. Mexican culture is vivid on these pages of terrifying tales. MC WL

36.2   Bauer, Marion Dane, editor. **Am I Blue? Coming Out from the Silence.** HarperCollins, 1994. 273 pp. ISBN 0-06-024253-1. Fiction.

This collection of sixteen original stories by authors such as William Sleator, Lois Lowry, and C. S. Adler all present honest and genuine portrayals of homosexuality. The characters are all either gay themselves or growing up with gay or lesbian friends or family members. Each one explores his or her life or the lives of others—a dying poet, a gay community, the death of a father's gay partner, and society's prejudice.

ALA Quick Picks for Young Adults, 1995

36.3   Brooks, Martha. **Traveling on into the Light and Other Stories.** Orchard Books, 1994. 146 pp. ISBN 0-531-06863-3. Fiction.

These eleven short stories all involve teenagers who are about to make important discoveries as they make their way into adulthood. There's Donald, an unappreciated artist; Niki, a young mother in an unhappy marriage; Jamie, who goes looking for his dead father; and Sidonie, who survives lost love. All these characters experience alienation and loss, but each finds hope for the future with the help and support of others.

ALA Best Books for Young Adults, 1995
ALA Quick Picks for Young Adults, 1995
School Library Journal Best Books, 1994

36.4   Carlson, Lori M., editor. **American Eyes: New Asian-American Short Stories for Young Adults.** Introduction by Cynthia Kadohata. Henry Holt, 1994. 144 pp. ISBN 0-8050-3544-3. Fiction.

After reading a manuscript by a Korean American that touched her heart, Carlson, curious about the diversity of perceptions Asian Americans bring to bear on the experience of coming of age, collected this set of stories illustrating the conflicts, choices, and experiences of young people re-envisioning the American way of life. MC

ALA Best Books for Young Adults, 1995

36.5   Cofer, Judith Ortiz. **An Island like You: Stories of the Barrio.** Orchard Books, 1995. 176 pp. ISBN 0-531-06897-8. Fiction.

Arturo says of himself, "Sometimes I just have to get out and walk." A grandmother yells at her grandchild, "You make me feel like a zero, a nothing." Teresa notes, "I can't swim very well, mainly because my eyesight is so bad that the minute I take off my glasses to get in the pool, everything becomes a blob of color and I freeze." The characters of Cofer's stories have problems and personalities with whom all readers can relate, but they sometimes have to come up with different solutions because they live in El Barrio of New York. So Sandi has to cope with the fact that her looks don't mesh with Latino notions of beauty, and the protagonist of "Arturo's Flight" has to cope with the fact that he is the object of ridicule because he has different dreams from those of his macho classmates. *An Island like You* allows readers to experience a different culture and to find parts of themselves in the characters as they deal with loss, sorrow, and the various tragedies of adolescence. MC

ALA Best Books for Young Adults, 1996
ALA Quick Picks for Young Adults, 1996
Booklist Editors' Choice, 1996
Notable 1995 Children's Trade Books in the Field of Social Studies

36.6   Cohen, Daniel. **Dangerous Ghosts.** G. P. Putnam's Sons, 1996. 86 pp. ISBN 0-399-22913-2. Fiction.

"Ghost"—the word conjures up scary images and spine-tingling feelings. In each of these stories Cohen gives the reader a different kind of ghost, from a corpselike child who haunts a sickroom to a woman who carries a basket containing her own head. ER

36.7   Conford, Ellen. **I Love You, I Hate You, Get Lost.** Scholastic Hardcover, 1994. 133 pp. ISBN 0-590-45558-3. Fiction.

In this group of seven hilarious stories, Conford crafts realistic characters. Dana gets stuck babysitting her little brother on what should have been a romantic evening. Howie is jealous because his best friend Bonnie keeps dating jerks. Laurel's father has already embarrassed her enough with his tacky carpet commercials; now he wants her to become Miss Floor Covering. They all know firsthand that being a teenager is tough, but sometimes it's also very funny. ER

ALA Quick Picks for Young Adults, 1995

36.8   Conrad, Pam. **Our House: The Stories of Levittown.** Illustrated by Brian Selznick. Scholastic Hardcover, 1995. 65 pp. ISBN 0-590-46523-6. Fiction.

Six stories of growing up in the post–World War II suburb of Levittown, New York, show that unique town from the 1940s to the 1990s. Generations of children are linked as one child's name scrawled in wet cement helps heal the pain of another's loss fifty years later, and as the invisible footprints we all leave are remembered in these stories. ER

36.9   Cramer, Alexander. **A Night in Moonbeam County.** Charles Scribner's Sons/Maxwell Macmillan, 1994. 197 pp. ISBN 0-684-19704-9. Fiction.

After jumping off a train while riding the rails, two teenage boys, Chas and Rail, land in Moonbeam County, where they meet a mysterious group of hoboes who tell them ten ghostly stories. The boys are drawn into a strange time and place, as the stories tell about foxes that talk, encounters with the devil, trips back in time, and painted souls. It's not until later that the boys realize how bizarre things are and how they fit into the stories.

36.10   Dann, Jack, and Gardner Dozois, editors. **Dinosaurs II.** Ace Books, 1995. 253 pp. ISBN 0-441-00285-4. Fiction.

Here are eleven tales of dinosaurs, from the pens of writers such as Clifford Simak, Allen Steele, and Isaac Asimov. Some frightening, some merely fascinating, these stories all allow the reader to review the past and speculate on the future, while rethinking the role of the dinosaur on Planet Earth.

36.11   Dozois, Gardner, and Sheila Williams, editors. **Isaac Asimov's Ghosts.** Ace Books, 1995. 225 pp. ISBN 0-441-00254-4. Fiction.

This is a collection of twelve short stories dealing with ghosts by various authors, all originally published in *Asimov's Science Fiction.* Thematically, many of the stories, most of which can be read in under an hour, describe the main character discovering meaning in life through an experience with death in some fashion. Some contain strong language and sexual situations.

36.12   Fiene, Pat, editor. **Expressions: Stories and Poems, Volume 2.** Contemporary Books, 1994. 150 pp. ISBN 0-8092-3648-6. Fiction.

Filled with short stories and poems written by contemporary authors such as Sandra Cisneros and Amy Tan, this anthology contains diverse works that appeal to teens. It is divided into three sections: "Beginning," "Building," and "Extending." Whether you enjoy mystery, comedy, or romance, you will find something here. After each section, a reflection and writing section follows. Part of Contemporary's Whole Language series. MC

36.13 Gallo, Donald R., editor. **Ultimate Sports: Short Stories by Outstanding Writers for Young Adults.** Delacorte Press, 1995. 334 pp. ISBN 0-385-32152-X. Fiction.

In these sixteen original sports stories written by respected young authors, readers are introduced to players of traditional sports, from basketball to football, and to those who prefer the challenges of less well-known sports, such as racquetball or yachting. But the stories are about more than playing the game; they are about relationships with friends, family, and oneself, responding to pressure, accepting responsibility, and learning more about the world by being open to whatever it has to offer. The stories are followed by brief biographies of their authors, almost all of whom are either former or current participants in the sports about which they write.

36.14 Gatti, Anne, editor. **Tales from the African Plains.** Illustrated by Gregory Alexander. Dutton Children's Books, 1994. 83 pp. ISBN 0-525-45282-6. Fiction.

Traditional stories retold never really grow old; instead, each new generation enjoys them all over again. This collection of traditional African tales deals with subjects from the fantastic and mythical to the ordinary business of everyday living. The paintings not only decorate the pages, they also bring the tales to life with brilliant color and traditional patterns. Readers of all ages will enjoy the stories and the illustrations. MC WL

36.15 Hartwell, David G., editor. **The Screaming Skull and Other Great American Ghost Stories.** Tor / Tom Doherty Associates, 1994. 217 pp. ISBN 0-812-55178-8. Fiction.

Be prepared to be scared as twelve of the most renowned American writers share their ghost stories. Instead of tame campfire stories, these stories fill your imagination with horror. All types of hauntings are available in one book, so there is something for every ghost lover. If you really like ghost stories then this book is for you, but we suggest you don't read it before going to bed!

36.16 Haslam, Alexandra R., and Gerald W. Haslam, editors. **Where Coyotes Howl and Wind Blows Free: Growing Up in the West.** University of Nevada Press, 1995. 201 pp. ISBN 0-87417-255-1. Fiction.

The editors have assembled a collection of legends, folktales, essays, and humorous stories of real people living real lives in the American West during the late nineteenth and early twentieth centuries. Each of the authors, many of them award winners, grew up in the West, and writes from firsthand knowledge and experience. This anthology represents life among the ethnically diverse peoples of the American West and could serve as a modern-day primary source for a sociological study of the region. MC

36.17   Jennings, Paul. **Unbearable! More Bizarre Stories.** Viking, 1995. 116 pp. ISBN 0-670-86262-2. Fiction.

These eight hauntingly amusing short stories involve bizarre creatures in bizarre situations with an unexpected twist at the end. A boy and smelly feet save a sea turtle and her eggs. A yellow parakeet comes back from the dead. A fox's fur locked in a secret closet is later rejuvenated with lemons from the lemon tree in the back yard. These stories as well as the others will leave readers laughing and entertained. WL

ALA Quick Picks for Young Adults, 1996

36.18   Jennings, Paul. **Uncovered! Weird, Weird Stories.** Viking, 1995. 134 pp. ISBN 0-670-86856-6. Fiction.

This collection of nine short stories explores family relations, growing up, and death, all with both humor and sensitivity. The characters in these stories often experience growth in inventive and surprising ways. One boy's wish is to see snow before his death. His supposedly severely retarded brother retreats to the attic to concoct a successful scheme to grant his brother's wish without his ever having to leave home. ER MC WL

36.19   Kafka, Franz. **Give It Up! and Other Short Stories by Franz Kafka.** Illustrated by Peter Kuper. Nantier Beall Minoustchine, 1995. 64 pp. ISBN 1-56163-125-6. Fiction.

In another fine graphic novel in the ComicsLit series, Kuper's black-and-white drawings evoke the alienation, dark humor, and frustration prevalent in the works of Kafka while injecting Kuper's own interpretations. (Fair warning: ComicsLit are their own literary form and cannot replace the original works!)

36.20   Kerr, Katharine, and Martin H. Greenberg, editors. **Weird Tales from Shakespeare.** Daw Books, 1994. 318 pp. ISBN 0-88677-605-8. Fiction.

This is a collection of short stories written by various authors involving Shakespeare in one way or another. They are entitled "weird" because these stories attempt to explain mysteries surrounding Shakespeare and his writing. Some of the settings are distinctly Shakespearean, others are very modern, but all of them allow the reader a new perspective on the Bard of Avon.

36.21   King, Stephen. **Nightmares and Dreamscapes.** Signet, 1994. 692 pp. ISBN 0-451-18023-2. Fiction.

Each of these twenty horror stories possesses a unique plot that fills the reader's mind with curiosity and imagination. The selections vary in style and include a set of chattering teeth coming to life to save a man's life and a man seeking revenge on another man by burying him and his car in a pit under the road. The book also includes a television script, a poem, and a nonfiction essay all written by King. Strong language.

36.22 Lee, Stan, editor. **The Ultimate Silver Surfer.** Byron Preiss Multimedia / Boulevard Books, 1995. 339 pp. ISBN 1-57297-029-4. Fiction.

Just the name "Marvel Comics" conjures up images of superheroes and their villainous adversaries battling it out in an intergalactic arena. This collection of fifteen stories highlights the Silver Surfer, cosmic defender of virtue, and his archenemies, Galactus, Thanos, and Mephisto. The first story gives background information on the Silver Surfer's origin, while the remaining stories are woven around themes of humanity's suffering and good versus evil. Accompanying each story is an illustration by a Marvel Comics artist.

36.23 Lyons, Mary E., editor. **Raw Head, Bloody Bones: African-American Tales of the Supernatural.** Aladdin Paperbacks, 1995. 77 pp. ISBN 0-689-80306-0. Nonfiction.

Fifteen scary African American folktales of the supernatural trace their roots to the strong storytelling tradition of Africa. Night doctors capture the unsuspecting for gruesome experiments; babies communicate with their mothers before they are even born; and Raw Head, a giant, sweats blood from his bald head. Recorded in several dialects reflecting their sources, these stories abound with tricksters, ghosts, monsters, and superhuman figures. ER MC WL

36.24 Macdonald, Caroline. **Hostilities: Nine Bizarre Stories.** Scholastic Hardcover, 1994. 131 pp. ISBN 0-590-46063-3. Fiction.

Have you ever experienced a bizarre or eerie incident that you could not logically explain but could never forget? This book presents nine such "bizarre" short stories that might not always scare you but will probably make you think twice about the strange things that happen to you. These are not traditional ghost stories but may leave the reader "haunted" anyhow. MC WL

36.25 Marks, Marlene Adler, editor. **Nice Jewish Girls: Growing Up in America.** Plume, 1996. 292 pp. ISBN 0-452-27397-8. Nonfiction.

Arranged by theme, this collection provides a well-balanced mix of fictional short stories, poetry, and autobiographical writings that explore the rich heritage of forty-five American Jewish writers. Some poignant, others humorous, the selections from Amy Bloom, Jane Yolen, Jane Schulzinger Fox, tova, Carolyn White, Erica Jong, and others shape a sense of what a Jewish girlhood is all about in terms of family connections, responsibilities, spirituality, and dating. MC

36.26 McGraw, Erin. **Lies of the Saints.** Chronicle Books, 1996. 195 pp. ISBN 0-8118-1315-0. Fiction.

From a radio talk show host whose ratings soar when her ex-husband becomes a regular caller, to a man who calls off his wedding because he thinks he has won a thirteen-million-dollar lottery prize only to find he was the victim of a hoax, to a family that struggles to cope with life and one another, this collection of short stories offers a sometimes humorous glimpse of usual people reacting to unusual circumstances.

36.27   Meyer, Carolyn. **Rio Grande Stories.** Gulliver Books / Harcourt Brace, 1994. 257 pp. ISBN 0-15-200548-X. Fiction.

Seventh-grade students at Rio Grande Middle School in Albuquerque write and sell a book about their heritage. All of the fifteen students' contributions to the book depict their different backgrounds. For example, Manuel Medina fears he will never learn to speak English and Rick Begay captures the history of the Navajo as told by his grandfather. Each student learns about the other students as well as themselves as a result of this school project. MC

36.28   Paterson, Katherine. **A Midnight Clear: Stories for the Christmas Season.** Lodestar Books, 1995. 212 pp. ISBN 0-525-67529-9. Fiction.

Although these twelve modern-day stories were originally written by this favorite author for her husband to use with his congregation on Christmas Eve, they are fitting for reading all year. A young boy befriends a homeless woman; in Communist China, a female scholar and a night watchman secretly read the Bible; a man on the way to see his dying father is robbed by a young hitchhiker; and in several stories, a baby is born. All the stories have beautiful titles, imaginative dialogue, unforgettable characters, and hopeful endings.

36.29   Resnick, Mike, Martin H. Greenberg, and Loren D. Estleman, editors. **Deals with the Devil.** Daw Books, 1994. 362 pp. ISBN 0-88677-623-6. Fiction.

The thirty-two stories in this collection relate deals made with the dark man himself. Some of the stories delve into horror, some into humor, and some into Hades itself. Each story has a different and sometimes unexpected twist to it which will surprise and entertain the reader.

36.30   Reynolds, Marilyn. **Beyond Dreams.** Morning Glory Press, 1995. 189 pp. ISBN 1-885356-00-5. Fiction.

Six short stories deal with problems often facing teens: a sense of failure, teen motherhood, abuse, grief and loss, the consequences of drunk driving, abortion, immigrant status, racism, and aging relatives. For those who have read *Too Soon for Jeff*, by the same author, also in the True-to-Life Series from Hamilton High, some of the same characters reappear since the setting is the same Southern California high school. ER

36.31   Sauerwein, Leigh. **The Way Home.** Illustrated by Miles Hyman. Farrar, Straus and Giroux, 1994. 118 pp. ISBN 0-374-38247-6. Fiction.

This collection of six short stories presents "snapshots" of the American West from 1853 to the present and helps the reader understand what it means to be an American. Each of the main characters is involved in the pursuit of freedom, either personal or political. Stories include a tale of a boy who meets the captured warrior Geronimo as well as a tale of two slaves escaping to freedom by riverboat. MC

36.32 Sherman, Josepha, editor. **Orphans of the Night.** Walker, 1995. 162 pp. ISBN 0-8027-8368-6. Fiction.

These thirteen tales of mythical creatures were borrowed by well-known authors for young people from folklore from around the world. While preserving the original legend, the stories set their demons in modern times, admittedly among many contemporaries who doubt their existence. The stories are more fantastic than gory or gruesome. Meet a Njuggle from the Shetland Islands, a Sidi-kur from Mongolia, an Ixtabay from Belize, and a Doppelganger from Germany, among others. Remember this title for Halloween! WL

36.33 Shusterman, Neal. **MindQuakes: Stories to Shatter Your Brain.** Tor Books / Tom Doherty Associates, 1996. 114 pp. ISBN 0-812-55197-4. Fiction.

Ten short stories, each easily read in one sitting, are contained in this collection of "Twilight Zone"–type pieces. Examples? A Christmas tree comes to life looking for revenge; a son and a daughter play a sinister prank on their father's new girlfriend; an autistic child paints pictures that can take people through time. At the conclusion of each of the stories, the author includes a section describing how he came up with the idea. ER

36.34 Soto, Gary. **Local News.** Scholastic, 1994. 144 pp. ISBN 0-590-48446-X. Fiction.

Gary Soto does it again. Soto takes the everyday events in young people's lives and creates thirteen authentic stories that are appealing to young adult audiences of different cultures and experiences, although they are all grounded in his own background as a young Mexican American man growing up in California. MC

36.35 Stanley, G. E. **Happy Deathday to You and Other Stories to Give You Nightmares.** Avon Flare Books, 1995. 113 pp. ISBN 0-380-77741-X. Fiction.

Mandy Styles finds and sends out some old, humorous greeting cards that carry a lot more than messages. Elgin Dougherty is forced to become a "catcher in the stairwell" for a ghost-boy who keeps jumping from the stairway. And Little Jess uses his evil powers to make his birthday revenge come true. These are just some of the strange situations found in this collection of eighteen stories. ER

36.36 Tashlik, Phyllis, editor. **Hispanic, Female and Young: An Anthology.** Piñata Books, 1994. 217 pp. ISBN 1-55885-072-4. Fiction.

This collection of short stories fills a gap in Latino literature. The book was compiled and partly written by a group of teenage girls who, being Latina themselves, noticed a need for feminine Hispanic literature. Some of the stories are the teenagers' own and some are contributed by authors the girls contacted and interviewed. MC

ALA Quick Picks for Young Adults, 1995

36.37 Taylor, Theodore. **Rogue Wave and Other Red-Blooded Sea Stories.** Harcourt Brace, 1996. 184 pp. ISBN 0-15-201408-X. Fiction.

Master of the adventure novel, Taylor here shows that he is equally adept in the short story genre. The tales in this collection all revolve around the power of the sea and are about the people who travel for diverse reasons over the ocean waters of the world.

36.38 Testa, Maria. **Dancing Pink Flamingos and Other Stories.** Lerner, 1995. 115 pp. ISBN 0-8225-0738-2. Fiction.

"Sal Lombardi walks down the center aisle of the cathedral, places a rose on Dominic's coffin, and all I can think of is how much I hate him," begins the title story in this volume of nine stories exploring the struggles of young people who seem to have all the odds stacked against them. Crime, violence, and a lack of hope about the future darken these stories, but the characters find hope, connection with others, and the sense of self that allows them to save themselves from despair. Ultimately the stories become stories of triumph rather than of tragedy.

ALA Best Books for Young Adults, 1996
ALA Quick Picks for Young Adults, 1996

36.39 Turner, Megan Whalen. **Instead of Three Wishes.** Greenwillow Books, 1995. 132 pp. ISBN 0-688-13922-1. Fiction.

Each of the seven short stories in this collection involves fantasy and magic found in ordinary places. A small town is overrun with tourists after a leprechaun is sighted. A boy is cursed with a nightmare and every night views how others perceive him through a snake with a mirror. A factory worker becomes friends with a ghost and joins her in her world. All the stories end with a surprise to intrigue readers and take them into the world of the supernatural.

36.40 Weis, Margaret, editor. **Fantastic Alice.** Ace Books, 1995. 291 pp. ISBN 0-441-00253-6. Fiction.

Fans of *Alice in Wonderland* will delight in these tales by modern fantasy writers, which bring back the grinning cat, the hookah-smoking caterpillar, the Mad Hatter, and other denizens of Wonderland in all new, wild and weird, updated situations. Some are touching, some are amusing, some are frightening—but all are entertaining.

36.41 Westall, Robert. **Shades of Darkness.** Farrar, Straus and Giroux, 1994. 310 pp. ISBN 0-374-36758-2. Fiction.

These eleven short stories build an eerie sense of justice for characters who meet with life's dark side. Higginson stumbles upon a supposedly abandoned house while cutting school one day. In a small, dying coal town, Pastor Martin Williams is asked to schedule one funeral a month in advance of the death. Lonely Chas McGill finds companionship with a World War I soldier who "lives" behind a great wardrobe. Will these characters do the right thing or become victims of revenge?

36.42 Whitcher, Susan. **Real Mummies Don't Bleed: Friendly Tales for October Nights.** Pictures by Andrew Glass. Sunburst / Farrar, Straus and Giroux, 1994. 119 pp. ISBN 0-374-46209-7. Fiction.

Five spooky and bizarre short stories present interesting characters and plots. For example, Annie traps a pet witch who, through a purple dream, grants her a wish for a horse. Readers will also meet a paper-bag genie, a talking toad, a one-eyed dog and a parrot, and a Halloween night that involves hieroglyphics. ER

36.43 Wilson, Budge. **The Dandelion Garden and Other Stories.** Philomel Books, 1995. 168 pp. ISBN 0-399-22768-7. Fiction.

Can a dandelion, a canoe trip with your father, or a trip to the beach change your life forever? A charming brother, an enchanting new girl at school, and a concerned minister are a few of the characters the reader meets in this collection of ten stories that shows how seemingly unimportant people and events in our lives can have lasting consequences.

36.44 Wilson, Budge. **Mothers and Other Strangers.** Harcourt Brace, 1996. 194 pp. ISBN 0-15-200312-6. Fiction.

In this superb collection of short stories, Wilson investigates women's relationships and insights, often looking back at youthful experiences from the vantage point of age. Totally engaging for readers mature enough to be ready to accept that the simple passage of time does not guarantee wisdom, freedom from pain, or complete benevolence, these masterfully crafted stories are sure to win much favorable attention.

36.45 Yolen, Jane. **Here There Be Witches.** Illustrated by David Wilgus. Harcourt Brace, 1995. 117 pp. ISBN 0-15-200311-8. Fiction.

This third book in the "Here There Be . . . " series contains a variety of stories and poems about witches, wizards, and warlocks. The book opens with a poem about Hansel and Gretel and continues with stories involving a young boy waiting to grow up to be a warlock and the spell cast by a face sewn within the cloth given to a princess. The book is illustrated with pencil drawings. ER

36.46 Young, Richard, and Judy Dockrey Young, editors. **Ozark Ghost Stories.** August House, 1995. 207 pp. ISBN 0-87483-410-4. Fiction.

Storytellers have the art of weaving tales, legends, folklore, and ghost stories to mesmerize their listeners. The Youngs are performing storytellers in the Ozark region who have compiled a collection of favorite ghost stories for readers to enjoy. This collection ranges from traditional stories about haunted places to urban legends, and ends on a humorous note with ghost jokes and light-hearted ghostly tales. MC

36.47   Zweifel, Karyn. **Covered Bridge Ghost Stories.** Crane Hill, 1995. 206 pp. ISBN 1-881548-23-6. Fiction.

Covered bridges have a mystique of their own, partly due to their unique architecture and the folklore that claims they contain spirits from the past. These thirteen stories set at the sites of actual covered bridges located around the United States provide regional tales of mystery and legend. Included with the stories is information about, and directions to, the bridges themselves.

36.48   Zweifel, Karyn. **Southern Vampires: Thirteen Deep-Fried Bloodcurdling Tales.** Crane Hill, 1995. 130 pp. ISBN 1-881548-14-7. Fiction.

These thirteen stories, set in the southern United States, explore the existence of vampires. Twelve of the stories are based on some historical fact with embellishment by the author. These stories, rich in atmosphere, combine the intrigue of the vampire creature with the romanticism of the South.

Titles Annotated in Other Chapters Related to Short Stories

Applegate, Katherine, Ellen Conford, Alane Ferguson, and Lee Wardlaw. *See You in September*. Romance.

Asher, Sandy. *A Senior Class Yearbook: Out of Here*. School.

Bruchac, Joseph, and Gayle Ross (told by). *The Girl Who Married the Moon: Stories from Native North America*. Myths.

Charyn, Jerome, ed. *The New Mystery: The International Association of Crime Writers' Essential Crime Writing of the Late Twentieth Century*. Mysteries.

Clark, Mary Higgins, ed. *Bad Behavior*. Mysteries.

Conford, Ellen, Ellen Leroe, Jane McFann, and Jean Thesman. *A Night to Remember*. Romance.

Finnis, A., ed. *Bone Meal: Seven More Tales of Terror*. Horror.

Finnis, A., ed. *The Cat-Dogs*. Horror.

Giovanni, Nikki, ed. *Grand Mothers: Poems, Reminiscences, and Short Stories about the Keepers of Our Traditions*. Poetry.

Kipling, Rudyard. *The Jungle Book: The Mowgli Stories*. Classics.

Lee, Stan, ed. *The Ultimate Spider-Man*. Fantasy.

Pedersen, Ted. *True Fright: Trapped beneath the Ice! and Other True Stories Scarier than Fiction*. Adventure.

Resnick, Mike, and Martin H. Greenberg, eds. *Sherlock Holmes in Orbit*. Mysteries.

Serling, Carol, ed. *Return to the Twilight Zone*. Horror.

Spariosu, Mihail I., and Benedek Dezső. *Ghosts, Vampires, and Werewolves: Eerie Tales from Transylvania*. Myths.

Stepto, Michele, ed. *African-American Voices*. Diaries.

Varley, John, and Ricia Mainhardt, eds. *Superheroes*. Fantasy.

Wrede, Patricia C. *Book of Enchantments*. Fantasy.

Wynne-Jones, Tim. *Some of the Kinder Planets: Stories by Tim Wynne-Jones*. Humor.

Yolen, Jane. *Here There Be Unicorns*. Poetry.

37 Sports and Sports Figures

"The will to win is not nearly so important as the will to prepare to win."

Bobby Knight

"Racing and hunting excite man's heart to madness."

Lao-tse

37.1   Bennett, James. **The Squared Circle.** Scholastic Hardcover, 1995. 247 pp. ISBN 0-590-48671-3. Fiction.

Basketball is Sonny Youngblood's passion. One of the best high school players in the country, he is recruited by SIU in the hopes that he will take them to the NCAA championships. At the university, Sonny begins to question whether his passion for basketball can withstand the obstacles of his free-spirited older cousin, the financial needs of the SIU basketball program, and his own tormented childhood memories. The book takes the reader to an unexpected climax in which Sonny makes a dramatic decision about his future and whether he will continue with his college career with or without basketball.

ALA Best Books for Young Adults, 1996

37.2   Blais, Madeleine. **In These Girls, Hope Is a Muscle.** Warner Books, 1995. 266 pp. ISBN 0-446-67210-6. Nonfiction.

This book about a girls' state championship basketball team joins the ranks of inspirational sports literature. A true story, it is told by a writer who blends accomplished reporting with an instinct for the telling detail in her description of the players and coaches. The book may be unique among sports books in that it is a documentary focusing on an entire season with a girls' basketball team and the community that nurtured and celebrated it.

37.3   Boga, Steve. **The Lunch Bowl.** High Noon Books, 1994. 44 pp. ISBN 0-87879-922-3. Fiction.

Ronnie first meets the new kid, David Strong, after David's incredible catch in the "Lunch Bowl" football game. David seems to have everything, even Katie, who has been Ronnie's friend since first grade. Ronnie is small and not athletic, but he is funny and becomes a successful radio announcer. Although they are high school friends, Ronnie is jealous of David until a car crash changes things—all told in nine short chapters. ER

37.4   Boga, Steve. **Side Kick.** High Noon Books, 1994. 44 pp. ISBN 0-87879-993-1. Fiction.

Fran, the rebel teenager, hates her parents, gets caught smoking pot after her parents split up, and has a smart, pretty younger sister. Tired of the constant fights, Fran's father sends her to boarding school where she discovers she is a natural at soccer. Her life changes, but her father's drinking still keeps her parents apart. Will she get to play in the world championships? ER

37.5   Christopher, Matt. **Fighting Tackle.** Illustrated by Karin Lidbeck. Little, Brown, 1995. 147 pp. ISBN 0-316-14010-4. Fiction.

Because of a growth and weight spurt, Terry is moved from his beloved position of defensive safety to offensive tackle on his football team. Unable to convince his coach to move him back to his former position, Terry is determined to earn the position back by improving his speed. At the same time, Terry's younger brother Nicky, who has Downs Syndrome, is practicing for the Special Olympics. Nicky's speed angers Terry, who has always supported his younger brother. Readers watch Terry learn to balance his own needs with those of his brother. ER

37.6   Christopher, Matt. **Shoot for the Hoop.** Little, Brown, 1995. 110 pp. ISBN 0-316-14125-9. Fiction.

This fast-paced and easy-to-read novel follows Rusty Young's struggle to learn to live with his recently diagnosed diabetes. Realistic explanations of symptoms, effects, and treatment of the disease are provided incidentally as Rusty attempts to bring his life back to normal. With the help of a coach who has his own physical limitations, Rusty works to rejoin his basketball team. ER

37.7   Dygard, Thomas J. **Game Plan.** Puffin Books, 1995. 220 pp. ISBN 0-14-036970-8. Fiction.

With the final big football game of the season just one week away and Barton High's coach disabled after a car accident, Beano Hatton, student manager and "nerd extraordinaire," steps in to coach the team. Not exactly your stereotypical football hero, but quite intelligent and clever, Beano applies his wits to game strategy and managing the rebellious quarterback, resulting in a satisfying, if not surprising, conclusion. ER

37.8   Dygard, Thomas J. **The Rebounder.** Puffin Books, 1996. 180 pp. ISBN 0-14-037702-6. Fiction.

After a devastating accident, Chris Patton decides to quit playing basketball and hides his former court successes from his new peers after transferring to Hamilton High. But Coach Doug Fulton recognizes the former star and feels that with Chris on his team, it could be of championship quality. Can he help Chris rebound from his past as well as on the court?

37.9   Dygard, Thomas J. **Running Wild.** Morrow Junior Books, 1996. 208 pp. ISBN 0-688-14853-0. Fiction.

Who would have thought that senior Pete Holman, who was always cutting classes, smoking at school, and even getting into trouble with the law, would end up a football star? Given the choice between a night in jail and joining the team, he even surprises himself when his interest in the play book doesn't fade, and he finds out how to use his natural ability. When his old gang, who can't understand the thrill of succeeding on the field, jeopardize his chance to play by stealing his play book, he learns what it really means to be a part of a team. ER.

37.10   Evans, Jeremy. **Adventurers: Skateboarding.** Crestwood House / Macmillan, 1993. 48 pp. ISBN 0-89686-822-2. Nonfiction.

If you are a novice or are interested in taking up skateboarding this book offers an easy-to-read summary of the sport. Included is information about street skating, ramp skating, tips and techniques, and safety aspects. A glossary of terms is included and a color photograph or diagram can be found on nearly every page. This book is one in a series of at least a dozen books about "challenging but accessible outdoor activities" from this publisher. ER

37.11   Evans, Jeremy. **Adventurers: Surfing.** Crestwood House / Macmillan, 1993. 48 pp. ISBN 0-89686-824-9. Nonfiction.

If you are a novice surfer or have a curiosity about this sport this book offers a simplified look at surfing. The history of surfing, types of boards, techniques, and international competition are covered, and safety is stressed throughout the book. At least one color photograph or diagram enlivens each page. This book is another in a series of at least a dozen books about "challenging but accessible outdoor activities" from this publisher. ER

37.12   Fundamental Sports series. Lerner, 1995. 64 pp. Photographs by Andy King. Nonfiction.

Coleman, Lori. **Fundamental Soccer.** ISBN 0-8225-3451-7.

Krause, Peter. **Fundamental Golf.** ISBN 0-8225-3454-1.

Miller, Marc. **Fundamental Tennis.** ISBN 0-8225-3450-9.

These titles accomplish their goal of providing information to the novice about the history, rules, and basics of various sports. Chapters on scoring, technique, and vocabulary are also included, and the easy-to-follow explanations are illustrated by color photographs of players in action, making these texts useful introductions to today's popular sports. ER

Fundamental Soccer:
ALA Quick Picks for Young Adults, 1996

37.13 Galt, Margot Fortunato. **Up to the Plate: The All American Girls Professional Baseball League.** Lerner, 1995. 96 pp. ISBN 0-8225-3326-X. Nonfiction.

In 1943 Coach Wrigley of the Chicago Cubs brought together the best female ball players in the country to form the All American Girls Baseball League. This story about their twelve successful seasons, individual careers, and impressive base-stealing and pitching includes photographs from players' scrapbooks. They played professional ball with muscle, competitive spirit, and determination, but had a skirted uniform, a dress code, and chaperones and became a casualty of more rigid expectations for women after World War II.

37.14 Gibson, Bob, and Lonnie Wheeler. **Stranger to the Game.** Penguin Books, 1996. 286 pp. ISBN 0 14 01.7528 8. Nonfiction.

From his early years in Nebraska to his major league pitching career in St. Louis, the events of Bob Gibson's life are chronicled in this recollection. A soft-spoken man, Gibson became a fierce competitor on the field, viewing opposing batters as the enemy in his total determination to win. Several pages of black-and-white photographs are included. Some strong language. MC

37.15 **Good Days, Bad Days.** Puffin Books, 1995. 119 pp. ISBN 0-670-84686-4. Nonfiction.

This official NFL book is a collection of anecdotes from fifteen of football's most famous players, such as Troy Aikman, Gary Clark, Jerry Rice, and Deion Sanders. These players recount some of their best memories and worst tragedies in the game of football. Lessons applicable to any walk of life can be learned from each of the stories. The good times reflect the benefits of hard work; the bad times create character. ER

37.16 Green, Carl R., and Roxanne Ford. **Deion Sanders.** Crestwood House / Maxwell Macmillan, 1994. 48 pp. ISBN 0-89686-840-0. Nonfiction.

Deion Sanders gained fame playing professional baseball and pro football simultaneously. Dual sports are nothing new to Deion. In college at Florida State University he competed in baseball, football, and track within the same year. This book details Deion's flashy style including diamonds, black leather, and expensive "toys," his sometimes-criticized "pranks," which have cost him tens of thousands of dollars in team fines, and his generosity. There's never a dull moment with "Prime Time" Deion. From the Sports Headliners series. ER MC

37.17 Green, Carl R. **Jackie Joyner-Kersee.** Crestwood House / Maxwell Macmillan, 1994. 48 pp. ISBN 0-89686-838-9. Nonfiction.

As a young girl in East St. Louis, Jackie Joyner excelled at academics, basketball, and track. Joyner went to UCLA in 1980 with an athletic scholarship in basketball, yet she achieved her greatest fame as a heptathlete. Jackie does it all: running, javelin, long jump, hurdles, and shot put. The book chronicles Jackie's ability to consistently exceed each of her own records and limits as she wins one gold medal after another in the heptathlon. Upon finishing this book from the Sports Headliners series you too will want to follow Joyner's future accomplishments. ER MC

37.18   Gutman, Bill. **Emmitt Smith: NFL Super Runner.** The Millbrook Press, 1995. 42 pp. ISBN 1-56294-501-7. Nonfiction.

Emmitt Smith was born to a hardworking family in Pensacola, Florida. His grandfather described him as a "blessing to the family"; he has also been a blessing to the game of football. He began playing at the age of seven, and by the time he was a freshman in high school, he was the star running back. Smith broke fifteen school records while playing in one game for the University of Florida. In addition to being an outstanding athlete, Emmitt Smith is a man who values family, sportsmanship, and hard work. ER MC

37.19   Gutman, Bill. **Larry Johnson: King of the Court.** The Millbrook Press, 1995. 43 pp. ISBN 1-56294-502-5. Nonfiction.

Larry Johnson grew up in the housing projects in South Dallas. At a young age he earned the respect of his peers and even the hard-core drug dealers in his neighborhood. Johnson became star of Skyline High School's varsity basketball team during his freshman year, and his skill coupled with his desire to be a team player won him the respect of teammates throughout his career. From college basketball player of the year to the NBA, Larry Johnson continues to be a man of principle. ER MC

37.20   Gutman, Bill. **Reggie White: Star Defensive Lineman.** The Millbrook Press, 1994. 47 pp. ISBN 1-56294-461-4. Nonfiction.

In addition to his accomplishments on the football field, Reggie White also takes seriously his life off the field. Ordained a Baptist minister at seventeen, White believes strongly in himself as a role model for young sports fans. Although he dropped out of college to turn professional, eventually he did successfully complete his degree. Reggie White's good works outside of football earn him as much praise as do his athletic exploits on the gridiron. ER MC

37.21   Gutman, Dan. **World Series Classics.** Viking, 1994. 241 pp. ISBN 0-670-85286-4.

In this great book for baseball fans, Gutman overviews the 1912, 1924, 1947, 1975, and 1991 World Series. Black-and-white photographs, newspaper clippings, box scores, and trivia highlight the book. Wonderful details and insights bring the games and players to life. True baseball fans will be interested to note the differences in the game from 1912 to 1991. Whether you have been a fan of baseball forever or are new to the game, this is a must read.

37.22   Holbrook, Mike. **Adventurers: Snorkeling.** Crestwood House / Macmillan, 1993. 48 pp. ISBN 0-89686-823-0. Nonfiction.

If you have ever considered taking up snorkeling, this book would be a good place to start. A simple look at equipment, safety, techniques, and marine life is included with at least one color photograph or diagram on each page. A glossary of terms is also provided to help the novice. This book is one in a series of at least a dozen books about "challenging but accessible outdoor activities" from this publisher. ER

37.23   Judson, Karen. **Sports and Money: It's a Sellout!** Enslow, 1995. 112 pp. ISBN 0-89490-622-4. Nonfiction.

Are youngsters suffering injuries from overtraining? Is college athletic recruitment out of control? Are professional athletes overpaid? This volume of the Issues in Focus series explores the trend in American sports away from sportsmanship and the fun of the game to an obsession with winning and sports as big business, and provides a useful service in raising the issues for the reader to ponder.

37.24   Klass, David. **Danger Zone.** Scholastic Hardcover, 1996. 232 pp. ISBN 0-590-48590-3. Fiction.

Jimmy Doyle and Augustus LeMay both make the American "Dream Team" for basketball. An intense, and destructive, rivalry develops between them during their training period, which is inflamed by the fact that Jimmy is white and Augustus is African American. Once they are in Italy and Augustus and other team members face racial taunts on the court, however, Jimmy is forced to take a stand in order to help make their team a success. ER MC

37.25   Klein, Aaron. **Deion Sanders: This is Prime Time.** Walker, 1995. 160 pp. ISBN 0-8027-8369-4. Nonfiction.

Two-sport superstars are rare and Deion Sanders is one of the rarest. Few have matched his exploits on the football field and the baseball diamond, or achieved his level of commercial fame. From his college days to today, Deion Sanders, known as "Prime Time," has worked to become a star. After you read this life story see if you can decide if it is football or baseball that Sanders loves the most. ER MC

37.26   Krone, Julie, with Nancy Ann Richardson. **Riding for My Life.** Little, Brown, 1995. 212 pp. ISBN 0-316-50477-7. Nonfiction.

Julie Krone was the first woman jockey to win the Belmont Stakes, the first to win five races in one day, and the first to compete in a Breeders'

Cup Race. She has had to fight harder and ride better to stand her ground against the men in horse racing, and her story is one of loneliness, depression, a drug problem, and a near-fatal accident. In this autobiography, Krone tells how, through it all, her strong will and her determination to succeed in a man's world drove her to be the best.

37.27 Lipsyte, Robert. **Jim Thorpe: Twentieth-Century Jock.** HarperTrophy / HarperCollins, 1993. 103 pp. ISBN 0-06-446141-6. Nonfiction.

Lipsyte tells the story of Jim Thorpe, who has been called the greatest all-around athlete in history and who was named Male Athlete of the Half-Century by the Associated Press. He has also won Olympic gold medals in the decathlon and the pentathlon. Through Thorpe's story, Lipsyte tells how Native Americans were treated as second-rate citizens, both in Indian boarding schools and on the playing field. Thorpe is a valuable role model to young people because he overcame these obstacles and the disgrace of losing his gold medals. ER MC

37.28 Manes, Stephen. **An Almost Perfect Game.** Scholastic Hardcover, 1995. 162 pp. ISBN 0-590-44432-8. Fiction.

Jake loves visiting his grandparents. They always go to see his favorite baseball team, the Shoppers. These trips to the ballpark have become a tradition for Jake and his brother, and for Jake, the best part is trying to keep a perfect scorecard. Jake loves to keep track of each play, until he finds out that his scorecard might have magical powers. Suddenly, Jake is controlling plays through his card. Finally, Jake finds that he cannot control the card, his predictions are backfiring, and the Shoppers are losing. Jake must learn to control the magic scorecard or the Shoppers will lose their final game of the season. ER

37.29 McKissack, Patricia C., and Fredrick McKissack, Jr. **Black Diamond: The Story of the Negro Baseball Leagues.** Scholastic Hardcover, 1994. 184 pp. ISBN 0-590-45809-4. Nonfiction.

African Americans are a familiar part of major league baseball today, but for nearly a century they were shut out. Their response was to form their own leagues, and this book takes the reader through the history of the Negro Baseball Leagues, focusing on the leagues' cast of colorful characters and stars while detailing the Negro Leagues' rise (in the late 1800s) and fall (several years after the desegregation of the major leagues in 1947). MC

Notable 1994 Children's Trade Books in the Field of Social Studies

37.30 Mullen, Chris, with Brian Coleman. **The Young Basketball Player.** Dorling Kindersley, 1995. 45 pp. ISBN 0-7894-0220-3. Nonfiction.

An encyclopedia of basketball, this very visual book presents the history of the game and court, the basics of play and rules, league information, and useful addresses. Many diagrams, photographs, and helpful captions make this a valuable resource for the basketball novice who wants to learn basics or for the experienced player or fan who needs reference information. ER

37.31 Murrow, Liza Ketchum. **Twelve Days in August.** Avon Flare Books, 1995. 187 pp. ISBN 0-380-72353-0. Fiction.

Before twins Alex and Rita Beekman arrived in town, Todd O'Connor's life was soccer-filled and issue-free. But when Alex, a gifted athlete, captures a top spot on the soccer team, some envious teammates spread rumors about Alex's sexual orientation. Humiliated by taunts that his relationship with Alex is more than casual, Todd fails to challenge his teammates' bigotry. Only Todd's uncle, who has experienced discrimination firsthand, can give him the courage to "do the right thing."

37.32 Myers, Walter Dean. **Slam!** Scholastic, 1996. 266 pp. ISBN 0-590-48667-5. Fiction.

At seventeen, Slam just *knows* he can be one of the lucky ones, a basketball player whose talents on the court can transport him from the inner city to the big-time arenas. But he also knows that his less-than-ideal grades and his quick, hot temper will be problematic, as his coach is quick to point out. In this fast-paced sports story, Myers describes the tensions, fears, and dreams of a young man facing a future he didn't anticipate and having to decide whether he is strong enough to make the story end the way he wants it to end. MC

Coretta Scott King Award, 1997

37.33 Parks, Deborah. **Climb Away! A Mountaineer's Dream.** Silver Burdett Press, 1996. 142 pp. ISBN 0-382-39093-8. Nonfiction.

Climb Away! is not a how-to book, but is rather the personal narrative of Deborah Parks, who realized her dream of mountain climbing. Her tales from the trails tell the triumphs and sometimes tragedies of mountain climbers who have aimed high.

37.34 Plowden, Martha Ward. **Olympic Black Women.** Illustrated by Ronald Jones. Pelican Publishing Co., 1996. 174 pp. ISBN 1-56554-080-8. Nonfiction.

Brief biographies chronicling the achievements of African American women's participation in the modern Olympics are provided here within the context of Olympian history. Such greats as Wilma Rudolph, Florence Griffith Joyner, and Jackie Joyner-Kersee are featured. Information on athletic organizations, a listing of the African American women who have participated in the modern Olympics, and a glossary are also included. ER MC

37.35 Rappoport, Ken. **Shaquille O'Neal.** Walker, 1994. 115 pp. ISBN 0-8027-8294-9. Nonfiction.

At seven-foot-one and three hundred pounds, Shaquille O'Neal stands out in a crowd even on NBA courts. Ironically, Shaquille means "little one" in Arabic. Tidbits such as this are sprinkled throughout this biography of the basketball and media star. The book traces O'Neal's life from his childhood years in Newark, New Jersey, to his sometimes stormy relationship with his army drill sergeant, to his forty-million-dollar contract with the Orlando Magic. Large type and a section of glossy photographs make the book easy to read. ER MC

37.36   Rivers, Glenn, and Bruce Brooks. **Those Who Love the Game: Glenn "Doc" Rivers on Life in the NBA and Elsewhere.** HarperTrophy / HarperCollins, 1995. 221 pp. ISBN 0-06-446174-2. Nonfiction.

Former New York Knicks star Glenn "Doc" Rivers and Newbery Honor author Bruce Brooks team up in this book to deliver more than a simple sports biography. Rivers speaks candidly about a number of issues concerning his life on and off the basketball court, including sensitive issues such as money and racism. Brooks provides valuable insight while allowing Rivers's true voice to shine through. ER MC.

ALA Best Books for Young Adults, 1995

37.37   Sports Great Books series. Enslow. Nonfiction. 64 pp.
         Aaseng, Nathan. **Sports Great John Stockton.** 1995. ISBN 0-89490-598-8.
         Harrington, Denis J. **Sports Great Jim Kelly.** 1996. ISBN 0-89490-670-4.
         Knapp, Ron. **Sports Great Mario Lemieux.** 1996. ISBN 0-89490 -596-1.
         Knapp, Ron. **Sports Great Steffi Graf.** 1995. ISBN 0-89490-597-X.
         Rappoport, Ken. **Sports Great Wayne Gretzky.** 1996. ISBN 0-89490-757-3.
         Rekela, George. **Sports Great Anfernee Hardaway.** 1996. ISBN 0-89490-758-1.
         Savage, Jeff. **Sports Great Karl Malone.** 1996. ISBN 0-89490-599-6.
         Sherrow, Victoria. **Sports Great Pete Sampras.** 1996. ISBN 0-89490-756-5.
         Sullivan, Michael J. **Sports Great Barry Bonds.** 1995. ISBN 0-89490-595-3.
         Sullivan, Michael J. **Sports Great Shaquille O'Neal.** 1995. ISBN 0-89490-594-5.
         Thornley, Stew. **Sports Great Dennis Rodman.** 1996. ISBN 0-89490-759-X.

In the Sports Great Books series, readers are introduced to the accomplishments of some of today's most famous athletes in basketball, football, tennis, and hockey. The goals they set for themselves, the triumphs and tragedies they experience, and the situations that help them achieve their successes are inspirations for all young athletes. ER MC

37.38   **The Sports Illustrated 1995 Sports Almanac.** Little, Brown, 1995. 797 pp. ISBN 0-316-80860-1. Nonfiction.

This comprehensive overview of the past year in sports includes everything from baseball and football to motor sports and horse racing. Amateur, college, and professional athletics are covered by journalistic reports, rosters, and charts. The text is accessibly segmented, and the statistics are coherently organized for the sports fan, who will have no difficulty interpreting the contents.

37.39   Sports Top 10 series. Enslow. 48 pp. Nonfiction.

Bjarkman, Peter C. **Top 10 Baseball Base Stealers.** 1995. ISBN 0-89490-609-7.

Bjarkman, Peter C. **Top 10 Basketball Slam Dunkers.** 1995. ISBN 0-89490-608-9.

Harrington, Denis J. **Top 10 Women Tennis Players.** 1995. ISBN 0-89490-612-7.

Knapp, Ron. **Top 10 Basketball Centers.** 1994. ISBN 0-89490-515-5.

Knapp, Ron. **Top 10 Basketball Scorers.** 1994. ISBN 0-89490-516-3.

Knapp, Ron. **Top 10 Hockey Scorers.** 1994. ISBN 0-89490-517-1.

Lace, William W. **Top 10 Football Quarterbacks.** 1994. ISBN 0-89490-518-X.

Lace, William W. **Top 10 Football Rushers.** 1994. 0-89490-519-8.

Rappoport, Ken. **Top 10 Basketball Legends.** 1995. ISBN 0-89490-610-0.

Riley, Gail Blasser. **Top 10 NASCAR Drivers.** 1995. ISBN 0-89490-611-9.

Sullivan, Michael J. **Top 10 Baseball Pitchers.** 1994. ISBN 0-89490-520-1.

Thornley, Stew. **Top 10 Football Receivers.** 1995. ISBN 0-89490-607-0.

Beginning with statistics that show how each of the athletes chosen for the Top 10 qualifies for this honor, and following with thumbnail sketches of each athlete's career, these books detail the best in basketball, football, baseball, hockey, tennis, NASCAR driving, and more. From old-timers like Sandy Koufax to current stars like Michael Jordan, each book includes a short biography and brilliant color photographs of the greatest athletes who ever pitched, passed, rushed, scored a goal, or grabbed a rebound. ER MC

37.40   Strachan, Gordon. **Getting Started in Soccer.** Sterling, 1994. 80 pp. ISBN 0-8069-0834-3. Nonfiction.

What's a corner shot? What's a header? What is the role of the halfback? The goalie? Here is a slim, easy-to-follow volume that will answer those questions for budding soccer players while helping them better understand the game. Strachan provides concise instructions on all aspects of the game, from the importance of a positive attitude to the more advanced skills for experienced players. ER

37.41 Sullivan, Michael J. **Chris Mullin: Star Forward.** Enslow, 1994. 104 pp. ISBN 0-89490-486-8. Nonfiction.

"Gym rat," star Golden State Warriors basketball player, and Olympic gold medal winner, Chris Mullin is an exceptional individual. His life story is interspersed with fact boxes, statistics, and black-and-white photographs of Chris doing what he does best—making basketball shots. Many people who know Chris have contributed their thoughts about what makes him so remarkable in this book from the Sports Reports series. ER

37.42 Sullivan, George. **Pitchers: Twenty-Seven of Baseball's Greatest.** Atheneum / Maxwell Macmillan, 1994. 74 pp. ISBN 0-689-31825-1. Nonfiction.

A very good historical introduction detailing the relative significance of pitchers since the beginning of baseball leads off this lineup of biographies of all-star major league pitchers. The articles outline the career history and highlights of each of the twenty-seven players, accompanied by good game photographs and baseball card reproductions. Four pages of all-time pitching records wrap up this fact-filled, lively volume, a great choice for fans of our national sport. ER

ALA Quick Picks for Young Adults, 1995

37.43 Vancil, Mark. **NBA Basketball Basics.** Sterling, 1995. 127 pp. ISBN 0-8069-0927-7. Nonfiction.

There is no wasted space in this book. Clear, concise, well-organized instruction is provided on all the fundamental skills of the game. Good supporting photographs are provided, as well as a useful section on the rules.

37.44 Wright, Bob. **Fast Break.** High Noon Books, 1994. 44 pp. ISBN 0-87879-990-7. Fiction.

Kelly and Deke have perfected the fast break on their winning basketball team. Their trouble begins when Kelly shows off with one second left in a game. Although warned by the coach not to be a "hot dog," Kelly again shows off and is benched. He leaves the gym in anger, but a gambler pays him to tell the coach he is sorry. Now with Kelly back on the team, the gambler wants him and Deke to lose the championship game, in this short book with a surprise ending. ER

37.45 Wright, Bob. **Strike Zone.** High Noon Books, 1994. 44 pp. ISBN 0-87879-991-5. Fiction.

This short book is narrated by Bill Train, the baseball pitcher of the Edison High School "Egg Rolls," a winning team in Martinez, California. On the team with him are Hilly, a girl who throws a funny pitch no one can hit, and Jimmy, the catcher. Bill loves the game but has problems with the grouchy coach, Mr. Tarp, who used to play for the New York Yankees. ER

37.46   Wright, Branson. **Rookie Season: A Year with the West Michigan Whitecaps.** William B. Eerdmans, 1995. 206 pp. ISBN 0-8028-7057-0. Nonfiction.

This book reads like a series of articles that together tell about the successful 1994 season of the West Michigan Whitecaps, when the "Caps," a minor league baseball team in Grand Rapids, smashed the all-time Class A season attendance record. Written for baseball fans by a journalist who covered the games, this account includes photographs, player profiles and statistics, as well as stories about players' families, their coaches, and their fans.

37.47   Young, Ken. **Cy Young Award Winners.** Walker, 1994. 152 pp. ISBN 0-8027-8300-7. Nonfiction.

Sandy Koufax, Bob Gibson, Dwight Gooden, and Roger Clemens have all won the Cy Young Award, given annually to the best pitcher in each major league. The author has profiled these and six other pitchers, and has supplemented the text with black-and-white photographs and statistics. ER

Titles Annotated in Other Chapters Related to Sports and Sports Figures

Bonner, Staci. *Now Hiring: Sports*. College.

Chimits, Xavier, and François Granet. *Williams Renault Formula I Motor Racing Book*. Airplanes.

Chronicle of the Olympics 1896–1996. History.

Daytona 500: The Men and Machines of Speedweeks '94. Airplanes.

Hamley, Dennis. *Death Penalty*. Mysteries.

Lipsyte, Robert. *The Chief*. Choices.

Lynch, Chris. *Iceman*. Family.

Owens, Thomas S. *Collecting Baseball Memorabilia*. Recreation.

Paulsen, Gary. *Father Water, Mother Woods*. Diaries.

Powell, Randy. *Dean Duffy*. Choices.

Powell, Randy. *The Whistling Toilets*. Friendships.

Ryan, Joan. *Little Girls in Pretty Boxes: The Making and Breaking of Elite Gymnasts and Figure Skaters*. Drugs.

Voigt, Cynthia. *The Runner*. Choices.

38 Television, Movies, and Entertainment

"If it weren't for the fact that the TV set and the refrigerator are so far apart, some of us wouldn't get any exercise at all."

Joey Adams

38.1   Day, Nancy. **Sensational TV: Trash or Journalism?** Enslow, 1996. 112 pp. ISBN 0-89490-733-6. Nonfiction.

Are talk shows, news magazines, and tabloid newspapers news, entertainment, or exploitation for profit? Does television offer factual news that the public needs to know or does the quest for higher ratings influence the networks to seek out the sensational and the lurid? The history of journalism, the American public's viewing preferences, the ethical responsibilities of the media, and the future of television news are explored here as the author seeks to find the line between trash TV and informative news, in this volume from the Issues in Focus series.

38.2   Friedman, M. J. Lois and Clark: The New Adventures of Superman series. HarperPaperbacks / HarperCollins. Fiction.
   Deadly Games. 1996. 133 pp. ISBN 0-06-101063-4.
   Exile. 1996. 150 pp. ISBN 0-06-101062-6.

Set in the fictional city of Metropolis, these titles, based on the *Lois and Clark* television show, extend the adventures of Superman into print. Each book includes a section of black-and-white television cast photographs. ER

38.3   Gibson, William. **Johnny Mnemonic.** Ace Books, 1995. 164 pp. ISBN 0-441-00234-X. Fiction.

In the twenty-first-century, a mnemonic is a high-tech smuggler, carrying information in a computer chip implanted in the head. Johnny is a pro, but he's in trouble now, having overloaded his capacity. Although he is anxious to get the data downloaded before his brain fries, the deal goes bad when a ruthless and powerful international gang tries to intercept the information and eliminate Johnny. The book includes both the original story written in 1981 and the new screenplay, both containing much violence.

38.4   Hansberry, Lorraine. **A Raisin in the Sun: The Unfilmed Original Screenplay.** Edited by Robert Nemiroff. Foreword by Jewell Handy Gresham-Nemiroff. Introduction by Margaret B. Wilkerson. Commentary by Spike Lee. Signet, 1994. 206 pp. ISBN 0-451-18388-6. Fiction.

This screenplay, complete with an eight-page photograph insert, contains the original, uncut version of *A Raisin in the Sun* that Hansberry intended for the cinema. After reading it and then renting the 1961 movie, Spike Lee writes in his commentary, "It seems to me all the cuts had to deal with softening a too defiant black voice. I found the parts that were cut to be some of the most interesting parts of the screenplay." ER MC

38.5   Hill, Elizabeth Starr. **Curtain Going Up!** Viking, 1995. 131 pp. ISBN 0-670-85919-2. Fiction.

In this sequel to *Broadway Chances*, Fitzi Wolper and her family are all actors in the hit musical *Crowd Scene*, which has been nominated for several Tony awards. Fitzi tries to get a romance started with Hark Hiller, one of the show's leading characters. However, Fitzi's life becomes rather strained as both Mark and Clement Dale, her grandfather, are rivals for the same Tony Award–Best Featured Actor in a Musical.

38.6   Jones, K. Maurice. **Spike Lee and the African American Filmmakers: A Choice of Colors.** The Millbrook Press, 1996. 160 pp. ISBN 1-56294-518-1.

Contemporary movie audiences are probably familiar with the films of Spike Lee. What they probably don't know is that Lee follows in the footsteps of many talented African American directors. Jones chronicles the emergence of these talents, using interview and research data to support his analysis of the issues influencing the ways African Americans have been portrayed and have portrayed themselves throughout the history of film in the United States. MC

38.7   Sherrow, Victoria. **Violence and the Media: The Question of Cause and Effect.** The Millbrook Press, 1996. 160 pp. ISBN 1-56294-549-1. Nonfiction.

Violence in television, movies, music, and video games is discussed here using very up-to-date examples from TV shows, movies, and performances by groups of the 1990s. Sherrow also discusses solutions for dealing with the presence of such violence, and she includes an index, source notes, places to contact for more information, pictures, and crime statistics to support her arguments.

38.8   Thompson, Peggy, and Saeko Usukawa. **Hard-Boiled: Great Lines from Classic Noir Films.** With an introduction by Lee Server. Chronicle Books, 1995. 124 pp. ISBN 0-8118-0855-6. Nonfiction.

This book captures famous lines from the film noir era, full of slang and humor that readers will enjoy. Many reproductions of posters and photographs of Hollywood history supplement the text, which is filled with such great lines as this gem: "If I always knew what I meant, I'd be a genius." ER

Titles Annotated in Other Chapters Related to Television, Movies, and Entertainment

Lipsyte, Robert. *Arnold Schwarzenegger*. Autobiography.

Littke, Lael. *The Watcher*. Horror.

Maxwell, Will N., ed. *The Country Music Guide to Life*. Religion.

Powell, Stephanie. *Hit Me with Music: How to Start, Manage, Record, and Perform with Your Own Rock Band*. College.

Rees, Dafydd, and Luke Crampton. *Encyclopedia of Rock Stars*. Reference.

Riley, Gail Blasser. *Wah Ming Chang*. Autobiography.

Schuman, Michael A. *Bill Cosby*. Autobiography.

Vitkus-Weeks, Jessica. *Now Hiring: Television*. College.

39 War

"War loves to seek its victims in the young."

Sophocles

*"In the name of human good
our killing and our hate destroy."*

Frederick Douglass

39.1   Beatty, Patricia. **Jayhawker**. Beech Tree, 1995. 214 pp. ISBN 0-688-14422-5. Fiction.

Sixteen-year-old Elijah Tully grows up quickly in the service of the Jayhawkers, the abolitionist underground of Kansas, just before the Civil War. Devoted to his family's staunch antislavery beliefs, he becomes a messenger and goes undercover among the proslavery bushwhackers of Missouri. Cameos of historical figures like the charismatic John Brown add to the reality of the personal sacrifice and tense emotion that led to the Civil War.

39.2   Brainard, Cecilia Manguerra. **When the Rainbow Goddess Wept.** Dutton, 1994. 216 pp. ISBN 0-525-93821-4. Fiction.

This novel is an intriguing combination of themes of youth, war, and the oral tradition of the Filipino people. An adolescent girl named Yvonne tells the story of her family's struggle through the Second World War. Interwoven with legends of the merciful rainbow goddess, Bongkatolan, Yvonne's life teaches the reader about the Filipino people and their culture. MC WL

39.3   Carter, Peter. **The Hunted.** Farrar, Straus and Giroux, 1994. 326 pp. ISBN 0-374-33520-6. Fiction.

Italy surrenders to the Allies in July 1943 but the hunt for Jews continues. Corporal Vito Salvani is eagerly waiting to return home from southern France when he is thrown onto a life-or-death flight with an orphaned Jewish child, Judah. Their exploits and adventures vividly portray the horrors of war and the courage of people in the quest for survival.

39.4   Denenberg, Barry. **Voices from Vietnam.** Scholastic Hardcover, 1995. 251 pp. ISBN 0-590-44267-8. Nonfiction.

This book is a poignant and very personal presentation of the longest war in American history. Told in the words of those who served in Vietnam, the sequential, concise account from 1945 to 1975 emphasizes the human element of the war while also reporting its historical origins and the political decisions that shaped it. A chronology, a glossary, and a bibliography are included. MC

ALA Best Books for Young Adults, 1996
Booklist Editors' Choice, 1996

39.5 Devaney, John. **America Triumphs: 1945.** Walker, 1995. 208 pp. ISBN 0-8027-8328-7. Nonfiction.

This is the final volume in a series that has received positive reviews from librarians and educators. Each book covers one year of World War II, beginning in 1941. The author, who died in 1994, shares his soldier's perspective and passion in bringing this era to life for today's students. Included are biographical information, black-and-white photographs, a chronology, maps, and a list of further readings. ER

39.6 Martin, Joseph Plumb. **Yankee Doodle Boy: A Young Soldier's Adventures in the American Revolution Told by Himself.** Edited by George F. Scheer. Illustrated by Victor Mays. Holiday House, 1995. 192 pp. ISBN 0-8234-1176-1. Nonfiction.

At fifteen, Connecticut farm boy Joseph Martin had been waiting a year to enroll in the Continental Army. Expecting a six-month hitch, he served in the Revolutionary War from 1776 until 1783. Joseph encamped at Valley Forge, marched to Yorktown, stormed Cornwallis's fortifications, and watched the British Army lay down its arms. During those years he endured the cruelest hardships, yet he formed a close brotherhood with his fellow soldiers. Joseph had no formal schooling, yet this narrative of his adventures is spellbinding, and his genuine and dryly humorous personality will endear him to the reader.

39.7 McKissack, Patricia, and Fredrick McKissack. **Red-Tail Angels: The Story of the Tuskegee Airmen of World War II.** Walker, 1995. 136 pp. ISBN 0-8027-8292-2. Nonfiction.

This treatment of the Tuskegee Airmen story provides unique photographs and personal interviews to further enhance readers' understanding of a significant episode of American and African American history. MC

39.8 Ousseimi, Maria. **Caught in the Crossfire: Growing Up in a War Zone.** Walker, 1995. 120 pp. ISBN 0-8027-8363-5. Nonfiction.

Five backdrops to recent or current violence are made painfully real by restrained yet disturbing text and dramatic black-and-white photographs interwoven with statements from young victims—survivors, to some degree, of unimaginable horrors. Information explaining the conflicts in Lebanon, El Salvador, Mozambique, and Bosnia-Herzegovina, as well as, closer to home, the street violence in Washington, D.C., is supplied without talking down to the audience, making this appropriate for a wide age range. ER MC

ALA Best Books for Young Adults, 1996

39.9 Qualey, Marsha. **Come in from the Cold.** Houghton Mifflin, 1994. 219 pp. ISBN 0-395-68986-4. Fiction.

Jeff and Maud are seventeen and living in Minnesota in 1969. Their separate lives are affected by tragic events brought about by the Vietnam War: Maud's sister purposely stays in a building blown up by her underground group and Jeff's brother, a Marine, is killed in the war. Jeff and Maud's friendship begins when they meet at a protest rally and the narrative follows their decisions about smoking pot, having sex, and joining a commune.

ALA Best Books for Young Adults, 1995
IRA Teacher's Choice Award, 1996

39.10 Reuter, Bjarne. **The Boys from St. Petri.** Translated by Anthea Bell. Dutton Children's Books, 1994. 215 pp. ISBN 0-525-45121-8. Fiction.

> "We'll dangle Hitler from a rope
> And right beside him Ribbentrop . . . "

Adolescent banter taunts the Nazi troops occupying Denmark in 1943. These pranks perpetrated by "the boys from St. Petri" are intended to annoy the Nazis. But what begins as mere mischief escalates into sabotage, and the bond among the young men is strengthened, threatened only by the secrets kept by Lars, one of the "boys." The momentum of suspense and intrigue is intensified as the story unfolds in this fictional novel based on actual events. WL

ALA Best Books for Young Adults, 1995
Mildred L. Batchelder Award, 1995

39.11 Salisbury, Graham. **Under the Blood-Red Sun.** Delacorte Press, 1994. 246 pp. ISBN 0-385-32099-X. Fiction.

According to Tomi's father, Hawaii is a good place for their Japanese family, but in the fall of 1941 he's beginning to feel the hatred and distrust aimed at his ethnic group in general. They are poor but proud, acutely sensitive to honor, and Tomi's grandfather declares that the Japanese bring shame with their attack on Pearl Harbor. With their loyalty in question, the tough times are just beginning. ER MC

ALA Best Books For Young Adults, 1995
ALA Notable Book for Children, 1995
Booklist Editors' Choice, 1995
Notable 1994 Children's Trade Books in the Field of Social Studies
IRA Teacher's Choice Awards, 1995

39.12 Van Dijk, Lutz. **Damned Strong Love: The True Story of Willi G. and Stefan K.** Translated by Elizabeth D. Crawford. Henry Holt, 1995. 138 pp. ISBN 0-8050-3770-5. Fiction.

The mature theme of a teenage boy discovering his sexual orientation is sensitively handled and placed in the horrific setting of the German occupation of Poland. When Stefan falls in love with a German soldier his shame comes not from taunts of "queer" but from being labeled a traitor. It is his homosexuality that causes his arrest by the Nazis, but it is his treatment thereafter that is largely the focus of the novel. MC WL

ALA Notable Books for Children, 1996

39.13   Warren, James A. **Cold War: The American Crusade against World Communism, 1945–1991.** Lothrop, Lee and Shepard, 1996. 279 pp. ISBN 0-688-10596-3. Nonfiction.

Extremely complex international dynamics are effectively handled here on a level appropriate for young adults. The Cold War involved many nations, but essentially pitted the superpowers, the United States and the USSR, in an ideological conflict with global impact. From delicate top-level negotiations down to the anti-Communist paranoia of ordinary citizens, all under the pall of nuclear capabilities, fear and distrust shaped a period of fifty years. The text includes a chronology, a bibliography, notes, a record of federal expenditures, and an index.

39.14   Westall, Robert. **Gulf.** Scholastic, 1996. 98 pp. ISBN 0-590-22218-X. Fiction.

The life of a middle-class English family named Higgins is disrupted as the younger son, Andy, goes into temporary trancelike states and begins speaking strange languages. As the Persian Gulf War begins and his behavior becomes even more bizarre, his brother Tom questions whether the family and Andy can survive. Is Andy insane, or a victim of a telepathic "mystery of nature" as he slips deeper and deeper into the identity of an Iraqi soldier in the desert war?

39.15   White, Ellen Emerson. **The Road Home.** Scholastic Hardcover, 1995. 469 pp. ISBN 0-590-46737-9. Fiction.

The ugly realities of war force Rebecca Phillips to don a dispassionate facade to be able to endure her torturous days working in a field hospital in Vietnam. Returning home to less than a hero's welcome, Rebecca realizes the challenges of reconnecting with emotions long buried. Depression propels her on a personal quest to find and repair the broken pieces of her life. *The Road Home* provides the conclusion to Rebecca's story, which is chronicled throughout the award-winning four-book Echo Company series.

ALA Best Books for Young Adults, 1996

39.16   White, Richard. **Jordan Freeman Was My Friend.** Four Walls Eight Windows, 1994. 223 pp. ISBN 0-941423-73-5. Fiction.

The unlikely trio of eleven-year-old Billy Latham, ex-slave Jordan Freeman, and Tom Wansuc, a Pequot Indian, play an important role in this historical novel. The fervor of patriotism runs through these three and many of the other residents of Groton, Connecticut, as they join forces to build Fort Griswold to fend off a British invasion. On September 6, 1781, Benedict Arnold and nine hundred soldiers storm the fort and massacre the Connecticut Militia. Not only is this a story brimming with adventure and excitement, but it is a story of patriotism, loyalty, and friendship that transcends ethnic barriers. ER MC

39.17 Williams, Eric. **The Wooden Horse.** BBC / Parkwest, 1994. 264 pp. ISBN 0-563-36901-9. Fiction.

An innocent-looking wooden vaulting horse constructed by POWs in a German prison camp is the perfect cover for one of the most dangerous and daring escapes of World War II. British prisoners are able to dig a tunnel to freedom and conceal their work as their fellow prisoners exercise on the vaulting horse overhead. Eric Williams tells his story in this true account of an important moment in history.

39.18 Wisler, G. Clifton. **Mr. Lincoln's Drummer.** Lodestar Books / Dutton, 1995. 131 pp. ISBN 0-525-67463-2. Fiction.

Bravery and courage come in all sizes and at all ages. This historical novel tells the story of courageous young men, the drummer boys, who marched first into Civil War battles. The particular focus of this tale is Willie Johnson, who is too young to fight in the Civil War, yet who manages to be selected as a drummer boy. His courage and determination in battle earn him the attention of President Abraham Lincoln, who awards him the Congressional Medal Of Honor. Wisler's account of this true story brings history to life. ER

39.19 Wisler, G. Clifton. **Thunder on the Tennessee.** Puffin Books, 1995. 153 pp. ISBN 0-14-037612-7. Fiction.

Willie Delamer is proud of his father and of the family motto: "Delamers always stand in the first line of battle." When his father is asked to command a brigade of Texans fighting for the Confederacy, fifteen-year-old Willie joins him. Like his courageous father, Willie is unwilling to run from responsibility. Yet as they engage in battle after battle with equally determined Union troops, ending in the heartbreakingly destructive Battle of Shiloh, their commitment to kin and country is sorely tested.

Titles Annotated in Other Chapters Related to War (Note: See all titles in Holocaust)

Archer, Jules. *A House Divided: The Lives of Ulysses S. Grant and Robert E. Lee.* Autobiography.

Azuela, Mariano. *The Underdogs: A Novel of the Mexican Revolution.* Classics.

Binstock, R. C. *Tree of Heaven.* Historical Fiction.

Boyd, James. *Drums*. Classics.

Colman, Penny. *Rosie the Riveter: Women Working on the Home Front in WW II*. History.

DeFord, Deborah H., and Harry S. Stout. *An Enemy among Them*. Historical Fiction.

Denenberg, Barry. *When Will This Cruel War Be Over? The Civil War Diary of Emma Simpson*. Diaries.

Deschamps, Hélène. *Spyglass*. Autobiography.

Holland, Isabelle. *Behind the Lines*. Historical Fiction.

Kent, Deborah. *The Vietnam War*. History.

Kent, Zachary. *World War I*. History.

Kerr, M. E. *Linger*. Family.

Kronenwetter, Michael. *The Peace Commandos*. Political Science.

Mead, Alice. *Adem's Cross*. Choices.

Mettger, Zak. *Till Victory Is Won: Black Soldiers in the Civil War*. History.

Morin, Isobel V. *Days of Judgment: The World War II War Crimes Trials*. History.

Murphy, Claire Rudolf. *Gold Star Sister*. Death.

Pushman, Muriel Gane. *We All Wore Blue*. Autobiography.

Shelley, Rick. *The Buchanan Campaign*. Science Fiction.

Silverman, Jerry. *Songs and Stories from the American Revolution*. Arts.

Stein, R. Conrad. *World War II in Europe*. History.

Sullivan, George. *Matthew Brady: His Life and Photographs*. Autobiography.

Yep, Laurence. *Hiroshima*. Historical Fiction.

Zeinert, Karen. *Elizabeth Van Lew: Southern Belle, Union Spy*. Autobiography.

Zeinert, Karen. *Those Incredible Women of World War II*. Autobiography.

40 Westerns and the Old West

"Go west, young man, and grow up with the country."
Horace Greeley

"Now that we've fought and lied and sweated and stolen and hated as only the disappointed strugglers in a bitter dead little western town know how to do, what have we got to show for it?"
Willa Cather

40.1   Bonner, Cindy. **Looking after Lily: A Novel.** Algonquin Books of Chapel Hill, 1994. 324 pp. ISBN 1-56512-045-0. Fiction.

For fans of westerns, this is a mature love story set in the Wild West, complete with gunfights, American Indians, outlaws, and falling for the wrong woman. Two of Haywood Beatty's brothers were killed in a shootout with vigilantes, and now, after escaping a charge of murder himself, he is asked by his jailed brother "Shot" to look after Shot's pregnant wife. Quite a tall order for a twenty-year-old petty criminal!

ALA Best Books for Young Adults, 1995

40.2   Granfield, Linda. **Cowboy: An Album.** Ticknor and Fields, 1994. 96 pp. ISBN 0-395-68430-7. Nonfiction.

Contrary to the Hollywood image, the life of a real cowboy over a century ago was far from glamorous. Dirty, tedious, and extremely hard, the Wild West wore most men out before their thirtieth birthdays. Richly illustrated, well written, and thoroughly researched, this book describes the life, clothes, accoutrements, myths, and legends of cowboys in both the United States and Canada, taking care to note the role of African and Native Americans and women in the frontier from its beginnings, through its heyday, to the present.

ALA Quick Picks for Young Adults, 1995
Notable 1994 Children's Trade Books in the Field of Social Studies

40.3   Green, Carl R., and William R. Sanford. **Allan Pinkerton.** Enslow, 1995. 48 pp. ISBN 0-89490-590-2. Nonfiction.

Allan Pinkerton was America's first great detective. Green and Sanford use maps, pictures, an index, a glossary, and extensive notes to delve into Pinkerton's life and background. They glorify neither outlaws nor law officers in this revealing account of an important part of the history of the United States.

40.4   Green, Carl R., and William R. Sanford. **Butch Cassidy.** Enslow, 1995. 48 pp. ISBN 0-89490-587-2. Nonfiction.

Robert LeRoy Parker, who became known as Butch Cassidy, was born to a homesteading family in Utah. He was a rebellious youngster who had early brushes with the law. Despite his skill with horses, he rejected honest work in favor of joining a gang of robbers. After a prison term, Butch established his most notorious relationship, with the "Wild Bunch Gang" and the "Sundance Kid." Part of the Outlaws and Lawmen of the Wild West series. ER

40.5   Green, Carl R., and William R. Sanford. **The Dalton Gang.** Enslow, 1995. 48 pp. ISBN 0-89490-588-0. Nonfiction.

Green and Sanford tell the colorful story of the Dalton brothers and the Wild West. The gang seems to come to life through the use of pictures and maps. The facts are presented, and the authors make the point that crime does not pay: only one gang member, Emmett Dalton, lived to an old age. Part of the Outlaws and Lawmen of the Wild West series.

40.6   Green, Carl R., and William R. Sanford. **Doc Holliday.** Enslow, 1995. 48 pp. ISBN 0-89490-589-9. Nonfiction.

In this volume, part of the Outlaws and Lawmen of the Wild West series, authors Green and Sanford attempt to set the record straight about the legendary Doc Holliday. Doc Holliday was born John Henry Holliday in pre–Civil War Georgia. As a young man he learned dentistry and returned home to practice. Unfortunately, he was soon diagnosed with tuberculosis and encouraged to go west to a warmer, drier climate. There Doc Holliday acquired a reputation as a hard-gambling, hard-drinking gunslinger, a life that climaxed with his role in the shootout at the O.K. Corral. ER

40.7   Green, Carl R., and William R. Sanford. **Judge Roy Bean.** Enslow, 1995. 48 pp. ISBN 0-89490-591-0. Nonfiction.

Judge Roy Bean was one of the most colorful characters in the history of the Wild West. Authors Green and Sanford attempt to sort out fact from fiction in this biography, from the Outlaws and Lawmen of the Wild West series, of the "hanging judge" who never really hanged anyone. Judge Roy Bean represents a time and place where people made up the law as circumstance dictated. ER

40.8   Green, Carl R., and William R. Sanford. **The Younger Brothers.** Enslow, 1995. 42 pp. ISBN 0-89490-592-9. Nonfiction.

The Younger brothers were born into a wealthy family, so it is surprising that they became such ruthless outlaws of the Wild West. When their loyalty to the Confederate Army brought hard times to their family both during and after the Civil War, the brothers turned to the gunslinger's trade out of bitterness and revenge, and they were very good at it. Green and Sanford's book, part of the Outlaws and Lawmen of the Wild West series, tells the story of these brothers, their partnership with the James brothers, their rise to fame, and their ultimate fall. ER

40.9   Gregory, Kristiana. **Jimmy Spoon and the Pony Express.** Scholastic Hardcover, 1994. 128 pp. ISBN 0-590-46577-5. Fiction.

Jimmy Spoon, seventeen and bored with his predictable life, answers an advertisement for "expert riders willing to risk death daily." Hired by the Pony Express, he finds all the excitement he can handle and some he'd rather not. Determined to fulfill his one-year commitment, none-theless, Jimmy anxiously waits for the day he can return, not to the family he left, but to the people and the place that made his life the happiest. ER

40.10   Katz, William Loren. **Black Women of the Old West.** Atheneum Books for Young Readers, 1995. 84 pp. ISBN 0-689-31944-4. Nonfiction.

Farmers, businesspeople, teachers, ranchers, community leaders, wives, mothers, and human rights activists are some of the titles that describe the African American women who settled the early American frontier. Biographical sketches and historical photographs give life to these for-gotten women, whose contributions to American history are a tribute to their gender, their ethnic group, and their country. ER MC

40.11   Lavender, David. **The Santa Fe Trail.** Holiday House, 1995. 64 pp. ISBN 0-8234-1153-2. Nonfiction.

It is the last rather than first page which moves the reader most in this book. A photograph of wagon ruts made by thousands of people mov-ing west which remain a century later brings history to life. The linear passage of people from the East to Santa Fe as they seek opportunity is frequently interspersed with illustrations, making this text a worthwhile addition to the study of the American Southwest. ER

40.12   Malone, Mary. **Will Rogers: Cowboy Philosopher.** Enslow, 1996. 128 pp. ISBN 0-89490-695-X. Nonfiction.

"I never met a man I didn't like," is a saying closely identified with Native American humorist Will Rogers, and most of his fans felt the same way about him. In this volume from the People to Know series, Malone describes how Rogers turned the cowboy skills he learned on his father's ranch into a lifelong career entertaining audiences from vaudeville to Hollywood. Rogers's homespun philosophy made him a favorite with people from average citizens to presidents of the United States. ER MC

40.13   Miller, Brandon Marie. **Buffalo Gals: Women of the Old West.** Lerner, 1995. 88 pp. ISBN 0-8225-1730-2. Nonfiction.

This short book pulls no punches in describing the hard life of women in the West in the mid-1800s. The hopes, dreams, and tragic realities of the lives of white, African American and Native American women are documented here through quotations from diaries, letters, and photographs. Every aspect of life is covered, from arriving in the West by wagon train, to building sod homes, to trying to keep faith in God, to securing an education, to finding a job outside the home—whether it be as a leader in the business community, a farmer, a dance-hall singer, or a prostitute. The text is fascinating and sometimes poignant, providing a wonderful overview of the cultural history of women in the time period.

Notable 1995 Children's Trade Books in the Field of Social Studies

40.14   Morris, Juddi. **The Harvey Girls: The Women Who Civilized the West.** Walker, 1994. 101 pp. ISBN 0-8027-8302-3. Nonfiction.

It is said that while Winchester rifles and Colt pistols tamed the West, the Harvey Girls civilized it. Their role as waitresses and models of female decorum was created by Fred Harvey, an English immigrant who saw an opportunity to make a fortune (which he did) upgrading the deplorable food service along the burgeoning railroad lines. This story, simply written, largely from memories narrated by former Harvey Girls, outlines a moving piece of Americana. ER

ALA Quick Picks for Young Adults, 1995

40.15   Taylor, Theodore. **Walking up a Rainbow.** Harcourt Brace, 1994. 307 pp. ISBN 0-15-294512-1. Fiction.

Susan Carlisle is an extremely resourceful young woman of fourteen. Left orphaned and in debt in 1919, she schemes her way to the West to sell the sheep her father left behind. On her way, Susan finds both trouble and victory in a multitude of ways. The story is told from Susan's point of view as well as the point of view of the man Susan sets her sights on marrying.

Titles Annotated in Other Chapters Related to Westerns and the Old West

Rees, Elizabeth M. *Plainsong for Caitlin.* Romance.

Appendix A: Award-Winning Books

Among the many ways there are of finding good books to read, the following awards and recognitions are also helpful. We have included major awards for poetry, fiction, drama, and nonfiction for young readers and adults, given from 1994 to 1997, as well as descriptions of some other useful booklists.

Jane Addams Award

The Jane Addams Award, established in 1953, is given annually to the book for young people that most effectively promotes peace, social justice, world community, or equality of the sexes and of all races. It is given by the Women's International League for Peace and Freedom and the Jane Addams Peace Association.

1994   Levine, Ellen. *Freedom's Children: Young Civil Rights Activists Tell Their Own Stories*. Avon.
1995   Freedman, Russell. *Kids at Work: Lewis Hine and the Crusade against Child Labor*. Clarion Books.
1996   Taylor, Mildred D. *The Well: David's Story*. Dial Books for Young Readers.

Mildred L. Batchelder Award

Given annually (unless no book is deemed worthy) to a United States publisher, the Batchelder Award honors the most outstanding book originally published in a language other than English or a country other than the United States. Established in 1968, it is given by the Association for Library Service to Children of the American Library Association.

1994   Farrar, Straus and Giroux: *The Apprentice,* by Pilar Molina Llorente. Translated from the Spanish by Robin Longshaw.
1995   Dutton Children's Books: *The Boys from St. Petri,* by Bjarne Reuter. Translated from the Danish by Anthea Bell.
1996   Houghton Mifflin: *The Lady with the Hat,* by Uri Orlev. Translated from the Hebrew by Hillel Halkin.
1997   Farrar, Straus and Giroux: *The Friends,* by Kazumi Yumoto. Translated from the Japanese by Cathy Hirano.

Booklist's Top of the List

The "Top of the List," initiated in 1991, represents the selections made by the staff of *Booklist* of the very best of their "Editor's Choice" annual lists. The complete lists may be found in *Booklist* each January 15.

1994   **Youth Fiction**
Temple, Frances. *The Ramsay Scallop*. Orchard Books / Richard Jackson.

Youth Nonfiction
Bachrach, Susan D. *Tell Them We Remember: The Story of the Holocaust*. Little, Brown.

1995   **Youth Fiction**
Morpurgo, Michael. *The War of Jenkins' Ear*. Putnam / Philomel.

Youth Nonfiction
Giblin, James Cross. *When Plague Strikes: The Black Death, Smallpox, AIDS*. HarperCollins.

1996   **Youth Fiction**
Pullman, Philip. *The Golden Compass*. Alfred A. Knopf.

Youth Nonfiction
Fleischman, Sid. *The Abracadabra Kid: A Writer's Life*. Greenwillow Books.

Boston Globe—Horn Book Award

Given annually since 1967 by *The Boston Globe* and *The Horn Book Magazine,* these awards are conferred in three categories: outstanding fiction or poetry, outstanding nonfiction, and outstanding picture book.

1994   **Fiction Award**
Williams, Vera B. *Scooter*. Greenwillow Books.

Fiction Honors
Fine, Anne. *Flour Babies and the Boys of Room 8*. Little, Brown.
Fox, Paula. *Western Wind*. Orchard Books.

Nonfiction Award
Freedman, Russell. *Eleanor Roosevelt: A Life of Discovery*. Clarion Books.

Nonfiction Honor Books
Marrin, Albert. *Unconditional Surrender: U. S. Grant and the Civil War*. Atheneum.
Levy, Constance. *A Tree Place and Other Poems*. Margaret K. McElderry Books.

1995   **Fiction Award**
Wynne-Jones, Tim. *Some of the Kinder Planets*. Orchard Books.

Fiction Honors
Hickman, Janet. *Jericho*. Greenwillow Books.
Nelson, Theresa. *Earthshine: A Novel*. Orchard Books.

Nonfiction Award
Bober, Natalie. *Abigail Adams: Witness to a Revolution*. Simon and Schuster.

Nonfiction Honors
Harris, Robie H. *It's Perfectly Normal: Changing Bodies, Growing Up, Sex and Sexual Health*. Illustrated by Michael Emberley. Candlewick Press.
Murphy, Jim. *The Great Fire*. Scholastic.

1996   **Fiction Award**
Avi. *Poppy*. Illustrated by Brian Floca. Richard Jackson / Orchard Books.

Fiction Honors
McGraw, Eloise. *The Moorchild*. Margaret K. McElderry Books.
White, Ruth. *Belle Prater's Boy*. Farrar, Straus and Giroux.

Nonfiction Award
Warren, Andrea. *Orphan Train Rider: One Boy's True Story*. Houghton Mifflin.

Nonfiction Honors
Bruchac, Joseph. *The Boy Who Lived with the Bears, and Other Iroquois Stories*. Illustrated by Murv Jacob. HarperCollins.
Geisert, Bonnie. *Haystack*. Illustrated by Arthur Geisert. HoughtonMifflin / Lorraine.

Andrew Carnegie Medal

This medal, first given in 1937 to commemorate the centenary of the birth of Andrew Carnegie, is awarded annually by the British Library Association to an outstanding children's book written in English and first published in the United Kingdom.

1994   Swindells, Robert. *Stone Cold*. Hamish Hamilton.
1995   Breslin, Theresa. *Whispers in the Graveyard*. Methuen.
1996   Pullman, Philip. *Northern Lights*. Scholastic Ltd.
1997   Burgess, Melvin. *Junk*. Andersen Press.

International Board on Books for Young People Honor List

Established in 1956, this list is published every two years to recognize books published in countries all over the world that represent the best in literature for young readers. Listed below are recent honorees from the United States.

1994   **Text Award**
Paterson, Katherine. *Lyddie*. Dutton Children's Books.

Illustrator Award
Bedard, Michael. *Emily*. Illustrated by Barbara Cooney. Doubleday.

Translation Award
Orlev, Uri. *The Man from the Other Side*. Translated by Hillel Halkin. Houghton Mifflin.

1996   **Text Award**
Cushman, Karen. *Catherine, Called Birdy*. Clarion Books.

Illustrator Award
Johnson, James Weldon. *The Creation*. Illustrated by James E. Ransome. Holiday House.

Translation Award

Jimenez, Juan Ramón. *Platero y Yo (Platero and I).* Translated by Myra C. Livingston and Joseph F. Dominguez. Clarion Books.

International Reading Association Children's Books Award

Given annually since 1975, this award honors the first or second book of an author, from any country, who shows unusual promise. Titles listed here are winners in the older readers category.

1994   Toll, Nelly. *Behind the Secret Window: A Memoir of a Hidden Childhood during World War Two.* Dial Books.

1995   Krisher, Trudy. *Spite Fences.* Delacorte Press.

1996   Alder, Elizabeth. *The King's Shadow.* Farrar, Straus and Giroux.

1997   Haddix, Margaret Peterson. *Don't You Dare Read This, Mrs. Dunphrey.* Simon and Schuster.

Coretta Scott King Award

These awards and honor designations have been given annually since 1969 to African American authors and illustrators for books that are outstanding inspirational and educational contributions to literature for children and young people. They are given by the Social Responsibilities Round Table of the American Library Association.

1994   **Author Award**

Johnson, Angela. *Toning the Sweep.* Orchard Books.

Author Honor Books

Thomas, Joyce Carol. *Brown Honey in Broomwheat Tea.* Illustrated by Floyd Cooper. HarperCollins Children's Books.

Myers, Walter Dean. *Malcolm X: By Any Means Necessary.* Scholastic.

Illustrator Award

Feelings, Tom. *Soul Looks Back in Wonder.* Written by Tom Feelings, with contributions by Maya Angelou, Askia Toure, and Langston Hughes. Doubleday.

Illustrator Honor Books

Cooper, Floyd. *Brown Honey in Broomwheat Tea.* Written by Joyce Carol Thomas. HarperCollins Children's Books.

Ransome, James. *Uncle Jed's Barbershop.* Written by Margaree King Mitchell. Simon and Schuster.

1995   **Author Award**

McKissack, Patricia C., and Frederick McKissack. *Christmas in the Big House, Christmas in the Quarters.* Edited by John Thompson and Ann Reit. Scholastic.

Author Honor Books

Woodson, Jacqueline. *I Hadn't Meant to Tell You This.* Edited by Wendy Lamb. Delacorte Press.

McKissack, Patricia C., and Frederick McKissack. *Black Diamond: The Story of the Negro Baseball Leagues.* Edited by Ann Reit. Scholastic.

Illustrator Award

Ransome, James E. *The Creation*. Written by James Weldon Johnson. Edited by Margery Cuyler. Holiday House.

Illustrator Honor Books

Shaffer, Terea. *The Singing Man*. Written by Angela Shelf Medearis. Edited by Margery Cuyler. Holiday House.

Cooper, Floyd. *Meet Danitra Brown*. Written by Nikki Grimes. Edited by Susan Pearson. Lothrop, Lee and Shepard Books.

1996 **Author Awards**

Hamilton, Virginia. *Her Stories*. Illustrated by Leo and Diane Dillon. Blue Sky / Scholastic.

Author Honor Books

Curtis, Christopher Paul. *The Watsons Go to Birmingham—1963*. Delacorte Press.
Williams-Garcia, Rita. *Like Sisters on the Homefront*. Lodestar.
Woodson, Jacqueline. *From the Notebooks of Melanin Sun*. Blue Sky / Scholastic.

Illustrator Award

Feelings, Tom. *The Middle Passage: White Ships / Black Cargo*. Written by Tom Feelings. Dial Books.

Illustrator Honor Books

Dillon, Leo, and Diane Dillon. *Her Stories*. Written by Virginia Hamilton. Blue Sky / Scholastic.

Pinkney, Brian. *The Faithful Friend*. Written by Robert D. San Souci. Simon and Schuster.

1997 **Author Award**

Myers, Walter Dean. *Slam!* Scholastic.

Author Honor Book

McKissack, Patricia C., and Fredrick L. McKissack. *Rebels against Slavery: American Slave Revolts*. Scholastic.

Illustrator Award

Pinkney, Jerry. *Minty: A Story of Young Harriet Tubman*. Written by Alan Schroeder. Dial Books for Young Readers.

Illustrator Honor Books

Christie, Gregory. *The Palm of My Heart: Poetry by African American Children*. Edited by Davida Adedjouma. Lee and Low.

Ruffins, Reynold. *Running the Road to ABC*. Written by Denize Lauture. Simon and Schuster Books for Young Readers.

Saint James, Synthia. *Neeny Coming, Neeny Going*. Written by Karen English. BridgeWater Books.

NCTE Award for Excellence in Poetry for Children

Established in 1977, this award is presented every three years to a living American poet for an aggregrate body of work for children ages three to thirteen.

1991 Valerie Worth. Major works: *Small Poems* (1972, Farrar, Straus and Giroux) and *All the Small Poems* (1987, Farrar, Straus and Giroux).

1994 Barbara Esbensen. Major works: *Cold Stars and Fireflies: Poems for the Four Seasons* (1984, HarperCollins Children's Books); *Words with Wrinkled Knees* (1987, HarperCollins Children's Books); and *Who Shrank My Grandmother's House? Poems of Discovery* (1992, HarperCollins Children's Books).

1997 Eloise Greenfield. Major works: *For the Love of the Game: Michael Jordan and Me* (1997, HarperCollins Children's Books); *Night on Neighborhood Street* (1991, Dial Books for Young Readers); and *Honey, I Love: And Other Love Poems* (1978, HarperCollins Children's Books).

NCTE Orbis Pictus Award for Outstanding Nonfiction for Children

This award commemorates the work of John Comenius, *Orbis Pictus: The World in Pictures,* published in 1657 and historically considered to be the first book actually planned for children. The selection committee chooses one outstanding nonfiction book each year on the basis of accuracy, organization, design, writing style, and usefulness for classroom teaching.

1994 **Award**

Murphy, Jim. *Across America on an Emigrant Train.* Houghton Mifflin / Clarion Books.

Honor Books

Brandenburg, Jim. *To the Top of the World: Adventures with Arctic Wolves.* Walker.

Brooks, Bruce. *Making Sense: Animal Perception and Communication.* Farrar, Straus and Giroux.

1995 **Award**

Swanson, Diane. *Safari Beneath the Sea: The Wonder World of the North Pacific Coast.* Sierra Club Books.

Honor Books

Dewey, Jennifer Owings. *Wildlife Rescue: The Work of Dr. Kathleen Ramsay.* Boyds Mills Press.

Freedman, Russell. *Kids at Work: Lewis Hine and the Crusade against Child Labor.* Houghton Mifflin / Clarion Books.

McKissack, Patricia C., and Fredrick L. McKissack. *Christmas in the Big House, Christmas in the Quarters.* Edited by John Thompson and Ann Reit. Scholastic.

1996 **Award**

Murphy, Jim. *The Great Fire.* Scholastic.

Honor Books

Pringle, Laurence. *Dolphin Man: Exploring the World of Dolphins.* Atheneum.

Colman, Penny. *Rosie the Riveter: Women Working on the Home Front in World War II.* Crown.

1997 **Award**

Stanley, Diane. *Leonardo da Vinci.* Morrow.

Honor Books

Blumberg, Rhoda. *Full Steam Ahead: The Race to Build a Transcontinental Railroad*. National Geographic Society.

Freedman, Russell. *The Life and Death of Crazy Horse*. Holiday House.

Osborne, Mary Pope. *One World, Many Religions: The Ways We Worship*. Alfred A. Knopf.

John Newbery Medal

The Newbery Medal and honor book designations have been given annually since 1922 to the most distinguished contributions to children's literature published in the United States during the preceding year. The authors must be citizens or residents of the United States. The award is given by the Association for Library Service to Children of the American Library Association.

1994 **Medal**

Lowry, Lois. *The Giver*. Houghton Mifflin.

Honor Books

Conly, Jane Leslie. *Crazy Lady!* HarperCollins Children's Books.

Yep, Laurence. *Dragon's Gate*. HarperCollins Children's Books.

Freedman, Russell. *Eleanor Roosevelt: A Life of Discovery*. Houghton Mifflin / Clarion Books.

1995 **Medal**

Creech, Sharon. *Walk Two Moons*. HarperCollins.

Honor Books

Cushman, Karen. *Catherine, Called Birdy*. Houghton Mifflin / Clarion Books.

Farmer, Nancy. *The Ear, the Eye and the Arm*. Richard Jackson / Orchard Books.

1996 **Medal**

Cushman, Karen. *The Midwife's Apprentice*. Clarion Books.

Honor Books

Coman, Carolyn. *What Jamie Saw*. Front Street.

Curtis, Christopher Paul. *The Watsons Go to Birmingham 1963*. Delacorte Press.

Fenner, Carol. *Yolanda's Genius*. Margaret K. McElderry Books.

Murphy, Jim. *The Great Fire*. Scholastic.

1997 **Medal**

Konigsburg, E. L. *The View from Saturday*. Jean Karl / Atheneum.

Honor Books

Farmer, Nancy. *A Girl Named Disaster*. Richard Jackson / Orchard Books.

McGraw, Eloise. *Moorchild*. Margaret K. McElderry Books.

Turner, Megan Whalen. *The Thief*. Greenwillow Books.

White, Ruth. *Belle Prater's Boy*. Farrar, Straus and Giroux.

Scott O'Dell Award for Historical Fiction

Established in 1981, the Scott O'Dell Award is given to a distinguished work of historical fiction for children or young adults. The author must be a citizen or resident of the United States, the work must be written in English and published in the United States, and the story must be set in the New World (North, South, or Central America). The award is given annually (if a worthy book has been published) by the Advisory Committee of the Bulletin of the Center for Children's Books.

1994   Fleischman, Paul. *Bull Run*. HarperCollins.
1995   Salisbury, Graham. *Under the Blood-Red Sun*. Delacorte Press.
1996   Taylor, Theodore. *The Bomb*. Harcourt Brace.
1997   Paterson, Katherine. *Jip: His Story*. Lodestar.

National Book Award for Young People's Literature

Beginning in 1996, the National Book Awards, administered by the National Book Foundation, have included a category for Young People's Literature, with an emphasis on literary merit.

1996   Martinez, Victor. *Parrot in the Oven: Mi Vida*. HarperCollins / Joanna Colter Books.

Booklists

In addition to recognition awarded to a handful of selected titles, several organizations issue annual lists of recommended books. While such lists are too lengthy to include in this volume, we include descriptions of the booklists that would be of interest to readers of *Books for You*, and indicate how to obtain these booklists.

American Library Association Notable Children's Books

The Notable Children's Book Committee of the Association for Library Service to Children, a division of the American Library Association, selects notable books each year on the basis of literary quality, originality of text and illustrations, design, format, subject matter of interest and value to children, and likelihood of acceptance by children. The complete list of Notable Children's Books appears yearly in the March 15 issue of *Booklist*, a journal published by the American Library Association.

American Library Association Best Books for Young Adults

The Young Adult Library Services Association of the American Library Association each year chooses the fiction and nonfiction titles that best satisfy the criteria of good literary quality and popular appeal to young adult readers. The complete list is published each year in the April 1 issue of *Booklist*, or you may receive a copy by sending a self-addressed stamped business-size envelope to YALSA, 50 E. Huron Street, Chicago, IL 60611.

American Library Association Quick Picks for Young Adults

The ALA's Young Adult Library Services Association also publishes a list each year of books with high appeal to young adult readers who, for whatever reason, do not like to read. The complete list is published each year in the April 1 issue of *Booklist,* or you may receive a copy by sending a self-addressed stamped business-size envelope to YALSA, 50 E. Huron Street, Chicago, IL 60611.

International Reading Association

The International Reading Association each year asks children, young adults, and teachers to vote on a list of books recommended by recognized sources such as *Booklist, Horn Book,* and *Journal of Reading.* The top vote-getters in each group are listed in IRA journals each year and may also be obtained from the IRA directly. The complete list of Children's Choices appears yearly in the November issue of *The Reading Teacher,* the Young Adults' Choices appear in the November issue of *Journal of Reading,* and the Teachers' Choices appear in the November issue of *The Reading Teacher.* Single copies of any of the lists may be obtained at no charge by sending your request along with a stamped (4 oz.), self-addressed 9" x 15" envelope to The International Reading Association, Order Department, 800 Barksdale Road, P.O. Box 8139, Newark, DE 19714-8139.

Notable Children's Trade Books in the Field of Social Studies

A Book Review Committee appointed by the National Council for the Social Studies, in cooperation with the Children's Book Council, selects books published in the United States each year that (1) are written primarily for students in grades K–8, (2) emphasize human relations, (3) represent a diversity of groups and are sensitive to a broad range of cultural experiences, (4) present an original theme or a fresh slant on a traditional topic, (5) are easily readable and of high literary quality, and (6) have a pleasing format and, when appropriate, illustrations that enrich the text. The complete list of these notable books appears yearly in the April / May issue of *Social Education,* the journal of the National Council for the Social Studies. Single copies may be obtained at no charge by sending a stamped (3 oz.), self-addressed 6" x 9" envelope to the Children's Book Council, 568 Broadway, Suite 404, New York, NY 10012. (In 1994, the date on the list was changed to coincide with the current calendar year. Prior to 1994, the date on the list was for the previous calendar year, the year in which the books were published. Thus, while there is no list labeled Notable 1993 Children's Trade Books in the Field of Social Studies, there has been no interruption in the listing. The 1993 books appear on the 1994 list.)

Outstanding Science Trade Books for Children

Each year a book review panel appointed by the National Science Teachers Association and assembled in cooperation with the Children's Book Council selects a list of outstanding books for young readers that present substantial science content in a clear, accurate, and up-to-date way. Each book is also evaluated on its freedom from gender, ethnic, and socioeconomic bias, and on the quality of its presentation of material. The complete list of outstanding science books is published each spring in the March issue of *Science and Children.*

School Library Journal's **Best Books of the Year**

The Book Review Editors of *School Library Journal* annually choose the best among the thousands of new children's books submitted to the journal for review during the preceding year. Books are selected on the basis of strong story line, clear presentation, high-quality illustration, and probable appeal to young readers. The complete list is published each year in the December issue of the journal.

Other Sources of Information

Lists and descriptions of other awards, prizes, and lists can be found at the front of recent editions of *Children's Books in Print,* an annual publication of R. R. Bowker, and at the Children's Book Awards web site maintained by David K. Brown at the University of Calgary, Alberta, at http://www.ucalgary.ca/~dkbrown/ awards.html.

Appendix B: Multicultural Titles

The books listed here reflect diverse cultures, both American and international. Entries are organized by author, title, a short form of the chapter name, and cultural reference. (If no specific cultural reference is given, the text includes varied characters or perspectives.)

Able, Deborah. *Hate Groups.* Political Science.

Achebe, Chinua. *Things Fall Apart.* Classics. Nigeria.

Adams, Carmen. *The Claw.* Horror. African American.

Adler, Bill, Jr. *Tell Me a Fairy Tale: A Parent's Guide to Telling Magical and Mythical Stories.* Myths.

Adoff, Arnold, editor. *My Black Me: A Beginning Book of Black Poetry.* Poetry and Drama. African American.

Alicea, Gil C., with Carmine DeSena. *The Air down Here: True Tales from a South Bronx Boyhood.* Diaries. Latino American.

Allen, Paula Gunn, and Patricia Clark Smith. *As Long as the Rivers Flow: The Stories of Nine Native Americans.* Autobiography. Native American.

Alvarez, Julia. *In the Time of the Butterflies.* Historical Fiction. Dominican Republic.

Andryszewski, Tricia. *Immigration: Newcomers and Their Impact on the United States.* Political Science.

Antush, John V., editor. *Nuestro New York: An Anthology of Puerto Rican Plays.* Poetry and Drama. Latino American.

Ashabranner, Brent. *A New Frontier: The Peace Corps in Eastern Europe.* History. Eastern Europe.

Ashby, Ruth, and Deborah Gore Ohrn, editors. *Herstory: Women Who Changed the World.* History.

Atkin, S. Beth. *Voices from the Streets: Young Former Gang Members Tell Their Stories.* Diaries.

Avila, Alfred. *Mexican Ghost Tales of the Southwest.* Short Stories. Mexican American.

Ayer, Eleanor H., with Helen Waterford and Alfons Heck. *Parallel Journeys.* Holocaust. Jewish.

Bachrach, Susan D. *Tell Them We Remember: The Story of the Holocaust.* Holocaust. Jewish.

Baldwin, Joyce. *DNA Pioneer: James Watson and the Double Helix.* Autobiography. African American.

Banfield, Susan. *Ethnic Conflicts in Schools.* School.

Banks, Russell. *Rule of the Bone: A Novel.* Choices. Jamaican American.

Barber, Nicola, and Mary Mure. *The World of Music.* Arts.

Barboza, Steven. *Door of No Return: The Legend of Gorée Island.* History. African American.

Barr, Roger. *The Importance of Malcolm X.* Autobiography. African American.

Beals, Melba Pattillo. *Warriors Don't Cry: A Searing Memoir of the Battle to Integrate Little Rock's Central High.* Autobiography. African American.

Beatty, Paul. *Joker, Joker, Deuce.* Poetry and Drama. African American.

Begay, Shonto. *Navajo: Visions and Voices across the Mesa.* Poetry and Drama. Navajo.

Benedict, Helen. *Bad Angel.* Choices. Dominican Republic.

Bennett, James. *Dakota Dream.* Choices. Dakota.

Bennett, Martin (retold by). *West African Trickster Tales.* Myths. West African.

Bennett, William J., editor. *The Book of Virtues for Young People: A Treasury of Great Moral Stories.* Religion.

Bernier-Grand, Carmen T. *Poet and Politician of Puerto Rico: Don Luis Muñoz Marín.* Autobiography. Puerto Rico.

Bernotas, Bob. *Branford Marsalis: Jazz Musician.* Autobiography. African American.

Binstock, R. C. *Tree of Heaven.* Historical Fiction. Japan and China.

Bjarkman, Peter C. *Top 10 Basketball Slam Dunkers.* Sports.

Bjarkman, Peter C. *Top 10 Baseball Base Stealers.* Sports.

Blue, Rose, and Corinne J. Naden. *People of Peace.* Autobiography.

Boas, Jacob. *We Are Witnesses: Five Diaries of Teenagers Who Died in the Holocaust.* Holocaust. Jewish.

Bode, Janet, and Stan Mack. *Heartbreak and Roses: Real Life Stories of Troubled Love.* Dating.

Bosse, Malcolm. *Deep Dream of the Rain Forest.* Adventure. Borneo.

Bosse, Malcolm. *The Examination.* Adventure. China.

Bosse, Malcolm. *Tusk and Stone.* Adventure. India.

Boyd, Candy Dawson. *Fall Secrets.* Arts. African American.

Boyko, Carrie, and Kimberly Colen, compilers. *Hold Fast Your Dreams: Twenty Commencement Speeches.* Diaries.

Brainard, Cecilia Manguerra. *When the Rainbow Goddess Wept.* War. Philippines.

Bredeson, Carmen. *Henry Cisneros: Building a Better America.* Autobiography. Mexican American.

Brown, Kevin. *Malcolm X: His Life and Legacy.* Autobiography. African American.

Bruchac, Joseph (told by). *Flying with the Eagle, Racing the Great Bear: Stories from Native North America.* Myths. Native American.

Bruchac, Joseph, and Gayle Ross (told by). *The Girl Who Married the Moon: Stories from Native North America.* Myths. Native American.

Bunkley, Anita Richmond. *Black Gold.* Romance. African American.

Burks, Brian. *Runs with Horses.* Historical Fiction. Apache.

Campbell, Eric. *The Shark Callers.* Adventure. Papua New Guinea.

Carlson, Lori M., editor. *American Eyes: New Asian-American Short Stories for Young Adults.* Short Stories. Asian American.

Carlson, Lori M., editor. *Cool Salsa: Bilingual Poems on Growing Up Latino in the United States.* Poetry and Drama. Latino American.

Carter, Alden R. *Dogwolf.* Choices. Native American.

Case, Dianne. *92 Queens Road.* Family. South Africa.

Casey, Maude. *Over the Water.* Family. Ireland.

Castañeda, Omar S. *Imagining Isabel.* Choices. Guatemala.

Charbonneau, Eileen. *In the Time of the Wolves.* Historical Fiction. Native American.

Charbonneau, Eileen. *Honor to the Hills.* Historical Fiction.

Charyn, Jerome, editor. *The New Mystery: The International Association of Crime Writers' Essential Crime Writing of the Late Twentieth Century.* Mysteries.

Child, John. *The Rise of Islam.* Religion. Islamic.

Chin, Steven A. *The Success of Gordon H. Chong and Associates.* Arts. Chinese American.

Choi, Sook Nyul. *Gathering of Pearls.* Choices. Korea.

Chong, Denise. *The Concubine's Children.* Autobiography. Chinese Canadian.

Christiansen, C. B. *I See the Moon.* Choices. Norwegian American.

Chu, Daniel, and Bill Shaw. *Going Home to Nicodemus: The Story of an African American Frontier Town and the Pioneers Who Settled It.* Autobiography. African American.

Clark, Mary Higgins, editor. *Bad Behavior.* Mysteries.

Cofer, Judith Ortiz. *An Island like You: Stories of the Barrio.* Short Stories. Latino American.

Cohen, Barbara. *David.* Autobiography. Israel.

Cohen, Barbara, and Bahija Lovejoy. *Seven Daughters and Seven Sons.* Myths. Middle East.

Cohen, Daniel. *Cults.* Religion.

Cole, Michael D. *Vostok 1: First Human in Space.* Science. Former Soviet Union.

Cooper, Michael L. *Bound for the Promised Land: The Great Black Migration.* History. African American.

Cox, Vic. *The Challenge of Immigration.* Political Science. American.

Crawford, Peter. *Nomads of the Wind: A Natural History of Polynesia.* History. Polynesia.

Creeden, Sharon. *Fair Is Fair: World Folktales of Justice.* Myths.

D'Aguiar, Fred. *The Longest Memory: A Novel.* Historical Fiction. Guyana.

Dalkey, Kara. *Little Sister.* Historical Fiction. Japan.

Danticat, Edwidge. *Breath, Eyes, Memory.* Choices. Haitian American.

Darin-Smith, Kate. *Exploration into Australia.* History. Australia.

Davidson, Sue. *A Heart in Politics: Jeannette Rankin and Patsy T. Mink.* Autobiography.

Davis, Ossie. *Just like Martin.* Choices. African American.

de Vries, Anke. *Bruises.* Family. Netherlands.

de Trevino, Elizabeth Borton. *Leona: A Love Story.* Historical Fiction. Mexico.

DeFord, Deborah H., and Harry S. Stout. *An Enemy among Them.* Historical Fiction. German American.

Denenberg, Barry. *Voices from Vietnam.* War.

Deschamps, Hélène. *Spyglass: An Autobiography.* Autobiography. France.

Desetta, Al, editor. *The Heart Knows Something Different: Teenage Voices from the Foster Care System.* Diaries.

Dickinson, Peter. *Shadow of a Hero.* Choices. Eastern Europe.

Dorris, Michael. *Sees behind Trees.* Choices. Native American.

Draper, Sharon M. *Tears of a Tiger.* Death. African American.

Duong Thu Huong. *Paradise of the Blind.* Choices. Vietnam.

Duvall, Lynn. *Respecting Our Differences: A Guide to Getting Along in a Changing World.* Human Rights. American.

Eady, Cornelius. *You Don't Miss Your Water: Poems.* Poetry and Drama. African American.

Eliot, Alexander. *The Global Myths: Exploring Primitive, Pagan, Sacred, and Scientific Mythologies.* Myths.

Evans, Jeremy. *Motocross and Trials.* Airplanes.

Farmer, Nancy. *The Ear, the Eye and the Arm.* Science Fiction. Zimbabwe.

Feder, Harriet K. *Mystery of the Kaifeng Scroll: A Vivi Hartman Adventure.* Mysteries. Turkey.

Feelings, Tom. *The Middle Passage: White Ships / Black Cargo.* Arts. African / African American.

Ferber, Elizabeth. *Yasir Arafat: A Life of War and Peace.* Autobiography. Palestine.

Ferris, Jean. *Signs of Life*. Death. Lascaux (France).

Fiene, Pat, editor. *Expressions: Stories and Poems, Volume 2*. Short Stories.

Filipović, Zlata. *Zlata's Diary: A Child's Life in Sarajevo*. Diaries. Bosnia-Herzegovina.

Fireside, Harvey, and Sarah Betsy Fuller. *Brown v. Board of Education: Equal Schooling for All*. Political Science. African American.

Fleet, Robert C. *Last Mountain*. Fantasy.

Fleming, Robert. *The Success of Caroline Jones Advertising, Inc.: An Advertising Success Story*. Autobiography. African American.

Frank, Ben G. *A Travel Guide to Jewish Europe*. Recreation. Jewish.

Franklin, Paula A. *Melting Pot or Not? Debating Cultural Identity*. Human Rights. American.

Fremon, David K. *Japanese-American Internment in American History*. History. Japanese American.

Friedman, Ina R. *Flying against the Wind: The Story of a Young Woman Who Defied the Nazis*. Holocaust. German.

Friedman, Carl. *Nightfather*. Holocaust. Netherlands.

Gaarder, Jostein. *Sophie's World: A Novel about the History of Philosophy*. Mysteries. Norway.

Gaines, Ernest J. *A Lesson before Dying*. Friendships. African American.

García, John. *The Success of Hispanic Magazine: A Publishing Success Story*. Autobiography. Latino American.

Garden, Nancy. *Dove and Sword: A Novel of Joan of Arc*. Historical Fiction. France.

Garland, Sherry. *Cabin 102*. Choices. Arawak.

Garland, Sherry. *Indio*. Adventure. Pueblo.

Gatti, Anne, editor. *Tales from the African Plains*. Short Stories. African.

Gay, Kathlyn. *Keep the Buttered Side Up: Food Superstitions around the World*. Myths.

Gellman, Rabbi Marc, and Monsignor Thomas Hartman. *How Do You Spell God? Answers to the Big Questions from Around the World*. Religion.

Gibson, Bob, and Lonnie Wheeler. *Stranger to the Game*. Sports. Africa.

Gillam, Scott. *Discrimination: Prejudice in Action*. Human Rights.

Giovanni, Nikki, editor. *Grand Mothers: Poems, Reminiscences, and Short Stories about the Keepers of Our Traditions*. Poetry and Drama. African American.

Glaser, Isabel Joshlin, editor. *Dreams of Glory: Poems Starring Girls*. Poetry and Drama.

Gleason, Judith, editor. *Leaf and Bone: African Praise-Poems*. Poetry and Drama. Africa.

Glenn, Mel. *Who Killed Mr. Chippendale? A Mystery in Poems*. School.

Glover, Denise M., editor. *Voices of the Spirit: Sources for Interpreting the African-American Experience*. Reference. African American.

Goldin, Barbara Diamond. *Bat Mitzvah: A Jewish Girl's Coming of Age*. Religion. Jewish.

Gonzales, Doreen. *Alex Haley: Author of Roots*. Autobiography. African American.

Goodman, Joan Elizabeth. *Songs from Home*. Family. Italy.

Goodrich, Norma Lorre. *Ancient Myths*. Myths.

Gordon, Ruth, editor. *Pierced by a Ray of Sun: Poems about the Times We Feel Alone*. Poetry and Drama.

Green, Carl R. *Jackie Joyner-Kersee*. Sports. African American.

Green, Carl R., and Roxanne Ford. *Deion Sanders*. Sports. African American.

Green, Roger Lancelyn. *Tales of the Greek Heroes: Retold from the Ancient Authors*. Myths. Greece.

Griffin-Pierce, Trudy. *The Encyclopedia of Native America*. Reference. Native American.

Gunesekera, Romesh. *Reef*. Choices. Sri Lanka.

Gutman, Bill. *Reggie White: Star Defensive Lineman*. Sports. African American.

Gutman, Bill. *Larry Johnson: King of the Court*. Sports. African American.

Gutman, Bill. *Emmitt Smith: NFL Super Runner*. Sports. African American.

Haggard, H. Rider. *She*. Classics. Egypt.

Hague, Michael, editor. *The Book of Dragons*. Myths.

Hajdusiewicz, Babs Bell. *Mary Carter Smith: African-American Storyteller*. Autobiography. African American.

Haldeman, Jack C., II, and Jack Dann. *High Steel*. Science Fiction. Native American.

Hamilton, Virginia. *Arilla Sun Down*. Choices. African/Native American.

Hansberry, Lorraine. *A Raisin in the Sun: The Unfilmed Original Screenplay*. Television. African American.

Hansen, Joyce. *The Captive*. Historical Fiction. African American.

Harjo, Joy. *The Woman Who Fell from the Sky: Poems*. Poetry and Drama. Native American.

Harrington, Denis J. *Top 10 Women Tennis Players*. Sports.

Harris, Jacqueline L. *The Tuskegee Airmen: Black Heroes of World War II*. History. African American.

Hartnett, Sonya. *Wilful Blue*. Death. Australia.

Harvey, Karen D., editor; Lisa D. Harjo, consultant. *American Indian Voices*. Poetry and Drama. Native American.

Haskins, James. *The Scottsboro Boys*. Human Rights. African American.

Haskins, Jim. *Black Eagles: African Americans in Aviation*. Autobiography. African American.

Haskins, Jim. *The Harlem Renaissance*. History. African American.

Haskins, Jim, and Joann Biondi. *From Afar to Zulu: A Dictionary of African Cultures*. Reference. Africa.

Haslam, Alexandra R. and Gerald W. Haslam, editors. *Where Coyotes Howl and Wind Blows Free: Growing Up in the West*. Short Stories.

Herda, D. J. *Furman v. Georgia: The Death Penalty Case*. Political Science. African American.

Herda, D. J. *Thurgood Marshall: Civil Rights Champion*. Autobiography. African American.

Herman, Charlotte. *What Happened to Heather Hopkowitz?* Religion. Jewish.

Herman, Spring. *R. C. Gorman: Navajo Artist*. Autobiography. Navajo.

Hermes, Jules. *The Children of Morocco*. History. Morocco.

Hewett, Lorri. *Soulfire*. Choices. African American.

Hiçyilmaz, Gaye. *The Frozen Waterfall*. Friendships. Turkey.

Hinojosa, Maria. *Crews: Gang Members Talk to Maria Hinojosa*. Diaries.

Hobbs, Will. *Kokopelli's Flute*. Adventure. Native American.

Hockenberry, John. *Moving Violations: War Zones, Wheelchairs, and Declarations of Independence*. Autobiography.

Hodge, Merle. *For the Life of Laetitia*. School. Trinidad.

Hoig, Stan. *Sequoyah: The Cherokee Genius*. Autobiography. Cherokee.

Holliday, Laurel, compiler. *Children in the Holocaust and World War II: Their Secret Diaries*. Holocaust.

Hoobler, Dorothy, and Thomas Hoobler. The American Family Album series. Diaries. African American, Chinese American, Irish American, Italian American, and Mexican American.

Hughes, Langston. *The Block: Poems*. Poetry and Drama. African American.

Hughes, Libby. *Colin Powell: A Man of Quality*. Autobiography. African American.

Hunter, Mollie. *A Stranger Came Ashore*. Family. Shetland Islands (Scotland).

Irwin, Hadley. *Jim-Dandy*. Historical Fiction. Native American.

Jenkins, Lyll Becerra de. *Celebrating the Hero*. Family. Colombia.

Jenkins, Lyll Becerra de. *So Loud a Silence*. Choices. Colombia.

Jennings, Patrick. *Faith and the Electric Dogs*. Animals. Latino American.

Johnson, Angela. *Humming Whispers*. Family. African American.

Johnson, Venice, editor. *Voices of the Dream: African-American Women Speak*. Diaries. African American.

Jones, K. Maurice. *Say It Loud! The Story of Rap Music*. Arts. African American.

Jones, K. Maurice. *Spike Lee and the African American Filmmakers: A Choice of Colors*. Television. African American.

Jones, Hettie. *Big Star Fallin' Mama: Five Women in Black Music*. Autobiography. African American.

Jordan, Michael. *I Can't Accept Not Trying: Michael Jordan on the Pursuit of Excellence*. Religion. African American.

Jordan, Sherryl. *Wolf-Woman*. Animals. New Zealand.

Karas, Phyllis. *The Hate Crime*. School. Jewish American.

Katz, Jane, editor. *Messengers of the Wind: Native American Women Tell Their Life Stories*. Autobiography. Native American.

Katz, William Loren. *Black Women of the Old West*. Westerns. African American.

Kessler, Lauren. *Stubborn Twig: Three Generations in the Life of a Japanese American Family*. Autobiography. Japanese American.

Kherdian, David. *The Road from Home: The Story of an Armenian Girl*. Autobiography. Armenian American.

Kherdian, David, editor. *Beat Voices: An Anthology of Beat Poetry*. Poetry and Drama.

Killingsworth, Monte. *Circle within a Circle*. Choices. Chinook.

Kimmel, Eric A. *Bar Mitzvah: A Jewish Boy's Coming of Age*. Religion. Jewish.

Kimmel, Eric A. (retold by). *The Adventures of Hershel of Ostropol*. Myths. Jewish.

Kipling, Rudyard. *The Jungle Book: The Mowgli Stories*. Classics. India.

Klass, David. *Danger Zone*. Sports. African American.

Klein, Aaron. *Deion Sanders: This Is Prime Time*. Sports. African American.

Kort, Michael G. *China under Communism*. History. China.

Kort, Michael G. *Yitzhak Rabin: Israel's Soldier Statesman*. Autobiography. Israel.

Kramer, Barbara. *Alice Walker: Author of The Color Purple*. Autobiography. African American.

Kreischer, Elsie Karr. *María Montoya Martínez: Master Potter*. Autobiography. Mexican American.

Krisher, Trudy. *Spite Fences*. Choices. African American.

Kuklin, Susan. *Irrepressible Spirit: Conversations with Human Rights Activists*. Diaries.

Kuraoka, Hannah. *Missing!* Mysteries. Japanese American.

Laird, Christa. *But Can the Phoenix Sing?* Holocaust. Jewish.

Lang, Paul. *The English Language Debate: One Nation, One Language*. Language.

Lasky, Kathryn. *Beyond the Divide*. Historical Fiction. Amish.

Lasky, Kathryn. *True North: A Novel of the Underground Railroad*. Historical Fiction. African American.

Lawlor, Laurie. *Shadow Catcher: The Life and Work of Edward S. Curtis*. Autobiography. Native American.

Lawlor, Veronica. *I Was Dreaming to Come to America: Memories from the Ellis Island Oral History Project*. Diaries.

Lawrence-Lightfoot, Sara. *I've Known Rivers: Lives of Loss and Liberation*. Autobiography. African American.

Lee, Gus. *China Boy*. Family. Chinese American.

Lee, Marie G. *Saying Goodbye*. Friendships. Korean American.

Leroux, Gaston. *The Phantom of the Opera*. Classics. France.

Lester, Julius (as told by). *The Last Tales of Uncle Remus*. Classics. African American.

Lester, Julius. *Othello: A Novel*. Classics. African.

Levine, Ellen. *Anna Pavlova: Genius of the Dance*. Arts. Russian.

Levinson, Nancy Smiler. *Turn of the Century: Our Nation One Hundred Years Ago*. History.

Levitin, Sonia. *Escape from Egypt*. Religion. Jewish.

Levoy, Myron. *A Shadow like a Leopard*. Friendships.

Lewis-Ferguson, Julinda. *Alvin Ailey, Jr.: A Life in Dance*. Autobiography. African American.

Lipstadt, Deborah E. *Denying the Holocaust: The Growing Assault on Truth and Memory*. Holocaust. Jewish.

Lipsyte, Robert. *The Chief*. Choices. Native American.

Lipsyte, Robert. *Jim Thorpe: Twentieth-Century Jock*. Sports. Native American.

Llorente, Pilar Molina. *The Apprentice*. Historical Fiction. Italy.

Llywelyn, Morgan. *Brian Boru: Emperor of the Irish*. Historical Fiction. Ireland.

London, Jack. *White Fang*. Classics. Native American.

Lyons, Mary E., editor. *Raw Head, Bloody Bones: African-American Tales of the Supernatural*. Short Stories. African American.

Macdonald, Caroline. *Hostilities: Nine Bizarre Stories*. Short Stories. New Zealand.

MacDonald, Fiona. *A Sixteenth Century Mosque*. Arts. Islamic.

Mahy, Margaret. *The Other Side of Silence*. Family. New Zealand.

Malone, Mary. *Maya Lin: Architect and Artist*. Autobiography. Chinese American.

Malone, Mary. *Will Rogers: Cowboy Philosopher*. Westerns. Native American.

Mancini, Salvatore. *On the Edge of Magic*. Poetry and Drama.

Mann, Kenny. African Kingdoms of the Past series. History. Africa.

Marcus, Leonard S., editor. *Lifelines: A Poetry Anthology Patterned on the Stages of Life*. Poetry and Drama.

Marks, Marlene Adler, editor. *Nice Jewish Girls: Growing Up in America*. Short Stories. Jewish.

Marsden, John. *Letters from the Inside*. Friendships. Australia.

Marsh, Graham, and Barrie Lewis, editors. *The Blues: Album Cover Art*. Arts. African American.

Martell, Hazel Mary. *Food and Feasts with the Vikings*. History. Viking.

Martin, Rafe. *Mysterious Tales of Japan*. Myths. Japan.

Matas, Carol. *The Burning Time*. Historical Fiction. France.

McCall, Nathan. *Makes Me Wanna Holler: A Young Black Man in America*. Autobiography. African American.

McCormick, Anita Louise. *Native Americans and the Reservation in American History*. History. Native American.

McKissack, Patricia C., and Fredrick McKissack, Jr. *Black Diamond: The Story of the Negro Baseball Leagues*. Sports. African American.

McKissack, Patricia C., and Fredrick L. McKissack. *Christmas in the Big House, Christmas in the Quarters*. History. African American.

McKissack, Patricia C., and Fredrick L. McKissack. *Rebels against Slavery: American Slave Revolts*. History. African American.

McKissack, Patricia, and Fredrick McKissack. *Red-Tail Angels: The Story of the Tuskegee Airmen of World War II*. History; War. African American.

McKissack, Patricia, and Fredrick McKissack. *The Royal Kingdoms of Ghana, Mali, and Songhay: Life in Medieval Africa*. History. Africa.

Mead, Alice. *Adem's Cross*. Choices.

Meltzer, Milton, editor. *Frederick Douglass: In His Own Words*. Diaries. African American.

Menzel, Peter. *Material World: A Global Family Portrait*. Family.

Merino, José Maria. *Beyond the Ancient Cities*. Historical Fiction. Spain.

Merino, José María. *The Gold of Dreams*. Adventure. South America.

Mettger, Zak. *Till Victory Is Won: Black Soldiers in the Civil War*. History. African American.

Meyer, Carolyn. *Gideon's People*. Religion. Amish.

Meyer, Carolyn. *Rio Grande Stories*. Short Stories. Latino American.

Meyer, Carolyn. *Drummers of Jericho*. Human Rights. Jewish.

Michelson, Maureen, editor. *Women and Work: In Their Own Words*. Diaries.

Mikaelson, Ben. *Countdown*. Adventure.

Mikkelsen, Nina. *Virginia Hamilton*. Autobiography. African American.

Mohr, Nicholasa. *In My Own Words: Growing Up inside the Sanctuary of My Imagination*. Autobiography. Puerto Rico.

Monceaux, Morgan. *Jazz: My Music, My People*. Autobiography. African American.

Mori, Kyoko. *The Dream of Water: A Memoir*. Autobiography. Japan.

Mori, Kyoko. *One Bird*. Family. Japan.

Morrison, Toni. *The Bluest Eye*. Classics. African American.

Murphy, Barbara Beasley. *Fly Like an Eagle*. Family. Native American.

Myers, Christopher A., and Lynne Born Myers. *Forest of the Clouded Leopard*. Choices. Borneo.

Myers, Walter Dean. *The Glory Field*. Family. African American.

Myers, Walter Dean. *Slam!* Sports. African American.

Nall, Jasper Rastus. *Freeborn Slave: Diary of a Black Man in the South*. Autobiography. African American.

Namioka, Lensey. *April and the Dragon Lady*. Family. Chinese American.

Napoli, Donna Jo. *Song of the Magdalene*. Religion.

Narayan, Kirin. *Love, Stars, and All That*. Romance. Asian American.

Newman, Richard, and Marcia Sawyer. *Everybody Say Freedom: Everything You Need to Know about African-American History*. History. African American.

Newman, Gerald, and Eleanor Newman Layfield. *Racism: Divided by Color*. Human Rights.

Nolan, Han. *If I Should Die before I Wake*. Holocaust. Jewish.

Novas, Himilce. *Everything You Need to Know about Latino History*. History. Latino American.

Okimoto, Jean Davies. *Talent Night.* Choices. Japanese American.

Old, Wendie. *Marian Wright Edelman: Fighting for Children's Rights.* Autobiography. African American.

Oliver, Marilyn Tower. *Gangs: Trouble in the Streets.* Political Science.

Orlev, Uri. *Lydia, Queen of Palestine.* Holocaust. Jewish Romanian.

Orlev, Uri. *The Man from the Other Side.* Holocaust. Jewish Polish.

Ousseimi, Maria. *Caught in the Crossfire: Growing Up in a War Zone.* War.

Ovid. *The Poems of Exile.* Classics. Rome.

Oz, Amos. *Soumchi.* Adventure. Israel.

Panzer, Nora, editor. *Celebrate America in Poetry and Art: Paintings, Sculpture, Drawings, Photographs, and Other Works of Art from the National Museum of American Art, Smithsonian Institution.* Poetry and Drama.

Parry, Glyn. *Monster Man.* Adventure. Australia.

Paterson, Katherine. *Jip: His Story.* Choices. African American.

Paterson, Katherine. *Rebels of the Heavenly Kingdom.* Historical Fiction. China.

Paulsen, Gary. *Dogsong.* Adventure. Inuit.

Paulsen, Gary. *Sentries.* Choices. Ojibway.

Paulsen, Gary. *Winterdance: The Fine Madness of Running the Iditarod.* Adventure.

Pausewang, Gudrun. *Fall-out.* Choices. Germany.

Pausewang, Gudrun. *The Final Journey.* Holocaust.

Pepper, Dennis. *The Oxford Book of Animal Stories.* Animals.

Petersen, P. J. *Liars.* Mysteries.

Philip, Neil, editor. *Earth Always Endures: Native American Poems.* Poetry and Drama. Native American.

Philip, Neil, editor. *Singing America.* Poetry and Drama. Native American.

Philip, Neil, editor. *Songs Are Thoughts: Poems of the Inuit.* Poetry and Drama. Inuit.

Philip, Neil (retold by). *The Arabian Nights.* Classics. Arabia.

Picard, Barbara Leonie (retold by). *Tales of the Norse Gods.* Myths. Viking.

Plotkin, Mark J. *Tales of a Shaman's Apprentice: An Ethnologist Searches for New Medicines in the Amazon Rain Forest.* Science. South America.

Plowden, Martha Ward. *Famous Firsts of Black Women.* Autobiography. African American.

Plowden, Martha Ward. *Olympic Black Women.* Sports. African American.

Porte, Barbara Ann. *Something Terrible Happened: A Novel.* Family.

Power, Susan. *The Grass Dancer.* Family. Dakota.

Poynter, Margaret. *Marie Curie: Discoverer of Radium.* Autobiography. Poland and France.

Price, Susan. *Ghost Dance: The Czar's Black Angel.* Fantasy.

Rapp, Adam. *Missing the Piano.* School.

Rappaport, Doreen. *The Sacco-Vanzetti Trial.* Political Science. Italian American.

Rappoport, Ken. *Shaquille O'Neal.* Sports. African American.

Ray, Karen. *To Cross a Line.* Holocaust. Jewish.

Rees, Dafydd, and Luke Crampton. *Encyclopedia of Rock Stars.* Reference.

Rees, Bob, and Marika Sherwood. *The Black Experience: In the Caribbean and the U.S.A.* History. African American.

Rekela, George. *Sports Great Anfernee Hardaway.* Sports. African American.

Reuter, Bjarne. *The Boys from St. Petri.* War. Danish.

Riley, Gail Blasser. *Wah Ming Chang: Artist and Master of Special Effects.* Autobiography. Chinese American.

Rinaldi, Ann. *Broken Days.* Historical Fiction. Native American.

Rinaldi, Ann. *Hang a Thousand Trees with Ribbons: The Story of Phillis Wheatley.* Historical Fiction. African American.

Riordan, James (retold by). *Korean Folk-tales.* Myths. Korea.

Rivers, Glenn, and Bruce Brooks. *Those Who Love the Game: Glenn "Doc" Rivers on Life in the NBA and Elsewhere.* Sports. African American.

Rochman, Hazel, and Darlene Z. McCampbell, editors. *Bearing Witness: Stories of the Holocaust.* Holocaust. Jewish.

Rosenberg, Liz. *Heart and Soul.* Friendships. Jewish American.

Rosenberg, Maxine. *Hiding to Survive: Stories of Jewish Children Rescued from the Holocaust.* Holocaust. Jewish.

Ruby, Lois. *Steal away Home.* Historical Fiction. Quaker and African American.

Rumbaut, Hendle. *Dove Dream.* Choices. Chickasaw.

Rutberg, Becky. *Mary Lincoln's Dressmaker: Elizabeth Keckley's Remarkable Rise from Slave to White House Confidante.* Autobiography. African American.

Rutledge, Len. *Maverick Guide to Malaysia and Singapore.* Recreation. Malaysia and Singapore.

Salisbury, Graham. *Under the Blood-Red Sun.* War. Japanese American.

Sanford, William R. *Quanah Parker: Comanche Warrior.* Autobiography. Comanche.

Sauerwein, Leigh. *The Way Home.* Short Stories.

Sawyer, Kem Knapp. *Refugees: Seeking a Safe Haven.* Human Rights.

Say, Allen. *The Ink-Keeper's Apprentice.* Arts. Japan.

Schiff, Ellen, editor. *Awake and Singing: Seven Classical Plays from the American Jewish Repertoire.* Poetry and Drama. Jewish American.

Schiff, Ellen, editor. *Fruitful and Multiplying: Nine Contemporary Plays from the American Jewish Repertoire.* Poetry and Drama. Jewish American.

Schon, Isabel, editor. *Contemporary Spanish-Speaking Writers and Illustrators for Children and Young Adults: A Biographical Dictionary.* Reference. Hispanic.

Schraff, Anne. *Women of Peace: Nobel Peace Prize Winners.* Autobiography.

Schuman, Michael A. *Bill Cosby: Actor and Comedian.* Autobiography. African American.

Shusterman, Neal. *Dissidents.* Adventure. Former Soviet Union.

Sidel, Ruth. *Battling Bias: The Struggle for Identity and Community on College Campuses.* Human Rights.

Silverman, Jerry. *Just Listen to This Song I'm Singing: African-American History through Song.* Arts. African American.

Sinclair, April. *Coffee Will Make You Black.* Choices. African American.

Sleator, William. *Dangerous Wishes.* Adventure. Thailand.

Smith, Karen Patricia, editor. *African-American Voices in Young Adult Literature: Tradition, Transition, Transformation.* Reference. African American.

Smith, Roland. *Thunder Cave.* Adventure. Kenya.

Smith, John David. *Black Voices from Reconstruction 1865–1877.* History. African American.

Soto, Gary. *Canto Familiar.* Poetry and Drama. Latino American.

Soto, Gary. *Jesse.* Choices. Latino American.

Soto, Gary. *Local News.* Short Stories. Latino American.

Soto, Gary. *Summer on Wheels.* Friendships. Latino American.

Southgate, Martha. *Another Way to Dance.* Arts. African American.

Spariosu, Mihail I., and Benedek Dezső. *Ghosts, Vampires, and Werewolves: Eerie Tales from Transylvania.* Myths. Romania.

Spencer, William. *Islamic Fundamentalism in the Modern World.* Religion. Islamic.

St. George, Judith. *To See with the Heart: The Life of Sitting Bull.* Autobiography. Dakota.

Staples, Suzanne Fisher. *Dangerous Skies.* Friendships. African American.

Staples, Suzanne Fisher. *Haveli.* Adventure. Pakistan.

Stefoff, Rebecca. *Mao Zedong: Founder of the People's Republic of China.* Autobiography. China.

Stefoff, Rebecca. *Nelson Mandela: Hero for Democracy.* Autobiography. South Africa.

Stefoff, Rebecca. *Saddam Hussein: Absolute Ruler of Iraq.* Autobiography. Iraq.

Stein, R. Conrad. *The Mexican Revolution, 1910–1920.* History. Mexico.

Stepto, Michele, editor. *African-American Voices.* Diaries. African American.

Stolz, Mary. *Cezanne Pinto: A Memoir.* Historical Fiction. African American.

Sullivan, Michael J. *Sports Great Shaquille O'Neal.* Sports. African American.

Sullivan, George. *Slave Ship: The Story of the Henrietta Marie.* History. African American.

Sutton, Roger. *Hearing Us Out: Voices From the Gay and Lesbian Community.* Diaries.

Świebocka, Teresa, editor; English edition by Jonathan Webber and Connie Wilsack. *Auschwitz: A History in Photographs.* Holocaust. Jewish.

Symynkywicz, Jeffrey B. *Germany: United Again.* History. Germany.

Symynkywicz, Jeffrey. *Václav Havel and the Velvet Revolution.* Autobiography. Former Czechoslovakia.

Tarpley, Natasha, editor. *Testimony: Young African-Americans on Self-Discovery and Black Identity.* Diaries. African American.

Tashlik, Phyllis, editor. *Hispanic, Female and Young: An Anthology.* Short Stories. Latina American.

Tate, Eleanora E. *A Blessing in Disguise.* Family. African American.

Taylor, Mildred D. *The Well: David's Story.* Family. African American.

Taylor, Theodore. *The Bomb.* Historical Fiction. Marshall Islands.

Taylor, Theodore. *Sweet Friday Island.* Adventure.

Temple, Frances. *The Ramsay Scallop.* Historical Fiction. Haiti.

Temple, Frances. *Taste of Salt: A Story of Modern Haiti.* Choices. Haiti.

Temple, Frances. *Tonight, by Sea.* Adventure. Haiti.

Thomas, Joyce Carol. *When the Nightingale Sings.* Choices. African American.

Thomas, Roy Edwin, compiler. *Come Go with Me: Old-Timer Stories from the Southern Mountains.* Diaries.

Thornley, Stew. *Sports Great Dennis Rodman.* Sports. African American.

Thornley, Stew. *Top 10 Football Receivers.* Sports.

Thornton, Yvonne S., M.D., as told to Jo Coudert. *The Ditchdigger's Daughters: A Black Family's Astonishing Success Story.* Autobiography. African American.

Trahant, Lenora Begay. *The Success of the Navajo Arts and Crafts Enterprise: A Retail Success Story.* Arts. Navajo.

Turner, Glennette Tilley. *Running for Our Lives.* Historical Fiction. African American.

Turner, Don. *Maverick Guide to Bali and Java.* Recreation. Indonesia.

Uchida, Yoshiko. *The Invisible Thread.* Autobiography. Japanese American.

van der Rol, Ruud, and Rian Verhoeven, in association with the Anne Frank House. *Anne Frank: Beyond the Diary: A Photographic Remembrance.* Holocaust. Jewish.

Van Dijk, Lutz. *Damned Strong Love: The True Story of Willi G. and Stefan K.* War. Germany.

Velásquez, Gloria. *Juanita Fights the School Board.* School. Latina American.

Vick, Helen Hughes. *Walker's Journey Home.* Historical Fiction. Native American (Sinagua).

Villaseñor, Victor. *Walking Stars: Stories of Magic and Power.* Autobiography. Mexican American.

Visual Dictionary of Ancient Civilizations, The. History.

Walker, Barbara K., compiler. *Laughing Together: Giggles and Grins from around the Globe.* Humor.

Walker, Paul Robert. *Giants! Stories from around the World.* Myths.

Walter, Mildred Pitts. *Second Daughter: The Story of a Slave Girl.* Historical Fiction. African American.

Wangerin, Walter, Jr. *The Crying for a Vision.* Choices. Native American (Dakota).

Wartski, Maureen. *Candle in the Wind.* Choices. Japanese American.

Watkins, Yoko Kawashima. *My Brother, My Sister, and I.* Family. Japanese American.

Werlin, Nancy. *Are You Alone on Purpose?* Friendships. Jewish.

West, Dorothy. *The Wedding.* Family. African American.

White, Richard. *Jordan Freeman Was My Friend.* War. African American.

Williams, Gregory Howard. *Life on the Color Line: The True Story of a White Boy Who Discovered He Was Black.* Autobiography. African American.

Williams, Michael. *The Genuine Half-Moon Kid.* Family. South Africa.

Williams-Garcia, Rita. *Like Sisters on the Homefront.* Family. African American.

Wilson, Erlene B. *Money for College: A Guide to Financial Aid for African-American Students.* College. African American.

Wolfson, Evelyn. *From Abenaki to Zuni: A Dictionary of Native American Tribes.* Reference. Native American.

Wood, Nancy. *Dancing Moons.* Poetry and Drama.

Woodson, Jacqueline. *Autobiography of a Family Photo: A Novel.* Family. African American.

Woodson, Jacqueline. *From the Notebooks of Melanin Sun.* Family. African American.

Woodson, Jacqueline. *I Hadn't Meant to Tell You This.* Family. African American.

World in Our Hands, A: Written, Illustrated, and Edited by Young People of the World in Honor of the Fiftieth Anniversary of the United Nations. Diaries.

Wormser, Richard. *American Islam: Growing Up Muslim in America.* Religion. Islamic.

Wright, Richard. *Rite of Passage.* Adventure. African American.

Wynne-Jones, Tim. *Some of the Kinder Planets: Stories by Tim Wynne-Jones.* Humor. Canada.

Yep, Laurence. *Dragon Cauldron.* Fantasy. Chinese American.

Yep, Laurence. *Dragon War.* Fantasy. Chinese American.

Yep, Laurence. *Hiroshima.* Historical Fiction. Japan.

Young, Richard, and Judy Dockrey Young, editors. *Ozark Ghost Stories.* Short Stories.

Yumoto, Kazumi. *The Friends.* Friendships.

Appendix C: World Literature Titles

The books listed here include those written by authors from countries other than the United States, Canada, or Great Britain, as well as anthologies of world literature. Entries are organized by author, title, a short form of the chapter name, and country or region.

Achebe, Chinua. *Things Fall Apart*. Classics. Nigeria.

Adler, Bill, Jr. *Tell Me a Fairy Tale: A Parent's Guide to Telling Magical and Mythical Stories*. Myths. Varied.

Alvarez, Julia. *In the Time of the Butterflies*. Historical Fiction. Dominican Republic.

Avila, Alfred. *Mexican Ghost Tales of the Southwest*. Short Stories. Mexico.

Ayer, Eleanor H., with Helen Waterford and Alfons Heck. *Parallel Journeys*. Holocaust. Germany.

Azuela, Mariano. *The Underdogs: A Novel of the Mexican Revolution*. Classics. Mexico.

Barnes-Murphy, Frances (retold by). *The Fables of Aesop*. Myths. Greece.

Bennett, Martin (retold by). *West African Trickster Tales*. Myths. West Africa.

Boas, Jacob. *We Are Witnesses: Five Diaries of Teenagers Who Died in the Holocaust*. Holocaust. Germany.

Bond, Nancy. *Truth to Tell*. Family. New Zealand.

Brainard, Cecilia Manguerra. *When the Rainbow Goddess Wept*. War. Philippines.

Campbell, Eric. *The Shark Callers*. Adventure. Papua New Guinea.

Case, Dianne. *92 Queens Road*. Family. South Africa.

Castañeda, Omar S. *Imagining Isabel*. Choices. Guatemala.

Charyn, Jerome, editor. *The New Mystery: The International Association of Crime Writers' Essential Crime Writing of the Late Twentieth Century*. Mysteries. Varied.

Choi, Sook Nyul. *Gathering of Pearls*. Choices. Korea.

Cohen, Barbara, and Bahija Lovejoy. *Seven Daughters and Seven Sons*. Myths. Iraq.

Craft, M. Charlotte (told by). *Cupid and Psyche*. Myths. Greece.

Creeden, Sharon. *Fair Is Fair: World Folktales of Justice*. Myths. Varied.

Danticat, Edwidge. *Breath, Eyes, Memory*. Choices. Haiti.

de Vries, Anke. *Bruises*. Family. Netherlands.

de Trevino, Elizabeth Borton. *Leona: A Love Story*. Historical Fiction. Mexico.

Deschamps, Hélène. *Spyglass: An Autobiography*. Autobiography. France.

Duong, Thu Huong. *Paradise of the Blind*. Choices. Vietnam.

Eliot, Alexander. *The Global Myths: Exploring Primitive, Pagan, Sacred, and Scientific Mythologies*. Myths. Varied.

Filipović, Zlata. *Zlata's Diary: A Child's Life in Sarajevo*. Diaries. Bosnia-Herzegovina.

Friedman, Ina R. *Flying against the Wind: The Story of a Young Woman Who Defied the Nazis*. Holocaust. Germany.

Friedman, Carl. *Nightfather*. Holocaust. Netherlands.

Gaarder, Jostein. *Sophie's World: A Novel about the History of Philosophy.* Mysteries. Norway.

Gatti, Anne, editor. *Tales from the African Plains.* Short Stories. Africa.

Gay, Kathlyn. *Keep the Buttered Side Up: Food Superstitions around the World.* Myths. Varied.

Giovanni, Nikki, editor. *Grand Mothers: Poems, Reminiscences, and Short Stories about the Keepers of Our Traditions.* Poetry and Drama. Varied.

Gleason, Judith, editor. *Leaf and Bone: African Praise-Poems.* Poetry and Drama. Africa.

Goodrich, Norma Lorre. *Ancient Myths.* Myths. Varied.

Gordon, Ruth, editor. *Pierced by a Ray of Sun: Poems about the Times We Feel Alone.* Poetry and Drama. Varied.

Green, Roger Lancelyn. *Tales of the Greek Heroes: Retold from the Ancient Authors.* Myths. Greece.

Gunesekera, Romesh. *Reef.* Choices. Sri Lanka.

Hague, Michael, editor. *The Book of Dragons.* Myths. Varied.

Hartnett, Sonya. *Wilful Blue.* Death. Australia.

Hartnett, Sonya. *Sleeping Dogs.* Family. Australia.

Haskins, Jim, and Joann Biondi. *From Afar to Zulu: A Dictionary of African Cultures.* Reference. Africa.

Hodge, Merle. *For the Life of Laetitia.* School. Trinidad.

Holliday, Laurel, compiler. *Children in the Holocaust and World War II: Their Secret Diaries.* Holocaust. Varied.

Jansson, Tove. *Moominpappa's Memoirs.* Fantasy. Finland.

Jenkins, Lyll Becerra de. *Celebrating the Hero.* Family. Colombia.

Jenkins, Lyll Becerra de. *So Loud a Silence.* Choices. Colombia.

Jennings, Paul. *Unbearable! More Bizarre Stories.* Short Stories. Australia.

Jennings, Paul. *Uncovered! Weird, Weird Stories.* Short Stories. Australia.

Jordan, Sherryl. *Wolf-Woman.* Animals. Australia.

Kimmel, Eric A. (retold by). *The Adventures of Hershel of Ostropol.* Myths. Ukraine.

Kuklin, Susan. *Irrepressible Spirit: Conversations with Human Rights Activists.* Diaries. Varied.

Leroux, Gaston. *The Phantom of the Opera.* Classics. France.

Lipstadt, Deborah E. *Denying the Holocaust: The Growing Assault on Truth and Memory.* Holocaust. Israel.

Llorente, Pilar Molina. *The Apprentice.* Historical Fiction. Spain.

Lyons, Mary E., editor. *Raw Head, Bloody Bones: African-American Tales of the Supernatural.* Short Stories. Caribbean.

Macdonald, Caroline. *Hostilities: Nine Bizarre Stories.* Short Stories. Australia.

Mahy, Margaret. *The Other Side of Silence.* Family. Australia.

Marsden, John. *Letters from the Inside.* Friendships. Australia.

Martin, Rafe. *Mysterious Tales of Japan.* Myths. Japan.

Merino, José María. *Beyond the Ancient Cities.* Historical Fiction. Spain.

Merino, José María. *The Gold of Dreams.* Adventure. Spain.

Michelson, Maureen, editor. *Women and Work: In Their Own Words.* Diaries. Varied.

Orlev, Uri. *Lydia, Queen of Palestine.* Holocaust. Israel.

Orlev, Uri. *The Man from the Other Side.* Holocaust. Israel.

Ovid. *The Poems of Exile*. Classics. Rome.

Oz, Amos. *Soumchi*. Adventure. Israel.

Parry, Glyn. *Monster Man*. Adventure. Australia.

Pausewang, Gudrun. *Fall-out*. Choices. Germany.

Pausewang, Gudrun. *The Final Journey*. Holocaust. Germany.

Philip, Neil (retold by). *The Arabian Nights*. Classics. Arabia.

Philip, Neil, editor. *Songs Are Thoughts: Poems of the Inuit*. Poetry and Drama. Greenland and North America.

Picard, Barbara Leonie (retold by). *Tales of the Norse Gods*. Myths. Norway.

Reuter, Bjarne. *The Boys from St. Petri*. War. Denmark.

Riordan, James (retold by). *Korean Folk-tales*. Myths. Korea.

Rochman, Hazel, and Darlene Z. McCampbell, editors. *Bearing Witness: Stories of the Holocaust*. Holocaust. Varied.

Say, Allen. *The Ink-Keeper's Apprentice*. Arts. Japan.

Schon, Isabel, editor. *Contemporary Spanish-Speaking Writers and Illustrators for Children and Young Adults: A Biographical Dictionary*. Reference. Varied.

Sherman, Josepha, editor. *Orphans of the Night*. Short Stories. Varied.

Spariosu, Mihail I., and Benedek Dezsö. *Ghosts, Vampires, and Werewolves: Eerie Tales from Transylvania*. Myths. Romania.

Stein, R. Conrad. *The Mexican Revolution, 1910–1920*. History. Mexico.

Świebocka, Teresa, editor; English edition by Jonathan Webber and Connie Wilsack. *Auschwitz: A History in Photographs*. Holocaust. Poland.

Temple, Frances. *The Ramsay Scallop*. Historical Fiction. Haiti.

Temple, Frances. *Taste of Salt: A Story of Modern Haiti*. Choices. Haiti.

Temple, Frances. *Tonight, by Sea*. Adventure. Haiti.

van der Rol, Ruud, and Rian Verhoeven, in association with the Anne Frank House. *Anne Frank: Beyond the Diary: A Photographic Remembrance*. Holocaust. Netherlands.

Van Dijk, Lutz. *Damned Strong Love: The True Story of Willi G. and Stefan K.* War. Germany.

Verne, Jules. *Journey to the Center of the Earth*. Classics. France.

Walker, Paul Robert. *Giants! Stories from around the World*. Myths. Varied.

Walker, Barbara K., compiler. *Laughing Together: Giggles and Grins from around the Globe*. Humor. Varied.

Watkins, Yoko Kawashima. *My Brother, My Sister, and I*. Family. Japan.

Williams, Michael. *The Genuine Half-Moon Kid*. Family. Australia.

World in Our Hands, A: Written, Illustrated, and Edited by Young People of the World in Honor of the Fiftieth Anniversary of the United Nations. Diaries. Varied.

Yumoto, Kazumi. *The Friends*. Friendships. Japan.

Appendix D: How to Order Books

Because of the frequency with which telephone numbers and e-mail addresses change, and because many teachers and librarians find it easiest to deal directly with bookstores or distributors, we have not listed publishers' addresses here. Current information on publishers' addresses can be found in *Books in Print* and in *Literary Market Place*, both published annually by R. R. Bowker; through reference libraries; and on the World Wide Web. The following distributors, who exhibit frequently at NCTE conferences and conventions, are also good sources for books:

Econo-Clad Books
Box 1777
2101 N. Topeka Boulevard
Topeka, Kansas 66608
(913) 233-4252

Houghton Mifflin
222 Berkeley Street
Boston, Massachusetts 02116
(617) 351-5000

Penguin USA
375 Hudson Street
New York, New York 10014

Perma-Bound
Vandalia Road
Jacksonville, Illinois 62650
(217) 243-5451

Random House
201 E. 50th Street
New York, New York 10022
(800) 726-0600

Scholastic, Inc.
555 Broadway
New York, New York 10012
(800) 392-2179

Sundance Publishers
P.O. Box 1326
Littleton, Massachusetts 01460
(508) 486-9201

William Morrow and Company
1350 Avenue of the Americas
New York, New York 10019
(800) 843-9389

Author Index

Subject Index

To avoid duplication, subject index terms that correspond to chapter titles are not included unless they contain entries from other chapters.

Title Index

Editors

Lois T. Stover is a former teacher of senior and junior high school English and drama who currently serves as chair of the Educational Studies Department at St. Mary's College of Maryland, where she teaches methods courses, educational psychology, and "The Child in America," all using young adult literature. She is past editor of the "Young Adult Literature" column for *English Journal*, and has written numerous articles on young adult literature for professional publications such as *The ALAN Review* and the Adolescent Literature as a Complement to the Classics series. Her most recent books are *Young Adult Literature: The Heart of the Middle School Curriculum* (1996) and *Presenting Phyllis Reynolds Naylor* (1997).

Stephanie F. Zenker is currently with the Office of Gifted and Talented Education of the Baltimore County Public Schools in Towson, Maryland, and is an instructor for the Department of Secondary Education at Towson University. She served as a middle and high school English chair and teacher before moving into the field of gifted education. She is a member of the National Council of Teachers of English and of the National Association for Gifted Children, on whose Professional Development Committee she serves.

Committee on the Senior High School Booklist

Lois Stover, *Co-chair,* St. Mary's College of Maryland, St. Mary's City, Maryland

Stephanie Zenker, *Co-chair,* Baltimore County Public Schools, Towson, Maryland

Jonathan Aaron, MacDonough School, Owings Mills, Maryland

Kathy Baker, Southern High School, Baltimore, Maryland

Tina Baran, Chesapeake High School, Baltimore, Maryland

Elizabeth Benzinger, Chesapeake High School, Baltimore, Maryland

Scott Borgerding, Eastern Technical High School, Baltimore, Maryland

Andrew Brown, Chesapeake High School, Baltimore, Maryland

Jeffrey Brown, Landon School, Bethesda, Maryland

Carla Buckley, Bethesda, Maryland

Karen Casanova, Arnett J. Brown Middle School, Baltimore, Maryland

Linda Channell, Towson State University, Towson, Maryland

Cellestine Cheeks, Towson State University, Towson, Maryland

Helena Cook, Washington, DC

Joan Cooper, Stemmers Run Middle School, Baltimore, Maryland

Lisa Cunningham, Upper Marlboro, Maryland

JoAnne Dement, Chesapeake High School, Baltimore, Maryland

Darien Fisher-Duke, Brookland Middle Schools, Richmond, Virginia

Diane Freeman, Arvada West High School, Arvada, Colorado

Mary Fulton, Peebles High School, Peebles, Ohio

Jan Gerard, Stemmers Run Middle School, Baltimore, Maryland

Howard Gradet, Forest Park High School, Baltimore, Maryland

Ilene Hammet, Howard County Public Schools, Howard County, Maryland

Mary Ann Hartshorn, North Harford High School, Harford County Schools, Maryland

Lin Hill, Albemarle High School, Charlottesville, Virginia

Ginger Huller, North Harford Middle School, Pylesville, Maryland

Kathy Icenogle, Caravel Academy, Bear, Delaware

Bruce Ickes, Chesapeake High School, Baltimore, Maryland

Kathy Jepsen, Meade Senior High School, Fort George G. Meade, Maryland

Laurie Jones, Edgewater, Maryland

Rebecca Joseph, Southeast Middle School, Baltimore, Maryland

Rita Karr, Sykesville Middle School, Sykesville, Maryland

Connie Kihm, Towson State University, Towson, Maryland

Laura Klein, Albemarle High School, Charlottesville, Virginia

Susan Kreh, Baltimore County Public Library, Reisterstown, Maryland

Carol Maid, George Fox Middle School, Pasadena, Maryland

Kafila Malik, J. S. Chick Elementary School, Kansas City, Missouri

Terry Martin-Minnoch, Presbytery of Baltimore, Baltimore, Maryland

Sara Mix, MacDonough School, Owings Mills, Maryland

Mary Murray, Randallstown High School, Randallstown, Maryland

Heather Neville, Garrison Forest School, Owings Mills, Maryland

Judy Pardew, North Harford Middle School, Pylesville, Maryland

Penny Parker, Woodlawn High School, Baltimore, Maryland

Joe Pazourek, Dundalk High School, Baltimore, Maryland

Marilynn Revelle, Yarmouth, Maine

Jill Sarnese, Owings Mills, Maryland

Stephanie Shauck, Towson State University, Towson, Maryland

Patricia Simon, Franklin Elementary School, Baltimore County, Maryland

Joseph Stover, Maryland Arts Council, Baltimore, Maryland

Kathryn Surchek, Albemarle High School, Charlottesville, Virginia

Debbie Taylor, Enoch Pratt Library, Baltimore, Maryland

Jo Tyson, North Harford Middle School, Pylesville, Maryland

Tricia Uppercue, Fallston High School, Fallston, Maryland

D. Michelle Voelker, Towson State University, Towson, Maryland

Danyka Wolfkill-Hoffman, Bel Air High School, Bel Air, Maryland

Edd Zenker, Baltimore County Public Schools, Maryland

Connie Zitlow, Ohio Wesleyan University, Delaware, Ohio

This book was typeset in Palatino and Helvetica by Electronic Imaging.
Typefaces used on the cover were University Roman and Palatino.
The book was printed on Chesapeake Offset 50-pound paper by Port City Press, Inc.